31232000182768

MAY   2002

D1564160

The Companion
to African Literatures

The Companion to African Literatures

Editors

Douglas Killam
&
Ruth Rowe

Consultant Editor
Bernth Lindfors

Associate Editors
Gerald M. Moser
Alain Ricard

James Currey
OXFORD

Indiana University Press
BLOOMINGTON & INDIANAPOLIS

First published in 2000 in the United Kingdom by

James Currey
73 Botley Road
Oxford
OX2 0BS

and in North America by

Indiana University Press
601 North Morton Street
Bloomington, Indiana 47404-3797

British Library Cataloguing in Publication Data
The companion to African literatures
    1. African literature (English) – History and criticism
    2. African literature (English) – Dictionaries
    I. Killam, G. D. (Gordon Douglas)   II. Rowe, Ruth
820.9'96

ISBN 0-85255-549-0

Library of Congress Cataloging-in-Publication Data
The companion to African literatures / editors, Douglas
    Killam, Ruth Rowe.
      p. - cm.
    ISBN 0-253-33633-3 (cloth : alk, paper)
    1. African literature (English)--Bio--bibliography Dictionaries.
2. African literature (English) Dictionaries.   3. Authors, African-
-Biography Dictionaries.   4. Africa--In literature Dictionaries.
I. Killam, G. D. II. Rowe, Ruth.
PR 9340.C65 1999
820.9'96'03--dc21
[B]
                                    99-30001

1 2 3 4 5 04 03 02 01 00

Typeset in 8/9 Bembo by Long House, Cumbria, UK
Manufactured in the United States of America

Contributors

The editors and publishers would like to thank the following contributors on whose work the entries are based.

Evelyn Accad
Funso Aiyejina
Ayo Akinwale
Adetayo Alabi
Peter Alexander
Yaw Asante
Chris Awuyah
C. Azuonwe
E.A. Babalola
Fola Babayode
Richard Bailey
F. Odun Balogun
Jacqueline Bardolph
Tina Barsby
Richard Bartlett
Ulli Beier
Mary C. Bill
Elizabeth Blakesley
Charles Bodunde
Duncan Brown
Thomas Bruckner
Charlotte Bruner
Noverino Canonici
B. Chandramohan
Anthony Chennells
Neville Choono
Austin Chukwu
George Elliot Clarke
Stewart Crehan
James Currey
Geoffrey Davis
Margaret Daymond
Pietro Deandrea
Neloufer De Mel
Claire L. Dehon
Gaurav Desai
Teresa Dovey
Ann Dry
Chris Dunton
Jill Eagling
Afam Ebeogu
Arlene A. Elder
Isaac I. Elimimian
Onuora Ossie Enekwe
Dennis F. Essar
Ezenwa-Ohaeto
Robert Elliot Fox
Anne Fuchs
Susan VanZanten Gallagher
Colin Gardner
Richard Gaylard
James Gibbs
Gitahi wa Gititi
Daniel Gover
Pumla Dineo Gquola
Ina Grabe
Stephen Gray

M.M. Green
Gareth Griffiths
John Gruesser
Farida Abu-Haidar
Frederick Hale
Russell G. Hamilton
Geoffrey Haresnape
Muhammed Haron
Temple Hauptfleisch
Christopher Heywood
Yvette Hutchison
Emilia Ilieva
Belinda Jack
Alex Johnson
J. A. Kearney
Daya Khandoo
Adele King
A.H.M. Kirk-Greene
Dirk Klopper
Sue Kossew
Jane Koustas
Marcia Leveson
Deserée Lewis
Cecily Lockett
Clayton G. MacKenzie
Craig MacKenzie
Obi Maduakor
R. Marais
Paola Marchionni
D.I. Mathumba
Tom Matshakaylie-Ndlovu
T.O. McLoughlin
M. McMurtry
David Medalie
Cheryl Ann Michael
Peter Midgley
Yemi Mojola
David Chioni Moore
Gerald M. Moser
P.T. Mtuze
Khalid Al-Mubarak
Venu Naidoo
Obioma Nnaemeka
Alfred Ndi
Jonathan Ngate
Chinyere L. Ngonebu
Dumisani Ntshangase
Sarah Nuttall
Chimalum Nwankwo
C.O. Nwodo
Kalu Ogbaa
S.E. Ogude
Tanure Ojaide
Chidi Okonkwo
Tayo Peter Olafioye
Modupe Olaogun
Gloria Nne Onyeoziri

Damian U. Opata
Oyekan Owomoyela
Fiona Paterson
Richard Peck
Ernest Pereira
Abioseh Porter
Emmanuel Quarcoo
Sam Raditlhalo
Pauline Rewt
Alain Ricard
Sheila Roberts
Henriette M. Roos
Adrian Roscoe
Keith Sambrook
Elaine Savory
Paul A. Scanlon
F. Schulze-Engler
Jamie S. Scott
Mabel D. Segun
Stephen Serafin
Govind N. Sharma
Carol Sicherman
Pamela J. Smith
Gaele Sobott-Mogwe
Kelwyn Sole
Blandine Stefanson
Graham Stewart
Philip Stewart
Lindy Stiebel
C.F. Swanepoel
Neil ten Kortenaar
Alan Thorold
Farouk Topan
Iroha Udeh
Maurice Vambe
H.P. van Coller
Bruno van Dyk
Helize van Vuuren
Johan van Wyk
Malvern Van Wyk Smith
Flora Veit-Wild
Nick Visser
Jean-Marie Volet
Jean-Philippe Wade
F. Wako
Chris Wanjala
Barry J. Ward
Hein Willemse
Peter Williams
Catherine Woeber
Brian Worsfold
Derek Wright
Dan Wylie
Chantal Zabus
Hans Zell
Rino Zhuwarara
Opportune Zongo

Guide to Readers

The Companion to African Literatures is an alphabetically organized, comprehensive guide to work written in English or widely available in translation from other languages. There are separate entries for selected African language literatures, with an emphasis on works available to readers of English.

Cross-referencing: ★Asterisks are used before the first appearance of a word within each entry to indicate that a separate related entry appears elsewhere in *The Companion*.

There are entries in the following categories:

Authors writing in English. Author entries include biographical information, details of major publications, and comment on their critical reputation.

Authors who write in an African or non-African language, but some of whose work is available in English translation.

Selected works of an author, giving brief descriptive entries.

Language entries distinguish *The Companion* from other reference works to the literature of the African continent. Selected African languages with published literatures (Gikuyu, Hausa, Igbo, Krio, Malagasy, Ndebele, Pidgin, Shona, Sotho, Swahili, Tsonga, Xhosa, Yoruba and Zulu). Entries on works which are written in Afrikaans, Portuguese (see *Lusophone Literature*), and French (see the *Novel, Francophone*), but which are mostly available in translation.

Themed entries as listed below are **further sub-divided alphabetically by region** (East Africa; South-Central Africa, South Africa and West Africa), categories which reflect differences in the literatures as shaped by their colonial and post-colonial experiences. (The literatures of North Africa, when available in translation from Arabic and French into English, are described through individual author entries).

Literary genres and sub-genres: Drama, the Novel, Poetry, the Short Story, Popular Literature, Oral Tradition and Folklore, Anthologies, Biography and Autobiography, Children's Literature, Literary Magazines

Relations between literature and extra-literary influences: Religion and Literature (Christianity, Islam, and Traditional African Religions), Politics and Literature, War Literature, Censorship, Women in Literature

Selected list of topics and themes:

African Writers Series
African-American Literature
African-British Literature
African-Canadian Literature
African-Caribbean Literature
Africanist Discourse
Afrikaans
Anglo-Boer War
Anthologies
Apartheid
Biography and Autobiography
Black Atlantic
Black Consciousness
Bushmen in South African Literature
Censorship
Drama
Feminism and Literature
Francophone-Anglophone Literary Relations
Gay and Lesbian Sexuality in Literature
Gikuyu Literature
Hausa Literature
Igbo Literature
Krio
Literary Criticism
Literary Magazines
Literary Theory
Maghrebi Literature
Malagasy
Mauritius
Ndebele Literature

Negritude
Nigeria-Biafra War
Novel, the
Onitsha Popular Market Literature
Oral Tradition and Folklore
Orature
Pidgin Literature
Poetry
Politics and Literature
Popular Literature
Prison Literature in South Arica
Publishing in Sub-Saharan Africa
Religion and Literature
— Traditional Religions and Literature
— Christianity and Literature
— Islam and Literature
Réunion
Shaka in African Literature
Shona Literature
Short Story
Sotho Literature
Swahili Literature
Tsonga Literature
War Literature
Women in Literature
Writing Systems in Africa
Xhosa Literature
Yoruba Literature
Zulu Literature

Country–Author Guide

Algeria
Mohammed Dib
Assia Djebar
Touati Fettouma

Angola
Agostinho Neto

Benin
Félix Couchoro

Botswana
Bessie Head

Cameroon
Mongo Beti
Calixthe Beyala
Yodi Karone
Simon Njami
Ferdinand Oyono
Guillaume Oyono-Mbia

Central African Republic
Blaise N'Djehoya

Congo-Zaïre
Kama Kamanda
Sony Labou Tansi

Côte d'Ivoire
Bernard Dadié
Ahmadou Kourouma

Egypt
Andrée Chedid
Fathy Ghanem
Tewfiq al-Hakim
Naguib Mahfouz
Nawal el Saadawi

Ethiopia
Sahle Sellassie

Gambia
Lenrie Peters
Tijan M. Sallah

Ghana
Joseph Wilfred Abruquah
Kobena Eyi Acquah

Ama Ata Aidoo
Kofi Anyidoho
Ayi Kwei Armah
R.E.G. Armattoe
Kofi Awoonor
Mohammed Ben-Abdallah
J. Benibengor Blay
Yaw M. Boateng
Kwesi Brew
J. E. Casely-Hayford
Ottobah Cugoano
Joe de Graft
Michael Francis Dei-Anang
Cameron Duodu
Ferdinand Kwasi Fiawoo
Asare Konadu
B. Kojo Laing
Bill Okyere Marshall
Atukwei Okai
Martin Owusu
Kobina Sekyi
Francis Selormey
Efua Sutherland
Asiedu Yirenkyi

Guinea
Camara Laye
Williams Sassine

Kenya
Jared Angira
Khadambi Asalache
Francis Imbuga
Samuel Kahiga
Leonard Kibera
Muthoni Likimani
Charles Mangua
Ali A. Mazrui
Micere Githae Mugo
Meja Mwangi
Stephen N. Ngubiah
Ngugi wa Thiong'o
Rebeka Njau
Grace Ogot
Mwangi Ruheni
M. G. Vassanji
Godwin Wachira
Charity Waciuma
Kenneth Watene
Miriam Were

Lesotho
Thomas Mofolo
A. S. Mopeli-Paulus

Liberia
Bai T. J. Moore

Madagascar
Jean-Joseph Rabéarivelo
Jacques Rabémanajara

Malawi
Steve Chimombo
Frank Chipasula
Aubrey Kachingwe
Legson Kayira
Ken Lipenga
Jack Mapanje
Felix Mnthali
Edison Mpina
Anthony Nazombe
David Rubadiri

Mali
Amadou Hampâté Bâ

Mauritius
Edouard Maunick

Morocco
Tahar Ben Jelloun
Driss Chraïbi

Mozambique
Mia Couto
Lina Magaia

Namibia
Joseph Diescho
Dorian Haarhoff

Nigeria
Chinua Achebe
Catherine Obianuju Acholonu
Remi Aduke Adedeji
Frank Aig-Imoukhuede
Funso Aiyejina
Christie Ade Ajayi
Tolu Ajayi
Zaynab Alkali

T. M. Aluko
Elechi Amadi
Ogbuefi Nwagu Aneke
I.N.C. Aniebo
Seinde Arogbofa
Biyi Bandele-Thomas
J. P. Clark Bekederemo
Chinweizu
Michael J. C. Echeruo
T. Obinkaram Echewa
Obi B. Egbuna
Cyprian Ekwensi
Buchi Emecheta
Ossie Enekwe
Olaudah Equiano
D. O. Fagunwa
Tunde Fatunde
Harry Garuba
James Ene Henshaw
Chukwuemeka Ike
Eddie Iroh
Festus Iyayi
Duro Ladipo
Theresa Ekwutosi Meniru
S. Okechukwu Mezu
John Munonye
Pol Nnamuzikam Ndu
Emeka Nwabueze
Martina Awele Nwakoby
Nkem Nwankwo
Flora Nwapa
Onuora Nzekwu
Olu Obafemi
Odia Ofeimun
Olu Oguibe
Molara Ogundipe-Leslie
Wale Ogunyemi
Tanure Ojaide
Gabriel Okara
Christopher Okigbo
Akomaye Oko
Onookome Okome
Ifeoma Okoye
Isidore Okpewho
Ben Okri
Tayo Peter Olafioye
Kole Omotoso
Tess Akaeka Onwueme
Dillibe Onyeama
Dennis Osadebay
Naiwu Osahon
Femi Osofisan
Niyi Osundare
Sonny Oti
Helen Ovbiagele

Femi Oyebode
Segun Oyekunle
Ola Rotimi
Ken Saro-Wiwa
Mabel Segun
Zulu Sofola
Bode Sowande
Wole Soyinka
Ibrahim Tahir
Amos Tutuola
Obiora Udechukwu
Ada Ugah
Kalu Uka
Adaora Lily Ulasi
Rosina Umelo
Mamman Jiya Vatsa
Adebayo Williams
Sa'ad Zungur

Rwanda
Alexis Kagame

Senegal
Mariama Bâ
Alioune Diop
Birago Diop
Cheikh Anta Diop
David Diop
Malick Fall
Aminata Maiga Ka
Sembene Ousmane
L. S. Senghor

Sierra Leone
Adelaide Casely-Hayford
Gladys Casely-Hayford
Syl Cheney-Coker
William Conton
R. Sarif Easmon
Lemuel A. Johnson
Yulisa Amadu Maddy
Abioseh Nicol

Somalia
Nuruddin Farah

South Africa
Lionel Abrahams
Peter Abrahams
Tatamkhulu Ismail Afrika
Stephen Black
Douglas Blackburn
Harry Bloom
Elleke Boehmer
Dugmore Boetie

H. C. Bosman
Breyten Breytenbach
André Brink
Dennis Brutus
Guy Butler
Roy Campbell
Stuart Cloete
Sydney Clouts
J. M. Coetzee
Jack Cope
Patrick Cullinan
R. N. Currey
Achmat Dangor
H. I. E. Dhlomo
R. R. R. Dhlomo
Modikwe Dikobe
Menán du Plessis
Ahmed Essop
J. Percy Fitzpatrick
Athol Fugard
Sheila Meiring Fugard
Perceval Gibbon
Nadine Gordimer
Stephen Gray
Mafika Pascal Gwala
Bessie Head
Christopher Hope
Noni Jabavu
Dan Jacobson
Ingrid Jonker
A. C. Jordan
Farida Karodia
Gibson Kente
Keorapetse Kgositsile
Daniel P. Kunene
Mazisi Kunene
Ellen Kuzwayo
Alex La Guma
Douglas Livingstone
Donald Maclennan
Sindiwe Magona
Matsemele Manaka
Umaruiddin Don Mattera
James Matthews
Mzwakhe Mbuli
Zakes Mda
Gcina Mhlophe
Ruth Miller
Sarah Gertrude Millin
Bloke Modisane
Casey 'Kid' Motsisi
Es'kia Mphahlele
Mbuyiseni Mtshali
Mothobi Mutloatse
Mbulelo Mzamane

Nat Nakasa
Njabulo Ndebele
Lauretta Ngcobo
Mbongeni Ngema
Mike Nicol
Lewis Nkosi
Arthur Nortje
Alan Paton
Sol T. Plaatje
William Plomer
Thomas Pringle
Alfred Temba Qabula
Lesego Rampolokeng
Richard Rive
Sheila Roberts
Olive Schreiner
William Charles Scully
Sipho Sepamla
Mongane Wally Serote
Francis Carey Slater
Pauline Smith
Can Themba
Gladys Thomas
Miriam Tlali
Laurens van der Post
Christopher van Wyk
B. W. Vilakazi
Ivan Vladislavić
Stephen Watson
Zoë Wicomb
Peter Wilhelm

Sudan
Tayeb Salih

Tanzania
Agoro Anduru
Abdulrazak Gurnah
Ebrahim N. Hussein
Peter Palangyo
Prince Kagwema
Gabriel Ruhumbika

Tunisia
Albert Memmi

Uganda
Austin Bukenya
Barbara Kimenye
Bonnie Lubega
Lubwa p'Chong
John Nagenda
Peter Nazareth
Richard Carl Ntiru
Okello Oculi
Okot p'Bitek
John Ruganda
George Seremba
Eneriko Seruma
Robert Serumaga
Taban lo Liyong
Bahadur Tejani
Timothy Wangusa

Zambia
Dominic Mulaisho

Zimbabwe
N. H. Brettell
Samuel Chimsoro
Shimmer Chinodya
Edmund Chipamaunga
A. S. Cripps
Tsitsi Dangarembga
John Eppel
Chenjerai Hove
Wilson Katiyo
Doris Lessing
Nevanji Madanhire
Dambudzo Marechera
Timothy O. McLoughlin
Charles Mungoshi
Solomon Mutswairo
Geoffrey Ndhlala
Emmanuel Ngara
Stanley Nyamfukudza
Freedom Nyamubaya
Kristina Rungano
Stanlake Samkange
Ben Sibenke
T. K. Tsodzo
Lawrence Vambe
Yvonne Vera
Andrew Whaley
Paul Tiyambe Zeleza
Musaemura Zimunya

Acknowledgements

We owe a special debt of gratitude to Bernth Lindfors who, with typical collegiality and professionalism, read the manuscript, suggesting corrections, elaborations and further entries as well as suggesting the names of colleagues who could contribute to making *The Companion* more comprehensive.

The selection of entries derives from the advice of experts in the field, freely offered in the initial planning stages of *The Companion*. We are indebted to Craig MacKenzie, Charlotte Bruner, Emilia Ilieva, Gititi wa Gitahi, Anthony Chennels and Johan van Wyk.

Similarly, as the List of Contributors reveals, entries have been prepared by distinguished scholars and critics of African literature.

We want to thank Alain Ricard and Gerald Moser, who read the entries on Francophone and Lusophone literatures, making helpful suggestions and providing additional entries.

We would like to acknowledge the assistance given by Olga Griffin in the initial stages of the preparation of the manuscript.

We wish to acknowledge the support given by the University of Guelph.

We also wish to acknowledge substantial grants from the Social Sciences and Humanities Research Council of Canada which made the preparation of this work possible.

Lastly we wish to record the exceptional contribution of the typesetter Katherine Kirkwood and of the editors Mike Kirkwood and Lynn Taylor; without their informed, concerned and dedicated work the whole project might never have been completed.

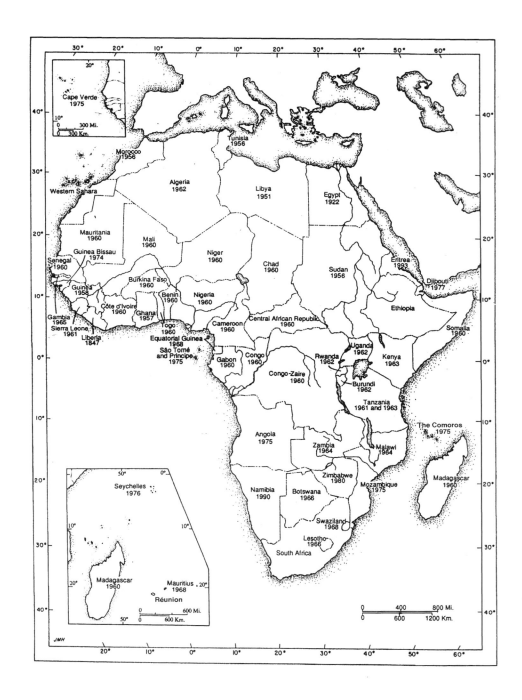

Map 1 African nations, with dates of independence

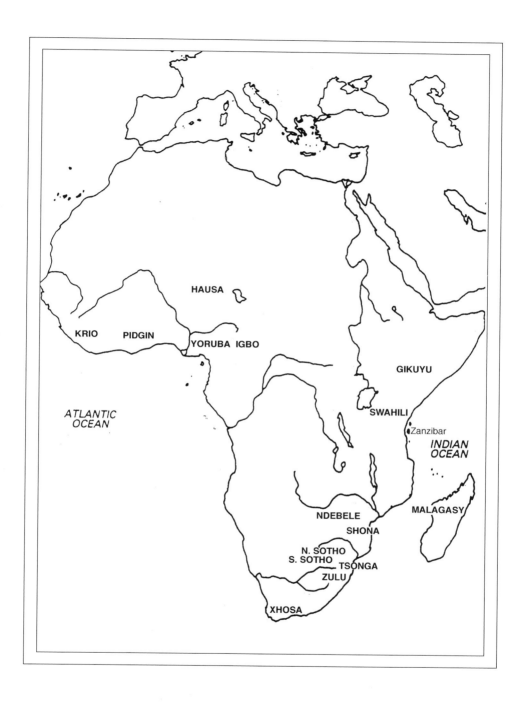

Map 2 African languages with entries in *The Companion*

A

ABRAHAMS, Lionel (1928-), South African poet, editor, and critic, has lived all his life in Johannesburg, South Africa, the subject and locale of much of his writing. He was educated at Damelin College and the University of the Witwatersrand and had private tuition in writing from Herman Charles ★Bosman. Since 1952 Abrahams has edited seven volumes of Bosman's work (1952-7); several literary journals, among them *The Purple Renoster* and *Sesame*; and anthologies of South African writing. Co-founder of Bateleur Press and a champion of new writers, he has been awarded two honorary doctorates and the Medal of the English Academy of South Africa.

His four published volumes of poetry, *Thresholds of Tolerance* (1975), *The Journal of a New Man* (1984), *The Writer in Sand* (1988), and *A Dead Tree Full of Live Birds* (1995), range in content from the political and the personal to culture and cosmology. The mode is descriptive, speculative, or argumentative and the style is various, though mainly in free verse; the work relies considerably on cadence and sound play. *The Celibacy of Felix Greenspan* (1977), an autobiographical 'novel in eighteen stories', was reissued in North America in 1993. The mode is realistic, and the prose is at its simplest and most persuasive when forced to mimic the paucity and obliqueness of childhood. The stories of later life are typically organized around ironical epiphanies. Abrahams is an indefatigable champion of cultural standards, and his polemical essays are an important contribution to literary debate. *A Reader* (1988), a miscellany of his work, was published as a tribute for his sixtieth birthday. *A Writer in Stone* (1998), a collection of stories, essays, and poems by South African writers, was published to celebrate his seventieth birthday.

ABRAHAMS, Peter (1919-), South African novelist and essayist, was born in Vrededorp, Johannesburg. After attending school and college intermittently he worked for a time as a seaman before settling in Britain to fulfil his ambition to be a writer. As a result of an assignment in Jamaica he moved his family permanently to Kingston in 1959, where he continued his career as a novelist, editor, and political commentator.

Although Abrahams had to leave South Africa in order to find his identity as a writer, much of his fiction returns there as he works out his understanding of race. *Song of the City* (1945) and *★Mine Boy* (1946), both influenced by his early interest in marxism, were among the first African novels to represent the experi-

ence of rural migrant workers facing the racial discrimination and alienation of the industrialized city. These two novels, along with two volumes of poetry, *Here, Friend* (ca.1940) and *A Blackman Speaks of Freedom* (1941), a collection of sketches, *Dark Testament* (1942), and *The ★Path of Thunder* (1948), a novel about the illegal love affair between a 'coloured' (mixed-race) man and a young white woman, are often seen to comprise the first stage of Abrahams' career, characterized by an optimistic vision of a world without colour prejudice where individual freedom takes precedence over politics.

The second stage of Abrahams' career, marked by his increasing concern with the history and politics of race, includes the novel *Wild Conquest* (1950), *Return to Goli* (1953), which is a book of essays, and his autobiography, ★*Tell Freedom* (1954). *Wild Conquest*, a historical novel, attempts to trace the origin of racial conflict in South Africa to the Great Trek of 1836, when Afrikaners and Africans struggled over the fate of the land. The lingering hope at the end of *Wild Conquest*, that individual attitudes towards colour could still transcend prejudice, gave way to the bitterness and anger of the essays in *Return to Goli*, written after a six-week return to South Africa. *Tell Freedom*, which followed quickly on *Return to Goli*, confirmed the reputation he had established with *Mine Boy* as an artist who was also a witness to the black experience in South Africa.

The third phase of Abrahams' career begins with the publication of *A Wreath for Udomo* (1956). With this novel and its successor, *This Island Now* (1966), he widens the scope of his examination of the politics of race as he shifts his settings to West Africa and the Caribbean respectively, anticipating the difficulties and trade-offs of the movement from colonialism to independence.He returns briefly to the South African setting of the earlier novels in *A Night of Their Own* (1965). *The View from Coyoba* (1985), which draws on a century-and-a-half of black history in Africa, the Caribbean, and North America, consolidates the achievements of Abrahams' career and his politics in its vision of freedom for blacks from the prison of western cultural expectations.

An important part of Abrahams' achievement has been the encouragement and example he provided as one of the first black African writers of the 1950s and 60s to others, including Chinua ★Achebe and ★Ngugi wa Thiong'o. The development of his thought over his writing career indicates how African literature has attempted to deal with power, race, and culture during the past half-century.

ABRUQUAH, Joseph Wilfred (1921-), Ghanaian novelist. Educated at Mfantsipim School, a Methodist school in what was then Gold Coast, King's College, London, and Westminster College, London, Abruquah broke into the literary market of 1960s Ghana with his autobiographical first novel *The Catechist* (1965), an account of the narrow religious environment into which he was born. Although the novel was ignored by academic critics trained in the methods of European criticism, it was followed by a second, entitled *The Torrent* (1968), whose young protagonist, Josiah Afful, is among the 'bush boys' whom expatriates transform into black Europeans. The book expresses concern for the loss of African values and culture. Abruquah abandoned work on a third novel in 1972 and has published nothing since.

ACHEBE, Chinua (1930-), Nigerian novelist, was born in Ogidi, Nigeria and educated at the local Church Missionary Society primary school, at Government College, Umuahia, and University College, Ibadan. In 1954 he became a talks producer for the Nigerian Broadcasting Corporation, rising to Director of External Broadcasting in 1961 and remaining with the corporation until the 1966 massacre of Igbos in Northern and Western Nigeria. After the outbreak of the *Nigeria-Biafra war (1967-70), Achebe served in the Biafran diplomatic service. In 1971, he founded *Okike: Journal of New African Writing* and for the next decade nurtured it while holding a succession of teaching posts at universities in the USA and at the University of Nigeria, Nsukka. He has been awarded the prestigious Nigerian National Merit Award and the Order of the Federal Republic. He has published short stories: *Girls at War and Other Stories* (1972); children's stories: *Chike and the River* (1966), *The Drum* (1977), *The Flute* (1977), and *How the Leopard Got His Claws* (with John Iroaganachi, 1976); poetry: *Beware, Soul Brother and Other Poems* (1971; issued in the US as *Christmas in Biafra and Other Poems*, 1973), which won the 1972 Commonwealth Poetry Prize; essays: *Morning Yet on Creation Day* (1975) and *Hopes and Impediments: Selected Essays, 1965-1987* (1988); political commentary: *The Trouble with Nigeria* (1983); and five novels:*Things Fall Apart* (1958),*No Longer at Ease* (1960),*Arrow of God* (1964), *A *Man of the People* (1966), and *Anthills of the Savannah* (1987).

Achebe's writing explores the processes and consequences of Africa's transformation through its historic encounter with Europe. Recognizing the relationship between European imperialism and European myths of Africa, Achebe conceives his writing as a counter-discourse through which he participates in Africa's quest for self-reconstruction. His early theories of literature, described in 'The Role of the Writer in a New Nation' (*Nigeria Magazine*, No. 81, 1964) and 'The African Writer and the English Language' (*Transition* 4.18, 1965), have their parallels in his early cultural-nationalistic short stories and the novel *Things Fall Apart*, which challenges the image of Africa in such racist fiction as Joyce Cary's *Mister Johnson* and Joseph Conrad's *Heart of Darkness*. Over the years, he has amplified those early arguments on several occasions, from his controversial 1975 Chancellor's Lecture on racism in *Heart of Darkness* to a 1989 interview with Bill Moyers (*A World of Ideas*, ed. Betty Sue Flowers, 1989) to the 1993 Ashby Lecture at Cambridge University, England. There is, therefore, a remarkable continuity in his creative, theoretical, and political writing. With continuity goes contemporization: the elaboration of character and situation archetypes from earlier works in a contemporary context to suggest the recurrence of certain patterns in history and human behaviour.

Together Achebe's novels span the period from the Berlin Conference of 1884-5, which unleashed Europe's scramble for Africa, to the sham decolonization of the 1960s and the neo-colonial realities of the present day. Yet despite challenging the racial myths behind the scramble and presenting its profound consequences for Africa, the novels also contain it within the dynamics of Africa's history and explore the role played by fundamental transformations from oral ethnic cultures to literacy and nation-state cultures. The novels thus fall into two broad categories: the 'ethnic' novels, *Things Fall Apart* and *Arrow of God*, and the 'national' novels, *No Longer at Ease, A Man of the People*, and *Anthills of the Savannah*. Achebe's interest in literacy goes beyond African novelists' conventional opposition of traditional to Western education. For him, writing contemporizes the oral raconteur's function of conserving, interpreting, and transmitting communal history. The district commissioner's book in *Things Fall Apart* demonstrates the relationship between control of the written word and the ability to impose one's version of history or reality on others. Writing is thus crucial to social reconstruction, for, as a sage argues in *Anthills of the Savannah*, 'only the story ... can [save] our progeny from blundering like blind beggars into the spikes of the cactus fence'. The first three novels feature characters who propose to write a book, while the last two are conceived as works by writer-protagonists. The language and expository devices reflect this development along an orality-literacy continuum as Achebe moves from peasant-farmer protagonists to priests (the intellectual elite of oral culture) and university graduates, in that order.

As part of his debunking of colonialist myths of Africa in the ethnic novels, Achebe explores problems of creation, maintenance, and absence of order. Both novels are set in Igboland, but while the inhabitants of

Umuofia in *Things Fall Apart* have a common ancestry, the nine-village Umuaro in *Arrow of God* comprises separate though culturally related clans that have federated themselves to withstand common enemies. By foregrounding the rituals and institutions developed for ordering the pre-colonial universe, the novels seek to rescue the people's history from the denigrating historiography by which the colonial enterprise had been rationalized. Thus, the consultative assemblies in both plots parallel Achebe's non-fictional challenge to western claims that democratic ideals are peculiarly western. Umuaro's federation-by-mutual-consent is also contrasted with Europe's forcible amalgamation of diverse peoples to serve imperial interests. Ultimately, the collapse of both societies arises from a combination of colonialist aggression and inherent flaws, notably Umuofia's branding of certain people as ritually impure and the fierce competition among the different villages of Umuaro, which the colonizer exploits.

Unlike the ethnic cultures, colonial and neo-colonial states in the national novels lack structures of order, and the novels explore the problems of evolving such structures. Action in these novels alternates between ethnic settings and the anarchic national capital city. *No Longer at Ease*, set in the last days of colonial rule, highlights the problems of such contradictions. Individuals and ethnic groups in the capital city abandon all morality in their competition for national resources, and predatory politics subverts national priorities, a development prefigured in *Arrow of God* in Nwodika's move from Umuaro to Okperi, the seat of the colonial regime, to compete for opportunities generated by the administration. In *A Man of the People*, Chief Nanga, a national politician, urges Odili to re-enact Nwodika's part on behalf of the tribe. The tragedy of the post-colonial state is therefore partly traced to colonialism's destruction of traditional normative structures and the concomitant lack of interest in creating viable alternatives.

It is instructive that even in the national novels, Achebe's principles of order are derived not from Western institutions but from the moral universe of the rural novels, namely, the cult of the deity Idemili. Idemili's balance of power with justice contrasts sharply with Chief Nanga's abuse of ministerial power in *A Man of the People* and the president's ruthless drive for absolute power without accountability in *Anthills*. The army's overthrow of the government at the end of these novels is therefore not a solution but a new dimension to the problem, for the army lacks moral authority. Achebe offers a glimpse of an alternative in a symbolic naming ceremony at Beatrice Okoh's flat at the end of *Anthills*. A female baby has just been born. Not only do Beatrice and her friends (a cross-section of the society) ignore family elders, they also give the female child a male name. The name, Amae-chine, which translates as 'may the path never close', expresses Achebe's Igbo culture's dread of anarchy, symbolized in the choking of a derelict homestead by weeds. Their act is self-validating, particularly since, despite her education, Beatrice contemporizes both Idemili and the priestess Chielo of *Things Fall Apart*. The implication, therefore, is that a genuine moral order can be constructed only by the ordinary people retrieving their destiny from anarchic leaders and obsolete customs. This conclusion is consistent with the central role assigned in the novel to members of those social classes, notably women and the urban proletariat, marginalized by colonial and neo-colonial culture. In the task of re-creation, the writer's role is to keep alive the memory of the past and visions of the struggle ahead.

ACHOLONU, Catherine Obianuju (1951-), Nigerian literary critic, playwright, and poet, was born in Orlu, Nigeria and attended secondary schools in Orlu before gaining a master's degree and a Ph.D. from the University of Dusseldorf, Germany. She has taught at Alvan Ikoku College, Owerri since 1978. Inspired by the traditional narratives and poetry of her Igbo people, Acholonu has published both plays and poetry. Although she has written three books of poems for schoolchildren, she is better known for two poetry collections, *Nigeria in the Year 1999* (1985) and *The Spring's Last Drop* (1985), and the plays *Into the Heart of Biafra* (1985), based on the *Nigeria-Biafra war experience, and *Trial of the Beautiful Ones* (1985), which incorporates myths and legends. Another play, *The Deal and Who Is the Head of State* (1986) confirms her desire to address topical issues. Of her critical writing, her most controversial work is an anthropological study entitled *The Igbo Roots of Olaudah Equiano* (1989), in which she claims to have traced the surviving descendants of *Equiano's father. In *Motherism* (1994) she interrogates Western feminism and examines the concept of motherhood in Nigerian cultural affairs.

ACQUAH, Kobena Eyi (1952-), Ghanaian poet, was born in Winneba, in the Central Region of Ghana, and educated at the University of Ghana, Legon and the Ghana Law School. A legal and investment consultant, he also contributes to Ghana's public life in such organizations as the Copyright Board, the W.E.B. Dubois Centre for Pan-African Culture, and the Ghana Book Development Council.

Though some of his short stories and essays have appeared in print, Acquah is best known for his poetry, which has been anthologized, translated, reviewed, dramatized, broadcast, and read to large audiences worldwide. His publications include *The Man Who Died* (1984), *Music for a Dream Dance* (1989), *Rivers Must Flow*, and *No Time for a Masterpiece* (1995).

He dramatizes the nightmare that independence has become for Ghanaians and Africans, as well as the plight of oppressed black people the world over, in poetry influenced by the history, folklore, proverbs, idioms, riddles, and drum language of his people as well as his personal Christian faith. While lamenting the brutalities that go with oppression and insisting that oppressed peoples take their destinies into their own hands, his priestly voice cautions moderation in the quest for justice and equality, and insists on reason and forgiveness, not vengeance. While documenting human suffering, the poetry insists on hope and redemption, not doom.

ADEDEJI, (Alu)Remi Aduke (1937-), Nigerian children's writer, was born in Okemesi in western Nigeria. She gained BA and MA degrees, has taught at the Polytechnic, Ibadan, is a member of the International Board on Books for Young People (IBBY), and is the associate editor for *Bookbird* in Nigeria. She started writing storybooks for African children after discovering that the only books available for pleasure reading for readers between six and thirteen were alien to African culture. Many of her stories are Nigerian folktales in which the tortoise features prominently. Her books range widely in subject and complexity, from *The Fat Woman* (1973), stories about simple life experiences aimed at young children, through a series about a village child named Tunde Ojo and his social world, to *Dear Uncle* (1986), stories about contemporary Nigerian family life intended for older children.

African Child, The (1954) A novel by *Camara Laye, translated from the French (*L'Enfant noir*, 1953), and also published in English as *The Dark Child* (1954). One of francophone Africa's earliest and still most widely read novels, it also achieved renown with its near-immediate English translation. A first-person, semi-autobiographical tale, *The African Child* tells the story of its narrator, who remains nameless almost throughout, from about six to eighteen. Born to a respected family of blacksmiths, the young boy is raised first near the mountainous region of Guinea. He learns his people's traditions, the magic of the forge and of snakes. His youth is idyllic, though the young boy is introspective and bookish. After traditional initiation rites, the growing boy goes to the sea-coast capital Conakry to enrol in French schools and live with his uncle. School is difficult, and causes him to grow distant from his traditions, as he becomes more French in outlook. At the end of the novel, he gets on a plane for still more schooling in France. A gently told coming-of-age story which also details beliefs, stories, and traditions of the Malinke people, *The African Child* has long been popular with African, European, and American audiences. While many

readers have praised its sensitive, lyrical style, others have criticized it for failing to portray or protest at the French colonial presence in Guinea at that time. Still others have suggested that a reading informed by Malinke or Mande sources shows that a middle-ground interpretation is best of all.

African Image, The (1962) A study by Ezekiel (now Es'kia) *Mphahlele. In the first study by a black critic of the presentation of Africans in fiction by Europeans and by white South Africans, Mphahlele addresses, through his consideration of the fiction, the wider and pressing issue (in its time) of the value and implications of Africans pursuing and gaining a 'European' education. The book is widely regarded as opening the serious critical discussion of an emerging African literary tradition and the place of this writing in the educational agendas of African countries. Mphahlele also addresses the issue of the value of *negritude in the context of problems of education in the widest sense facing post-independence African countries.

AFRICAN LANGUAGES AND LITERATURES [See GIKUYU; HAUSA; IGBO; KRIO; MAGHREBI; MALAGASY; NDEBELE; PIDGIN; SHONA; SOTHO, NORTHERN; SOTHO, SOUTHERN; SWAHILI; TSONGA; XHOSA; YORUBA; ZULU]

African Tragedy, An (1928) A novel by R.R.R. *Dhlomo. While it is no masterpiece, this simple, moralistic tale of the disasters that befall urbanized Africans does represent the first time African hardships were depicted in a realistic way. It is the story of Robert Zulu, who is lured into evil ways on the mines. Dhlomo, who worked on the mines, was well equipped to comment on the subject. It is a classic example of mission-inspired literature.

AFRICAN WRITERS SERIES was started by Heinemann Educational Books in London in 1962. The Series Editor for the first 100 titles was Chinua *Achebe, after which he was called Founding Editor. There were very few paperback series in British publishing at that time beyond Penguin and Pan. The use of the Penguin orange for covers of the novels was cheeky but successful and the series became known in Africa as 'the orange series'. Poetry, plays and political autobiography were also included. The writer Edward Blishen said that it did for African literature what Penguin did for him when he was young; introduced him to a new world of writing.

The first Heinemann editor Van Milne got it off to a flying start with two reprints of novels by Achebe and, very soon, a new first novel by the Makerere student *Ngugi wa Thiong'o. Kaunda's autobiography was among the first titles and he was later joined by Odinga Odinga, Nelson Mandela, and

Olusegun Obasanjo. From early on there were anthologies of verse and prose introducing new voices from the intoxicating time of Africa's independence.

Keith Sambrook took over Van Milne's job at Heinemann. Chinua Achebe and he were faced with the problem that there was little previously published work by African writers. The publishing convention was that paperback series provided texts of books originally published in hardback by general publishers. But very few books by Africans had been published by British or American publishers or in English-speaking Africa. Writers from the Caribbean had begun to be published by London publishers such as Andre Deutsch. Parisian publishers had been more enterprising in the 1950s, and translations of Mongo *Beti, Ferdinand *Oyono and *Sembene Ousmane were to become bigger sellers in the Series than they ever were in French.

Chinua Achebe and Keith Sambrook seized the opportunity to encourage new work. The Series became famous because of its active role in encouraging writers with first publication in paperback. They often also issued books in hardback to get them reviewed in London Sundays and weeklies. The market in Africa was almost entirely for educational textbooks. With independence more secondary schools were being built and universities were being founded. The West African Examination Council (WAEC) and the East African Examination Council (EAEC) were taking over from the Cambridge Overseas and actively looked for African writers to prescribe.

Just after the *Nigeria-Biafra war started in 1967 James Currey went to Heinemann with a major reponsibility to edit the Series; he had been running the Three Crowns Series, started by Rex Collings at Oxford University Press, which gave first British publication to Wole *Soyinka and other playwrights and poets. With Achebe's quiet but firm encouragement the African Writers Series included all the very best writing from the continent and was not inhibited over sex, religion and politics, subjects which at that time were considered unsuitable for a school list in Britain. The Lady Chatterley trial had only recently taken place in London. The writing of Ayi Kwei *Armah and Tayeb *Salih was added to the list. The Series, though run by an educational company, was providing a startling revelation to Africans of the full range of their own literary creativity.

Ngugi agreed to take over the editorship from Achebe at No. 100 in 1972 but then realised that the responsibility might interfere with his own creative writing. So the younger editors in the Heinemann African companies began to play a more active role. Aig Higo, Managing Director in Ibadan and himself a poet, Akin Thomas in Ibadan, and Henry Chakava, Simon Gikandi, and Laban Erapu in Nairobi made sure that the Series was truly African. In this triangle

of Ibadan, Nairobi, and London nobody had the veto. A book was accepted if any one of the editors backed it with his own literary judgement and the reports of his team of readers. There was almost total agreement over the choice of novels and collections of short stories. Selection of poetry depended upon the very strong push of individuals; it could become, as with Jack *Mapanje's work in Malawi, the last line of defiance against the censor. Plays depended on a few people who could visualise the plays in production, not just under the old proscenium arch but off the back of trucks, in the open air and in the townships of South Africa out of sight of the police. James Currey's connections with South African writers in exile as well as with writers in the country made books available that could not have appeared in South Africa; David Philip in Cape Town found legal loopholes to enable writers such as Alex *La Guma to evade South African Customs.

This rich outpouring of new writing fed on itself and gave people all over Africa hope of publication. Manuscripts in various states of clarity, even in handwriting, poured into the offices in Ibadan, Nairobi and London. A substantial proportion were sent out for report. If the reports were modestly encouraging they were circulated to the two other offices in the triangle. Most manuscripts had to be turned down but there was an active policy of letting the writers see reports.

The commodity price hike of the late 1970s meant that Nigerian education was awash with oil revenues, Zambia had the benefits of copper sales and Kenya the 'black gold' of coffee, much of it smuggled from Amin's Uganda. Heinemann, under the imaginative chairmanship of Alan Hill, allowed publication to grow as talent emerged. Output peaked at 22 titles in one year and for several years some 15 were published; not many for a whole continent, but unmatched in British and African publishing history. The financial strength of the Series helped. Bessie *Head's A Question of Power was turned down by Gollancz, her original publishers, because she refused to work on it further. Heinemann accepted without requiring a word to be changed; so she set to work to strengthen it. The orange African Writers Series paperback edition got far more reviews than the hardback. Literary critics in London and New York were now looking first to the Series to introduce them to the new writing from Africa.

The Series was riding on a high. There were piles of the orange books in university booksellers. Container loads were floating into Apapa docks. It had, as one teacher said, become 'the most stolen series in Africa'. Something like eighty per cent of the books were sold in Africa, about ten per cent in North America and ten per cent in Britain and the rest of the world. But the Nigerian foreign exchange crashed in April 1982. Sales to Africa disappeared. Debts hung on. The corporate accountants started demanding the decimation of the Series. James Currey went to start up his own imprint in 1984. Keith Sambrook joined him soon afterwards. There were 270 books in the Series including titles by all three African Nobel prize winners, Wole ★Soyinka, Nadine ★Gordimer and Naguib ★Mahfouz.

In the mid-1980s Heinemann had four different owners. Fortunately the Series was allowed to continue, although with a ration of some three new titles each year, with Adewale Maja-Pearce as Series Editor and Abdulrazak ★Gurnah as Series Consultant. Two-thirds of the titles have been put out of print. Without the work of John Watson in building up Heinemann sales in the United States the damage could have been worse. The Series remains the main source of the canon of African literature. M. G. ★Vassanji's The Gunny Sack and Shimmer ★Chinodya's Harvest of Thorns were Commonwealth Prize winners. The poems collected in The Chattering Wagtails of Mikuyu Prison reflect on Jack ★Mapanje's detention without trial in Banda's Malawi. The Seven Solitudes of Lorsa Lopez, translated from French at last introduced ★Sony Labou Tansi to an English audience. And Wangui wa Goro translated ★Ngugi's Matigari from ★Gikuyu.

AFRICAN-AMERICAN LITERATURE

Though the African presence in North America pre-dates the trans-Atlantic slave trade, African-American literature begins with the oral performances with which African slaves relieved, when possible, the physical and psychological horrors of their lives. Written literature did not emerge until the eighteenth century, principally because slaves were forbidden by statute to acquire literacy or any intellectual equipment that might engender a rebellious consciousness of self-worth. Significantly, as Darwin Turner has observed, the first written literature comes from northern and eastern states, where slaves had a modicum of educational opportunity. Earliest examples were in verse: Lucy Terry's 'Bars Fight, August 28, 1746' (1746), describing an Indian attack, and Jupiter Hammon's 'An Evening Thought: Salvation by Christ, with Penitential Cries' (1760). The first critically acclaimed African-American, however, is Phillis ★Wheatley, enslaved to a Boston tailor, whose elegies and devotional lyrics were published as Poems on Various Subjects, Religious and Moral (1773).

Hammon's and Wheatley's predicament illustrates the limitations of writing in bondage and has been paradigmatic of African-American writing ever since. Fully aware of the racial myths justifying slavery, Hammon in his 'Address to Negroes in the State of New York' (1787) exhorts his people to conduct themselves properly. For her part, Wheatley obviously realizes that any criticism of slavery would alienate her master's good will; she appeals instead for a recognition of the humanity of Africans and subtly challenges European colour symbolism in her poem 'On being brought from Africa to America'.

From the late eighteenth century, African-American writing increased from a trickle to a continuous stream. Much of it consisted of real-life accounts of ex-slaves and fugitive slaves supported by the abolitionist movement. Notable examples are Olaudah ★Equiano's The Interesting Narrative of the Life of Olaudah Equiano, or Gustavus Vassa, the African Written by Himself (1789), Frederick Douglass's autobiography, Narrative of the Life of Frederick Douglass, an American Slave (1845), subsequently enlarged and revised, and Martin Robinson Delany's The Condition, Elevation, Emigration, and Destiny of the Colored People of the United States (1852).

In the nineteenth century a succession of novelists and playwrights painfully forged a literary tradition that expressed the dilemma arising from a recognition of their African heritage and their American destiny. Anger, self-assertion, and indictment of historical wrongs intermingled with a desire for acceptance by the dominant white society. The evils of slavery and the problems of miscegenation are centres of interest in William Wells Brown's Clotel; or, the President's Daughter (1853), the first full-length novel by an African-American, and his play The Escape (1858), while Martin Delany's Blake; or, the Huts of America portrays slavery as institutionalized economic plunder. The economic disadvantages of America's racial caste system are foregrounded in Frank Webb's The Garies and Their Friends (1857). Towards the end of the century, Charles Waddell Chestnutt's fiction portrays racial prejudice as a deterministic force blighting African-American lives. Of his novels, The House Behind the Cedars (1900) explores the peculiar problems of 'passing' (the attempt by a near-white mulatto to pass as white) while historically based The Marrow of Tradition (1901) explores the implications of the re-institutionalization of racism after a brief period of progress following the civil war. Between 1899 and 1908, the energetic Baptist minister Sutton Griggs wrote five novels that began by advocating 'race patriotism' and separatism (Imperium in Imperio, 1899) and ended with a search for racial reconciliation (Pointing the Way, 1908). Ellen Watkins Harper achieved considerable success with her abolitionist poetry and her novel on the caste question, Iola LeRoy (1892). One of the most prominent writers of the period was the poet and novelist Paul Laurence Dunbar, best known for his comic dialect verse, romantic themes, and artistic exploitation of his black heritage. The self-denigration in many of Dunbar's works contrasts sharply with his nationalist tributes to African-American heroes ('Frederick Douglass') and his celebration of Ethiopia ('Ode to Ethiopia'), which anticipates mid-twentieth century *negritude poetry. Despite publishing his first book of poetry in 1892, Dunbar did not gain national attention until recommended by William Dean Howell, in the introduction to *Lyrics of Lowly Life* (1896), as the first 'Negro' to 'evince innate artistic talent'.

The last decade of the nineteenth century and the early decades of the twentieth witnessed the emergence of an articulate African-American middle class and intelligentsia, a massive African-American migration to the cities, and a politically activist leadership under W.E.B. DuBois and James Weldon Johnson. The struggle for racial justice was pursued on both political and literary fronts. DuBois and Johnson were also writers, and Johnson reveals in his autobiography (*Along this Way*, 1933) that his work was influenced by his 'realization of the importance of the American Negro's cultural background and his creative folk-art, and … the superstructure of conscious art that might be reared upon them'. This new consciousness was a major contributor to what became known as the Harlem Renaissance of the 1920s and 30s.

With its huge African-American population and proximity to the cultural centres of New York City, Harlem in upper Manhattan attracted many intellectuals and artists from various parts of America, Africa, and the African diaspora and developed into a cosmopolitan community of composers, musicians, essayists, novelists, playwrights, and poets. Members of the Harlem School heeded Alain Locke's call for 'the New Negro' (*The New Negro*, 1925) to become a 'collaborator and participant in American civilization'. Harlem culture was characterized by pride in blackness and the African heritage. Among its notable literary achievements were Countee Cullen's *Color* (1925) and *The Ballad of the Brown Girl* (1927), Jean Toomer's *Cane* (1923), Langston Hughes's *The Weary Blues* (1926), and Claude McKay's *Home to Harlem* (1928) and *Banjo* (1929), with the work of James Baldwin coming later.

The Harlem phenomenon was also part of a global climate of anti-imperialist agitation in the colonized world and western youth's rebellion against establishment values. This largely explains its amalgam of black nationalism, rebellion without ideological foundation, and negritude-style adoption of western stereotypes of black culture as exotic. Robert A. Bone's observation that the writers were 'more interested in interpreting Negro culture than in pleading the cause of racial justice', making Harlem 'a place of love and laughter, not of struggle and oppression', is an unintended indictment. The protagonists of such novels as McKay's *Home to Harlem* and *Banjo* are rebels rather than revolutionaries, though Langston Hughes's *Not Without Laughter* (1930) shows that joy and laughter are compatible with sociopolitical responsibility.

African-American writing was sharply refocused on urgent issues of racial oppression by the American stock market crash of 1929 and the ensuing global economic depression. The mood of the times is eloquently captured in Arna Bontemps' *Black Thunder* (1936), which deals with a slave rebellion in Virginia, while Zora Neale Hurston's *Moses, Man of the Mountain* (1939) satirically explores the African-American experience through analogy with the biblical Jews' experience in Egypt. Among the greatest works of the period is Richard Wright's *Native Son* (1940), a brutally realistic novel that links the violence in African-American life to the psychological deformity inflicted on African Americans by racial oppression. Ralph Ellison's *Invisible Man* (1952) has become a classic of modern American literature for its treatment of similar themes in the context of the quest for identity and acceptance in a society that resolutely denies African-American reality. This period also witnessed the first award of the Pulitzer Prize to an African-American poet, Gwendolyn Brooks, for her volume *Annie Allen* (1949). James Baldwin explored topical psychological and social issues such as homosexuality and father-son relations (*Go Tell It on the Mountain*, 1953, *Giovanni's Room*, 1956, and *Another Country*, 1962) as well as race relations (*The Fire Next Time*, 1963). Lorraine Hansberry's *A Raisin in the Sun* (1959), a portrayal of a black family's struggle against ghetto existence, was enthusiastically received by establishment critics, although the play was denounced by many black critics as politically naive.

The civil rights and *Black Consciousness movements of the 1960s and 70s had their literary complement in the search for a black aesthetic. Ideologically, the black aesthetic was closer to Malcolm X (*Autobiography of Malcolm X*, 1965) and Eldridge Cleaver (*Soul on Ice*, 1967) than to the mainstream politics of Martin Luther King, Jr. Among the vanguard of the movement for a black aesthetic was the playwright and essayist Imamu Amiri Baraka (formerly LeRoi Jones), whose play *Dutchman* (1964) represents his idea of the role of the black artist in America, which is 'to aid in the destruction of America as he knows it'. Less stridently, Toni Morrison's *The Bluest Eye* (1970) explores the personality-warping impact of racial denigration through the heroine, Pecola, who earnestly prays for blue eyes, a very appropriate subject for the era when Euro-American chemical factories produced skin-whitening creams and hair-straightening shampoos for Africans. Alex Haley's highly successful *Roots* (1976) integrates fiction, racial history, and genealogical lore into a powerful exploration of the 'roots' of the African-American predicament in America. Other important novelists include Ishmael Reed, Gloria Naylor (*The Women of Brewster Place*, 1982), and John Edgar Wideman, whose *Philadelphia Fire* (1990) probes the depths of black ghetto life. Toni Cade Bambara, who was active in civil rights and community development programmes, edited *The Black*

Woman (1970), a literary-political anthology of poems, stories, and essays. Her novels *The Salt Eaters* (1980) and *If Blessing Comes* (1987) address both racial and black women's problems from a realization 'that [writing] was a perfectly legitimate way to participate in struggle'. In drama, Charles Fuller (*A Soldier's Play*, 1982) and August Wilson (*Fences*, 1987) mediate African-American reality to a broader audience, as do Ntozake Shange's books, for example *For Colored Girls Who Have Considered Suicide, When the Rainbow Is Enuf* (1975), a long poem, and *Sassafras, Cypress, and Indigo* (1982), a novel.

African-American women writers have been particularly successful since the 1970s, winning wide critical and commercial success. The crowning point has been Toni Morrison's winning the 1993 Nobel Prize for literature. From their experience of treble victimization (as blacks, women, and black women), they bring invaluable female perspectives to their portrayal of significant racial and human experience. However, their success owes as much to artistic merit as to aggressive promotion by publishers and establishment critics, to whom gender is both commercially profitable and ideologically serviceable for smothering uncomfortable questions of race relations.

Contemporary black women's writing stresses gender contradictions, rape (often incestuous), and other forms of male-on-female violence. Maya Angelou's nationalistic *I Know Why the Caged Bird Sings* (1969), Toni Morrison's *The Bluest Eye*, and Alice Walker's *The Color Purple* (1982) all portray female protagonists who are raped by male villains. This is only one aspect of African-American women's writing, however. Walker has revealed that her 'attachment to William Faulkner was rudely broken' by discovery of his racism, and her *The Third Life of Grange Copeland* (1970) probes the possibilities of heterosexual harmony. Toni Cade Bambara declared that she worked 'to celebrate struggle, to applaud the tradition of struggle in our community'. Like Richard Wright's *Native Son* and *Lawd Today* (1963), black women's writing achieves psychological complexity by exploring the violence in the larger contexts of American culture and race relations.

The psychological complexity is often ignored in criticism, however. While western critics concentrate voyeuristically on the formulaic ingredients of violence and sexual aberrations, black feminist critics eagerly embrace the role of insiders exposing unsavoury family truths. Black feminist criticism often uncritically adopts western anthropological theories of gender relationships in black cultures. Rephrasing a thesis first formulated by the International Monetary Fund, it frequently substitutes patriarchy for colonialism and neo-colonialism as the root of women's dehumanization in black societies.

Black feminist criticism is also better understood alongside another fairly recent development in African-American writing, minority discourse, as a product of the sweeping transformation of academic discourse under post-modernism. Though ostensibly contesting western ethnocentrism, minority discourse not only adopts Eurocentric reference points but also encourages profligate theorizing for its own sake. Some black feminist essays betray similar self-contradictions. Polemical criticism aside, however, African-American women scholars have made enormous contributions to the study of African-American culture.

African-American literature emerged as a literature of self-assertion and self-definition, and has grown by negotiating the cultural tastes and vested interests within the dominant Euro-American culture. These conditions have not changed fundamentally over the centuries.

AFRICAN-BRITISH LITERATURE Although African-British writing began in the eighteenth century with autobiographies of freed slaves, imaginative literature among Britons of African ancestry and Africans resident in Britain has blossomed since the mid-twentieth century. Writing by Afro-Caribbean Britons belongs more properly with West Indian-British literature, exceptions being rap and dub poetry, which can be shown to be based on the African oral tradition.

Best known among the slave narratives published in Britain are Briton Hammon's *A Narrative of the Uncommon Sufferings, and Surprizing Deliverance of Briton Hammon, A Negro Man* (1760), Ukawsaw Gronniosaw's *A Narrative of the Most Remarkable Particulars in the Life of James Albert Ukawsaw Gronniosaw, an African Prince, as Related by Himself* (ca.1770), Ignatius ★Sancho's *Letters of the Late Ignatius Sancho, an African* (1782), Ottobah ★Cugoano's *Thoughts and Sentiments on the Evil and Wicked Traffic of the Slavery and Commerce of the Human Species* (1787), and Olaudah ★Equiano's *The ★Interesting Narrative of the Life of Olaudah Equiano, or Gustavus Vassa, the African, Written by Himself* (1789). The writers were not all male: among female writers was Mary Prince, who published her autobiography in 1831. A version edited by Thomas Pringle is entitled *The History of Mary Prince, a West Indian Slave*. Next came Mary Seacole's *Wonderful Adventures of Mrs. Seacole in Many Lands* (1857). Towards the close of the century came Peter Thomas Stanford's *From Bondage to Liberty: Being the life story of the Rev. P.T. Stanford* (1889).

These accounts cover various experiences, from the dehumanizing cruelty of slavery and the hypocrisy of Christianity-professing enslavers to the predicament of being black in eighteenth- and nineteenth-century Britain, which was rapidly building prosperity on black people's labour and resources. African-born writers like Gronniosaw, Equiano, and Cugoano reveal some childhood memories of their origins. Nationalistic and abolitionist consciousness was also strongest among them, and their writing was part of the campaign against the enslavement of Africans. Conversely, the 'wonderful adventures' of Mary Seacole, born (1805) to a Scottish army officer and a free Jamaican black woman, resound with patriotic sentiments appropriate to her privileged life sheltered from the common lot of black people in Britain.

These narratives assume greater importance in the larger context of those historical periods, for even in the so-called Age of Enlightenment people could seriously ask whether blacks were humans. In John Newton's memorable image, slaves bound for America in slave ships were packed 'like books upon a shelf'. The significance of this transformation from shelved books into creators of books was not lost on the autobiographers: titles of their narratives proudly proclaimed that the author was 'an African', 'a Negro', or 'an African slave', with some pointedly adding that the account was 'written by himself'.

These narratives are also significant as precursors of the self-affirmation themes that agitated African literature in the nationalistic 1950s and 60s. The ex-slaves insistently redefine the African self through affirmation rather than negation: as *black* rather than *non-white*, *African* rather than *non-European*. They challenge the racial myths used to rationalize slavery and, later, colonialism. Long before Chinua *Achebe and his followers, Equiano subverts Europe's racialist colour symbolism by observing that in his own *Igbo culture it is the European 'albino' complexion that is considered abnormal. Furthermore, not only does Equiano's veneration of his own mother anticipate the 'Mother Africa' trope in mid-twentieth-century *negritude writing, it also reflects the honoured status of mothers and the female principle in many African cultures, contrary to the revisionist anthropological accounts in gender studies programmes.

Among Afro-British writers of the present age, the best known are probably Buchi *Emecheta and Ben *Okri, while Gabriel Gbadamosi is attracting increasing critical attention. A rare case is Sierra Leone-born Ernest Marke, who arrived in Britain as a stowaway in 1917 and for years supported himself through menial jobs in various English cities before producing his only book, the autobiographical *In Troubled Waters* (1975), which offers a rare glimpse into mid-twentieth century Afro-British life.

An Igbo born in Lagos in 1944, Buchi Emecheta followed her husband to Britain in 1962. In 1974, she gained a degree in sociology from the University of London. She has written more than a dozen novels and children's stories. Often drawing upon personal experience, she strives to interpret and redefine women's social roles by portraying heroines struggling for self-actualization against negating forces of male and racial prejudice, sometimes in the broader context of Europe's oppression of Africa. Her writing has been strongly influenced by her academic training. By her own account, her training in sociology inclines her to approach writing in terms of developing a concept: such 'concepts' include cultural clash in *Second Class Citizen* (1974), population control and polygamy in *The Joys of Motherhood* (1979), slavery in *The Slave Girl* (1977), the predicament of Caribbean immigrants in Britain in *Gwendolen* (1989), the importance of the female principle in *The Rape of Shavi* (1983) and *Destination Biafra* (1982). This 'sociological' approach encourages novels with oversimplification of complex issues and excessive dependence on European colonialist anthropological accounts of African cultures. However, *Kehinde* (1996) seriously explores the eponymous heroine's personality development in the context of contradictions between European-style abortion on demand and African beliefs in reincarnation.

Nigerian-born Ben Okri emigrated to Britain in 1978 for university education. His fiction includes the novels *Flowers and Shadows* (1980), *The Landscapes Within* (1981), *The *Famished Road* (1991), which won the Booker Prize, and a collection of short stories, *Incidents at the Shrine*. In the tradition of post-independence critical realism, *Flowers and Shadows* and *The Landscapes Within* explore the crises of nation-building in modern Nigeria. With *The Famished Road*, Okri enters the realm of mythic reconstruction of the vicious cycles of progress and retrogress that have blighted Africa's neo-colonial history. The controlling image here is the *abiku*, the spirit child who in West African myth goes through cyclic birth and death to torment the parents. Okri thus follows a long tradition also exploited by Achebe in *Things Fall Apart* and Cyprian *Ekwensi in *Iska* (1966). But the immediate literary influence is Wole *Soyinka's treatment of the recurrence of evil in such poems as 'Abiku', 'Death in the Dawn', and 'Idanre'.

Cambridge-educated Gabriel Gbadamosi, born of Irish/Nigerian parents in 1961, writes poetry and plays. Much of his writing has been done with the aid of fellowships and Arts Council grants, including a Winston Churchill Fellowship that took him to West Africa to observe indigenous drama. Gbadamosi's poems have appeared in *The New Poetry 1968-1988* (1988) and *The Heinemann Book of African Poetry in English* (1990). Among his plays, some produced but not yet published, are *No Blacks, No Irish*; *Shango*; *Abolition*; *Eshu's Faust*, and a television play, *Friday's Daughter*. His work, notably *Eshu's Faust*, experiments with a synthesis of western and African dramaturgy. First produced in 1992 at King's College, Cambridge, *Eshu's Faust* attempts to reinterpret the European Faust archetype through Eshu, the Yoruba trickster god. Though the experiment was unsuccessful, its effects depending more on lively Yoruba drumming and dance performed by a professional troupe than on the development of dramatic conflict, it revealed the possibilities of such multicultural experiments.

Many Afro-British writers are academics. Nigerian-born E.B. Asibong has published a slim volume of poetry, *Infolding* (1979), suitable for younger readers. Abdulrazak Gurnah, a Tanzanian born in Zanzibar, teaches literature at the University of Kent, Canterbury. He is more prolific, with five novels: *Memory of Departure* (1987), *Pilgrims Way* (1988), *Dottie* (1990), *Paradise* (1994), and *Admiring Silence* (1996), which reworks the themes of cultural conflict and problems of development through an anti-realist text revealed by a self-conscious, self-subverting narrator.

Worsening race relations and bleak economic prospects led to the emergence of anti-establishment poetry, often designated as rap and dub poetry, among inner-city Afro-Britons in the 1970s and 80s. Structurally, the poetry is extensively conditioned by the psychodynamics of the spoken word and live performance. While light-hearted word games follow the staccato rhythms of rap, more serious examples are characterized by rigorously controlled rhythmic repetition, syntactic balancing, antithesis, and other rhetorical devices adapted from oral poetry.

Like the slave narratives, much of this writing was initially self-published, usually in slim volumes like Ghanaian-born Rauf Adu's thirty-one page *The Rise and Rise of General Gun* (1981). More find outlet in such anthologies as *News for Babylon* (ed. James Berry, 1984), *Angels of Fire: An Anthology of Radical Poetry in the '80s* (eds Sylvia Paskin, Jam Ramsay, Jeremy Silver), *Apples and Snakes* (1984), and David Orme and Martin Glynn's *Doin Mi Ed In: Rap Poems* (1993). However, writers like Milton Smalling, John Agard, Linton Kwesi Johnson (who coined the expression 'dub poetry'), and Benjamin Zephaniah have had their work accepted by established publishers. Johnson chose to start his own recording label (LKJ Records) in 1981 to free himself from the asphyxiating hold of major recording companies.

First-generation dub and rap poetry expresses the anger and defiance of Afro-Britons in combative verse that recalls the slave narratives, mid-twentieth century negritude poetry, South African resistance poetry of the 1970s and 80s, and Nigerian Afro-beat as exemplified by the lyrics of Fela Anikulapo-Kuti since the 1970s. Such militancy is evident in such titles as Milton Smalling's *Living on the Edge of Paradise* (1982), *Fighting Spirit* (1983), and *The Battlefield* (1986); Linton Kwesi Johnson's *Inglan is a Bitch* (1980), and John Agard's *Mangoes & Bullets: Selected and New Poems 1972-84* (1985) and *Laughter Is an Egg* (1990). Readers acquainted with negritude poetry will recognize the black-affirmation theme of Lemn Sissay's 'Airmail to a Dictionary' in Orme and Glynn's anthology, with its

deliberate accumulation of positive attributes for the word 'black'.

Perceived improvements in inner-city conditions, the emergence of a black middle class, and black representation in government have mellowed radical revolutionary fervour. For example, whereas an early poem by Linton Kwesi Johnson, 'Di Great Insohreckshan', deals with the 1981 riots by Afro-Caribbean Britons, the more recent 'Mi Revalueshanary Fren' focuses on eastern Europe. Similarly, with Zephaniah's growing popularity, his incorporation into the middle class is evident in the movement from *The Dread Affair* (1984) and *Job Rocking* (in *Black Plays: Two*, ed. Yvonne Brewster, 1989) to *Talking Turkeys* (1994), a cultivated protest in which the Rastafari sentiment of 'peace and love' governs the poet's ironical critiques of a broad spectrum of issues, including multiculturalism ('Multi-Culture'), the dinosaur craze ('Drivosaurus Rex'), the environment ('Solidarity'), and fox hunting ('A Killer Lies'). Martin Glynn's 'Machoman' (in Orme and Glynn's anthology) comments on the pervasive culture of violence in western society. In John Agard and Grace Nichols' *A Caribbean Dozen: Poems from Caribbean Poets* (1994), which includes five Afro-British poets, and in Nichols' own *Give Yourself a Hug* (1994), protest is subordinated to celebrations of Caribbean life. These poems fall outside the dub and rap tradition.

One conclusion might be that despite some significant achievements, Afro-British writing is hardly free from the constraints under which the eighteenth-century slave narratives emerged. While academic and other university-educated writers broadly reflect the cultural theories that prevail at any given time in Western academia, inner-city writing begins as anti-establishment expression of the plight of ethnic minorities who constitute Great Britain's third-world underbelly, but develops towards conventional protest as successful practitioners become incorporated into the dominant culture. Without a fundamental change in the social context of the literature, this pattern is set to continue into the foreseeable future.

AFRICAN-CANADIAN LITERATURE African and Afro-Canadian literature in English evolved from the same event, namely the epochal collision between European and African civilizations, a cataclysm that precipitated the enslavement of millions of Africans over four centuries, their dispersal to Europe and North and South America, and the colonial (and post-colonial) exploitation of their descendants. This heritage of strife, struggle, and survival has left its imprint in both African and Afro-Canadian literatures, most indelibly in their intense interest in recovering histories and in their privileging of the mode of documentary realism. Even more significantly, both literatures bear the resonant influence of Pidgin or Africanized

Englishes – that is, the Creole discourses arising from the complex Babel of tongues engendered by the slave trade and the colonial era. In both contexts, the British lexicon was annexed to African grammatical forms and speech patterns. Afro-Canadian writer Marlene Nourbese Philip describes this transatlantic process and its importance in the remarkable introduction to her book *She Tries Her Tongue, Her Silence Softly Breaks* (1989) as a rupture in the 'traditional' grammar, syntax, and literary meaning of English that explains the inherent creative tension between the written and the oral that animates all African literatures.

Yet African and Afro-Canadian literature share more than blood, sentiment, and the effort to naturalize an imposed language; they also share *ur*-texts written in the eighteenth century by two religious leaders who had escaped slavery in America, namely Baptist David George and Methodist Boston King. Along with 3,500 fellow black loyalists who rallied to the crown during the American Revolution, both men were settled, following the American victory, in Nova Scotia in 1783. Nine years later, having failed to receive adequate allotments of land and provisions, they voyaged, along with 1,188 other disenchanted black 'Nova Scotians', to Sierra Leone. George's dictated memoir, *An Account of the Life of Mr. David George, from Sierra Leone in Africa...* (1793), recounts his spiritual strivings in three lands and on two continents and anatomizes and excoriates the Sadean horrors of the 'peculiar institution'. King's autobiographical article, 'Memoirs of the Life of Boston King, a Black Preacher, Written by Himself during His Residence at Kingswood School' (1798), surveys similar territory. Both men's works echo the themes of the first Anglo-African texts, namely *Letters* (1782) by Ignatius ★Sancho, *Thoughts and Sentiments on the Evil of Slavery* (1787) by Ottobah ★Cugoano, and the *Interesting Narrative* (1789) by Olaudah ★Equiano.

Though African and Afro-Canadian literature issue from a common matrix of concerns, they have matured independently of one another, for Canada's anti-black immigration laws prohibited entry for Africans (and other blacks), thus disrupting any effective transoceanic contact until 1967, when the last racial restrictions were abolished. Nevertheless, Afro-Canadians did not forego their African inheritance during the decades of disconnection, for black Christian denominations titled themselves pointedly 'African Baptist', or 'African Methodist Episcopal', or 'African Orthodox'. In the 1920s, Afro-Canadians in Montreal, Toronto, and Cape Breton exalted the Harlem-centred Universal Negro Improvement Association of Jamaican racialist Marcus Garvey, whose slogan, 'Africa for the Africans', and self-styled provisional African government-in-exile manifested his movement's implacably black nationalist and pan-Africanist orientation.

Pan-Africanism, the idea or advocacy of the catholic solidarity and spiritual union of peoples of black African descent, remains a potent ideology in Afro-Canadian literature, surviving particularly in the black nationalist ideal of 'Afrocentrism', that is, the notion that the cultural, philosophical, and religious education of people of black African descent must coalesce around their African 'essence'. A revelatory source of pan-Africanist/black nationalist thought is Algerian psychologist and black liberation theorist Frantz Fanon. His books *Peau noire, masques blancs* (1952; *Black Skin, White Masks*, 1967) and *Les Damnés de la terre* (1961; *The Wretched of the Earth*, 1963) are veritable bibles for many African and Afro-Canadian writers. Fanon's influence colours writings by Austin Clarke, whose essay *Public Enemies: Police Violence and Black Youth* (1992) accents black antipathy for white Canadians' 'polite' racism, while his selection of short fiction *Nine Men Who Laughed* (1986) regards immigrants as pseudo-slaves. Poet Dionne Brand attacks neo-colonialism in several texts, notably *Primitive Offensive* (1982), *Chronicles of the Hostile Sun* (1984), which deals with the October 1983 US-led invasion of Grenada, and *No Language Is Neutral* (1990), which was nominated for the 1990 Governor-General's Award for poetry. *Comment faire l'amour avec un nègre sans se fatiguer* (1985; *How to Make Love to a Negro*, 1987), by Haitian-born Dany Laferrière, explores inter-racial sex with language that seems to evoke Fanon. Pan-Africanism appears in the race-conscious poetry of Maxine Tynes in her book *Borrowed Beauty* (1987).

Pan-Africanism takes religious form in Afro-Canadian literature in three ways: the espousal of an anti-Occident Islam (as in Laferrière's *Comment faire l'amour avec un nègre sans se fatiguer*), the invocation of traditional African deities (as in writings by Brand and Nourbese Philip), and the espousal of Rastafarianism, the Jamaica-originated faith that considers the late Haile Selassie I of Ethiopia as the messiah and Africa as the Promised Land (as in the works of some dub or oral-performance poets). In contrast, Frederick Ward, a Bahà'ì, insists upon the spiritual oneness of humanity in his novels *Riverlisp* (1974), *Nobody Called Me Mine* (1977), and *A Room Full of Balloons* (1981).

Africa itself has inspired or informed a host of Afro-Canadian works. In her darkly satiric novel *Looking for Livingstone: An Odyssey of Silence* (1991), Nourbese Philip interrogates the ethnocentric assumptions of European imperialism. Fantasy novelist Charles R. Saunders details the adventures of Imaro, his African hero of Herculean strength, in three popular works: *Imaro* (1981), *Imaro II: The Quest for Cush* (1984), and *Imaro III: The Trial of Bohu* (1985). In her play *Afrika Solo* (1990) playwright Djanet Sears dramatizes her persona's simultaneous discovery of Africa and of self. The main setting of *Some Great Thing*

(1992), a comic novel by Lawrence Hill, is Winnipeg, but Cameroon, whose population is mainly black and francophone, appears as the instructive racial and linguistic opposite of a hate-prone Canada.

The single black African writer to excavate Afro-Canadian history, albeit obliquely, is Sierra Leone's Syl *Cheney-Coker. His magical realist novel The *Last Harmattan of Alusine Dunbar (1990) relates in part the landing of black loyalist pioneers at the mythical village of Malagueta (a Sierra Leonian version of Colombian writer Gabriel García Márquez's Macondo), and their efforts to build a nation. The same motif also colours Cheney-Coker's Concerto for an Exile (1973), in which Nova Scotia becomes a descriptor of madness.

If African writers have seldom felt compelled to imagine Afro-Canadian history, they have assisted, nonetheless, the current efflorescence of Afro-Canadian literature. For example, the journal Black Images (1972-4), published in Toronto, was founded in part by Ghanaian Jojo Chintoh. South African native Harold Head edited the anthology of African-Canadian literature Canada in Us Now (1976), which he introduces as a spiritual return to a symbiosis of artist and community.

Several Africans, though perhaps only briefly resident in Canada, buttress anthologies and bibliographies of Afro-Canadian writers. Kenyan F.E.M.K. Senkoro has published a few sparse lyrics in English; Nigerian (Biafran) author Samuel Udochukwu Ifejika's novel The New Religion (1973) denounces materialism and greed in post-civil war Nigeria. Two South Africans are especially important. Poet Arthur *Nortje, in his posthumously published Dead Roots (1973), offers twenty sharply metaphorical poems treating his time in Canada, sketching a bleak, Waste Land-sterile portrait of Toronto in 'Quiet desperation'. Rozena Maart won the prestigious Journey Prize in 1992 for the best short story published in a Canadian literary journal for her story 'No Rosa, No District Six' (Fireweed 32, 1991). Ghanaian-Jamaican poet Kwame Dawes, whose book of poems Progeny of Air (1994) won the Forward Poetry Prize for best first collection, also resided briefly in Canada.

Among African writers who have made Canada their home, three have attracted international attention. Zimbabwean-Malawian Paul Tiyambe *Zeleza has published two collections of fiction, the highly acclaimed *Night of Darkness (1976) and The Joys of Exile (1994), and a starkly written novel, Smouldering Charcoal (1992), reminiscent of the social-realist style of Afro-American author Richard Wright. South African native and African National Congress representative Archie Crail was a Governor-General's Award nominee in 1992 for his short-story selection The Bonus Deal (1992). Nigerian Molara *Ogundipe-Leslie, a highly respected academic and poet, is the author of Sew the Old Days and Other Poems (1985), a

milestone in Anglo-African women's poetry.

Other African-born Afro-Canadian writers of note include Kenyan Jane Tapsubei Creider, author of The Shrunken Dream (1992), a novel; Zimbabwean Yvonne *Vera, whose first book was the story collection Why Don't You Carve Other Animals? (1992); and South Africans Dee September, the author of a chapbook of poems, Making Waves (1979), Nonqaba ka Msimang, whose short story 'Lady in Waiting' won a prize in a competition sponsored by the Swedish International Development Agency in 1985, and Kwanza Msingwana, whose stories appear (with others by Nancy Chong and Martha Kofie) in Only Mountains Never Meet (1993).

Non-black African writers have also propelled the growth of Afro-Canadian literature. The London-born, partly South African-educated South Asian writer Réshard Gool (pseud. Ved Devajee) autopsied South African life in his novels Price of Admission (1970), Nemesis Casket (1979), and Cape Town Coolie (1990). South African-South Asian Farida *Karodia has published three works of fiction, *Daughters of the Twilight (1986), Coming Home and Other Stories (1988), and A Shattering of Silence (1993), that explore South African or Mozambican situations. Kenyan-South Asian M.G. *Vassanji chronicles East Indian-East African life in his critically popular works The *Gunny Sack (1989), No New Land (1991), Uhuru Street: Short Stories (1992), and The *Book of Secrets (1994). Zimbabwean-Chinese artist Laiwan comments on her African identity in her visuals and writing in distance of distinct vision (1992). South African-South Asian Bridglal Pachai, a historian, tells of his quest for freedom and fulfilment in South Africa and Nova Scotia, thus reversing, at least geographically, the odyssey of George and King, in his memoir, My Africa, My Canada (1989).

African and Afro-Canadian literature share similar histories, interests, philosophies, and even, on occasion, writers. Certainly native African participation has added weight, stature, and lustre to Afro-Canadian literature. Yet African writers are but slightly represented in Afro-Canadian anthologies. The first such collection, One Out of Many: A Collection of Writings by 21 Black Women in Ontario (1975), edited by Liz Cromwell, lists one African writer. Harold Head's Canada in Us Now presents three African writers out of its twenty contributors. Lorris Elliott's anthology Other Voices: Writings by Blacks in Canada (1985) numbers one African writer among its forty-two contributors. Ann Wallace offers one African writer in her selection Daughters of the Sun, Women of the Moon: Poetry by Black Canadian Women (1990). Ayanna Black includes two African writers out of the fifteen gathered in Voices: Canadian Writers of African Descent (1992) and six out of twenty in her Fiery Spirits: Canadian Writers of African Descent (1994). (Unfortunately, sketchy bibliographies and skimpy biographies mar all of the aforementioned collections.) Work by George and King appears in *Fire on the Water: An Anthology of Black Nova Scotian Writing*, 2 vols. (1991-2), edited by George Elliott Clarke. *Prism International*, a journal, juxtaposes works by Syl Cheney-Coker, Kofi ★Awoonor of Ghana, and Niyi ★Osundare of Nigeria with works by Brand, Nourbese Philip, and Claire Harris in a special issue linking West African and Afro-Canadian writers (22.4, 1984). Among bibliographies, Lisette Boily's 'Contemporary Canadian First Nations Writers and Writers of Colour: A Working Bibliography' (*West Coast Line* 28.1-2, 1994) is the most comprehensive. Lorris Elliott's *Bibliography of Literary Writings by Blacks in Canada* (1986) and *Literary Writings by Blacks in Canada: A Preliminary Survey* (1988), though inaccurate and outdated, are useful preliminary research guides for Afro-Canadian literature. In terms of general historical material, James W. St. G. Walker's typescript paper, 'African Canadians: The Peoples of Canada: An Encyclopedia for the Country' (1993) provides a readable digest of Afro-Canadian experience and its African connections.

AFRICAN-CARIBBEAN LITERATURE Since the population of the Caribbean is mainly of African descent, the cultural links between the African continent and the Caribbean archipelago, including the northern coast of South America, are very strong, various, and complex. But three important facts must frame the study of connections between Africa and the Caribbean: that slavery and colonialism systematically attacked African cultural identity over hundreds of years, even to the point of recruiting people of African ancestry who had internalized rejection of Africa; that distance and separation cause cultural changes even without any sustained onslaught on original cultural identity; and that the Caribbean is a genuinely multicultural space in which syncretism and sheer inventiveness reconstitute all cultural elements. But African identity and culture form the sustaining underground that gave the poorest and most dispossessed African majority in the Caribbean strength to resist and to survive slavery, colonialism, racism, and poverty. However, in a 1966 essay, the Barbadian writer George Lamming could confidently say that the concept of Africa had not yet permeated the West Indian consciousness, by which he meant the intellectual West Indian consciousness. He did see clearly Africa's centrality in the West Indian literary imagination. Lamming's essay is very important in considering African-Caribbean literary connections: in it he explores the ambiguities towards and attachments to Africa in Caribbean literary texts by Vera Bell, Eric Roach, and Derek Walcott. He notes that even white and Indo-Caribbean writers such as Geoffrey Drayton, Samuel Selvon, and V.S. Naipaul can include explicit or implicit reference to Africa, since the model of resistance and the emphasis on the poor or the peasantry in Caribbean literature derives from the African example. Lamming dates anglophone Caribbean literature from the riots of 1937, which expressed a political response to old grievances and influenced the first generation of Caribbean writers. Lamming's point, then, is that in many ways Caribbean literature grew up focused on decolonization and the ending of a grossly inequitable society in which African identity too often meant disenfranchisement and poverty. In many ways, then, Caribbean literature is an African-centred literature.

Written texts are only, of course, one kind of Caribbean verbal artistry, and they are nurtured and informed by other kinds of cultural activity. African elements in Caribbean culture have by now, more than thirty years after Lamming wrote his essay, been examined extensively. Because of the work of linguists who have painstakingly tracked the survival of African words and phrases in Caribbean cultures, we know that Caribbean creoles are languages formed by the creative amalgamation of English or French or Spanish or Dutch (or more than one of these) with African languages (and, in the case of Trinidad and Guyana, Indian words as well). A long battle, now virtually won, between those who thought of Creole as 'dialect' or 'bad' English and those who saw it as the full and legitimate expression of a people's history, situates Caribbean language forms politically. It remains to ensure that creoles are standardized and analysed so that differences in facility can be understood and codes established not only for the formal educational system but also for writers, who have had to invent their own orthography and who will creatively renew creoles by working both within and against the conventions. There is a great deal of justified pride in the discovery that Caribbean creoles, so central to oral and written literatures, were built out of a long-treasured submerged connection with Africa as well as an enforced and evident connection with Europe. Language remains a great source of African connection for Caribbean writers: Merle Collins, in the preface to her novel *Angel* (1987), acknowledges as helpful a doctoral dissertation on African language influences on Creole languages.

Africa also remained in the songs, dances, and symbolic languages of such cults as the Shango cults of Trinidad or the relatively recent Rastafarian religion and culture, which began in Jamaica, as well as in the survivals of African religions such as obeah, the cults celebrating African gods, and *voudou* in Haiti. Original African religions were driven underground and fragmented, very often by the planters' practice of separating people of similar language and culture in order to discourage communication in their first languages. Opinions differ about possible concentrations of people of one nation or language, but many people point to a significant Ashanti/Coromantee culture in Jamaica, a Yoruba culture in Trinidad, and an Igbo culture in Barbados, though people from many of the West African coastal and inland areas were brought to the Caribbean during slavery. With the slaves came not only language and religion but also storytelling traditions such as the Anancy tales of the Akan people, known in the Caribbean often as 'Nancy stories' and retold in demotic English to be appropriate for the conditions that faced peoples of African descent during enslavement and colonialism in the so-called New World. Andrew Salkey's *Anancy's Score* (1973) retells the old stories. Mythological figures such as the West African Watermaid reappear in Caribbean folktales, which, like their West African equivalents, often have a ritualistic opening and closing exchange between storyteller and audience. Africa also remained in the rhythms of calypso and reggae and in music's primacy as an art form. Even language, in African cultures, is music, just as the drum became language: in the Caribbean, musical talent fuses with language talent constantly. ★Orature has always been the primary verbal tradition of African culture, a tradition to which the Caribbean has remained very largely true. African rhythms and syncopation predominate in Caribbean performance poetry. The tradition of calypso clearly owes a good deal to African satirical songmaking and, according to such historians of calypso as Gordon Rohlehr and Hollis Liverpool (the Mighty Chalkdust), can be seen to have come into being in Trinidad solely through the agency of African-Caribbean people who resisted colonialism and sustained their links with their ancestral past. Though calypso is no longer an exclusively Trinidadian form, the source of calypso lies in the urban yards of Port of Spain and the *jamette* culture of the poor outsiders to colonial city life. They became the creative bridge between plantation survivals of African musical forms of resistance and contemporary calypso. Jamaican forms of orature, whether represented by Louise Bennett's Creole poems or by reggae and dub, have similarly built on African forms and made of them contemporary popular expression. Oral poets like the late Michael Smith, Jean 'Binta' Breeze, Mutabaruka, John Agard, and Linton Kwesi Johnson or calypsonians like Sparrow, Spoiler, and Chalkdust focus on specific forms, for example dub or calypso, in the tradition of African oral poets, often using call and response structures and, in the case of calypsonians, sometimes extemporizing. Such oral poems may function as rhetorical statements of self, locating and constructing a persona for the world: this tradition has roots in the *griot* traditions of West Africa. In general, verbal arts in the Caribbean are most popular when they are oral, and even written literature draws heavily on orature in order to convey authentically the life of the ordinary Caribbean man or woman.

Theatre and drama, while often reflecting European influences, as in the form of the verbally oriented play, also frequently strongly incorporate such popular cultural elements as Creole language, forms of music and dance, satirical comedy, and masking, all of which can be traced to African roots. St. Lucia poet Derek Walcott, although often more European in his choice of poetic form than for example the Barbadian poet Kamau Brathwaite, portrays Creole-speaking Caribbean peasants as central characters in his early plays and makes much use of the masking tradition in *Dream on Monkey Mountain* (1972) and *Tijean and his Brothers* (1972). Walcott's poem 'A Far Cry From Africa' (*In a Green Night*, 1962) articulates poignantly the position of many middle-class Caribbean people trying to work out their relationship with Africa and Europe. Jamaican Dennis Scott in *An Echo in the Bone* (1985) and Rawle Gibbons from Trinidad have both used African-derived rites in their plays, and Gibbons has contributed in 'I, Lawah' (unpublished) to the development of Carnival theatre, a theatre that understands not only the cultural forms of Carnival but its place in the history of resistance to oppression in Trinidad and Tobago. Carnival drew on European festival traditions, but clearly in many of its forms and functions as well as its historical and political significance it is an African-centred festival. Sistren, the women's theatre company from Jamaica, uses masking strongly in its *Bellywoman Bangarang*, a play scripted from improvisation that makes use of language and events from actors' lives and from their society, i.e. that of working-class black people in Kingston.

Literature as written text has been very important in the representation of African-Caribbean connections. George Lamming constructed an important moment in the collective imagination of the Caribbean when in *Season of Adventure* (1970), he created Fola, who discovers her African roots through the ceremony of souls, which she at first resists. The great poet Kamau Brathwaite has contributed immensely to the realization of African connections. Like other Caribbean writers and scholars such as O.R. Dathorne (*The Scholar Man*, 1964), Neville Dawes, Denis Williams (*Other Leopards*, 1963), and Oliver Jackman (*Saw the House in Half*, 1974), he spent time in Africa as a young man, an experience that contributed enormously to his adult consciousness of the Caribbean. From his first poetic trilogy, *The Arrivants* (1973), an epic of the cultural journey of peoples of African descent from Africa to the so-called New World and then to England, his work has been very important for the whole African world, but perhaps even more for Barbados, where African survivals were for years ignored by official Barbadian culture. In essays such as *Contradictory Omens* (1974) Brathwaite began to explore the nature of Caribbean cultural identity. He would eventually write of African tonality beneath

English-language Christian hymn singing in small Barbadian country religious meetings and of African rhythms in which people might march behind military bands. He recognized that the 'little tradition', as he put it, of Africa was submerged beneath the so-called great tradition of dominant Europe more deeply in Barbados than in other islands. But poets like Brathwaite and the Barbadian oral poet Bruce St. John, who pioneered performance poetry in Barbadian Creole built on a tonality directly surviving from African influences, have done a great deal to liberate African sources in Barbadian identity and culture. M. Nourbese Philip explores African identity for a woman in her work, and, especially in 'Discourse on the Logic of Language' (*She Tries Her Tongue, Her Silence Softly Breaks*, 1989), relates the experience of slaves being silenced for speaking their own tongue to the poet's agony now in discovering how to get past the anguish that is English. Jamaican Lorna Goodison's poem 'To Us All Flowers Are Roses' (*Selected Poems*, 1992) invokes African place-names in Jamaica, affirmations of connection to history and the continent; at the same time the poem recognizes other influences in Jamaica's complex history.

Paule Marshall, born in New York of Barbadian parents, reproduces the Barbadian voice in her work. Her *Praisesong for the Widow* (1983) tells of a widowed, affluent African-American woman who finds her African roots in the island of Carriacou in the Caribbean. Here she finds African dance and ritual have been preserved and with them a sense of ancestry. Erna Brodber, a Jamaican novelist influenced by Kamau Brathwaite, portrays a rural Jamaican community in *Jane and Louisa Will Soon Come Home* (1980). Brodber, a Rastafarian since 1976 and an academic sociologist very much aware of the racial and cultural complexity of Caribbean identity, describes folk traditions, largely African in source but also European, as a source of healing and security for a young woman making the difficult transition from girl to woman. Earl Lovelace's fiction expresses the African storytelling tradition and the importance of remaining true to the community and to history. His novel *The Wine of Astonishment* (1982) portrays the Spiritual Baptists of a village called Bonasse. Like Paule Marshall, Lovelace often observes that relative wealth or education can alienate a person from the African-centred values of the village. *Jestina's Calypso* (1984) explores in the form of the play the true beauty of a person that lies below the surface: Jestina must battle male stereotyping of female attractiveness affected by colonial/Western and racist images that construct light-skinned women as more beautiful than dark.

African culture, within the continent and in the rest of the world, has many modes and requires only that an inheritance of African forms and a consciousness of Africa as centre be important elements in whatever new forms are created. Caribbean music now influences African popular music, just as jazz and the blues from African America have done. Caribbean culture absorbs and transforms elements from all world cultures as they are present and influential in the region. Of these, African culture is central and both re-creates other cultural elements and is re-created itself as Caribbean. The living continuity with Africa feeds Caribbean creativity. Caribbean literature, both oral and written, affirms Africa as source and as symbol of the courage and determination of a people to survive the attempt by colonialism and racism to annihilate their culture and force them to forget the huge number of souls who died in the middle passage and on the plantations.

AFRICANIST DISCOURSE From the time of Homer to the present, Westerners have reached out to the African continent and brought it back as language, in the process revealing more about themselves and their culture than about Africans and theirs. 'Africanist discourse', a term coined by Christopher Miller, refers to a discourse at odds with itself, projecting the West's desires on the perceived blank slate of Africa. Building on the work of Michel Foucault and Edward Said, Miller in *Blank Darkness* cites an array of Western and Eastern accounts of Africa from the *Iliad* through Leo Africanus and beyond to support his assertion that 'Africa is conceived of as a void and unformed prior to its investment with shape and being by the Christian or Islamic outside'. As a product of the Euro-American imagination, with all its fantasies and fears, Africanist discourse regards Africa ambivalently, resulting in favourable and/or unfavourable depictions of the continent.

Three major interlocking conventions of Africanist discourse are binary oppositions, image projection, and evolutionary language. The oppositions are a manifestation of the West's ambivalence towards Africa. It is either a dream or a nightmare and is often both; or the West is one thing – good, reasonable, bright – while Africa is its opposite – evil, irrational, dark. Secondly, regarding Africa as a blank space, Africanist writers have used many different images in describing the continent – a heart, a swamp, a question mark – no one more appropriate than the other, each used to mould the perceived formlessness of Africa into a shape recognizable to the Western eye. In his aggressively imperialist travel book *My African Journey* (1908), Winston Churchill provides a classic example of Africanist ambivalence and image projection when he uses the phrase 'a curious garden of sunshine and nightshade' to assert that Africa is both beautiful and meretriciously poisonous. Finally, there is the tendency on the part of Africanist writers to describe Africans and Africa as lagging behind Westerners and the West in development – Africans are children, the continent is prehistoric, the people and the land recall an era the West experienced centuries ago.

In *The Myth of Africa* (1977) Dorothy Hammond and Alta Jablow contend that twentieth-century literature elaborates rather than alters the image of Africa found in accounts of the continent from 1530 until the end of the nineteenth century. What they refer to as 'the dark labyrinth' becomes the modern extension of the myth of the dark continent, and they cite Joseph Conrad's *Heart of Darkness* (1902), one of the most influential and controversial literary works about Africa, as the first example of it. In these works, according to Hammond and Jablow, rather than seeking answers to geographical mysteries or attempting to bring 'civilization' to Africans, the European comes to Africa to learn about himself or herself and escape 'civilization', becoming a better person as a result of the experience with the African labyrinth. Although this general description corresponds fairly well with Conrad's Marlow, Conrad also depicts the situation of the European who fails to follow Ariadne's thread in Kurtz, the Westerner run amok. The first in-depth treatment of the European fear of 'going native', Conrad's novella uses Africa as a metaphor for a condition of unlimited power and lack of external restraint that tests the basic beliefs of a Westerner, thus originating a whole tradition of narratives in which expatriates come to Africa to escape the limitations of European society and test themselves in what are regarded as more elemental conditions. Edgar Rice Burroughs's Tarzan novels, beginning with *Tarzan of the Apes* (1912), sold prodigiously, making him, by some estimates, among the bestselling authors in history. The ability of Burroughs, who never visited the continent, to market his fantastic Africa attests to the pervasiveness of Africanist discourse among the general public.

From 1885 to 1914, the period during which Churchill's, Conrad's, and Burroughs's works were published, the age of high imperialism for Europeans in Africa prevailed. The first date corresponds with the Treaty of Berlin, which diplomatically regulated and legitimized the scramble for Africa, the second with the commencement of the First World War, which has been seen by many historians as the event symbolically marking the death of the old order. Although the beginning of the end of colonialism did not occur until the 1950s, and many assert that a form of imperialism exists today, unselfconscious high imperialism was questioned during the years between the world wars. Even though African leaders and authors such as Kwame Nkrumah and Chinua *Achebe openly challenged the accuracy and deplored the effects of Euro-American depictions of the continent, Africanist writing continued largely unaltered until the 1960s and only in the 1980s began to be subverted and, in some cases, abandoned.

From the 1930s to the early 1960s, Evelyn Waugh, Graham Greene, Joyce Cary, Saul Bellow, and others largely ignored the political realities of Africa. The mostly reactionary novels inspired by the Mau Mau revolt in Kenya in the 1950s and Margaret Laurence's *This Side Jordan* (1960), which predicts a bright future for the new Africa, were significant exceptions to the apolitical nature of western writing during the twilight of colonialism. More openly political than their predecessors, Africanist writers of the late 1960s and 1970s such as Paul Theroux, Shiva and V.S. Naipaul, Martha Gellhorn, and John Updike regarded post-colonial Africa as a hopeless combination of failed colonialism and indigenous corruption. In contrast to Conrad and Greene, who depicted Europeans in Africa as heroic figures with tragic flaws, Euro-American writers in the post-colonial era have often depicted expatriates as powerless and even inept individuals. During the 1980s certain Western writers, most notably Helen Winternitz, Jonathan Raban, Maria Thomas, T. Coraghessan Boyle, Peter Dickinson, and William Duggan, either actively subverted the established conventions of Africanist writing, or, more boldly, rewrote the history of African-European relations during the pre-colonial and colonial eras in order to reverse Africanist discourse by focusing on events that belie its continuity.

AFRIKA, Tatamkhulu Ismail (1921-), is the adopted name of a South African poet and novelist who was born in Egypt and brought to South Africa by his parents when he was still a young child. He has held a variety of jobs ranging from copper miner in Namibia to musician in a local band. His first publication was a novel, *Broken Earth* (1940), which appeared at a time when he was serving in the South African forces. During active service in North Africa, he was taken captive and held as a POW for three years. After his return to South Africa, he became involved in anti-*apartheid activism as a member of the then outlawed African National Congress and was arrested by the minority white South African government in 1964, the year of his conversion to Islam. As a founder member of the Al-Jihaad organization, he vehemently opposed the government when it declared the traditionally black District Six, Cape Town, a white area. In 1987 he was banned for five years from writing and public speaking.

Ironically, it was at this time that Afrika began to write again. Poems reflecting his experience of prison and of apartheid's oppression were published in literary magazines such as *Contrast* and *New Coin* and were eventually collected in *Nine Lives* (1991) and *Dark Rider* (1992). His late efflorescence won wide recognition from the South African literary establishment with a CNA Debut Prize (1991), the English Academy of Southern Africa's Olive Schreiner Prize (1992) and Thomas Pringle Award (1991 and 1993), and the SANLAM Literary Award (1994). Since the advent of a majority elected democratic government, he has published a second novel, *The Innocents* (1994), and three further collections of verse, *Maqabane* (1994), *Flesh and the Flame* (1995), and *The Lemon Tree and Other Poems* (1995). His non-materialistic way of life and ascetic temperament give him access to the poorer members of South African society, on whose behalf many of his poems speak naturally and easily. He combines wry observation with an intense lyrical streak.

AFRIKAANS Afrikaans is one of the major languages in South Africa and Namibia. It can be traced to the intermittent contact between the indigenous Khoi people and European and other visitors and shipwreck survivors, particularly after 1652 and the founding of a Dutch refreshment settlement at the Cape of Good Hope, when officials of the VOC (Vereenigde Oostindische Compagnie, the Dutch East India Company) encountered the Khoi people in situations of negotiation and barter. The population of the settlement increased steadily, first with the arrival of slaves from Ceylon, India, Indonesia, Madagascar, Malaya, Mozambique, and West Africa in 1658 and thereafter with the immigration of French, Germans, and Portuguese. These migrations gave rise to a heterogeneous society characterized by various religions, widespread multilingualism, and a need for secondary proficiency or second-language interaction. Dutch became the minority primary language, used in economic and social interaction between the speakers of this miscellany. In the decades following the establishment of the settlement several interlectal varieties developed: those spoken by the aboriginal Khoi people, those spoken by the slaves, and lastly those varieties spoken by the increasing number of European settlers.

Miscegenation also contributed to the development of Afrikaans. Sexual unions were established between the Khoi and the slaves, the Khoi and the Europeans, and the slaves and the Europeans. Slaves who had been freed, known as free blacks, learned to speak Dutch as one of the prerequisites for manumission.

The interlectal varieties of Dutch were disseminated throughout southern Africa by the movement of people. Groups of Khoi people and free blacks migrated during the seventeenth and eighteenth centuries from the Cape settlement to the vast arid expanse of the northern Cape, southern Namibia, and the plains of the central region. With the expansion of the Cape Colony white settlers also established themselves in the eastern Cape. At the beginning of the nineteenth century these people became disaffected with the policies of the new British colonial power and trekked towards the northern savannah inland

region and the subtropical east coast.

Theories on the origins of Afrikaans have led to intense debate among linguists and historians. Although Afrikaans is distinguishable from Dutch, the two are, especially in their standardized varieties, mutually intelligible, a fact that led earlier researchers to regard Afrikaans as a logical continuum of seventeenth-century Dutch. Although standard Afrikaans retains notable Dutch and German characteristics in its syntax, morphology, and lexicon, other languages such as Khoi, Malay, French, Portuguese, various African languages, and especially English profoundly influenced its structure.

Three broad theories have been advanced to explain the development of Afrikaans: the first proposes that Afrikaans is the outcome of the continuation of Dutch varieties, the second that Afrikaans resulted from the blending of the different languages at the Cape, and the third that both the continuation of Dutch varieties as well as the newly established learner varieties brought about the formation of Afrikaans.

Early instances of written Afrikaans date back to the early nineteenth century and consist mainly of farcical renditions written by journalists or travellers of the learner varieties spoken by free blacks and slaves. The deliberate codification of Afrikaans began as a way of making religious literature available to adherents of Islam and later to Christian converts of mixed descent. Cape Dutch or Afrikaans, as well as Dutch, were used regularly in *De Bode van Genadendal* (established in 1859), a periodical aimed at black Christian converts that published poetry, stories, and reports on church matters by white and black readers. The Afrikaans-only newspaper *Patriot* was published in 1876 as the standard-bearer of a small band of emerging Afrikaner nationalists, the Fellowship of True Afrikaners, a movement that was met with derision in some quarters.

The codification of Afrikaans in the *Patriot* tradition began in 1874 and accelerated after 1915. Scholars with decidedly Afrikaner nationalist leanings, schooled in Dutch, founded the South African Academy for Language, Literature and Arts, which undertook responsibility for the standardization of the Afrikaans language. They followed the prestige norms of Dutch and the variety, also referred to as eastern Afrikaans, spoken by white, middle-class northerners. The two other varieties, namely southwestern Afrikaans and northwestern Afrikaans, which originated as interlects among free blacks, slaves, and the Khoi, were not taken into account during the first or subsequent standardization efforts and were heavily stigmatized in public life, education, and the media. Standardization aided the creation of a new imagined community, the Afrikaners, who mobilized around the political fallout from the *Anglo-Boer war (1899–1902), which included calls for the recognition of

Afrikaans as an official language along with English. This goal was reached in 1925.

Afrikaans became increasingly associated with Afrikaner nationalism and the National party, whose policies, based on white privilege and the statutory formalization of the discriminatory colonial customs of previous governments, led to an election victory in 1948 and the formalization of *apartheid. From the outset the government elected in 1948 took steps to expand the use of Afrikaans throughout the civil service, the courts, and education. Thirty years later Afrikaans was thoroughly institutionalized. In 1976 resentment against the National party administration culminated in a prolonged uprising against the introduction of Afrikaans as a language of instruction for non-native speakers, and Afrikaans became commonly known as the language of the oppressor. Among other factors, the policies of the National party and the practices of Afrikaner nationalist cultural bodies led to sharp divisions in the Afrikaans speech community, and a major part of that community, its non-white speakers, was alienated from forthright identification with the language. Similarly, other non-native speakers who had previously shifted to Afrikaans also dissociated.

For the majority of South Africans Afrikaans was closely identified with apartheid. Faced with this negative image of the language, Afrikaner intellectuals, linguists, and ordinary speakers feared that Afrikaans would not survive into the future. Several professional, cultural, language, and community organizations among Afrikaans speakers attempted to foster a new image, typified by calls to make the language more 'friendly' and to recognize the previously neglected varieties. When the National party was unseated by the African National Congress in the 1994 election, the new interim constitution replaced the 1925 provision of two official languages with a new policy that recognizes eleven official languages.

In Namibia an early form of Afrikaans was established around the end of the eighteenth century when the Oorlams Khoikhoi and later groups of people from mixed extraction called the Basters migrated north across the Orange River. Although the history of written Afrikaans in this territory is rather sketchy, Afrikaans correspondence from around 1850 and correspondence between leaders of aboriginal groups and German missionaries exists. The best known piece of early Namibian Afrikaans-Dutch is the collection of papers known as *The Diary of Hendrik Witbooi*, written by a Nama chieftain towards the end of the nineteenth century. At independence in 1990 English became Namibia's only official language and the preferred language of educational instruction, although provision is made for the limited use of mother-tongue instruction in the early stages of primary school. However, Afrikaans continues to be used as the lingua franca in the main towns in the southern and central regions of the country, and Afrikaans newspapers, magazines, videos, films, and books are imported from South Africa.

Notwithstanding the intricacies of historical explanation, Afrikaans as a living language continues to be modified by its proximity to other southern African languages. Contemporary Afrikaans borrows heavily from English for terminology in all spheres of technology, communication, politics, and entertainment. With political transformation under way, some linguists are proposing a thorough restandardization of Afrikaans to include the varieties spoken by mainly black Afrikaans speakers. This move, they argue, will reduce the obstacles to mother-tongue education and literacy. It will also facilitate the reappropriation of Afrikaans by previously disaffected groups.

The colonial phase of Afrikaans literature – that is, publications written in Dutch and its varieties – spans almost four centuries, from the latter part of the fifteenth to the end of the nineteenth century. The most important texts in the colonial period were *Daghregisters* [day registers], travel records, and diaries. The prototypical and best *Daghregister* was written by Jan van Riebeeck (1619-77), the first Dutch commander in the Cape. Travel records that followed the conventions of the sixteenth century were compiled in strict accordance with certain topological questions, were often fictionalized to resemble those of such classical authors as Herodotos and Plinius, and were typical of the 'discourse of the other'. André *Brink alludes to these records in his novel *Inteendeel* (1993).

Few literary works of merit were published in the colonial period, with the exception of those by Pieter de Neyn, who wrote several topical poems in Dutch during his brief stay at the Cape (1672-4). T.F. Burgers (1834-81, later president of the Transvaal) wrote in the vein of Hildebrand, and the popular D'Arbez (pseudonym of J.F. van Oordt, 1856-1918), who wrote in Dutch, incorporated many Afrikaans linguistic forms. Some of the earliest Afrikaans texts were an anonymous song, a dialogue by Louis Henry Meurant (1860), and comic poems by F.W. Reitz (1870).

The decolonization phase in the development of Afrikaans literature follows the colonial period. Its three stages, appropriation, nationalism, and emancipation, are not necessarily chronological, and examples of the first stage can still be found in contemporary Afrikaans literature. Broadly speaking, however, they fall into successive periods. The first, appropriation, dates from the founding of Die Genootskap van Regte Afrikaners [the community of true Afrikaners] in Paarl in 1875, whose members soon established a press and published the *Patriot* and a magazine, *Ons Klyntji*. D.F. du Toit (Oom Lokomotief), C.P. Hoogenhout, A. Pannevis, and S.J. du Toit were the driving forces; S.J. du Toit and Jan Lion Cachet, author of the novel *Sewe duiwels en wat hul gedoen het*

(1907), are widely regarded as the group's best writers. Although they were motivated by nationalistic ideals and exploited indigenous literary forms, they were deeply indebted to European literature (especially Dutch and English) for models and forms, which they ardently copied, adapted, or even 'translated': F.W. Reitz produced a rendition of 'Tam o' Shanter' and later Jan F.E. Celliers adapted Percy Shelley's 'The Cloud'.

Appropriation gradually developed into ethnic nationalism after the Anglo-Boer war of 1899-1902, when a brutal second period of anglicization encouraged Afrikaners to popularize Afrikaans-Dutch. Such poets as Jan Celliers, Totius (pseudonym of Jacob Daniel du Toit), and Eugène Marais, whose poem 'Winternag' (1905) for many marks the beginning of Afrikaans literature proper, and the versatile C.J. Langenhoven were fervently nationalistic; even the cosmopolitan C. Louis Leipoldt, one of the earliest poets of merit in Afrikaans and a transgressor of the traditional frontiers of nationalism and religion, wrote nationalistic poems. In prose writing the two dominant traits were realism, with Jochem van Bruggen as the most important exponent, and romanticism, with D.F. Malherbe as its most typical representative. Nationalism appeared in farm novels, adventure stories, and historical novels. M.E.R. (M.E. Rothmann) initially published youth literature and short stories with convincing characterization and a keen sense of human interaction typical of her later (and better) work. Sociological problems pertaining to the Afrikaner played an important part in the dramas of J.F.W. Grosskopf.

The first real period of radical change and renewal in Afrikaans literature began in the 1930s with the publication of Die ryke dwaas (1934) by W.E.G. Louw and Alleenspraak (1935), a collection of poems by his elder brother, N.P. Van Wyk Louw. In the tradition of the great men of letters the poet was seen as a lonely seer whose only allegiance was to language and literature. This period of romanticism relates closely to European romanticism and the well-known 'Tagtigers' [poets of the 80s] in Dutch literature. Some writers, notably the Louw brothers, cultivated a militant, if idealistic, nationalism. Van Wyk Louw established himself as the most important Afrikaans poet up to that time, and he ranked above his contemporaries (with the possible exception of D.J. Opperman) for the next three decades. Although the poetry of this period was in some respects derivative, the fundamental break with the existing tradition brought Afrikaans poetry to a new level. Van Wyk Louw was described as a great 'European' poet and in 1948 received an honorary doctorate from the University of Utrecht, renowned for the reticence with which it bestows such honours. Elisabeth Eybers later emigrated to Holland, where she continued to write in Afrikaans

and was eventually awarded the P.C. Hooft prize for Dutch literature, one of the most prestigious literary awards in Holland.

During this period fiction began to incorporate the mystic attachment to the soil and the almost pantheistic experience of God in nature that characterize what usually is called the farm novel. This genre blends the two most important modes of earlier Afrikaans prose writing, namely romanticism and realism, reaching its pinnacle in the novels of C.M. van den Heever, Somer (1935) and Laat vrugte (1939). Jan van Melle's novel Bart Nel (1936) remains one of the best novels in Afrikaans.

The final flourishing of this period occurs in the sober poems of Van Wyk Louw's Gestaltes en diere (1942) and W.E.G. Louw's Adam en ander gedigte (1944). D.J. Opperman's Heilige beeste (1945), stark and expressive, marks the final break with nationalist romanticism. Other important poets of this era are S.J. Pretorius and Ernst van Heerden, who developed into a major poet in the 1970s and 80s, when he published his best work.

A characteristic of the nationalist period was the proliferation of popular literature. For example, book clubs published novels with idealized rural settings, in effect trivializing the genre of the farm novel. The impasse to which prose writing and drama had come during this period prompted Van Wyk Louw's influential articles on the necessity for renewal in Afrikaans prose writing in 1957-9, later published as Vernuwing in die prosa (1961).

The stage of emancipation in the decolonization phase of Afrikaans literary history is usually associated with the movement of the 'Sestigers', although this period also provides some striking examples of appropriation. The name Sestiger alludes to the fact that this group of writers published important work in the 1960s and that the most influential of them identified with a magazine called Sestiger. The renewal that characterizes emancipation began in 1955 with Peter Blum's Steenbok tot poolsee, which, together with Krokos (1958) by Boerneef (pseudonym of I. W. van der Merwe) and Tristia (1962) by Van Wyk Louw, shows the influence of experimental European poetry, notably that of the 'Vijftigers' in Holland.

Two books by Étienne Leroux, Die eerste lewe van Colet (1955) and Na'va (1972), delimit the emancipation stage and indicate the centrality of prose writing. Together with Jan Rabie's Een-en-twintig (1956), Leroux's first novel marked a break with the Afrikaans prose tradition. Several of the Sestiger writers lived in Paris for many years and were deeply indebted to contemporary French philosophy. Within a few years such key words as 'alienation', 'detachment', 'existentialism', 'the outsider', and 'exile' were part of Afrikaans literature. Following a period of establishment of the new movement, three important books were published in 1962: Van Wyk Louw's *Tristia* and the novels *Sewe dae by die Silbersteins* by Étienne Leroux and *Lobola vir die lewe* by André Brink. Among other poets of the emancipation stage, Breyten *Breytenbach remained unaligned with any Afrikaans literary movement. Although Breytenbach is the most untypical of Afrikaans poets, with a field of reference steeped in Buddhism and European experimental poetry, his poetry is at the same time archetypically Afrikaans and reflects an uncanny mastery of the language.

Drama is often regarded as the least prominent of the three classical genres in Afrikaans literature, perhaps because relatively few plays have been published. However, the townships produced vibrant community theatre for many decades, and many good plays, by among others P.G. du Plessis and Christian Barnard, were produced at festivals and on television. Du Plessis's first play, *Die nag van Legio* (1969), was influenced by Artaud's theatre of cruelty, although *Siener in die suburbs* (1971) is a rehash of the social drama of the 1920s. The tendency to allude to the literary tradition is also evident in plays by Pieter Fourie and later Reza de Wet, who have been the most prominent playwrights in Afrikaans during the 1980s and 90s.

In the two decades following the emancipation stage, traumatic political events such as South Africa's involvement in Angola and the Soweto riots of 1976 contributed to an artistic shift in emphasis towards Africa as topological, philosophical, and ideological concept. André Brink's banned novel *Kennis van die aand* (1973) introduced this phase, Leroux's *Magersfontein, O Magersfontein!* (1976) widened the divide between writer and government – illustrated in tragicomic fashion by Breytenbach's imprisonment – and Elsa Joubert's *Die swerfjare van Poppie Nongena* (1978) became the icon of that troubled time. *Mahala* (1971) by Christian Barnard was an important novel, and J.C. Steyn's *Op pad na die grens* (1976) initiated the 'frontier' literature that blossomed in the 1980s.

During this period of overt political commitment, younger writers such as Alexander Strachan ironically demanded freedom from all demands. Like the poets of the 1930s (also in reaction to the demands for 'committed' literature), they wanted freedom of expression and the liberty to write on any topic. This approach gave rise to disconcertingly realistic 'reports' of the border war in Namibia and Angola and suburban unrest. Étienne van Heerden, Alexander Strachan, and Koos Prinsloo, the heirs of apartheid, startlingly assessed their traumatic youth. Violence became a motif in Afrikaans prose writing, notably in the work of P.J. Haasbroek and John Miles. Yet one of the best books of the 1980s, *Die kremetartekspedisie* (1981) by Wilma Stockenström, is almost detached in tone. It defeats easy categorization, even of temporal and spa-

cial setting. Stockenström is also an important poet, whose exploration of Africa and its mythology simultaneously critiques the Afrikaans canon and rediscovers the language itself. Fresh language also features prominently in the poetry of J.C. Steyn, whose work is akin to that of A.G. Visser in the 1920s and 30s.

Although Sheila Cussons began publishing in 1947 her volumes of poems were only published after 1970. Because she lived outside South Africa for many years and was deeply influenced by Roman Catholicism and mysticism, her poetry differs from that of her contemporaries but conjoins with that of the later Van Wyk Louw. Other important poets of this era are T.T. Cloete, who made his debut in his sixties, and Antjie Krog.

After 2 February 1990 Afrikaans literature began to reveal an almost obsessional struggle with a personal and collective past. While the 1960s were the heyday of modernism, the latter part of the 1980s and the 1990s clearly demonstrate all the attributes of postmodernism, including fragmentary and experimental surface structure and a characteristic play of language. The intellectual hypotheses of modernism gave way to scepticism, and epistemological questions were replaced by ontological ones. Parody, intertextuality, reflexivity, and fictionalization are major components of this movement. Étienne Leroux's *Onse Hymie* (1982) initiated the post-modern phase, which reached an early culmination in Strachan's novel *Die jakkalsjagter* (1990).

A preoccupation with history is a feature of the Afrikaans literary tradition, in its modern guise appearing at the extremes of nostalgia and parody. Hennie Aucamp's early writing is almost nostalgic, but his later work becomes increasingly parodic, culminating in a critical appraisal of his homoerotic existence that is almost self-parody. In his realistic portrayal of the gay life he is the forerunner of a subgenre culminating in the works of Koos Prinsloo, who died of AIDS in 1994. *Toorberg* (1986) by Étienne van Heerden is one of a number of parodies of the farm novel since 1962 that suggest an ideological position against apartheid. The best parodic novels of the 1990s are *Triomf* (1994) by Marlene van Niekerk and *Karolina Ferreira* (1993) by Lettie Viljoen. The novels of Karel Schoeman, one of the most prolific writers in Afrikaans since his career began in 1965, often reflect the important characteristics of the stages of Afrikaans literary history since the 1960s. *'n Lug vol helder wolke* (1967) is typical of the 1960s, *Na die geliefde land* (1972) is an apocalyptical novel, and *Hierdie lewe* (1994) is an example of historiographic metafiction much more like postmodernism than is commonly recognized. His novel *'n Ander land* (1984), widely regarded as one of the best novels ever written in Afrikaans, recalls the novels of the late nineteenth century and ostensibly detaches itself from the traumatic political reality of South

Africa in the bleak period of the state of emergency. As in the case of Leroux and Stockenström, Schoeman defies categorization, as do the best authors and books.

Age of Iron (1990) A novel by J.M. *Coetzee. Like two of Coetzee's earlier novels, *Foe and *In the Heart of the Country, Age of Iron has a woman narrator. The dates 1986-9 are given at the conclusion of her narrative, indicating that the novel describes the period of its own writing, and it is to this period that the title alludes. This age is characterized on one hand by the South African state's claim to absolute power and on the other hand by the harsh and self-sacrificial resistance of black youth. Elizabeth Curren, the narrator, is a retired classics lecturer who is dying of cancer; her profession suggests the humanist tradition from which her discourse originates. Her stance is is very close to the position taken by Nadine *Gordimer in her essays 'The Essential Gesture' and 'Living in the Interregnum'. She thinks of setting herself alight in front of the Houses of Parliament but, judging this gesture through the eyes of her domestic worker, Florence, she realizes it would be a futile and self-serving attempt to find redemption. Instead she seeks redemption in loving 'the unloveable': an obdurately militant young black man who ignores her words. The entire novel is addressed to her daughter, who is living in voluntary exile in America; the tenuous and marginal nature of her discourse is indicated by the fact that she entrusts the delivery of this letter to her daughter to a derelict alcoholic who is her only companion during the last days of her life.

AIDOO, Ama Ata (1942-), Ghanaian playwright, poet, novelist, short-story writer, and critic, was born at Abeadze Kyiakor, near Dominase, in Ghana. She attended the Wesley Girls' High School at Cape Coast in the Central Region of Ghana and gained a BA at the University of Ghana, Legon (1964). While at university, she participated in writers' workshops at the School of Drama and produced her first two plays when she was still an undergraduate. After graduation, she moved on to the creative writing programme at Stanford University in the USA, and since then she has taught as a research fellow at the Institute of African Studies, University of Ghana, worked as a lecturer at the University of Cape Coast, Ghana, and has been a visiting lecturer at various universities in Africa and the USA. She was Secretary for Education in the military government of Flt. Lt. Jerry Rawlings in the early 1980s. Since her resignation she has lived in exile, first in Zimbabwe, where she worked as a freelance writer, and then in the USA, where she lives and lectures. Her second novel, *Changes: A Love Story* (1991) won a Commonwealth Writers Prize.

Aidoo is perhaps the most versatile of Ghanaian writers; she is as comfortable with the novel and short story as she is with drama and poetry, and she has written for children. Her published works in drama are *The *Dilemma of a Ghost* (1965) and *Anowa* (1970); two collections of short stories are entitled *No Sweetness Here* (1970) and *The Girl Who Can and Other Stories* (1996); and she describes her first novel, *Our Sister Killjoy* (1977), as a fiction in four episodes with verse-prose style. She has also published two volumes of poetry, *Someone Talking to Sometime* (1985) and *An Angry Letter in January* (1992). Her two published works for children are *The Eagle and the Chickens and Other Stories* (1989) and *Birds and Other Poems* (1989).

Aidoo does not merely lament Africa's fate, past, present, and even future, by bringing her sceptical intelligence to an examination of her place within an unbroken continuum of a history of colonialism and neo-colonialism; as one of black Africa's foremost feminists she considers the oppression of modern African women in all spheres of human activity. Two of her most frequently anthologized essays deal with the fate of Africa and its women: 'No Saviours' first appeared in *The New African* as an introduction to Ghanaian novelist Ayi Kwei *Armah's *The *Beautyful Ones Are Not Yet Born*, and 'To be an African Woman Writer – Overview and Detail' first appeared in *Criticism and Ideology* (1988), edited by Kirsten Holst Petersen.

Aidoo's dramatic art and her other work make extensive use of the oral roots of African literature, particularly the art of storytelling. For her the western idea of separating art into disconnected genres is unreal in the African context of orality because the storyteller's art is demonstrably a combination of poetry, acting, and narrative plot. Her art is therefore a synthesis of all the elements of *orature – community participation, music and dancing, and the general atmosphere – that characterize communities in which members are supportive of one another.

Her interest in traditional form translates to a vision of the future of African literature that includes a renewal of the fundamental unity of the vast continuum of verbal discourses. She insists, forcefully and successfully, that the liberation of the continent is inextricably linked with the liberation of its people. Arguably, she has no equal in the African literary tradition as an exponent of the reinvention of Africa and of the re-imaging and re-imagining of its women.

AIG-IMOUKHUEDE, Frank (1935-), Nigerian poet. Born at Edunabon, near Ife, Nigeria, he attended Igbobi College, Lagos and University College, Ibadan and worked with the Nigerian Broadcasting Corporation, the Lagos *Daily Express*, the federal Ministry of Information, and the Nigeria Arts Council. He is best known for his *Pidgin poems, published in such pioneer literary journals as *Black Orpheus* and *The Horn* and in his major collection *Pidgin Stew and*

Sufferhead (1982). His choice of Pidgin results from a quest for a home-grown medium of literary expression, an artistic vision he shares with Gabriel ★Okara, the Nigerian poet who experiments with transliteration.

One of Aig-Imoukhuede's tasks in *Pidgin Stew and Sufferhead* is to defend the Pidgin medium against the negative view that its comic associations make it unsuitable for serious subjects. In the title poem, 'Pidgin Stew', he explains that the comic style works within the satirical mode to expose corruption, especially where a totalitarian political structure makes the survival of overtly political literature impossible. His Pidgin poems describe experiences with attention to detail, and the voice in his narrative poems represents the ordinary person victimized by the conflicting social and political forces of his society.

AIYEJINA, Funso (1949-), poet and short-story writer, was born in Ososo, Edo State, Nigeria, and holds degrees from the University of Ife, Nigeria (BA), Acadia University, Nova Scotia, Canada (MA) and the University of the West Indies, Trinidad (Ph.D.). He taught at the University of Ife (now Obafemi Awolowo University) and since 1990 has taught at the University of the West Indies in Trinidad. In 1995-6, he was Fulbright Lecturer in Creative Writing at Lincoln University in Jefferson City, Missouri.

Aiyejina's short fiction has appeared in *Okike* and his stories and plays have been broadcast over the radio in Nigeria and England. He has published poems in various journals, including *Opon Ifa*, *Okike*, *West Africa*, *Greenfield Review*, and *Trinidad and Tobago Review*; his work has also been widely anthologized. His first book of poems, *A Letter to Lynda* (1988), which won the Association of Nigerian Authors Prize in 1989, explores indigenous idioms and images.

AJAYI, Christie Ade (1930-), Nigerian children's writer, was born in Ile-Oluji, Nigeria and educated in Nigeria, the UK, and the USA. As a teacher and writer, she has long been concerned about the learning needs of Nigerian schoolchildren. Her many published books, including titles such as *Ade, Our Naughty Little Brother* (1975), *Emeka and His Dog* (1982), and a host of others, aim to help pre-schoolers and beginners develop basic vocabulary and acquire reading skills easily and naturally through stories and illustrations relevant to the African child.

AJAYI, Tolu(walogo) (1946-), Nigerian fiction writer and poet, was born in Ijebu-Ode, Ogun State. Educated in Nigeria and the UK, he qualified as a physician at University of Liverpool Medical School in 1970 and specialized in psychiatry at Memorial University of Newfoundland, Canada. His medical experience informs his novel *The Year* (1981), which was followed by a second novel, *The Lesson* (1985), and a thriller, *The Ghost of a Millionaire* (1990). His collection of stories *Eyes of the Night* (1992) incorporates 'Family Planning', which won the 1990 BBC World Service short story competition, but his poetry collections *Images of Lives* (1992) and *Motions and Emotions* (1993) received mixed reviews. *After a Bad Moon* (1995) is a collage of experimental stories.

Aké: The Years of Childhood (1981) The autobiography of Wole ★Soyinka. Although some aspects of his interpretation of traditional social organization have been criticized, *Aké* is among Soyinka's most popular and highly praised work. It deals with the first decade of his childhood, the ten years leading up to and through the Second World War and ending just as he is enrolled in grammar school. Especially notable are Soyinka's portraits of his parents, two exceptionally talented and strong-willed individuals, and the vivid sense of place the book reveals, apparent already in its title and subtitle, which identify the years of childhood with Soyinka's birthplace. Above all, perhaps, the book owes its success, its profoundly endearing quality, to the gently ironic stance Soyinka sustains in evoking the child's sense of himself.

ALKALI, Zaynab (1950-), Nigerian novelist, was born in Biu, Nigeria, gained undergraduate and graduate degrees in English at Bayero University, Kano, and has taught English and African literature at Bayero University and the University of Maiduguri. Alkali's novels include *The Stillborn* (1984), which won the Association of Nigerian Authors award for prose fiction in 1985, and *The Virtuous Woman* (1987). The novels express her concern for the condition of African women in patriarchal African cultures. The protagonists, Li in *The Stillborn* and Nana Ai in *The Virtuous Woman*, contest their subservient position in society in various ways. They offer images of African women that contrast with those of colonial literature in works such as Joseph Conrad's *Heart of Darkness*, in which African women suffer the alienation of racism and sexism, and of earlier Nigerian novels such as Chinua ★Achebe's ★*Things Fall Apart*, in which women are forever located on the home front as cooks and housewives. The assault on patriarchy, however, is incomplete: the characters remain determined by institutionalized patriarchy.

ALUKO, T(imothy) M(ofolorunso) (1918-), Nigerian novelist, trained in civil engineering and town planning both in Nigeria and at Imperial College, London and rose in the Nigerian public service from colonial officer in 1950 to permanent secretary in the Ministry of Works and Transport at the time of his departure from the civil service in 1966. From

22

then until his retirement in 1978 he pursued a career as an academic, earning a doctorate in municipal engineering in 1976. He received several awards and honours including Officer, Order of the British Empire (OBE) in 1963 and Officer, Order of the Niger (OON) in 1964.

Aluko's short stories appeared in the late 1940s, but he attracted general interest only when his first novel, ★One Man One Wife, was published in Nigeria in 1959. The book is a controversial invective on Christians in conflict with traditionalists in southern Nigeria. Inspired by its modest literary success he produced his outstanding novel One Man, One Matchet (1964), which satirizes the colonizer's programme for rural economy and social integration. Aluko's other satirical works are Kinsman and Foreman (1966), Chief the Honourable Minister (1970), His Worshipful Majesty (1973), Wrong Ones in the Dock (1982), A State of Our Own (1986), and Conduct Unbecoming (1993). One of Nigeria's earliest writers of English prose fiction, Aluko maintains a consistent enthusiasm for humour and caricature. His fiction focuses on the commonplace evils of Nigerian society, such as bribery, ignorance, poverty, and vandalism, expressing scepticism about expatriate colonial officers as well as the educated or 'been-to' Africans who replaced them after independence. Although scholars do not consider his accomplishments equal to those of Chinua ★Achebe or Wole ★Soyinka, his best work, specifically One Man, One Matchet, is grounded in an intimate knowledge of Nigerian, particularly Yoruba, culture. His models are conservative English storytellers, particularly the humorists, from Charles Dickens to C.P. Snow. In 1994 he published his autobiography, My Years of Service, an account of his activities as an engineer and university teacher.

AMADI, Elechi (1934-), Nigerian novelist and playwright, was born in a small village near Port Harcourt in Rivers State, Nigeria. Like other writers from a rural eastern Nigerian background, he was educated at Government College, Umuahia; later he studied mathematics and physics at University College, Ibadan (B.Sc. Hons. 1959). He has had a varied career as a teacher and principal, a soldier, a civil-service administrator, and writer-in-residence at Rivers State College.

Amadi is from the Ekwerre people of eastern Nigeria. His three novels The ★Concubine (1966), The ★Great Ponds (1969), and The Slave (1978) form a trilogy that represents religion not only as part of social existence but also as the foundation of human values and relationships, without which individuals and communities lack balance. Divinity is necessary for a sustained tradition, defined in the fictional community as a prescribed code of conduct by and for village farmers. Unfortunately, however, the ancestral rules of the community infringe on the rights (i.e. the free-

dom) of individuals, as in the case of Ihuoma in The Concubine. Except in his last novel and the plays with urban settings, Amadi projects a sense of tragic loss in his description of the failure of individual human relationships within an established community.

Critics have applauded Amadi's writing for its lucidity and realism. Some of those same critics, however, have expressed misgivings about his apparently merely sociological interest in the ways the lives of local inhabitants have been threatened by forces such as Western imperialism, education and Christianity. It is perhaps easy to mistake Amadi's elegant restraint as a lack of profound and passionate concern.

Amadi has also published Estrangement (1986) and four plays: Isiburu (1973), The Road to Ibadan (1974), The Dancer of Johannesburg (1977), and Peppersoup (1977). His most important non-fiction work is Sunset in Biafra (1973), his account of his participation in the ★Nigeria-Biafra war as a Federal Army officer, twice a Biafran prisoner and once again a Federal officer and administrator. He has also written Ethics in Nigerian Culture (1982).

ANDURU, Agoro (1948-92), Tanzanian short-story writer. Born in a village on the eastern shores of Lake Victoria in what is now Tanzania, Anduru was educated at local schools. The story of his thirst for education, made obsessive under the uncertain condition of partial deafness, is told in the autobiographical 'Without Despair', which forms part of A Bed of Roses and Other Writings (1989). Despite his handicap, he trained and worked as a radio journalist. His first short stories appeared in Tanzania's weekly newspaper Sunday News in the 1970s. Temptation and Other Stories (1981), This Is Living and Other Stories (1982), and indeed all his writings exhibit an interest in various aspects of everyday city life in Tanzania and have a clear didactic purpose. They expose the indiscriminate pursuit of material wealth, moral laxity, and the preference for superficial relationships and appeal, sometimes melodramatically, for honesty, decency, loyalty, friendship, and love.

ANEKE, Ogbuefi Nwagu (ca. 1916-90). Aneke was the exponent of an indigenous system of syllabic writing, the Nwagu Aneke ★Igbo script, which he claimed to have created sometime in 1960 by copying marks on leaves of trees in the forest and ascribing syllabic sounds to them with the aid of ancestral spirits. He was, by his own reckoning, born two years before the great influenza of 1918, at Umuleri in the Anambra River area of Anambra State, Nigeria. He succeeded by birth to the traditional medical profession at an early age and became a renowned diviner and, by inheritance, a wealthy landowner. He took the highest title of his community, Ogbuefi [killer-of-cows], and was quite prosperous before the alleged series of visions and encounters with ancestral spirits that resulted in his sudden acquisition of a complete system of signs for representing his native Umuleri dialect of Igbo on paper.

The script lacks diacritical marks, numerals, punctuation marks, word boundaries, and characters for vowels and syllabic nasals, but it follows the consonant-vowel (CV) structure of basic Igbo syllables and has a set of 256 characters representing the complete Igbo syllabary. In the writing, syllables are combined to create words and words are strung together to form sentences. Although it runs from left to right as in the roman script, it does not appear to have been influenced by any alien system. The existence of evidence of earlier users of the same script, however, suggests that this *writing system is much older than Aneke claimed.

Aneke spent several years in a frustrating struggle to call attention to the value of his script and the message for humankind he says was entrusted to him by his spirit-visitors. During this time, he sold off all his land, sank into abject poverty, and was shunned as a lunatic by his relatives and neighbours, who could not understand how an unlettered person could spend so much time every day making quaint marks on paper in the name of writing. However, after the *Nigeria-Biafra war (1967-70), people began to take him more seriously when he surprised the village by reading from his books accurate records of meetings, decisions, and contributions made by his people during the war. A number of press reports called the attention of the academic community to him, and a Nwagu Aneke research project was set up at the University of Nigeria. Appointed a writer-in-residence in the Institute of African Studies at the University of Nigeria, Nsukka in recognition of his resourcefulness and dedication to the revival and promotion of what he called 'traditional knowledge which the Igbo people lost because of the coming of Europeans', Aneke produced a copious assortment of texts in more than two hundred exercise books in the script. The texts range from diaries and memoirs to local history, political theory, social criticism, theology, philosophy, and prophetic reflections on the condition of modern Nigeria and the wider black world. Composed in a poetic language reminiscent of the rhetoric of the Old Testament prophecies, a selection of his writings, edited by Donatus Nwoga, was published under the title *The Scriptures of an African Visionary: Ogbuefi Nwagu Aneke* (1992).

ANGIRA, Jared (1947-), Kenyan poet. At the University of Nairobi Angira studied commerce and edited the seminal literary magazine *Busara*, in which some of his early poetry first appeared. His poetry collections include *Juices* (1970), *Silent Voices* (1972), *Soft Corals* (1973), *Cascades* (1979), *The Years Go By*

(1980), and *Tides of Time: Selected Poems* (1996). A lyrical and philosophical poet who often laments the 'great self-deception' suffered by many who vainly think they know themselves best (as in 'An Evening Liberetto'), he also subtly fuses searing satire and humour about the delusions and senseless arrogance of people, especially politicians. In 'No Coffin, No Grave', a pompous politician who dreams of a great funeral for himself is assassinated in a nightclub and is ironically left on the streets to be eaten by vultures. Several poems reflect the disillusionment that came with the betrayal of the hopes for independence and reveal in their ironic tone a deeply committed radical for whom poetry is an instrument of mass political mobilization against a visionless and irresponsible elite.

ANGLO-BOER WAR For Britain and its white dominions the Anglo-Boer war (1899-1902) was the culmination of Victorian imperial endeavour. Britain's imperial rivals saw the conflict as a rapacious excursion to appropriate South Africa's mineral wealth, and the Boer republics as enclaves of heroic pastoral and patriarchal virtues. Everywhere humanitarian, pacifist, socialist, and feminist organizations rallied to the pro-Boer cause, outstanding proponents being W.T. Stead and Olive *Schreiner. The black majority of South Africa remained conspicuously marginalized in these controversies, though not in the conflict itself.

Much of the pro-British poetry that came out of the war was versified propaganda, but some of it anticipated Wilfred Owen's concept of 'the pity of war', notably H.D. Rawnsley's *Ballads of the War* (1900), Henry Newbolt's *The Sailing of the Long Ships* (1902), Rudyard Kipling's *The Five Nations* (1903), Thomas Hardy's *Poems of the Past and Present* (1902), and T.W.H. Crosland's *The Five Notions* (1903). Poetry protesting at the war is well represented in William Watson's *For England* (1904), *Songs of the Veld* (1902), Perceval *Gibbon's *African Items* (1903), Kingsley Fairbridge's *Veld Verse* (1909), and Alice Buckton's *The Burden of Engela* (1904), a remarkable articulation of empathy with the Boers.

Among soldier and journalist poets at the front the better were G. Murray Johnstone ('Mome'), *The Off-Wheeler Ballads* (1902); Harry Graham ('Coldstreamer'), *Ballads of the Boer War* (1902); and Edgar Wallace, *Writ in Barracks* (1900). The Australians A.D. Paterson, Henry Lawson, and Harry ('Breaker') Morant wrote sharply dissident poems about the conflict. Boer experience of the war inspired the early Afrikaans poets J.F.E. Celliers, Eugène Marais, J.D. du Toit, and C. Louis Leipoldt. In Europe spirited poetry in the Boer cause came from François Coppee, Edmond Rostand, and Sully Prudhomme in French, Willem Kloos and Albert Verwey in Dutch, and Friedrich Lienhard and Ludwig Thoma in German.

The war inspired some 150 novels, ranging from imperialist romance by Ernest Glanville, Bertram *Mitford, and G.A. Henty to several texts more sensitive to the issues involved: Richard Dehan (pseud. for Clotilde Graves), *The Dop Doctor* (1910); Owen Rhoscomyl (pseud. for Owen Vaughan), *Old Fireproof* (1906); Anna Howarth, *Nora Lester* (1902); Douglas *Blackburn, *A Burger Quixote* (1903); W.C. *Scully, *The Harrow* (1921); and Stuart *Cloete, *Rags and Glory* (1963). Kipling's enigmatic Boer war stories appeared in *Traffics and Discoveries* (1902).

Memorable personal reminiscences of the war include Emily Hobhouse's *The Brunt of the War and Where It Fell* (1902), Johanna Brandt's *The Petticoat Commando* (1913), C.R. de Wet's *Three Years War* (1902), Winston Churchill's *London to Ladysmith via Pretoria* (1900), M.H. Grant's *Words by an Eyewitness* (1901), C.G. Dennison's *A Fight to a Finish* (1904), Deneys Reitz's *Commando* (1929) – this last an unusually vivid, haunting memoir – and the almost sole surviving black account of the war, *The *Mafeking Diary of Sol T. Plaatje* (1973; 1999).

ANIEBO, I.N.C. (1939-) Born in Awka in Anambra State of Nigeria, Aniebo joined the Nigerian army after his secondary education. He was a commissioned officer before he joined the Biafran army as one of its pioneer officers. Discharged from the army after the *Nigeria–Biafra war (1967-70), he went to the USA for his undergraduate and graduate degrees. He is currently a teacher of creative writing in the University of Port Harcourt, Nigeria.

Aniebo began publishing short stories in the 1960s in journals, magazines, and newspapers; some were collected later as *Of Wives, Talismans and the Dead* (1983) and *Man of the Market: Short Stories* (1994). By the time his two novels, *The Anonymity of Sacrifice* (1974) and *The Journey Within* (1978), were published his technical control was well established. The themes of marital conflict and infidelity, the vicissitudes of human relationships, the cultural conflict between Africa and Europe, and the human cost of artificial social structures resonate in both the stories and the novels.

The Anonymity of Sacrifice, one of the earliest novels on the Biafran experience, narrates with earthy lucidity the story of two soldiers fighting on the Biafran front. The novel unmasks the anonymity of 'the unknown soldier' to reveal the war's human dimension: the principles and private motives that propel individuals to action and the reasons for certain choices as personal concerns dovetail with those of the nation. *The Journey Within*, as do the short stories, identifies Aniebo with an African authenticity that is embodied in traditional Igbo life and values. Distancing himself from characters who are confused by the clash of African and European values, he privileges

characters who remain resilient in spirit and positive in action in spite of that contact. His effective use of cinematic narratological techniques singles him out as a structural strategist in the art of storytelling.

Anowa (1970) A play by Ama Ata *Aidoo. Based on an old Ghanaian legend about a young woman who decides against her parents' wishes to marry the man she loves, the play is an examination of the dangers of individualism in a culture that values communality. The characters of the woman, Anowa, and her lover, Kofi, allow Aidoo to explore the necessity for flexibility and openness in relationships. It ends when both Anowa and Kofi choose suicide over further involvement with each other and the rest of the world.

Anthills of the Savannah (1986) A novel by Chinua *Achebe. Set in the imaginary West African country of Kangan, which to all intents and purposes is Nigeria, the novel continues the examination of political conditions in a representative post-colonial country initiated in *A *Man of the People* (1966). Here Achebe is concerned with the consequences of military rule in a country where democratic processes have been hopelessly violated, where political chaos has been replaced by megalomania, where constitutional means have come to an impasse. Through dramatic encounters and the ruminations of the principal characters, Achebe dismisses such external factors as international finance capitalism as accounting for Kangan's political problems, demonstrating that the problem with Kangan is a total lack of leadership. The novel is a study of how power corrupts and of how corrupt power destroys itself. In that faint but predictable certainty lies hope. The novel is also concerned with the role of story and storytelling in a society in which oral wisdom is threatened by technology. For Achebe, stories both consolidate gains made by a people and, through new versions of old stories, mediate change by providing a different order of reality.

ANTHOLOGIES

East Africa: East Africa's leading anthologists include David Cook, Chris L. Wanjala, Lennard Okola, and Robert Green, who have been based at Makerere University, University of Nairobi and University of Dar es Salaam. David Cook, who was the first Professor of Literature and English in East Africa, edited *Origin, East Africa: A Makerere Anthology* (1965), *Poems from East Africa* (1971) (with David *Rubadiri), and *In Black and White: Writings from East Africa with Broadcast Discussions and Commentary* (1976). He nurtured such writers as *Ngugi wa Thiong'o, Jonathan Kariara, and John *Ruganda by publishing them in the Department of English magazine, *Penpoint*, and by introducing them to the reading market through the anthologies.

Lennard Okola edited *Drum Beat: East African Poems* (1967), the first anthology of East African poetry to contain poems drawing from African literary traditions. Others were modern and experimental. Chris L. Wanjala, Professor of Literature at Egerton University, edited *Faces at Crossroads: A 'Currents' Anthology* (1971), *Singing with the Night: A Collection of East African Verse* (1974), *The Debtors: Plays from East Africa* (1977), and *Attachments to the Sun* (1980) (with Douglas Blackburn and Alfred Horsfall). The first three were published under the Students' Book Writing Scheme of the East African Literature Bureau, which also published *Just a Moment, God! An Anthology of Verse and Prose from East Africa* (1970), edited by Robert Green. Other poetry anthologies published by the East African Literature Bureau include *Sleepless Nights* (1975) by S.N. Waititu and Y.G. Obasa and *Flashpoints* (1976) by Peter Waithaka and Sam Mbure. *Pulsations: An East African Anthology of Poetry* (1974), edited by Arthur Kemoli and published in the Book Writing Scheme, introduced poets who were to publish their poems in later anthologies. These included Bahadur *Tejani, Jared *Angira, and Amin Kassam. The anthology also included poets from National Teachers' College, Kyambogo, Uganda, whose verse came from rural popular culture and had been selected from a student magazine, *Nanga*, and edited by the controversial British author Denis C. Hills.

Agencies that have prepared and published anthologies include government institutions such as the Kenya Institute of Education, which has produced *The Winner and Other Stories* (1994) and two earlier anthologies, *The Stranger and Other Stories* (1989) and *Chameleon's Second Delivery* (1985). The British Council, Nairobi, an agency of the British government, has edited and published three anthologies of poems from Kenyan schools: *Youthful Voices* (1992), *Search for a New Tomorrow* (1993), and *The Secrets of Wisdom* (1994). Other publishers of anthologies are East African Educational Publishers: *Boundless Voices: Poems from Kenya* (1988), ed. Arthur I. Luvai, and *Tender Memories: Poems and Short Stories* (1989), ed. A. Luvai, W. Kabira, and M. Muluka; Longman, Kenya: *An Anthology of East African Poetry (1988)*, ed. A.D. Amateshe; and Heinemann Kenya.

Among the most anthologized East African writers are Ngugi wa Thiong'o, Joseph Kariuki, John Ruganda, David Rubadiri, Jared Angira, Grace *Ogot, Jonathan Kariara, Joseph G. Mutiga, *Taban Lo Liyong, Samuel N. Mbure, and Benjamin Onyango Ogutu. Jonathan Kariara is the author of a number of poems in *Origin, East Africa*, contributed to *Modern African Prose* (1964), and co-edited *Introduction to East African Poetry* (1977) with Ellen Kitonga. Joseph G. Mutiga, whose poems look to the spiritual past and grieve over the replacement of the African God by the God 'hidden in a dubious Bible', has poems in *Drum Beat* and *Origin, East Africa*. Joseph Kariuki's poems are included in *Modern Poetry from Africa* (1963), edited by Ulli Beier and Gerald Moore. Samuel Mbure, whose family could not afford to allow him to complete his formal schooling, has published poems in *Nexus* and been broadcast in the African Poetry programme of the Voice of Kenya.

South Africa: South Africa has had a significant English-speaking population since the eighteenth century. The beginnings of a literary culture can be traced to the settlers of 1820, many of whom gravitated to the coastal towns and embarked on printing, publishing, and bookselling ventures. Thomas *Pringle and Robert Greig were among the pioneers in this field, and by 1828 R.J. Stapleton could put together an anthology, *Poetry of the Cape of Good Hope*, selected from local periodicals. Alexander Wilmot's *The Poetry of South Africa* (1887), though it demonstrates the failings of much colonial work of the period, stands as the first solid collection. The first anthology to point to the beginnings of an indigenous poetic tradition was Francis Carey *Slater's authoritative *Centenary Book of South African Verse* (1925). Its successor, the *New Centenary Book of South African Verse* (1945, also compiled by Slater), was soon eclipsed by Roy Macnab and Charles Gulston's more enterprising selection, *South African Poetry: A New Anthology* (1948), which was also the first to include the work of a black poet, H.I.E. *Dhlomo.

The anthologies that followed these early examples, Guy *Butler's *A Book of South African Verse* (1959) and Jack *Cope and Uys Krige's *Penguin Book of South African Verse* (1968), reflected poetic developments in South Africa following the Second World War; the latter volume also incorporates translations of Afrikaans and black poetry. This eclecticism characterizes several more recent anthologies, such as *SA in Poësie/SA in Poetry* (1988), ed. Johan van Wyk *et al.*, and the *Penguin Book of Southern African Verse* (1989), ed. Stephen *Gray. Whereas Butler's anthology went some way towards defining a literary canon, Michael Chapman's *A Century of South African Poetry* (1981) gave due emphasis to the emergence of significant black poets. Cosmo Pieterse (in *Seven South African Poets*, 1971) and James *Matthews (in *Black Voices Shout!* 1974) had already focused on the work of black writers; during the 1980s several more such anthologies were published, including *The Return of the Amasi Bird: Black South African Poetry 1891-1981*, edited by Tim Couzens and Essop Patel, and *Voices from Within*, edited by Chapman and Achmat *Dangor (both 1982). Protest and satire aimed at the *apartheid system gave rise to anthologies such as *I Qabane Labantu: Poetry in the Emergency/Poësie in die Noodtoestand* (1989), edited by Ampie Coetzee and Hein Willemse, and *Black Mamba Rising* (1986), edited by Ari Sitas, which features 'South African Worker Poets in the Struggle'. Two collections focusing on women writers are Nohra Moerat's *Siren Songs* (1989) and Cecily Lockett's *Breaking the Silence* (1990).

Anthologies of short stories followed a similar pattern of development from Eurocentric to Afrocentric concerns, as early pioneering tales of exploration and adventure in a hostile environment gave way to an increasingly sympathetic engagement with the indigenous peoples and problems of the country. If E.C. Parnwell's *Stories of Africa* (1930) is largely redolent of colonial values, *Veld-Trails and Pavements* (1949), by H.C. ★Bosman and C. Bredell, and *Quartet: New Voices from South Africa* (1963), by Richard ★Rive, suggest a shift of focus. Most anthologies of short fiction have been limited in scope by being compiled for the schools market; however, Jean Marquard's *A Century of South African Short Stories* (1978) offered a more representative selection; it was updated by Martin Trump in 1994. Among other collections devoted to black writing are Mothobi ★Mutloatse's *Forced Landing, Africa South: Contemporary Writings* (1980) and Mbulelo ★Mzamane's *Hungry Flames and Other Black African Short Stories* (1986). Feminism informs Ann Oosthuizen's *Sometimes When It Rains* (1987), Lindiwe Mabuza's *One Never Knows: An Anthology of Black South African Women Writers in Exile* (1989), and Annemarie van Niekerk's *Raising the Blinds: A Century of South African Women's Stories* (1990).

The first notable anthology of South African plays, *Six One-Act Plays by South African Authors* (1949, no editor), was the product of a competition run by the Federation of Amateur Theatrical Societies of South Africa. Later selections, energized by the renewal of South African drama dating from the 1960s, include Ernest Pereira's *Contemporary South African Plays* (1979), Stephen Gray's *Theatre One* (1978) and *Theatre Two* (1981), Robert Kavanagh's *South African People's Plays* (1981), *South African Theatre: Four Plays and an Introduction* (1984), edited by Temple Hauptfleisch and Ian Steadman (which juxtaposes English, Afrikaans, 'black', and 'alternative' drama), Stephen Gray's *Market Plays* (1986) (plays staged at the Johannesburg Market Theatre), and *Woza Afrika!* (1986), by Duma Ndlovu. More recently Gray published a new selection, *South African Plays* (1993), and John Kani compiled *More Market Plays* (1994).

Among the anthologies that cut across genres are Roy Macnab's *Towards the Sun* (1950), *South African Writing Today* (1967), edited by Nadine ★Gordimer and Lionel ★Abrahams, and Gray's *Writer's Territory* (1973). *A Land Apart* (1986), edited by André ★Brink and J.M. ★Coetzee, incorporates translations of African writers, and *From South Africa: New Writing, Photographs and Art* (1987), by David Bunn and Jane Taylor, specifically focuses on the concept of political emergency in art. Narrower in scope are Mothobi

Mutloatse's *Reconstruction: 90 Years of Black Historical Literature* (1981) and, from a feminist perspective, *LIP from Southern African Women* (1983), edited by Susan Brown et al., and *Women in South Africa: From the Heart* (1988), by Seagang Tsikang and Dinah Lefekane.

Festschrift publications, selections of critical essays, and popular compilations of stories and articles dealing with travel, exploration, wildlife, sport, and folklore have proliferated in recent years, as have anthologies aimed at juvenile readers. Whereas sociopolitical imperatives have been the *raison d'être* for a considerable number of the anthologies published before 1990, political developments in the post-apartheid period and shifts of perspective may well change the direction of South African writing and, consequently, the nature of future anthologies.

South–Central Africa: The first anthology of Rhodesian poetry was John Snelling's *Rhodesian Verse: 1888-1938* (1938), in which only A.S. ★Cripps's poems stand out from Georgian musings and ballads about exile on the imperial frontier. Its most remarkable feature is Cripps's introduction, which attacks Rhodesian racism, looks forward to future anthologies where poems by black poets will appear, and celebrates the absence in the anthology of 'post-war anti-traditional' verse. Rhodesian poets' rejection of English modernism can be seen again in Snelling's *A New Anthology of Rhodesian Verse* (1950). D.E. Finn's *Poetry in Rhodesia: 75 Years* (1968) shows considerable development. Finn had access to poems from the periodicals *Rhodesian Poetry* and *Two Tone*, both of which encouraged technically innovative poems and published poetry by black and white writers. T.O. ★McLoughlin's *New Writing in Rhodesia* (1976) was the first anthology to place short stories and a play alongside recently published poems. His selection drew overwhelmingly on black writers. Kizito Muchemwa's *Zimbabwean Poetry in English* followed in 1978, and he argued on the evidence of his selection that black poets writing in English possessed a distinctive voice. After Zimbabwean independence, Mudereri Kadhani and Musaemura ★Zimunya published their important anthology *And Now the Poets Speak* (1981), which was the first locally published body of protest, resistance, and war poetry; its final section consists of poems celebrating the founding of the new nation. Alec Pongweni's *Songs That Won the Liberation War* (1982) provides the ★Shona original and an English translation of songs sung during the liberation war by guerillas and popular bands. The texts are linked by brief commentaries. The most historically complete anthology remains Colin and O-Lan Style's *Mambo Book of Zimbabwean Verse in English* (1986). It includes English translations of traditional Shona and ★Ndebele poetry, a selection from the poets available to Snelling, and poems by both black and white poets writing after 1950. Musaemura Zimunya also edited *Birthright: A Selection of Poems from Southern Africa* (1989), which includes verse in English and in English translation from the frontline states of Angola, Botswana, Lesotho, Malawi, Mozambique, Swaziland, Tanzania, Zambia, and Zimbabwe. In 1990 T.O. McLoughlin produced a new anthology of short stories, *The Sound of Snapping Wires*, in which stories by A.S. Cripps, Doris *Lessing, Charles *Mungoshi, and Tsitsi *Dangarembga appear with stories by lesser-known writers. In 1994 the Zimbabwean Women Writers organization published a large selection of poems and short stories written in English by their members in *Anthology*, edited by Norma Kitson. The organization is preparing companion anthologies in Ndebele and Shona.

West Africa: Two main anthologizing practices relating to the selection of materials and to the purposes of the anthologies are revealed by West African poetry anthologies of the 1970s. The dominant selection method focuses mainly on the re-publication of existing poems by established authors; the chief purpose is the arrangement of texts into a literary historical format. The use of published works as materials for poetry anthologies is exemplified in major African poetry collections such as *A Selection of African Poetry* (1976), edited by Kojo Senanu and Theo Vincent, Wole *Soyinka's *Poems of Black Africa* (1975), and *Modern Poetry from Africa* (1963 and new editions), edited by Gerald Moore and Ulli Beier. In *Poems of Black Africa*, the editor acknowledges 'the permission of the poets and their respective publishers to reprint the poems in [the] anthology'. Donatus Nwoga's *West African Verse* (1965) is a good example of an earlier West African poetry anthology in which the works of published poets are used to construct a literary historical scheme reflecting phases of literary and social development. Nwoga's anthology captures the historical point of the transition from the colonial period to the post-colonial, and his arrangement of materials into sections of pioneer poets and modern poets generates one of the most convenient ways of categorizing poetry in Africa. The selection of poems from such pioneer poets as Dennis *Osadebey and Gladys *Casely-Hayford has the merit of reflecting one phase in the development of West African poetry: the first significant effort at fashioning artistic skill to make poetry respond to social and political functions. The inclusion of *negritude poets like L.S. *Senghor registers an important landmark in which writers struggle for self-awareness, identity, and assertion. Also, poems chosen from the dominant West African poets such as Soyinka, Lenrie *Peters, and Christopher *Okigbo mark a period in which African poets reach a level of technical competence and social awareness.

Another type of West African poetry anthology introduces the work of poets from a particular country. An example is *Messages: Poems from Ghana* (1971), edited by Kofi *Awoonor and G. Adali-Mortty. The anthology is tangible evidence of Ghanaian poetry from the viewpoint of the more established poets. Although the poems of Kofi Awoonor and others in the anthology still show the influence of oral traditions, many of the poems express the new themes of social and political problems, often in a scathingly satirical mode.

The publication in the 1980s of two poetry anthologies in Nigeria set a new direction in compiling materials for anthologies. These anthologies are *Voices from the Fringe* (1988), edited by Harry *Garuba, and *Rising Voices* (1991), edited by David Cook, Olu *Obafemi, and Wumi Raji. (Two African poetry anthologies initiated by the BBC, *Summer Fires*, 1983, and *The Fate of Vultures*, 1989, are not dissimilar.) None of the poems in *Voices from the Fringe* or *Rising Voices* had ever been published, and both anthologies shift the focus from the more established poets to relatively new ones. The anthologies also mark the first appearance in print for many of their contributors. Not only do the two books represent a departure from typical practice in mode of selection, purpose, circumstances of production, and vision, but they also indicate a fairly homogeneous group of writers existing in the same literary historical phase. Earlier anthologies, containing the published work of poets from several literary traditions, provide a picture of literary historical movements.

Voices from the Fringe and *Rising Voices* contain the work of poets who may be described as a new generation of Nigerian writers. Many of the voices in the anthologies would not have emerged so readily from the frustrating experience of trying to publish an individual poetry collection. The collective nature of the anthology form enables these poets to pull resources together in order to realize the text. Details of the preliminary activities leading to the publication of these anthologies show that each poet had full knowledge of the processes of the production of the texts. Unlike the editors of the much older West African anthologies, editors of the new anthologies kept the contributing poets informed of their interaction with the publishers. Where it was necessary to co-fund production with the publishers, contributors were contacted for decisions. The result is a production system in which writers participate in the actual production processes.

The conditions for the involvement of poets in the technical production and transmission of their works have been initiated by emergent literary associations, which are conscious of the problems of publication and determined to search for alternative media for transmitting creative products. Most of the poems that eventually appear in new anthologies have undergone critical evaluation in literary meetings, which are often the arena of poetry readings, criticism, and exchange among poets.

A close reading of each of the new West African poetry anthologies indicates textual evidence of literary works realized through readings, performances, and criticism. An alternative literary tradition gradually emerges from the new West African poetry anthologies: poets' collective response to shared experience. This collective force in art production appears first in literary organizations and is then transferred into anthology form, which technically permits the existence of a community of writers and acts as the provenance of their poetry harvests.

ANYIDOHO, Kofi (1947-), Ghanaian poet, was born in Wheta in the Volta Region of Ghana and was educated at the University of Ghana, Legon (BA), Indiana University (MA), and the University of Texas (Ph.D.). He taught primary, middle, and secondary school in Ghana before moving into a university career. He is Professor of Literature in the English Department as well as Director of the School of Performing Arts of the University of Ghana. He has received several awards for his poetry, including the Valco Fund Literary Award, the Langston Hughes Prize, the BBC Arts and Africa Poetry Award, the Fania Kruger Fellowship for Poetry of Social Vision, Poet of the Year (Ghana), and the Ghana Book Award. He was elected a fellow of the International Academy of Poets in 1974. Some of his poems have been translated into Italian, German, Dutch, and Slavic.

Anyidoho's poetry has appeared in journals and anthologies world wide. His four published books of poetry are *Elegy for the Revolution* (1978), *A Harvest of Our Dreams* (1985), *Earthchild* (1985), and *Ancestral-Logic and Caribbean Blues* (1993). Though rooted in the traditions and culture of the Ewe people of Ghana, the major themes and concerns of his poetry have been public, political, and social. In its oracular quality it compares, especially in its presentation of the poet-cantor, to the poetry of Kofi ★Awoonor, Christopher ★Okigbo and Atukwei ★Okai. Although his poetry is elegiac in tone, it also reveals that within a traditional African ontological context the tragic cannot be divorced from the comic, life and death exist on an indistinguishable continuum, and sorrow and joy occupy the same revolving axis. In spite of the mournful tone of 'From Christianborg to Ussherfort' (in *A Harvest of Our Dreams*), for example, Anyidoho can assert 'We will gather again the unfinished harvest/of lost seasons and.../a basketful of songs for our festival of peace'. Noticeably characteristic of his themes is his concern with the communal welfare, as is evident in his use of the first person plural pronoun in the lines quoted here.

The source of Anyidoho's poetry is anger: righteous indignation at the rape, the brutalization, and the dehumanization that he perceives as the hallmark of European colonization of Africa and its peoples, anger at the venality and ineptitude of the majority of post-independent African leaders. He makes his preoccupation with the plight of post-independent Africa explicit in 'HouseBoy' (in *A Harvest of Our Dreams*): 'The dreams of Fanon's wretched of the earth/condense into storms in our mourning sky'. His poetry, best seen in performance, insists on the redemptive transformation of the lives of black people all over the world.

APARTHEID On the 1948 general election hustings in South Africa, Dr D.F. Malan presented the all-white electorate with a policy he called 'apartheid', whereby the multiple ethnic groups in the Union of South Africa would develop separately. The Nationalist party victory on the apartheid ticket ensured white South African domination over the black, 'coloured' (mixed race), and Asian majority. It also meant that the West could maintain influence over gold, diamond and uranium deposits and over the strategically significant Cape sea route.

A clear affront to democratic principles, South Africa was ejected from the Commonwealth in 1961, and that same year an all-white referendum transformed the Union of South Africa into a republic. Under Dr. Hendrik Verwoerd and successive Nationalist party prime ministers, white domination over the so-called 'non-whites' or 'non-Europeans' was consolidated. The Sharpeville massacre (1960), the Soweto uprising (1976), and township violence across the republic throughout the 1980s were flashpoints in an era of violent state oppression. However, by the early 1990s, years of economic sanctions, a sports boycott, and guerilla warfare perpetrated principally by Umkhonto we Sizwe, the military wing of the African National Congress, combined with unexpectedly swift events in Europe in the late 1980s to make apartheid unviable. Soviet bloc disintegration, symbolized by the fall of the Berlin Wall in 1990, ended the Cold War. By April 1994, the first all-race elections had been held in South Africa and ANC leader Nelson Mandela elected president. Like European colonialism, apartheid had been consigned to the history books.

Apartheid's skin-colour discrimination caused black (African, coloured and Asian) and white South African experiences to differ intrinsically, thereby precluding a single, national South African literature. While socially and economically privileged whites lived in a conspiracy of ignorance in their pseudo-democracy, Africans, coloureds, and Asians were subjected to three versions of the police-state oppression of a totalitarian regime. As a result, distinct subliteratures developed, the differences between them becoming more marked as apartheid oppression and *censorship intensified – despite the potentially unifying effect of the resolutely non-racial political approach of the Congress movement and, for blacks, the emphasis on the unity of the oppressed in the *Black Consciousness philosophy which dominated the 1970s.

In broad terms, black South African writing focused on the daily suffering of black communities and their resistance to the injustices of the apartheid regime, institutionalized subjugation of blacks having muted other universal topics such as gender. Sol T. *Plaatje and other forerunners laid a foundation, but it was in the nature of colonial repression, with its periodic pogroms and 'clampdowns', to stratify the generations of resistance and inhibit the development of a resistance culture. Not until the 1950s did a distinct black South African literature begin to take shape. Witty, acerbic articles and short stories appearing in *Drum magazine, Golden City Post, and The Classic attracted a large black urban readership and served as a springboard for many writers, among them Bessie *Head, Arthur Maimane, Todd Matshikiza, James *Matthews, Bloke *Modisane, Casey *Motsisi, Es'kia *Mphahlele, Nat *Nakasa, Lewis *Nkosi, Henry Nxumalo and Can *Themba. By the 1960s, however, the verve and humour of 'the Drum decade' had been beaten out of black creative writing and the Sharpeville massacre aftermath had forced many writers into exile.

In the 1970s resistance to apartheid was rekindled by the *Black Consciousness movement under the inspirational leadership of Steve Biko and by the black labour movement in the wake of the Durban strikes of 1973; this resistance ignited in the Soweto uprising of 1976. With the labour movement forced to build slowly, picking its way through repressive industrial legislation, and the Black Consciousness political organizations all banned in October 1977, a space opened for literature as a medium of popular resistance to apartheid. These were the years of *Staffrider magazine and the Staffrider Series – story collections, novels, books of poetry and anthologies that drew on work first appearing in or advertised through the magazine. Literature had always been a strand in Black Consciousness attempts to inspire a political renaissance by returning to black social and cultural roots. In the Staffrider period the new writing moved decisively beyond protest as black writers addressed themselves to township readers rather than to the sympathetic liberal public in white South Africa and abroad. Publishing ventures – in fields such as literacy, education and popular history as well as literature – attempted to create new networks of communication (book clubs, youth associations and semi-clandestine street-to-street selling rather than bookshops), bringing writers

and readers together in a new space that would come to be known as people's culture.

Despite several writers' attempts to write novels about the Soweto uprising (Miriam *Tlali in Amandla, Mongane *Serote in To Every Birth Its Blood, Sipho *Sepamla in A Ride on the Whirlwind, Mbulelo *Mzamane in The Children of Soweto and Mothobi *Mutloatse in Mama Ndiyalila), the strength of black South African prose incontestably remained in the short story, now adapted to giving political counsel (Mtutuzeli Matshoba's stories winning a special place in township folklore) but also devoted to the 'rediscovery of the ordinary', Njabulo *Ndebele's phrase for a process he detected in the stories of Joel Matlou and sought to cultivate in his own. In this way resistance to apartheid broadened into a search for identity and the cultural resources to sustain the struggle and build the future.

The first wave of Black Consciousness writing had announced itself in poetry rather than prose, with Sipho Sepamla, Mongane Serote, and Mafika *Gwala as the central figures. Post-Soweto, Sepamla became mainly a prose writer and director of cultural projects, Serote wrote long poems from exile that tracked his internalization of the struggle as an activist, Gwala extended his visceral and varied output from the heart of the troubled township of Mpumalanga, where he had formed one of the writers' groups typical of the new period, and poets like Christopher *van Wyk and Achmat *Dangor published their first collections. As literally hundreds of 'instant poets' sought to emulate these forerunners on the page, the hugely successful performance poetry of Ingoapele Madingoane and others provided a significant new dimension which combined literary skill and activism to redefine the traditional role of the oral poet.

A low-key but increasingly significant aspect of black literature in the closing decades of apartheid was the emergence of a sense of its history and trajectory. Interest in oral traditions, the republication of pioneering writers like Plaatje and H.I.E. *Dhlomo and the recognition and celebration of the 'Drum decade' were all aspects of a process that proceeded at the academic level (with Es'kia *Mphahlele now returning as a professor of African literature) but also at the grassroots, through cultural workshops, journalism and publishing.

If a space for 'people's culture' in which literature participated had emerged by the beginning of the 1980s, the phrase itself really belongs to the next period of resistance to apartheid, in full swing from the mid-1980s and extending to the dismantling of the regime in the 1990s. In this period black literature was recontextualized by the revival of organized political opposition spearheaded by the United Democratic Front and the Congress of South African Trade Unions, both clearly identified with the exiled liberation movement led by the African National Congress. Worker poetry and plays spoke to black workplace audiences with the enspiriting directness that township-based writers had achieved, while 'people's poets' like Mzwakhe *Mbuli sounded the keynotes on Congress-aligned political platforms.

If the emergence – decade by lost decade, then as an energized political force – of a 'literature against apartheid' has to be understood primarily as a phenomenon involving black writers and readers/audiences, there remains the ironic consideration that internationally the literary challenge to apartheid is most closely identified with white writers – such as Alan *Paton, Nadine *Gordimer, Athol *Fugard, or J.M. *Coetzee – who are sometimes perceived as courageous and heroic figures despite their increasingly searching explorations of the deeply ambiguous role of the writer who sets out to represent the lives of subaltern others.

Apartheid has been 'a great provoker' of creative writing. The post-apartheid period could witness the continuation of apartheid's racially defined discourses. Alternatively, it could herald the articulation of an all-race, national discourse in which the politics of the text is seen to open onto a dimensional space unimaginable within the more confining prison-house of apartheid.

ARMAH, Ayi Kwei (1939-), Ghanaian novelist, was born to Fanti-speaking parents in Sekondi-Takoradi, the twin harbour city and capital of the Western Region of Ghana. He had his early education at Achimota School, near Accra, after which he worked as a Radio Ghana scriptwriter, reporter, and announcer. At the age of nineteen he went to the USA as a scholarship student and acquired post-graduate degrees from Harvard and Columbia. His life has been centred on his literary work, especially on the retrieval of the African past for the re-invention of post-colonial Africa. He has lived and worked in every region of the continent and has taught at universities in North America, including Massachusetts and Wisconsin. A resident of Dakar, Senegal, he combines the writing of fiction with professional translation and university teaching in literature and creative writing. He is perhaps the most provocative and versatile prose stylist of the second generation of anglophone African writers as well as the most significant Ghanaian novelist to date.

Armah is a scholar, a critic, a university professor, essayist, poet, and short-story writer, but his reputation derives from his novels. He has written and published six novels: The *Beautyful Ones Are Not Yet Born (1968), an unflinching exposé of government corruption; *Fragments (1970), in which he deploys the autobiographical mode to expose and lament the giddying suffocation of a post-colonial African society

(represented by Ghana); *Why Are We So Blest? (1972), which, while excoriating post-colonial African leadership for its privileging of European culture, encapsulates a vision of the contemporary world; *Two Thousand Seasons (1973), which Wole *Soyinka calls a 'visionary reconstruction' of the African past; The *Healers (1978), a fictional re-creation of Akan society; and *Osiris Rising (1995), which borrows its narrative structure from the Isis-Osiris myth cycle to tell a story of love, death, and the promise of creative renewal in modern Africa.

In an essentially autobiographical article, 'One Writer's Education' (West Africa, August 1985), Armah identifies himself not simply as an Akan, an Ewe, a Ghanaian, and a West African, but 'most significantly as an African'. His concern to work for change in Africa has made him perhaps not only the most controversial but also the most polemical African writer. In Armah's Africa, revolutionaries are the only creators, an ideological position that has elicited the wrath of both African and foreign critics. But although those critics have taken him to task for his position on race, it is pertinent that The Beautyful Ones and Fragments lambast not whites but the corrupt African leadership. Like his compatriot Ama Ata *Aidoo, he sees Africa as a 'community without unity', and his writing, particularly in Two Thousand Seasons, stridently insists on a community with unity. Critics have also commented on the Western influences on Armah's thought and style. Although such influences are undeniable, his concerns in all his work are African, and his art, like that of many committed artists, demonstrates a synthesis between style and subject matter.

ARMATTOE, R(aphael) E(rnest) G(rail) (1913-53) Ghanaian poet. Born in Keta, in the Volta Region of Ghana, Armattoe was educated in Togo and Ghana, where he wrote his first poems, and in Europe, where he trained as a physicist. He identified with Togolese nationalism and is today claimed as a Togolese writer by younger scholars. His wide-ranging intellectual interests included anthropology and European philosophy; he wrote profusely, but published little. His collected poems are entitled Between the Forest and the Sea (1950). The modern African nationalists who fought for independence for Gold Coast were critical of the attitudes towards black Africans in Deep Down the Black Man's Mind (1954), in which he expresses his alienation from his homeland. He did not, however, spare white European cultures his disparagement; he described the British as great literary people but 'obtuse minded'. He died prematurely while visiting Hamburg.

AROGBOFA, Seinde (1940-), Nigerian dramatist, was born in Oka and educated at Victory College,

Ikare and the University of Ibadan. His four plays, *Trapped* (1983), *Agidi Sours* (1985), *The Socialite* (1988), and *Wives and Mothers* (1989), are social satires directed at men trapped in lecherous schemes, husbands who take wives for granted, indecisive educated women caught awkwardly in the transition from tradition to modernity, hypocritical and corrupt public and religious officials, ostentatious public display, the violence and immorality that accompany the get-rich-quick mentality, and indiscipline at all levels of society. However, the pessimism and despair of satire are countered by the moral optimism encouraged by human acts of kindness. Although the early plays show weakness in the characterization of women, slavish adherence to classical dramatic forms, insufficient humour, and lack of objective distance between the playwright and his materials, succeeding plays become more realistic, believable, and entertaining. Traditional cultural elements such as the *oriki* (praise names), proverbs, Ifa divinatory poetry, music, dance, and song enhance dialogue, plot, and stage action and appeal strongly to the popular audience for whom Arogbofa predominantly writes.

Arrow of God (1964; rev. 1974) A novel by Chinua *Achebe. The novel develops the theme, initiated in Achebe's first novel, *Things Fall Apart* (1958), of the impact on Igbo traditional life of British imperial-colonial rule. Set in eastern Nigeria during the period of the entrenchment of colonial rule, it tells the tragic story of Ezeulu, chief priest of the god Ulu, who in trying to reconcile the demands of his god and his quest for personal power brings calamity on himself, his family, and his clan and inadvertently fosters the hegemony of Christianity. Achebe's style is characterized by a clear narrative, a plain yet highly allusive English, and the use of local imagery and folk literary materials. His vision is at once neutral, ironic, and tragic in a novel that deals with problems of traditionalism and ritual under stress from modernism and the emulation of western concepts and ideals.

ASALACHE, Khadambi (1934-), Kenyan novelist and poet, was born in northern Kenya to a family of poor herdsmen. Exposed, through contacts with his peers, to the benefits of Western-style education in post-colonial Kenya, he struggled hard to overcome the poverty and deprivations of his childhood and to see himself through primary school and the equivalent of a high-school education. He subsequently fought his way into the Royal College, Nairobi, where he studied art and architecture. Brought up as a herdsman in an environment of inter-communal feuds during his early school days, his only novel, *A Calabash of Life* (1967), and a sprinkling of poems in various journals and anthologies take the reader further back to pre-colonial Kenya, where such feuds often grew into

open warfare. He left Kenya in 1960 to settle in London after a tour of Rome, Geneva, Vienna, and London and has held a number of teaching positions since. His only volume of verse, *Sunset in Naivasha* (1973), published in London, explores the situation of an exile who meditates on a world to which he can never return. Although *A Calabash of Life* received a fair amount of favourable critical notice shortly after its publication, not much has been heard in recent years from Asalache. Nevertheless, he has a place among the pioneers of modern Kenyan literature in English.

AWOONOR, Kofi (Nyedevu) (1935-) (formerly known as George Awoonor-Williams), Ghanaian poet, novelist, and critic, was born in Wheta, Ghana, studied at Achimota School, the University of Ghana, the University of London, and at the State University of New York at Stony Brook, where he gained a Ph.D. in English and Comparative Literature. Having served as Chair of the Department of Comparative Literature at SUNY Stony Brook, Head of the Department of English and Dean of the Faculty of Arts at University of Cape Coast, he was appointed Ghana's ambassador to Brazil in 1985 and to Cuba in 1989. He has also served as Ghana's representative in the United Nations. He has been a contributing editor to *Transition* and received the National Book Council Award for poetry in 1979.

Awoonor is known for his use of traditional Ewe folklore and poetry in his writing. His first volume of poetry, *Rediscovery* (1964, published under the name George Awoonor-Williams), was followed by *Night of My Blood*, a co-edited volume of Ghanaian poetry (*Messages: Poems from Ghana*), and his novel *This Earth, My Brother* (all 1971). The versatile Awoonor also published two short plays, *Ancestral Power* and *Lament* (1972), before returning to poetry with his third volume *Ride Me, Memory* (1973). In 1974 he turned to translation of Ewe poetry with *Guardians of the Sacred Word*, a work featuring the oral poetry of Henoga Vinoko and Komi Ekpe. Shortly after returning to Ghana from the USA he was arrested for aiding a political fugitive, and some of his subsequent works, including *The House by the Sea* (1978) and *Until the Morning After: Collected Poems* (1987), contain poetic and narrative accounts of his experiences as a prisoner in Ghana's Ussher Fort prison. Although his poems cover a number of broad topics such as the effects of colonialism, the African personality, and the corruption of African politicians, they remain highly personal and autobiographical. *Night of My Blood*, for example, deals with his physical and psychological separation from his early life in Africa and the Western influences upon his life. In *Ride Me, Memory* he writes of his experiences in the US, where he discovers a connection between the sufferings of African-

Americans and Africans. *The House by the Sea* ranges from his wandering through America, his return to Ghana and his imprisonment, to his vision of the future. *This Earth, My Brother* covers many of the same themes as his poetry. Like the author, the novel's protagonist, Amamu, finds himself unable to come to terms with conditions in Ghana after independence. And, like his countryman Ayi Kwei *Armah, Awoonor is distressed by the corruption and hypocrisy of post-independence Ghana and seeks to discover some way to reconcile expectations and realities. His second novel, *Comes the Voyager at Last*

(1992) is a mythic tale of the return of a slave from the New World to his native land. Awoonor's role as critic and teacher is best seen in his book *The Breast of the Earth: A Critical Survey of Africa's Literature, Culture and History* (1975). This ambitious volume, containing useful essays on African writers, music, oral literature, arts, and politics, reflects the concerns for African traditional culture present in Awoonor's poetry and fiction. He has also written books of political commentary: *The Ghana Revolution: A Background Account from a Personal Perspective* (1984) and *Ghana: A Political History from Pre-European to Modern Times* (1990).

B

BÂ, Amadou Hampâté (1901-91) The work of Hampâté Ba, as he is usually called, is central in West African writing. As a historian, a theologian, an ethnographer, a novelist and autobiographer, as well as a linguist and an ambassador, he has been present on all fronts of cultural development in the second half of the century. Born in Bandiagara, Mali to a pre-eminent Fula Muslim family he was trained in a francophone primary school and became a junior clerk in colonial administration. At the same time he completed his Muslim upbringing by following the teachings of Tierno Bokar, a Muslim mystical master. He became involved in collecting texts for historical and ethnographic research when he was seconded to IFAN, the French colonial research institute based in Dakar, with branches all over West Africa. His first publications are joint works with colonial historians and ethnographers; in the 1960s his stature rose as he became Director of the new Malian Institute for Research in Human Sciences and an Ambassador to UNESCO. He is credited with coining the now famous phrase: 'the death of an old man is like the burning of a library' in praise of both old age and oral tradition. He produced a series of texts in Fula, edited, transcribed and translated with fellow scholars (*Koumen*, 1961 with Germaine Dieterlen; *Kaîdara*, 1968, with Lilyan Kesteloot) and himself authored some of the classic mystical stories (*Njeddo Dewal*, 1985). His work as a guardian of oral tradition became well known, but he was at the same time, paradoxically, a Muslim scholar trying to bridge the gap between cultures.

His only novel *L'Etrange destin de Wangrin* (1973; trans. *The Fortunes of Wangrin*, 1999) is a masterpiece of picaresque humour. It narrates in a vivid language the adventures of an interpreter who is a crook and embodies much of the ambiguous position of many African middlemen in the first half of the century.

In his later years he retired to Abidjan, concentrating on Muslim teaching, preaching an open minded Islam, in dialogue with the world, Christianity and African religions. At the same time he prepared an autobiography, *Amkoullel, l'enfant peul* (1991) which has become a bestseller because of his combination of authentic ethnographic knowledge with a gentle humour and unrelenting energy.

BÂ, Mariama (1929-81), Senegalese novelist writing in French. Between the publication of her first novel in 1979 and her death just two years later, Bâ gained a considerable international readership. The impact of that first novel, *Une si longue lettre* (*So Long a Letter*, 1981) rests partly on its intrinsic quality. It is, however, also a pioneering work, as Bâ was among the very first female novelists from sub-Saharan Africa to explore the experience of Muslim African women (another Senegalese writer, Aminata Sow-Fall, produced her novel *La Grève des Bàttu*; *The Beggar's Strike*, 1981, in the same year). Although she denied that *So Long a Letter* was closely autobiographical, the essential outlines of her heroine's life correspond to Bâ's own. Born in Dakar, Senegal, the daughter of a civil servant (later, Senegal's first minister of health), Bâ was to marry a parliamentarian, from whom she separated after bearing nine children. A primary schoolteacher and later schools inspector, Bâ became a prominent activist in what were essentially apolitical Senegalese woman's associations. She had written little before her novel *So Long a Letter*, which in 1980 won the first Noma Award for writing published in Africa and soon appeared in more than a dozen translations.

Bâ died, after a long illness, shortly before the publication of her second novel, *Un chant écarlate* (1981; *Scarlet Song*, 1986). Less a pioneering work than *So Long a Letter* in the sense that its subject matter is familiar from earlier novels, *Scarlet Song* deals with marriage across cultures, demonstrating how the difficulties of a young Frenchwoman, Mireille, in adjusting to an African value system and the inability of her Senegalese husband, Ousmane, to adapt to a syncretic life lead to the breakdown of their marriage. Despite a certain deterministic rhetoric, the novel vividly describes Ousmane's increasingly blatant neglect of Mireille and his emphatic re-insertion in his own culture.

Bacchae of Euripides, The (1973) A play by Wole *Soyinka. Commissioned by the National Theatre of Great Britain in 1971, this 1973 adaptation presents a fifth-century Hellas plagued with slave labour and state-controlled Eleusinian mysteries in need of the cathartic and democratizing force of a foreign god, Dionysus, who appears in this version of the play as the younger brother to Ogun, the Yoruba deity. Juxtaposing humorous levity with snippets from Nietzsche and Frazer, Soyinka subtly hints at the Afro-Asiatic roots of Greek civilization. The conclusion he reaches about the martial puritanism of Attica equally applies to contemporary Nigeria's state corruption.

BANDELE-THOMAS, Biyi (1967-), Nigerian

poet, playwright, and novelist, was born in Kafan-chan, northern Nigeria, studied drama at Obafemi Awolowo University, Ile-Ife (1987-90), and lives in London, writing and working for several periodical publications and the BBC. He has written a collection of poetry, *Waiting for Others* (1989), which won the British Council Lagos Award; six plays, *Rain* (1989), winner of the International Student Playscript Com-petition, *Marching for Fausa* (1993), *Resurrections* (1994), *Two Horsemen* (1994), which was selected as the Best New Play at the London New Play festival in 1994, *Death Catches the Hunter,* and *Me and the Boys* (1995); two novels, *The Man Who Came In From the Back of Beyond* (1991) and *The Sympathetic Undertaker and Other Dreams* (1991); and several plays for radio and television. In 1997 his stage adaptation of Chinua *Achebe's *Things Fall Apart* was performed in Leeds and London.

Bandele-Thomas's satirical novels are a wild and angry portrait of contemporary Nigerian politics, of its all-consuming corruption and overall militarism. Sev-eral stories fold into one another, ensnaring the reader in a nightmare labyrinth. The heroes are fragile vic-tims unwilling to bend to that nightmare reality. In *The Man Who Came In*, a teacher relates the story of his life to one of his pupils, the narrator. An unfinished novel within the novel turns out to be the life story of one of the teacher's childhood friends, a criminal who invests the profits from illegal drug dealing in arms to wage a guerilla war against the corrupt misalliance of politicians and the military. After he is shot dead he becomes a sort of moral guide for the teacher's pupil. *The Sympathetic Undertaker* is in some ways a continua-tion of the first novel. Underlying the pessimism that is a feature of the plays as well as the novels, however, is hope for an end to the derangements that humanity suffers.

Beadle, The (1926) A novel by Pauline *Smith. Although Smith's other fiction is set in South Africa's arid Little Karoo, the story of Andrina du Toit and Aalst Vlokman unfolds in the Aangenaam Valley. The novel deals with self-righteousness and forgiveness. Andrina is unaware that she is the illegitimate daugh-ter of the Beadle, Aalst Vlokman, a harsh and bitter man unable to forget the sin that led to her birth. When Andrina becomes pregnant and disappears from the valley, Aalst Vlokman is tormented with concern for her, and when he finds her, he fears she will reject him. But the novel revises the idea of sin as a perma-nent condition. When Aalst Vlokman arrives at the home of the compassionate old man who has given Andrina shelter, she calls on him to come and see his grandson, referring to him as *Oupa* or grandfather. Aalst Vlokman, who at the beginning of the novel had no one to call friend and no on he dared call child, is now embraced into the small family. Although sin is a

source of sorrow and pain, deep joy comes to those who repent.

Beatification of Area Boy, The (1995) A play by Wole *Soyinka. Soyinka's most significant play since the mid-1970s was premiered in Britain while the play-wright was living in self-imposed exile. A large-scale work in episodic form (Soyinka gives it the sub-title 'A Lagosian Kaleidoscope'), the play gradually coa-lesces into a composite picture of the increasingly harsh conditions under which Nigerians lived during the military regimes of the 1980s and 90s. Set in a street traders' area outside a smart Lagos supermarket, a series of vivid vignettes touch seamlessly and with-out thematic forcing on realities such as street crime, slum clearance, ritual murder, the corruption of the military, and the *Nigeria-Biafra war, all of this punc-tuated with astringent satirical songs. It climaxes in a large set-piece scene, a disastrous society wedding, which recalls the famous denouement of Soyinka's 1967 play * *Kongi's Harvest.*

Beautyful Ones Are Not Yet Born, The (1968) A novel by Ayi Kwei *Armah. In Armah's first novel 'the man', a railway clerk, inertly observes the physical and moral corruption pervading Accra, which Armah immerses in arresting excremental imagery. Kwame Nkrumah's nationalist ideals have waned quickly without changing the quality of life for the majority, and a feverish urge to consume characterizes the élite, represented by the minister Koomson. The man, both fascinated and repelled by the gaudy luxury he observes, refuses bribes and therefore meets the hostil-ity of his shallow colleagues and his spiritless wife. He has abandoned all hope for the future. His only friend, 'the Teacher', similarly condemns himself to waste his brightness in a secluded existence. Armah's uncom-promisingly bleak vision generated a great deal of crit-ical controversy and prompted comparisons with European existentialism.

BEDIAKO, Kwabena Asare [See KONADU, (Samuel) Asare]

BEKEDEREMO, J(ohn) P(epper) Clark (1935-), Nigerian poet and playwright; originally published under the name of J. P. Clark. Born of both Urhobo and Ijo ancestral origins, Bekederemo received his early education at the Native Administration School and the prestigious Government College in Ughelli, and his BA degree in English at the University of Ibadan, where he edited various magazines including the *Beacon* (1956-) and *The Horn* (1957-). Upon grad-uation from Ibadan in 1960, he worked as an informa-tion officer in the Ministry of Information in the old Western Region, as features editor of the *Daily Express*, and as a research fellow at the Institute of

African Studies, University of Ibadan. He was for several years a professor of English at the University of Lagos, a position from which he retired in 1980. In 1982 he founded, with his wife Ebun Odutola (a professor and former director of the Centre for Cultural Studies at the University of Lagos), the Pec Repertory Theatre in Lagos. A widely travelled man, Bekederemo has, since his retirement, held visiting professorial appointments at several institutions of higher learning, including Yale and Wesleyan University in the USA.

Poetry is the genre in which he is probably most successful as an artist. His poetic works are *Poems* (1961), a group of forty lyrics that treat heterogeneous themes; *A Reed in the Tide* (1965), occasional poems that focus on the poet's indigenous African background and his travel experience in America and other places; *Casualties: Poems 1966-68* (1970), which illustrates the horrendous events of the *Nigeria–Biafra war; *A Decade of Tongues* (1981), a collection of seventy-four poems, all except 'Epilogue to Casualties' (dedicated to Michael Echeruo) previously published in his earlier volumes of verse; *State of the Union* (1981), which highlights his apprehension about the sociopolitical events in Nigeria as a developing nation; and *Mandela and Other Poems* (1988), which deals with the perennial problem of ageing and death. His poetic career spans three literary pedigrees: the apprenticeship stage of trial and experimentation, exemplified by such juvenilia as 'Darkness and Light' and 'Iddo Bridge'; the imitative stage, in which he appropriates such Western poetic conventions as the couplet measure and the sonnet sequence, exemplified in such lyrics as 'To a Fallen Soldier' and 'Of Faith', and the individualized stage, in which he attains the maturity and originality of form of such poems as 'Night Rain', 'Out of the Tower', and 'Song'. While his poetic themes centre around violence and protest (*Casualties*), institutional corruption (*State of the Union*), the beauty of nature and the landscape (*A Reed in the Tide*), European colonialism ('Ivbie' in *Poems*), and humanity's inhumanity (*Mandela and Other Poems*), he draws his imagery from the indigenous African background and the Western literary tradition, interweaving them to dazzling effect. Although he is fascinated by the poetic styles of Western authors, particularly G.M. Hopkins, T.S. Eliot, W.B. Yeats, and W.H. Auden, he has cultivated an eloquent, penetrating, and descriptive voice of his own.

Bekederemo's dramas include *Song of a Goat* (1961), a tragedy cast in the Greek classical mode in which the impotence of Zifa, the protagonist, causes his wife Ebiere and his brother Tonye to indulge in an illicit love relationship that results in suicide; *The Masquerade* (1964), a sequel in which Dibiri's rage culminates in the death of his suitor Tufa; *The Raft* (1964), in which four men drift helplessly down the Niger aboard a log raft; *Ozidi* (1966), an epic drama rooted in Ijaw saga; and *The Boat* (1981), a prose drama that documents Ngbilebiri history. Although his plays have been criticized for leaning too much on the Greek classical mode (especially the early ones), for their thinness of structure, and for unrealistic stage devices (such as the disintegration of the raft on the stage in *The Raft*), they challenge and engage the audience with their poetic quality and their uniting of the foreign and the local through graphic imagery.

Bekederemo's contribution to other genres includes his translation of the *Ozidi Saga* (1977), an oral literary epic of the Ijaw; his perceptive critical study *The Example of Shakespeare* (1970), in which he articulates his aesthetic views about poetry and drama; and his journalistic essays in the *Daily Express*, *Daily Times*, and other newspapers. He is also the author of the controversial *America, Their America* (1964), a travelogue in which he criticizes American society and its values. While the furore generated by *America, Their America* early catapulted him into the international literary limelight, the damage this work and *Casualties* have done to his reputation seems permanent: in both works he infuriated and alienated a large audience and some influential critics. Bekederemo has maintained that he portrayed events as he saw them.

As one of Africa's pre-eminent and distinguished authors, he has, since his retirement, continued to play an active role in literary affairs, a role in which he is increasingly gaining deserved international recognition. In 1991, for example, he received the Nigerian National Merit Award for literary excellence, received an honorary doctorate from the University of Benin, and saw publication, by Howard University, of his two definitive volumes, *The Ozidi Saga* and *Collected Plays and Poems 1958-1988*.

BEN JELLOUN, Tahar (1944-), novelist, essayist, and poet writing in French, was born in Morocco and raised in Fès, Tangiers, and Rabat, where he read philosophy. A member of the leftist Union of Moroccan Students who staged the 1965 student uprising, he was drafted into the army after the Moroccan government reintroduced compulsory military service as a means to subdue rebellious youth. He wrote his first poem, 'L'Aube des dalles', while in El Hajeb's and Ahermoumou's military barracks between 1966 and 1967. When he returned to civilian life in 1968, he took up a teaching position in Tétouan; later he was transferred to Casablanca, where he wrote the draft of his first novel, *Harrounda* (1973), and contributed to Abdellatif Lâabi's literary journal *Souffles*. Since 1971, the date of the publication of *Hommes sous linceul de silence*, he has lived in Paris. He has published an anthology of Moroccan poetry, *La Mémoire future: Anthologie de la nouvelle poésie du Maroc* (1976), short stories, and poems, but he is best known for his novels, including *Moha le fou, Moha le sage* (1978), *La Prière de l'absent* (1981), and *La Nuit sacrée* (1987; *Sacred Night*, 1989), for which he was awarded the Prix Goncourt.

His work has been influenced to a large extent by the exile and solitude he experienced both in Morocco and France. *La Réclusion solitaire* (1976), *La Plus haute des solitudes* (1977), and *Hospitalité française* (1984) explore the isolation and alienation that have accompanied immigration from North Africa to France over the last thirty years. In *L'Ecrivain public* (1983) and *L'Enfant de sable* (1985; *Sand Child*, 1987), solitude and anguish relate to characters' alienation from their own selves as much as from society. Solitude is also at the centre of *Jour de silence ... Tanger* (1990), the story of an elderly man 'forgotten by time and flouting death'. A critique of the relationship between men and women in *Maghrebi societies runs through all of Ben Jelloun's work, from his first novel *Harrounda* through to *Les Yeux baissés* (1991) and a recent collection of short stories, *Le Premier amour est toujours le dernier* (1995).

While Ben Jelloun has remained in touch with his roots and his own experience, recent novels show an enlargement of his interest in human dignity and social justice, reaching beyond the Moroccan experience. *L'Homme rompu* (1994) is dedicated to Indonesian novelist Pramoedya Ananta Toer and deals with the theme of corruption, and the short stories of *L'Ange aveugle* (1992) explore and reflect on life in the south of Italy. *Les Raisins de la galère* (1996) encapsulates the wisdom of a writer who remains lucid and who shows no sign of slowing down his attack on injustice and intolerance.

BEN-ABDALLAH, Mohammed (1944-), Ghanaian dramatist. Of mixed North African and Ghanaian descent, Mohammed Ben-Abdallah was born in Kumasi. He was educated and had early work experience in Accra, Kumasi, and Legon; later he went abroad to earn postgraduate qualifications in theatre at the Universities of Georgia and Texas in the USA. He returned in 1982 with a doctorate, already a playwright and director, to teach at the School of Performing Arts, University of Ghana, Legon. During the next ten years he held ministerial-level offices in culture and education in the Rawlings government and was the first Chair of the National Commission on Culture. In office he implemented programmes that he believed in, not hesitating to do so even though they were controversial or unpopular.

Ben-Abdallah the playwright cannot be dissociated from Ben-Abdallah the teacher or the political activist, and his concerns embrace classroom, national, and continental issues. For example, in response to the needs of schools, he wrote children's plays based on Ananse stories; he is also a pan-Africanist who draws

on the work of Frantz Fanon, and he is deeply concerned to encourage the use of African languages. His plays examine historical, political, and social issues in typically robust, frequently controversial, sometimes salacious fashion. Recent Ghanaian history provides the background to *The Trial of Mallam Ilya* (1987), regional tensions surface in *The Verdict of the Cobra* (1987), supernatural power plays a role in *The Witch of Mopti* (1989), and the controversy about the origin of the Ashanti nation makes its presence felt in *The Fall of Kumbi* (1989). The plays incorporate ritual, dance, and music, and the storytelling conventions that frequently provide structural elements connect his work to a national tradition. In an introduction to one of his collections, he writes of authentic African theatre as that which has meaning for its target audience, and, somewhat idealistically, calls for a theatre that would 'break down barriers' and appeal across a broad spectrum.

The passing years and experience of high office have undoubtedly affected Ben-Abdallah's creative vision. For example, *Land of a Million Magicians* (1993), which he wrote and directed for a summit of the Non-Aligned Movement, is based very loosely on Bertolt Brecht's *Good Woman of Setzuan*. A narrator who becomes involved in the action, the presentation of the variety of cultural traditions within the nation, and the concern with a major issue, in this instance strategies for development, are characteristic of the playwright's interests and his ability to make a theatrical impact. But there is another aspect to the playwright as well; the contrast between the plays' endings, upbeat for the production, downbeat for the published text, hints at his continuing search for answers to perennial questions. This restless search, combined with the seriousness of the issues he tackles and the boldness of his theatrical conception, makes him the major Ghanaian playwright of his generation.

BETI, Mongo (pseud. of Alexandre Biyidi) (1932-), novelist writing in French. Educated in Cameroon and France, Beti taught in French *lycées* until 1994. As an outspoken critic of Ahmadou Ahidjo and Paul Biya, the first two presidents of Cameroon, he was permitted to visit his country only briefly in 1961 and 1991. Beti's literary career falls into two parts: before independence in 1960 and after. In the pre-independence period he published a short story, 'Sans haine, sans amour' (1952), and a novel, *Ville cruelle* (1954), under the pen-name of Eza Boto, and as Mongo Beti *Le Pauvre Christ de Bomba* (1956; *The *Poor Christ of Bomba*, 1971), *Mission terminée* (1957; *Mission to Kala*, 1964), and *Le Roi miraculé* (1958; *King Lazarus*, 1960). In these anti-colonial novels, the principal characters are ordinary young men who try to achieve success on their own terms in a society in which the old represent a disintegrated traditional Africa and the young acquire useless knowledge in French schools for travels that lead nowhere. The contribution of these novels to the growing opposition to colonialism made them literary models and their author known internationally. In this period Beti and his colleague Ferdinand *Oyono strongly influenced the trend to realism in the African *novel in French. Today, university professors in Africa teach these novels in preference to more recent and more subversive materials, perpetuating the hope that as blacks succeeded in freeing themselves from whites, so they can free themselves from any oppressive regime.

Between 1960 and 1994, Beti taught and participated in the political life of Rouen where he lived while paying close attention to Cameroonian affairs. When his pamphlet *Main basse sur le Cameroun* (1972), which is critical of the lack of freedom, the one-party system, and the relationship between government and French profiteers, was seized by the French authorities, he returned to fiction to spread his ideas. In *Perpétue ou l'habitude du malheur* (1974; *Perpetua and the Habit of Unhappiness*, 1978), the life of a bright young girl is a metaphor for the fate of the Cameroonian populace under Ahidjo: dominated by tyrants, they witness the destruction of their dreams and ambitions. *Remember Ruben* (1974; trans. 1980) recalls Ruben Um Nyobé, a national hero killed in 1958, in a story of young revolutionaries who fail to overthrow the government. In *La Ruine presque cocasse d'un polichinelle* (1979; *Lament for an African Pol*, 1985) the young revolutionaries succeed in deposing an unfit chief. In *Les Deux Mères de Guillaume Ismaël Dzewatama, futur camionneur* (1983) and *La Revanche de Guillaume Dzewatama* (1984), a white woman encourages her husband and his son to resist the corrupt régime, expressing an optimism that disappears in *L'Histoire du fou* (1994), in which Cameroon has reached a level of degradation that no government can redress. After having fought corruption and injustice in his novels and in articles published in *Peuples noirs, peuples africains*, the journal he edited between 1978 and 1991, Beti despairs of ever seeing economic or political improvement in Cameroon. He has now retired from his teaching position and lives in Cameroon, where he has opened a bookshop.

BEYALA, Calixthe (1961-), novelist writing in French, was born in Douala, Cameroon to a poor family and completed her secondary and university studies in France and Spain. She has lived in Paris since 1984. Undoubtedly the most prolific as well as the most feminist of French-language African writers, Beyala published six novels and one pamphlet by the age of thirty-four. Her first two novels, *C'est le soleil qui m'a brûlée* (1987) and *Tu t'appelleras Tanga* (1988), are set in the poor quarters of an unidentified African country and address the oppression of young women by their families as well as by men. Forced into prostitution at an early age, they find succour only in close friendships with other women. *Seul le diable le savait* (1990) is a longer, more ambitious, but perhaps less successfully plotted work with elements of an African magical realism. More recent novels, set at least partly in Europe, have brought Beyala considerable attention in France. *Le Petit prince de Belleville* (1992; *The 'Little Prince' of Belleville*, 1995), her best-known work, is the story of a young boy, born in France to African parents, who observes with considerable humour the follies of his family and of the population of an immigrant quarter of Paris. A sequel, *Maman a un amant* (1993), is narrated by the same young boy. In 1994 *Assèze, l'Africaine*, the story of a Cameroonian girl who makes her way to Paris, was awarded the Prix Tropiques. As in her earlier work, Beyala portrays what it means to be an African female through two characters, one manipulative, one passive. *Lettre d'une Africaine … ses soeurs occidentales* (1995) is an outspoken defence of 'feminitude', feminism based on both difference and equality, with an emphasis on the ways in which African and western women must unite. Beyala has been accused of plagiarizing other African writers and considerable heat has been generated by these allegations, put forward after she won the Grand Prix du Roman de l'Académie Française in 1996.

BIAFRA [See NIGERIA–BIAFRA WAR]

BIOGRAPHY AND AUTOBIOGRAPHY
East Africa: Biography and autobiography are dominated by prison notes, petitions, diaries, character sketches, travel accounts, and letters that tell stories of childhood in African villages and European estates, first encounters with European life at school, mission centres, urban centres and overseas, and dreams and visions for the future. The origins of prose and the spoken word in East Africa, these life stories are political tracts didactic in nature. Early examples of autobiography include *An African Speaks for His People* (1934) by Permenas Githendu Mockerie, the story of school days in a Kenyan village, and *Child of Two Worlds* (1964), Mugo Gatheru's dream of a warrior. Early biographies include a character sketch of Ham Mukasa of Buganda by Catherine Sebuliba (Uganda), which first appeared in *The Uganda Journal* (23.2) in 1959, and a character sketch of Mwalimu Julius Kabarage Nyerere, which appears in Tom Mboya's *Freedom and After* (1963).

Among autobiographers, politicians dominate the field. In *Suffering without Bitterness* (1967), Jomo Kenyatta relates his identification with the nationalist struggle for freedom in Kenya. Other political autobiographers include Harry Thuku, who records his life and trade union activities in *An Autobiography*

(1970), and Bildad Kaggia, whose *Roots of Freedom, 1921-1963* was published in 1975. Tom Mboya, an early crusader for African independence, Kenyatta's close associate in Kenya, and an observer of personalities, relates the story of his growing political commitment and his role in Kenyan political life in his autobiography *Freedom and After.* J.M. Kariuki, a disciple of Kenyatta, was detained by the colonial governor of Kenya in 1953 and later made a name for himself in politics. He records his vision of an emancipated Kenya and his experiences in detention in his autobiography, *'Mau Mau' Detainee* (1963), re-released with an afterword by ★Ngugi wa Thiong'o in 1994. Other titles on the Mau Mau theme in this genre include Waruhiu Itote's *Mau Mau General* (1967), Joram Wamweya's *Freedom Fighter* (1971), journalist Henry Muoria's *I, the Gikuyu and the White Fury* (1994), and Gakaara wa Wanjau's *Mwandiki wa Mau Mau ithaamrio-ini* (Gikuyu,1983; *Mau Mau Author in Detention*, 1988).

South Africa: In the twentieth century autobiographical writing, like prison literature, became a prominent and vital literary form in South Africa, largely as a result of sociopolitical tensions in the multicultural, multi-ethnic society. South African autobiography is characterized by its use of motives such as racial conflict, class differences, language issues, the dispossession of land, exile, religion (Christianity versus traditional beliefs), political imprisonment, and ★apartheid laws. Among the works of special interest are three autobiographies from the significant literary decade of the 1950s – Peter ★Abrahams' ★*Tell Freedom* (1954), Ezekiel (Es'kia) ★Mphahlele's ★*Down Second Avenue* (1959), and Bloke ★Modisane's ★*Blame Me on History* (1963) – Nelson Mandela's *Long Walk to Freedom* (1994), Alan ★Paton's two volumes of autobiography (see below) and J.M. ★Coetzee's recent *Boyhood: Scenes from Provincial Life* (1997).

Autobiographical writing before the twentieth century is mainly in the form of diaries and journals. In the pre-colonial and colonial period (1488-1910), a vast library of diaries, journals, and travel journals were written by the agents of colonization. In *Before van Riebeeck: Callers at South Africa from 1488 to 1652* (1967), R. Raven-Hart collected fragments of pre-colonial travel journals, beginning with the first sighting of the Cape of Good Hope by Bartholomeu Dias in 1488 and ending with Jean-Baptiste Tavernier resting at the Cape for a month in 1549. The *Dag Verhaal van Eerw. Erasmus Smit – 1815* [The Journal of the Rev. Erasmus Smit – 1815] (1956) relates the experiences of a Dutch missionary among the 'wild Bushmen' at Toornberg. It suggests an extraordinary lack of cultural sensitivity to the Cape ★Bushmen or /Xam's language, customs, and beliefs. The fragmented 'Personal History' of the /Xam man

//Kabbo, narrated orally to Wilhelm Bleek (recorded in Specimens of Bushmen Folklore, 1911) is poignant. Although heavily mediated (from /Xam to English, from oral text to written), //Kabbo's narration of his capture and journey to Cape Town and his longing to return home gives insight into a marginalized people and their experience of enforced colonization.

Also stemming from the colonial period are the numerous diaries and journals of the settlers of 1820, British citizens who emigrated to the eastern frontier of the Cape Colony to form a buffer zone against the Xhosa. Examples of these texts are H.H. Dugmore's *The Reminiscences of an Albany Settler* (1871), W.C. ★Scully's *Reminiscences of a South African Pioneer* (1913), Francis Carey ★Slater's *Settler's Heritage* (1954), and Jeremiah Goldswain's *Chronicle* (vols. 1 and 2, 1946 and 1949).

The ★Anglo-Boer war (1899-1902) produced many autobiographical texts with a communal sociopolitical focus. Examples are Johanna Brandt's *The Petticoat Commando; or, Boer Women in Secret Service* (1913), Deneys Reitz's *Commando: A Boer Journal of the Boer War* (1929), the war diary of Afrikaans poet Totius (pseudonym of D.F. du Toit), *Vier-en-sestig dae te velde. 'n Oorlogsdagboek* [Sixty-four days in the battlefields: a war diary] (1977), and Sarah Raal's Boer cowgirl's adventures in battle, *Met die Boere in die veld* [With the Boers in the battlefields] (1937). Sol T. ★Plaatje surveyed the war as an outsider in the ★*Mafeking Diary of Sol T. Plaatje* (1973; 1999). Of interest also is Winston Churchill's Boer war journal, *London to Ladysmith via Pretoria* (1900), relating his capture by the Boers and subsequent escape.

In the early twentieth century C. Louis Leipoldt described life as medical doctor in far-flung parts in *The Bushveld Doctor* (1937). In *The Way Out* (1946) the flamboyant Afrikaans literary figure Uys Krige vividly portrays his escape through the mountains of Italy as a German prisoner of war in 1944.

Subsequent to the Afrikaner Nationalist takeover in 1948 and the period of apartheid that followed, Afrikaans autobiographical writing dwindled, to be replaced between the 1940s and 1970s by reports of travels to Europe and elsewhere and, in the case of Elsa Joubert, other parts of Africa. English language writers such as T.V. Bulpin (*The Ivory Trail*, 1954) and Laurens ★van der Post (*Venture to the Interior*, 1952, *The Lost World of the Kalahari*, 1958, and *The Heart of the Hunter*, 1961) practised travel writing with a focus on romantic adventures in unknown parts. Both M.E. Rothman, in her memorable autobiography *My beskeie deel: 'n Outobiografiese vertelling* [The measure of my days: an autobiographical narration] (1972), and Alan Paton, author of ★*Cry the Beloved Country* (1949), in *Towards the Mountain* (1980) and *Journey Continued* (1988), reflect on contemporary sociopolitical tensions of the time as well as on the development and formation of the self. *Paulina Dlamini: Servant of Two Kings* (ed. H. Filter and S. Bourquin, 1986) is a heavily mediated (orally given) autobiography of a Zulu woman who first served the Zulu king Cetshwayo and later became a Christian convert. Reinventing himself as a man of action, the Durban-born poet Roy ★Campbell dubbed his romantically dramatized *Light on a Dark Horse* (1951) an 'autobuggeroffery'. In contrast with Campbell's vibrant style the autobiographies of William ★Plomer (*The South African Autobiography*, 1984) and Guy ★Butler (*Karoo Morning*, 1977, and *Bursting World*, 1983) seem somewhat bland. Godfrey Moloi records the vicissitudes of township life in *My Life: Volume One* (1987; reworked into *My Life: Volumes One and Two*, 1991). In *Brief Authority* (1960) Charles Hooper focuses on sociopolitical upheaval after the expropriation of two 'black spots'. In *My Traitor's Heart* (1990) Rian Malan confronts his Afrikaner roots and attempts to make sense of the violent sociopolitical realities of his country.

The 'coloured' Afrikaans voice, representing communities whose life histories have been recorded in English only by Peter Abrahams and Richard ★Rive, is heard in fictional texts with strongly imbedded autobiographical aspects: Abraham Philips's *Die verdwaalde land* [The lost land] (1992) and A.H.M. Scholtz's *Vatmaar: 'n Lewenddagge verhaal van 'n tyd wat nie meer is nie* [Take it: a lively story of a time that is no more] (1995).

The autobiographies of Sarah Gertrude ★Millin (*The Night Is Long*, 1941 and *The Measure of My Days*, 1955), Petronella van Heerden (*Kerssnuitsels*, 1962), and Eve Palmer (*The Plains of the Camdeboo*, 1966) have white women as central subjects, as does Lynn Freed's *Home Ground* (1986), with its striking sense of place in the descriptions of her childhood's colourful Durban. In contrast, black women autobiographers Noni ★Jabavu (*Drawn in Colour: African Contrasts*, 1960 and *The Ochre People: Scenes from a South African Life*, 1963), Ellen ★Kuzwayo (*★Call Me Woman*, 1985), Sindiwe ★Magona (*To My Children's Children*, 1990 and *Forced to Grow*, 1992), and Emma Mashinini (*Strikes Have Followed Me All My Life*, 1989) all tend to focus less on the individual self as separate identity and more on self versus sociopolitical tensions. The pejorative racial phrase *Coolie Doctor* (1991), which Goonarathnam Goonam takes as her title, expresses the tension between herself (as Indian Durbanite) and apartheid society. Life stories based on a strong antiapartheid theme are Norma Kitson's *Where Sixpence Lives* (1987), Winnie Mandela's *Part of My Soul* (1985), Helen Joseph's *Side by Side* (1986), and Mary Benson's *A Far Cry* (1989).

Among political life histories, autobiographies of important black leaders are often co-authored; these include *Freedom for My People: The Autobiography of Z.K. Matthews: Southern Africa 1901 to 1968* (1981),

Albert Luthuli's *Let My People Go* (1962), and Nelson Mandela's best-selling *Long Walk to Freedom* (1994).

Many autobiographers have included stories of their childhoods in their life stories. Peter Abrahams is often seen as the pioneer of black South African autobiography with *Tell Freedom*, the story of his coming-to-consciousness as poverty-stricken coloured Afrikaans child and later aspiring English writer. Similar stories of childhood-under-apartheid characterize Ezekiel Mphahlele's *Down Second Avenue*, Richard Rive's '*Buckingham Palace', District Six* (1986), Mark Mathabane's *Kaffir Boy: Growing out of Apartheid* (1986), Don ★Mattera's *Memory Is the Weapon* (1987), and Jay Naidoo's *Coolie Location* (1990). The Afrikaans writer F.A. Venter tells of his isolated and poverty-stricken formative years as a farmboy in the well-wrought *Kambro-kind* [Kambro Child] (1979), while dramatist Athol ★Fugard describes growing up in Port Elizabeth in *Cousins: A Memoir* (1994).

Autobiography is an important source of sociopolitical history. *Blame Me on History* by Bloke Modisane portrays the depersonalization of black people under the structural violence of apartheid. Naboth Mogatle's title signifies the same indifference: *Autobiography of an Unknown South African* (1971). Trevor Huddleston's *Naught for Your Comfort* (1956) describes conditions in the townships where he worked as priest during the 1950s before deportation. Worker-poet Alfred Temba ★Qabula calls *A Working Life: Cruel beyond Belief* (1989) a 'testament' of his life as factory worker (the prose is interspersed with worker poems composed for the political struggle). Of conservative Afrikaans background, ANC politician Carl Niehaus describes his rebellious and questioning youth in *Om te veg vir hoop* [To fight for hope] (1993). Planned sabotage cost him a prison sentence for high treason. As an octogenarian, the dissident Afrikaans religious leader Beyers Naudé (long under house arrest and banned from preaching) recently published *My land van hoop* [My land of hope] (1996).

Several texts offer fragmentary autobiography. Two promising young black writers who died prematurely, Can ★Themba and Nat ★Nakasa, both wrote for ★*Drum* magazine in the 1950s. Themba's *The Will to Die* (1972) and Nakasa's *The World of Nat Nakasa* (ed. Essop Patel, 1993) bear testimony to difficult times and wasted lives. *Liberation Chabalala: The World of Alex ★La Guma* (1993) offers a fragmented journal of life under apartheid by the gifted novelist. In 1990 the exiled novelist Bessie ★Head's autobiographical writings were published as *A Woman Alone* (ed. Craig Mackenzie).

Two important South African writers have written of exile. Breyten ★Breytenbach's *Seisoen in die paradys* (1976; *A Season in Paradise*, 1980), a diary-cum-travel journal interspersed with poems, describes a trip to South Africa on a ninety-day visa (1972-73) from exile in Paris. The subsequent *Return to Paradise* (1993) is a rather unstructured narrative of a later journey in 1991. Breytenbach's post-modernist prison memoir, *True Confessions of an Albino Terrorist* (1984), can be seen as a confessional text and therapeutic exercise in dealing with the fragmented selves of author and subject. In 1984 Es'kia Mphahlele published *Afrika My Music* about his years in self-imposed exile; this sequel to *Down Second Avenue* tells how he chose to return his country of birth, rejecting the condition of placelessness.

South-Central Africa: From the mid-nineteenth century, European missionaries, prospectors, and hunters published accounts of their experiences in what is now Zimbabwe. With only occasional exceptions these narratives produce their protagonists as, on the one hand, men of science observing with detachment the people, flora, and fauna of the interior and, on the other, as heroes of imperial romances able to confront and subdue with gun or Bible savage nature and savage people. David Livingstone's books dominated the missionary narratives and Frederick Courtenay Selous' those of the hunters. William Charles Baldwin's *African Hunting* (1863) influenced Selous, and Edward Mohr's account, translated as *To the Victoria Falls of the Zambesi* (1876), and the missionary Thomas Morgan Thomas's *Eleven Years in Central South Africa* (1873) are important examples. Frank Oates's posthumous *Matabeleland and the Victoria Falls* (1881) reveals uncharacteristic doubts in the author about his ability to play the heroic role. With the publication in the late 1940s of the Oppenheimer series, it became possible to compare letters and journals with published books. The most important of these are *The Matabeleland Journals of Robert Moffat*, the letters and journals of John and Emily Moffat, *The Matabele Mission* (both 1945), and *The Northern Goldfield Diaries of Thomas Baines* (1946). The missionaries reveal doubts about their vocation, quarrel with their fellow agents, and make racial judgements, and Baines acknowledges a shared humanity with blacks and seems happy to forgo his share in an imperial destiny, attitudes impossible to accommodate in the imperial or missionary romance. The same distinction between people's private reflections and public productions of themselves can be found in the letters written to friends and superiors by members of the Jesuit Zambesi mission in *Gubulawayo and Beyond*, ed. M. Gelfand (1968), and the selection of reports and letters edited for French supporters of the mission in *Journey to Gubuluwayo*, ed. R. Roberts (1979).

After the British South Africa Company occupied Mashonaland in 1890, autobiographies of soldiers, settlers, or early administrators identify the writer as part of the glorious epic whose successful end was the founding and development of Southern Rhodesia.

These include A.G. Leonard's *How We Made Rhodesia* (1896), F.R. Burnham's often untrue *Scouting on Two Continents* (1927), and Frank Johnson's *Great Days* (1940). Women's autobiographies recalling the early period, R. Blennerhassett's and L. Sleeman's *Adventures in Mashonaland* (1893) and the highly inventive *Melina Rorke: Told by Herself* (1939), are no different from the male narratives in their conception of the civilizing and nation-building mission in which settlers were involved. An exception to the celebration of Rhodesia's progress is Stanley Portal Hyatt's *The Old Transport Road* (1914), which attacks progress for destroying romance.

The first autobiographies of blacks in English were mediated through whites and owe as much to H. Rider Haggard and Bertram Mitford as to the purported narrator. A.A. Campbell's *Mlimo* (1911) is an example.

Later a narrative of domestic life begins to dominate white autobiography. The poverty of settlers on the farms in the 1920s and 30s is recalled in Hylda Richards's *Next Year Will Be Better* (1952). Daphne Anderson's *The Toe-Rags* (1989) recollects an even starker settler poverty during the 1930s. Doris ★Lessing's *Under My Skin* (1994) deals partly with the ruined hopes of her family during the same period. Her autobiography identifies some of the models for the fictional people and events in the first four volumes of her series of novels *Children of Violence*. Lessing's *Going Home* (1957) describes what was to be her last visit to Rhodesia before being declared a prohibited immigrant, and in *African Laughter* (1992) she rediscovers the country in which she had been raised after Zimbabwean independence allowed her to return.

Autobiographies by prominent politicians were a development in the 1960s. White liberals use the form to suggest alternative positions to the increasingly hostile racial polarization that followed the collapse of federation. Sir R. Welensky's *Welensky's 4000 Days* (1964) and Sir R. Tredgold's *The Rhodesia That Was My Life* (1968) are examples. Polemical autobiographies by supporters of UDI include Brigadier A. Skeen's *Prelude to Independence* (1966). The modern African nationalist autobiography was pioneered in Rhodesia by Nathan Shamuyarira. In his *Crisis in Rhodesia* (1965), he traces his growing disillusionment with a multiracial political option as the early liberalism of the federation was replaced by an intransigent white racism. From 1956 to 1963 he was editor of *The African Daily News*, and his part in the events of those years is recalled with the authority of a man in a position of considerable influence. The first four chapters of the 1968 edition of Ndabaningi Sithole's *African Nationalism* are autobiographical, and like Shamuyarira, he produces his own experience as typical and extrapolates from it to comment on the disabilities of

41

blacks in Rhodesia. Radical white autobiographies of this period include Judith Todd's *The Right to Say No* (1972), which describes her arrest, imprisonment, and detention during 1971 and 1972, and Peter Niesewand's *In Camera* (1972), which provides the details of his trial, from which reporters were excluded. Lawrence *Vambe's *An Ill-fated People* (1972) and *From Rhodesia to Zimbabwe* (1976) are probably the most important black autobiographies produced from Rhodesia. Several writers use autobiography to trace the growth of their nationalist consciousness. Didymus Mutasa's *Rhodesian Black behind Bars* (1974) recalls the inspiration of Guy Clutton-Brock for his generation of nationalists and the Tolstoyan socialism of the Cold Comfort Farm Society. Stanislaus Made's *Made in Zimbabwe* (1980) describes the typical struggle for education blacks routinely endured. Maurice Nyagumbo's *With the People* (1980) recalls the politics of southern African black resistance from the perspectives of a migrant worker. Nyagumbo's memories include his numerous clashes with settler authority and years of detention and imprisonment after he became a nationalist leader. Joshua Nkomo's *Nkomo: The Story of My Life* (1984) recounts the multiple influences from traditional spiritual authority to trade unionism on a turbulent political career, from which he emerged as Zimbabwe's vice-president.

White autobiography since independence includes Kenneth Skelton's account of his years as Anglican bishop of Matabeleland, *Bishop in Smith's Rhodesia* (1985), and his opposition to UDI, which brought him into conflict with the authorities. Bruce Moore-King's *White Man, Black War* (1988) successfully interposes a fragmented narrative with more conventional autobiographical narration to recall the routine brutality of Rhodesian troops during the liberation war. His book is a bitter indictment of the settler ideology that so conditioned young whites like Moore-King that they were left without the conscience to question what they were doing. Peter Godwin's *Mukiwa* (1996) re-creates with pathos and humour the tug of opposing loyalties that complicated the identity of many whites growing up in Rhodesia.

A large number of Rhodesian and Zimbabwean novels are fictionalized autobiography. Terence Ranger in *Are We Not Also Men?* (1995) has drawn attention to the autobiographical content in Stanlake *Samkange's *The Mourned One* (1975) for example, and personal experience is fictionalized in novels as different from one another as Ndabaningi Sithole's *The Polygamist* (1972) and Shimmer *Chinodya's *Dew in the Morning* (1982).

West Africa: Following the letters and memoirs of Ignatius *Sancho in his *Letters of the Late Ignatius Sancho, an African* (1782), the earliest known autobiography is the Nigerian ex-slave's account *The Interesting Narrative of the Life of Olaudah *Equiano, or Gustavus Vassa the African, Written by Himself* (1789), abridged by Paul Edwards as *Equiano's Travels* (1967). The second generation of autobiographies came a century-and-a-half later when nationalist agitators against British rule wrote about their lives. The best known are Kwame Nkrumah's *Ghana* (1957) and those by four Nigerians: Obafemi Awolowo's *Awo: The Autobiography of Chief Obafemi Awolowo* (1960), *My March through Prison* (1985), and *The Travails of Democracy and the Rule of Law* (1987); *My Life* (1960) by Ahmadu Bello; *Fugitive Offender* (1965) by Anthony Enahoro; and *My Odyssey* (1970) by Nnamdi Azikiwe. The *Nigeria-Biafra war, 1967-70, inspired a spate of memoirs by soldiers including *Reminiscences* (1989) by David Akpode Ejoor.

One of the best autobiographies, *The Time Has Come* (1989) by Nigerian pioneer diplomat John Mamman Garba, was published posthumously. *Our Unforgettable Years* (1983) and *Our International Years* (1988) by Simeon Adebo and *Diplomatic Soldiering* (1987) by Joe Garba are also by Nigerians, while *The Symbol of Liberia* (1961) was written by a Liberian diplomat, C.L. Simpson. An internationally reputed Nigerian jurist, Akinola Aguda, wrote *Flashback* (1989).

West African creative writers have written childhood autobiographies including the children's classic *My Father's Daughter* (1965) by Nigerian Mabel *Segun, the internationally acclaimed *Aké: The Years of Childhood* (1981) by Nobel laureate Wole *Soyinka, and *Kossoh Town Boy* (1960) by Robert Wellesley Cole of Sierra Leone. The Nigerian novelist Buchi *Emecheta has written a life account, *Head Above Water* (1986).

Many West African biographies portray politicians, especially heads of state. Three notable ones about Nkrumah and his contemporaries are Peter Omari's *Kwame Nkrumah: The Anatomy of an African Dictatorship* (1970), *The Life and Times of Dr. J.B. Danquah* (1974) by L.H. Ofosu-Appiah, and *In My Father's House* (1992) by Kwame Anthony Appiah, son of Joe Appiah. Nigerian biographies include John Paten's *Ahmadu Bello, Sardauna of Sokoto, Values and Leadership in Nigeria* (1986); J. Elaigwu's *Gowon* (1985); Trevor Clark's *A Right Honourable Gentleman: The Life and Times of Alhaji Sir Abubakar Tafawa Balewa* (1991), and Chidi Amuta's *Prince of the Niger* (1992), about Babangida.

Two religious leaders and an educationist are the subjects of *The Life and Works of Othman dan Fodio* (1975) by Ismail Balogun, *Holy Johnson, Pioneer of African Nationalism (1836-1970)* (1970) by E.A. Ayandele, and C.O. Taiwo's *Henry Carr: An African Contribution to Education* (1975). Two protagonists in the Nigerian civil war, Emeka Ojukwu and Chukuma Nzeogwu, are highlighted in Frederick Forsyth's

Emeka (1982) and Olusegun Obasanjo's *Nzeogwu* (1987). A Nigerian journalist who was killed by a parcel bomb in 1986 is immortalized in *Born to Run: The Story of Dele Giwa* (1987) by Dele Olojede and Onukaba Adinoyi-Ojo. Two women are portrayed in Jean Boyd's *The Caliph's Sister: Nana Asma'u 1793-1865, Teacher, Poet and Islamic Leader* (1987) and Justus Akinsanya's *An African 'Florence Nightingale': A Biography of Chief (Dr.) Mrs. Kofoworola A. Pratt* (1987).

Most West African biographies focus on the pains and agonies of a subject who struggles for education. Ezenwa-Ohaeto's *Chinua Achebe: A Biography* (1997) gives a detailed account of Chinua ★Achebe's formative years and his rise to the status of 'father of African literature'. Biographies that involve a politically active subject concentrate on the troubled paths by which the subject reaches the peak of the political structure. In West Africa, the political careers of such personalities as Nnamdi Azikiwe, Kwame Nkrumah, Obafemi Awolowo, and Ladoke Akintola have made exciting material for biographers. A biography of any one of those eminent figures has a way of attracting details about the others.

The nationalist activities of these West African politicians agitated the colonial establishment and sensitized the grassroots towards self-rule. The evidence of the relevance of early West African biographies shows in the ease with which they inhabit existing popular literature. Literary critic Adrian Roscoe, for instance, locates a tendency to deify Azikiwe in Okenwa Olisah's *Many Things You Must Know about Ogbuefi and Republican Nigeria*, a title from the ★Onitsha market literature. Like other biographies focused on early West African nationalists, it records the protagonist's intense desire for education, a project which is often accomplished through a sojourn in the West.

Two biographies stand out among the many West African examples. The first, Victor Ladipo Akintola's *Akintola: The Man and the Legend* (1982), was written to reveal the significant events in the life of Samuel Ladoke Akintola, the Nigerian politician who was assassinated during the January 1966 coup. The second, Wole ★Soyinka's *Isarà: A Voyage around 'Essay'* (1989), is remarkable for its appropriation of the techniques of fiction to its non-fiction purposes. Both books show the journey as a dominant theme in West African biography.

Like most biographers, Victor Akintola reveals the events that shape the personality of his subject, situating his work within the genre by recounting Akintola's experience as a voyager whose interest in travelling was a source of knowledge. He captures the enduring will of his subject as he struggles against the harshness of winter in Britain to emerge with the knowledge that would later assist him in his political career. Akintola's text describes the political climate and the nationalist movement that characterized the pre-independence period in West Africa. Through his journeys and political manoeuvring the subject relates to such political activists as Nkrumah, Jomo Kenyatta, Ahmadu Bello, the Sardauna of Sokoto, and Abubakar Tafawa Balewa, Nigeria's first prime minister. There is a tragic irony in this biography that derives from the portrait of the protagonist as a victim of the political formation he helped to cultivate. Akintola's assassination was the climax of the political disruption evidenced in the trial and incarceration of the renowned politician Obafemi Awolowo.

Wole Soyinka's *Isarà* is sophisticated in its admixture of fact and fiction. In the preface, Soyinka informs the reader that he has fictionalized character, time, and place to elevate his biography beyond mere history. Released from historical underpinnings, characters and events in *Isarà* can be interpreted according to their symbolic or literary functions within the text. Soyinka's text reveals the compelling voyage of the enthusiastic protagonist, who emerges from the experience as a man of knowledge and vision. The text's literariness shows in the way its symbolism helps to develop the theme of the voyage.

BITEK [See OKOT P'BITEK]

BIYIDI, Alexandre [See BETI, Mongo]

BLACK, Stephen (1880-1931), South African dramatist and novelist, was born in Claremont, Cape Town and was educated at Saint Saviour's Upper Boys' High School and at Diocesan College. He won many athletic awards and the Rhodes Prize for Literature (1904). He wrote three novels and worked as a journalist, but he is best known as a founder of South African drama.

Black worked as an actor-manager and wrote popular plays with which he and his company toured from the Cape to what was then Rhodesia. Although many of the texts have been lost, the Africana Collection of the South African Library, Cape Town and the Johannesburg Public Library's Strange Collection retain unpublished texts. Three of his most significant plays are *Love and the Hyphen* (1908, revised 1928-9), *Helena's Hope, Ltd* (1910), and *Van Kalabas Does His Bit* (1916). They display his best qualities, which are a journalist's inquisitiveness, a superb ear for dialogue, and a performer's comic timing and sense of the theatrical. Meticulously observed satires on all layers of Cape society, the plays are at the same time useful records of social mores and uses in a society in which racial contact and interracial relations played a large part.

Black lived in London between 1913 and 1915 and France from 1918 to 1927, marketing his work, writing, and negotiating foreign rights for his repertoire. He toured refurbished versions of his plays in South Africa from 1916 to 1917 and again in 1928 with a new company.

BLACK ATLANTIC A recent, widely discussed, and probably durable name for a very old idea, denotes that broad cultural zone surrounding the Atlantic Ocean in which peoples of African descent now live. The black Atlantic includes most of sub-Saharan Africa, many regions in Latin America, the entire Caribbean, much of North America, and several parts of Western Europe. The concept 'black Atlantic' also serves as a label or description for items in that zone, as in, for example, 'black Atlantic writer' or 'black Atlantic novel'.

Until about the 1400s, the five Atlantic regions of Western Europe, Africa, South America, the Caribbean, and North America were largely isolated from each other. At times, slow migration, trade, and travellers did produce some links, but in general these regions, each of them containing much diversity, could be conceived of as distinct. Beginning in the mid-1400s, however, first Portuguese, then Spanish, and then many other explorers began to criss-cross the broad Atlantic zone. Columbus's 1492 voyage was important, but even more significant was the 1516 start of the European slave trade to the 'new world'. Over the next three centuries more than ten million black Africans were dragged in chains to North and South America and the Caribbean, forming the basis of the great Afro-diasporic populations in those regions. More recently, a smaller number of Afro-diasporic peoples have migrated from the Americas, the Caribbean, and Africa into different parts of Europe.

Over time, these diasporic black Atlantic populations formed rich cultures based on at least four contributions: their diverse (and then blended) African origins; their contacts with native or 'Indian' populations; their resistance to and interplay with dominant European and white new-world cultures; and local developments in each community. African coastal cultures (and to some extent those in Africa's interior) were also affected by such encounters. Almost as soon as these new cultural formations began to develop, a selected set of travellers and influences began to move back and forth across the black Atlantic. From the sixteenth to the eighteenth centuries these connections were sporadic, but beginning in the nineteenth century the frequency of exchanges across the black Atlantic increased. Importantly, also, the directions of the exchanges grew more diverse. In the middle decades of the twentieth century, for example, Harlem Renaissance poets such as Langston Hughes became important influences on the West African philosophy of ★negritude. Caribbean theorists such as Frantz Fanon played important roles in pan-African political discussions. Many intellectuals from across the entire zone took up residence and met in London or Paris. Countless books were produced by intellectuals who travelled from one region to another.

'Mainstream' European and white new-world cultures were also profoundly affected by these formations. The real or imagined existence of enslaved, 'primitive', or 'savage' blacks played large 'contrasting' roles in the development of western theories of rationality and freedom. And in the new world, the very idea that a white person was white also required some real or imaginary other called the black.

Despite these many black Atlantic interlinkings, however, until recently most scholars still thought of each of the five regions as relatively separate, and within each region many also felt that it was possible to discuss white literature, culture, and philosophy on its own, as if it were separable from what was black. In 1993, however, the black British sociologist and cultural theorist Paul Gilroy, building on the growing sense of many scholars that something was wrong with such a model, sharply changed the picture. In his book *The Black Atlantic*, Gilroy labelled this complex interlinked zone 'the black Atlantic' and argued that this massive area should be thought of as a single space. More precisely, he argued that because there existed such a dense network of exchanges all across the zone, it could usefully be discussed, for certain purposes, as just one place. Gilroy makes two important notes about his proposal. The first is that his 'Atlantic' isn't simply restricted to the world of blacks. Rather, Gilroy suggests that blacks and whites in all parts of the Atlantic are unthinkable without each other. Black culture often resists or speaks in counterpoint to white life and culture, at the same time as the involvement of whites in slave trades, slave systems, and, more recently, in racially defined societies make white culture dependent on the black. The second important note about Gilroy's black Atlantic concept is that it has no single centre. Contradicting Afrocentric theories, for example, Gilroy does not claim that Africa is the sole origin of black Atlantic culture. Nor would he claim with Eurocentrists that Europe is the basic source of its dynamic. Instead, the black Atlantic concept suggests that each part, in varying ways, has impact on all the others. America influences Africa influences the Caribbean influences Europe.

Gilroy's concept of the black Atlantic provides a compact and useful name for a complex real-world configuration. In literary studies, for example, the label 'black Atlantic' adds rich dimensions to canonical writers such as Joseph Conrad, Nadine ★Gordimer, and William Faulkner, who, because of their fundamental bi- or tri-cultural perspectives, cannot be described only as British, South African, or American whites. Perhaps the best way to illustrate the black Atlantic concept, however, is simply to list, in a way that only scratches the surface, some of the sets of major figures that can be linked across the zone: Pablo Picasso and central African sculpture; V. Y. Mudimbe and the Greek and Latin classics; Solomon ★Plaatje and W.E.B. DuBois; *Ngugi wa Thiong'o and Frantz Fanon; Aimé Césaire and Léopold S. *Senghor; Léopold Senghor and French ethnography; Charlotte Brontë and Jean Rhys; Maryse Condé and the Salem witch trials; Michelle Cliff and Bessie *Head; Miles Davis and Hugh Masekela; Derek Walcott and European poetry; negritude and Surrealism; Jamaican reggae music and an imagined Ethiopia; T.S. Eliot, jazz, and Edward Kamau Brathwaite; Wole *Soyinka, Henry Louis Gates, Jr., and Kwame Anthony Appiah; and, individually, the African 'been-to' novel and travelling African writers such as M. G. *Vassanji, Buchi *Emecheta, and Bernard *Dadié. In each case noted, important cultural influences have passed, in all directions, from one geography to another. If all of these connections were drawn on just one map, they would indicate a zone so richly interlinked that it would be difficult to label any single writer, novel, or artistic movement on that map as only 'African', say, or 'Caribbean'. Rather, they would all be, in different ways, more compellingly labelled 'black Atlantic'.

Whether Paul Gilroy's contribution will last as long is a separate question. On the one hand, Gilroy's 1993 book has been acclaimed for its prose style, readings of figures such as Richard Wright and W. E. B. DuBois, analyses of contemporary music, treatment of links between blacks and Jews, refusals of ethnocentrism, assessments of the European black Atlantic, genealogy of modernity, and more. At the same time, however, many other commentators have found Gilroy's formulations disappointing. Some have accused Gilroy of focusing too much on aesthetic and philosophical issues, while avoiding fuller treatment of the pain and suffering of blacks. Others have attacked him for avoiding economics, and for focusing on a few élites and some aspects of popular music when he should be denouncing the imbalances that still exist in the system. Finally, and most importantly from an African perspective, Gilroy's version of the black Atlantic pays little attention to Africa itself. Clearly Gilroy prefers to discuss the USA, the UK, and the anglophone Caribbean, and while he has regretted his neglect of the Hispano- and Luso-Afro diaspora, his exclusion of Africa itself has caused him much less concern. Of course, it is easy to critique a suggestive book about a diverse zone by pointing out where more could have been said. And, equally, one would not want to attack Gilroy's neglect of Africa in order to promote some now-discredited single, essential 'Africa' as the 'real origin' of the black Atlantic. Yet, at the same time, the broader black Atlantic culture has depended crucially on Africa as place, Africa as source of peoples and cultural traditions, Africa as focus of both diasporic and white imaginations, and, indispensably, on Africans themselves. Without Africa, the black Atlantic would be nothing.

These reservations about Gilroy's specific formulations, however, will not turn 'the black Atlantic' into a useless concept. There is, in sum, a multiple-centred, massively networked, quatro-continental and archipelagic cultural formation in the world today: the black Atlantic. It is neither African, American, Caribbean, nor European, nor solely black nor solely white, but is rather all of these at once and more. The black Atlantic has existed since the fifteenth century, has expanded greatly in the twentieth, and will continue to add energy to the world in the next, more global epoch. Few cultural producers, products, or movements on the Atlantic Ocean's shores are fully understandable without this concept.

BLACK CONSCIOUSNESS IN SOUTH AFRICA
The first organized opposition to *apartheid by black people after the crackdown of the early 1960s, Black Consciousness was a philosophical, cultural, and quasi-political movement that emerged among intellectuals at the segregated universities and theological colleges at the end of that decade. During the 1970s Black Consciousness was, as an influence, far and away the most important expression of black discontent with apartheid inside South Africa.

Its philosophy and ideology initially took hold among a relatively small group of urban youth and students, those who, generally speaking, had been historically most susceptible to the influence of white culture and consequently most attracted to a self-conscious rediscovery of their African roots. In the face of apartheid's divisive and exclusive racial policies and the continuing oppression of blacks within the country, black intellectuals and artists felt keenly a desire to identify with their own people. The ideology arose among a younger generation who regarded the means of combating segregation used by black organizations and individuals in the past – civil disobedience, protest at specific injustices, upliftment through education, and so on – as suspect and ineffective and who were thus groping for new forms of action. Through a number of organizations such as the South African Students' Organization (founded in 1969), the Black People's Convention (1972), Black Community Programmes (1973), the Black Women's Federation (1975), and the South African Students' Movement (which took on an increasingly Black Consciousness direction after 1972), it sought throughout the 1970s to enlarge its support base and draw black people into its ambit of influence.

Black Consciousness constructed its appeal on a rejection of assimilation, pride in one's African cultural heritage, and a determination to emancipate blacks on a number of levels. Unlike previous forms of black resistance in South Africa, it had emerged by the mid-1970s as a counter-ideology expressly aimed at delegitimizing the South African government. It is important to note that its adherents displayed a variety of political convictions. The diffuse nature of its influence proved in many ways to be a strength rather than a weakness; it allowed people to acknowledge and come to grips with the feelings of inferiority and psychological dismemberment apartheid practices had inculcated in them both as individuals and as a group.

All those who identified with Black Consciousness, nevertheless, shared common attitudes and ideas in varying degrees. Black Consciousness divided the country into two sharply distinguished groups: white 'haves' and black 'have-nots'. It maintained that white domination had served to denigrate past and present African civilization and had stereotyped blacks as backward and passive. It stressed that black liberation was the burden of black people themselves, who must learn to articulate their own grievances and perspectives rather than allow them to be represented by anyone else, even sympathetic whites. However, Black Consciousness was perceived by many of its early ideologues as a transient strategy that would disappear once it had served its purpose of allowing black people to meet whites on equal terms, rather than an overweening racial view of the world.

The demand for psychological and political liberation went hand in hand with what were regarded as positive black values, such as a humanistic and communalistic approach to life, a distaste for commercialism and consumerism, and a preoccupation with the rediscovery of black history and culture. A distinct 'African personality', humane and democratic, was seen as a bastion against exploitative social and economic relationships imported from the West.

Drawing on such precepts, Black Consciousness stressed the need for unity (under the rubric of 'blackness') of all people in South Africa who were oppressed because of their skin colour. Thus, the term encompassed Africans, 'coloureds' (individuals of mixed race) and Indians. This postulated unity was to encompass all black concerns, political and otherwise, excluding only those black people irretrievably locked into the apartheid system such as Homeland leaders, community councillors, acquisitive businessmen, and others who effectively gave their allegiance to the workings of apartheid and who were excoriated as 'non-whites' and 'sell-outs'. Each person or group of people in the black community became identified as 'part of the solution or part of the problem'.

Black Consciousness's highlighting of identity and experience naturally lent itself to expression in creative cultural activity. Cultural revival was on the agenda of Black Consciousness from the beginning, so it was no surprise that fine art, music, drama, and literature were seen as important media for its expression. A revival and burgeoning of black art took place in the 1970s that can largely be attributed to its influence and that in turn helped to spread its message. With 'a place among the people' black cultural forms demonstrated the common links between blacks and forged a common cultural identity.

With the exception of those educated outside of South Africa, the generation of writers, artists, and performers who emerged in this period were only minimally influenced by black literature from the period before the Sharpeville massacre of 1960, most of which had been banned. Thrown back on their own resources, they built a literary and artistic tradition to suit their needs through experiments in content and form. In line with the general thrust of the ideas to which they gave their allegiance, the Black Consciousness writers who emerged in the 1970s saw the need to articulate black viewpoints and opinions through their work. Writers saw themselves as assisting the breakdown of a symbolic order associated with white domination and created a literature that was predominantly political in its subject matter and effects.

Art and politics were seen as inseparable: literature and other cultural forms of expression were regarded as having the potential to fulfil important roles in social liberation because of the extremely circumscribed nature of normal political expression allowed in other areas. Most importantly, however, from its beginnings Black Consciousness cultural activists and artists saw their primary goal as the conscientization of their racial community. Emphasizing the need for social commitment, they chose to take sides and fully participate in the social struggles against apartheid, placing their art at the service of social change. Generally speaking, they also wished to change their readers and audiences into active participants in the struggle for liberation. Writers and artists who did not position their work in such a manner were castigated for not demonstrating truthfully the oppressive nature of township life.

In literature, the relationship between writer and reader was seen as one of dynamic interaction. Black Consciousness activists saw themselves as the spokespeople of the black community and gave their work the task of exposing the miseries of life under apartheid and finding solutions. Despair and reaffirmation were therefore interwoven in their work. In line with the idea that writers should at all times be prepared to learn from ordinary black people, in the early 1970s much more emphasis was placed on forms that were immediately accessible to audiences, such as drama and performance poetry, than on publication; towards the end of the decade, there were still those who believed that any writer who published at all was politically suspect.

At the same time, somewhat paradoxically, the use of African languages in creative expression was regarded with suspicion because of their association in these writers' minds with the ethnically divisive policies of apartheid. Most of the proponents of Black Consciousness in the 1970s favoured the use of an

English that was redolent with the *flytaal* patois used in the townships. They downplayed the demand for a grammatically correct English in their utterances, which the poet Mafika ★Gwala described as a 'myth of the first order'.

Black writers and literary critics also began to search for and argue about the need for more relevant critical tools in the assessment of black art and literature. In a situation in which critics of South African literature were overwhelmingly white, Black Consciousness adherents pointed out that the reception of black literature was often conducted by those who were in general unfamiliar with the experiences, assumptions, and judgements of people in the townships. Such critics were perceived as enslaved to Eurocentric notions about art that denied the sociopolitical determinants and consequences of local artistic praxis. In response, Black Consciousness literary commentators strove to discover and articulate more authentically 'African' aesthetic criteria. Such criteria and models of artistic behaviour were often sought in traditional and oral literature. For example, assertions were made by commentators such as Mafika Gwala that modern black poets derived their sense of the socially committed, democratic, and educative function of literature from the model of the pre-colonial praise poet, the *imbongi*.

It was vital to Black Consciousness thought that the dynamic and reciprocal social link between cultural producers and consumers be maintained. Instead of 'protesting' to sympathetic white and overseas audiences, black writers and performers were required to supply 'positive messages' to black audiences and readers. The notion was widely promulgated that they and their audiences partook in a collective 'black experience' and racial collective consciousness, which they sought to transform into what they regarded as more politically efficacious forms. Thus short-story writer Mbulelo ★Mzamane could speak of his attempts to create a new collective consciousness, which he related to Black Consciousness. Consequently the writing that came out of Black Consciousness saw its purpose as normative and transformative. It attempted, in other words, to force a new conception of subjectivity among individuals in the community as a whole, who could thereupon begin to identify and join together with those other blacks who perceived the need for similar solutions to the problem of apartheid.

Throughout the 1970s, Black Consciousness remained the hegemonic form of political opposition and cultural expression of black people in opposition to apartheid. It caused not only some of the most visible and significant forms of overt opposition to the government (such as the Soweto uprising of 1976-7), but also produced highly significant and enduring creative work by a number of South African writers who subscribed to its values and beliefs, of whom Mongane Wally ★Serote, Mtutuzeli Matshoba, Miriam ★Tlali, Matsemela ★Manaka, Mafika Gwala, and Sipho ★Sepamla are perhaps the best known. With the advent in the 1980s of the vision and rather different priorities of newly emerged non-racial political organizations such as the United Democratic Front and the movement of the black trade unions into the political and cultural arenas, its predominance diminished. However, its legacy remains. It spawned a plethora of writers and drama groups, gave birth to its own literary journal, ★*Staffrider*, and influenced the direction not only of black but also white South African literature in ways which have not yet been fully explored or recognized.

Black Docker, The (1986), a novel by ★Sembene Ousmane, translated from the French (*Le Docker noir*, 1956). This short novel, Sembene's first, dates from the first generation of francophone African novels. Set in the southern French port city of Marseilles, it tells of Diaw Falla, a Wolof immigrant from then-colonized Senegal. Falla struggles to earn a living as a dock worker and to write novels, despite the racist obstacles he finds in both fields. The novel opens with Falla's trial for murder in a Paris court, then flashes back to the origins of his crime. While Falla was struggling along with his African compatriots in Marseilles, a successful young French author named Ginette offered to show his manuscript to publishers. But then she published the book as her own, to great acclaim. Under psychological stress, Falla goes to Paris to confront her, and she is killed during the ensuing violent struggle. At the end of the novel, Falla is found guilty and sentenced to life. *The Black Docker* sketches a painful and multi-faceted portrait of African immigrant life in France, full of economic and emotional strife. Critics have suggested that the text's many sub-plots about romance, labour agitation, other African immigrants, a tragically botched abortion, and more cause the book to cohere less well than it might. The fact that Sembene began his own writing career in Marseilles as a dock worker adds a partly but not wholly autobiographical element.

Black Orpheus [See LITERARY MAGAZINES, West Africa]

BLACKBURN, Douglas (1857-1929), novelist, was a left-wing British journalist who lived in the Transvaal Republic and Natal between 1892 and 1908. His seven novels include a trilogy, *Prinsloo of Prinsloodorp: A Tale of Transvaal Officialdom by Sarel Erasmus* (1899), *A Burgher Quixote* (1903), and *I Came and Saw* (1908), which gently satirizes the Transvaal Boers in their contests with British imperialism. *Kruger's Secret Service, by One Who Was in It* (1900), an ironic portrait of the Rand, is scathing about the militarism of Cecil Rhodes. *Richard Hartley, Prospector* (1904) parodies the colonial adventure romance. His masterpiece, *Leaven: A Black and White Story* (1908), the first 'Jim Comes to Joburg' (rural–urban migration) novel, exposes mining capitalist exploitation, colonial violence, and the corrupting influence of the 'civilizing mission' on Africans. *Love Muti* (1915) is one of the first examples of the 'love across the colour bar' theme. His autobiography is entitled *Secret Service in South Africa* (1911).

Blame Me on History (1963) The autobiography of Bloke ★Modisane. The author takes stock of his life just before leaving South Africa for exile in England. After quitting his job as a reporter for ★*Drum*, Modisane walks among the ruins of Sophiatown, the black township in Johannesburg where he grew up (it was felt by the designers of ★apartheid to be too close to the white city). He recalls incidents from his own life, including the murder of his father, who was buried in a coffin bearing the son's name. The narrative conveys the jazzy, cosmopolitan character of the township as well as the ambivalence that Modisane felt for it and for the white world that attracted him and punished him. The text is abstract and interiorized and the structure is inchoate, but these features succeed in conveying Modisane's difficulties in making sense of himself and the world under apartheid.

Blanket Boy's Moon (1953) A novel by Atwell Sidwell ★Mopeli-Paulus. The novel, written in collaboration with Peter Lanham, was a great popular success for its dramatization of the causes and prosecution of ritual medicine murder in rural Lesotho and for its depiction of the township life of migrant workers in Johannesburg. Mopeli-Paulus puts on the record the nature of Lesotho life and customs, the policies and practices of the British administration, and the conditions in which migrant mine workers found themselves in South Africa.

BLAY, J. Benibengor (1915-), Ghanaian writer of fiction, poetry, and drama. Blay's numerous novelettes, stories, plays, and books of verse are of the order of ★Onitsha market chapbooks, most of them published under his own imprint, Benibengor Book Agency (Aboso), or by Stockwell (Ilfracombe, England). Born in Half Assini, Western Ghana, he was educated at the Regent Street Polytechnic, London. In 1958, he was elected a member of the Ghanaian National Assembly and later became Minister of Arts and Culture under President Kwame Nkrumah, who wrote an introduction to his book of verse *Ghana Sings* (1965).

Blay's books are generally platitudinous and heavily moralistic, dealing with the hackneyed themes of tradition and change in post-colonial Ghana. But following European and Onitsha market chapbook romance formulae, they have appealed strongly to adolescents at school and the less educated reading public since the early 1940s. Many of his titles remained in print or underwent several reprints into the late 1970s. The novelettes include *Emelia's Promise and Fulfilment* (*n.d., ca.* 1944), *Dr. Bengto Wants a Wife* (1953), *After the Wedding* (1967), and *The Story of Tata* (*ca.* 1976). The collections of stories include *Be Content With Your Lot* (1947, a collection of his early stories), *Operation Witchcraft* (1956), and *Tales for Boys and Girls* (1966). Of the several volumes of verse *Thoughts of a Youth* (1967) combines the texts of *Immortal Deeds* (1940), *Memoirs of the War* (1946), and *King of the Human Frame* (1947) in one volume. He also published a biography entitled *Legend of Kwame Nkrumah* (1973).

Blood Knot, The (1961) A play by Athol ★Fugard. The action of the play operates on at least two levels: the interaction between two 'coloured' (mixed-race) half-brothers, one of whom is dark-skinned and the other light-skinned enough to 'pass for white'; and the conflict between their ideas about their future. The lighter-skinned brother, Morrie, is serious and wants to save money to buy a farm. Zachariah is desperate to meet a woman. Following Morrie's advice to begin with a pen-pal, Zachariah enters a prolonged communication with Ethel, a white woman, but casting aside all caution, he lies about their condition and invites Ethel to visit them. Finally, with bitterness, Zachariah must confront the fact of his dark skin. The tensions and disappointments of the play are dispersed when, later, Ethel writes to Zachariah to tell him she is engaged to another man. The brothers return to their former life with relief.

BLOOM, Harry (1913-81), South African journalist and novelist. He was educated at the University of the Witwatersrand and worked as an advocate in Johannesburg until his self-imposed exile to England in 1963. His first novel, *Transvaal Episode* (originally published as *Episode*, 1956), was banned because the South African authorities believed it had the potential to disturb race relations and endanger the safety of the state. It is the story of an uprising in the fictional township of Nelstroom in the aftermath of the 1952-3 African National Congress defiance campaign. Bloom was denied an exit permit to travel to England to receive the British Authors' Club Prize for the best novel of 1956 for *Episode*. Bloom's second novel, *Whittaker's Wife* (1962), was completed while he was serving a three-month detention in prison. He also wrote the book for *King Kong: An African Jazz Opera* (1961), the tragedy of a boxer from the black ghetto, which reached a multiracial audience both locally and internationally.

BOATENG, Yaw M. (1950-), Ghanaian novelist and playwright, was born in Kumasi, Ghana and educated in Cape Coast and at Kumasi University of Science and Technology and the Swiss Federal Institute of Technology, Zurich. His first play was the historical *Katier* (1972), which was produced on Ghana Television. *The Return* (1977), a novel set in the nineteenth century, follows the story of Seku Wattara, a warrior who rises from obscurity to a position of influence as a general in the Asante army. His brother Jakpa, whom he once left for dead, comes to Asante as a Muslim scholar; discovering that Seku Wattara is still alive, Jakpa plots revenge. The novel is an exploration of the tragedy of Africans who sold each other into slavery for the benefit of Europeans.

BOEHMER, Elleke (1961-), South African novelist, was born in South Africa of Dutch parents and educated there and, as a Rhodes Scholar, at Oxford University. Now resident in Britain, she teaches at the School of English at Leeds University. She has published two novels, *Screens against the Sky* (1990) and *An Immaculate Figure*, both set in South Africa, and *Colonial and Post-Colonial Literature* (1995), a history of the writing of empire and of writing that grew out of opposition to it.

Both of her novels take as their central metaphor the enclosure and impassivity of white South Africa. She avoids representing black lives, at least as central protagonists. As a feminist writer, she is concerned to portray women's stories in particular and to redefine what she has referred to as a largely male southern African literary context. In *Screens Against the Sky* the passivity of the central character is shown to be as much a product of her white consciousness as of her exclusion in gendered terms from a male public and political world. The central character of *An Immaculate Figure* is again a victim of her white vision but also of the way men manipulate her, harnessing her beauty to the furthering of their material aspirations.

Boesman and Lena (1969) A play by Athol *Fugard. A 'coloured' (mixed-race) couple are evicted from their shantytown home and take to the road. But this is nothing new: they are used to trudging along from place to place, carrying all their possessions on their backs. The action of the play (performed on a totally empty stage) is restricted to a night of explosive confrontation between Boesman and Lena, and of fear when an old African who shares their campfire dies unexpectedly. The interlocking themes of the play explore the nature of poverty and homelessness, the apparent need of the oppressed to oppress in turn, and the importance of claiming personal freedom within conditions that discourage it.

BOETIE, Dugmore (1920-66), Boetie published only one book, the autobiographical novel *Familiarity Is the Kingdom of the Lost* (1969). Described as an 'experimental autobiography', the novel is a sardonic picaresque narrative based on Boetie's life from the 1920s to the 1950s. Orphaned after murdering his abusive mother, the picaro inhabits the extreme margins of black South African urban township life as a 'legless, homeless and passless' thief, con man, and perpetual prisoner. The political criticism of such things as as the cruel absurdities of the laws regulating African urban labour or the inferior status of African soldiers fighting in the Second World War, for example, never extends to political engagement. The solutions are relentlessly individual: surviving in an uncaring racist society by cunning manipulation. Unlike a later generation of *Black Consciousness writers, Boetie is unconcerned with his African identity; indeed, the influence of American popular culture (films, comics, jazz) is more prominent. The book's imperative of physical survival makes it refreshingly free of liberal moral concern over township delinquency. The playwright Barney Simon edited the text and contributed an epilogue that casts doubt on the novel's claim to be autobiographical.

Book of Secrets, The (1994) A novel by M.G. *Vassanji. Pius Fernandes, a retired Goan teacher living in Dar es Salaam, stumbles upon the diary of Alfred Corbin, an English colonial officer in East Africa. The diary, written in 1913 and found in 1988, unravels for Fernandes secrets that lead him into an engagement with his community's history in East Africa, its colonial tensions, and his own achievements and failures. The narrative structure of the novel comprises excerpts from Corbin's diary, Fernandes's comments on them, and the story of his investigations into their events and those of his own life. There are also excerpts from Fernandes's personal notebook. Through the diary Fernandes learns of the relationship between the Shamsi community of Kikono, a border town between Kenya and Tanganyika, and its colonial masters, and of his own link with that community as he comes to terms with his unrequited love for a pupil, Rita, whose life touches the lives described in the diary. Some of the diary's secrets unravel to clarify incidents and histories of the community, but there are others that remain out of reach or unresolved. So it is with this particular reconstruction of history that, spanning almost a century, takes the reader through the colonial confrontation in East Africa, its diverse communities, its aspirations to independence, and its ideas of modernity.

BOSMAN, H(erman) C(harles) (1905-51), short-story writer, was born of middle-class parents in a bilingual (English and Afrikaans) home outside Cape Town. He spent most of his life in Johannesburg, where he had a public-school type education and trained as a teacher at the University of Witwatersrand. His first – and as it turned out last – posting was to the remote Groot Marico district on the Botswana border, a dustbowl then devastated by the *Anglo-Boer war. This became the locus of most of the 150 short stories on which his reputation is based.

In 1926 he was sentenced to hang for having killed his stepbrother but was reprieved. As chronicled in his harrowing gothic memoir, Cold Stone Jug (1949), he served his prison term until released in 1930. In the same year his first great story, 'Makapan's Caves', using his frequent mouthpiece, the backveld storyteller Oom Schalk Lourens, appeared in The Touleier, the first of several literary journals for which he acted as literary editor. In London in the late 1930s he produced such characteristic stories as 'Mafeking Road', which examines the power of empire as it affects marginalized, colonized people. During the Second World War he was editor of a pro-United party newspaper in Pietersburg in the Northern Transvaal, which he used as the setting of his novels Jacaranda in the Night (1947) and Willemsdorp (not published until 1977). The novels developed his scathing critique of puritan Afrikaner exclusivity as the Nationalist party rose to power and initiated the *apartheid era. Although Bosman died too soon to be categorized as an anti-apartheid writer, there can be no doubt that his sharp, humane handling of such crucial issues as the injustice of the Immorality Act forbidding so-called mixed relationships and of the migrant labour system enforcing population dispersals was characteristic of his generally anti-segregationist views. Although he was never a partisan, his natural anarchism and sympathy with the communist press nevertheless ensured he was always able to use satire to stir up important issues.

The only collection of his work put together by himself was *Mafeking Road (1947), which contains twenty-one stories that have come to enjoy classic status. Although promoted by Roy *Campbell, who broadcast some of them on the BBC, his stories did not find a British publisher until as late as 1963, when William *Plomer introduced a second selection, Unto Dust, assembled by Bosman's pupil Lionel *Abrahams. Not until another South African-born partisan, the poet David Wright, took up the Bosman cause and showed that Bosman was hardly a Boer hick could the oeuvre be said to have made some impact outside South Africa. A collection by Abrahams of Bosman's late journalism, A Cask of Jerepigo (1957), began what became a Bosman craze, or even cult, within South Africa. In a society where humorists writing from within are rare, Bosman has become a favourite national property and is the only major figure all of whose works remain in print. Makapan's Caves and Other Stories (1987), edited by Stephen *Gray, is a

cross-section of his short fiction. Bosman's influence is widely felt in South African writing.

BRETTELL, N.H. (1908-1991). English-born poet N.H. Brettell emigrated to Zimbabwe (then Rhodesia) in 1930. Two volumes of poetry, Bronze Frieze (1950) and Season and Pretext (1975) established him as a significant southern African poet, and he wrote an autobiography, Side-Gate and Stile (1981). Selected Poems appeared posthumously (1994). He twice won Rhodesia's PEN literary prize (1972, 1978).

Brettell's reputation has grown slowly because of his (in his own words) 'tardy, reluctant, indolent' approach to his craft and a casual humility born of living always on 'the blurred edges of solitude'. Despite the slight oeuvre, poet Douglas *Livingstone has called Brettell 'the undoubted giant of poetry in southern Africa, and probably this continent'. A potentially dangerous primitivism is held from sentimentality by awareness of Africa's concomitant harshness. His characteristic voice is ambivalently melancholy, his diction latinate but leavened with Zimbabwean and English dialect, his varied stanza forms rigorously controlled.

BREW, (Osborne Henry) Kwesi (1928-), Ghanaian poet. Born of a Fante family in central Ghana, Kwesi Brew was brought up after the death of his parents by a British guardian who introduced him to books. After his early education in Ghana, Brew was among the first BA graduates from the University College of the Gold Coast in 1951. Later he served both colonial and independent governments in district commissions, and after independence in diplomatic posts in Europe.

While still a student, Brew participated in college literary activities and experimented with prose, poetry, and drama; after graduation he won a British Council poetry competition in Accra, and his poems appeared in the Ghanaian literary journal Okyeame as well as several important African anthologies. Shadows of Laughter (1968), a collection of his best early poems, reveals a thematic interest unusual for an African poet: the value of the individual compared with that of society as a whole. In poems such as 'The Executioner's Dream', which views with something like horror some of the rituals of traditional African life, he suggests that society, in an attempt to purge itself of the ills of life, robs the individual of dignity. African Panorama and Other Poems (1981) draws upon the sights and sounds of rural and urban Africa. In his collection Return of No Return (1995), he pays tribute to the American writer Maya Angelou and to Ghanaians who may have helped reshape his Eurocentric views into Afrocentric ones.

BREYTENBACH, Breyten (1939-), South African

poet, prose writer, and painter, was born in Bonnievale in the Western Cape and studied fine art at the University of Cape Town. He left South Africa for Paris in the early 1960s, and when he married a Vietnamese he was not allowed to return. He co-founded Okhela [Zulu: ignite the flame], a resistance group fighting *apartheid in exile. On an illegal trip to South Africa in 1975, he was betrayed, arrested, and sentenced to nine years of imprisonment for high treason. Released in 1982 as a result of massive international intervention, he returned to Paris and lived alternately in Paris and Gorée, Senegal, where he founded and headed a fine art workshop for African artists. His work includes numerous volumes of poetry, novels, and essays, many of which are in Afrikaans, many translated from Afrikaans to English, and many published originally in English. He has won five CNA (Central News Agency) Awards. He recently returned to South Africa to take an appointment in creative writing at the University of Natal.

Breytenbach's writing is best described as an artist's constant search for his own identity. This search has much to do with his biography as an exile, political activist, cosmopolitical 'vagabond' between worlds, 'bastard' bred on different cultures. The search is first and foremost a personal one but provides the reader with a deeply felt and accurately drawn insight into the destructive efforts any inhuman régime exerts on any of its individuals, even if they happen to live in the relative safety of exile. His poetry as well as his prose has always been marked by a combination of Kafkaesque scepticism and a celebration of life; images connect surreal worlds to the harsh and brutal realities of apartheid, magical realism to critical realism. His is not the direct ideological onslaught nor the quick and easy answer, but the delicate scalpel of a neurosurgeon constantly engaged in a search for the mad spots on the brain of the human species.

BRINK, André (1935-), South African novelist, playwright, and essayist, was born in Vrede, a small South African town in the Orange Free State, into an Afrikaans family. Because of his father's work as a magistrate, the family moved every four or five years during his childhood, living in a series of small, mostly Afrikaner villages in the interior. His parents were both supporters of the ruling Nationalist party, and his upbringing was strictly conservative and Calvinist. He graduated from Potchefstroom University in 1959 with MA degrees in both English and Afrikaans, did postgraduate work at the Sorbonne in the early 1960s, and gained a doctorate at Rhodes University, Grahamstown, where he taught for thirty years. In 1991 he became Professor of English at the University of Cape Town. He has been the recipient of many literary prizes, both within and outside South Africa, the most notable being the Martin Luther King Memorial

Prize, the Prix Médicis Étranger, and the South African CNA (Central News Agency) Award, which he has received three times (for both English and Afrikaans works). His work has twice been on the short list for the Booker Prize (for An *Instant in the Wind and for *Rumours of Rain), and he was awarded the Légion d'Honneur in 1982 and made an Officier de l'Ordre des Arts et des Lettres by the French government in 1987.

Brink's experience in Europe before his return to South Africa in 1961 exposed him to contemporary trends in European literature and radicalized his politics partly by clarifying his perception of the Sharpeville massacre, which occurred during his time abroad. In the mid-1960s he and a number of other South African writers (notably Breyten *Breytenbach) who had been abroad, mostly in Paris, formed the 'Sestigers' [1960-ers] movement, which sought to inject techniques of European experimental writing into traditional Afrikaans realism. Existentialism was a particularly important influence. His writing during this period, which was solely in Afrikaans, tended to avoid under the influence of the Sestiger creed the sociopolitical realities of South Africa in its attempt to break taboos and become more cosmopolitan. However, when he returned to Paris in 1968 intending to settle there, the student revolts that year led to his reassessment of the responsibilities of the writer in society and his realization that his place was in South Africa as witness and recorder.

His return to South Africa in the late 1960s marked a different approach to his writing, and he began to explore his love-hate relationship with the Afrikaner in *apartheid South Africa. His first openly political novel, Kennis van die Aand (1973), caused a sensation within rigidly conservative Afrikaans society for its political and its sexual content. The novel was banned in 1974 under tough new censorship laws applied in this instance for the first time to an Afrikaans work, a response that demonstrated the strength of reaction by the Afrikaans establishment to criticism by their own kind. As a result of being cut off from his Afrikaans readership, Brink translated this novel into English as *Looking on Darkness (1974), entering what he called a 'new medium', that of the English novel that could attract an overseas readership. He continued the practice with his subsequent novels. The process of translation differs for each novel according to its own principles and the relationship between the two languages within the text. Language itself thus becomes a part of the political message: A Chain of Voices (1982), for example, in the original manuscript uses English for the black characters and Afrikaans for the Afrikaner characters so that, in dialogue between them, they literally do not understand each other. More recently, rather than translating, he writes in both languages simultaneously.

All Brink's novels since the 1970s have been firmly based within a South African political context. His work attempts to rethink and revise Afrikaner history in order to understand the present, as in *An Instant in the Wind* (1976), *A Chain of Voices, The First Life of Adamastor* (1993), and *On the Contrary* (1993); to explore the nature of political action or inaction, as in *The Wall of the Plague* (1984), *States of Emergency* (1988), and *An Act of Terror* (1991); to analyse what he sees as both the positive and negative aspects of the Afrikaner, as in *Rumours of Rain* (1978) and *A *Dry White Season* (1979); and, an underlying theme in most of the novels, to come to terms with the responsibility of the writer or artist within a repressive political regime, as in *Looking on Darkness* (1974). Experimentation with form is evident in many of his novels, some of which have been described as post-modernist. A prolific writer, he has written seventeen novels, twelve of which are available in English. His work includes a number of plays and short stories written in Afrikaans and numerous translations of literary works into Afrikaans. An edition of his critical writings was published as *Mapmakers: Writing in a State of Siege* in 1983.

Despite his international popularity (his work has been translated into more than twenty languages) and three nominations for the Nobel Prize for Literature, his reputation within South Africa is less secure than those of his fellow novelists of note, Nadine *Gordimer and J.M. *Coetzee. This uncertainty is partly attributable to the perception that his work is uneven, unsophisticated or overwritten, a view shared by some international critics, and partly to a clumsiness or awkwardness of expression that results from his translations. Certainly some of his books are less successful than others: *An Act of Terror*, for example, is unnecessarily long and repeats many of the themes he has tackled more succinctly elsewhere.

In post-apartheid South Africa, Brink is a strong supporter of the ANC and the government of national unity. Despite the lessening of the influence of Afrikaans, which is no longer an official language, he is optimistic about its future as a language of the people and about the continuing role for white writers within South Africa.

BRUTUS, Dennis (1924-), South African poet, was born to South African parents in Zimbabwe (then Rhodesia), and as a young child moved with them to South Africa. After taking a BA degree at the University of Fort Hare in 1947, he taught in schools for fourteen years and became involved in the struggle against *apartheid, particularly in the realm of sport. During an eighteen-month term in the prison on Robben Island his first volume of poems, *Sirens Knuckles Boots* (1963), was published in Nigeria. In 1966 he left South Africa with his family on an exit permit. He lived in London and the USA, travelling widely to campaign against apartheid: he played a crucial role in the decision by the International Olympic Committee to exclude South Africa from the Olympic Games. He has taught at Northwestern University, the University of Texas, and the University of Pittsburgh in the USA.

Brutus has published a number of volumes since the first, including *Letters to Martha and Other Poems from a South African Prison* (1968), *Poems from Algiers* (1970), *Thoughts Abroad* (1975), *Strains* (1975), *China Poems* (1975), *Salutes and Censures* (1984), *Airs and Tributes* (1989), and *Still the Sirens* (1993). *A Simple Lust* (1973) and *Stubborn Hope* (1978) are collections, though they also contain previously unpublished poems. As a poet Brutus offers a striking and original combination of the radical and the traditional. His main subject is the ugliness of oppression and the human and social need to resist, but his characteristic tone is lyrical, meditative, analytical, revealing an affinity for such poets as John Donne, G.M. Hopkins, and Robert Browning. The most effective of his earlier poems are complex and sometimes elaborate; after the experience of prison the style becomes austere, colloquial, and resonant. The poems are carefully crafted and scrupulously precise in their charting of emotion; they never lapse into crude propaganda, even when they portray the poet as torn painfully between human love and love of his country. Brutus came to be regarded outside South Africa as the most powerful voice from the land of apartheid. In retrospect, his poems also provided a premonition of the emotional maturity and magnanimity of the ANC's assumption of political power.

Within South Africa itself Brutus is still not well known: unlike the poetry of Mbuyiseni *Mtshali, Mongane Wally *Serote, and Sipho *Sepamla, his was not allowed to feature in school and other anthologies in the later years of the apartheid era. By the time his work was officially unbanned in 1990 and he began to pay visits to South Africa, readers had become less interested in the tribulations of the previous era, and indeed he himself seemed a visitant from the past. There can be little doubt, however, of his stature as one of South Africa's most important poets. His most memorable poems are those about or closely related to his concrete experiences as an opponent and a victim of apartheid. But as a citizen of the world and as a person deeply concerned with human and cultural rights and freedoms he has continued to write thoughtful, delicately crafted, sometimes haunting lyrical poems.

BUKENYA, Austin (1944-), Ugandan novelist, poet, and playwright, was born in Masaka, Uganda, educated in Uganda, Tanzania, and the UK, and has taught at Makerere University and at Kenyatta University, Kenya. His novel *The People's Bachelor* (1972), a satire, criticizes extravagance and pretentiousness among African elites. *The Bride* (1984), a play, similarly attacks the elites, deriding the simplistic representation of African folk common in African writing. His research on oral literature has been published as *Understanding Oral Literature* (1995).

Burger's Daughter (1979) A novel by Nadine *Gordimer. As the title suggests, Rosa Burger struggles to define herself as separate from her father Lionel, a dedicated worker for racial justice in South Africa who died as a martyr imprisoned by the racist regime. Unable to abandon the principles of a lifetime as Burger's daughter to achieve personal happiness, Rosa eventually accepts her role as her father's successor. She realizes that there is no life for her without responsible action.

This novel provided the focus of one of the greatest legal cases against South African *censorship.

BUSHMEN IN SOUTH AFRICAN LITERATURE The aboriginal inhabitants of southern Africa were hunter-gatherers whose names for themselves were derived from the languages they spoke. The most southern group, now extinct, was called the /Xam (around the Cape and its hinterlands); others were the /Auni, Xatia, =Khomani, =Kunkwe (all four in what is now the Kalahari Gemsbok Park), //Ku //e (in what is now the Free State), Seroa (in present-day Lesotho), !Ga !ne (in present-day Transkei) and //Xegwi (at Lake Chrissie in the eastern Transvaal). In Namibia Ju is still spoken among the Ju/'hoasi (or !Kung). The contact with European culture that came with colonialism brought intercultural conflict, war, hybridization, and disease, an onslaught that resulted in the decimation of most of these indigenous groups, the death of many of their languages, and the loss of most of their culture. Remnants of these first peoples are still eking out a living in Angola, Namibia, Botswana, and parts of South Africa, mostly as an economically and politically powerless underclass.

The appellation 'Bushman' is derived from the Dutch *boschjesman*, meaning 'man living in the bushes', a name given to these first inhabitants by the Dutch settlers. Although 'Bushman' has long been considered a pejorative racial epithet, the equally negative connotation of 'San' (meaning 'vagabond', a name given by the pastoralist Khoi people) has reconciled many researchers to the use of 'Bushman'. The study of these early inhabitants relies on the vestiges of their culture that remain in the form of rock art (painting and engraving) and oral traditions. A shift in the concept of what constitutes literature reveals the rock art as the earliest form of writing (or 'dream writing', as it has been called) in southern Africa. This shift further suggests that South African literature has its roots not only in African oral traditions, nor in printed texts in Afrikaans or English, but also in the much older Bushman oral traditions. Ironically, our only knowledge of extinct oral traditions is through written records; the performative aspect that is quintessentially part of oral tradition is absent.

In the South African context, the study of oral traditions at the interface with writing is of necessity also a study of the interrelationship between colonized and colonizer, since it was in the records of missionaries, travellers, and scientists that elements of the oral cultures were first recorded. The mediating influence of translation, unequal power relationships, and cultural differences, for example, always intervenes in our understanding of and access to these oral cultures. As in most colonial situations, it is precisely the colonial powers represented by the recorder/author that contributed to the demise of the first people and their culture. Anyone interested in the study of these cultures is inevitably confronted with a problem: can representatives of the vanquishers speak legitimately for extinct peoples? What is the status of utterances by representatives of vanquishers about extinct peoples? Various attitudes are visible in the early records, ranging from outsiders enjoying the spectacle of the exotic, mythologizing and fantasizing about indigenous people (an example is the fixation in the eighteenth and nineteenth centuries on the hypothetical 'genital apron' of Khoikhoi women), to patronizing and/or philanthropic involvement, especially by missionaries.

For the colonial period of Southern African history (1652-1910), eighteenth- and nineteenth-century explorer journals, missionary reports, historiography, fiction, and poetry are sources of European representations of the subcontinent's first peoples. The travel journals of W.H.C. Lichtenstein (*Travels in Southern Africa in the Years 1803, 1804, 1805 and 1806*, 2 vols., 1929 and 1930), Robert Gordon (*Cape Travels, 1777 to 1786*, 2 vols., 1988), and François Le Vaillant (*Travels into the Interior Parts of Africa*, 2 vols., 1790 and 1791) reveal outsiders' views of the Bushmen as exotic people. Among missionaries, Robert Moffat (*Missionary Labours and Scenes in Southern Africa*, 1842), the *Dag Verhaal van Eerw. Erasmus Smit −1815* [The journal of the Rev. Erasmus Smit − 1815] (1956) and John Philip's *Researches in South Africa* (2 vols., 1828) offer a mixture of complacent superiority, insight into religious beliefs, and attacks on colonial racism.

In the realm of historiography, G.M. Theal's *Ethnography and Condition of South Africa Before A.D. 1505* (1919) contains a section on 'The Bushmen or Aborigines of South Africa' which describes rock art and includes four /Xam narratives. In *History of South Africa (1691-1795)* (1888), a colonial historical narrative, Theal describes in graphic detail the extinction of the Bushmen as a result of the colonists' system of commando warfare.

Among fictional representations of Bushmen, Thomas *Pringle's 'Pangola: An African Tale' (1831) is the story of a Bushman captured as a child. In Edward Kendall's *The English Boy at the Cape* (1835) the protagonist is saved in the wilderness by a beautiful Bushman girl: the mixture of sexual attraction and repugnance he experiences when first meeting the girl suggests the typical colonial fantasy about native subaltern women.

In Pringle's poem 'Afar in the Desert' the Bushman is incommunicative, almost part of the landscape: 'Afar in the Desert I love to ride,/ With the silent Bush-boy alone by my side...'. In the 'Song of the Wild Bushman' (1825) Pringle attempts to articulate the Bushman's perspective. Speaking as 'lord of the Desert Land' the Bushman challenges the 'cruel White Man' who wants him to 'crouch beneath the Christian's hand'. In 'The Bushman' (1827) Pringle describes the dying moments of a Bushman murdered in his 'secret lair'. This sonnet illustrates the threat to the continued existence of the Bushmen by 'the proud Christian-men' at whose hands he dies.

For the early twentieth-century, anthropological writing, recordings of folklore, fiction, and writing for children are the principal sources for representation of Bushmen. George Stow's *The Native Races of South Africa* (1905) accentuates the antiquity of the Bushmen as first inhabitants of South Africa and identifies all latecomers as intruders, turning the tables on colonial perceptions of the Bushmen as degenerate 'thieves', 'vagabonds' and even 'vermin'. Schapera's *The Khoisan Peoples of South Africa: Bushmen and Hottentots* (1930) challenged colonial ideas even further with its focus on culture and ethnography.

Although the /Xam (or Southern Cape Bushmen) became extinct around the turn of the twentieth century, their oral tradition, albeit mediated in written format, is what has become best known about them. That knowledge comes through the work of Wilhelm Bleek and Lucy Lloyd (*Specimens of Bushmen Folklore*, 1911, and posthumously published articles in the journal *Bantu Studies*, 1930-7) and Bleek's daughter, Dorothea (*A Bushman Dictionary*, 1956, *The Mantis and His Friends*, 1924). Bleek and Lloyd offered samples of the /Xam's oral tradition under different headings: mythology, fables, legends, poetry, and history. They attempted to approximate the mnemonic quality of oral storytelling by retaining repetition, parallelism, and the cyclical structure that avoids rounded-off endings.

Central to all these narratives, which are built around the trickster figure of the supernatural mantis, is the ease with which metamorphosis or transmogrification occurs (shaman into lion, mantis into hartebeest, human into animal or even vegetable form). The /Xam informants (as Lloyd calls them) describe a

world in which human beings lived in close relationship with nature and had intimate knowledge of the habits of animals and the behaviour of natural elements and planets. Rain as life-giver, central to many narratives, is described as gendered, according to the nature of the rain: if soft and pleasant it is a 'she-rain'; if ferocious and hard it is a 'he-rain', often depicted as the dangerous rain bull who is inclined to elope with young maidens. One of the roles of medicine men or shamans is also as rainmakers.

Under the rubric of personal history Bleek and Lloyd's main informant, //Kabbo (whose name means 'Dream'), offers fragmented testimony about his life. These fragments are particularly interesting for the glimpse they offer of an earlier, ostensibly free nomadic life, in contrast to his life in *prison under colonial power.

In *Boesman-Stories* [Bushman stories] (4 vols., 1919-21) G.R. von Wielligh provides some missing links between Bleek and Lloyd's fragmented narratives and a clearer historical context, although the simplistic style he used reduces the scientific value of his work and he also edited out the intensive repetition characteristic of oral style.

Fictional narratives of the period in which Bushman characters feature include *Dwaalstories* [Trance/wandering stories] (1927) by Eugène Marais, stories about shamans, metamorphosis, and the rain bull told in a style that recalls oral traditions. Although Marais tells the name of his informant, old Hendrik, he also says that he reconstructed the narratives from memory, rather than having recorded them where he heard them. This format raises the issue of authorship: for decades, Afrikaans literary critics considered the narratives to be the moving and poetical responses of Marais himself, attributing authorship to the white writer and ignoring the proper cultural heritage of the stories. The stories suggest a romanticizing perspective, but his introduction alerts the reader to Bushmen trance stories as a separate genre in which animals play a pivotal role.

The practice of presenting Bushman folklore as children's literature began when Wilhelm Bleek's daughter Dorothea prepared a posthumous publication of creation myths and animal stories, *The Mantis and His Friends: Bushman Folklore* (1924), leaving out the original /Xam texts and much of the repetition and giving the narratives a more digestible, less scientific form. The impression of a children's book is strengthened by Dorothea Bleek's patronizing introduction describing the Bushman as 'all his life a child'. The presentation of Bushman folklore in children's books continued throughout the twentieth century.

Throughout the *apartheid period, anthropological writing, fiction, poetry, and autobiography continued to provide textual representations of Bushmen. The mushrooming scientific interest of the last half of the twentieth century has resulted in a plethora of anthropological publications about the Bushmen. E. Marshall Thomas's anthropological journal of two expeditions among the !Kung (later renamed Ju/'hoasi), *The Harmless People* (1959), is remarkably isolationist and romanticized, a stance also evident in the work of later American researchers, such as *Kalahari Hunter-Gatherers: Studies of the !Kung San and their Neighbours* (1976), edited by Richard B. Lee and Irven DeVore, Richard B. Lee's *The !Kung San: Men, Women, and Work in a Foraging Society* (1976), and Richard Katz's *Boiling Energy: Community Healing among the Kalahari Kung* (1982).

A corrective to the isolationist approach came in the revisionist studies of Edwin N. Wilmsen (*Land Filled with Flies: A Political Economy of the Kalahari*, 1989) and Robert J. Gordon (*The Bushman Myth: The Making of a Namibian Underclass*, 1992). Another important scholarly contribution to the field is Alan Barnard's *Hunters and Herders of Southern Africa: A Comparative Ethnography of the Khoisan Peoples* (1992). Of more interest to the literary critic is Roger Hewitt's *Structure, Meaning and Ritual in the Narratives of the Southern San* (1986) and M.G. Guenther's *Bushman Folktales: Oral Traditions of the Nharo of Botswana and the /Xam of the Cape* (1989). In *Women Like Meat: The Folklore and Foraging Ideology of the Kalahari Ju/'hoan* (1993) Megan Biesele discusses the Ju/'hoasi, especially the women, and their folklore, discovering a scabrous and bawdy element in the contemporary Ju/'hoasi tales that is absent in Bleek and Lloyd's /Xam collection.

Studies of rock art and the role of trance dancing, which are important for a fuller understanding of the /Xam narratives and culture, have flourished in the twentieth century. The most persuasive theory about the function of rock art in /Xam (and Bushman) society is formulated in *Seeing and Believing: Symbolic Meanings in Southern San Rock Paintings* (1981) by David Lewis-Williams.

Laurens *van der Post's books about the world of the Bushmen include travelogues (*The Lost World of the Kalahari*, 1958, *The Heart of the Hunter*, 1961), Kalahari novels (*A Story like the Wind*, 1972, *A Far-off Place*, 1974), lectures (*The Dark Eye in Africa*, 1955, *The Creative Pattern in Primitive Africa*, 1957), a mystical tale (*A Mantis Carol*, 1975), and autobiography (*A Walk with a White Bushman*, 1986). Van der Post's forcing of the /Xam narratives into a Jungian framework in *The Heart of the Hunter* produces strange interfaces of orality and literature.

J.J. van der Post (1927-71), who lived and hunted with Bushmen in the Xeiseb-Epukiro region of Namibia, wrote a string of thirteen adventure novels in Afrikaans featuring Bushmen protagonists from whose amazed perspective he presents white culture. Other works of fiction focusing on or featuring Bush-

men in this period include J.M. *Coetzee's 'The Narrative of Jacobus Coetzee' (in *Dusklands*, 1974) and *Maru* (1971) by Bessie *Head, in which an orphaned Masarwa girl's romance is the central theme, explored through Maru's consciousness of her people as social outcasts in the predominantly black community. In Wilma Stockenström's *Die kremetartekspedisie* (1981; *The Expedition to the Baobab Tree*, 1983) a mythical Bushman presence is acknowledged at the end as the protagonist searches for her origins in Africa.

Poetry of the period often imaginatively reworks stereotyped knowledge of the Bushman. Sydney *Clouts's striking poem 'Firebowl' (in *One Life*, 1966) has 'Kalahari Bushman fires flowing/in the hollows of the desert', while images of the Bushmen in Elizabeth Marshall Thomas's *The Harmless People* inspire some of the poems in *Photographs of Bushmen* (1974) by Peter Strauss. Stephen *Watson's collection *Return of the Moon: Versions from the /Xam* (1991) rewrites the mainly prose narrations in the Bleek and Lloyd collection, offering an informative introduction and copious footnotes to explain the cultural context in which the poems belong.

Of the autobiographical texts of the period, Marjorie Shostak's *Nisa: The Life and Words of a !Kung Woman* (1981) juxtaposes lengthy commentary with the American author with the translated life story by the !Kung woman Nisa.

BUTLER, Frederick Guy (1918-) South African poet, dramatist, short-story writer, historian, autobiographer and critic, was born and educated in the Eastern Cape town of Cradock. Like Olive *Schreiner, he never lost his affinity for the harsh beauty of the Karoo and his simple upbringing, which he described in the first of his three volumes of autobiography, *Karoo Morning* (1977).

In 1938 he graduated from Rhodes University, receiving his MA in English the following year. In 1940 he married Jean Murray Satchwell, but left South Africa in August to fight in the Second World War. He studied at Brasenose College, Oxford, receiving his Honours degree in English in 1947. His eight years as student and soldier are chronicled in the second volume of his autobiography, *Bursting World* (1983). On his return to South Africa he lectured in English at the University of the Witwatersrand. In 1951 he moved to Grahamstown as Senior Lecturer at Rhodes, and a year later was made Professor and Head of English. He retired in 1987, when he was appointed Emeritus Professor and Honorary Research Fellow. Butler has received honorary D.Litt degrees from the universities of Natal, the Witwatersrand, South Africa and Rhodes.

His early plays on the encounter between Boer and Briton, *The Dam* (1953), which received the Van Riebeeck Tercentenary Foundation Award, and *The*

Dove Returns (1956), were performed under the aegis of the National Theatre Organization. Another play, *Demea*, was begun in the 1950s, but because it called for a non-racial cast, it could not be performed before 1990, when it was staged and published. Butler has an eminent reputation in Eastern Cape history, particularly of the 1820 Settlers, who provide the inspiration and subject matter for much of his literary work. For the 150th anniversary celebrations in 1970 *Richard Gush of Salem* (1982) was performed, like the earlier Settler play, *Take Root or Die* (1970), and *Cape Charade or Kaatjie Kekkelbek* (1968), at the newly-built Rhodes Theatre. Butler has pointed out to detractors of the 'Settler myth' that as Alan ★Paton suggests, the South African land itself expresses the commonality between its people, binding them together in their fight against the elements.

The engagement with both drama and history has enriched poetry with a mythic dimension and the rhythms of living speech. His work is a sustained endeavour to distinguish and synthesize the two strains of 'Europe' and 'Africa', each roughly represented by the narrative poems published twenty years apart, *On First Seeing Florence* (1968), a major symphonic poem begun in 1945, and *Pilgrimage to Dias Cross* (1987), begun in 1971. Africa is seen as a place where white English-speakers strive to come to terms with themselves, a testing ground for their beliefs. But Africa also represents a state of mind in which the poetic imagination tries to find a habitation, an idea which also informs the third volume of his autobiography, *A Local Habitation* (1991). The struggle to articulate and reconcile contending forces, and be true to experience, infuses Butler's poetry with tension, but also with a serenity and unforced naturalness.

He has brought out four volumes of lyric poetry, the first being *Stranger to Europe* (1952), which concentrates on his experience of the war; it was re-published with poems of a more South African nature in 1960. *South of the Zambezi* (1966), *Selected Poems* (1976), which won the CNA Literary Award and was re-published with more poems in 1989, and *Songs and Ballads* (1978) earth his experience firmly in South Africa, yet draw their inspiration from Wordsworth, Yeats and Eliot. Many poems deal with parting, failure or self-denial, and are responsible to a deep religious vision. The early poems, including the finely crafted war poems, assert themselves with youthful arrogance, while the most recent are not so sure of themselves and focus on solitary figures, who sense that stillness may be the only response to the enigma of this world.

This meditative poetry has been attacked by radical critics, who have also accused him of 'Butlerism', a colonial and separatist mentality, in his striving to lead English-speaking South Africans towards an awareness of their own identity and heritage. Yet Butler sees the encounter of different South African cultures as exciting, producing both a symbiosis and tension, and he has also modified some rather outlandish views over the years. He has, moreover, always believed in literature's role in the creation of a united nation of distinct and complementary languages and cultures. In defiance of the trend of fellow white South African poets like Sydney ★Clouts who left throughout the decade of exodus in the post-war years for the heart of civilization ('Europe') which nurtured their intellect, Butler chose to stay where his roots were ('Africa'), and so has kept contact with the source of what has fashioned his soul.

C

Cairo Trilogy by Naguib *Mahfouz: three novels published in 1956–7, following the life of a Cairo family through three generations from 1917 to 1944. The hero of *Palace Walk* Ahmad Abd al-Jawad, and his wife Amina are regarded by Egyptians as archetypal figures. In *Palace of Desire,* attention focuses on their sons, the sensual Yasin and the intellectual Kamal, who is an autobiographical portrait of Mahfouz. In *Sugar Street* the grandchildren grow up and are drawn into the conflict between the Muslim Brotherhood and the communists. These books, in which Mahfouz says he set out to write 'a history of my country and of myself', are generally regarded as his greatest work.

Call Me Woman (1985) The autobiography of Ellen *Kuzwayo. The book is testimony to the resilience of its author, who overcomes personal adversity to become a community leader and inspiration to many women. Her own search for a place to call home intersects with the wider history of displacement and dispossession experienced by black people in South Africa. The personal trauma of a disastrous marriage and separation from her sons is doubled by the trauma of detention without trial. Throughout she is at pains to point to the typicality of her experience. The book celebrates the achievements of black women in South Africa in the face of their double exclusion (as women and as blacks). Feminist critics have explored the tensions and ambiguities inherent in Kuzwayo's attempt to define a feminist position while at the same time subscribing to what sound like rather stereotypical views of femininity and womanhood.

CAMARA LAYE (1928–80), Guinean novelist who wrote in French, was born in Kouroussa, Upper Guinea, in what was then French West Africa. (Laye's first or given name is in fact Laye, and his family name is Camara, but he always referred to himself as 'Camara Laye'.) He was born into a lineage of Malinke (or Mande) blacksmiths and goldsmiths, and during his childhood in Kouroussa and his mother's birth village of Tindican, he absorbed the traditional and not yet heavily French-influenced culture of his people. Though he attended both the Koranic and the local French elementary school in Kouroussa, his 'break' did not occur until he travelled at age fourteen to Conakry, the distant coastal capital of Guinea, to continue his education. He did well there, and succeeded in his vocational studies in motor mechanics. In 1947, aged nineteen, he travelled to a relatively cold and lonely Paris to continue studies in mechanics. There he also worked at the Simca automobile factory, in Les Halles food market, and took further course work in engineering and towards the *baccalauréat.*

All of this changed in 1953, with the publication of his first novel, *L'Enfant noir* (*The African Child*, 1954), a gentle, touching, apparently non-radical, highly autobiographical story, which narrates in the first person a Guinean boy's life from his earliest childhood in the village of Kouroussa through his development in Conakry until his departure for France. The book won the Prix Charles Veillon in 1954. *L'Enfant noir* was followed quickly by the very different *Le Regard du roi* (1954; *The Radiance of the King*, 1956). This second book reverses the classic theme of the African who travels to Europe and becomes unsettled, since it concerns a white man, Clarence, who has come to Africa to seek his fortune; he fails and then embarks on an increasingly strange and alienating quest towards the southern jungles in search of recognition by the African king. With these two novels – among the very earliest major works in francophone African literature – Camara Laye vaulted into fame on both continents. In 1956 he returned to Africa, first to Dahomey (now Benin), then Gold Coast (now Ghana) and then to newly independent Guinea, where he held a series of government posts. In 1965 he left Guinea for Dakar, Senegal as a result of political troubles, never to return. In 1966 his third novel, *Dramouss* (*A Dream of Africa*, 1968), appeared; it continues the autobiographical account of *L'Enfant noir* but in a much more bitter mood, emphasizing the political critique of a Guinean regime grown corrupt. It may safely be classified with the late 1960s wave of African 'novels of disillusionment'. In 1978 his fourth and final work appeared: *Le Maître de la parole – Kouma Lafôlô Kouma* (*The Guardian of the Word*, 1980). It is a rendering – the author terms himself 'the modest transcriber and translator' – of the month-long 1963 narration by the traditional Malinke *griot* (traditional storyteller) Babou Condé, of the famous Soundiata (or Sundiata or Sunjata) story: that of the legendary thirteenth-century founder of the powerful empire of Old Mali. Camara Laye died in Dakar of a kidney infection.

Laye's literary legacy is mixed. *L'Enfant noir* is widely recognized as one of the early landmarks in contemporary African writing, insofar as it was among the earliest works of great international renown. It was, for example, published in English in 1954 by Farrar, Straus and Giroux. *L'Enfant noir* remains extremely widely taught, read, translated, and critiqued in several languages. At the same time, some critics have downgraded the book for its lack of political edge. *Le Regard du roi* has attracted nearly as much critical attention for its rich, labyrinthine plot, its 'white reversal', and its resonance with Kafka and other Euro-modernist writers. *Dramouss* has only rarely been addressed and is very infrequently taught or read. *Le Maître de la parole*, finally, has received some but not much critique, partly because of the limited number of specialists studying the interfaces between African ★orature and literature and between African literature and history. Though his life's literary output was not massive, Laye will always be remembered as a pioneering figure in African literature in European language. At least three of his four works will continue to animate readers both young and old, and scholars both admiring and critical, in Africa, in Europe, and elsewhere, for many decades to come.

CAMPBELL, Roy(ston) (1901-57), South Africa's most widely recognized poet, also gained a reputation as a critic, autobiographer, and controversialist. Born in Durban in 1901 into the family of a wealthy physician, he was educated there before sailing for Oxford in 1919 in a vain attempt to gain admission to Merton College, where he hoped to read English. Unable to learn enough Greek for entrance to the university, he went to London, where he moved on the fringes of the literary and artistic world of the capital. In 1922 he met and married the painter Mary Garman; the couple moved to the Welsh village of Aberdaron, where Campbell completed a long and extraordinary poem, *The ★Flaming Terrapin* (1924).

Buoyed by the success of *The Flaming Terrapin*, Campbell returned to South Africa in 1924 and there founded South Africa's first bilingual literary and political journal, *Voorslag*. The journal's attacks on the colour bar, as ★apartheid was then known, embarrassed its financial backer, who forced Campbell's resignation as editor. It was during the period of artistic and political engagement when he worked on *Voorslag* that Campbell wrote many of the lyrics he was to publish in *Adamastor* in 1930, which depict white South African racial attitudes as not just morally wrong but politically suicidal. Before his return to Europe at the end of 1926 he also wrote a number of vivid epigrams and a long satire, *The Wayzgoose* (1928), an attack on white South African mediocrity and complacency.

On their return to England, the Campbells rented a cottage in Kent in 1927 and that same year met Vita Sackville-West, with whom Mary Campbell had an affair. This is the turbulent background to *The Georgiad* (1931), the long satirical poem attacking Sackville-West and all her friends, in particular the

Georgian poets (hence the title). All Campbell's enemies are gathered together for a weekend house party at the Nicolsons' home; after being allowed to exhibit all their weaknesses and follies, they are shown up by contrast with a real artist, Campbell himself in disguise. The volume did Campbell more harm than he realized at first, for the Nicolsons and their friends formed a powerful literary coterie that from then on had an interest in downplaying or ignoring his work. Of more lasting poetic value than *The Georgiad* was the next volume of verse he published, *Adamastor*, which confirmed his status as a poet of high talent. As the 1930s wore on, critics spoke of him in the same breath as W.H. Auden and Stephen Spender.

Having moved to France in 1928, he published *Flowering Reeds* (1933). French influence shows not just in that volume, but in the fine translations and adaptations from such writers as Arthur Rimbaud and Charles Baudelaire that he included; from this point on translations were to play a large part in Campbell's writing. In Spain, where he moved in 1933, he finished an autobiography, *Broken Record* (1934) and began revising the strange and difficult sonnet sequence he had written in his last year in France and was to publish under the title *Mithraic Emblems* (1936). Forced out of Spain by the civil war, the Campbells moved in 1937 to Portugal, where he worked steadily at a long poem in defence of Franco's Nationalists, writing most of it in a mere two weeks in March 1938. It was published as *Flowering Rifle* (1939), and with the appearance of this five-thousand-line poem Campbell's relations with his fellow writers in English (already strained by *The Georgiad*) were finally broken. *Flowering Rifle* convinced all who read it that Campbell was a fascist; it was a slur from which he was never fully to free himself.

During the war, he began a translation of the poems of St. John of the Cross, which he was to work on intermittently for years and to publish in 1951. Campbell served with the British forces in East Africa and produced some fine war poems, published in *Talking Bronco* (1946). After the war he lived in Portugal, where he was killed in car crash.

CASELY-HAYFORD, Adelaide (1868-1960), prose writer, was born of Fanti and English parents and studied in Sierra Leone and England and later lived in Sierra Leone. As one of Africa's pioneer writers in English, she, along with Mabel Dove Danquah, was among the first to reach an international audience and used her influence as the wife of the distinguished diplomat Joseph Ephraïm Casely-Hayford to benefit Africa in general and African women in particular, especially in women's education. Her story 'Mista Courifer', discovered by Langston Hughes and anthologized in *An African Treasury* (1960), is a lightly ironic portrait of a Sierra Leone elitist who apes everything British; it and the autobiographical *Reminiscences* (1953) reveal a sense of herself as African that was unusual in a Creole culture that privileged its British heritage.

CASELY-HAYFORD, Gladys (1904-50), poet and short-story writer, was born in Ghana but was taken early to England for medical care and was educated in Europe. She returned to Freetown, Sierra Leone in 1926 to help her mother, Adelaide *Casely-Hayford, with her girls' vocational school. In the 1930s she spent a few years in Europe, joined a Berlin jazz group, and travelled in the USA. She was, like her parents, a pioneer West African writer, and intensely aware of herself as African. That awareness informs the language and rhythms of such poems as 'Rejoice' and 'Nativity', which celebrate blackness. Although she was not widely published before her death, during the 1960s her poems were often anthologized. She also wrote poems in *Krio, some of which were published as *Take Um So* (1948), a pamphlet.

CASELY-HAYFORD, Joseph Ephraïm (1866-1930) Lawyer and politician from the Gold Coast, he is the author of *Ethiopia Unbound* (1911), a novel which is one of the first texts of fiction produced in English in West Africa. His book shows the clear influence of E. Blyden and W.E.B. Du Bois, and is first a vigorous defence of black people and critical of Christianity, a religion dominated by white people, whereas its origin could be, according to him, traced back to Ethiopia. *Ethiopia Unbound* is the story of Kwamankra and his friend Whitely who move from London to the Gold Coast, which permits a satirical presentation of the colonial milieu. Stories and songs, sometimes in Fanti, are included in the narration as well as poems in Victorian English. It is an original book and the work of a distinguished intellectual, which deserves to stand as an African literary landmark.

CENSORSHIP

East Africa: Censorship of literature in East Africa has been primarily politically motivated; however, the proliferation of sexually explicit popular fiction since the early 1970s has invoked moral standards as a further consideration. Although the debate about the power of such writing to influence human behaviour and attitudes continues, in Tanzania the government has on occasion taken strict prohibitive action. Thus it banned, temporarily, Osija Mwambungu's (*Prince Kagema's) novel *Veneer of Love* (1975), Charles *Mangua's *Son of Woman* (1971), and David G. Maillu's books.

Censorship takes various forms. The most overt is the imposition of bans. In 1977 Kenyan authorities withdrew the licence for performances of *Ngugi wa Thiong'o's and Ngugi wa Mirii's Gikuyu play

Ngaahika Ndeenda [I will marry when I want], which remained outlawed until 1994. In 1982 the Kamiriithu Theatre Group was refused permission to perform publicly Ngugi's play *Maitu Njugira* [Mother sing for me], and later police demolished Kamiriithu's people's theatre. *Muntu by Joe *de Graft and the Swahili plays *Kilio cha Haki* [The cry for justice] by Alamin Mazrui and *Kilio* [The cry] by students of Nairobi School were prohibited around the same time. Stage productions were reported stopped as recently as July 1995. In 1987 Ngugi's *Gikuyu-language novel *Matigari* (1986) was withdrawn from the Kenyan market. The book is now available in bookshops.

The detention or imprisonment of writers is also a kind of censorship. In Uganda the founder-editor of *Transition* magazine, Rajat Neogy, was detained in the late 1960s and subsequently put on trial by president Milton Obote. Although acquitted, Neogy could no longer function in that country, and *Transition* ceased publication in Uganda.

In a region with a relatively undeveloped reading culture, the exclusion of certain authors from the school syllabus amounts to censorship. In Kenya, the integration of literature as a subject in the school system into 'English' in the 1980s led to a drastic decrease in the number of local books as set texts. Thus, since 1988 none of Ngugi's books has been offered for study.

Grossly uneven competition, in which the economically disadvantaged East African countries cannot resist cultural domination from outside, in effect censors local production. The situation recalls the 1976 controversy that arose between the foreign management of the Kenya National Theatre and the Ministry of Social Services over the National Theatre's repertoire during a time of symbolic national significance. The former finally conceded to having two Kenyan plays run for a total of eight days (two foreign shows ran for thirty-one).

'Cheap literature has proliferated at the expense of serious literature', says *Taban lo Liyong (*Sunday Nation*, 30 July 1995). This particular censorship of 'serious' literature is a result of both the exclusively market-determined orientation of local publishers towards mediocre popular taste and the entrenchment of such a taste by the second-rate products of Western popular culture that flood East Africa. Commercial considerations also persuade local publishers to avoid the risk of publishing new authors, thus censoring their works and hampering the growth of national literature. In Uganda, Timothy *Wangusa talks of hundreds of manuscripts by indigenous writers awaiting publication.

Lastly, there is the phenomenon of self-censorship. Some decide not to write for fear of persecution. Others, like Hilary Ng'weno of Kenya, are ready to delimit 'the sphere of an author's operation'. The dependence of local artists on foreign publishers, theatre owners, and donors also leads to self-imposed censorship, manifested in the tendency to create within the foreign tradition or within the foreigners' notion of African art.

East African writers have learned to subvert censorship by resorting to allegory, humour, and satire. Examples of such works are Francis *Imbuga's play *Betrayal in the City* (1976), John *Ruganda's *The Floods* (1980), Cyprian Karamagi's novel *Bulemu the Bastard* (1980), and Wahome Mutahi's *Three Days on the Cross* (1991). Paradoxically, perhaps, censorship sometimes serves as the enemy that some claim art needs to flourish. In prison in 1978 for the production of *Ngaahika Ndeenda*, Ngugi wrote his novel *Devil on the Cross* (1982).

South Africa: The production and distribution of books and films as well as the mounting of public entertainments in South Africa is controlled by the Publications Act of 1974, which came into effect on 1 April 1975. Previously, censorship had been imposed through the Suppression of Communism Act (1950) and the Publications and Entertainment Act (1963). The former, together with its successor, the Internal Security Act (1976), was a powerful instrument of control, since it empowered the state to suppress literature deemed to be communist or produced by an unlawful organization (such as the banned African National Congress) and to impose bans not only on persons but also on all their utterances and writings. Together with the vast corpus of laws required to impose *apartheid, this legislation severely restricted freedom of expression and, in the 1950s and 60s, led to the banning, exile, and even suicide of writers. Black writers in exile found themselves listed and their work banned, thus rendered unavailable in South Africa. Publishing the work of a banned person constituted a criminal offence. A whole generation – that of Dennis *Brutus, Todd Matshikiza, James *Matthews, Es'kia *Mphahlele, Nat *Nakasa, and Lewis *Nkosi – was silenced and the intellectual isolation of the country took on serious proportions.

The Publications Act set up a Directorate of Publications, committees to review books, films, and entertainments, and a Publications Appeal Board, while abolishing the right of appeal to a court of law. Members of the public, customs officers, the police, or publishers submitted publications for examination to the directorate, which did not hear evidence or consider legal representation before reaching a decision. The committees' findings were relayed by the directorate to interested parties. If a publication was found to be 'undesirable', both its distribution and its possession could be made an offence. Decisions were published periodically in the *Government Gazette* specifying the nature of the undesirability, the broadly

defined criteria for which were set out in section 47 (2) of the act. A publication was considered 'undesirable' if it was found to be indecent, obscene, or blasphemous; to bring 'any section of the inhabitants of the Republic into ridicule or contempt'; to be 'harmful to the relations between any section of the inhabitants of the Republic'; or to be 'prejudicial to the safety of the State, the general welfare, or the peace and good order'.

Although the act made provision for an appeal against the decision of a publications committee, few writers availed themselves of the opportunity, since they rejected the whole system; some appeals were allowed, however. Censorship caused writers and publishers inordinate financial losses and denied readers access to important works. The extent of the devastation of cultural and intellectual life is revealed by the statistics. Of the 1,944 publications and objects (including films) submitted in 1976 alone, 1,141 were judged 'undesirable' and 726 'not undesirable'. After the Soweto uprising of 1976, the censors intensified their activities.

The first work of Afrikaans literature to be banned was André *Brink's *Kennis van die Aand* (*Looking on Darkness*, 1974) in 1973, to be followed, controversially, in 1977 by Étienne Leroux's CNA (Central News Agency) Award-winning *Magersfontein, O Magersfontein* (1976), which went on, while banned, to win the prestigious Hertzog Award. A volume of poems by Breyten *Breytenbach, *And Death White as Words* (1978), was banned while the poet was serving a prison sentence.

It was, however, black writers who were mainly affected. Gibson *Kente's play *Too Late* (1975) and Sipho *Sepamla's poetry collection *The Soweto I Love* (1977) were banned, as was Miriam *Tlali's *Muriel at Metropolitan* (1975), regarded as containing derogatory remarks about Afrikaners. Khayalethu Mqayisa's play *Confused Mhlaba*, in a famous case, failed on appeal. When Ravan Press founded the *Staffrider* series as a much-needed outlet for new black writing, eight of the first thirteen volumes were banned, among them Mtutuzeli *Matshoba's *Call Me Not a Man* (1979), Mothobi *Mutloatse's anthology *Forced Landing* (1980), Daniel P. *Kunene's *A Seed Must Seem to Die* (1981), Mbulelo *Mzamane's *The Children of Soweto* (1982), and Mongane Wally *Serote's *To Every Birth Its Blood* (1981). Literary magazines such as *Donga* and *Staffrider* were frequently banned.

The furore that followed the bannings in 1979 of Brink's *A *Dry White Season* (1979) and Nadine *Gordimer's *Burger's Daughter* (1979) caused the directorate to appeal against decisions of its own committees. Brink's clandestinely published novel (advance copies were distributed through the post in an effort to circumvent the censors) dealt with the raising of Afrikaner political consciousness and with deaths in

60

detention. *Burger's Daughter* was banned under all five categories of the act, the author standing accused of 'launch(ing) a blistering and full-scale attack on the Republic of South Africa'. Her response, *What Happened to Burger's Daughter*, (1980) was an outspoken and detailed critique of the censorship system. The banning of major works inevitably caused a crisis with which Professor J.C.W. van Rooyen, appointed to the chair of the Publications Appeal Board in 1980, had to contend. Under his administration, a new dispensation was implemented, incorporating three major changes: a committee of experts was appointed to advise on literary merit (with the aim of averting conflict between government and the literary establishment); 'undesirability' was to be defined on the basis of the 'probable reader' rather than the 'average man'; and the criteria were to be interpreted more realistically. In the field of literature, the practical effects were that few works were banned; previously banned works were re-published; a work could no longer be banned on the basis of isolated passages only; greater tolerance was exercised towards the expression of political grievances by blacks; and the practice of banning future issues of controversial journals was abandoned. Under what Gordimer sceptically termed 'censorship's new deal' and especially during successive states of emergency the focus switched to the media and oppositional political organizations.

The aim of censorship was to facilitate the policy of apartheid, to contain the potentially explosive force of literary creativity, and to thwart political debate. Writers were harassed, publishing became a precarious enterprise, academic work was hampered. The changes introduced by F.W. de Klerk in 1990 reversed the trend towards greater control. In the new South Africa, the censorship laws are being revised.

South–Central Africa: The anxiety about obscenity that motivated the earliest censorship legislation in Zimbabwe has resurfaced throughout the century. Given the political power of settler ideology until Zimbabwe's independence in 1980, this anxiety could be attributed to a moral agenda to maintain standards of decency among the whites and to protect the blacks from the supposed corrupting influences of Western media, be they films, magazines, or books. This however does not explain the continuing focus by the censorship board of Zimbabwe on indecent and obscene materials well into the 1990s. The notable variation arises during the period of UDI (1965-79) when the Rhodesia government introduced legislation to control the media, particularly the press, while the board of censors, caught up in the climate of civil war between the settlers and nationalist groups, took the predictable step of banning literature that dealt with the plight and aspirations of the black majority or African nationalism.

The earliest legislation was the Obscene Publications Act of 1912, which aimed 'to prevent the making, importation, sale, exhibition, or possession of indecent or obscene books, pictures, prints and other articles'. The most serious offence was the making or importation of such material, an offence that carried a fine of up to 250 pounds. The fine for possessing the material was only ten pounds. The controlling authority was left in the hands of two people, the officers in charge of the town police in Bulawayo and Salisbury. Until 1932 they were the official censors.

At the start of the First World War censorship was introduced for security reasons, with the main thrust on postal and other communications with 'a foreign country' and particularly German persons or businesses. The experience seems to have galvanized government into a new sense of national security because by the late 1920s the Ministry of Defence had introduced a 'controller' of censorship whose task was to monitor postal services, radio, press, books, and photographs. This threat of censorship was strengthened as the Second World War loomed and led to the wartime legislation of the period 1939-45.

Censorship of films dates from 1917, when the government agreed to be guided by the Transvaal board of censors, who would send their weekly lists giving two categories of film, those suitable for European audiences and those for 'coloured persons and natives'. In 1927 these latter films were also vetted by a non-governmental organization, the American Board of Missions in Johannesburg. This sensitivity to material available to blacks is apparent again in the next major censorship legislation, the Entertainments Control and Censorship Act (1932), which included among its targets 'posters of low class travelling shows, posters being exported from Russia and elsewhere', which were forbidden, especially to 'natives'.

In response to the growing variety of media technology as well as the development of entertainment in the urban centres, the government introduced the first board of censors in 1932 to be appointed by the minister of home affairs. Racial and religious issues seem implicit in their brief to prohibit material that might bring 'any section of the public into ridicule or contempt'.

In the increasing political tensions within Southern Rhodesia after the Second World War censorship became a political tool of government wielded most obviously against the press. The Subversive Activities Act (1950), designed at first to tackle communist literature, ended up giving comprehensive powers to prohibit printed material of all kinds. In the early 1960s under the Law and Order Maintenance Act government was able to prosecute or ban newspapers, their editors, and writers for causing 'alarm and despondency'. As UDI broke in November 1965, censors armed with the Emergency Powers (Control of Publications) Act entered newspaper offices and censored newspapers while they were being set up. Some papers protested by appearing with blank spaces, but that was quickly forbidden. The Constitutional Council found in March 1966 that the regulations contravened the Bill of Rights in the constitution, particularly 'the individual's fundamental right to freedom of expression'. In 1967 a new act, the Censorship and Entertainment Control Act, replaced previous censorship legislation and was the basis for censorship until independence. A board of censors was appointed by the minister of law and order, as well as an appeals board, and lists of banned material were published regularly. Hundreds of books and magazines were censored during the 1970s, mainly for sexual or nationalist content.

Although the 1967 act continued in operation for three years into independence there was a major shift in policy in 1980 with the unbanning of scores of books by Zimbabwean writers prohibited during UDI. Works by writers like Canaan Banana, Wilson *Katiyo, Lamont, Doris *Lessing, Charles *Mungoshi, Garikai Mutasa, Solomon *Mutswairo, Stanlake *Samkange, Ndabaningi Sithole, and Lawrence *Vambe became available in Zimbabwe, some of them for the first time. Musical lyrics by Thomas Mapfumo and Frederick Zindi were also released. The work of the censors for the previous twenty years was undone at a stroke. The first moment of awkwardness was the banning of Dambudzo *Marechera's Black Sunlight in 1981 on grounds of obscenity. The book was unbanned in 1982 after an appeal, but the case ironically pointed to future trends.

Since the Censorship and Entertainment Control Amendment Act (1983) censorship seems to have reverted to its 1912 role of moral guardian against indecent and obscene materials. Dozens of magazines as well as posters, postcards, and calendars are banned every year for their sexual content. The number of books banned for the same reason has dropped dramatically to less than half the pre-independence levels, and virtually no books of political interest have been banned since 1980. The focus is highlighted by an incident in 1996, when the censorship board vetted Flame, a Zimbabwean film about women in the liberation war, which was suspected of offending against the obscenity laws. The film was passed, though some wanted it banned because they claimed it demeaned those who fought in the armed struggle. Later in 1996 the board attempted, on the grounds of its inherent obscenity, to ban any material the gays and lesbians of Zimbabwe might want to display on their stand at the Zimbabwe International Book Fair.

Much more attention has been given since independence to releasing books banned during UDI: these vary from seventeen in 1981 to eighty in 1986. A good number of these are of political interest, such as

Lenin for Beginners and V.S. Naipaul's Guerrillas, but the majority are what were previously thought obscene, such as John Cleland's Fanny Hill and Henry Miller's Tropic of Cancer.

West Africa: Censorship is directed mostly at journalists and media houses rather than at writers and books, since the former make more impact in a subregion where there is mass illiteracy and most people restrict their reading to newspapers and periodicals. Journalists are subjected to various kinds of harassment including physical assault, arrest and detention without trial, death threats, and even murder. Sometimes spouses and children are detained in place of absent journalists.

Nigerian journalists who have been detained during the 1990s include Dan Agbese, Ray Ekpu, and Yakubu Mohammed, all of Newswatch magazine, who were detained in April 1994 following an interview with a retired brigadier-general who was critical of the military regime and then granted presidential 'pardon'. In Ghana, harassment was so effective that for a decade Ghanaian journalists maintained what the head of state Flight Lieutenant Jerry Rawlings himself referred to as 'the culture of silence'. This silence was broken in 1991, and in 1992 an attempt to transfer eleven outspoken critics of the state-owned Daily Graphic was strongly resisted by the Ghana Journalist Association. The Sierra Leone government also began to silence critical journalists. After a new law had reduced the number of newspapers from thirty-six to eleven, security agents started arresting and interrogating journalists, including Ibrahim Seaga-Shaw, editor of New Oracle. In 1993 the draconian decree was repealed. Since the bayonetting of Charles Gbenyon, editor-in-chief of Liberian Television, in President Samuel Doe's executive mansion in 1984 and the murder by parcel bomb of Nigerian investigative journalist Dele Giwa, editor-in-chief of Newswatch, in 1986, there have been no reports of censorship-associated killings.

Foreign journalists are not exempt from harassment. In April 1994 Wall Street Journal reporter Geraldine Brooks, who was reporting a story about the violence in Ogoniland, Nigeria in connection with which the crusading writer Ken *Saro-Wiwa was 'executed', was arrested, held incommunicado for several days, and deported. In August of that year two CNN journalists were also deported.

Censorship weapons used against media houses include oppressive licensing laws and decrees, confiscation of their publications, printing of fake progovernment editions, police siege, temporary closure, and proscription. Ghana's licensing laws of 1963, 1973, and 1989, Nigeria's Official Secrets Act of 1962, decrees 4 (1984) and 43 (1993), Liberia's decree 88A of 1984, and Sierra Leone's press guidelines of 1994, with their stringent registration conditions or veto on certain publications, were all aimed at curtailing freedom of the press. Whole editions of magazines such as *The News* and *Tell* in Nigeria were confiscated on several occasions in 1993 and 1994, leading to what became known as 'guerilla journalism' when the management of *The News* temporarily replaced it with *Tempo*, which was published and printed in shifting locations.

Nigeria has used the proscription weapon freely, with nineteen newspapers and magazines proscribed in 1994. Ten of them belonged to the Concord Group owned by detained Moshood Abiola, widely regarded as the winner of the 1992 presidential elections, whose annulment by the military sparked unrest in the country.

Chaka (1931) A novel by Thomas *Mofolo, translated from the Sesotho (*Chaka*, 1925). The result of many years of research by its writer, the chronicle of the life of *Shaka, a notable Zulu king, still represents an achievement in South African fiction. In the style of tragedy, Mofolo describes the rise and fall of his hero, whom he presents as a noble figure tragically lured by the desire for power. A relentless and despotic leader, Shaka subjugates most of the neighbouring tribes, but the price of this success is a Faustian pact in which he agrees to kill his wife. The tyrant's inevitable downfall is inextricably linked to his life: he is threatened by his enemies as well as his own brothers, from whom he initially wrested the chieftainship. The brothers eventually kill him, thus vindicating the evil he has sown. Mofolo's psychological and philosophical insights into Shaka are unique. Daniel P. *Kunene made a new translation of *Chaka* in 1981.

CHEDID, Andrée (1920-), novelist, poet, and playwright writing in French, was born in Egypt of Lebanese descent. She wrote the first of twenty volumes of verse while she was a student at the American University in Cairo. She has also written ten novels as well as a number of plays, of which the best-known is *Bérénice d'Egypte* (1981). She has won many prizes: for the whole sweep of her work, the Grand Prix of Belgium in 1975, three French prizes for her poetry, the Prix Goncourt for the short story. In 1991, the journal *Sud* devoted an issue to her entitled *Andrée Chedid, Voix multiple*.

Chedid refuses barriers: geographic, temporal, linguistic. Her fiction flows easily between France and Egypt: an early novel, *L'Autre* (1969), and the film made from it display the human bond between a modern Egyptian and a European brought together by an earthquake. History, both ancient and modern, relationships, and romantic love are recurring themes in both fiction and drama, and her plays often com-

bine mime, poetry, masque, and music. Some of her novels are *Sommeil délivré* (1952; *From Sleep Unbound*, 1983); *Le Sixième jour* (1960; *The Sixth Day*, 1987), also a film; *La Maison sans racines* (1985; *The Return to Beirut*, 1989); and *L'Enfant multiple* (1989; *The Multiple Child*, 1995). Her positive spirit and her unique perspective, denying constraints of time and place, are evident in all her work.

CHENEY-COKER, Syl (1945-), poet and novelist, was born in Freetown, Sierra Leone. He studied at the universities of Oregon and Wisconsin, USA, and in 1988 was a visiting writer in the International Writing Program at the University of Iowa, USA. He works as a journalist in Freetown.

Cheney-Coker's four volumes of poetry, *The Road to Jamaica* (1969), *Concerto for an Exile* (1973), *The Graveyard Also Has Teeth* (1980), and *The Blood in the Desert's Eyes* (1990), emerge from the Creole culture of his native Sierra Leone, where the images, patterns, and techniques of indigenous African oratory are far less influential than those of European culture. As a result, African themes such as the slave trade and its consequences for the people of Sierra Leone, his own Creole roots, the destruction of the natural environment, and the internecine wars of independent Africa are yoked with references to Greek mythology, Goya, Breughel, Shakespeare, Blake, and Vivaldi. Recurring motifs and images are drawn from nature in its most disgusting forms, and he combines images with a deliberate disregard for syntax, punctuation, and word order. Christian motifs seem to coagulate into a synonym for the world's failures, and his anger gains strength and passion from a deeply felt commitment to the suffering masses of Africa toiling for the luxury goods of their new rulers. Cheney-Coker's only novel, *The *Last Harmattan of Alusine Dunbar* (1990), which won a Commonwealth Writers Prize, is an account of the history of Sierra Leone in the magic realist style.

Children of Gebelawi (1959; trans. 1981) by Naguib *Mahfouz is an allegorical novel in five parts, four of whose heroes re-live in a Cairo alley the lives of Adam, Moses, Jesus and Muhammad. The fifth represents the scientist, whose activities bring about the death of their ancestor Gebelawi. The novel has been banned ever since its serialization in 1959, being considered by many to be blasphemous. Mahfouz claims on the contrary that it is deeply religious.

CHILDREN'S LITERATURE
East, West and South-Central Africa: The term African children's literature, suggesting a canon of writing defined by the age of its audience, is in some respects problematic. In the pre-colonial tribal environment stories experienced by children were com-

municated orally and were firmly rooted in the secular and religious mores of the tribe. Many of the traditional recitatives of clan lore – folk legends, songs, riddles, ancestral sagas, cautionary anecdotes, heroic panegyrics – were integral to the life of the community as a whole and not restricted simply to the domain of childhood. Nonetheless, several factors have nurtured the relatively recent development in Africa of a substructure of story type which may be referred to as children's literature. Among such factors may be numbered the rapid reorientation, this century, of educational provision along Western lines, with its emphasis on reading and writing and its redefinition of schooling as a formal process outside the immediate jurisdiction of the tribe; the growing prioritization throughout modern Africa of written, rather than spoken, modes of narrative transmission; and the dominance, through colonialism, of European languages and their literary substructures and categorizations in so-called anglophone, francophone, and lusophone Africa from the nineteenth century onwards.

While these circumstances have done much to legitimize the term 'African children's literature', there remains at least one definitive difficulty. A good deal of writing, inside and outside Africa, traverses the boundaries between childhood and adolescence, and the even wider terrain between childhood and adulthood. In Western repertoires, Daniel Defoe's *Robinson Crusoe* and Mark Twain's *The Adventures of Tom Sawyer* are conspicuous illustrations; in Africa, *Ngugi wa Thiong'o's *Weep Not, Child* and Ben Chirasha's *Child of War* (1985) are equally persuasive, if not parallel, examples. For present purposes, and with this in mind, children's literature will be regarded as literature targeted primarily, but not always exclusively, at adolescent and/or pre-adolescent youth. The discussion focuses on writing in English.

The ascent to prominence of a group of gifted African writers in English in the 1950s and 1960s reasserted the inherent accomplishment and confidence of literary traditions which, though temporarily obscured by colonialism, stretched back three thousand years and more to the classical literatures of north Africa. The Nigerian poet Tanure *Ojaide has rightly identified the sense of utilitarian obligation generally felt by African artists towards the societies that have nurtured them. The education of children is a particular focal point for such concerns, and one that many African authors have addressed proactively through public service, sometimes as high officials in ministries of education; through theoretical and practical treatises on the teaching of young people; through personal testaments of childhood experience, as with Wole *Soyinka's autobiographical *Aké: The Years of Childhood* (1962); and, of course, through literary works for African youth, often written contemporaneously with internationally esteemed 'adult' output.

Ama Ata *Aidoo, perhaps Africa's most distinguished female writer, has produced an engaging collection of poetry for children, *Birds and Other Poems* (1992). Amos *Tutuola's 'bush of ghosts' novels, sagas of fantastic and magical childhood adventure, span a twenty-year period of his career. Chinua *Achebe's children's story *Chike and the River* was published in 1966, the same year as his masterpiece *A *Man of the People*. During the period immediately following the publication of *Petals of Blood* (1977), Ngugi produced two works of children's fiction, *Nyamba Nene and the Flying Bus* (1986) and *Nyamba Nene's Pistol* (1986), both translated into English by Wangui wa Goro. In volume, Cyprian *Ekwensi's children's fiction constitutes a substantial and important dimension of his wider literary achievements. At the heart of all such work lies the desire to provide African children with an Afrocentric view of the world, one that may balance and rectify the cultural, ideological, and other content of non-African texts.

The revivification in written form of the oral tales that once occupied such a seminal place in the African child's communal upbringing has provided the strongest impetus for the authorship, collection, and recapitulation of children's stories in English during the last several decades. A plethora of works assembling traditional tales has sought to reaffirm essentially rural tribal oral traditions – ironically, but perhaps not coincidentally, at a time when Africa has been rapidly urbanizing. Collections ranging from C.L. Vyas's *Folk Tales from Zambia* (1973) to L. Farrant's *Fables from Kenya* (1990) have recast the familiar myths and tales of African tribal legend. Many are somewhat formulaic, though a few have adopted more inventive approaches to their subject material. An unusual example, intermingling traditional form and contemporary context, is Sarah F. Oppong's *Around the African Fire* (1994). The setting is contemporary England: students from Uganda, Kenya, Cameroon, Nigeria, and Ghana each take it in turn to tell a story in which the heroic figures include Hare, Tortoise, and Spider. Such works have tended to be produced as collections of short fiction rather than as novels, reflecting the episodic nature of oral story traditions. This genre may have been entrenched further by the shortage of books in post-colonial schools, a context in which teachers often took on the role of oral disseminators, reading *to* classes rather than reading *with* them. The myriad Ananse stories of Ghana, for example, lend themselves particularly well to this approach. S.Y. Manu's *Six Ananse Stories* (1993) and J. Osafoa Dankyi's several anthologies (*Ananse Searches for a Fool, The Pot of Gold Dust, and The Discovery of Palm Wine*) are notable among these.

Other authors have moved outside the short-story domain, developing novels or novellas which retain the structures and some of the story elements of tradi-

modernist, then his novels introduce a new dimension into post-modernism: that of ethics. Drawing on European novelists and European theorists such as Jacques Derrida, Michel Foucault, and Jacques Lacan, Coetzee succeeds in translating their ideas and theories into the situation and tradition within which he writes in South Africa. The self-reflexivity of his novels is a means of scrutinizing the assumptions of the discourses that are available to him in this context, while not denying his inevitable imbrication in a tradition of white South African writing; it is also a means of drawing attention to the question of positionality, authority, and agency, always asking 'Who writes? Who takes up the position of power, pen in hand?'

Early criticism of Coetzee's novels by both liberal and marxist critics in South Africa did not understand the radical self-reflexivity of his writing, and took him to task for failing to represent accurately the historical conditions of oppression under apartheid. Coetzee has consistently refused to comment on the meaning of his novels, or to declare overtly his political affiliations. He has said that he is alienated by all political language, by 'language that lays down the law, that is not provisional, that does not as one of its habitual motions glance back sceptically at its premises'.

Since the late 1980s there has been a growing body of theoretically informed criticism produced by critics within and outside South Africa that locates the novels in the contexts of post-modernity and post-coloniality. A 1990 bibliography lists approximately five hundred items of commentary on Coetzee, including books, anthologies, journal articles, reviews, and interviews. The volume of critical commentary has continued to escalate since then, and Coetzee has received numerous awards: for *Dusklands,* the Mofolo-Plomer Prize; for *In the Heart of the Country,* the CNA (Central New Agency) Award; for *Waiting for the Barbarians,* the Geoffrey Faber prize, James Tait Black Memorial prize, the University of Cape Town book award, and the CNA Award; for *Life & Times of Michael K,* the Booker-McConnell Prize, the Jerusalem prize, the Prix Femina Étranger and the CNA Award; for *Age of Iron,* the *Sunday Express* Book of the Year award and the University of Cape Town book award, and for *Master of Petersburg,* a Commonwealth Writers Prize. Coetzee received an honorary Doctorate of Letters from the University of Strathclyde in 1985 and from the State University of New York at Buffalo in 1989. In 1988 he was nominated for the Nobel Prize and elected Fellow of the Royal Society of Literature and, in 1990, was made an honorary Fellow of the Modern Languages Association of America.

Coetzee is also a literary critic, a translator, a commentator on popular culture, and a reviewer, having published approximately two hundred items in these various fields. *White Writing: On the Culture of Letters in South Africa* (1988), is a collection of critical essays about the European invention of South Africa. *Doubling the Point: Essays and Interviews* (1992) gathers his major critical writing from 1970 to 1990; each of its eight sections is introduced with an interview between Coetzee and the editor, David Attwell, who describes the book as in a sense Coetzee's autobiography. Coetzee's autobiographical memoir, *Boyhood: Scenes from Provincial Life,* was published in 1997.

Collector of Treasures, The (1977) Short stories by Bessie *Head. The issues arising in the village of Serowe, Botswana include the impact of western civilization on the traditional way of life, the fecklessness of men in the village, and the hardships endured by women. The stories engage on the levels of both narrative and theme with the texture of village life. Accordingly, some of the stories are retellings of traditional tales, while others attempt to capture the contemporary mix of gossip, local lore, and oral history that constitutes the cultural fabric of the largely oral community of Serowe.

Concubine, The (1966) A novel by Elechi *Amadi. With *The Great Ponds* (1969) and *The Slave* (1978), *The Concubine* forms an epic trilogy. Set in the Niger Delta in pre-colonial times, the novel portrays rural village life in Erekwi (Ikwerre), where social morality and interaction revolve around ancestor worship and other ideals of local fishing communities. The protagonist is Ihuoma, good, beautiful and dignified who suffers the curse of a sea god. But the supernatural aspect of Ihuoma's character remains hidden from her lovers, all of whom die soon after marriage. She thus symbolizes fate in a society where European values do not disturb the old truths, and which is orderly and predictable unless the gods are wronged.

Conservationist, The (1974) A novel by Nadine *Gordimer and joint winner of the Booker Prize. Mehring, the conservationist of the title is a wealthy South African industrialist. Pleased with his perception of himself as a preserver of the landscape and traditions of rural South Africa on his hobby farm outside Johannesburg, he in fact actively perpetuates white masculine privilege. Both Mehring and the text itself are haunted by the nameless black man from the nearby location who has died and is buried on the farm; for Mehring the man symbolizes the uncertainty and lack of control that lie too close to the surface of his carefully ordered life.

CONTON, William (Farquhar) (1925-), novelist and short-story writer, was born in Bathurst, now Banjul, in the Gambia to educated, middle-class parents and had primary education in Gambia, Guinea, and Sierra Leone. Upon his return to Sierra Leone from England, where he had his secondary and university education, he served first as principal of the government secondary school in Bo and for many years afterwards as Chief Education Officer of the Sierra Leone government.

The publication of *The African* (1960) ranks Conton among the first group of modern African writers to emerge in the 1950s and 1960s. In addition to *The African*, which has been translated into Arabic, Russian, and Hungarian and has had two American editions, he has written many short stories as well as an African history textbook that has been used widely in African schools.

Since its first publication, *The African* has received little more than mere mention from African critics, who cite it as an example of the 'black Victorian' novel, and Euro-American critics, who view it as a novelty, an apprentice novel at best. These criticisms are not without basis, particularly since the novel's bent for a distinctively British linguistic elegance sets it apart from other African novels characterized by the distinctive language of the oral tradition. The novel chronicles the coming of age of Kisimi Kamara, a gifted young boy, his initiation into Western education and culture from primary and secondary school in Songhai to university in England, and his engagement on his return to Africa in the political liberation of his people from British colonial rule. With an obvious political axe to grind, *The African* is designed to show the shattering effect of Europe on the African psyche. The labouredness of this preoccupation and the heavy-handed use of the English language weaken the novel's plausibility and effectiveness, despite its rich display of humour.

COPE, Jack (Robert Knox) (1913-91), South African novelist, short-story writer, poet, and editor, was born in Natal, South Africa and attended boarding school in Durban, afterwards becoming a journalist on the *Natal Mercury* and then a political correspondent in London for South African newspapers. At the outbreak of the Second World War, in a state of some disillusionment, he returned to his father's farm and, while working at various jobs, took up creative writing. During the following four decades Cope published eight novels, more than a hundred short stories, and three collections of poetry, the last one in association with C.J. Driver. For twenty of those years, beginning in 1960, he edited *Contrast*, a literary magazine bilingual in English and Afrikaans. He co-edited *The Penguin Book of South African Verse* (1968) with Uys Krige and, as general editor throughout much of the 1970s, produced the Mantis editions of southern African poets. In 1980 he moved to England, where he published *The Adversary Within: Dissident Writers in Afrikaans* (1982) and his *Selected Stories* (1986).

Cope's first novel, *The Fair House* (1955), considers the Bambata Rebellion of 1906 in an attempt to account for the later racial and political conditions in his country. Later novels, including *The Golden Oriole* (1958), *Albino* (1964), and *The Rain-Maker* (1971), chronicle the white man's destruction of black culture and the ensuing struggle by the blacks to regain their pride and identity. However, it is as a short-story writer that Cope demonstrated his finest talent. His stories evoke, according to Alan *Paton, 'with a few words the scents and sounds and colours of our country'. In 'A Crack in the Sky' (*The Tame Ox*, 1960) and 'Power' (*The Man Who Doubted and Other Stories*, 1967) his moral vision is clear; his third collection, *Alley Cat and Other Stories* (1973), contains darker themes such as those of alienation and loneliness. Among Cope's main achievements was his influence on South African literature during the 1960s and 1970s, important years in the struggle against *apartheid.

COUCHORO, Félix (1900-1968) Born in Ouidah, a well-known slave trading town on the coast of Dahomey, now Benin, Félix Couchoro attended mission school and received primary education before starting work as a Catholic primary school teacher. In 1929 he published in Paris a novel *L'Esclave*, which has the distinction of being the second novel published in French by an African. His success did not get much attention since his work, heavily influenced by colonial novels and campaigning for true assimilation in Africa, was not in tune with the beginnings of the Parisian and intellectual *negritude movement; it was nonetheless a pioneering work for its time and Couchoro became a well-respected and active journalist in the Dahomean press, one of the most critical of colonial administration at the time. In 1941 he moved to Togo and became active in the Togolese nationalist movement. He published a second novel locally in 1941 (*Amour de féticheuse*) and a third one in 1950 (*Drame d'amour à Anecho*). These achievements made him famous within Togo but did not bring him any recognition from outside. Couchoro was closely watched and probably little liked by the colonial police. He had to flee to Gold Coast in 1954 after denouncing colonial repression. He came back to Togo after the Nationalist victory in 1960 and started a new career publishing serial novels in the Togolese daily newspaper. He produced eighteen novels, more than 3,000 pages, depicting a universe of junior clerks, civil servants, traders and pretty girls, in a style borrowed from popular European fiction, Bible stories and mixed with French local usage. He had a wide readership in Lomé and represents the closest francophone attempt at a local literary production, part *Onitsha, part *Ekwensi, part Benibengor Blay. His first novel has been reprinted and is now part of the common literary heritage of Benin and Togo.

COUTO, Mia (1955-), Mozambican poet and short-story writer, writing in Portuguese. A member of Mozambique's ruling party, Frelimo, Couto was born in Beira and had just begun his journalism career when he was drawn into the war of independence against Portugal under Frelimo. After the war, he became the director of the Mozambique Information Agency (AIM) and editor of the government-owned daily newspaper, *Notícias*. While in government service, he began to publish short stories and contribute articles to newspapers. He later quit government service to take a degree and pursue a career in environmental biology, but continued to produce radical journalism and fiction. In two collections of his short stories, *Vozes anoitecidas* (1986; *Voices Made Night*, 1990) and *Cada homen e uma raca* (1990; *Every Man Is a Race*, 1994), he juxtaposes narrative motifs and folk magic from the oral tradition with events that mirror the festering social wounds of post-war Mozambique. From the juxtaposition, post-war realities assume the eeriness of folktale while the fantasies of folktale resolve themselves into parables for satiric refigurations of present-day realities. Thus, in 'The Day Mabata-bata Exploded' (*Voices Made Night*), the motif of an exploding ox from popular folktale merges into the reality of an ox deliberately stuffed with explosives and ruthlessly left by armed bandits for unsuspecting peasants. By and large, Couto's admixture of folk fantasy and graphic descriptions of the violence, poverty, and ignorance of both the peasantry and the inane bureaucracy enables him to combine his loyalty to Frelimo with veiled criticism of its dictatorial tendencies and the apparently widening gap between its officials and the masses who supported it wholeheartedly during the revolutionary war.

Other notable work by Couto, yet to be translated into English from the Portuguese, includes *Cronicando* (1991), a collection of journalistic essays originally published in newspapers and magazines, *Terra Sonâmbula* (1992), a novel, and *Estórias Abensonhadas* (1994), a collection of short stories.

CRIPPS, A(rthur) S(hearly) (1869-1952), poet, novelist, and essayist, came to present-day Zimbabwe as an Anglican missionary in 1901, determined to fight for racial freedom and equality under the overarching power of one God after reading Olive ★Schreiner's *Trooper Peter Halket of Mashonaland* (1897). Born in Tunbridge Wells, England and educated at Charterhouse and Trinity College, Oxford, Cripps had published a volume of poetry, *Primavera* (1890) with Lawrence Binyon, before embarking for Africa. His collection *The Black Christ* (1902), completed in England before his experience of Africa, contains poems that appear fairly conventional and hymnal in quality but possess a unique power forged by Cripps's libertarian philosophy, missionary zeal, and transparent love for Africa (especially 'The Black Christ', 'In

Deserto' and 'To the Veld').

Besides *The Black Christ*, Cripps published several other volumes of poetry, among them *Titania and Other Poems* (1900), *Lyra Evangelistica: Missionary Verses of Mashonaland* (1909), including poems regarded as typical of his career; *Lake and War: African Land and Water Verses* (1917); and *Africa: Verses* (1939), the most comprehensive volume of his poetry. He also published two novels, *The Brooding Earth* (1911) and *Bay-Tree Country* (1913); two collection of folkloric short stories, *Faeryland Forlorn: African Tales* (1910) and *Cinderella of the South: South African Tales* (1918); and an assortment of general prose, including missionary travel journals and pamphlets on political topics. With the title invoking the image of white settlers as the wicked who flourish in a desert land like the green bay tree of the Bible, *Bay-Tree Country* uses the forced-labour scandal of 1911 as a backdrop for attacking white settler exploitation of indigenous Africans, a position further pursued in his essay *An Africa for Africans: A Plea on Behalf of Territorial Segregation Areas and Their Freedom in a Southern African Colony* (1927).

Cry, the Beloved Country (1948) A novel by Alan ★Paton. The story is fairly simple, but the mode of its narration creates a fable of social transformation arising out of crime, degradation, death, and despair. The main character, Stephen Kumalo, an aging minister of religion in Ndotsheni, Natal, receives a letter that takes him from the countryside to the cesspits of Johannesburg in search of his son, who has disappeared. The year is 1946, and the Reverend Kumalo encounters for the first time African resistance to white laws in the form of a squatter camp outside Johannesburg and the boycott of subsidized buses, which have raised their fares. Although Kumalo must return to Natal unable to help his son, who has killed a white man in the course of a burglary, the story ends more hopefully when his drought-stricken country receives help from a white man, the father of the man whom Kumalo's son has killed.

CUGOANO, Ottobah (b.1757) was kidnapped at the age of two from his native Ajumako, in what is now the Central Region of Ghana, and enslaved in the West Indies. Taken to England, educated by one Alexander Campbell, and baptized, he married an English woman and had a family. He was an active member of the London Committee for the Abolition of the Slave Trade, and in 1787 he wrote to Edmund Burke and George III urging them to stop the slave trade.

Cugoano's *Thoughts and Sentiments on the Evil of Slavery* (1787) is his first-hand account of the traumatic experience of being dislocated from family and auctioned, a heart-wrenching tale of suffering on plantations and, eventually, freedom. He assumes a moral position as he censures Western and Christian institutions for condoning and profiting from slavery. In an apparent paradox, Cugoano also affirms the liberating power of formal education and Christianity. He tends in *Thoughts* to censure the negative activities of the church while affirming the positive values of genuine Christianity, an attitude that has been taken up with passion by Richard Wright and *Ngugi wa Thiong'o. In a language as vitriolic as Ayi Kwei *Armah's in *Two Thousand Seasons*, Cugoano condemns African slave hunters, 'who were the first cause of [his] exile and slavery'. But Cugoano insists that the European is ultimately responsible for the slave trade.

Although *Thoughts* is autobiographical, Cugoano assumes a public voice to speak to the collective experience of black people. Thus, writing was for Cugoano what it became for Frederick Douglass and Harriet Jacobs, a public act, an act of empowerment, a way to raise the voice of the voiceless millions of oppressed black people throughout the world. Cugoano questions the preposterous argument of pro-slavery advocates that Africans are the descendants of Ham who suffer from Noah's curse and who therefore may be enslaved. His statement that neither skin colour nor texture of hair can determine a person's character and morality resonated in the sentiments and convictions of Martin Luther King, Jr., nearly two hundred years later.

As a typical slave narrative, *Thoughts* served well to rally support for the anti-slavery movement. However, by refuting aspersions about black people and by questioning Europe's imperial quest in Africa, Cugoano's narrative inaugurates a tradition of protest and anti-colonial writing. *Thoughts* anticipates the struggles of black people for liberation, justice, and equality in the twentieth century.

CULLINAN, Patrick (Roland) (1932-), South African poet and biographer, was born in Pretoria and attended Charterhouse School and Oxford University in the UK before returning to South Africa where he was for many years a sawmill operator in the Eastern Transvaal. With Lional *Abrahams he founded the journal *The Bloody Horse: Writings and the Arts* (1980) and the Bateleur Press. Through the journal (the title taken from a poem by Roy *Campbell) Cullinan sought to re-establish the fact of poetry as art.

Cullinan's poetry collections include *The Horizon Forty Miles Away* (1973), *Today Is Not Different* (1978) and *Selected Poems, 1961–1991* (1992). The volume *The White Hail in the Orchard* (1984) contains what Cullinan calls 'Versions' by which he means translations from the poetry of Eugenio Montale. Cullinan accepted the fact that writers ought to be involved in the struggle against *apartheid while acknowledging that, in his view, it is difficult to create a fully satisfactory political poem.

Cullinan has taught at the University of the Western Cape. He has also published a biography of Robert Jacob Gordon, a Dutch traveller and soldier, *Robert Jacob Gordon 1743–1795: The Man and His Travels at the Cape* (1992).

CURREY, Ralph Nixon (1907-), South African poet, has lived and taught in England since the early 1920s. A veteran of the Second World War, during which he served in the British Royal Artillery, Currey was born in Mafeking and left South Africa at fourteen to go to school in England and to Wadham College, Oxford.

Currey's poetry is rooted in his war experience and the challenges of living between two worlds, the Africa of his birth (evoked in his fifth volume of poetry, *The Africa We Knew*, 1973) and his 'English homeland'. His four earlier volumes of poems are *Tiresias and Other Poems* (1940), *This Other Planet* (1945), *Indian Landscape: A Book of Descriptive Poems* (1947), and *Formal Spring: Translations of French Renaissance Poems* (1950). In addition to these, he has published a dramatic poem for the radio, *Between Two Worlds* (1947); broadcast a radio feature on the BBC, *Early Morning in Vaaldorp* (1961); edited *Letters and Other Writings of a Natal Sheriff, Thomas Phipson, 1815-1876* (1968); and written a critical study, *Poets of the 1939-1945 War* (1967), as well as publishing poems in journals and anthologies. *Vinnicombe's Trek* (1989) records the pioneering history of Currey's church-building grandfather who composed simple verse when on horseback. Among other honours and awards, Currey won the Viceroy's Poetry Prize (1945, shared with Anthony Delius) and the South African Poetry Prize (1959). He was elected Fellow of the Royal Society of Literature in 1970.

D

DADIÉ, Bernard (1916–), playwright and novelist writing in French. Born in Côte d'Ivoire, where he spent his youth, he qualified in 1939 as a civil servant in the colonial administration and worked at Dakar's Institut Fondamental d'Afrique Noire until 1947. Upon his return to Abidjan, he became actively involved with his country's independence movement, for which he became the press attaché. His subsequent sixteen-month imprisonment for demonstrating against the colonial power is related in detail in *Carnet de prison* (1981). From 1957 until his retirement from government in 1985, he held many senior ministerial offices, including that of Côte d'Ivoire's minister for culture. Unlike most writers of his generation who gave up literary activities as they reached high-ranking positions at the time of independence, Dadié not only continued writing but also kept alive his early humanist ideals of social justice and respect for people of all walks of life.

As a student Dadié wrote two plays, one of which, *Assémien Déhylé*, was performed in 1936 in Dakar by fellow students and a year later in Paris, at the 1937 Colonial Exposition. From this time and throughout his literary career, theatre remained for him the genre par excellence, capable of breaking political deadlocks and overbearing government attacks against civil liberties. Particularly noteworthy are *Monsieur Thôgô-Gnini* (1970; trans. 1985), written and performed in Abidjan at the height of the 1963 political unrest; *Béatrice du Congo* (1970), staged at the Avignon Festival in 1971; *Les Voix dans le vent* (1970); *Iles de tempête* (1973); and *Mhoi-Ceul* (1979).

Versatile in his use of literary genres, Dadié gained literary recognition soon after his liberation from prison with *Afrique debout* (1950), a book of verse that was followed by an autobiographical and no less successful novel, *Climbié* (1956; trans. 1971). Other novels include *Un Nègre à Paris* (1959; *An African in Paris*, 1994), and *Patron de New York* (1964; *One Way: Bernard Dadié Observes America*, 1994), which received the Grand Prix Littéraire d'Afrique Noir, *La Ville où nul ne meurt* (1968; *The City Where No One Dies*, 1986), and *Commandant Taureault et ses nègres* (1980). Dadié has also published traditional tales such as *Le Pagne noir* (1955; *The Black Cloth*, 1987) as well as short stories, for example in *Les Jambes du fils de Dieu* (1980).

Dance in the Sun, A (1956) A novel by Dan *Jacobson, published in one volume with Jacobson's novella *The *Trap* (1955) in 1957. From the beginning the narrative hints at danger or at least profound discomfort when two university students on a hitchhiking vacation in South Africa are forced to look for lodging in an isolated place named Mirredal. When they are grudgingly offered a night's accommodation in a large, rambling, shuttered, overfurnished house they encounter a family drama involving sexuality and race. The narrative is characterized by images of the sun, which becomes a complex symbol. The sun dominates the natural setting and reduces and shrivels whites and their settlements; it is tolerable only to the indigenous black people. The whites' fear and rejection of the sun is part of their inability to accept and be part of the African earth itself. Thus they remain forever strangers on the continent and strangers to themselves, punished by a furious sun they cannot escape in spite of shuttered, cluttered houses.

Dance of the Forests, A (1963) A play by Wole *Soyinka. This immensely ambitious play was written for Nigeria's independence celebrations, although it was not accepted as an official entry by the organizing committee for that event. Drawing on Yoruba myth, in particular the complex of attributes associated with specific gods (such as Ogun's combination of creative passion and violence), Soyinka here builds a multi-stranded plot and employs music, dance, and masquerade in order to comment on the historical sources of Nigeria's contemporary reality. As Forest Head calls ancestors to life to celebrate the present, no idealized version of the past is discovered but rather a legacy of oppression, violence, and martyrdom. An extended flashback establishes parallels between lives from the past and the actions of living characters such as the modern-day whore, Rola, and the tyrant of a royal court, Madam Tortoise. The play's vision of Nigeria's future prospects emerges in a series of climaxes that are vividly compelling and yet have proven endlessly difficult to interpret.

DANGAREMBGA, Tsitsi (1959-), Zimbabwean novelist and dramatist, was educated at the Universities of Cambridge and Zimbabwe, where she studied medicine and psychology, and is best known for her novel *Nervous Conditions* (1988), set in 1960s colonial Rhodesia. A female *Bildungsroman*, the novel is a harrowing indictment of sexual and cultural imperialism that exposes the stultifying power of colonial assimilation. In addition to *Nervous Conditions*, which won a Commonwealth Writers Prize, Dangarembga has published a play, *She No Longer Weeps* (1987), about a young student who becomes pregnant in the city and makes good, though at great personal cost, in the teeth of her lover's and family's rejection.

DANGOR, Achmat (1948-), South African poet and prose writer, was born and educated in Newclare, Johannesburg and has worked in the business world and for various NGOs. Politically active, he was banned between 1973 and 1978. During the 1970s he was a member of Black Thoughts and in the 1980s of COSAW (the Congress of South African Writers).

Dangor's prose collection *Waiting for Leila* (1978) won the Mofolo-Plomer Prize and he has published a play, *Majiet* (1986), and a novel, *The Z Town Trilogy* (1989), but is best known as a poet. A regular contributor to such publications as *New Nation* and ★*Staffrider* and well represented in anthologies such as *The Return of the Amasi Bird* (1982) and *Modern South African Poetry* (1984), his two collections are *Bulldozer* (1983) and *Private Voices* (1992), which won the BBC prize for African poetry. In 1997 he brought out *Kafka's Curse: A Novella and Three Other Stories*, another award-winning collection.

Daughter of Mumbi (1969) A novel by Charity ★Waciuma. The Mau Mau emergency in Kenya is the setting for this autobiographical story of childhood and adolescence. Waciuma is herself a daughter of transition: from her storyteller grandfather she learned love and respect for Kikuyu lore, and from her health-inspector father and her mother, a district counsellor, she learned to conciliate cultural differences, even those between the local indigenous 'witch doctors' and the practitioners of western 'scientific' medicine. With candour, clarity, and good humour, Waciuma paints an endearing portrait of herself, her family, and the Kikuyu customs that shaped her life.

Daughters of the Twilight (1986) A novel by Farida ★Karodia. Fourteen-year-old Meena narrates an account of the petty daily indignities as well as the major discriminatory acts of ★apartheid. In a two-year period, the Abdul family suffers forced eviction and resettlement, the downgrading of educational opportunities, and the sadistic brutality of some Afrikaner neighbours who know they can act with impunity. The father of the family, a Muslim immigrant, is Asian, the mother 'coloured' (mixed race). Meena's beautiful, wilful seventeen-year-old sister Yasmin and their grandmother, Nana, have built up a household and family store in an area now reclassified for whites. Dispossessed, harassed, with Yasmin raped and impregnated, they struggle on despite deprivation, empowered by Nana's faith and Meena's hope for a better future.

DE GRAFT Joe (Joseph Coleman) (1924-78),

Ghanaian dramatist and poet. With a name that suggests the centuries of contact between Europe and Africa, Joe de Graft was born and initially educated in Cape Coast. After gaining a degree in English at University College, Achimota, he returned to Mfantsipim School in Cape Coast as a teacher and became deeply involved in drama. His career was devoted to teaching, but he was also passionately committed to the theatre and was often able to combine the two.

From Mfantsipim, de Graft was recruited to help Efua ★Sutherland set up programmes at the Drama Studio in Accra and the School of Music and Drama, Legon. Between 1962 and 1969, he worked not only as a teacher but also as an adaptor, writer, director, and all round man-of-the-theatre, contributing to the national theatre movement and the establishment of drama education at the University of Ghana. In 1969, failing to get expected support at Legon, he moved to Nairobi, first to a UNESCO appointment in language teaching and then to a university post in drama. His collection of poems, *Beneath the Jazz and Brass* (1975), was published while he was in East Africa. He returned to Ghana to take up a professorship in 1977, the year before his death.

De Graft's writing is partly to be seen in relation to the Western tradition: ★*Sons and Daughters* (1964) is a 'well-made play' in which the villains are neatly exposed; ★*Through a Film Darkly* (1970), a much more complex drama and one that de Graft worked on over an extended period, has links with Pirandello; ★*Muntu* (1977) is a wide-ranging historical pageant incorporating myth, folk songs, drums, storytelling, and formal exchanges; and *Mambo* (produced 1978 but unpublished) is a response to *Macbeth*. However, the issues his plays raise grew directly out of his own experience; they include the importance of the arts in national life, the damaging effects of racism, and the violence of some African leaders during the 1970s. The affection in which he is held by ex-students shows his commitment as a teacher.

Death and the King's Horseman (1975) A play by Wole ★Soyinka. The play examines transition and change, self-sacrifice, and loyalty to a long-established ideal in the face of inevitable cultural transformation. According to the author's note, it is based on events that took place in 1944 in Oyo, Western Nigeria, when British authorities intervened in a traditional burial ritual on the death of the Alafin of Oyo, preventing a faithful servant, the Alafin's Master of Horse, from following his master by committing suicide. The British Resident had the Horseman arrested, whereupon the Alafin's son fulfilled the servant's role by killing himself. The play uses these events to reveal not only the strength of Nigerian/Yoruba religious belief but, more forcefully, the arrogance of the British colonial administration as a whole and of the individuals, both men and women, who comprised it.

Dedan Kimathi (1974) A play by Kenneth *Watene. The action of the play unfolds in Kenya in late 1956, i.e. after several years of unequal struggle between the Mau Mau freedom fighters and the colonial military forces. This historical moment is transformed into a critical point in the life of the protagonist, whose strength, courage, and hope have been stretched to the limit. The admission of vulnerability inherent in such a perspective does not deny Dedan Kimathi the stature of a nationalist hero; neither does it deprive him of the legendary qualities popularly attributed to him. However, it has contributed to a perception of him as a human being endowed with human weaknesses.

DEI-ANANG, Michael Francis (1909-77), Ghanaian poet, playwright, and novelist, was born at Mampong-Akwapim, Ghana and attended Achimota College, Ghana and the University of London before entering the civil service, where he served in several ministries in the colonial and post-colonial periods. He was one of the main pillars in Kwame Nkrumah's African Secretariat, which was mainly concerned with the liberation of the rest of Africa still under colonial rule. He was arrested and detained for two months after the fall of Nkrumah in 1966.

Dei-Anang's deep interest in oral poetry and the traditional myths and legends of the Akan people is revealed in the traditional themes of his poems in English, which were the first creative works by an African to be published in Ghana. His first collection, *Wayward Lines from Africa* (1946) was followed by *Africa Speaks* (1959), which contains a useful introductory essay on African poetry. His poems also appeared in *Okyeame* and *An African Treasury*, an anthology of the 1960s edited by Langston Hughes, the outstanding black American writer, who visited Ghana at the time of independence. Dei-Anang's later collections were *Ghana Semitones* (1962) and *Ghana Glory: Poems on Ghana and Ghanaian Life* (1965), the latter co-authored with Yaw Warren and introduced by Kwame Nkrumah. *Okomfo Anokye's Golden Stool* (1960), a drama in three acts based on an Ashanti legend, was produced by the Masquers' Theatre, University of Chicago, in 1961 and staged by actors from the University of Ghana during the silver jubilee celebrations of Asantehene in August 1995. The earlier *Cocoa Comes to Mampong: Brief Dramatic Sketches Based on the Story of Cocoa in the Gold Coast* (1949) is more didactic. After 1966, Dei-Anang left Ghana for the USA, where he taught at a college in Brockport.

Detained: A Writer's Prison Diary (1981) A memoir by *Ngugi wa Thiong'o. On 30 December 1977 Ngugi was detained for publishing *Ngaahika Ndeenda*

(1977; *I Will Marry When I Want*, 1982), an experiment in community theatre in which he projects the Mau Mau guerillas who fought for Kenyan independence as heroes and patriots and the home guards who resisted them as traitors. The diary discusses the conception and writing of *I Will Marry* and of the ideology behind the Kamiriithu experiment in general. He reflects randomly on his work, his country's social and political history, the personalities that make that history, and a whole range of issues including the language question. He attacks capitalism, neo-colonialism, and imperialism and comments on the novel he was writing while in prison, *Devil on the Cross* (1982), and the character of Wariinga, the novel's female hero. While Ngugi is critical of university intellectuals for their inconsistency ('they talk progressive and act conservative'), he has high praise for the great nationalist J. M. Kariuki, murdered for his populist views in 1975.

Devil on the Cross (1982) A novel by *Ngugi wa Thiong'o, translated from the Gikuyu (*Caitaani Muthuraba-ini*, 1980). The novel deals with the overall effect of the exploitation of Kenyans through the collusion of corrupt Kenyans with the international entrepreneurial comprador bourgeoisie. The related themes Ngugi treats in the novel are the alienation of the people from the land, the destruction of a productive Kenyan peasantry, and the exploitation of labour through the coercive methods of state, church, and police. Ngugi's principal purpose goes beyond the mere description and dramatization of these civil and political problems. He seeks to show through the experiences of his principal characters, Wangari, Muturi, Gatuiria, and Wariinga, what actions can be taken to counteract oppressive and exploitative methods of the state to return the means and rewards of production to the people, the rightful owners. Ngugi achieves his effect here (as in his other writings) by a reliance on coincidence, exaggeration, and melodrama, especially in the scenes devoted to the Devil's Feast, where Christianity is ruthlessly satirized. Wariinga, whom Ngugi refers to as 'my Wariinga', is the true hero of the novel. She is the vehicle who acts on behalf of the people in executing a representative of the oppressor class, thus consummating her symbolic role in the novel and revealing Ngugi's contempt for those Kenyans who collude with external oppressors or who, seeing the vicious exploitation of their people and deploring it, nevertheless fail to act. The novel was a popular success in Kenya, selling some 13,000 copies in three successive printings. It is also estimated that perhaps 100,000 people heard the novel when it was read aloud.

DHLOMO, H(erbert) I. E. (1903-56), South African journalist, playwright, and poet, was born in Siyamu, Edendale and educated in the sheltered missionary environment of Adams College, where he eventually graduated as a teacher. Dhlomo took to journalism at an early stage of his life, and it is in this field that he left his mark as one of the most important literary figures of the 1930s and 40s. In 1937, he became the first African librarian at the Carnegie Bantu Library in Johannesburg. After a series of disagreements with his employers, he left for Durban in 1941, where he was appointed as assistant editor of *Ilanga lase Natal* [The Natal Sun], a position he retained until his death. Although never one of the leaders, he was always active in the African National Congress, particularly as a driving spirit behind the formation of the Youth League in 1946.

Dhlomo's creative work, written mainly after 1936, sought to articulate his theories on African literature. His oeuvre includes at least nine plays and numerous poems. *The *Girl Who Killed to Save: Nongquase the Liberator* (1936), the only one of his plays to be published during his lifetime, was the first anglophone play to be published by a black South African and takes as its subject matter the events surrounding the vision of Nongquase, the Xhosa prophet, and the subsequent cattle killing of 1857. The play is very much of the 'missionary literature' genre, but Dhlomo outgrew such colonial subservience in his later work. Of his poems, the best known is *The *Valley of a Thousand Hills* (1941), a carefully constructed work that contrasts the harmony of nature and the cruelty of human society. His complete creative output appeared posthumously in *Collected Works* (1985).

Dhlomo's importance as a critic rests on the fact that he advocates the use of Western styles, but only as far as they can enhance the existing African tradition. The view that only Africans can truly express the African soul finds expression in his uncompleted play 'The Expert', a scathing criticism of white liberalism and missionary intervention in African affairs.

Based purely on his creative output, it would be difficult to characterize Dhlomo as an original talent. His dramas are unwieldy, with a thoroughness and attention to detail more reminiscent of a novel than of theatre. This is, however, in line with his own feeling that Africans first had to produce 'literary drama' before they could produce plays for the stage. His poetry often lapses into the sentimental, with forced rhymes and stilted language that at its worst is a poor imitation of Victorian models and at its best reveals rare insight. Finally, though, Dhlomo's oeuvre reveals a talent that might, with sufficient encouragement, have produced work of great merit. As far as his journalism is concerned, there is no doubt that Dhlomo's essays on African art are among the most valuable pieces of South African literary history.

DHLOMO, R(obert) R(olfes) R(eginald) (1901-71), South African novelist. Rolfes Dhlomo, the elder brother of H.I.E. *Dhlomo, was born in Siyamu, Edendale, educated at the Ohlange Institute, and graduated as a teacher from the American Mission Board School in Amanzimtoti. He became a regular contributor to *Ilanga lase Natal* [The Natal Sun], a bilingual newspaper, and later to a Transvaal newspaper, *Bantu World*. He worked as a mine clerk in Johannesburg before joining the staff of *Ilanga*; later he became the editor. Dhlomo is known primarily as the author of a series of Zulu historical novels based on the lives of nineteenth-century African leaders: *U-Dingane* (1936), *U-Shaka* (1937), *U-Mpande* (1938), *U-Cetshwayo* (1952) and *U-Dinizulu* (1968). He also wrote *An *African Tragedy* (1928), the first English novella by a black South African, and contributed a number of English short stories to *Sjambok*, a literary journal (1929-31). In 1951, he became the first recipient of the Vilakazi Memorial Award.

The short stories written for *Sjambok* are incisive, with a journalistic style. 'The Death of Masaba', written in 1929, reflects an intimate knowledge of mining conditions and provides an historical perspective not to be found in any report or history of the period. The short stories also indicate to what extent the African writer of the 1920s and 30s was concerned with presenting a realistic picture of life around him rather than trying to create lasting literary artefacts. He returned to the theme of conflict between rural and city life in the Zulu-language *Indlela Yababi* [The evil one] (1946). Here he looks again at the effects of township life on African morale, but with far greater maturity than in *An African Tragedy* or the *Sjambok* stories. Although Dhlomo's writing is characterized by the many pitfalls of early black writing, such as a tendency towards the moralistic and blatant imitation of Victorian prose, he is a writer of note, but his English writing has received little critical attention.

DIB, Mohammed (1920-), Algerian novelist and poet writing in French, was born in Tlemcen, Algeria. From 1939 to 1951 he worked in a variety of occupations before establishing a literary career. Expelled from Algeria in 1959 for his outspoken political stance, he settled in France, where he continues to reside.

Dib emerged at the forefront of the modern wave of Algerian literature in French with the publication of his panoramic trilogy of pre-revolutionary Algeria: *La Grande maison* (1952), *L'Incendie* (1954), and *Le Métier à tisser* (1957). Following his expulsion from Algeria, he merged the social commentary of his early fiction with experimental forms of expression in *Qui se souvient de la mer* (1962; *Who Remembers the Sea*, 1985), *Cours sur la rive sauvage* (1964), *La Danse du roi* (1968), and *Habel* (1977). Dib departed from the realistic depiction of post-revolutionary Algeria portrayed in *Dieu en Barbarie* (1970) and *Le Maître de chasse* (1973) with his recent enigmatic trilogy, *Les Terrasses d'Orsol*

(1985), *Le Sommeil d'Éve* (1989), and *Neiges de marbre* (1990). His first collection of poetry, *Ombre gardienne* (1961), was followed by *Formulaires* (1970), *Omneros* (1975), *Feu beau feu* (1979), and *Ô vive* (1987). A prolific and constructive *Maghrebian writer in French, Dib continues to penetrate the Algerian past as a means to illuminate the possibilities of liberation and rebirth.

DIESCHO, Joseph (1955-), one of Namibia's very few native-born novelists, was raised in a rural village near the Roman Catholic mission of Andara in northern Namibia. He graduated in political science and law from Fort Hare University before going on to study in Germany and the USA for his post-graduate degrees.

His two novels, *Born of the Sun* (1988) and *Troubled Waters* (1993), both have Namibian settings. *Born of the Sun*, partly autobiographical, is set in the early 1960s and traces the growth of political consciousness in Muronga, who leaves the idyllic village of Kake in eastern Kavango to work on the mines. The work ends with the possibility of homecoming for the exiled hero still in the distant future. Set in 1974, *Troubled Waters* is a novel of transition, focusing on two young people who are distanced from their roots as a result of political change. There is a vision of a fractured tribal society, and always present are the guerilla fighters of the Namibian war. *Troubled Waters* reveals a penetrating political understanding and signifies a quantum leap in Diescho's development as a writer. Diescho has also edited a collection of Namibian folktales.

DIKOBE, Modikwe (pseud. of Marks Rammitloa) (1913-), novelist and poet. He went to live in Johannesburg at the age of ten, left school without finishing, and attended night classes run by the African Communist party while working at a variety of jobs. Following the bus boycott (1942) and the squatters' movement (1946), he became involved in the trade union movement. He was detained for three months and then banned in the early 1960s; as a 'listed' person, he could not publish under his own name. He published some journalism and a volume of poetry (*Dispossessed*, 1983), but his reputation as a writer rests on his novel, *The *Marabi Dance*, begun in the 1950s, finished in 1963, and finally published, after passing through various hands, by Heinemann in 1973. The novel's examination of the urban black working class is encapsulated within its many sub-narratives, many of which deal with the urban experiences of rural migrants.

Dilemma of a Ghost, The (1965) A play by Ama Ata *Aidoo. The play investigates the requirements for successful or fulfilling interpersonal and intercultural relations. The main character, Ato, a Ghanaian student, is married to a black American woman, Eulalie, and the story examines their illusions about each other's character and culture, focusing on their return to Ghana and their struggle as they face the social, physical, and psychological realities of living in Africa. The play ends with a verbal and physical confrontation between Ato and Eulalie and a sharp commentary from Ato's mother that speaks to the individual's responsibility for maintaining communication with others.

DIOP, Alioune (1910-80) Born in Saint Louis, Senegal, into a Muslim family where French was spoken, young Alioune went to French school and recieved his literary baccalaureat in 1931. He studied philosophy at the University of Algiers, where he met Albert Camus, and found himself in France during the World War II. Diop converted to Catholicism and briefly worked in colonial administration at the end of the war.

He created the journal *Présence Africaine* in 1947 with an editorial committee including, among many famous intellectuals, Jean-Paul Sartre, Albert Camus and André Gide. In 1949, he created the publishing house Présence Africaine, which had the distinction of publishing Aimé Cesaire's *Discours sur le colonialism* (1955, trans. *Discourse on Colonialism*, 1972). Many of the editorial pieces in the journal were written by him, as well as seminal pieces such as *Niam n'goura* ('Eat in order to live' - Fula proverb) (1947), the definition of his cultural project and his introduction to P. Tempels, *Bantu Philosophy: Niam M'paya* ('Eat in order to fatten' - Fula proverb) (1949). A rigorous, modest and energetic man, he was the driving force behind the movement to organize black intellectuals which started in 1956 with the *Premier Congrès des écrivains et artistes noirs* (First Congress of Black Writers and Artists) and with the creation of the Society of African Culture of which until his death he was general secretary. This movement culminated in the Dakar festival of 1966; and Alioune Diop continued to work to keep African intellectuals independent from political pressures. He initiated the Second World Black and African Festival of Arts and Culture in Lagos in 1977. His correspondence, manuscripts, and collected texts, when published in volumes will be central pieces in the history of African literature in the twentieth century and especially in the definition of a new African intellectual and artist.

DIOP, Birago (1906-89), Senegalese re-creator of traditional folktales, poet and autobiographer writing in French, was born in Ouakam, then a small village near Dakar. The child of a traditional homemaker and a master mason who worked at the nearby French military post, Diop received a mixed traditional and French primary education. In 1920, aged fourteen, he travelled north to Saint Louis, Senegal to attend the renowned lycée Faidherbe. His literary formation was then and always would remain dual: rich troves of traditional tales, oral histories, and genealogies told to him by family members and nearby storytellers, and the classics of French and European literature and fables. In the late 1920s he travelled to France for one year of military service and then began several years of veterinary training in Toulouse and Paris, where he met L.S. ★Senghor, Léon Damas, and other pioneering francophone literary figures. From the mid-1930s to 1958, excepting the war years spent in Paris, Diop travelled widely all across French colonial Africa as a veterinary officer, taking time to collect folktales at every opportunity. From 1960 to 1964, he served as the first Senegalese ambassador to newly independent Tunisia. In 1964 he returned to Dakar and had a private veterinary practice until his retirement in 1979. From 1979 until his death in 1989, he devoted himself to his memoirs and to leadership in several Senegalese writers' organizations.

Diop's literary career began as early as 1925, when he started writing poetry in French, but his breakthrough into public consciousness was not until 1947, when he published *Les Contes d'Amadou Koumba* (1947), one of the landmark works of contemporary African letters. *Les Contes* is a collection of nineteen stories, all apparently as told to Diop by the family *griot* (traditional storyteller, oral historian, and genealogist) Amadou Koumba, whom Diop met while posted in Kayes, near the intersection of present-day Senegal, Mauritania, and Mali. Diop followed this work with the collections *Les Nouveaux contes d'Amadou Koumba* (1958; *Tales of Amadou Koumba*, 1966, includes texts from both collections of stories), *Contes et lavanes* (1963), the shorter *Contes d'Awa*, and the play *L'os de Mor Lam* (both in 1977). Diop's tales are, like many renderings of traditional oral tales the world over, by turns moral, didactic, and entertaining, and feature animal, human, and supernatural characters and events. Trickster hares, lazy crocodiles, difficult hyenas, and sharply drawn humans abound. Though he presents the bulk of his work as the faithful repetition of traditional tales, it is clear that great art on the part of their transcriber has been required: an art that translates, reshapes, and recasts each tale for consumption in written form, and that directs these tales towards generally non-local audiences while preserving local essence. These seminal collections of West African tales have sustained a broad range of interpretive approaches by critics, who have often addressed the religious, political, and philosophical dimensions of the tales. Diop's tales have been translated into more than a dozen languages and have served functions ranging from the entertainment and instruction of children to the illumination of West African traditions to the illustration of universal human culture.

In contrast to his folktales, Diop's poetry – principally his 1960 *Leurres et lueurs*, a collection of poems dating from 1925 – has received comparatively less attention. In 1978 he began publishing a remarkable five-volume autobiography or series of memoirs extending from his birth through 1989: *La Plume raboutée* (1978), *A rebrousse-temps* (1982), *A rebrousse-gens* (1985), *Du temps de...* (1986), and *Et les yeux pour me dire* (1989). Such an extended first-person recounting of a richly lived life is, it seems, without parallel in contemporary African letters. Though these memoirs have received scant critical attention, they are engagingly written and remarkably detailed and should serve as an invaluable resource for students of twentieth-century francophone West African history generally, and of the multi-faceted political, scientific, colonial, and finally literary figure of Birago Diop in particular.

DIOP, Cheikh Anta (1923-86) The work of Cheikh Anta Diop has had tremendous influence on African contemporary thought. Trained as a historian as well as a nuclear physicist, Diop was very active in the student nationalist movement in France in the 1950s. His doctoral thesis in history was not accepted by the Sorbonne because of its strong iconoclastic views: it claimed to demonstrate the links between Egypt and Black Africa, especially Senegal. It was nonetheless published and had a great influence on Egyptology, changing the traditional views of a great divide between Egypt and the rest of Africa (*Nation nègre et culture*, 1954). The debate was continued in the *UNESCO General History of Africa, Volume II*, which presents a balanced view of the discussion on the origins of Ancient Egyptians. Diop's wide-reaching claims have been criticized, as have his all-embracing approach to human sciences, and its questionable methodology particularly in linguistics. But the fecundity of his hypothesis has been demonstrated in many areas: it stimulated Meroitic studies and had a great heuristic importance. During his career as a Professor of History in Dakar and as head of a carbon dating laboratory he was able to continue his task of building up a cursus of classical African antiquities.

DIOP, David (1927-60), Senegalese poet, was born in Bordeaux, France, of a Senegalese father and Cameroonian mother. As an adolescent Diop displayed the intellectual verve – and suffered the physical ill health – that characterized his entire short life. His single poetry collection ★*Coups de pilon* (1956; *Hammer Blows*, 1973), in which he articulates a cause that is anti-colonialist and pan-Africanist (with its sights ranging beyond Africa to Suez, Hanoi, Atlanta), confirmed his already significant reputation in francophone African nationalist circles, a reputation bolstered by his move to Guinea in 1958, which affirmed his support for Sékou Touré's stand against French neo-colonialist hegemony. Diop died tragically, with his second wife and two children, in a plane crash.

Divorce, The (1977) A play by Wale ★Ogunyemi. A full-length comedy, this is one of the most frequently performed English-language plays in Nigeria. The plot, in turns farcical and satirical, deals with a businessman's mistaken belief that his wife is adulterous. The play is at its most attractive when satire and farce combine, as in the portrayal of an incompetent policeman. A Pidgin-speaking character, the houseboy Patrick, is especially popular with audiences. The play has, however, attracted criticism on the grounds of male chauvinism.

DJEBAR, Assia (pseud. of Fatima Zohra Imalayen) (1936-), Francophone writer from the ★Maghreb, also film-maker and academic. Born in Cherchel, Algeria, she was educated in Algeria, and later in France where she obtained a degree in history. During the Algerian war of independence (1954-62) she taught at the universities of Rabat and Tunis and worked also as a journalist. Djebar has since lived and worked in France and the United States. She published her first novel, La Soif, in 1957, followed a year later by another novel, Les Impatients. Both works, which appeared during the Algerian war, concentrate on social issues. Djebar tackled the theme of the war in her novels, Les Enfants du nouveau monde (1962) and Les Alouettes naïves (1967). Because of the criticism Algerian authors received for writing in French, Djebar did not write any more novels until the 1980s, but published a volume of poetry and a play. She made two films in Arabic. La Nouba des femmes du Mont Chenoua, shown at the Venice Biennale (1979), won a prize. Before resuming novel-writing, Djebar published a collection of short stories, Femmes d'Alger dans leur appartement (1980; Women of Algeria in their Apartment, 1992), where she explores the world of Algerian women, a theme she was to take up again in later works. In L'Amour la fantasia (1985; Fantasia, 1989), the first volume of her Algerian quartet, she presents two histories running concurrently, that of Algeria and the life story of her central character which is loosely autobiographical. In the second volume, Ombre sultane (1987, A Sister to Scheherazade, 1988), the two female characters, one traditional the other emancipated, represent the two faces of Algerian women and stress the importance of female bonding, explored also in Loin de Médine (1991; Far from Madina 1994), a novel set in the early days of Islam. Djebar rarely experiments with the French language, but in her latest novels she has begun to introduce Arabic and, occasionally, Berber words and expressions. Recent events in Algeria have not gone unnoticed by Djebar. In Le blanc de l'Algerie (1995) she pays tribute to the victims of religious fundamentalists. In Oran, langue morte (1997) she focuses on Algerian women, both at home and abroad, who are living through some of the worst times Algeria has witnessed in its recent history.

DJOLETO, (Solomon Alexander) Amu (1929-), Ghanaian novelist and poet, was educated at Accra Academy, St. Augustine's College, and at University College of the Gold Coast. He joined the Ministry of Education in the 1960s as a classroom teacher and education officer and later studied textbook development at the Institute of Education, University of London, returning to Ghana to become an editor of the Ghana Teachers' Journal. He is the author of three popular novels, The Strange Man (1967), Money Galore (1975), and Hurricane of Dust (1987), all of which focus on social and economic life. In The Strange Man he recounts the life of Mensah in colonial and post-colonial Ghana; Money Galore satirizes the corruption at every level of post-independence Ghana; and Hurricane of Dust deals with Ghana under military misrule. His poems appear in the anthologies Voices of Ghana (1958) and Messages: Poems from Ghana (1970) and have been collected in Amid the Swelling Act (1992). As a director of Ghana's Book Development Council and an advisor on educational reform, Djoleto has made an important contribution to Ghana's literary culture. He has also written books for young readers: Obodai Sai (1990), Twins in Trouble (1991), and The Frightened Thief (1992).

Down Second Avenue (1959) Autobiography by Ezekiel (now Es'kia) ★Mphahlele. This account of growing up in an impoverished family in a black ghetto in South Africa is a powerful, sensitive, passionate, often angry re-creation of the struggle of a sensitive and highly intelligent child to gain an education in conditions that explicitly forbid it. While the life displayed in the writing is highly personalized and redolent of reminiscences of close family life, the work also suggests that the experiences conveyed here, the conditions of near poverty, the denial of civilized potentials, are typical of the experience of a large number of South Africans. What ultimately makes the book a classic of its kind is the tribute it pays to the resilience of the human spirit, the capacity to survive and prevail over the most appalling conditions.

DRAMA
East Africa: Michezo ya Kuigiza, or theatre and drama, in East Africa relate to rituals, ceremonies, storytelling, drumming and dance, and to the practicality and spirit of the East African peoples. Before the advent of Europeans in East Africa, court dramatists worked in the Kabaka's palace in Buganda. That tradition finds contemporary expression in the dramatic works of Robert ★Serumaga, Byron Kawadwa, Nuwa Sentongo, and Elvania Namukwaya Zirimu, who, at least in sentiment, perpetuate pro-royalist theatre in East Africa. Christian schools and churches used drama to teach the 'Great Tradition' of English culture, which was reinforced by the establishment of English

studies at Makerere University College, Kampala, in the 1950s.

East African drama and theatre follow two traditions: classical theatre is in English; popular theatre in indigenous languages uses song and dance to reach its audience. *Ngugi wa Thiong'o's *Gikuyu-language plays of the 1970s have had a galvanizing effect on East African drama; his efforts to make his work more accessible to mass audiences helped Kenyan theatre to break from imperialist traditions, symbolized by the Kenya National Theatre.

Many East African plays have evolved around legendary figures (Lwanda Magere, Gor Mahia), freedom fighters (Waiyaki, Kinjeketile, Elijah Masinde), and political personalities: examples are Kenneth *Watene's *Dedan Kimathi (1974), The *Trial of Dedan Kimathi (1976) by Ngugi and Micere Githae *Mugo, and James Irungu and James Shimanyula's The Black Prophet (1982), a play about Elijah Masinde. In these plays rebels are heroes and the white man is a forbidding oppressor. Freedom fighters liberate Africa from a colonialism in which African ways symbolize barbarism and backwardness, Western ways progress and enlightenment. Some plays advocate a middle course, suggesting that some African traditions are not worth retaining. These include Watene's My Son for My Freedom, The Haunting Past, and The Broken Pot, published in one volume in 1973. Watene's moderate approach to historical issues in his play Dedan Kimathi motivated Ngugi and Micere Githae Mugo to write The Trial of Dedan Kimathi as a rejoinder.

There are several well-known East African playwrights writing in English. Robert Serumaga's published plays include A Play (1967), Majangwa: A Promise of Rains (1974), and The Elephants (1971). A mime, Renga Moi (1975), is rendered in four indigenous Ugandan languages. John *Ruganda is the author of Covenant with Death, which appeared with Black Mamba in a volume of that name in 1973, followed by The Burdens (1972), The Floods (1980), and Echoes of Silence (1986). Ngugi's English-language plays are collected in This Time Tomorrow (1970); the three one-act plays are The Rebels, The Wound in the Heart, and the title play, which was first written for radio and broadcast on the BBC African Service in 1967. His play The Black Hermit (1968) was staged in Kampala in 1962 as part of Uganda's independence celebrations. Rebeka *Njau, who is also a novelist and a journalist, published The Scar in the journal Transition in 1963. Francis *Imbuga's published plays include The Fourth Trial (1972), The Married Bachelor (1973), Betrayal in the City (1976), Game of Silence (1977), The Successor (1979), Man of Kafira (1984), Aminata (1988), and The Burning of Rags (1989). Cliff *Lubwa p'Chong, a Ugandan, is the author of Generosity Kills and The Last Safari (1975), the latter inspired by *Okot p'Bitek's long poem *Song of Lawino. Some playwrights, such as Micere

Githae Mugo, Henry Kuria, or Nuwa Sentongo, have earned their reputations more as actors than as writers.

The drive in East Africa is to indigenize drama and theatre, as well as literature. Important conferences on African writing, drama, and theatre in Europe and Africa from the 1950s through the 1980s provided a basis for a theory of indigenous literature and drama and offered advocacy for developing and indigenizing theatre in Africa. Theatre and drama critics, protesting at the alienation of African dramatists, commend experimentation with language that aims to bridge the gap between dramatist and audience. East African drama is changing from a literary genre to a tool of social and political education.

South Africa: Although the first documented performances of drama in English in South Africa were Shakespearean and Restoration classics mounted at the African Theatre (founded 1801) by officers of the garrison during the British occupation of the Cape, followed by the productions of successive touring companies, it is Stephen *Black, active in 1908-1917 and 1928-1929, who has often been regarded as the first South African dramatist. An actor-manager, he wrote and produced satirical comedies which, in spite of their obvious debt to such as Sheridan and Wilde as well as to the familiar models of Victorian and Edwardian melodrama and music hall, nevertheless contrived to develop a uniquely South African style. This was characterized by the incorporation of locally understood, topical references updated for each performance, by the development of a range of recognizably South African stock characters such as the colonial maiden, the Boer patriarch, and the gullible native, as well as by skilful exploitation of the growing distinctiveness of South African English. Not all of Black's work has survived, since he took no steps to have it published. His best known plays are Love and the Hyphen (1908), *Helena's Hope, Ltd (1910), The Flappers (1911), and The Uitlanders (1911).

A determining factor of South African theatre history since the 1930s has been the emergence of an urban black culture, an early manifestation of which was the foundation in 1932 of the Bantu Dramatic Society by H.I.E. *Dhlomo, whose aim was to encourage indigenous drama on African themes. Dhlomo's own dramas sought to view rural tribal history in the light of contemporary urban black experience. Of the nine that have survived complete, two (both written before 1936) concern Xhosa history: The *Girl Who Killed to Save: Nongqause the Liberator (the first published play by a black South African), which argues unconvincingly that the national suicide of the Xhosa was ultimately beneficial since it facilitated their modernization, and Ntsikana. Dingane (1937) and Cetshwayo (1936) are tragedies, much more disillusioned in tone, on the Zulu struggle against the British; *Moshoeshoe* (1937) is a romance evoking a pre-colonial state of freedom through a depiction of the communal life of the Basotho; while *The Living Dead, The Pass (Arrested and Discharged), The Workers*, and *Malaria* (1939-1941) address urgent contemporary social themes with increasing bitterness. Dhlomo, who is now recognized as an important early theorist and critic, has been credited with inaugurating an African-centred, non-colonialist drama and should be regarded as a forerunner of the *Black Consciousness theatre of the 1970s.

During the *apartheid era (1948-1990) the various directions taken by theatre were largely determined by state-imposed measures: those companies favoured by the regime were lavishly funded, while those deemed oppositional struggled to survive against the combined effects of the pass laws, the segregation of venues, and censorship. In the first category were the four state-funded performing arts councils established in 1963 in succession to the National Theatre Organization (1947 1961), one for each province; often designated by their acronyms, these were CAPAB in the Cape, NAPAC in Natal, PACOFS in the Orange Free State, and PACT in the Transvaal. One critic (Stephen *Gray) has dubbed them ' "cultural bunkers" [...] where ballet, opera and music could thrive for whites alone and without controversy' but concedes that their performance standards were 'often extremely accomplished'. In the second category were the many initiatives towards an alternative, non-racial theatre undertaken between the late 1950s and the mid-1970s. Among these were the foundation of Union Artists together with the African Music and Drama Association and the Rehearsal Room at Dorkay House, Johannesburg (1961), where English-speaking and urban African performers including Athol *Fugard, Gibson *Kente, and Barney Simon could work together; Fugard's collaboration with the Serpent Players in New Brighton township (from 1963); the setting up of the influential Workshop '71 by Robert McLaren (1971); the opening of the multiracial Space Theatre in Cape Town by Brian Astbury, Yvonne Bryceland, and Fugard (1972); the formation by Barney Simon and Mannie Manim of The Company (1974) and later of the Market Theatre (1976), which soon made its stages available to many theatrical initiatives; and the emergence of the Junction Avenue Theatre Company (from 1976).

Athol Fugard, whose theatrical career now spans four decades, is indubitably the major figure in the history of South African drama. His large body of work includes the early Sophiatown 'township' plays, *No-Good Friday* (1958) and *Nongogo* (1959); a searing analysis of the psychological consequences of racial division, *The Blood Knot* (1961), his first major success produced at Dorkay House; the political plays on apartheid themes workshopped with the Serpent

Players, *Sizwe Bansi is Dead* (1972) and *The Island* (1973), which initiated a life-long association with actors John Kani and Winston Ntshona, and together with *Statements after an Arrest under the Immorality Act* (1972), all performed at the Royal Court in London, laid the foundations for an international reputation; the unsparingly autobiographical *'Master Harold'... and the Boys* (1982); his celebration of artistic creativity through the life and work of the sculptor Helen Martins in *The Road to Mecca* (1984); and the plays with which he sought with varying degrees of success to address the problem of political violence in South Africa (*My Children, My Africa!* 1989), the need for reconciliation (*Playland*, 1992), and the emotional complexities of adjusting to social change (*Valley Song*, 1996). Fugard's plays, whose sparseness and economy of means owe much to Samuel Beckett, have been a barometer to the social evolution of his country, witnessing with deep sensitivity to the isolation of the human condition and to the myriad injustices of apartheid alike, profoundly responsive to the nuances of South African language use, and uniquely able to encapsulate conflict in scenes of enormous intensity.

The work of Robert McLaren's Workshop '71 has proved of seminal importance for future theatre practice, not only because of the quality of its work-shopped productions such as *Crossroads* (an adaptation of *Everyman*) and the prison play *Survival*, but also because, as McLaren says, '(it) opened up the theatre to the people's languages, suggested democratic ways of making plays and running companies and eventually came to embody in its aesthetic and in its practice the ideal of a non-racial, democratic South Africa'. Clearly, such experiences played a formative role in preparing a theatre for a post-apartheid society.

Barney Simon's own workshop productions, which include *Black Dog/In'emnyama* (1984), *Outers* (1985), *Born in the RSA* (1985), and *Score Me the Ages* (1989), are all characterized by consummate storytelling, an interest in biography, and a commitment to social authenticity, and are informed by an unerring sense of language. In *Born in the RSA*, for example, the personal dilemmas of political activism are allowed to emerge through seven interwoven life stories narrated directly to the audience. Simon also collaborated with Percy Mtwa and Mbongeni *Ngema on the remarkable *Woza Albert!* (1980), whose innovative performance style was much indebted to Grotowski's poor theatre, relying heavily on the actor's body and craft, using multiple character transformations, stripping props down to a minimum, and creating music through the orchestration of voices. Mtwa went on to write *Bopha!* (1986) and Ngema embarked on an international career with *Asinamali!* (1985) and the musical *Sarafina!* (1987), performed by his Durban-based Committed Artists group.

In seeking to articulate an alternative view of South African history the Junction Avenue Theatre Company drew on the experience of Workshop '71, developments in international theatre (Beckett, Brecht, Littlewood) and theory (Grotowski). Committed to a socialist world view and employing a performance style characterized by a delight in parody, pastiche, and caricature, the company explored the consciousness of the young white, dissident male (in *Fantastical History of a Useless Man*, 1976), dramatized the conflicting interests of the mining and liquor industries (in *Randlords and Rotgut*, 1978), and critically confronted the lived experience of non-racialism to the segregationist policy of apartheid in the story of the forced removal of an inner-city Johannesburg suburb (in the hugely successful *Sophiatown*, 1986). The company's highly experimental examination of the complex realities of the dying phase of apartheid in *Tooth and Nail* (1989), an arbitrarily arranged collage of some ninety-eight fragments, deployed a grotesque, expressionist style combining opera, ritual, and the puppetry of the Handspring Puppet Company which, although influential, proved too radically innovative for audiences.

There were, however, also those who sought not collaboration in multiracial theatre, but a more confrontational stance by blacks. Three companies that pioneered such a development in the 1970s, drawing their inspiration from the aims and ideology of the ★Black Consciousness movement, and some of whose work was written by members of its constituent organizations were subjected to constant harassment by the authorities: the Theatre Council of Natal (TECON) founded in 1969 memorably produced *Antigone in '71*, but its organizers were soon banned; the People's Experimental Theatre (PET) founded in Lenasia in 1973 aimed to encourage black creativity, but its leaders were detained and charged with staging revolutionary plays soon after its first production, Mthuli Shezi's *Shanti*; and the Music, Drama and Literature Institute (MDALI), founded in 1972, sought to inaugurate a national black cultural movement but folded when its leader, Molefe Pheto, was detained.

In the late 1970s a new generation of writers and performers began to emerge from the townships. Their work was indebted to the 'township musical', a genre inaugurated by *King Kong* (produced in 1959 with an all-black cast) and later taken up by the theatre entrepreneur Gibson Kente, whose shows *How Long?* (1971), *Too Late* (1973), and *Sikalo* (1976) enjoyed great success with the black township audiences for whom he exclusively performed. Some of them were Africanists, whose work remained ideologically oriented to the Black Consciousness movement. Among them were Matsemela ★Manaka and Maishe Maponya.

Manaka's experimental plays, as performed by the

Soyikwa Theatre group which he founded, are unusual for their innovative synthesis of the arts of drama, music, dance, and painting, their exploration of mime, and their increasing commitment to forms of African artistic expression long inaccessible to black South Africans. His early plays on socioeconomic conditions of black dispossession such as migrant labour and forced removals (*Egoli*, 1979; *Pula*, 1982; *Children of Asazi*, 1984) were followed by works that sought to develop a 'theatre for social reconstruction', symbolically demonstrating the fusion of European and African cultures (*Gorée*, 1989), defining an African identity (*Blues Afrika Café*, 1990), and celebrating the contribution of exiled artists to South African culture (*Ekhaya*, 1991).

Maponya, a playwright of outspoken radical commitment, was frequently the victim, together with his Bahumutsi Theatre Group, of harassment by the authorities (restriction of performances, withdrawal of passport). His plays constitute a fearless onslaught on the abuses of the apartheid system, whether it be the exploitation of industrial labour (*The Hungry Earth*, 1978), working conditions and racist practices in the health service (*Umongikazi/The Nurse*, 1982), or the harassment of writers in the form of banning, interrogation, and torture (*Gangsters*, 1984). Remarkable for their abundant theatricality, their indebtedness to Brecht (especially the didacticism of *The Measures Taken*), their innovative use of gesture and their frequent recourse to improvisation, Maponya's plays supplement dialogue with choral singing, gumboot dancing, and mimed sequences (as in *The Hungry Earth*), call upon actors to perform multiple roles (as in *Umongikazi/The Nurse*), and deploy telling juxtapositions of scenes (interrogation and literary recitation in *Gangsters*). The printed texts accordingly give little notion of the scenic impact.

Somewhat apart from the work of his contemporaries in style, themes, and performance history is that of Zakes ★Mda. Displaying an unusual refinement of language and conciseness of dialogue, abounding in satirical humour, and delighting in intellectual debate, the plays in Mda's two collections (*We Shall Sing for the Fatherland*, 1979 and *And the Girls in Their Sunday Dresses*, 1993) focus on the lives of ordinary people, viewing political issues in the context of personal experience, and are often preoccupied with neo-colonial abuses found in independent states such as Lesotho where Mda lived for many years. The radio play *Banned* (1982), for example, shows how squatter camp residents overcome the hopelessness of their situation and recognize the need to act. *Joys of War* (1989) is a careful handling of the issue of armed struggle which explores the moral nature of two soldiers' commitment and the social background out of which it is born. *And the Girls in Their Sunday Dresses,* written in 1988, is a lively two-hander depicting through multiple role-playing and comic banter the plight of two women queuing for days to buy rice; embedded within the witty satirizing of bureaucracy and corruption is a serious discusion of Lesotho's dependence on South Africa and the politics of gender informing women's social roles.

Three types of alternative theatre that came to the fore during the latter years of the apartheid era were workers' theatre, theatre for development, and theatre-in-education.

Workers' theatre emerged in the difficult years of successive states of emergency (1983-1987) largely in Natal and centred on the trade-union based Durban Workers Cultural Local (DWCL). Evolved as a collaborative venture between semi-literate factory workers, white intellectuals, and experienced theatre practitioners from groups like Junction Avenue, plays such as *The Long March*, *The Sun Shall Rise for the Workers*, and *Comment* sought to mobilize workers and raise political conscience by dramatizing their own experience of the labour struggle while at the same time exploiting African cultural sources (gumboot dancing, praise song, the Zulu language). Theatre for development, hitherto associated largely with the work of Zakes Mda and the Marotholi Travelling Theatre in Lesotho (on which he has published an important study, *When People Play People*, 1993) is also finding adherents in South Africa. Matsemela Manaka produced a literacy play, *Koma* (1986); Doreen Mazibuko toured a voter-education play, *Moments*, a practical exposition of the workings of democracy in the run-up to the 1994 elections; and Maishe Maponya embarked on his Winterveld project with uemployed squatter camp youth. An increasing body of work in theatre-in-education ranges in variety from the Handspring Puppet Theatre's involvement in science education to Matsemela Manaka performing *Julius Caesar* in Setswana and English in rural areas, and the Market Theatre Laboratory taking *Romeo and Juliet* to the riot-torn township of Sebokeng.

By the end of the apartheid era, a curious transposition had taken place: the alternative theatres had become the mainstream, and the state theatres, still wedded to a discredited ideology, found themselves marginalized. Both thus confronted a problem of redefinition: the alternative theatre needed to revise its artistic and political aims in view of the fact that the main target of its opposition, apartheid, no longer existed and other urgent issues were beckoning; the state theatres needed to transform themselves into non-racial institutions if they were to remain politically acceptable. At the same time, political changes began to be felt in theatre. In as far as the cultural boycott was lifted, censorship ended, exiles returned, and previously undreamt-of theatrical events could take place (for example the Johannesburg Civic Theatre opening with the Dance Theatre of Harlem),

the effects were positive. As the first signs of revised state and private-sector funding allocations became apparent, they were also potentially problematic.

This situation led to revised priorities, reallocated resources, and institutional change. Past achievements were reassessed and new creative principles formulated. The performing arts councils were reorganized; new opportunities opened up for black writers, performers, and managers; Eurocentrism in the arts was questioned; the cultural interests of the majority were to be addressed and indigenous art forms supported. Out of the welter of challenges posed by radical social and political change there began to emerge a variety of thought-provoking innovative responses in the theatre. A younger generation of playwrights dissected social transition: Sue Pam-Grant acutely registered social change in the decaying urban environment of inner-city Johannesburg in *Curl Up and Dye* (1989), while Paul Slabolepzsy, 'cartographer of the white male soul' and author of *Saturday Night at the Palace* (1982), penned a witty, satirical reversal of the 'Jim comes to Jo'burg' topos in *Mooi St. Moves* (1992), where it is the innocent white who learns the tricks of urban survival from the streetwise black.

The artist William Kentridge, working with the Handspring Puppet Company, used an eclectic and highly original mixture of puppetry, animated video film depicting charcoal drawings, and European and African music to transpose Büchner to the Transvaal in *Woyzeck on the Highveld* (1992), elaborating this innovatory style with *Faustus in Africa* (1995), which also incorporated Bulgakov and the work of the South African rap singer Lesego ★Rampolokeng. The same company's triumphant multimedia adaptation of Alfred Jarry's *Ubu Roi* in *Ubu and the Truth Commission* (1997, scripted by Jane Taylor) proved an intellectual and intertextual *tour de force*, a phatasmagoria of complex theatrical images that sought through the media of acting, puppetry, animated film, drawing, and music to force the audience to confront the issues of truth, forgiveness, and reconciliation then being urgently debated.

That there is much creative energy being released in post-apartheid South African theatre may also be demonstrated from the spectacular success (at the 1997 and 1998) Grahamstown Festivals of Brett Bailey and the Third World Bunfight's *iMumbo Jumbo The Days of Miracle and Wonder* and *Ipi Zombi?*, amateur township-based performances full of ritual and ceremony which, if nothing else, suggest that there are forms of theatrical performance emerging the like of which has not been seen before.

West Africa: Whereas the history of performance in Africa goes back to antiquity, the dramatic form, i.e. the staged play, is arguably in its predominant forms a product of the interaction between African traditions and colonial cultural imports. An interesting body of theoretical work that seeks to explore the boundaries between African ritual and the concept of drama is represented in *Drama and Theatre in Nigeria: A Critical Source Book* (1981), edited by Yemi Ogunbiyi. However, the term West African drama most often refers to a drama staged for a paying audience in a theatre building or taken on tour with simpler facilities, perhaps performed in the round in a village. Often, the drama is written primarily in the former colonial language, now a major lingua franca of the post-colonial nation. Anglophone West African drama had an immense flowering during the immediate post-colonial period and, like other forms of so-called new literatures in English, was stimulated by independence movements and by the cultural transitions of the first decades of independence. Anthony Graham-White's *The Drama of Black Africa* (1974) and Michael Etherton's *The Development of African Drama* (1982) both discuss the antecedents for West African drama in English. Ebun Clark's *Hubert Ogunde: The Making of Nigerian Theatre* (1979) examines the nature and contribution of Ogunde's establishment of professional musical theatre in the 1940s, a theatre that drew on both the European variety concert and the long tradition of theatre called *alarinjo* among the *Yoruba.

One of the best-known early West African plays is Ghanaian Kobina *Sekyi's satirical comedy *The Blinkards* (1915). The play was written in the period Sekyi spent at home after completing his first degree in England and before returning there for his legal training. During that time he re-immersed himself in his Akan-Fanti culture, favouring a return to the best of traditional values rather than colonial ones. Ghana, as the country became in 1957 at independence, also nurtured the dramatic talent of Efua *Sutherland. Sutherland was instrumental in the Ghana Drama Studio, which was set up by Kwame Nkrumah as part of his concentration on affirming cultural identity for the new Ghanaian state, as well as developing a touring company that worked largely in Twi, the language of the Ashanti. She rewrote and reinterpreted Euripides' *Alcestis* as *Edufa* (1967) and used the Anansesem tradition of folktales as a basis for *The *Marriage of Anansewa* (1975). In both plays, her attention to traditional material such as rituals and her sense of the applicability of some ancient Greek dramatic elements including the chorus to contemporary Ghana, along with her use of the European play form, show her to have something of the same impulse as Sekyi. However his political direction did not find expression in the use of traditional African theatrical elements in *The Blinkards*. In Nigeria, the exact contemporary of Efua Sutherland was James Ene *Henshaw, a prolific dramatist whose plays are rather Victorian. But his presence, like Sekyi's in Ghana, established an English-speaking drama which drew heavily on the forms

of English theatre of an earlier era for contemporary African social comment. His first volume of plays, *This Is Our Chance: Three Plays from West Africa* (1956) also included *The Jewel of the Shrine* and *A Man of Character* and was often reprinted. Raymond Sharif *Easmon, from Sierra Leone, combined playwriting and the practice of medicine, like Henshaw. His *Dear Parent and Ogre* (1964) and The *New Patriots* (1965) are, like Henshaw's works, well-structured plays.

The history of West African drama might be seen as a series of generational responses to history and culture on the part of playwrights. Obviously, dramatists who use the English language ally themselves with European influence to a greater or lesser extent. But it is important therefore to consider the ways in which dramatists draw on their African inheritance and change the shape of the European play, even while retaining English. The first generation of dramatists did a good job of producing a European play form prevalent in their day but used it to speak against the impact of colonialism on their culture. For example Sekyi dealt with the inherent irony of the situation by using Fante as well as English (indeed the play may well have been produced entirely in Fante, since Sekyi wanted to encourage linguistic proficiency in the language among the Western-educated middle class). But it was the generation that was educated under colonialism and matured about the time of independence, in the 1960s, that began serious experimentation with form.

The best-known of all West African dramatists is Wole *Soyinka, who won the Nobel Prize in 1986. Although he is a novelist, poet, and essayist as well as a dramatist, Soyinka's plays are what have won him world attention. He was already in his mid-twenties when Nigeria became independent in 1960, and his generation of Nigerian playwrights, including J.P. Clark *Bekederemo, Ola *Rotimi, Ime *Ikiddeh, Kalu *Uka, Zulu *Sofola, Yemi Ajibade, Uwa Udensi, and Wale *Ogunyemi, carved out a collective reputation. Many of these writers are Yoruba. The predominance of successful dramatists in Yoruba culture and successful novelists in Igbo culture in the post-colonial period has been a matter of interest to critics and commentators. Universities in Nigeria have been the crucible of much modern drama, especially since 1970, as Chris Dunton points out in his *Make Man Talk True: Nigerian Drama in English Since 1970* (1992), not only through departments of theatre arts (such as the famous one at Ibadan), but through the establishment of extra-mural theatre companies, tours, and the encouragement of drama groups in schools and colleges. It is striking that all ten of the playwrights Dunton discusses (Ola Rotimi, Zulu Sofola, Kole *Omotoso, Bode *Sowande, Femi *Osofisan, Tess *Onwueme, Olu *Obafemi, Tunde *Fatunde, Akanji Nasiru, and Segun *Oyekunle) are university educated and all but one (Oyekunle) have been or are university teachers.

Soyinka and his playwriting contemporary Clark Bekederemo were both associated with universities also, and Soyinka's shrines to Yoruba gods on the Ife campus were an important theatrical expression of his political and social views on the importance of living tradition in modern African life. Soyinka utilized Yoruba mythology extensively in his plays beginning with his first major work, A *Dance of the Forests (1963), which he wrote for the 1960 independence celebrations in Nigeria. Though he has been criticized for this tendency by the powerful marxist lobby within West African theatrical criticism, notably in the fine work of Biodun Jeyifo (The Truthful Lie: Essays in a Sociology of African Drama, 1985), it is through this material that Soyinka has established two directions in his plays: myth often provides a means of indirectly criticizing contemporary Nigerian politics and culture and it has also been a pedagogical tool, educating foreign audiences about the Yoruba world. He has thereby created more space for African writers in general by opening up an awareness of the riches of African traditions and modern contributions to world culture. Soyinka's first dramatic writing was satirical, and he has often written out of anger at fraudulence and used his comic range to effect for this purpose, for example in The Jero Plays (1973). His masterpiece, The *Road (1965), however, uses poetic images, and an almost absurdist sense of meaninglessness threatens his post-colonial characters. He tends to romanticize central male figures, as he does with the Elesin in his *Death and the King's Horseman (1963). Soyinka's strengths are in his command of language and his ability to juxtapose theatrical elements to produce fine dramatic tension (as when two egungun masks dance the tango to open a scene in Death and the King's Horseman). Where his plays are weakest is in occasional overwriting and lapses in theatrical pace, but they are generally of extraordinarily fine quality and also very varied.

Soyinka's theorizing about theatre and culture in the essays included in *Myth, Literature and the African World (1976) and Art, Dialogue and Outrage (1988) have contributed a good deal to the debates over form and political significance in West African drama. His use of tragedy, as well as the cultural significance of this term as Soyinka complexly views it, is discussed by Ketu Katrak (Wole Soyinka and Modern Tragedy, 1986). Critical Perspectives on Wole Soyinka, edited by James Gibbs (1980), and Research on Wole Soyinka, edited by James Gibbs and Bernth Lindfors (1993), are both useful introductions.

J. P. Clark Bekederemo began his playwriting career with *Song of a Goat, the title referring to the possible original meaning of the Greek word for tragedy. The play was first produced at the *Mbari

Club in the city of Ibadan, and was one of the important contributions that organization made to Nigerian theatre. His use of traditional material intensified in his adaptation of the Ozidi saga into a staged play, *Ozidi (1966), though this is less successful than his transcription and translation of the storytelling and community performance tradition (1977), the seven-day Ozidi saga, in Orua, in the Delta region of Nigeria. He made a film of one performance in Orua in 1964 with Frank Speed.

Ola Rotimi, who is the same generation as Soyinka and Bekederemo but did not emerge as a playwright until the 1960s, is a major theatrical presence, though he has been accused of spectacle and of failing to draw together all of the elements in his productions into a coherent whole. He studied in America, notably playwriting at Yale. His early comedy, Our Husband Has Gone Mad Again (1974), his historical dramas *Kurunmi (1971) and Ovonramwen Nogbaisi (1974), as well as If (1983), which deals with social injustice in the context of an election, Hopes of the Living Dead (1988), which dramatizes a lepers' rebellion, and the absurdist Holding Talks (1979) are quite different facets of this absolute man of the theatre.

Wale Ogunyemi, like Rotimi, has developed the historical drama, for which he did considerable research. Ijaye War (1970) deals with the Ijaye-Ibadan conflicts of the mid-nineteenth century and centres on the historical figure of Kurunmi, the Aare of Ijaye. His Kiriji (1976) deals with the Kiriji war of the last part of the nineteenth century, again about conflict between Ibadan and its neighbours, this time the Ekiti and Ijesa peoples. The name Kiriji came from the sound of cannons, used in this region for the first time in this war. These plays dramatize local history and offer the Nigerian audience a sense of the complexity of military and social conflicts and historical characters. Ogunyemi's other works include the music-dramas Obaluaye (1972) and Langbodo (1979).

Social conscience, sometimes constructed in radical, marxist terms, has been one strong facet of Nigerian response to the introduction of capitalism and the growing gap between rich and poor since independence. Femi Osofisan (Morountodun, 1982) and Bode Sowande (Farewell to Babylon, 1979) have both written about the Farmer's Revolt, the Agbakoya farmers' protest (1868-9). Osofisan has emerged as a major figure in Nigerian drama since 1970, and Morountodun is one of his best works, drawing together symbolism, theatricality, and a strong sense of social realism with a political intensity which weaves history and contemporary Nigeria together, as Soyinka does in A Dance of the Forests. Osofisan has written many plays, among them The Chattering and the Song (1977), Once Upon Four Robbers (1980), Midnight Hotel (1986), and Esu and the Vagabond Minstrels (1991). Sowande and Osofisan are both aware of intellectual aspects of dramatic forms and interested in moving towards a popular audience. Kole Omotoso's socialist dramas *The Curse* (1976) and *Shadows in the Horizon* (1977) established him as an effective dramatist, though he has given more time to his fiction. These are realistic plays of great theatrical and dramatic impact.

Zulu Sofola began to develop a woman's perspective on cultural issues in the early 1970s in her stage and television plays. There are only three women playwrights so far who are well known in Nigeria: Sofola, Tess Onwueme, and Stella Oyedepo. Sofola's radicalism is problematic; for example, in *The Sweet Trap* (1977), a group of university wives rebel against their husbands, but the play has disappointed some commentators, since the women are conciliatory in the end. Sofola argues that traditional roles for women are in some ways more powerful than contemporary ones, that marriage should be based on mutual respect, and that there are numerous realities for middle-class Nigerian women, rather than one single political direction. Tess Onwueme has experimented with many different forms and is often more explicitly and conventionally feminist than Sofola. In Ghana, Ama Ata *Aidoo, novelist and politician, produced two important plays: The *Dilemma of a Ghost* (1965), about cross-cultural tensions in a family, and *Anowa* (1970), based on a legend about a young woman who defies her parents in her choice of husband. Her sense of character, dramatic structure, and language is strongly informed by her consciousness of women's roles in modern African society, a characteristic she shares with the Nigerian women playwrights.

Ghanaian drama in the 1980s is perhaps best represented by Asiedu *Yirenkyi, whose collection *Kivuli and Other Plays* (1980) established him as an important voice in the social realist tradition.

Forms of drama are restricted very often in Muslim society in West Africa for religious reasons, but a notable example of a drama based in Muslim society is Umaru Ladan and Dexter Lyndersay's 1975 dramatic adaptation of the autobiographical novel *Shaihu Umar* by Sir Abubakar Tafewa Balewa.

Language is an important issue in relation to West African drama. The choice of English does not necessarily distance the dramatist from the general population of Nigeria, nor make him/her elitist or academic, especially with the possibility of writing truly nationally, for television. Dramatists may include songs, short speeches, or simply words or phrases in their first language, and whether or not these are translated after the text indicates whether their primary concern is with a local audience, a national, or an international one. Soyinka's plays, for example, which use Yoruba songs and phrases or Pidgin quite extensively, usually carry translations, as in the case of *The Road*.

The influences on West African drama are enormously various. The long-established theatrical tradi-

tions of the region remain crucially important in having established a sense of enjoyment and critical awareness for performance of all kinds in West African communities, whether urban or rural. To these traditions may be added the full range of available forms of world drama known to each dramatist. What makes the field of West African drama particularly interesting to the researcher of world drama is the rich continuum of creative experimentation and the use of non-verbal theatricality drawn from African traditions, such as particular forms of masking, dancing, drumming, singing, or ritual or symbolic gesture, which further the dramatist's purpose in the specific context of a local audience's communal memory and sense of identity. In addition, the collective contribution that West African drama has made to the decolonization process is enormous, given its re-visioning of western theatrical elements within a local frame of dramatic and sociopolitical reference.

Drum A *literary magazine, *Drum* was first produced in March 1951 in Cape Town as *African Drum* and published throughout South Africa. Following a cool reception, the magazine's proprietor, Jim Bailey, relocated to Johannesburg, changed the name to *Drum*, and replaced the white staff with a talented group of black journalists headed by a young editor from England, Anthony Sampson. At various times the *Drum* staff included Ezekiel *Mphahlele, Can *Themba, Bloke *Modisane, Nat *Nakasa, Lewis *Nkosi, and Casey *Motsisi. *Drum* became the largest-selling magazine in Africa, with editions in Nigeria, Ghana, East Africa, and Central Africa.

Although *Drum* is still published today, it is really to the 1950s that *Drum*'s significance within the South African journalistic, literary, and political spheres may be confined, since it was the most popular of the magazines of the time aimed at a black readership. But *Drum* was not merely a popular urban African magazine; it also published political articles and imaginative fiction, and featured outstanding exposés and investigative journalism. None of the other magazines at the time managed to offer the same combination.

The political articles that *Drum* was to publish dealt with the face-to-face manoeuvring of the newly elected Nationalists and the democratic opposition in the form of the Congress Alliance. The investigative journalism and exposés were, among other things, to reveal what life was like for people of colour within *apartheid South Africa, and they dealt with such issues as forced labour on white farms, prison conditions for blacks, and church apartheid. In the literary sphere, *Drum* was to act as a publishing outlet for people of colour when such opportunities were virtually non-existent elsewhere. This opportunity first appeared in April 1951 when *African Drum* called for entries to the Great African International Short Story

Contest; prizes were fifty pounds for the winning entry and four pounds for each publishable story. The contest was to prove an ongoing success, receiving 1,683 entries in its biggest year, 1957. Of the stories received between 1951 and 1958 (when *Drum* stopped publishing fiction) more than ninety were published, including (in addition to those writers mentioned earlier) stories by Richard *Rive, Alex *La Guma, Peter Clarke, and James *Matthews. In this way, *Drum* effectively established the story as the pre-eminent genre of black South African writers.

The publishing history of the imaginative fiction that appeared in *Drum* is interesting for what it reveals of the preoccupation of the writers and the mood of the new, mainly African proletariat. The early literary content, mainly translated folktales, soon gave way to something altogether more contemporary and urban. Compared with stories by such writers as R.R.R. *Dhlomo, Peter *Abrahams, and Mphahlele, such stories as Modisane's 'The Dignity of Begging' was jazzy and hip, featuring a freedom of language and outsider characters that were to hallmark many of the later *Drum* stories. In the context of the 1950s, this new style was provocative in its modernity and its mockery of received English at a time when the apartheid government wanted conformity from, and an ethnic identity for, its black population. Instead, what the *Drum* writers produced with their exuberant, subversive, confident language was a bee-bop of the typewriter that had its origins in Afro-America, African jazz, and *tsotsi-taal* (township slang).

The content and the style of the *Drum* stories from the 1950s are the most representative features of that writing, but they also account for the controversy that has characterized their reception. While some critics have seen the stories as escapist, seeking to ignore the daily suffering of the people of colour in favour of some Americanized landscape, others have relocated the stories to their informing locus and have recognized their ideological and literary function within that locus and, consequently, their value for South African literary studies. The informing locus within which these stories were written bears more than passing interest. For most of the stories, the context of their production was the township of Sophiatown, whose free-wheeling community identity failed to conform to apartheid's ideal of African society and marked it as 'black spot' in a white so-called group area. In 1957 it was razed and all its inhabitants dispersed to their own group areas – Africans to Meadowlands in what became Soweto – effectively breaking the back of the literary movement which had its origins there. *Drum* was banned between 1965 and 1968 and later sold. It continues to offer high-quality journalism.

Dry White Season, A (1979) A novel by André *Brink. In many ways this novel is a companion piece to the earlier *Rumours of Rain*. The novels represent the two faces of the Afrikaner, the 'ugly Afrikaner' or *apartheid apologist in *Rumours of Rain* and the dissident Afrikaner, the 'colonizer who refuses' in *A Dry White Season*. Both narrators encounter the 'dark side of history' in the form of visits to Soweto, a previously unknown territory for them in their sheltered white middle-class existences. The narrator of *A Dry White Season* is a writer of romantic fiction forced to confront reality when his friend, Ben du Toit, involves him in his Kafkaesque battle for justice against the authorities by asking him to safeguard his papers. With du Toit's 'accidental' death, the narrator (along with the reader) must repeat the dead man's journey from ignorance to enlightenment, increasingly implicated in the machinery of state control. Brink was influenced by Steve Biko's death to try to show in this novel that 'man can be rescued from his blindness and his follies'.

DU PLESSIS, Menán (1952-), South African novelist, is a resident of Cape Town, a city whose natural beauty she evokes in both *A State of Fear* (1983) and *Longlive!* (1989). Her political commitment is mirrored in her fictional concern with what constitutes appropriate action in a repressive society. While her realist style conveys a strong sense of place and time – Cape Town in the midst of the violent police action and popular protest of the 1980s – the novels focus primarily on her characters' inner struggle. The much-acclaimed *A State of Fear* (winner of two South African awards and well received internationally) is a first-person narrative of a teacher who attempts to combat her feelings of isolation in a deeply divided society by sheltering two politically involved pupils. The stylistically more experimental *Longlive!* reflects a clearer engagement with resistance politics, particularly protests against the 1985 state of emergency, and dramatizes some of the conflicts Du Plessis herself has grappled with: the ethical responsibilities of being a white South African, writing in English despite her Afrikaans background, and rejecting the notion of a 'female voice' while showing how notions of identity and history are particularly fraught for women of Afrikaans descent.

DUODU, Cameron (1937-), Ghanaian journalist, novelist, and poet, was born in eastern Ghana and educated at Abuakwa State College. After graduation he worked as a radio journalist for the Ghana Broadcasting Corporation from 1956 to 1960 and edited the Ghana edition of the South African magazine *Drum* from 1960 to 1965 and the prestigious Ghana *Daily Graphic* between 1967 and 1968. His only novel, *The Gab Boys* (1967), describes the aimless, impoverished lives of young men who seem cut off from the modernization taking place in Ghana and reflects Duodu's own frustrations with village life. Two of his poems, 'Return to Eden' and 'The Stranded Vulture', were published in the anthology *Messages: Poems from Ghana* (1970). After an unsuccessful attempt at election to public office and disillusioned with the Rawlings government, he moved in the 1980s to Britain to work as a freelance journalist.

Dusklands (1974) A novel by J.M. *Coetzee. Begun in the USA and completed on his return to South Africa in 1971, the novel comprises two apparently unrelated sections, the first set in the US and the second in southern Africa. Read allegorically, they are linked through their deconstruction of what Coetzee has referred to as the 'sciences of man', particularly the discourses of historiography and ethnography, and the way they have functioned to legitimate imperialism at different historical periods. The first section, entitled 'The Vietnam Project', comprises the first-person narrative of Eugene Dawn, a 'mythographer' employed by the US Department of Defense, and his intro-duction to the ironically titled 'New Life Project', a project of psychological warfare against the Viet Cong. The second section, 'The Narrative of Jacobus Coetzee', is made up of the fictional account of two journeys into the southern African interior by this frontiersman; a fictional 'Afterword' supposedly pro-duced by Dr. S.J. Coetzee, Afrikaner historian and (fictional) father of J.M. Coetzee; an appendix, which contains the only authentic historical document in the novel, the 'Deposition of Jacobus Coetzee (1760)', translated from the Dutch by his descendant, J.M. Coetzee; and a 'Translator's Preface', which deliber-ately obscures the historical/fictional nature of the documents that follow as well as the relationship among the different authors, fictional and real. The allegorical mode and the theme of the failed quest into an unknown colonial interior link *Dusklands* to Joseph Conrad's *Heart of Darkness* and Patrick White's *Voss*, although Coetzee goes further than these predecessors by both politicizing the metafictional mode and re-inserting it within history.

E

EASMON, R(aymond) Sarif (1913-), novelist, playwright, and short-story writer, was born in Freetown, Sierra Leone and was educated in Sierra Leone, Guinea, and at Newcastle University. As a physician he worked in government service until his aversion to corruption led him into private practice. The theme of corruption and bribery predominates in his writing.

Easmon's first play, *Dear Parent and Ogre* (1964), which won a playwriting competition in *Encounter* magazine, is about the nepotism and bribery prevalent in the Sierra Leone civil service. In *The New Patriots* (1965), a satirical play, many of the characters seem preoccupied with living a western lifestyle and speaking a language akin to Oxford English. His other work includes a novel, *The Burnt Out Marriage* (1967), and a collection of short stories, *The Feud and Other Stories* (1981). Although critics such as Ama Ata *Aidoo have described his work as dated and un-African, it shows a good sense of the comic.

ECHERUO, Michael J. C. (1937-) was born in Okigwi, eastern Nigeria and educated at the universities of Ibadan and Cornell, where he took his doctorate in English literature. He became a lecturer in English at the University of Nigeria, Nsukka and published poetry regularly in various journals as well as articles of literary criticism. Although no single volume of his poems has appeared, his best work has been anthologized widely, for example, the well-known 'Outsider' and 'Lullaby'.

ECHEWA, T. Obinkaram (1940-), Nigerian novelist, was born in Aba, Nigeria and was educated in Nigerian schools and American universities. Echewa has been an associate professor of English at Cheyney College in Pennsylvania, a contributor to *Time* and the *New York Times*, and a writer of stories, poetry, and articles for magazines such as *The New Yorker*, *America*, *Newsweek*, *West Africa*, and *Essence*. His first novel, *The Land's Lord* (1976), awarded the English-Speaking Union Prize, is an insightful and well-constructed philosophical exploration of the confrontation between Christianity and European colonizers on one hand and indigenous traditional culture and African people on the other. In his second novel, *The Crippled Dancer* (1986), the intrigues and feuds of village life reflect the tension between truth and falsehood, past and present, and reality and illusion. His third novel, *I Saw the Sky Catch Fire* (1990), is based on the famous women's riot of Aba, in which the colonial forces

were challenged and checked. Skilful characterization, succinct images, and an effective use of folk speech contribute to the success of the novels. He has also published a children's book, *The Ancestor Tree* (1994).

Edufa (1969) A play by Efua *Sutherland. Basing her play specifically on *Alcestis*, Sutherland sought to exploit the similarities between the world views of ancient Greece and contemporary Ghana. Although some of the most powerful moments in *Edufa* owe a debt to the Greek play, there are points at which local inspiration takes over and the Ghanaian playwright's abilities can be appreciated. For example, the presentation of the Chorus shows her feel for the way Ghanaians interact, and the character of Sekyi is drawn to appeal to a distinctively West African sense of humour. The ambitious text requires a firm directorial hand if the constituent elements are to be kept balanced.

Efuru (1966) A novel by Flora *Nwapa. Efuru is a strong woman in a traditional African society who is the avatar of the Goddess of the Lake. She is abandoned in turn by two husbands, overcomes the social and psychological adversity that this experience causes her, and returns to her father's home to devote her life to the celebration of the Goddess of the Lake and helping her neighbours. The novel contains a wealth of information about pre-colonial customs and tradition solidly interpolated into the dramatic text of the novel.

EGBUNA, Obi B(enedict) (1940-), Nigerian novelist, playwright, essayist, and short-story writer, was born in Ozubulu, Nigeria. As a scholarship student Egbuna studied in Britain, where he became involved in the Black Power movement. When in 1968 he was arrested, charged, and jailed for a plot to murder six policemen, the reputation he had by then earned as a writer generated solidarity demonstrations for his release.

Egbuna's first major work, *Wind Versus Polygamy* (1964), a novel and its stage adaptation, was Britain's entry at the First World Black Festival of Arts in Senegal in 1966. (The novel was re-published in 1974 with the title *Elina*.) Much of his early writing addresses racial issues: his play *The Anthill* (1965) and especially *Destroy This Temple* (1971), *The ABC of Black Power Thought* (1973), and *Daughters of the Sun and Other Stories* (1970) examine black-white encounters in a variety of forms. He published a second collection of stories, *Emperor of the Sea*, in 1974 and another novel, *The Minister's Daughter*, in 1975. Returning to Nigeria in the mid-1970s he became the director of the East Central State Writers' Workshop and a director of East Central Broadcasting's television service and published a collection of his essays for the newspaper *Renaissance* (Lagos) as *Diary of a Homeless Prodigal* (1978). After a military coup he went to the USA for graduate studies; he gained a Master's degree from the University of Iowa and a Ph.D. from Howard University (1986) and published a collection of stories, *Black Candle for Christmas* (1980), and two novels, *The Rape of Lysistrata* (1980) and *The Madness of Didi* (1980).

EKWENSI, Cyprian (1921-), Nigerian novelist, short-story writer, and chronicler of traditional tales, has had a long and successful career as a writer of popular fiction. Born in Minna, Niger State, he trained as a pharmacist and served in the Nigerian Medical Service. Later he became head of features in the Nigerian Broadcasting Services (1957); director of information of the federal Ministry of Information, Lagos (1961-6); and director of Information Services, Enugu (1966); he has also held the directorships of Star Printing and Publishing (1975-9) and *Eagle* magazine (1981). He received the Dag Hammarskjold International Award for Literary Merit in 1968.

Ekwensi's first full-length novel, *People of the City* (1954), established him as the first West African author of a major novel in English and marked an important development in African writing. A novel of manners, *People of the City* recounts the coming to political awareness of a young reporter and band leader in an emerging African country. His next full length novel, **Jagua Nana* (1961), tells the story of a socially ambitious prostitute. She falls in love with a young teacher, Freddie, whom she agrees to send to law school in England on the understanding that they will marry upon his return. The tragic potential of the arrangement is finally undermined by a contrived happy ending, but not before Ekwensi crafts in his heroine one of the most memorable characters in Nigerian literature. *Burning Grass* (1962), subtitled 'A Story of the Fulani of Northern Nigeria', portrays with anthropological accuracy the life of nomadic cattlemen through the adventures of Mai Sunsaye and his sons.

Beautiful Feathers (1963) reflects the nationalist and pan-Africanist consciousness of the pre-independence days of the 1950s and how the young hero's youthful commitment to this ideal leads to the disintegration of his family, thus underscoring the proverb implied in the title: 'however famous a man is outside, if he is not respected inside his own home he is like a bird with beautiful feathers, wonderful on the outside but ordinary within'. The *Nigeria-Biafra war naturally sensitized Ekwensi's restless imagination. *Survive the Peace*

(1976) interrogates the problematics of survival in the so-called peace. We witness the pathetic fate of James Odugo, a journalist who has survived the war only to be cut down on the road by marauding former soldiers. *Divided We Stand* (1980) was written in the heat of hostilities, much earlier than *Survive the Peace* though published later. It reverses the received wisdom that unity is strength, showing how ethnicity, division, and hatred bring about distrust, displacement, and war itself.

Jagua Nana's Daughter (1986) reveals Ekwensi's fascination with the Jagua Nana phenomenon. The novel re-visits the life of the notorious Jagua Nana of the earlier novel in the life of her daughter, Liza, unlike her mother an educated professional woman. This social elevation enables her to select her numerous lovers from the privileged class. An affair with a highly placed professional blossoms into marriage, thus guaranteeing her the security and protection she desires. In *King for Ever!* (1992), a satire on the desire of African leaders to perpetuate themselves in office, Sinanda rises to power from humble beginnings and thereafter aspires to godhead.

Ekwensi's strength as a writer, born of his personal experiences while working in northern Nigeria, is in his depiction of contemporary events of social and cultural importance. Though a popular and influential writer of what has been called the first wave of Nigerian writers, Ekwensi's standing with literary critics has not been very high. The most frequent criticism is that his novels do not speak in an authentic African voice, that they could have been written by any competent writer from Europe or America as easily as by a Nigerian. Ekwensi was writing for a book-buying public in the West that expected certain literary conventions and forms, and the style of his writing was no doubt influenced by these expectations. His understanding of plot and character is another source of criticism. His characters, it is asserted, even when they are involved in events of cultural significance, reveal only a superficial awareness, learning little or nothing of themselves in their quests. Individual readers must judge for themselves if these negative evaluations are correct, but it is nonetheless apparent that many of his novels lack consistent plots and drift towards the melodramatic. The general popularity of Ekwensi's fiction is not in question, however. Several decades of readers, both in the West and in Nigeria, have found entertainment and a realistic picture of the pleasures and hazards of Nigerian city life in his novels and short stories.

EMECHETA, Buchi (1944-), Nigerian novelist whose works are a leading example of *African-British literature, was born in Lagos, Nigeria to Igbo parents. She became a writer after she left Nigeria with her husband in the early 1960s for England, where she worked as a librarian. The marriage collapsed, and Emecheta was left with five children to support. She took a degree in sociology and began to write seriously. Her first two novels, *In the Ditch* (1972) and *Second-Class Citizen* (1974), are autobiographical, a response to the experience of living in England, specifically London, and learning to write out this traumatic period. Her next group of novels, *The Bride Price* (1976), *The Slave Girl* (1977), *The *Joys of Motherhood* (1979), *Destination Biafra* (1982), and *Double Yoke* (1982), are set in Nigeria. *The Rape of Shavi* (1983) is a futuristic parable about race relations set in a fictional African country. *Head Above Water* (1986) is Emecheta's autobiography, *Gwendolyn* (1989, published in the USA as *The Family*, 1990) takes place in Jamaica and London, and *Kehinde* (1994) is set in both London and Nigeria. She has also written television plays and children's books.

Emecheta's fiction has sought to account for the situation of African women in a changing world, whether it be colonial Nigeria, traditional Igboland, or contemporary London. A strong sociological element characterizes the fiction, which portrays economic, cultural, and political pressures on African women wherever they live. Emecheta has maintained residence in England for more than twenty years, and her perception of African culture has sometimes been seen as puzzlingly hostile, at least in the earlier novels. She has also often been seen by western feminists as a feminist writer, though she herself is hesitant about the term.

She is clearly aware of the importance of her journey as a writer: it has not been a rejection of Africa nor a simple acceptance of England but a story of coping with emotional stress, economic hardship, and migration and of the need to fit into a new society as well as to understand both personal and communal African history. It has also been a journey of learning to write: from the first novels, which are in many ways fictionalized autobiography, valuable but technically unsophisticated, to *The Joys of Motherhood* is a progression from first attempts at the novel form to a remarkable, powerful portrait of colonial Nigeria and the fate of a woman trying to stay loyal to traditional Igbo culture in a rapidly changing Lagos.

Emecheta's central female characters find the world prejudiced against their efforts to realize full humanity and protect and guide their children. *The Rape of Shavi*, on the other hand, tells a moral tale of the implications of Western intrusion on African culture. Here Shavi, the country, is raped rather than an individual woman. Emecheta herself knows how to survive and tell her story: her writing was among the first by African women to find international attention. Although much of Emecheta's fiction is realist, she often gives her major characters a sense of the spiritual heritage of African culture: this is particularly impor-

tant in *The Joys of Motherhood* and *Kehinde*. Emecheta's conception of tradition is complex, neither accepting nor rejecting entirely: her female central characters seek sustenance from their people's customs, but if that fails them they will turn to contemporary options.

ENEKWE, Ossie (1942-), Nigerian poet, fiction writer, and playwright, is a graduate of the University of Nigeria and Columbia University, where he was a fellow in the Writing Division (1972-4), and is a professor of theatre in the University of Nigeria. His published work includes *Broken Pots* (1977), poems, *Come Thunder* (1984), a novel, *Igbo Masks* (1987), nonfiction, *The Betrayal* (1989), a one-act play, and *The Last Battle and Other Stories* (1996). His short stories and poems are anthologized world-wide, several in translation. The Biafran experience is the main theme of his early writing; in his later work, his poetic vision is dominated by metaphors of liberation. The threnodic trend in *Broken Pots* gives way to defiant assertion and hope. His lyricism reflects his dedication to poetry as an oral art. His work is characterized by its commitment to human dignity.

EPPEL, John (1947-), Zimbabwean poet and novelist, was educated at the universities of Natal and Rhodesia. His first two books were awarded important South African prizes: the Ingrid Jonker Prize for his volume of poems *Spoils of War* (1989), and the M-Net Prize for fiction for the novel *D. G. G. Berry's Great North Road* (1992). He has published two further novels, *Hatchings* (1993) and *The Giraffe Man* (1994), and another volume of poetry, *Sonata for Matabeleland* (1995). Eppel's usual settings for his poetry and prose are Bulawayo and southern Matabeleland, which are re-created in remarkably different ways in his poetry and his prose. In his prose, city and bush are sites for farces enacted by grotesques and touched by magic realism. These provide the basis for satires directed at such disparate targets as settler nostalgia for Rhodesia, destructive educational systems, political and financial corruption in contemporary Zimbabwe, indifference to Matabeleland's fragile ecology, and Christian fundamentalism that masks a range of public and private immoralities. Eppel's poetry derives a great deal of its power from his close observation of the Matabeleland bush, which is evoked with singular precision. This objective detailing of landscape endows moments of personal inspiration with a public significance. In his later volume, poems that deal with a series of largely private experiences constitute an informal history of Matabeleland's last thirty years.

EQUIANO, Olaudah (*ca.* 1745-97), Nigerian autobiographer. The Igbo Equiano's two-volume autobiography, *The Interesting Narrative of Olaudah Equiano or Gustavus Vassa, the African, Written by Himself* (1789), or *Equiano's Travels*, is the first substantial and most accomplished African account of slavery and the African diaspora. Equiano was born in Essaka, possibly Isseke, in what is now eastern Nigeria, the youngest son of a devoted mother and titled father. He was kidnapped with and separated from his sister by African slave traders and experienced forms of African slavery that contrasted with his experience of European slavery. Traumatic separation from his family is registered as 'too painful to tell' silences or as abrupt shifts from plain, accessible language to a more artificial, sentimental language. Remembered Igbo boyhood is a powerful source of identity in the autobiography. Much of Equiano's life was spent aboard ships, where he distinguished himself as resourceful and hard working, mastering English, literacy, other useful skills, and earning money through petty trading. His treatment of relations with Europeans reflects his need to fashion a surrogate family and his ability to obtain essential survival skills and information from crewmen and others. While Equiano was spared relentless hardship by good luck and his own effort, he was witness to and chronicler of the harsh brutalities endured by other enslaved Africans. The Igbo concept of *chi* or personal fate underpinning his Christian faith steels him against the vicissitudes of slavery. He purchased his freedom at the age of twenty-one, continued to travel and trade, and became an effective abolitionist in Britain, where he married Susan Cullen and had two daughters. His work on behalf of fellow Africans was characteristically pragmatic and energetic, focused on alleviation of suffering and, on speaking tours, educating and persuading the British public against slavery. In his lifetime the narrative went through one American and eight British editions and was translated into Dutch, Russian, and German. Chinua *Achebe has described Equiano as his literary ancestor. His autobiography – testimony against the inhumanity of European slavery and in support of the dignity of African peoples – is a foundation of West African, Afro-British, and African-American writing. Equiano died in Britain.

ESSOP, Ahmed (1931-), South African short-story writer and novelist, was born in India and emigrated to South Africa as a child. He was educated at the Johannesburg Indian High School in Fordsburg and at the University of South Africa (BA, 1964) and taught English at schools in Johannesburg.

His first publication was *The Dark Goddess* (1959), which was followed in the 1960s by short stories and poetry published in South African periodicals. He has since published stories in *Staffrider* and in anthologies edited by Stephen *Gray, Mothobi *Mutloatse, and Robin Malan. His often moving and richly comic collection *The Hajji and Other Stories* (1978) received the Olive Schreiner Award; his first novel, *The Visitation* (1980), returns to the setting of the stories of *The Hajji*. *The Emperor* (1984) is another novel; *Noorjehan and Other Stories* (1990) and *The King of Hearts and Other Stories* (1997) collect further stories.

Ethiopia Unbound [See CASELY-HAYFORD, Joseph Ephraïm]

Experience, The (1970) A novel by Eneriko *Seruma. 'The experience' the protagonist of this novel undergoes, that of a black man determined to live in a white world, becomes the source of crucial discoveries and self-knowledge. Perhaps the most significant realization concerns the conflict of cultures. The text suggests that the issue may not be one of intrinsic divergence, but rather a combination of confusion, superficiality, and lack of intelligence.

Eye of the Earth, The (1986) Poems by Niyi *Osundare. In his third volume of carefully articulated and precisely focused poems, Osundare expresses his concern with nature, the rural landscape, and rural life, envisioning an earth dying through the activities of the 'rich and ruthless', who are endlessly preoccupied with weaponry and profits while millions starve. The poems present a revolutionary agenda that seeks to redirect the attention of rulers to saving the environment.

F

FAGUNWA, D(aniel) O. (1903-63), Nigerian novelist, born in Oke-Igbo, Nigeria. Fagunwa studied at St. Luke's School, Oke-Igbo and St. Andrew's College, Oyo, after which he taught in various institutions in Nigeria. His novels include *Ogboju Ode ninu Igbo Irunmale* (1938), translated from *Yoruba into English by Wole *Soyinka as *The *Forest of a Thousand Daemons* (1968), *Igbo Olodumare* (1949; *The Forest of God*, 1984; *The Forest of the Almighty*, 1986), *Ireke Onibudo* (1949), *Irinkerindo ninu Igbo Elegbeje* (1954; *Expedition to the Mount of Thought*, 1994), and *Adiitu Olodumare* (1961). He won the Margaret Wrong Prize for his writing in 1955 and was awarded the MBE in 1959.

Fagunwa is arguably the most widely known writer in the Yoruba language and certainly one of the most widely read. His work has influenced such contemporary Yoruba writers as Amos *Tutuola, whose stories follow Fagunwa's pattern. The enduring strength of his novels lies in his negotiation of a relationship between the ideals of African traditional religion and Christianity, but its memorable use of language, his unique ability to create lasting and powerful events, his descriptive ingenuity, and the complexity of his narratives contribute to his stature among Yoruba writers.

Fagunwa's novels follow the pattern of the traditional Yoruba folktale in which the storyteller, conscious of his audience and of the didactic function of storytelling in traditional Yoruba communities, narrates his story to a formally educated person, who is requested to write down the story for posterity so that others can learn from it.

The novels are set in the natural and human Yoruba world of kings and subjects, a world of fantasy and the supernatural, as well as a world of sages, who teach the protagonists. The trilogy, *Ogboju Ode ninu Igbo Irunmale*, *Igbo Olodumare* and *Irinkerindo ninu Igbo Elegbeje*, narrates the heroic journeys of the Yoruba hunters who are its protagonists. *Adiitu Olodumare* and *Ireke Onibudo* record the grass-to-grace life stories of the protagonists for whom the novels are named.

FALL, Malick (1920-78), Senegalese novelist and poet who wrote in French. Malick Fall's literary reputation rests principally on his novel *La Plaie* [The wound] (1967), first published by Albin Michel, Paris, and re-published in 1980 in a limited boxed edition by Nouvelles Éditions Africaines, Dakar. He also produced a volume of poems, *Reliefs* (1964), with an introduction by L.S. *Senghor. Fall worked in the Senegalese Department of Information before embarking on a career as a diplomat.

Reliefs is made up of poems written over a long and complex period of Senegalese history as the country moved from colonial rule to independence. The poems explore, from an individual, private perspective, the country's contemporary preoccupations and fears. *La Plaie* is one of the celebrated francophone African novels of the 1960s, one of a number of early, in part autobiographical novels in which the city comes to represent the new reality of life in a post-colonial, urban setting. The protagonist, Magamou, is drawn to the attractions of the city, is injured in a traffic accident, and survives as a beggar because of the pity inspired by the awfulness of his wound. But the wound also marks him as an outcast, a status that allows him peculiar insights into the society of which he is not part until later, when his sore heals.

Famished Road, The (1991) A novel by Ben *Okri and winner of the Booker Prize in 1991. Through the innovative use of such familiar images as the road and the *abiku*, the spirit child whose cyclical birth, death, and rebirth is a source of terror and pain for its family, Okri discusses the political fashioning and re-fashioning of Nigeria and many other African countries. The strength of the novel lies not just in these images but in how they are used. Language in *The Famished Road* is generally poetic, incantatory, descriptive, and local. It is a thoughtful representation of the sociopolitical and economic situation of many African countries, and even some other parts of the world.

FARAH, Nuruddin (1945-), Somali novelist. Farah comes from a nomadic tradition and his studies and employments have been nomadic on a global scale. Born in Baidoa in the Italian-administered south of Somalia, he grew up in the Ethiopian-ruled Ogaden and was educated in Ethiopia and Mogadishu and at the Punjab University of Chandigarh (1966-70) and the University of Essex (1974-6). About to return to Somalia in 1976, he learned that his recently published novel *A *Naked Needle* (1976) had fallen foul of the authorities (an earlier play and a novel extract in Somali had been declared seditious) and that a lengthy jail sentence awaited him. He spent the next three years in Rome and since 1980 has held positions at universities in Africa, Europe, and North America. For twenty years Farah did not return to his native Somalia, in which his own works were until recently banned. His preoccupying subject throughout his writing career, however, has been the oppression of his country by the clan-based dictatorship of General Siyad Barre, which held power from 1969 until 1991. Specifically, his novels pinpoint the lethal collusions of family and state authoritarianisms and of tribalism, Islam, and marxism and feature pioneering studies of the patriarchal subjection of women in the Horn of Africa.

His first novel, *From a Crooked Rib (1970), tells the story of Ebla, an illiterate but independent-minded nomadic woman of the colonial 1950s, and her city-bound flight from bartered marriages in a society where a woman's only alternative to being sold by others as a chattel-wife is to sell herself as a prostitute. A Naked Needle, his second novel, is set in Mogadishu during the period of Somali political alignment with the USSR that followed Barre's 1969 coup and is more experimental. It was followed by a trilogy, Variations on the Theme of an African Dictatorship, comprising the novels *Sweet and Sour Milk (1979), Sardines (1981), and Close Sesame (1983). The trilogy is Farah's most artistically mature and complex work.

Maps (1986), a novel set during the 1977 Ogaden war, breaks ambitious new ground. It unfolds a complex fable of personal, ethnic, and national identity through the relationship of Askar, an orphaned Ogadenese-Somali child, and his adoptive mother Misra, an Oromo woman from the Ethiopian highlands with whom he develops an excruciatingly close physical bond that overrides nationalistic hatreds (he even menstruates in sympathy with her). Born to two patriotic martyrs, Askar is the posthumous mythic offspring of Ogadenese nationalism, his orphaned life an analogue for his parentless nation, his personal history identified with that of his country. But his problematic straddling of boundaries – national, sexual, ontological – raises crucial questions about the nature of Somali identity and, in post-modern fashion, generates a puzzling indeterminacy about where metaphor and allegory end and where literal reality starts. Farah's more conventional seventh novel, Gifts (1992), is a love story that places a suitor's offerings against the backdrop of international aid to famine-struck countries. The novel subtly explores the complex psychology of donorship, its binding ties and dependencies, and the ways they change the relationship between giver and receiver. Secrets (1998) makes adroit use of myth and metaphor to explore the past and present of characters who are reunited on the eve of civil war.

Farah is perhaps Africa's most cosmopolitan, multiliterate, and multilingual writer (English, in which he writes fiction, is his fourth language), and he is widely regarded as one of the most stylish and intellectually complex of contemporary African novelists. He has said that he associates multiple viewpoints with tolerance, closure and omniscience with tyranny, and commentators have duly praised his fluid, open-ended

narratives, his intricate metaphoric textures, and his nonpartisan, compassionate commitment to human freedom. Farah was awarded the 1998 Neustadt International Prize for Literature.

FATUNDE, Tunde (1955-), Nigerian playwright, gained a BA in French from the University of Ibadan and an MA and Ph.D. in France. He combines university teaching, writing and directing plays, trade union activities, and journalism; his newspaper columns especially have made him well known as an activist intellectual. He has published five plays: Blood and Sweat (1985), first performed in 1983; No More Oil Boom (1985), staged in 1984; No Food, No Country (1985), performed in 1985; Oga Na Tief Man (1986), staged in 1985; and Water No Get Enemy (1989), staged in 1988. The plays are unique for having been written, in the playwright's words, for 'the general public with minimum level of formal education', and their purpose, as noted by Femi Shaka in his introduction to the third play, is 'to encourage a culture of resistance, struggle and liberation amongst our working people and their families'. To this end, plot, characterization, dialogue, and language are highly simplified and predictable. Subject matter is usually a class conflict, and in the confrontation that inevitably ensues, the proletariat always act with courage and unity, and they always win morally, or physically, or both. While the proletariat are always positively portrayed, bourgeois elites are always depicted as villains. Dialogue is carried out either in a stepped-down standard English or in Pidgin, Nigeria's unofficial lingua franca.

FEMINISM AND LITERATURE The growing awareness of the importance of women writers in Africa has been related to, and accompanied by, an emerging debate on difference. Specifically the differences are, on the one hand, between African women's experience and understanding and male-centred accounts of African tradition, and on the other hand, between the feminist movements of Europe and North America and the affirmation by African women of their own identity, practical needs, and aspirations. What is sometimes referred to as 'African feminism', or to use another term suggested by African-American author Alice Walker, 'womanism', involves an effort by African women to be fully involved, as equal partners, in both the struggle for the freedom and fulfilment of African people in the face of racism, colonialism, and oppression and the worldwide struggle by women against social, cultural, and political marginalization. One of the areas of this double-sided struggle has been the effort on the part of women authors and, more recently, a number of feminist critics and *literary theorists, to place on the centre stage of African literary history a new canon of writings by African women, along with the visions of history, of human identity, and of literary aesthetics that those writings represent.

Although the role of women in the production and performance of oral literature has been downplayed in traditional scholarship, recent studies show the centrality and expertise of women in the oral transmission of literature in many African cultures. One of the earliest written genres employed by African women is autobiography, as a means by which 'people write themselves into history'. Early women autobiographers include Adelaide *Casely-Hayford, Noni *Jabavu, author of *The Ochre People* (1963), and Nafissatou Diallo, author of *De Tilène au Plateau: une enfance dakaroise* (1975). In these autobiographies, an often self-effacing author–narrator uses her own life to tell the story of the larger society in which she lives, while affirming her own being by taking up for herself the written word.

Beginning in the 1960s and at an accelerated pace through the 1970s, women writers became more numerous and more widely read; in *Efuru* (1966), Flora *Nwapa presents an intensely personal narrative of a single, childless woman in relation to the myth of the watermaid; beginning with *Le Revenant* (1976), Aminata Sow Fall published five novels that combine social and political criticism with the creation of strong women characters committed to what they consider to be positive aspects of African cultural traditions. There has been an increasing awareness of the need to address the oppression of women both within traditional culture (for example by sexual mutilation, forced maternity, and polygamy) and by certain practices introduced by colonialism, including the economic exploitation of women among the rural and urban poor and the systematic attempt to under-educate women in relation to men. These social realities are not only exposed but often overcome through the working of fantasy, the marvellous, and the legendary, from *oral tradition into women's perception of their world. This exposure is reflected in the works of such authors as Ama Ata *Aidoo, Bessie *Head, Buchi *Emecheta, Werewere Liking and Calixthe *Beyala.

Many African women writers, including Grace *Ogot, Flora Nwapa, and Mariama *Bâ, were dismissed from the outset by critics of both African and European origin for their lack of formal skills and sometimes for their complicity with colonialist attempts to undermine African traditions. However, as the focus has shifted away from the concern with the 'image' of *women in African literature towards the self-representation of women through formal innovations that reflect a tradition of feminine and feminist discourse, more positive studies are being undertaken of the themes and narrative structures of these authors.

In South African literature a feminist tradition dates from Olive *Schreiner's novels of the late nineteenth century, while the work of Pauline *Smith,

Bessie *Head, Miriam *Tlali, Gcina *Mhlope, and Nadine *Gordimer has proved fruitful ground for feminist analysis. Yet many African women writers have resisted an unqualified identification with feminism. Although research on gender has gained prominence recently, a major task remains: the need to articulate a feminism properly appropriate to South African society in its sensitivity to issues of class, race, and diversity in women's experience.

FETTOUMA, Touati (1950-), francophone novelist of the *Maghreb, was born in Azazoa, a small mountainous village in the Kabylia region of Algeria. Her parents emigrated to France in 1951. Wanting to learn more about the country of her birth, she returned to Kabylia in 1975 and remained there for four years, working principally as a librarian in the University of Tiziüouzou in the capital of Kabylia. During this time she witnessed the racism and sexism to which Algerian women are subjected, and on her return to France she wrote about these experiences in her novel *Printemps Désespéré: Vies d'Algériennes* (1984; *Desperate Spring*, 1987), which has also been translated into German and Arabic. The novel, which is set principally in Kabylia, traces the lives of three generations of Algerian women, from that of the grandmother Sekoura, who is omnipresent throughout, to those of her numerous grandchildren, concentrating particularly on the latter generation. The suffering of women is paramount in this novel: young women are forced to marry partners chosen by their families, married women are beaten into submission by their husbands and exist only through their children, and career women are subjected to insults because they reject the traditional role assigned to them. Despite the bleakness of these lives, however, there is hope in the network of women's relationships, which provide mutual support and understanding.

FIAWOO, Ferdinand Kwasi (1891-1969), Ghanaian playwright. Ferdinand Kwasi Fiawoo's formal education in Togoland began late and was interrupted, so it was not until 1928 that, with the help of the African Methodist Episcopal Zion Church, he was able to travel to the USA to begin undergraduate work. During the next five years he gained three bachelor's degrees and an educational qualification.

From this period came *Toko Atolia*, which appeared, in the author's English translation from Ewe, as *The Fifth Landing Stage* in 1943, and which remains a significant landmark in Ghanaian writing for the stage. By 1943 Fiawoo had been ordained and had returned to the Gold Coast, now Ghana, where he had begun to play an important role in public life and had started work on a Ph.D.: profoundly loyal to his Anlo Ewe background, he worked throughout his life to unite Christian education with the best in African culture.

The Fifth Landing Stage clearly reflects Fiawoo's background, education, times, and concerns. The title, a reference to the place of execution of Anlo Ewe malefactors, immediately indicates the play's concern with social control, and the somewhat ponderous introduction and the five-act structure of the play suggest a desire to engage with classical and Shakespearean conventions. Some of the twenty-eight scenes that make up the play are very short, and the problem of maintaining momentum in performance poses such a challenge that some think the play should be read rather than acted. Though set out like a conventional twentieth-century European drama, the text is conceived by an author at home with the fluidity of the folk narrative and at ease with formal exchanges of ideas. The plot explores the relationship between the generations and shows how easy it is for evil to triumph – indeed the drama embodies a terrifying sense of the vulnerability of virtue. Ultimately, however, the villain is exposed and sent to the fifth landing stage, where the hero, an embodiment of Anlo Ewe virtues, shows compassion. The play's combative sense that the author's country folk were morally and culturally the equals of those who had come to preach to them provides conviction that triumphs over limitations of stagecraft.

Fisherman's Invocation, The (1978) Poems by Gabriel ★Okara and winner of a Commonwealth Writers Prize in 1979. This slim volume of thirty-three poems is traversed by the iconic riverbank, inspired by the Niger Delta. The much-anthologized 'Call of the River Nun' and the title poem, written respectively before (1957) and after independence (1963), chart the tribulations of nation-building through Ijaw (Ijo) imagery and echoes from Wordsworth and Hopkins. While wartime poems written from the Biafran civilian's point of view co-exist with meek love poems and 'culture-conflict' poems wavering between the drum and the concerto, the tone that prevails is gentle, melancholy, allegorical, and unfailingly Christian.

FITZPATRICK, (Sir) J. Percy (1872-1931), South African novelist, son of an Irish lawyer of fallen fortunes who settled in the Cape Colony and became a judge in the Supreme Court. His championship of the Uitlander [foreign] community in the early days of gold mining on the Witwatersrand placed him at the forefront of affairs leading to and following the ★Anglo-Boer war. His book *The Transvaal from Within* (1899) rallied English opinion behind their cause.

Fitzpatrick's best-known work, ★*Jock of the Bushveld* (1907), is about an exceptional dog among the ox-wagon teams plying between the Transvaal and Delagoa Bay (Lourenço Marques/Maputo), an animal story in a social and natural setting in the tradition of *The Jungle Book* and *White Fang* that reflects his admiration for the work of Bret Harte and Mark Twain.

Fitzpatrick first displayed his Anglo-South African attitudes in *Through Mashonaland with Pick and Pen* (1892), an ironic record of Lord Randolph Churchill's tour of Southern Africa. In his collection of sketches, *The Outspan: Tales of South Africa* (1897), he anticipated themes to be found in books as different as *Jock* and Joseph Conrad's *Heart of Darkness*.

Fixions and Other Stories (1969) Short stories by ★Taban lo Liyong. The stories draw from East African folk tradition. While such stories as 'The Old Man of Usumbura and His Misery' and 'The Story of Master Hare and His Friend Jumbe Elephant' are wholly original in treatment, critics have often noted correspondences between them and the writing of ★Okot p'Bitek of Uganda and Amos ★Tutuola of Nigeria. As with p'Bitek and Tutuola, lo Liyong transmutes traditional material into modern applications.

Foe (1986) A novel by J.M. ★Coetzee. A woman narrator, Susan Barton, attempts to rewrite Daniel Defoe's *Robinson Crusoe* to address the issue of both women and colonized people achieving authority over their own representation. Having been cast up on Cruso's island and then rescued by a passing ship, Susan tells her story in letters addressed to Mr. Foe, who is in hiding from the bailiffs. Supported by Foe, Susan takes up lodgings in London with Friday, whose tongue has been cut out and for whom she feels responsible since the death of Cruso en route for England. Foe stands for the Author who is to turn her story into a book, and she struggles with him over the truthful representation of her experience. She becomes increasingly preoccupied with Friday and the telling of his story, while she recognizes that 'the only tongue that can tell Friday's story is the tongue he has lost'. The novel concludes with an unnamed narrator describing the descent into a wreck in which the bodies of Foe, Susan, and Friday are found. This is the 'home of Friday', and from his mouth a slow stream flows out to the ends of the earth, perhaps pointing to a future time when the voices of previously colonized peoples will establish their own authority around the world.

Fools and Other Stories (1983) Impressive collection of stories by Njabulo ★Ndebele, some of which first appeared in *Staffrider* magazine, enjoying a significantly wide exposure to the readership – African, urban, politically usurped – that the stories both address and challenge. Set in the mining town location of Charterston, near Johannesburg, 'The Test', 'The Prophetess', 'Uncle', and 'The Music of the Violin' all centre around the consciousness of a boy growing up as a middle-class child in a largely impoverished community. The long title story deals with the relationship that develops between an idealistic young political activist and a disgraced schoolteacher. The stories are characterized by minutely realized evocations of the texture of life in a South African township under ★apartheid, and by an often profound meditation on the cultural resources for survival and resistance within such a community.

Footprints in the Quag (1989) Short stories by Miriam ★Tlali, published outside South Africa as *Soweto Stories*. Individual stories vividly depict the painful and difficult conditions of black women's lives and their 'tooth and nail fight for survival in the city. Tlali draws on proverbs and idioms from the indigenous Sesotho to indicate the continuing influence of traditional culture. While the loss of traditional values and support structures is regretted, a story like 'Mm'a-Lithoto [Mother of bundles] shows the extent to which these very traditions often work to repress and subordinate women. Women are shown both as strong and able to provide mutual support, and as isolated and vulnerable to sexual assault and domestic abuse. The final story makes an uncompromising statement about the need for equality in marriage. In the context of a literary culture that sees the anti-★apartheid struggle as paramount, these stories insist on the urgent need to focus on the situation of women.

Forest of a Thousand Daemons, The (1968) A novel by D. O. ★Fagunwa, translated by Wole ★Soyinka from the Yoruba (*Ogbojo Ode ninu Igbo Irunmale*, 1938). Perhaps Fagunwa's most widely read novel, *Forest* follows the pattern of the Yoruba folktale, as do his other novels. It also employs the structural motif of the journey as Akara-Ogun travels through the forest of a thousand daemons. Fagunwa's powerful narrative technique, his figurative use of language, his descriptive power, and his various anecdotes make this one of the classics of African literature.

Foriwa (1967) A play by Efua ★Sutherland. First performed in the Akan language in 1962, *Foriwa* is a busy, crowded play full of insights into life in Ghanaian villages that moves to a spectacular conclusion. The plot draws on the familiar West African story of the young woman who rejects local suitors and chooses a stranger. Sutherland retells the tale with style and individuality; her dramatic version throbs with life, contains both comic moments and satirical jibes, and asks pertinent questions for a new nation, such as 'What is a stranger?' The play, which condemns the small-mindedness and stultifying litigiousness that poison communities, ends with a coming together of the villagers, the presentation of gifts, and a performance by an Asafo company. This festive ending contains the promise that new life will flow into the village.

Fragments (1970) A novel by Ayi Kwei ★Armah. The novel continues Armah's exploration of post-independence Ghana. Baako Onipa returns from the USA with a creative writing degree, but a series of disappointments frustrates his visionary talent. He cannot satisfy the demands placed on him by his family and by society at large, whose 'cargo mentality' expects 'been-tos' to become carriers of material fortunes. Ghana's literary personalities similarly show a sterile interest in fund-hunting rather than in imaginative writing. When his scripts are rejected by the state broadcast company, Ghanavision, Baako resigns his position there. Despite the sympathy shown by his sensitive partner Juana, a Puerto Rican psychiatrist, and by his former art teacher Ocran, he suffers a nervous breakdown and ends up in a mental asylum. The first and last chapter utilize the interior monologue of Naana, Baako's grandmother, and frame the novel in a circular structure that corresponds to Naana's faith in the ancestral cycle of death and rebirth.

FRANCOPHONE-ANGLOPHONE LITERARY RELATIONS African works in English and French reflect historical differences between former British and French colonies. The works themselves and the history of their production suggest difference, cross-cultural insemination of ideas, and experiments and accomplishments involving common problems of literary production.

French policies of cultural assimilation led to the view that mastery of the colonist's language would give the colonized access to French civilization and recognition as part of an intellectual elite. The British preferred practical communication among peoples of different languages, so that more prominence was possible for new linguistic forms such as Pidgin English. The ★negritude movement among francophone writers was the reaction of an assimilated intellectual elite to the forgetting of previously held values and identity.

In literary discourse, these differences become what Alain Ricard calls 'linguistic consciousness' or the author's awareness of writing in the language of an other. Poetry in English moved from erudite efforts to appropriate the colonist's language to concerns with social realities, orality in poetic expression, and formal experimentation, while accepting English as a pragmatic vehicle of communication. Poetic theory and practice in French was strongly influenced by L.S. ★Senghor and was for some time hesitant in developing new and original forms. The work of Hubert Ogunde, and later Wole ★Soyinka, contributed to the growth of a popular African theatre in Nigeria, a theatre that used complex levels of language to address the relationship between English and African languages. African theatre in French grew out of the pedagogy of the École normale William Ponty, which formed to a large extent the first generation of African francophone dramatists. With the latest generation, including Werewere Liking, Zadi Zaourou, Francis Bebey, and *Sony Labou Tansi, these constraints have begun to break down, while francophone African cinema has achieved international recognition for its originality. The questioning of the African *novel as an example of perfectly learned English can be seen as early as 1951, with Amos *Tutuola's The *Palm-wine Drinkard, and there has subsequently been a tradition of reworking English by such novelists as Gabriel *Okara and Chinua *Achebe. The first French-language novel to question its own status as a French text was Ahmadou *Kourouma's *Les Soleils des indépendances* (1970). But Zégoua Nokan's *Violent était le vent* (1966) for example, which, while conservative in its use of French, attempts to incorporate representations of orality into the novel form, suggests the need for caution in stressing such contrasts.

Despite these differences, and beyond the unity that may underlie African civilization in general, African literatures in English and French have influenced each other. The Harlem Renaissance of the 1920s, with its interest in the notion of Africa as the mythical place of origin of black Americans, as reflected in much *African-American literature, contributed to the revalorization of African civilization of the negritude movement in Paris in the 1930s. Later, Richard Wright became acquainted with African intellectuals in Paris, including L.S. Senghor, Aimé Césaire, and Alioune *Diop. Although Wright's search for a meeting point between this group and other peoples of African origin was not widely supported, he did exert a profound influence on the francophone theorist Frantz Fanon.

More recently the international presence of Wole Soyinka, who has shown an awareness, though not a wholesale acceptance, of French literary theory, has helped spread the ideas of contemporary Nigerian literature to other African countries. There have also been African critics from English-speaking countries, for example Abiola Irele, who have long been known as specialists in francophone literatures. Critics such as Irène D'Almeida have stressed the need, in attempting to explain the nature and purpose of African feminism and women's writing, to discuss both francophone and anglophone authors from both sides of the Atlantic.

Perhaps the most significant sign of increasing communication between English and French-language African authors is the growing interest in the problem of the translation of African texts. Translation is seen as an exploration of the linguistic problems African authors face in dealing with their specific cultural situations.

More and more frequently, African texts reflect common concerns: *Sembene Ousmane's cinema in Wolof, *Ngugi wa Thiong'o's decision to write in *Gikuyu, Ahmadou Kourouma's trans-linguistic play in *Monnè, Outrages et Défis* (1990; *Monnew*, 1993), and

Chinua Achebe's self-reflexive, re-thinking intertextuality in *Anthills of the Savannah* (1987) are examples of the recent tendency of African literatures in French and English to move towards an originally African post-modern consciousness of language and history.

From a Crooked Rib (1970) A novel by Nuruddin *Farah. The title is from a Somali proverb: 'God created woman from a crooked rib; and anyone who trieth to straighten it, breakest it.' The novel describes the truth of the proverb in the life of Ebla, a Somali woman unlike the generality of Somali women, who are obedient to their subservient roles in traditional Somali society. Ebla sets off on a peripatetic life of self-discovery, moving from place to place, her personal integrity tested again and again as she encounters the Somali world beyond the narrow confines of her traditional home. On the journey she discovers not only a crass and corrupt world filled with greed, treachery, and betrayal but also her ability to maintain her personal integrity and a measure of the innocence that prompted her quest. She is not destroyed by the harsh world and experiences she encounters; rather she is strengthened by the education she receives through her experiences.

FUGARD, Athol (1932-), South African dramatist, was born in Middelburg, the son of an English-speaking father and an Afrikaans-speaking mother. After attending school in Port Elizabeth, he began but did not complete a BA course at the University of Cape Town. His position as South Africa's most prominent playwright owes a great deal to his ability to turn apparently regional and local themes into more universal metaphors for his deeply felt liberal concern with humanity and his existential struggle to understand his own life. Making use of a simple and direct form of neo-realism within a 'poor theatre' framework, he combines an actor's sensitivity for dialogue with a designer's eye for the powerful visual images generated during live performance, and he uses these qualities to explore relationships between two or three exquisitely drawn individuals.

In the first few years of his creative life Fugard held a variety of short-term jobs, among others as merchant seaman, writer for the South African Broadcasting Corporation, clerk in the native commissioner's court in Johannesburg, stage manager for the National Theatre Organization, freelance actor-director in Belgium under Tone Brulin, and finally as director of The Rehearsal Room, a performance space at Dorkay House in 1961. In 1964 Fugard settled in Port Elizabeth to become a full-time professional playwright. Since then, except for periodic stints as resident playwright and director at various places in the world, including a very creative period with the Yale Repertory Company, Fugard has remained and continued to work in his 'region', namely Eastern Cape province. In the mid-1980s he bought a house in the hamlet of Nieu Bethesda (the setting of *Road to Mecca*, 1984).

Fugard has been extremely influential in South Africa and in world theatre. There are primarily two reasons for this. First there is his political profile as an opponent of ★apartheid, one he shares with such individuals as Nadine ★Gordimer, André ★Brink and E'skia ★Mphahlele. Both his plays and his life experiences with the government and its agencies made him an important and very eloquent witness to the atrocities of racism and bigotry in the country. However, his prominence in this regard for a long time tended to obscure his other qualities as theatrical craftsman. In the 1990s, as political changes made apartheid an issue secondary to more pressing social and cultural needs, observers have increasingly recognized Fugard's role as a technical and thematic innovator in South African, and indeed world, theatre.

Fugard's career naturally falls into a number of identifiable periods distinguished by differing working methods and thematic concerns. Following some early experiments in Cape Town, his first prominent plays were short essays in realism, written for and performed by Fugard and friends in the black townships around Johannesburg and inevitably dealing with life in those areas. ★*No-Good Friday* (1977) and *Nongogo* (1977) are somewhat exploratory works, dealing with incidents in the life of a shebeen keeper and a whore respectively. The first major work was The ★*Blood Knot* (1963), dealing with two brothers, one black, the other mixed race, and their dreams. It is the quintessential Fugard play: a two-hander, set in a single room and exploring the love-hate relationship between two individuals bound together by something more than mere circumstance, with one other (often off-stage) character as catalyst for the tragic action. It is a pattern he was to follow with minor variations in virtually all the plays over the years, including such prominent works as ★*Hello and Goodbye* (1966), ★*Boesman and Lena* (1969), *The Island* (1974), *Statements after an Arrest under the Morality Act* (1974), *A Place with the Pigs* (1988), *The Road to Mecca*, and *Playland* (both 1994).

In the next phase Fugard returned to his home region of Port Elizabeth with what are possibly some of his most accomplished and enduring works. *Hello and Goodbye* and *People Are Living There* (1969) deal with the angst of the white urban dweller, while the superb *Boesman and Lena* deals with the world of two disenfranchised 'coloureds'. It is a realistic play set in a barren but identifiable landscape, where it explores the notion of freedom through the struggle of the two itinerants to understand themselves, their relationship with each other, and the world about them. It is a play that inevitably echoes some of the great works of this century (most notably *Waiting for Godot*), but that

remains unique by virtue of its close characterization and its geographical context.

At the beginning of the 1970s Fugard discovered Grotowsky and began working through improvisation. The result was a series of highly political workshop productions, including *Orestes* (1978), *Statements after an Arrest under the Morality Act*, *The Island*, and ★*Sizwe Bansi Is Dead* (published together in *Statements*, 1974). The latter two works in particular, co-authored with John Kani and Winston Ntshona, did much to consolidate his fame as political writer.

In 1975 Fugard reverted to scripted plays with the allegorical *Dimetos* (1977), followed by two personal views of apartheid society in *A Lesson from Aloes* (1981) and the compelling and highly autobiographical *'Master Harold'...and the Boys* (1982). His concern with personal freedom and the role of the artist inform *The Road to Mecca*, a superbly textured piece of work based on a true story. This was followed by *A Place with the Pigs*, and in 1989 he returned to the political arena and in a sense to improvisational work with *My Children! My Africa!* (1990), *Playland*, and the largely workshopped *My Life* (performed 1994). The latter four plays have tended to disappoint his followers, for they seem to display something of Fugard's own growing uncertainties about his place in the new society and the theatre of post-apartheid South Africa.

Besides filmed versions of many of the plays, Fugard has also written a number of film scripts, including *The Guest* (1977) and *Marigolds in August* (1982), both filmed by Ross Devenish. A novel, *Tsotsi*, appeared in 1980 and an autobiographical work, *My Cousin*, in 1995. He has received numerous awards over the years, including the Commonwealth Theatre Award and honourary doctorates from Rhodes University, Yale University, Georgetown University, the University of Cape Town and the University of the Witwatersrand.

FUGARD, Sheila Meiring (1932-), South African novelist and poet born in Birmingham, England, was eight when her parents moved to South Africa. She studied theatre at the University of Cape Town, where she began writing short stories, and is married to playwright Athol ★Fugard.

Fugard's first novel, *The Castaways* (1972), won the Olive Schreiner Prize in 1972. The second, *Rite of Passage* (1976) treats race relations in history. A similar intention, 'to see history afresh', inspired her book of poems *Threshold* (1975). Her second collection of poetry, *Mystic Things* (1981), emphasizes her continuing interest in fantasy and the mysterious. Her third novel, *A Revolutionary Woman* (1983), is set in the Karoo district of South Africa in 1920 and was inspired by her experience in India in 1981 and by what she learned about Indian history and belief.

G

GARUBA, Harry (1958-), Nigerian poet. The son of a school inspector regularly posted around south-western Nigeria, Garuba had a nomadic childhood that exposed him to many languages and ethnic groups and fostered in him a cosmopolitan world view. He went on to attend the University of Ibadan, where he gained his BA, MA, and Ph.D. and where he is a lecturer. He has published a one-act play (*Pantomime for Saint Apartheid's Day* in *Festac Anthology of Nigerian New Writing*, 1977) and edited *Voices from the Fringe: An ANA Anthology of New Nigerian Poetry* (1988), but he is best known as a poet with a disposition for the tender and the philosophical. His *Shadow and Dream and Other Poems* (1982) is marked by an alluring lyricism and an introspective depth, a combination that is uncommon in the usually declamatory poetry of many young African poets. The collection coheres around the metaphor of scars: scars as markers of both historical and contemporary struggles, especially the struggle to span the abyss that separates the dream of the song from its realization. One of Garuba's strengths as a poet is his ability to translate events – the experience of colonialism, civil war, student activism – into metaphors that are at once specific to their impetus and general enough to be ideational. Although he has published only one collection, because of its high quality he continues to be regarded as one of the most outstanding Nigerian poets writing in English.

GASHE, Marina, pseud. for Rebeka *Njau.

GAY AND LESBIAN SEXUALITY IN LITERATURE
There are close to a hundred literary texts by black African authors that include some reference to gay and/or lesbian sexuality. In some cases treatment is cursory, generally with gay/lesbian behaviour employed as subject matter to consolidate a text's thematic development, in, for example, a critique of colonialist brutalities. In other cases, such as Ama Ata *Aidoo's *Our Sister Killjoy* (1977), Rebeka *Njau's *Ripple in the Pool* (1975), or Thomas Mpoyi-Buatu's *La Réproduction* (1986), treatment of gay/lesbian sexual relations is more extended and plays a more dynamic function in relation to the text's thematic development. In a considerable majority of cases gay/lesbian behaviour is stigmatized as an essentially un-African perversion that is seen to emerge generally in situations of coercion and exploitation. Only in rare cases does a straightforward presentation of a gay/lesbian relationship emerge, detailed more or less sympathetically. One example here is D.N. Malinwa's short story 'Everything under the Sun', an account of the friendship between two manual workers, one of them gay. Published in 1969 in the anthology *Africa in Prose* (1969), the story drew the following comment from its editors, O. R. Dathorne and Willfried Feuser: 'what we liked about it was the simplicity, the absence of condemnation, the regard for the relationship on its own terms'.

However, with gay/lesbian behaviour more generally harshly stigmatized, there emerges a clear dominant ideology of the text, which very few African authors have challenged. Condemnation of gay/lesbian sexuality is reflected in the legislation of many African states (the African National Congress's Bill of Rights marks a notable exception to the general trend), in the speeches of politicians and heads of state, and in the press. One comment in the Lagos *Monthly Life* (4-5, May 1987) exemplifies hundreds of others: 'homosexuality is still largely a Euro-American perversion which has not yet had any foothold in Africa'. This view has been contested in, for example, an anonymous letter in *Transition* (17, 1964) that claims, somewhat quaintly, 'a tolerance in traditional ethic to the ways of men'. But official discourse overwhelmingly identifies gay/lesbian sexuality as an alien import, a view sustained in the majority of African literary texts that touch upon the subject.

To document the frequency of gay/lesbian behaviour in African societies and a widespread actual tolerance of it, albeit often a covert tolerance not willingly articulated, is not an especially difficult task, assuming the co-operation of reliable and articulate witnesses. Yet one major caveat must be entered here, and it is a crucial reference point for analysis of the treatment of the subject in literary texts: it is that Western modes of naming and of self-representation do not necessarily correlate closely to African modes. The recognition of incidents of gay/lesbian behaviour would not necessarily imply an acknowledgement of gay/lesbian orientation: the latter as a mode of self-representation may well seem eccentric or incomplete in many African contexts. Reference, therefore, to the absence of non-condemnatory treatment of gay/lesbian sexuality from discourse may have naively overlooked questions of naming, framing, and conceptualization in the situation of the African literary text.

The difference in modes of self-representation provides a partial explanation of the differences in kind that exist between the texts categorized above and treatments of gay/lesbian sexuality by white South African writers. South Africa is unique on the continent in having had, for years, a more or less open gay/lesbian scene – bars, support groups, campaign groups, and a gay/lesbian press. Germane to the discussion here is the fragmentation that nonetheless exists between white and black gay/lesbian communities, a matter documented by Mark Gevisser and Edwin Cameron in *Defiant Desire* (1994). In this context of relative openness, the highly respected and progressive Congress of South African Writers (COSAW) has sponsored an anthology of gay/lesbian writing, *The Invisible Ghetto* (1993). The work published here is by writers who would represent themselves as being gay or lesbian or bisexual, a self-identification very rare indeed among black African writers, at least outside South Africa. Whatever the problems of representation their own work poses, and they are discussed by Shaun de Waal in *Defiant Desire*, texts by Damon Galgut, Koos Prinsloo, Stephen ★Gray, and others establish a discourse on gay/lesbian sexuality very different from that offered elsewhere, a fact that might provide fuel to feed the crude assertion that gay/lesbian sexuality is a white thing.

The following is a brief resumé of references in texts by black African authors that stigmatize gay/lesbian behaviour as being alien to Africa, or exploitative, and usually both. Attempts by European gays or lesbians to seduce unwilling Africans are detailed by Kole ★Omotoso in *The Edifice* (1971), where the victim is a schoolboy, the aggressor a white schoolmaster, and by Kofi ★Awoonor in *This Earth, My Brother* (1971), where the houseboy, Yaro, leaves his white master 'because he wanted to turn him into a woman'. A successful seduction is predicated on the African victim's material poverty in Williams ★Sassine's *Wirriyamu* (1976) and in Jean-Clément Aoué-Tchany's *Du Folklore en enfer* (1990), in which an African woman accepts the advances of a Dutch woman in order to achieve material advance. In Wole ★Soyinka's *The ★Interpreters* (1965) the black American, Joe Golder, is characterized as a predatory homosexual whose rejected advances lead to the death of young Noah; while Soyinka's characterization is pejorative, he does explore Golder's social psychology in detail within the context of the novel's wider thematic development. Where gay/lesbian relationships are developed voluntarily, and not necessarily between Africans and whites, they are generally a mark of societal degeneration, often in the context of a critique of corrupt and totalitarian government, as in Mongo ★Beti's *Remember Ruben* (1974), ★Sony Labou Tansi's *L'État honteux* (1981), and Bernard Nanga's *Les Chauves-souris* (1980), in which the dictator Ahmadou Ahidjo's ruling party is caricatured as PDPUR (out-and-out pederast). In Soyinka's novel *★Season of Anomy* (1973), set during the ★Nigeria-Biafra war, pederasty is depicted

as a vice of the northern emirate courts, and thus externalized, through identification with a reactionary politics inimical to the healthy development of a just African society. To redress the balance, it is worth noting that Hausa poets such as Mu'azu Hadeja and Sa'ad ★Zungur attack homosexuality as a debilitating vice that weakens the (unstated: hegemonic) social and political cohesiveness of northern Nigeria. A deepening of the sense of gay/lesbian behaviour as unnatural occurs with the frequent depiction of it as a vice imposed on victims in the close confines of the prison, which in the South African situation, under ★apartheid, is itself identified as abnormal: in Gibson ★Kente's play *Too Late* (1974), in James ★Matthews's story 'A Case of Guilt' (1983), in a novel such as D.M. Zwelonke's *Robben Island* (1973).

Other texts offer a less pejorative treatment of gay/lesbian sexuality, even one that may be overtly sympathetic. In most of these cases, however, gay/lesbian sexuality can hardly be said to be adapted as a subject matter in its own right: rather there is a more or less strong binding of the subject to the text's wider thematic concerns, a function that requires the subject to be in some sense foregrounded or specialized. In, for example, Yulisa A. ★Maddy's novel *No Past, No Present, No Future* (1973) the character Joe is depicted as a more successful and admirable social personality than are his friends, despite his homosexuality. Yet Maddy's characterization here, as with Yambo Ouologuem's depiction of a homosexual relationship in *Le Devoir de violence* (1968; *Bound to Violence*, 1971), is actually dependent on the stereotype, in the sense that to characterize Joe as both homosexual and morally admirable is only fully effective thematically in a context in which that pairing of qualities is seen as absurd.

Calixthe ★Beyala, a writer described as having broadly a 'lesbian approach', writes sympathetically of her heroine's lesbian yearnings in *C'est le soleil qui m'a brulée* (1987); yet Ateba's need for tenderness and love in a corrupt and brutal society suggests these yearnings are no more than a mental escape, imperfect, sympathetic *faute de mieux*. Something of the same is true of *Ripples in the Pool*, in which Rebeka Njau characterizes Selina as both deranged and dangerous to others and yet meriting compassion as victim of a neo-colonial state in which the community has become venal, self-poisoning. Njau's treatment of Selina's seduction of the younger woman, Gaciru, reflects this tension: the loving care with which Gaciru responds to Selina is perverse and yet admirable. The structuring of this text renders it unusually transparent in its deployment of the lesbian relationship in the interests of the novel's commanding theme. A more wholly unpejorative treatment of lesbian sexuality is given in Aidoo's *Our Sister Killjoy*, in which Sissie, black and heterosexual, is able to respond sympathetically to the German lesbian Marija, and to perceive common ground between her own and Marija's respective social isolation. Once again, however, the thematic effectiveness of Aidoo's treatment of this relationship is predicated on the marking of Marija's nature as 'other', and a refusal to stigmatize this must register as paradox.

GBADAMOSI, Gabriel [See AFRICAN-BRITISH LITERATURE]

GHANEM, Fathy (1924-) Egyptian novelist, worked as a journalist and became editor of the Cairo newspaper *Sabah al-Khair*. His first novel, *The Mountain* (n.d.), satirizes a well-meant attempt to resettle Luxor peasants; in his later novels the background, as in *The *Man Who Lost his Shadow* (1966), is frequently the 'jungle world', as he describes the Cairo press and its Byzantine intrigues and obsessions. These two novels were translated into English by Desmond Stewart.

GIBBON, Perceval (1878-1926), novelist and short-story writer, was born at Trelech, Wales and educated at Old Mill School (London) and the Moravian School (Königsfeld, Germany). After two years' service in the merchant navy, he arrived in South Africa as a journalist shortly before the *Anglo-Boer war (1899-1902) and worked as a war correspondent for a syndicate of colonial papers; he then worked for the *Natal Witness*, the *Rand Daily Mail*, and the *Rhodesian Times*. In the decade before the First World War he travelled widely as a correspondent journalist while extending his reputation as short-story writer, novelist, and linguist. A war correspondent at most of the Allied fronts and later a major in the Royal Marines during the war, he was commissioned to write dispatches and an official documentary, *The Triumph of the Royal Navy* (1919). He retired to Guernsey, where he died unexpectedly when at the peak of his literary powers.

Gibbon's African writing embodies the partial acclimatization to Africa of a sensitive Briton steeped in the European tradition. *African Items* (1903), a volume of verse, has considerable literary historical value. *The Vrouw Grobelaar's Leading Cases* (1905) foreshadows H.C. *Bosman's Oom Schalk Lourens tales. *Souls in Bondage* (1904), dealing with problems of miscegenation, and *Salvator* (1908), about political intrigue in Mozambique, are less successful than his third novel, *Margaret Harding* (1911), whose concern with human relationships on a colonial farm and at a nearby TB sanatorium in the Karoo region of South Africa make it a unique successor to Olive *Schreiner's *The *Story of an African Farm* (1883). Some of the robust stories in *The Adventures of Miss Gregory* (1912) and *The Second-Class Passenger* (1913) have African settings; those of *Those Who Smiled* (1920) and *The Dark Places* (1926) are wholly Eurocentric.

Renewed interest in Gibbon as war correspon-

dent, feminist, and significant post-colonial author no doubt inspired such projects as John Smallcombe's film *An African Dream* (1988), clearly derived from *Margaret Harding* (re-issued in 1983), Janice Honeyman's stage adaptation *The Story of Margaret Harding* (1991), and Brian O'Shaughnessy's radio serial *Margaret Harding* (1996).

GIKUYU LITERATURE Gikuyu is the language of the Aagikuyu people of Kenya (called 'Kikuyu' in the colonial literature). The possible origins of the recent renaissance of Gikuyu-language literature include the protracted debate regarding the question of what languages African literatures should be written in – European, African, or both? – as well as the decolonizing impulse that led to Kenya's nominal independence and that continues to struggle for it. *Ngugi wa Thiong'o has been an inspiring force in more recent Gikuyu literature, as has the Kamiriithu Community Education and Cultural Centre (Limuru).

In the years following his flight from sure persecution by the Moi regime, Ngugi has been instrumental in the inauguration of the first-ever enduring Gikuyu-language journal, *Mutiiri: Njaranda ya Miikarire* [Keystone: a journal of cultural expression], three issues of which came out in 1994, the year it was established, from Ngugi's academic base in the USA. So far the journal has published poetry, short fiction, translations (*Swahili-Gikuyu, Spanish-Gikuyu), literary and cultural criticism, excerpts from prison memoirs, biography and autobiography, political commentary, and philosophical reflection by some of the best and most promising contemporary Gikuyu writers and translators: Gitahi wa Gititi, Cege wa Githiora, Kimani wa Njogu, Ngugi wa Mirii, Ngugi wa Thiong'o, Waithira wa Mbuthia, Maina wa Kinyatti, Gicingiri wa Ndigirigi, K. K. Gtiiri, Ngina wa Kiarii, Alice Wambui wa Githiora, Wairimu wa Ngugi, Wairimu wa Mirii, and Ndungi wa Mungai. *Mutiiri* has also taken up the task of generating and expanding political, technical/scientific, literary, and academic vocabularies to accommodate and integrate knowledge in the various fields of Kenyan and world cultures. The journal has, for example, published a series of articles in Gikuyu by Githogori on computer technology and the first part of a bibliography of Gikuyu-language writing between 1900 and the present by Ann Biersteker, a Yale professor of African languages.

Before 1900, Kiswahili was perhaps the only Kenyan language with a written tradition. Until the advent of the written alphabet and books, oral literature, or *orature, constituted not only the storehouse of philosophy, religious and cultural values, history, and memory, it also embodied the rhetorical means of anti-colonial resistance (politically charged symbolic stories, oral poetry, drama, songs, chants, slogans) deployed against the forces of colonialism seeking to destroy or weaken the cultures, languages, histories, and educational and religious institutions that formed the basis of self-perception for the colonized. The crucial importance of orature as the wellspring of literary, political, philosophical, cultural, and religious discourses and practices in past and contemporary Kenya, in indigenous languages or otherwise, has been well documented. Not surprisingly, when writing in Gikuyu begins, its inspiration is the oral tradition and its objective the recording and validation of that which is threatened by colonial onslaught as well as the attrition of time. Accordingly, straightforward short fiction, origin stories, legends, proverbs, poems, songs, riddles, folktales, novellas, general historical and anthropological accounts, primers, and dictionaries comprise the bulk of Gikuyu literature to date. Texts originally composed in Gikuyu by Gikuyu speakers range from Stanley Kiama Gathigira's 1933 account of the culture of the Aagikuyu, Miikarire ya Agikuyu [sic], published by the Church of Scotland Mission press at Tumutumu, to B. Mareka Gecaga's 1946 Kariuki na Muthoni [Home life in Kikuyu land], to the plays and novels of Ngugi wa Thiong'o in the 1980s.

Thanks to the practice of colonial and neocolonial appropriation of the cultural production of 'others', Gikuyu-language texts (not translations) abound whose authorship has persistently been attributed to European missionaries, administrators, and scholars, but whose real authors are Aagikuyu. The apparently disjointed and fragmentary nature of the content of such derivative texts, which western critics have repeatedly cited as evidence of the lack of a literary or aesthetic consciousness among so-called third-world cultures, is a product of the various forms of the scramble for Africa, which include the ferocious contests over the architecture and ownership of cultural goods. Chief among the appropriated Gikuyu texts is the most extended written version of the indigenous Gikuyu poetic tradition called gicaandi. Published as Ndai na Gicandi (Enigmi Kikuyu, 1973) under Vittorio Merlo Pick's name, its author-composer was John Kahora, who had received his formal schooling at the Catholic Mission in Limuru and his more abiding education from his own father, a competent gicaandi poet and muundu-mugo [medicine man]. Others texts include Ng'ano Ikumi na Ithano cia Gikuyu [Fifteen Gikuyu folktales] (1957), attributed to Wesley Sadler; Muthomere wa Gikuyu: Ng'ano [Gikuyu reader: stories], first published in 1943 under Robert MacPherson's name but deriving its material from Church of Scotland and Africa Inland Mission Kikuyu readers, and G. Barra's 1000 Kikuyu Proverbs (1939, bilingual), culled from subscriptions sent in by Gikuyu readers of the Consolata Catholic (Nyeri) Mission's monthly magazine, Wathiomo Mukinyu (established ca.1921).

Two of the most prolific literary figures currently writing in Gikuyu, Gakaara wa Wanjau and Ngugi wa

Thiong'o, are separated, as practitioners in the language, by at least thirty years. Ngugi wa Thiong'o is regarded in some quarters as the writer who brought Gikuyu-language literature to the attention of the rest of Kenya and the world with the 1977 open-air performances at Kamiriithu, Limuru, of the play Ngaahika Ndeenda (1980; I Will Marry When I Want, 1982; co-authored with Ngugi wa Mirii), and later with the publication of Caitaani Mutharaba-ini (1980; Devil on the Cross, 1982), and Matigari ma Njiruungi (1987; Matigari, 1989). However, Gakaara wa Wanjau had been publishing novellas and serialized stories since at least 1951, the year Ngwenda Unjurage was printed. Through Gakaara Book Service in Nairobi, he published and distributed in 1952 alone Ihu ni Riau?, Marebeta Ikumi ma Wendo, Muraata wa Mwene, and O Kirima Ngagua. After his imprisonment by colonial authorities (1952–62) for his alleged subversive activities in the Mau Mau movement, Gakaara resumed publishing both in Nairobi and at his Gakaara Press in Karatina, creating a number of *popular literature series both similar to and different from those characteristic of the *Onitsha market literature of Nigeria. Between approximately 1976 and 1985, his Gikuyu-language vehicle was Gikuyu na Mumbi, a magazine whose varied episodes narrated the exploits of a picaresque middle-aged man named Wa Nduuta who is constantly attracted by get-rich-quick schemes, illicit sexual liaisons, and spurious land deals, but whose now peasant, now working-class, now petty-bourgeois posturings lead him to act sometimes heroically, sometimes ignobly. In Wa Nduuta Hingo ya Paawa [Wa Nduuta in the days following the coup], Gakaara reflects seriously on the reasons for the nearly successful coup and the political repression that preceded and followed the events of 1982.

Gakaara's publication of his prison memoirs, Mwandiki wa Mau Mau Ithaamirio-ini (1983; Mau Mau Writer in Detention, 1986), along with his commitment to the development of the Gikuyu language (vocabulary, grammar, orthography, instructional materials) for use in schools and for cultural expression, business, agriculture, and the discussion of family and societal issues earned him the Noma Prize in 1984. As a native of the Central Province in Kenya, which formed part of the so-called White Highlands and where land theft, forced labour, and large-scale removals were rampant, Gakaara was increasingly drawn towards the expression of a nationalist sentiment in song collections of overtly political resistance, an account of the emergence of the Kenya Land and Freedom Army, and a call to combat colonialism without fear. Examples include Nyimbo cia Gikuyu na Mumbi (1952), Nyimbo cia Gukunguira Wiathi (1963), Agikuyu, Mau Mau na Wiathi, Parts I and II (1971), and Nyimbo cia Mau Mau (1989). In 1951-2, just before the declaration of a state of emergency by the British colonial government, Gakaara had already published *Mageria Noomo Mahota* [Without struggle success is impossible], translated from its previous title in Swahili, *Roho ya Kiume na Bidii kwa Mwafrika* (1948). The latter had been widely distributed in neighbouring Tanganyika, where it had struck a responsive chord.

Gakaara's concern to save elements of Gikuyu culture (riddles, aphorisms, songs, dances, customs, and social mores) coincides with his efforts to save the Gikuyu language itself from oblivion. Representative of this concern is the publication of, among many others, *Mihiriga ya Agikuyu* [Gikuyu clans] (1967, the revised and enlarged version of *Wikumie na Muhiriga Waku*, 1961); *Turwimbo na Tumathako twa Twana* [Songs and games for children] (1968); *Nyimbo cia Ihii* [Gikuyu youth dances] (1971); *Thooma Giigikuyu Kiega*, Series 1 and 2 [Teach yourself proper Gikuyu] (1980 and 1986, rev. 1988); and *Mwandikire wa Gikuyu Karing'a* [Authentic Gikuyu grammar and orthography] (1991); all have been well received by teachers, parents, and education officials for their creativity and relevance to learners' social environments. Related to this endeavour is *Ugwati wa Muthungu Muiru* [The danger posed by 'black Europeans'] (n. d.), Gakaara's critique of the colonial mentality among the Kenyan middle class.

Gakaara's commitment to keep the Gikuyu language a vibrant and dynamic means for the expression of contemporary life is echoed in Ngugi wa Thiong'o's publication, in the 1980s, of three children's stories in a series called *Adventures of Njamba Nene: Njamba Nene na Mbaathi i Mathagu* (*Njamba Nene and the Winged Bus*, 1982); *Bathitoora ya Njamba Nene* (*Njamba Nene's Pistol*, 1984), and *Njamba Nene na Cibu King'angi* (*Njamba Nene and the Cruel Colonial Chief*, 1986). All three stories focus on issues of social class; the content, meaning, and approaches to public education; and the relevance (or irrelevance) of language as a carrier of culture and useful knowledge.

The inter-relatedness of the literary and the journalistic is an important feature of Gikuyu letters. For example, African newspapers in colonial Kenya were almost entirely published in indigenous languages such as Gikuyu and Swahili and were banned in the period 1945-52. Two examples of Gikuyu newspapers of the early period include *Muiguithania* [The reconciler], sometimes edited by Jomo Kenyatta and appearing intermittently between 1920 and 1930, finally banned around 1939; and the monthly *Mumenyereri* [The caretaker], established in 1945, published and edited by Henry Muoria, which would eventually become the rhetorical vehicle of Gikuyu patriotism. The persistent political content (as well as the language) of earlier and contemporary Gikuyu literature is in many ways informed and undergirded by the pragmatic strategic use of the tools at hand; censored content or message simply found its expression in any and every accessible

text. Indeed, in the volatile and chaotic political climate in Kenya of the last twenty years, Gikuyu literary and social expression, like its counterparts, subsists mostly in disguise and in secret: in short-lived but stubborn magazines, pamphlets, mimeographs, plays and skits, cassette recordings of song lyrics encoded with political innuendo. All are part of the topos of Gikuyu literary production in the 1990s.

A logical by-product of continued political repression is the resurgence of prison memoirs. While most of these have so far been written and published in English, recent developments suggest that this genre now demands to be heard in native languages. Sections of Maina wa Kinyatti's prison memoirs have already been serialized in *Mutiiri*. Exile in its various forms continues to be both a theme and, in some cases, a somewhat more enabling space for literary creation than the unnerving climate of a police state. Writing from exile, Gitahi wa Gititi has recently demonstrated a remarkable technical and linguistic competence that places him among the most accomplished writers in Gikuyu. His poetry, short fiction, translation work, and political and cultural commentary combine a keen appreciation of traditional Gikuyu oral repertoire as well as a narrative style whose tone, tenor, symbolism, and eye for detail reflect both his profound respect for his 'mother's language' and his polyglot background.

Girl Who Killed to Save: Nongquase the Liberator, The (1936)
A play by H.I.E. *Dhlomo. The influence of missionaries on early African writers emerges from this dramatization of the great cattle killing of 1857, a traumatic event that represents the collapse of Xhosa resistance to colonial rule. Dhlomo's play emphasizes Nongquase's innocence, making her the victim of the villainous witchdoctor, Mhlakaza, and the chief, Sarile. Nongquase's great victory, in Dhlomo's eyes, was that she had cast off the chains of tribalism and embraced Christianity. As such, she is presented as a symbol of national pride for Africans in the twentieth century.

God's Step-Children (1924)
A novel by Sarah Gertrude *Millin. The first of Millin's 'trilogy of the Coloured Race' (the others are *King of the Bastards*, 1949 and *The Burning Man*, 1952) explores the theme of miscegenation, following the descendants of the Reverend Andrew Flood, a missionary, and his Khoikhoi wife. After four generations, the descendants are a people set apart, aware of belonging neither to the white settlers nor to any of the indigenous groups, and they curse their ancestor. Millin's attitude to her characters in this novel and elsewhere is ambivalent and complex. While she considered that being 'coloured' (mixed race) was a form of affliction, something approaching insanity, and while she clearly considered such people to be vastly inferior to 'purely

white' people, *God's Step-Children* suggests compassion for such disadvantaged groups. The heaviest blame falls on Andrew Flood, the ancestor who so thoughtlessly set the tragedy in motion. The novel's descriptions of landscape and people, its characterization, pace, tension, and use of imagery are all very good – Millin was without doubt a writer of talent. The pity is that she could not see beyond South Africa's simplistic social Darwinism.

God's Bits of Wood (1962) A novel by *Sembene Ousmane, translated from the French (*Les Bouts de bois de Dieu*, 1960). One of the greatest francophone African novels, this tells the story of the actual 1947-8 workers' strike along the French African railway from Dakar, Senegal to Bamako, Mali. Occurring in three widely spaced cities (Dakar, Thiès, and Bamako) as well as villages along the way, the novel follows the lives of a broad range of characters over the course of ten months. Many hardships are endured, and many are overcome. Workers, intellectuals, old men, young hotheads, strikebreakers, fallen women, honourable mothers, and more abound. French administrators and 'sellout' African religious and economic leaders are negatively portrayed. A dramatic 'women's march' from Thiès to Dakar is a highlight, as is the unscrupulous resistance of the French powers. The new African dependence on Western technology is richly explored, and, despite the substantial violence portrayed, the novel ends on a positive note, as the strike is settled. Stylistically, the book resembles great French naturalist/realist novels of the late nineteenth century such as those by Zola, and it is unusual among African novels of its era for its length and very large social scope. Almost all critics have praised the novel, noting its strong plot, overall coherence, progressive politics, and historical depth. The novel's fully drawn women characters have received particular attention.

Gods Are Not to Blame, The (1971) A play by Ola *Rotimi. A reconceptualization of Sophocles' *Oedipus* and an early example of many successful Nigerian adaptations of earlier plays, from Greek tragedy to medieval theatre to Brecht, Rotimi's best-known play is set in a Yoruba royal court in the pre-colonial period. The play transforms Oedipus into a king who condemns himself as unfit to rule through his own serious weaknesses of character: impatience, stubbornness, and ethnic distrust. The play has been criticized, especially within Nigeria, for the doubtful relevance of the Greek source to Yoruba political, social, and ideological realities, and for the viability of Rotimi's attempts to simulate a Yoruba-ized variety of formal English. Rotimi is, however, a master of stagecraft and in performance the play is undisputably gripping. It is part of a trilogy that includes *Kurunmi* (1969) and *Ovonrameme Nogbaise* (1971).

Going Down River Road (1976) A novel by Meja *Mwangi. All the characters in this novel of emergent post-colonial Kenyan society belong to the class of urban workers. Mwangi sets out to portray their life by focusing on a single well-defined episode that occurs among them. The action takes place on the site of a construction project that has offered temporary employment to several scores of hands. The degrading, exploitative conditions of labour and the defeatist attitude of the toiling crowd towards them create a sense of despondency, muted only by occasional flickers of defiance and fellow-feeling.

GORDIMER, Nadine (1923-), South African novelist and short-story writer, was born near Johannesburg, the daughter of Jewish immigrants to South Africa. Her formal education at a Catholic convent school was interrupted when she was kept at home for her health the year she was eleven. From then until she was sixteen she had a private tutor and was isolated from people her own age. She attended the University of the Witwatersrand for a year in 1945. Her education as a writer was the intense reading she did as a child and young woman and her growing consciousness of the society in which she grew up, which adopted formal *apartheid in 1948. Gordimer's early identification with England and English writers is evident in her choice of novel form, but her sense of placement became much more complex after she began to realize what her society meant. What has been very clear is that her growth as a South African and a woman has gone hand in hand with her commitment to being a writer.

Gordimer has published twelve volumes of short stories, beginning with *Face to Face* (1949) and including two books of selected stories, *Selected Stories* (1975) and *Why Haven't You Written: Selected Stories 1950-72* (1992); twelve novels, including *The Lying Days* (1953), *A World of Strangers* (1958), *Occasion for Loving* (1963), *The Late Bourgeois World* (1966), *A *Guest of Honour* (1971), *The *Conservationist*, *Burger's Daughter* (1979), *July's People* (1981), *A *Sport of Nature* (1987), *My Son's Story* (1990), *None to Accompany Me* (1994) and *The *House Gun* (1998); numerous essays on literature and politics, some of which are collected in *The Black Interpreters* (1973); *What Happened to Burger's Daughter; or, How South African Censorship Works* (1980); and *The Essential Gesture: Writing, Politics and Places* (1988). She has also collaborated with Lionel *Abrahams to produce *South African Writing Today* (1967) and with the photographer David Goldblatt for *On the Mines* (1973) and *Lifetimes: Under Apartheid* (1986). This immense body of work spans the period of apartheid from beginning to end. Though she has many times expressed her knowledge that the white South African writer is extremely handicapped by the limitations of class and race in this period of South

African history, she has become known internationally for her consistent attacks on the implications of apartheid. In 1991 she won the Nobel Prize for literature, becoming the third African writer to do so after Nigerian Wole *Soyinka and Egyptian Naguib *Mahfouz.

Gordimer has been controversial throughout her career, whether for the rulers of South Africa or for those who have found her significance difficult to accept, given that she is a white middle-class African able to write full-time and in security while so many black South African writers had to flee the country or were silenced. Her work has at times been banned in South Africa. She herself is fully aware of the contradictions of her situation, although on occasion her political sympathy for the black community has outweighed her artistic empathy with the forms chosen by black African writers. In *The Black Interpreters*, she expresses strong reservations about the work of Flora *Nwapa, for example, mainly because Nwapa does not write in the European tradition of the novel: Gordimer observes that Nwapa could not plot a novel or deal with theme but fails to see that Nwapa's *Efuru* (1966) is very effective when read in the context of African oral traditions and the mythology of the watermaid in Igbo culture. Whatever might finally be judged to be Gordimer's weaknesses, however, her determination to examine the nature of white identity in the South African context has contributed to the realization in the white world of the nature of apartheid and of the necessity to oppose and destroy it. And she has been true to the task she set herself: to stay and to write about white South Africa, particularly about the well-intentioned liberals who thought that being a good person was enough to change a constitutional establishment built on fascism. Acknowledging the different fates under apartheid of the white writer and the black writer, and knowing that some white South African writers, such as Breyten *Breytenbach and Jeremy Cronin, were tried and imprisoned, she has never placed herself in the company of those who have suffered imprisonment, torture, exile, and death, nor claimed the slightest sharing of experience with black South Africans. For herself, there was no direct involvement in political action beyond her work. Happily, she has seen her work validated.

Gordimer's fiction has explored her developing ideas on the interconnectedness of personal emotion, physical desire, and political conviction and action. In *The Lying Days* sexual privacy and intimacy are overcast by the Prohibition of Mixed Marriages Act of the early phase of apartheid. This first novel, while charting a very different stage of both South Africa and the female protagonist's white consciousness, has nevertheless important elements in common with her novel of the mid-1990s, *None to Accompany Me*. Sexuality is a powerful current that directs connections between

people, but sexual desire becomes part of a political landscape. Here, the setting is post-apartheid South Africa. Black South Africans become much more central as characters in Gordimer's later fiction, and correspondingly, white characters' anxieties about the implications for society of their personal consciences or their political conviction less important. Vera Stark, the central white female character, has a new dilemma to consider: her daughter makes a lesbian relationship, a solid, middle-class, professional and personal bond in the mould of old-fashioned bourgeois heterosexual marriage but as contemporary as any two-career relationship, and adopts a black child. Gordimer had created an equally politically incorrect career for Hillela in *A Sport of Nature*, who pursues political knowledge through sexual connections and lives her anti-apartheid politics via her personal life. She marries a black freedom fighter and after his assassination becomes the white wife of the General, later President, chair of the OAU, and honoured guest at the celebrations of a newly freed country explicitly a fictionalized South Africa with a black president and first lady. In *My Son's Story*, she tries a mixed-race young male narrative voice, and some reviewers resisted a white writer crossing over racial boundaries to appropriate identity. But Gordimer has always been a voyager in search of more honesty and equality in human relations.

Gordimer's observation of personal detail is often a politically devastating insight: in her use of the short story form, economy often produces extraordinarily complex layerings of significance as personal and political meet. In 'Happy Event', a white couple smile at one another, for example, and in that smile, 'Europe, leisure and the freedom of the money they had saved up were unspoken between them' (1978). Middle-class white life, constructing others out of a desire to feel decent, safe, or in control, is set against the realities of black lives in South Africa. Her importance as a writer has been understood mostly to be in her handling of the novel and story forms as political statement: she has developed an idiosyncratic style, moralistic, clear-sighted, wedded in form to the tradition of Tolstoy and George Eliot.

Grain of Wheat, A (1963) A novel by *Ngugi wa Thiong'o. Set in the days immediately preceding Uhuru celebrations in Kenya, the novel traces the experiences of four characters, Mugo, Gikonyo, Karanja, and Mumbi, in the independence struggle and especially their relationship to Kihiga, a hero of the revolution hanged by the colonial authorities. The political struggle in Kenya is revealed through the inner turmoil it creates in these intelligent, principled, and sensitive characters. The political theme of the novel is balanced by the dramatization of personal relationships that centre on the betrayal of people and ideals. The influence of Joseph Conrad, which Ngugi has acknowledged, is apparent in the novel where the sources of individual guilt are gradually revealed, then followed by expiation of various kinds. The novel ends with a forecast that in the post-independence period Kenyan will be pitted against Kenyan in the quest for political and economic ascendancy, a theme explored in Ngugi's subsequent writing.

Grass is Singing, The (1950) A novel by Doris *Lessing. Set in a British colony in Africa based on Rhodesia, where Lessing grew up, her first novel recounts the failure of a British farming couple in the isolated rural culture and their descent into madness and tragedy involving one of their African servants. By characterizing the initial decency of the husband in comparison to the harshness of the other farmers, Lessing depicts English colonialism as a culture that required a brutal relationship towards Africa and Africans in order to survive. When it went soft and vulnerable, as with Dick and Mary Turner, it self-destructed. *The Grass Is Singing* shows Lessing, even early in her career, able to integrate her political message into the personal lives of her characters.

GRAY, Stephen (1941-), South African critic, anthologist, novelist, and poet. Born in Cape Town, Gray was educated at the universities of Cape Town, Cambridge, and Iowa, and was Professor of English at the Rand Afrikaans University, Johannesburg before taking early retirement in 1992. Notable among his publications are editions of H.C. *Bosman's and Athol *Fugard's work, three Penguin anthologies of South African stories and poems, and four other volumes of South African drama; he has also published eight novels and an extensive output of poetry.

Between 1974 (*It's about Time*) and 1992 (*Season of Violence*) Gray published five volumes of poetry. Many of the poems offer clear, fresh readings of landscape and animal life. A far more troubling subject, however, is the role of the poet in a restricted society, in 'a country of words without dialogue' ('Chamber Music at Mount Grace'). In many of the poems Gray engages in a cruel candour, employing concatenations of images, historical references, and often scabrous punning as he interrogates South Africa's violent history. He identifies continuities of oppression and of resistance in that history (in the title poem and 'In Memoriam: C. Louis Leipoldt' from *Hottentot Venus*, 1979): the rewriting of history, both its recovery and its correction, can be said to be the commanding theme of much of Gray's work. In the title poem of *Apollo Cafe* (1990) he chronicles survival in a city of appalling violence and dazzling plenty (Johannesburg, 'In which I live save my soul'). In the late 1980s an increasingly brutal environment leads Gray to the harsh, breathless, truncated utterances of *Season of Violence*. After a break from poetry and the opportunity to take a retrospec-

tive in the *Selected Poems* (1994), the poems of the mid-1990s show a new range and depth, less scarred by the immediate present.

Among Gray's work for theatre is *Schreiner: A One-Woman Play* (1983), highly successful both in Britain and South Africa. The novels are extremely diverse in form. While an early work such as *Visible People* (1978) is impaired by its fragile and caustic humour, *John Ross: The True Story* (1987) is a revelatory account of relations between a group of British traders and the Zulu emperor Shaka. *War Child* (1991) is an account of a Cape childhood during the Second World War, an elegiac work with disturbing undercurrents. Two novels, *Time of Our Darkness* (1988) and *Born of Man* (1989), deal with homosexual relations; the first is a provocative and often moving account of a love affair between a white schoolmaster and a black schoolboy, which Gray powerfully contextualizes in the political situation of the 1970s, and the second employs scandalous comedy to dissect South African attitudes towards sexuality.

Great Ponds, The (1969) A novel by Elechi *Amadi, the second in his trilogy depicting life in an Ekwerre village before the arrival of the British. It succeeds *The Concubine* and is followed by *The Slave*. It tells the tragic story of the feud between two villages for the disputed ownership of 'great ponds' which are of crucial importance to their individual economic, social and religious security and even survival. It presents, as in all Amadi's writing, a dignified and measured picture of the delicate balances which govern human relationships in a largely oral community. It turns out at the end that Worijo, the plague which is overwhelming the villagers, is the Spanish influenza of 1919 although they have never seen a white man.

Guest of Honour, A (1971), a novel by Nadine *Gordimer. Unlike Gordimer's later novels, *A Guest of Honour* combines a love story with a narrative about the politics of nation-building in a social-realist mode. Bray is a former colonial administrator in the (unnamed) African country at whose independence ceremonies he is a 'guest of honour'. The love affair between Bray and Rebecca, a young white woman born and raised in Africa, is played out as the newly independent state slides into authoritarianism and neo-colonialism. The novel thus raises questions about the personal and the political, the private and the public, that Gordimer would continue to ask in subsequent novels.

Gunny Sack, The (1989) A novel by M.G. *Vassanji and winner of a Commonwealth Writers Prize. In an account of the lives of the Indian community in East Africa, a gunny sack with mementoes of the past is bequeathed by Ji Bai to her great-nephew Salim Juma, who grew up in Dar es Salaam but now lives in

Toronto. As Salim takes a cap, three padlocked books, a bloodstained shirt, etc., from the gunny, he reconstructs through family history and his own growth to manhood the migrant experience of the Indians in Dar es Salaam. While Salim pursues family anecdotes and mythology, his brother Sona, at university, prefers a more academic route to understanding their inheritance. Their queries, both imaginative and academic, are counterpoised throughout, pointing to alternative ways of finding out and writing about history. The novel's three sections, named after the women in Salim's life – Ji Bai the great-aunt, Kulsum his mother, and Amina his love – are Vassanji's acknowledgment of the pivotal roles played by women in keeping families together.

GURNAH, Abdulrazak (1948-), novelist and critic, was born in Zanzibar and at eighteen moved to England to complete his studies. His works are examples of *African-British literature. In 1980-82 he taught at the University of Kano, Nigeria and in 1982 received his Ph.D. from the University of Kent, Canterbury, where he has been teaching English literature since 1985. He has published five well-received novels and has edited *Essays on African Writing: A Re-evaluation* (1993) and *Essays on African Writing: Contemporary Literature* (1995).

Memory of Departure (1987) is a narration in the first person of the protagonist's coming of age in an unnamed East African coastal town at the time of independence. The novel's central concerns are coastal culture and how the dynamics of living in a small place influence the formation of a young person who eventually decides to leave. Some autobiographical elements present in his first novel also shape *Pilgrim's Way* (1988), which humorously recounts the experience of Daud, a Muslim student from Tanzania, in an English provincial town. In an utterly personal struggle for survival Daud, like the biblical David, fights against the philistine culture that marginalizes him, using his wit and writing imaginary letters while his Tanzanian past continuously haunts him. Racial tensions, questions of belonging, and the making of identity are addressed in *Dottie* (1990), the story of the eponymous black British heroine. *Paradise* (1994), shortlisted for the Booker Prize in 1994, fuses myth, storytelling, religions, and East African and European literary traditions to tell of Yusuf's rite of passage. On the East African coast at the time of European encroachment, the boy is pawned by his father to Uncle Aziz, a rich merchant he must accompany on dangerous trading expeditions to the interior. Central to the narration is the multi-dimensional symbol of the garden as paradise. In *Admiring Silence* (1996) a Zanzibari man marries an English woman and writes romantic tales of the Africa he remembers. Only when he returns to Zanzibar does he discover uncomfortable truths about his country and himself. In all his novels, Gurnah's main concern rests with rejected characters and the process by which they construct their own identity.

GWALA, Mafika Pascal (1946-), South African poet and sociocultural critic, was born in KwaZulu-Natal and brought up in Durban. He has spent much of his life in Mpumalanga, a predominantly working-class township near Durban, and has worked as a secondary school teacher, legal clerk, factory worker, publications researcher, and industrial relations officer. He has also lived in Johannesburg and in England, where he did research on adult education at the University of Manchester. He has published two volumes of verse: *Jol'iinkomo* (1977) and *No More Lullabies* (1982). He has also produced short stories and essays, edited *Black Review 1973*, a full-length survey of trends in the black community, and co-edited *Musho! Zulu Popular Praises* (1991), which includes two praise poems composed by Gwala himself.

Gwala emerged as a significant writer and theorist in the late 1960s and early 1970s, a crucial period in which, in response to the political and economic successes of the *apartheid regime, the thrust of *Black Consciousness began to stir new energies within South Africa's oppressed communities. He was closely associated with the black South African Students Organization, and, together with such writers as Mongane Wally *Serote, Mbuyiseni *Mtshali, and James *Matthews, wrote and encouraged others to think in a way that expressed the political, social, cultural, and emotional needs and aspirations of all those victimized by apartheid. His first volume contains many tangy, colloquial poems of suffering, anger, and resolute defiance, but he also offers a somewhat greater variety of themes and of poetic styles than the other poets of his school. Some poems are descriptive evocations, others touch on the contrasts and continuities between the urban-new and the rural-traditional. He also writes of love and of family relationships. He is acutely conscious of sound and movement, with a particular feeling for jazz rhythms. Throughout there is a focus on emotions and experiences with a human authenticity and power that will make them ultimately liberatory. In his second volume the political focus has begun to change; like many others Gwala moved away from Black Consciousness (which he sometimes characterized as a strategy rather than a philosophy) towards a more explicitly non-racial socialism. Some of the poems are more militant than those in the earlier volume, but the variety of themes continues, and in many poems a quiet, mature determination amounts to the birth of hope.

H

HAARHOFF, Dorian (1944-), Namibian poet and dramatist, was born in Kimberley, South Africa, but has naturalized as a Namibian citizen. He is a prolific and versatile writer who uses Namibian history as a point of departure for discovering a new Namibian identity; his work is also influenced by mythology and Jungian psychology. His poetry has been collected in a number of volumes, of which *Bordering* (1991) and *Aquifers and Dust* (1994) in particular deal with the Namibian experience and explore the physical and psychological frontiers encountered by those who share his dual history. The poetry is characterized by a vision sometimes wry and ironic, always compassionate. His plays, *Orange* (1988), *Skeleton* (1989), and *Guerilla Goatherd* (1990), display exciting departures from traditional theatrical forms. In addition to drama and poetry, Haarhoff has written short stories and children's books, including *Desert December* (1992), *Water from the Rock* (1992), and *Legs, Bones and Eyes* (1994). These stories are characterized by a search for identity and include a rite of passage.

HAKIM, Tewfiq (Husayn) al- (1898-1987), Egyptian playwright and novelist writing in Arabic. Al-Hakim was born in Alexandria and educated there and at law school in Cairo. Until 1934 he worked as a public prosecutor and a civil servant; thereafter he concentrated on writing. Although he wrote a few novels, a handful of poems, and essays on arts and literature, he is best known as a playwright. Of his many plays in Arabic, eleven were translated by William Hutchins as *Plays, Preface and Postscripts of Tewfiq al-Hakim*, 2 vols. (1981); a number of individual plays have been translated as well.

Hammer Blows (1973) Poems by David *Diop, translated from the French (*Coups de pilon*, 1956). This seminal collection of seventeen poems is essentially a propositional work of highly compacted imagery, language that communicates an electric tension, and accomplished cadence. In the eulogies to Africanity ('To a Black Dancer') Diop edges close to the negritudinist L.S. *Senghor's characteristic image clusters, but here the sense of African community and of the natural world combine to convey revolt as the most urgent of natural forces ('Together' and 'Africa'). Indeed, as early as 1948 Diop was reproached in print by Senghor for his 'violent expression of an acute racial conscience'. Diop excoriates the alienation of the neo-colonialist elite-in-training ('The Renegade'):

both this poem and 'Negro Tramp', dedicated to Aimé Césaire, who coined the term *negritude, are exhilarating examples of his visionary passion. At the same time, Diop's poetry is saturated with a joyous anticipation of the necessary future, Africa's true liberation, proposed in songs 'whose only guide is love' ('To My Mother'). The best-known poems, such as 'Africa', 'The Vultures', and 'The Renegade', fiercely reject colonialism and look forward to the birth of a genuinely non-neocolonial Africa. These are poems of virulent condemnation but also of celebration ('To a Black Dancer') and hope for a future when, in Africa, 'Spring will put on flesh under our steps of light' ('The Vultures').

HAUSA LITERATURE Hausa, the language of the Hausa-Fulani people of West Africa, is spoken by thirty million people in the western Sahel. The introduction of the Roman script into the Hausa emirates by the colonial authorities in 1911 was one of a succession of stimuli to the opening up of Hausa literature to a wider readership. Then in 1930 the Translation (later Literature) Bureau was established in Zaria and organized a Hausa literature competition for creative writing. Five prize-winning novels were published in 1934. Next, the *Hausa Journal* was started, changing its format and name in 1939 to a weekly newspaper, *Gaskiya ta fi Kwabo* [Truth is worth more than a penny]. Under the editorship of Abubakar Imam it was to become an influential vehicle in the promotion of Hausa thought and culture. As a complement to the adult education campaign of 1954-9, the Northern Region Literature Agency (NORLA) sponsored a large number of booklets focused on local history and biography and written in a range of major languages, including Fulani, Nupe, Kanuri, Tiv, and others, as well as Hausa. The creation of the Hausa Language Board in 1955 contributed to this cultural projection, and from the 1970s literary societies and local printing presses became a regular feature of Hausaland. In this latter day cultural expansion, other forces have contributed positively: radio, television, the output of the Northern Nigerian Publishing Company, and a vigorous enterprise in cassettes. Finally, the opening of departments or centres of Nigerian languages at such universities as Bayero and Ahmadu Bello has brought further encouragement to Hausa literature, as has the journal *Harsunan Nijeriya* [Nigerian languages] and the series of international Hausa conferences inaugurated in 1978.

For non-Hausa speakers, the corpus of Hausa literature may be usefully presented in six principal categories, spread over the oral as well as the written form (here considered only in the romanized script, *boko*, and not in *ajami* or Arabic script): tales and historical traditions, forms of verbal play such as proverbs and riddles, dramatic texts, poetry, fiction, and biography and autobiography. Tales [*tatsuniyoyi*] and historical traditions [*labarai*] are essentially oral in origin and performance, although major published collections in translation can be found, for example in R.S. Rattray, *Hausa Folklore, Customs, Proverbs,* (1913) and A.J.N. Tremearne, *Hausa Folktales* (1914). Further forms of verbal art include proverbial lore [*karin magana*]; riddles and tongue-twisters; praise epithets [*kirarai*] and praise songs, the former being shorter and bestowed on persons, places, animals, and objects (types of cars, for example), whereas the context of the latter is ceremonial (royal courts, political party leaders) and generally performed by professional singers and drummers. Useful collections in English include C.E.J. Whitting, *Hausa and Fulani Proverbs* (1942) and A.H.M. Kirk-Greene, *Hausa Ba Dabo Ba Ne: Five Hundred Hausa Proverbs* (1966).

Plays [*wasanni*], earlier associated with youth associations, today form the basis of modern drama, chiefly manifested on television and radio and in school and college stage performances. The first published play (1949) was a burlesque piece of public health propaganda called *Wasan Marafa* [Marafa's play] by Abubakar Tunau, though a collection, *Six Hausa Plays*, was put together by R.M. East in 1936. Among the best known are Alhaji Mohammed Sada's *Uwar Galma* [Mother of evil gossip] and Umaru Ladan's dramatized version of *★Shaihu Umar* by Abubakar Tafawa Balewa. A useful discussion of Hausa drama is contained in Umaru Ahmed and Bello Daura, *Introduction to Classical Hausa and the Major Dialects* (1970).

Poetry or verse [*wak'a*] may be distinguished from songs [*wak'ok'i*], though considerable overlap exists. The former, recited or intoned in a strictly defined form and replete with didactic Islamic precepts, today often reflects contemporary socioreligious problems. The latter is of looser structure, originally sung at farming or (by women) domestic work, and today taking the form of wide-ranging sociopolitical commentary, for example on prostitution, politics, or the ★Nigeria-Biafra war of 1967-70. Translations of single poems apart, extensive excerpts of both genres appear in two books by Mervyn Hiskett, *A History of Hausa Islamic Verse* (1975) and *An Anthology of Hausa Political Verse* (1977).

Fiction [*littafan hira*: 'books to while away the evening instead of leisured conversation'] is the youngest category of Hausa literature. Of the five novels that were written as part of the 1933 competition, all but one were very much in the storytelling mode of *The Arabian Nights*. The exception was *Shaihu Umar*, which substituted moral norms and admired conventions of conduct, both features resonant of classical Hausa poetry, for the adventurous fantasies and heroic deeds of standard Hausa stories. While few novels were written in Hausa and fewer still translated before the 1970s, two new genres have recently emerged. The contemporary suspense and, increasingly, love stories of popular culture are still primarily aimed at a domestic audience. Leading authors are Mohmed Tukur Garba, with his *The Black Temple* (1981) and *Stop Press: Murder!* (1983), and the prolific pseudonymous Dan Fulani, with *Hijack* (1979) and *The Fight for Life* (1982) along with his action-packed *Sauna* series for younger readers. These sometimes appear in a Hausa and an English edition. Other writers are making a name for Hausa literature in English in the wider world, where such novels as Ibrahim ★Tahir's *The Last Imam* (1984), Zaynab ★Alkali's *The Stillborn* (1984) and *The Virtuous Woman* (1987), and Labo Yari's *Climate of Corruption* (1978) are also being published abroad and are beginning to challenge the hitherto Hausa-excluding reputation of such internationally acclaimed first-generation Nigerian novelists as Chinua ★Achebe, Wole ★Soyinka and Cyprian ★Ekwensi.

Biography and autobiography have not yet elicited much enthusiasm or experiment in Hausaland, although three texts in translation have achieved sufficient status and external publication to merit mention. One is Mary F. Smith's classic record of the verbatim reminiscences of a Hausa woman at the turn of the century, *Baba of Karo: A Woman of the Muslim Hausa* (1954; Hausa *Labarin Baba*, 1991). The second is the autobiography of Sir Ahmadu Bello, founding premier of Northern Nigeria, *My Life* (1962; Hausa *Rayuwata*, 1964). Third is the unique family case of Maimaina, the chief of Askira in northeast Nigeria. His grandfather, Abega, had accompanied the explorer Heinrich Barth in western Sudan and thence to England in the 1850s. He himself was persuaded in the 1950s to write down his own memoirs. The two autobiographical narratives of Abega and Maimaina are brought together, in translation, in *West African Travels and Adventures* (1971), by Anthony Kirk-Greene and Paul Newman.

HEAD, Bessie (1937-86), South African novelist and short-story writer. Born in Pietermaritzburg's Fort Napier Mental Institution, her mother Bessie Amelia Emery (née Birch) having been placed there after becoming pregnant by a black man, Head grew up in foster care until the age of thirteen, when the welfare authorities placed her in an Anglican mission orphanage in Durban. There she received a secondary school education and trained as a teacher. Finding out very soon that teaching did not suit her temperament, Head moved into the world of journalism, working in the early 1960s in Cape Town and Johannesburg for a newspaper in the famous *Drum* stable. In 1961 in Cape Town she met and married fellow journalist Harold Head; their only child, Howard, was born in 1962. After the break-up of her marriage in 1964 she relinquished South African citizenship and took up a teaching post in Serowe, Botswana. She soon lost this job, was declared a refugee, and turned to market gardening and writing. Having been turned down before, Head was granted Botswanan citizenship in 1979. Plagued by ill health and mental instability, she died in Serowe with six published works to her name and an international reputation.

Head's first work, *When Rain Clouds Gather* (1968), deals with the flight from South Africa of a young black political activist, Makhaya Maseko, his resettlement in Botswana, and his marriage to a Batswana woman. With an underlying tone of romance, it describes the efforts of Makhaya and Gilbert Balfour, a young English agricultural expert, to establish co-operative farming in a village in southeastern Botswana. Despite its naive, naturalistic style and clumsy characterization, Head's first work contains some of the innovative qualities that would characterize her later work. It eschews a simplistic paradigm of racial conflict in southern Africa by constructing the possibility of inter-racial co-operation and friendship and tackles issues very real to an independent and developing Africa in a challenging and forceful way.

Head's second novel, *Maru* (1971), with its eponymous central character, is an altogether more complex work. It has a surface realism that describes the conflict between Maru and Moleka in their love for the same woman. They are both in line for the chieftaincy of their tribe, and Margaret is a Masarwa, a member of the despised Bushman race who for generations had been the slaves of Batswana. By scheming and manipulating, Maru eventually succeeds in winning Margaret from her original love for Moleka and marries her, an act that throws time-honoured Batswana prejudices into disarray. Beneath the novel's surface realism there is an allegorical struggle between human character types that assumes godlike proportions. The energy of the novel is located at this level: Margaret's racial oppression achieves a universal resonance, and Maru and Moleka become human archetypes whose natures draw them into an unavoidable conflict. The resolution of the novel is therefore both a sociopolitical statement and an authorial comment on a universal pattern which inexorably controls human events.

*A *Question of Power* (1974) is Head's most unusual and perplexing novel, but it is also the work that has received the most critical attention. Although all three of Head's novels have an autobiographical dimension, elements of *A Question of Power* are most conspicuously drawn from the life experience of the author.

After a disastrous early life in South Africa, the protagonist Elizabeth leaves on an exit permit for Motabeng village in Botswana, where she engages in co-operative gardening ventures with the local Batswana and an international group of volunteer workers. It is in this context that Elizabeth's mental breakdown occurs. The narrative constantly switches between her tormented consciousness and the 'real world' of the novel – the bustling village life, communal gardening, and the daily activities of Elizabeth and her son, so tangibly evoked as to suggest a re-creation of the realism of *Rain Clouds*. Elizabeth confronts in her consciousness universal powers of good and evil and struggles to attain a sense of human value amid her mental confusion. The novel charts the terrifying course of her breakdown and recovery and ultimately affirms the primary human values of decency, generosity, and compassion.

Head's collection of short stories, The *Collector of Treasures and Other Botswana Village Tales* (1977), is remarkable for its skilful evocation of aspects of Botswanan village life: tribal history, the missionaries, religious conflict, witchcraft, rising illegitimacy, and, most importantly, problems that women in the society encounter. Her social history *Serowe: Village of the Rain Wind* (1981) is composed of a series of transcribed interviews edited and prefaced by the author to constitute a portrait of Serowe village life. The historical novel *A Bewitched Crossroad: An African Saga* (1984) simultaneously describes the process towards the establishment of the British protectorate of Bechuanaland and tells the story of Sebina, a leader of a clan that is eventually absorbed into the Bamangwato nation.

Four texts have appeared posthumously. *Tales of Tenderness and Power* (1989) is a collection of mostly fictional short writings, while *A Woman Alone: Autobiographical Writings* (1990) collects together miscellaneous pieces Head wrote in both South Africa and Botswana. Randolph Vigne's *A Gesture of Belonging: Letters from Bessie Head, 1965-1979* (1991) is an important collection of letters interspersed with commentary. *The Cardinals: With Meditations and Stories* (1993) is a previously unpublished novella (which Head wrote in Cape Town in the early 1960s) and a set of shorter pieces.

Healers, The (1978) A novel by Ayi Kwei *Armah. Subtitled 'An Historical Novel', the narrative is set during the second Asante war (1873-4). In the Fante village of Esuano the protagonist Densu is unjustly accused of killing Prince Appia. He flees to the trustworthy healer Damfo, who cures the body and soul of Appia's mother and of the military leader of the Asante army, Asamoa Nkwanta, an historical figure. Nkwanta is shown the oppression inherent in royal power, as opposed to Damfo's long-term goal (already present in *Two Thousand Seasons*) of reuniting the African peoples. Nkwanta is betrayed by the royals and thus the English army conquers Kumasi. Back in Esuano, Densu is tried and dramatically exculpated by Appia's mother, who unmasks a plot by the ambitious Ababio. Eschewing material power as Damfo teaches, Densu rejects the offer to be nominated king.

Heavensgate (1962) Poems by Christopher ★Okigbo. The subtitle, 'Portrait of the Poet as a Young Boy', affirms the explicitly autobiographical nature of the volume. In his first full volume of poems, Okigbo, Western-educated in the Greek and Roman classics, returns, a 'prodigal', to seek information, inspiration, and forgiveness from 'mother Idoto', the avatar of his culture and the inspiration for his art. This volume and those that were to follow record a constant attempt at reconciling his African inheritance and his Western education. For him they were often antagonistic to each other, making the business of reconciliation even more difficult.

Helena's Hope, Ltd (1909) A play by Stephen ★Black. A variety of characters are caught up in the rapid changes of the twentieth century in South Africa when the agrarian economy gives way to a world in which cash is dominant. The title is the name of a gold mine in which the action of the play unfolds and ironically expresses the hopes of the various characters for quick riches. The play ran for six hundred performances and toured widely in South Africa.

Hello and Goodbye (1965) A play by Athol ★Fugard. In 1963 Hester Smit visits her brother Johnnie in the small shabby house he had shared with their father. Not only is Johnnie on crutches, he is also unemployed, subsisting on the money left to him by the father. To deflect Hester's demands for a share of the meagre inheritance, Johnnie pretends that the father has not in fact died but is lying very ill in the next room, and he brings out all the family's old possessions for Hester to search through. She can find no money, nor will Johnnie allow her to enter the next room to 'disturb' their father. The two lonely siblings, although forced into self-revelation as they agonize over their childhood, the harshness of their father, and the deprivation of their current lives, nonetheless choose to remain lonely. Johnnie, alone on the stage after Hester leaves, reveals that he has purposely assumed the crippled identity of their father.

HENSHAW, James Ene (1924-), Nigerian playwright, was born in Calabar, Nigeria. He began his writing career in Dublin, with *This Is Our Chance*, written for the Association of Students of African Descent and published, along with *A Man of Character* and *Jewels of the Shrine*, in 1956. The three plays published in *Children of the Goddess* (1964), including the

title play, *Magic in the Blood*, and *Companion for a Chief*, and the three earlier plays emphasize the clash of tradition and modernity. Their clearly defined conflicts make them accessible and interesting to young audiences, whose instruction is one of the playwright's concerns. Although *Jewels of the Shrine* is also ironic enough for the conflicts to be played out convincingly, Nigerian critics tend to dismiss Henshaw as a writer for juveniles. In later plays such as *Medicine for Love* (1964) and *Dinner for Promotion* (1967), characterization becomes more rounded, dialogue is more apt, and comedy adds vitality to the action. In *Enough Is Enough* (1976), about detainees during the ★Nigeria-Biafra war, increased psychological depth produces intense drama. In *A Song to Mary Charles* (1985), a biographical play about an Irish nun, Henshaw develops one of the liveliest characters in Nigerian theatre. Henshaw considers characterization the most important dramatic element.

Heroes (1986) A novel by Festus ★Iyayi and winner of a Commonwealth Writers Prize. The novel's importance as an account of the ★Nigeria-Biafra war lies not only in its innovative use of stream-of-consciousness as a narrative technique but also in its views about the war. Through the journalist Osime Iyere's development from naivety to political consciousness, Iyayi suggests that the war is an intra-class fight with the masses on both sides as victims.

HONWANA, Luís Bernardo [See LUSOPHONE LITERATURE; POLITICS AND LITERATURE, Angola and Mozambique]

HOPE, Christopher (David Tully) (1944-), South African-born novelist and poet. Born in Johannesburg, he grew up in Pretoria, studied at the universities of Natal and the Witwatersrand, and has been based in London since 1975. A recent edition of *New Writing* (Number 5, 1996) suggestively paired him with Peter Porter, the eminent Anglo-Australian writer of an earlier generation. Hope shares with Porter a background in advertising, a wordsmith's dexterity too canny and sophisticated to be called slick, a gift for satirical cameo and pastiche, and a colonial's devotion to metropolitan culture and polished, witty texts. Like Porter he is an ambivalent sojourner in a post-colonial age: an Anglo-South African whose credentials in either culture still have to be asserted in terms of the other.

Hope's first novel, *A Separate Development* (1980), has the feel of a fantasy autobiography: Harry Moto, white boy living black, finds unlikely routes through the strict ★apartheid enclaves that enable bizarre but nourishing visions, mirroring his creator's imaginative escape from the banality of white suburbia. *Kruger's Alp* (1984) remains Hope's tour-de-force: a dense and allegorical satire, it blends a transcendental remaking of Catholic boys' school fundamentalism (which also takes in a full scoop of other South African moralizing certitudes) with the deep history signalled in his title's reference to the exile of an Afrikaner saint (and to his mythical buried millions). He has followed this with *The Hottentot Room* (1986), the novella *Black Swan* (1987), *My Chocolate Redeemer* (1989), *Serenity House* (1992), *Love Songs of Nathan J. Swirsky* (1994), *Darkest England* (1996), and *Signs of the Heart* (1999). Hope's South African phantasmagoria returns in various guises in these works as, necessarily and increasingly, he raids a European hinterland for new material.

A significant poetic oeuvre includes *Cape Drives* (1974), *In the Country of the Black Pig* (1981) and *Englishmen* (1985), a long poem subsequently dramatized by the BBC. He has written books for children (like *Me, the Moon and Elvis Presley*, 1999), a good deal of documentary journalism which includes the travel book *Moscow! Moscow!* (1990), the early stories in *Private Parts* (1981) reissued with additions as *Learning to Fly* (1990), and a memoir (*White Boy Running*, 1988) which provides an interesting counterpoint to *A Separate Development*.

House Gun, The (1998) is a novel by Nadine *Gordimer. *The Independent*, London reviewer said that 'Nadine Gordimer provides a magnificent corrective to … the myth that the best writing comes out of the struggle against injustice.' Duncan Lindgard has shot dead Carl Jespersen with the 'house gun' which is kept to protect the young male and female sharers of a garden house in post-apartheid suburban Johannesburg. Duncan openly confesses to the crime, though not the reasons. South Africa still has capital punishment. The novel centres on the bleak helplessness of the parents – she a doctor, he a business man – and their inability to get through to their son on visits to prison. They wish to hire the best lawyer available, and the case is taken by Hamilton Motsamai, who proves to be one of Gordimer's most powerful and memorable characters. He builds up to the realization that this was not just a simple case of a heterosexual 'love triangle' relished by the reporters crowding the court-room.

House of Hunger (1978) Stories by Dambudzo *Marechera. The stories deal with the brutality the author experienced as a youth in Rhodesia, now Zimbabwe, the real and psychological violence of the independence struggle with its associated racism, and the nature of guerilla warfare in the context of Ian Smith's UDI (Unilateral Declaration of Independence). In telling his stories Marechera adopts a variety of literary personae: student, poet, nationalist, and academic.

Houseboy (1956) A novel by Ferdinand *Oyono,

translated from the French (*Une vie de boy*, 1956). Like other novels written in French during the 1950s, this one expresses its author's anti-colonialist sentiments while blending African literary traditions with European ones. Also like its contemporaries, it gives great importance to the theme of power, used as the axis around which the plot develops: French colonial officers exercise power without humanity while African characters accept their subjugation all too willingly. Remarkably enough, *Houseboy* represents authority in the same fashion as most novels from these regions do today when they speak of current situations: people in high places are immoral and have no legitimate claim to the power they hold, which they abuse and impose on passive or victimized characters through gratuitous violence. Such a literary tactic has its consequence on African realism, which is the mode favoured by such writers: it appears to be based more on the typical than on the particular.

HOVE, Chenjerai (1956-), Zimbabwean poet and novelist. Dambudzo *Marechera aside, Hove is probably the best known of recent Zimbabwean writers. Apart from his writing in Shona, he came to prominence first as a poet with *Up in Arms* (1982), *Red Hills of Home* (1985), and, in collaboration with Lyamba wa Kabika, *Swimming in Floods of Tears* (1983). However, he has since achieved greater success in prose: the first of two English novellas, *Bones* (1988), won the Noma Award. *Shadows* (1991), the second, was followed by a collection of essays, *Shebeen Tales* (1994) and a novel, *Ancestors* (1996). As writer-in-residence at the University of Zimbabwe and chair of the Zimbabwe Writers' Union, Hove has been active in the promotion of literature in Zimbabwe. In 1994 he was a visiting professor at Lewis and Clark College in Oregon, USA.

Although Hove's earlier poems trenchantly supported the guerilla war, they are less populist in structure and tone than most contemporary nationalist work, provoking accusations of excessive difficulty. Often his language is deliberately brutal, as in 'Remember Chimoio' (site of a Rhodesian forces massacre): 'the spade you threw/caught mashed bowels'. In 'Death of a Soldier', detail is more personalized: 'His stench harangued my bowels'. A hatred Hove found necessary for survival is transcended later in looser, more approachable poems that turn to broader issues of unfulfilled political promises and his own role as writer in a chaotic world. A slighter vocabulary, a repetition characteristic of oral forms, and extensive use of vernacular-based image and aphorism also characterize Hove's best work, *Bones*, a moving consideration of the ravages of war on rural folk. Here he combines modernist techniques with mellifluously repetitive, proverb-like sentences to create an almost delirious meditation on the destruction of traditional life. Similarly, *Shadows* extols the choice of suicide of two young lovers as their community is rent by violence from both sides in the war. Corrosive despair mixes powerfully with images of frangible beauty. Both novellas have been criticized for their diffuseness. While lacking narrative thrust or specificity of characterization, however, they finely evoke a beleaguered culture's collective interior monologue. In *Shebeen Tales*, Hove follows *Ngugi wa Thiong'o and Ayi Kwei *Armah in chronicling the conditions of the dispossessed. He indicts the post-independence government for its self-serving 'political monologue'. *Ancestors* is an evocative tale of a woman without speech or hearing who, lonely and unhappy, manages to communicate the plight of voiceless women by haunting a man living a century later.

HUSSEIN, Ebrahim N. (1943-), Tanzanian dramatist writing in *Swahili. Graduated from the theatre arts department of the University of Dar es Salaam, Tanzania's pre-eminent playwright has written *Alikiona* [He got his just desserts] (1970); *Kinjeketile* (1969); *Wakati Ukuta* [Time is like a brick wall] (1971); *Mashetani* [Demons] (1971); *Jogoo Kijijini* and *Ngao ya Jadi* (1976); *Arusi* [Wedding] (1980); and *Kwenye Ukingo wa Thim* [At the edge of Thim] (1988). He pursued further education in East Germany, returning to teach drama at Dar es Salaam. He later taught at the University of Nairobi.

Hussein has contributed importantly to the development of an authentic Tanzanian drama by probing issues of history and national integration (*Kinjeketile*, *Ngao ya Jadi*); rapid cultural change (*Wakati Ukuta*); social class polarities (*Mashetani*); ethnic chauvinism, greed, and corruption (*Thim*), and cultural and linguistic rejuvenation. He makes brilliantly innovative use of elements of orature, particularly in *Jogoo Kijijini* and *Ngao ya Jadi*. He amalgamates a Brechtian aesthetic, a command of classical Swahili texts, and his own proficiency as a poet to expand the linguistic, stylistic, and cognitive topos of drama and poetry in Swahili.

I

I Will Marry When I Want (1982) A play by *Ngugi wa Thiong'o (1977), translated from the Gikuyu (*Ngaahika Ndeenda*). The play exposes the exploitation of peasant people, represented by Kiguunda, a labourer and former freedom fighter for Kenyan's independence from colonial rule, his wife, Wangeei, and their daughter Gatoni, by foreign capitalists in league with the Kenyan entrepreneurial class, represented by Kioi, a wealthy business man, his wife Jezebel, and their son Muhuumi. A wedding is proposed between Gatoni and John Muhuumi, and when money is needed for a proper Christian wedding, Kiguunda mortgages his farm. But when Gatoni is found to be pregnant by John Muhuumi the wedding is called off. The bank forecloses on Kiguunda's land, his only valuable possession, and he is left homeless with a few useless European possessions. Christianity serves as the agent of capitalist exploitation. Here, as in his later work, Ngugi is relentless in exposing the duplicity and hypocrisy of the class of Westernized Kenyans. The satire is, perhaps, heavy handed, but it had the effect of mobilizing the peasant people who first saw the play performed at the Kamiriithu Cultural Centre. The play was closed down by Kenyan authorities when they saw its effect on an audience that identified with Kiguunda and his family.

Ibadan: the Pankelemes Years, a Memoir 1946–1965 (1994) Memoir by Wole *Soyinka. The mode of 'faction', defined by the author as 'the genre which attempts to fictionalize facts and events', allows Soyinka a degree of creative freedom in this account of his response to the social and political events that shaped Nigeria in the 1950s and 60s. Having returned to Nigeria from Leeds towards the end of 1959, when the country was at the threshold of independence, Soyinka was engaged in independent research into the origin of traditional drama at the University of Ibadan. He has captured the violence, the thuggery, and the burning of public buildings that characterized the politics of the years between 1960 and 1965 with the strange coinage 'pankelemes'. He was a major actor in the series of crises that engulfed the nation soon after independence, and the book ends with his arrest and trial for attempting to hold up the radio station at Ibadan during the 1964 elections. The book is important to an understanding of Soyinka's political activism and for the insight it affords into his early beginnings as a young dramatist.

Idanre (1967) Poems by Wole *Soyinka. Some of the shorter poems in this, Soyinka's first poetry collection, deal with issues of immediate and poignant concern: the brutality of the military, seen under the advancing shadow of civil war ('Ikeja, Friday, Four O'clock', 'Civilian and Soldier'), the birth of a stillborn child ('A Cry in the Night'), and, in a subject also treated memorably by J.P. Clark *Bekederemo, the appearance of a 'born-to-die' spirit child ('Abiku'). Even in these poems the sense of the immediate and the play of irony are underpinned by Soyinka's absorption in Yoruba myth, the focus of the collection's twenty-five-page title poem. 'Idanre' is a hugely complex work of almost frenzied inspiration in which Soyinka employs an account of an ascent of Idanre hill, east of Ife, to explore his own artistic inspiration, his debt to myth, and the condition of his society.

IGBO LITERATURE Igbo is the language of the Ibo people of Nigeria. Igbo literature – written and read – whether colonial, modern, or contemporary, developed out of Igbo traditional literature, which is comprised of such elements as folktales, folk songs and chants, proverbs, myths and legends, and ritual incantations, as well as folk dances and celebrations. Collectively these are known as oral literature or *orature.

Even before European missionaries and British colonial agencies introduced roman script into Igbo country, the first Igbo to write about Igbo life were those who, having learned the mystery of the written word in slavery, were able to give utterance to their deepest yearnings for their lost homes in Igboland by re-creating the aspects of Igbo life they could still remember. The first of such writings is *Equiano's *The Interesting Narrative of the Life of Olaudah Equiano, or Gustavus Vassa, the African* (1789), which became a model for the nineteenth-century slave narrative, other examples of which include narratives by Frederick Douglass, William Wells Brown, and Harriet Jacobs.

During the nineteenth century primers and dictionaries began to appear. A short Igbo vocabulary was attached to Dr. William Baikie's *Narrative of an Exploring Voyage up the Rivers Kwora and Benue in 1854* (1856), and in 1857 a Yoruba ex-slave turned scholar and missionary, the Reverend Adjai Crowther, published the *Isuama-Ibo Primer*. In 1882 Crowther published the *Vocabulary of the Ibo Language*, and in 1883 an Igbo-English supplement to the dictionary, titled *Oku-Ibo: Grammatical Elements of the Ibo Lan-*

guage, was published under the editorship of Rev. J.F. Schön, a German scholar and missionary. All of the literary experiments in Igbo eventuated in the translation of the Bible into Igbo, *Bible Nso*.

Following Britain's final colonization of Igboland in 1905, *Bible Nso* as well as various editions of the Schön and Crowther primers were taught at both churches and mission schools to the first Igbo Christian converts and pupils. In 1906, an Igbo-English dictionary manuscript was compiled with the help of the Honourable L.E. Portman, and in 1913, Northcote Thomas, a government anthropologist, published an *English-Igbo and Ibo-English Dictionary*. The Methodist church translated *The Pilgrim's Progress* into Igbo for use in their schools. Inspired and influenced by the available Ibo dictionaries, primers, and grammar books, as well as *Bible Nso*, the early Igbo graduates of the mission schools began their own writing, which the missionaries helped them to publish in London. Among the early Igbo literary classics are a collection of Igbo proverbs, folktales, and etiological animal tales titled *Akwukwo Ogugu Ibo* [Igbo primer] (1927); Peter Nwana's *Omenuko* (1933); Leopold Bell-Gram's *Ije Odumodu Jere* [Odumodu's travels] (1963); and N. Achara's *Ala Bingo* [Bingo land] (1963.)

The development of Igbo literature went hand in hand with the development of Igbo language and linguistics. Apart from Igbo being taught in schools as one of the three major Nigerian languages (with ★Hausa and ★Yoruba), between 1905 and 1939 Union Igbo was adopted as the official standard form of the language, followed by Central Igbo from 1939 through 1972; from 1973 Standard Modern Igbo has been in use. These educated or edited forms, as opposed to the various, often confusing dialects, were developed and promoted by governments, universities, and colleges, and by individual scholarship and research.

Igbo literature is classified into non-creative and creative writing. Non-creative literature refers to the stylized verbal art of the folk, such as folktales, proverbs, folk dances, traditional verses, and songs, whose 'artists', 'makers', or collectors, including storytellers, chanteurs, chorus leaders, or (in modern times) researchers cannot be considered as their original creators, performers, or writers. Rather, they are the instruments through which the collective folk culture is kept alive and handed down from one generation to another. The verbal arts include folk narrative, traditional verse, and folk drama.

Folk narrative embraces folktales, mythological tales, customs and institutions, and sententious sayings. Folktales are told to explain natural phenomena and the Igbo world view. Mythological tales narrate the founding and origins of Igbo communities, wars, folk heroes, and legends as well as metaphysical events. Customs and institutions include traditions, practices,

and social and ritual institutions of the Igbo. Sententious sayings, as stylized verbal forms, serve as rhetorical aids that succinctly reveal and teach Igbo moral and ethical codes as well as cosmological and traditional religious beliefs. They include proverbs, anecdotes, and riddles and tongue-twisters. Traditional verse is comprised of folk songs, poems, incantations, and dances. Although there are no recorded Igbo folk dramas, most rituals and celebrations, such as the masquerade plays, the war dance, and the naming of age-grades contain dramatic elements that include community and audience, stage, costuming and spectacle, representation, mime and dance, plot, and music that could be re-enacted as monthly, seasonal, and yearly dramatic performances.

Creative literature is comprised of works of imagination by known individual authors. Although Igbo creative literature is written in both English and Igbo, it falls within European and American literary forms and structures in the three major genres, prose fiction, poetry, and drama. However, the better-known Igbo creative writers, such as Chinua ★Achebe, Cyprian ★Ekwensi, John ★Munonye, Christopher ★Okigbo, Flora ★Nwapa, and Buchi ★Emecheta, have so successfully married their native Igbo narrative and creative techniques to the European forms that the hybrid texts they produce have attracted and retained a large world readership without losing their quality of Africanness. The catalyst in this literary experiment from Africa, indeed Igboland, is Achebe's ★*Things Fall Apart* (1958), which has been translated into thirty world languages and has sold about three million copies.

Prose fiction includes entertainment pamphlets, short stories, and novels, some of which are written in English and others in Igbo. Inspired by the English literary texts they read in school, Igbo secondary school drop-outs and graduates wrote pamphlets, didactic in tone, which were to entertain and instruct their readers in the moral norms and conduct of Igbo culture, as well as in the Christian morality they read from the Bible. The pamphlets are called ★Onitsha market literature because they were published by presses based in Onitsha and their primary sellers and readers were Onitsha traders. They also had educational value for the masses, especially those who couldn't afford a secondary-school education.

The Onitsha tradition also owes something to the short story form, and Cyprian Ekwensi, an early pamphleteer, helped to lay the foundation for the market series with his first collection of stories, *Ikolo the Wrestler* (1947). Achebe's short stories, *Girls at War* (1972) and *How the Leopard Got His Claws* (1976) came after the ★Nigeria-Biafra war, 1967-70. Other short stories were written in Igbo, including Chianakwalam's *Enwe a Naakpo Candu* (1951) and Ugochukwu's *Ebubedike na Igwekala* (1965).

The most significant Igbo contribution to African

literature is the novel. Although Ekwensi was the first Nigerian novelist in English, Achebe's *Things Fall Apart* was so richly structured and it so expertly romanticized Igbo culture and civilization that it became the prototype of the twentieth-century African novel, exemplified in the works of other Igbo novelists such as Elechi *Amadi, Buchi Emecheta, Chukwuemeka *Ike, John Munonye, Nkem *Nwankwo, Flora Nwapa, and Onuora *Nzekwu. Such texts were taught in the rapidly Africanizing departments of English in post-colonial African colleges and universities, and many have become familiar in American and British departments of English, African studies, and women's studies. There has also been some increase in the number of novelists writing in Igbo, such as Achara (*Elelia na Ihe O Mere*, 1964), John Munonye (*Aghirigha*, 1975) and Ubesie (*Ukwa Ruo Oge Ya O daa*, 1972).

Igbo writers have also made significant contributions to African poetry. Christopher Okigbo, for example, is called West Africa's best poet by Robert Wren in *Those Magical Years: The Making of Nigerian Literature at Ibadan: 1948-1966* (1991). Michael Echeruo has written two volumes of poetry, *Morality* (1968) and *Distanced* (1975); Donatus I. Nwoga edited *West African Verse* (1967), which includes poems by poets of both English and French expression, and Chinua Achebe published two volumes of poems, *Christmas in Biafra* (1973) and *Beware, Soul Brother* (1971). In addition, other Igbo poets appear in Gerald Moore and Ulli Beier's *Modern Poetry from Africa* (1963). Many volumes of poetry and songs have been published in Igbo, including *Akpa Uche: An Anthology of Igbo Verse*, edited by R.M. Ekechukwu (1975) and Emmanuel Obike's *Eke Une* (1975).

Igbo drama began with radio and television, which included such situation comedies as *Icheku* of the 1960s, *Zebuludaya* of the 1970s, and *The Village Headmaster* of the 1980s. However, from the late 1970s through the early 1990s, Igbo playwrights writing in both English and Igbo have emerged; their titles include Chukuezi's *Udo Ka Mma* (1974), Akoma's *Obidiya* (1977), Mezu's *Umu Ejima* (1977), as well as Tess *Onwueme's *The Broken Calabash* (1984), *The Reign of Wazobia* (1988), and *Go Tell It to the Women* (1992).

IKE, (Vincent) Chukwuemeka (1931-), Nigerian

novelist, was born in eastern Nigeria and educated at the University of Ibadan and at Stanford in the USA. As an educator, Ike has contributed to the intellectual and cultural development of Africa in important administrative positions at Nigerian universities and at UNESCO and as professor at the University of Jos. His novels include *Toads for Supper* (1965), which is set in a university and deals with love and the inherent problems that married couples from different ethnic

backgrounds encounter; *The Naked Gods* (1970), also set in a university, which highlights the corrupt practices in the appointment of a new vice-chancellor at Songhai University; and *Expo '77* (1980), in which secondary school students trying to gain admission to the university cheat in examinations. More recently, *Our Children Are Coming* (1990) deals with the problem of youth unrest and student revolt in colleges and universities in Nigeria: reacting to commissions of inquiry that exclude them, the students set up a counter investigation of their own. *The Search* (1991) is the story of the feverish patriotism of a detribalized intellectual, Ola, and his search for Nigerian unity. Ike's prose style encompasses dialogue, wit, and satire, which he employs to castigate corruption and the quest for inordinate power. The novels transcend historical, sociological, and political documentation and achieve comedy, tragedy, irony, and metaphor. He has also written *How to Become a Published Writer* (1991).

IMBUGA, Francis (1947-), Kenyan playwright,

novelist, and poet, was born in Maragoli, Kenya, where he received his primary and secondary education. He gained BA and MA degrees from the University of Nairobi and a Ph.D. from the University of Iowa, USA. In the 1970s he travelled to Wales, Ghana, and Nigeria to broaden his theatrical experience, and he has taught literature at Kenyatta University, Nairobi since 1979.

While still an undergraduate Imbuga began writing dramas for Kenyan television, and although most of those plays were commissioned, they served him well in his apprenticeship. His television scripts and ten published plays, including a Swahili translation in 1994 of *Betrayal in the City* (1976), have established him as Kenya's foremost playwright. 'Kisses of Fate' and *The Fourth Trial* (1972), among his earliest plays, and *The Married Bachelor* (1973), initially published as *Sons and Parents* in 1971 and revised as *The Burning of Rags*, focus on domestic experience. *Game of Silence* (1977) forms a thematic and stylistic transition to the political emphases of later plays: *Betrayal in the City*, *The Successor* (1979), and *Man of Kafira* (1984) explore the crises of leadership, nepotism, despotism, disillusionment, social unease, and resistance that have characterized Africa's post-colonial period.

Since Imbuga freely draws from well-known events and figures, he deliberately resorts to disguising devices, notably the play-within-play, the figure of the fool, humour, and anagram. But disguise has its limits, and theatrical compromises have drawbacks of their own, as exemplified by resolutions inconsistent with plot and character development in *Betrayal* and *Man of Kafira*. *Aminata* (1988) was written for the United Nations Decade for Women Conference held in Nairobi in 1985 and highlights Imbuga's identification with some aspects of the women's struggle. *Shrine of*

Tears, a novel published in 1993, and his poems, included in anthologies edited by A. D. Amateshe and A. I. Luvai, thematically resonate with his plays and amplify the resources of the theatre, notably alienation effects for the purposes of de- and re-familiarization and selective yoking of absurdism and idealism. Critics interpret some of the jesting in his plays and some of his plays' resolutions as evidence of cynicism. Imbuga has certainly contributed to the theatrical and cultural experience of his society; the quaintness and wordiness that sometimes characterize his English renditions of indigenous idioms do not profoundly detract from his achievement.

In the Ditch (1972) A novel by Buchi *Emecheta. Strongly autobiographical in its sources, the novel tells the story of Adah, who, having been deserted by her wastrel husband, sets out to make a life for herself and her young family, contained as it is by living in the 'Ditch', a council housing estate in London. Emecheta conveys a sense of the conditions, mostly appalling, in which the denizens of the Ditch live their lives. Adah feels ambiguous about her relations with other members of the estate. She feels both distance from them and yet a growing warmth for them as she recognizes their collective effort – of which she never fully becomes a part – to overcome poverty, racism, and the patronizing charity of the council that runs the estate. Adah struggles to escape the narrow social and cultural confines of the Ditch by using her education, her personal initiative, and her determination, and eventually she succeeds. The use to which she puts the education and experiences she dramatizes in *In the Ditch* are more fully explicated in Emecheta's autobiography, *Head Above Water* (1986).

In the Fog of the Seasons' End (1972) A novel by Alex *La Guma. Although some of La Guma's novels make an appeal for compassion as a way to reduce oppression, *In the Fog of the Seasons' End* presents civil war as the only means of destroying a seemingly indestructible totalitarian system. But before the novel reaches the decisive meeting of opposing forces, La Guma conducts us once again through the maze of *apartheid laws; through the multifarious indignities visited on black and 'coloured' (mixed race) people by the pass laws; into the horror of the Sharpeville massacre and its aftermath – the creation of the armed branch of the ANC; into the wholesale destruction of lives caused by the Group Areas Act; and through the hideously exploitative system of mine labour. The novel draws to a conclusion as freedom fighters head northward for guerilla training. The final message is hopeful: the fog created by the apartheid regime, a fog of the dead and the living dead of all skin colours, will be burned away when South Africa is liberated.

In the Heart of the Country (1978) A novel by J.M. *Coetzee. The narrator of Coetzee's second novel is a single woman, Magda, who lives with her father and their servants, Hendrik and Klein-Anna, on an arid and isolated South African farm. The novel is articulated in explicitly Freudian and Lacanian terms: Magda refuses to talk to her stepmother, while she alternates between desperate attempts to achieve the recognition of her father and violent fantasies of killing the father, who is the all-powerful representative of the law. These are followed by fantasies of rape by the servant, Hendrik, and a plea to his wife, Klein-Anna, to tell her who she (Magda) is, and to call her by her name. Magda is an intensely self-conscious narrator who describes herself as 'a hole crying to be whole'; her monologue is given in numbered segments, suggesting that it never achieves the continuity of narrative. Unable to imagine a response, Magda achieves neither self-realization nor self-transcendence. Read allegorically, the novel can be seen as Coetzee's re-reading of Olive *Schreiner's seminal novel, *The *Story of an African Farm* (1883).

Incidents at the Shrine (1986) Short stories by Ben *Okri. Narrated in lucid English with the occasional use of Pidgin in conversations, the eight stories in this collection are told from different points of view ranging from the first person to the omniscient narrator. The often humorous stories are set inside and outside Africa, and they focus on social, political, and economic issues such as traditional African religion, poverty, prostitution, armed robbery, loneliness, alienation, and the *Nigeria-Biafra war.

Instant in the Wind, An (1976) A novel by André *Brink. Recalling Australian Patrick White's novel *A Fringe of Leaves* (1976), *An Instant in the Wind* deals with the story of Eliza Fraser, a shipwrecked colonial woman, and her relationship with an escaped convict who promises to deliver her back to 'civilization' in exchange for his freedom. Brink's eighteenth-century version of this myth of contact is a romantic one, a rewriting of a period of early colonial history that in turn interrogates the contradictions of the present. By making the convict character, Adam Mantoor, a black slave and the female character, Elisabeth Larsson, a Dutch settler married to an explorer, Brink attributes historical significance to her final betrayal of him. He has described the novel as dealing with 'two modes of experiencing Africa'. Both characters are shown to be enslaved in their own way, marginalized by the colonial and patriarchal society from which they have temporarily escaped.

Interesting Narrative of Olaudah Equiano or Gustavus Vassa, the African, Written by Himself, The (1789) Autobiography by Olaudah *Equiano.

Interpreters, The (1965) A novel by Wole *Soyinka. The interpreters in Soyinka's first novel are a small group of male university graduates – a journalist, an engineer, an academic and an artist – based in or near Lagos, and the novel depicts their lives during the increasingly fractured and violent period leading up to the outbreak of the Nigeria-Biafra war. Soyinka's emphasis is both on the failings of a corrupt and dysfunctional state and on the various attempts made by his main characters to interpret their society and to find a way of living within it that does not imply abandoning all integrity. Criticized for the diffuseness of its plot, the apparent indeterminacy of its imagery, and the complexity of its language, the novel is nonetheless deeply incisive and offers a remarkably vivid portrait of a particular sector of Nigerian society in the early 1960s, especially in a number of memorable set-piece episodes: a revivalist church service, a farcical traffic jam, a university staff party.

IROH, Eddie (1946-), Nigerian novelist and children's writer, was born in Nigeria and served in the Nigerian army before joining the Biafran War Information Bureau and Reuters news service during the *Nigeria-Biafra war (1967-70). He has worked both in the UK and Nigeria as a journalist and magazine editor.

Iroh belongs to the second generation of Nigerian writers, who wrote about modern Nigerian city life. His first novel, *Forty-Eight Guns for the General* (1976), focuses on the activities of mercenaries who fought in the Nigeria–Biafra war. Under the leadership of Colonel Steiner, the mercenaries are projected as detached witnesses of the war, with a carefree attitude about who wins. His second novel, *Toads of War* (1979), shows how a corrupt civil servant tries to

protect himself by conscripting the main character, Odim, who knows the civil servant's secrets, into the army. The novel shows the sabotage of the war effort for personal gain. *The Siren in the Night* (1982) is a historical reconstruction of the war detailing Iroh's own experience of intimidation and ethnic loyalties in the aftermath. *Without a Silver Spoon* (1984) is a children's book about a child growing up in a poor family.

ISLAM [See RELIGION AND LITERATURE]

IYAYI, Festus (1947-), Nigerian novelist, was born in Benin City, Nigeria and studied in Nigeria, the USSR, and England, where he obtained a Ph.D. from the University of Bradford. One of the most politically committed African novelists, Iyayi was dismissed from the faculty of the University of Benin for his revolutionary political and labour activities. His novels include *Violence* (1979), *The Contract* (1982), and *Heroes* (1986), for which he earned a Commonwealth Writers Prize, and are comparable ideologically to those of *Sembene Ousmane and *Ngugi wa Thiong'o. The novels can be situated within the framework of class struggle. His protagonists, representatives of the working class, begin as innocent individuals but become more informed and politically conscious as they are exploited along class lines, and ultimately they champion the cause of the victimized. *Violence* and *The Contract* examine class and gender. *Heroes*, on the other hand, treats the *Nigeria-Biafra war as a class-based conflict that leaves the masses of the people exploited and stranded on both sides. The novel celebrates the war's unglorified victims. *Awaiting Court Martial* (1996), a collection of short stories, continues his acerbic critique of contemporary Nigerian society.

J

JABAVU, Noni (Helen Nontando) (1919-), South African autobiographer, was born in South Africa's Eastern Cape to a distinguished Xhosa family of journalists and educators whose histories she charts in *Drawn in Colour* (1960) and *The Ochre People* (1963). As a teenager, she left South Africa to study in London, where she remained, working as a writer and in television. Both in its overt concerns – its nostalgic evocation of her rural childhood and exposure of the dehumanization of *apartheid – and more obliquely, Jabavu's work reflects her disrupted life history, her sense of belonging to 'two worlds with two loyalties'.

Jabavu's 1955 visit to South Africa provides the focal point for her writing. *The Ochre People* highlights three different regional cultures, from her family home, Middledrift, and her uncle's farm at Tsolo, to the urban 'locations' of Johannesburg. Like *Drawn in Colour*, it combines autobiography with travel writing and broader family, social, and cultural history. In her account of various family visits, Jabavu moves beyond the personal style of autobiography to incorporate details of group experience and to document the breakdown in African family life consequent upon urbanization. The canvas of *Drawn in Colour* is broader, extending Jabavu's reflections beyond those of a returning exile to include her impressions of westernization in East Africa as well as her criticism of traditional notions of 'a woman's place' and her simultaneous refusal of the self-definition 'feminist'. Both of these works thus prefigure the use of autobiography by subsequent black South African women: as 'a peg on which to hang life and events in South Africa', as in Phyllis Ntantala's account of a similarly privileged early life (*A Life's Mosaic*, 1993), and in works rooted more in the struggles of contemporary urban women, such as Joyce Sikakane's *A Window on Soweto* (1977) and Ellen *Kuzwayo's *Call Me Woman* (1985).

JACOBSON, Dan(iel) (1929-), South African novelist and short-story writer, was born in Johannesburg and began his career as a distinctly South African writer. His early fiction, set in recognizable South African locales, explored not only *apartheid's destruction of human lives but also its effects as it resonates in the human psyche, encouraging treachery, paranoia, and denial. His output in those early years was considerable: two novellas, *The *Trap* (1955) and *Dance in the Sun* (1956), both deal with the ways racism, greed and treachery cripple and restrict the lives of whites, while the powerlessness of blacks forces them into falsity and degradation; *The Price of Diamonds* (1957), set in Kimberley, the city where Jacobson spent his boyhood, dramatizes with humour events surrounding some illicit diamonds; *A Long Way from London* (1958) is his first collection of stories; and *No Further West* (1959) is a collection of essays about his stay as a fellow at Stanford University. Throughout his career he has published short stories, essays, and critical articles.

Jacobson's first full-length novel, *The Evidence of Love* (1960), is also set partly in Kimberley. Much of the second half of the novel, about the love between a white woman and a 'coloured' (mixed-race) man, is set in London, where Jacobson had settled in 1954. His impressions of London, partly developed in this novel, were more fully expressed in a second collection of essays titled *Time of Arrival* (1964). In 1966 he brought out his last South African novel, *The Beginners*, which follows the lives of two generations of South African Jews. The novel also expresses the family's conflicting and conflicted loyalties, whether to South Africa, the new state of Israel, or Britain.

Jacobson's own interests in South African settings seemed to resolve themselves with the publication of *The Beginners*, and his subsequent fiction, apart from some short stories, was not set in South Africa. However, although he had abandoned South Africa as a locus for his work, the lifeless quality of some South African settings still found its way into his fiction, specifically in *The Confessions of Josef Baisz* (1977), where the characters and the action seem very recognizably South African although the country is named Sarmeda. Once again the novel is preoccupied with the nature of betrayal and its pleasures.

Jacobson continued to write essays, some about South African lives and some not. These were collected in *Time and Time Again* (1985). His literary-critical articles were collected in 1988 in *Adult Pleasures: Essays on Writers and Readers*. He returned to South African concerns in the novel *Hidden in the Heart* (1991), in which the protagonist, a man with a propensity for treachery, is an Afrikaner living in London. More demonstrably, his ongoing interest in the country of his birth is expounded in *The Electronic Elephant* (1994), a diverse and entertaining account of his travels through southern Africa following the Great North Road into Zambia. Retired as a professor from University College, London, Jacobson lives with his wife Margaret and continues writing in London.

Jagua Nana (1961) A novel by Cyprian *Ekwensi. This is the story of Jagua Nana (so named because she is sleek, like the Jaguar car), her life as a Lagos prostitute, and her hopeless love for a young and idealistic Freddie, years younger than herself and murdered while fighting an election battle. While there is much melodrama in the handling of the plot and while its episodic nature makes for some confusion, the novel offers serious comment on problems of urbanization and incipient political corruption as Ekwensi exposes the seamier side of Lagos life, its poverty and squalor, its pimps and prostitutes, its greedy and corrupt politicians. The episodes of the plot allow Ekwensi to comment on social issues that concern him as a serious critic of the quality of Nigerian life in the city.

JOHNSON, Lemuel A. (1941-), poet, was born of Sierra Leonean parents in Nigeria and educated in Sierra Leone and in the USA. A professor of English at the University of Michigan, Ann Arbor, he has also taught in his home country and in Mexico.

With its concern for genealogy, Johnson's is a poetic voice both of an individual and of a multitude who proudly proclaim as their motto 'we barter coinage for coin/and do not sink'. Therein lies the strength of *The Sierra Leone Trilogy* (1995), which in its celebration of Johnson's *Krio heritage takes us in successive stages back to the poet's youth and the early years of political independence in Africa in the 1960s (*Highlife for Caliban*, 1973); the Second World War and its legacies in the bodies and minds of West African soldiers such as Corporal Bundu (*Hand on the Navel*, 1978); and finally in *Carnival of the Old Coast* (1995), the centuries of trafficking in human bodies between Africa and the New World (with a few returns to Africa) and beyond that, to biblical times, to give voice to 'Our Lady of Silences', Hagar of the triangular relations with Abraham and Sarah. The tone is funny, ironic, serious, and tragic in turns in this poetry that, though learned, maintains a fine ear for the rhythm of spoken words as heard in the streets of Freetown, Sierra Leone. Hybridity has never been celebrated with a fuller sense of history and a new cultural and human geography. 'How to Breathe Dead Hippo Meat, and Live', the introduction to each volume of the trilogy, and Sylvia Wynter's afterword to the first volume, 'The Poetics and the Politics of *Highlife for Caliban*,' provide a sure way to navigate through these poems. Johnson has also written numerous essays on African literature and has published *Shakespeare in Africa (and Other Venues): Import and the Appropriation of Culture* (1998).

JONKER, Ingrid (1933-65), South African poet who wrote in Afrikaans, was born in the rural area of Douglas, northern Cape, and educated at a girls' high school in Wynberg, where some of her earliest poetry appeared in the school magazine. She never attended a university.

By the age of sixteen Jonker was corresponding with the poet D.J. Opperman and publishing regularly in family magazines such as *Die Huisgenoot*. Her first book of poems, *Ontvlugting* [Escape] (1956), is characterized by its use of the distich form and by images of death and the passing of childhood. When her second book, *Rook en Oker* [Smoke and ochre] (1963), with its free verse and sensual, surrealist imagery, won the Afrikaanse Pers-Boekhandel Prize she became one of the Sestigers, a group that included Breyten *Breytenbach, André *Brink, Adam Small, and Bartho Smit, who were challenging conservative Afrikaans literary norms. A collection of early poems and poems written at the end of her life, *Kantelson* [Toppling sun] (1966) was published following her early death by drowning. Her *Versamelde Werke* [Collected works] (1975, 1983, and 1994) includes her prose, drama, and interviews. Her poems were translated by Jack *Cope and William *Plomer and published as *Ingrid Jonker: Selected Poems* (1988), and the Ingrid Jonker Prize for promising young poets in English and Afrikaans was instituted. At the opening of South Africa's first democratically elected parliament, President Nelson Mandela read 'The Child who Was Shot Dead by Soliders in Nyanga', a translation of her prophetic poem 'Die Kind'.

JORDAN, A(rchibald) C. (1906-68), South African novelist, was born in Mbokothwana, Transkei, educated at the Lovedale Institution and at St. John's College, Umtata, and gained a Ph.D. at Fort Hare University in 1956. As a result of political pressure, Jordan was forced to leave South Africa on an exit permit in 1961; he settled in the USA, where he was a professor of African languages and literature. *The Wrath of the Ancestors* (1980), Jordan's only novel, originally appeared in Xhosa as *Ingqumbo Yeminyanya* in 1940. His other work includes a collection of African folktales, published posthumously in 1973 as *Tales from Southern Africa*, and a critical study entitled *Towards an African Literature: The Emergence of Literary Form in Xhosa* (1972).

JOURNALS (See LITERARY MAGAZINES]

Journey Within, The (1978) A novel by I.N.C. *Aniebo. The relationships of two married couples living in the same urban environment are juxtaposed. The marriage between Christian and Janet is seen as a failure essentially because the woman apes European romanticism and female independence in her attitude to her weak and womanizing husband. Nelson's and Ejiaka's marriage is seen as a success because it is based on an Igbo connubial respect founded on unquestionable patriarchal dominance. The four major characters probe their hidden selves, in the process revealing to the reader the texture of their psychological disposi-tions. Within the framework of the narrative montage, the past and the present intersect, and the characters' inner journeys are symbolized by the train, whose ani-mated winding contours represent humanity's groping search for explanations of human experience.

Joys of Motherhood, The (1979) A novel by Buchi *Emecheta. Set in Nigeria in the 1930s and proceed-ing to the period of independence from colonial rule, the narrative follows Nnu Ego, who leaves her village with her husband to become part of the immigrant society of Lagos, the capital city and seaport. Emecheta deals with the shifting world of colonial Nigeria, where rural traditions and certainties give way to a cosmopolitan, competitive, and uncertain multiracial society. Nnu Ego's struggle is against the heartless world of Lagos and specifically against poverty and the selfish behaviour of her husband and then her child-

ren. The irony of the title relates to her struggle to give her children a good education, her one solid purpose in life. Once it is achieved, they reject her and she dies disillusioned and unrecognized.

July's People (1981) A novel by Nadine *Gordimer. Long before the orderly transition to majority rule in South Africa in the 1990s, Gordimer imagined in *July's People* the very real possibility of a far more violent revolution. The Smales, a privileged white family of four – husband, wife, two young children – escape an embattled Johannesburg by fleeing to the distant rural home of their house servant July, where they are dependent on July's extended family for their very lives. In the Smales' attempt to regain control and in the uncertainty about their fate as their hiding place is disclosed, the novel projects its sense that the white minority has not yet come to terms with the impera-tive for change.

K

KA, Aminata Maiga (1940-), Senegalese novelist writing in French. Born in Saint-Louis-du-Sénégal, Ka studied in Senegal, France, and the USA. After living in many countries in Africa, Europe, and North America, she returned to Dakar in 1976. Married to Senegalese author Abdou Anta Ka and mother of a large family, she works with the Ministry of National Education.

Ka began writing in the 1980s, following the deaths of her mother and of fellow writer and friend Mariama *Bâ. Her first work, published in 1985, consisted of two novellas: in *La Voie du Salut*, a promising magistrate is betrayed by the husband she saw as a partner in life and dies from the shock of the betrayal; in *Le Miroir de la vie*, a powerful minister's family is pulled apart by opposing social and political visions, while its exploited servant girl commits suicide to defy the 'dishonour' of an unjust imprisonment. The novel *En votre nom et au mien* (1989) explores the ramifications of the marriage of a young woman and a wealthy old man.

In all her work, against the backdrop of a disoriented neo-colonial society, Ka emphasizes the victimization of women, whether as high-placed noblewomen whose happiness is destroyed by their family's fragmentation and their misunderstanding of that fragmentation's causes, or as women whose sincere desire to establish partnerships with men is met with deceit and betrayal. Her tragic stories and incisive political vision assure her place in the tradition of African feminism and women's writing.

KACHINGWE, Aubrey (1926-), Malawian novelist and short-story writer, received his early education in Malawi and Tanzania. He has worked as a journalist and in public relations in East Africa, West Africa, and the UK.

Kachingwe's novel *No Easy Task* (1966) is about the struggle for independence in a fictional African country, Kwacha. The narrative unfolds through the eyes of the journalist, Jo Jozenzi. Kachingwe brings his journalistic experience to his exploration of the tensions and rapprochement between the newspapers and politics. The pride of the people who come from all walks of life to participate in the politics of an emergent nation radiates through the novel. Kachingwe's short stories have been published in literary magazines at home and abroad.

KAGAME, Alexis (1912-1981) Rwandan philosopher and poet, was born into a family close to the reigning dynasty in Rwanda. He was educated in a seminary and became a Catholic priest in 1941. He started collecting dynastic poetry very early thanks to his access to the royal court. He also translated these texts into French, and his linguistic and ethnographic work is the only written collection of dynastic texts in Rwanda. As a historian his approach was unusual, writing history primarily for his own people. He also wrote poetry in his own language, Kinyarwanda, and produced texts such as *Indyesha birayi*, 1949 (which can be read as a satirical poem of more than 2,000 verses, praising pigs, instead of cows as so much praised in oral poetry), and even translated some of his poems into French. His major poetic work is his *La Divine pastorale* (1952), a long poem in 24 cantos which remains unequalled in the genre of African Christian poetry.

In the 1950s as a professor of theology he produced a synthesis of his works in a thesis on *La philosophie bantu rwandaise de l'être* (1955) a daring attempt to merge Bantu world views – if such a synthetic concept can have relevance – and classic scholastic philosophy. He saw ideas as being reflected in a static linguistic system or 'cattle regiments' that reflect social groupings (1961). He completed his poetic and philosophical work by combining history and poetry in his translations of the praise names of Rwandese *armées bovines* (1961). His ample knowledge of traditional oral poetry informed his own work and he tried to transfer this understanding of these original sources into French. His enormous work has yet to be edited, but he stands as one of the founders of philosophical and religious reflection of African traditions as well as a master of contemporary Rwandese poetry.

KAHIGA, Samuel (1946-), Kenyan novelist and short-story writer, was born in the Central Province of Kenya. He graduated in fine art and design from the University of Nairobi and later studied film production. He has worked as a television producer, a composer, and a contributor to Kenya's *East African Standard*.

At a time when other Kenyan writers were producing their major works of social commitment, Kahiga showed a preference for the personal, intimate, and amusing side of life. *The Girl from Abroad* (1974) and *When the Stars Are Scattered* (1979) are love stories, unusual in African literature, though they also touch on social, cultural, moral, and religious issues. The short stories in *Flight to Juba* (1979) go a step further towards sheer entertainment, while *Lover in the Sky* (1975) has all the characteristics of popular fiction.

Kahiga's once singular interest in themes of universal relevance has made him a model in a literature increasingly heading in this direction. His novel *Paradise Farm* (1993) explores humanity's capacity for suffering and compassion, but the seriousness of the subject is subverted to the extent that the book takes the form of the thriller. In an entirely different vein, *Dedan Kimathi: The Real Story* (1990) is a historical novel that offers a reassessment of the Mau Mau movement in Kenya and of one of its most outstanding and controversial personalities.

Kalasanda (1965) Short stories by Barbara *Kimenye. The setting of the eight short stories in this collection is Kalasanda, an imaginary village in the kingdom of Buganda, and the main characters are the most striking personalities in a community of 'ordinary people who seldom hit the headlines' but who actually are 'the backbone of the country'. Each story presents with sustained humour a different segment of Kalasanda life, and collectively they combine to produce the impression of indestructibility and fullness.

KAMANDA, Kama (1952-), poet and novelist writing in French, was born in Luebo, in what was then Belgian Congo, and fled with his family during the civil war to Léopoldville (now Kinshasa), where he studied classics at a Jesuit college. He became a journalist, obtained a diploma in political science, and participated in the literary and political life of Zaïre. Exiled in 1977 because of his political views, he studied law at Liège, Belgium and in Strasbourg, France. He resides in Belgium.

Kamanda's poetry, novels, and folktales illustrate the dual influences of European education and Bantu tradition. As L.S. *Senghor noted in his preface to Kamanda's *Les Contes du griot* (1988), he brings an original and modern voice to African literature. Animism, the oral tradition, and African folklore combine with the beauty of the French language and literary heritage.

Seven collections of Kamanda's poetry, in which the celebration of Africa and the anguish of exile and solitude are recurring themes, have earned international recognition. *Chants de brumes* (1987), *L'Exil des songes* (1992), and *Les Myriades des temps vécus* (1992) were honoured by the Académie française. *La Somme du néant* (1989) won the Prix Louise Labbé. He recently published *Les Vents de l'épreuve* (1993) and *L'Étreinte des mots* (1995). Kamanda's reputation as a storyteller was established with *Les Contes du griot, Les Contes des veillées africaines* (1985), and *La Nuit des griots* (1991), which was awarded the Grand Prix littéraire de l'Afrique noire. *Lointaine sont les rives du destin* (1994) was his first novel. Kamanda's work has been widely translated and appears in English in American, British, and Indian literary journals.

KANE, Cheikh Hamidou [See RELIGION AND LITERATURE, Islam and Literature; NOVEL, Francophone]

KARODIA, Farida (1942-), novelist and short-story writer, was born in Aliwal North, South Africa, graduated from Coronationville Teacher Training College in 1961, and taught in Johannesburg and later in Zambia. When the government of South Africa withdrew her passport in 1968, she emigrated to Canada, where she supported herself with teaching and other jobs while studying and writing fiction and radio drama. Only in 1994 did she return to South Africa.

Though she draws on her own varied background, Karodia is not limited in scope or genre. Her first novel, *Daughters of the Twilight* (1986), reflects her South African childhood and the limits on education and domicile for non-whites under *apartheid. Her collection of short stories, *Coming Home and Other Stories* (1988), shows her skill and versatility in depicting protagonists of various ethnic groups: a Boer girl, a black teacher, a 'coloured' (mixed race) mother, a white employer. She has also written about Canada, and after a visit to India in 1991 she wrote and filmed *Midnight Embers*, released by Farida Films in 1992. Like Buchi *Emecheta and Flora *Nwapa, whose novels describe rape and massacre in the *Nigeria-Biafra war, Karodia finds a unique fictional theme in Mozambique. *A Shattering of Silence* (1993) depicts the kidnapping and enslavement of children. After her return from exile, she produced a collection of long and short stories set in South Africa, *Against an African Sky and Other Stories* (1995).

KARONE, Yodi (1954-), novelist, was born in France to a Cameroonian family in political exile and spent much of his youth in North Africa, where his father practised medicine. He obtained university degrees in literature and economics. *Le Bal des caïmans* (1980) is set in Cameroon and based on an actual trial of a revolutionary leader and a bishop during Ahmadou Ahidjo's rule. Their two stories, told in parallel chapters, include descriptions of prison torture and of the politically inspired courtroom proceedings. A similar two-part structure is used in *Le Nègre de paille* (1982), which won the Grand Prix littéraire de l'Afrique noire, to describe the reality and the dream life of a man returning from imprisonment. The following novel, *La Recherche du cannibale amour* (1988), is set partly in Paris and describes the life of an artist. *Les Beaux Gosses* (1988), a story of criminality and corruption in Abidjan, is filled with details of brutal sex and sordid night life. Karone's taste for vivid descriptions of violent action shows the influence of one of his masters, Chester Himes, just as his surrealistic scenes show his debt to another acknowledged master, Boris Vian. He is one of the most inventive and original of the younger generation of Cameroonian novelists.

KATIYO, Wilson (1947-), novelist and film maker, was born at Mutoko, Southern Rhodesia, now Zimbabwe, and educated at Fletcher High School. Following harassment by the police he completed his education in England; he returned to Zimbabwe at independence but now lives in France. His first novel, *A Son of the Soil* (1976), a classical decolonization narrative, uses the memories and experiences of the family of the protagonist, Alexio, to show the links between the initial armed resistance to settlers and the Zimbabwean liberation war. In the novel land takes on both political and spiritual dimensions. In the sequel, *Going to Heaven* (1979), the Rhodesian forces brutally murder Alexio's family, and he escapes to England with the help of a white couple. The presence in the narrative of whites who sympathize with the black struggle made the novel a relevant text for the policy of reconciliation that followed Zimbabwean independence. Katiyo gained a wide audience for his work when *A Son of the Soil* was chosen as a set text for the national 'O' level English examinations.

KAYIRA, Legson (1942-), Malawian novelist. The facts of Kayira's early life are legendary: a Tumbuka born and educated in Nyasaland (now Malawi), he walked as a young man from there to Khartoum, Sudan, a distance of 3,200 kilometres, seeking opportunities for further education. He found them, and studied in the USA and at Cambridge, England. His first book was the autobiographical *I Will Try* (1965), and he has written four novels: *The *Looming Shadow* (1968), *Jingala* (1969), *The Civil Servant* (1971), and *The Detainee* (1974).

Kayira's early work was non-political, painting a portrait of rural Malawi and revealing him as an observer of everyday, undramatic life. Certainly it contrasts strongly with, for example, the Malawian protest poetry of Steve *Chimombo, Frank *Chipasula, or Felix *Mnthali. The light tone of the first two novels begins to shift, however, with *The Civil Servant*, in which the gently comic vision darkens to address social issues such as the export of labour to South Africa. In *The Detainee*, written after a visit to Malawi at the height of the Banda era, the mode is satire. The texts also reveal a sharpening skill with dialogue and characterization and an ability to tease out fully their ironic potential. Old Jingala, the hero of the novel of that name, is one of the best comic portraits in all African literature, a man whose stopped watch poignantly symbolizes the passing of a whole way of life before the encroachments of central government and party politics.

KENTE, Gibson (1932-), South African composer-arranger and playwright, was born in the Eastern Cape. He revolutionized urban African popular theatre through the 1960s.

As a director for Union Artists, Dorkay House, Kente learned the craft of musical theatre, producing *Manana, the Jazz Prophet* (1963) and *Sikalo* (1966), a musical that blended African gospel and township jazz. In these plays Kente concentrated on social and communal rather than political issues, thus reflecting the African daily experience while formulating a new theatrical language for the townships' first mass audience. In 1967 he formed a company and presented *Life* (1968) and *Zwi* (1970). By 1974 he had three travelling theatre companies without state subsidy. Low admission prices and an eclectic and accessible style of theatre contributed to his success. From 1973 Kente was greatly influenced by the *Black Consciousness movement. He was caught between the public's increasing demand for political expression and the authorities' threat of shutting him down. Influenced by Athol *Fugard, John Kani, and Winston Ntshona he produced *How Long, I Believe*, and *Too Late* (1974-6), political melodramas attacking *apartheid.

Following his detention and release (1976-7) for attempting to film *How Long*, Kente's work varied from pure entertainment in *Can You Take It?* (1977), a Broadway-style township love story, to *La Duma* [It thundered] (1978) and *Mama and the Load* (1980), dramatizations of the conflict between political pressures and family/community solidarity. Kente influenced playwrights such as Mbogeni *Ngema, Matsemela *Manaka, and Maishe Maponya by creating a form that reflects black experience.

KGOSITSILE, Keorapetse (1938-), South African poet, trained as a journalist but taught for many years at the University of Dar es Salaam, the University of Nairobi, and the University of Gaborone. He spent most of the 1960s in political exile all over the world, including the USA, where he was in compatriotic as well as intellectual contact with Es'kia *Mphahlele, Dennis *Brutus, both Daniel P. and Mazisi *Kunene, and others. In the 1970s, he entered the writing programme of Columbia University in New York and worked for *Black Dialogue* magazine in the same city. In 1985, he left Botswana for a long exile when South Africa invaded his host country. His works include *Spirits Unchained* (1969), *For Melba* (1970), *My Name is Afrika* (1971), *The Present Is a Dangerous Place to Live* (1974), *Places and Bloodstains* (1975), *The Word Is Here* (1980), and *When the Clouds Clear* (1990). A volume of his collected poems, entitled *Heartprints* (1980), was published in Germany. He lives in South Africa.

KIBERA, Leonard (1942-83), Kenyan novelist and short-story writer, was born at Kibete, Kenya, attended high school at Embu, and studied at the University of California and at Stanford University in the USA. He taught at the University of Zambia and at Kenyatta University, Kenya from 1976 until his death. His first publication was a book of short stories, *Potent Ash* (1968), which he wrote with his brother, Samuel *Kahiga. The book explores the guilt, betrayal, and failure of the Mau Mau, a familiar theme among such Kenyan writers as *Ngugi wa Thiong'o, Godwin *Wachira, and Grace *Ogot. Several of the stories have been anthologized, especially 'The Spider's Web', which points an accusing finger at Kenya's elite for the state of Kenya since independence. His only novel, *Voices in the Dark* (1970), questions with dark humour why most of the Mau Mau soldiers who fought for independence are left to beg and die forgotten by the roadside. Kibera has also written several articles of criticism.

KIKUYU [See GIKUYU LITERATURE]

KIMBUGWE, Henry S. [See SERUMA, Eneriko]

KIMENYE, Barbara (1930-), Ugandan children's writer and short-story writer. Born in England, Barbara Kimenye studied in a convent in Yorkshire and trained as a nurse in London. On going to East Africa, she changed her profession to journalism and started writing fiction.

Kimenye is best known as a writer of children's adventure stories, some of them having risen to the rank of classics. Her first publications in this genre were *The Smugglers* (1966), and *Moses* (1967), the first of a series about the escapades of a Kenyan schoolboy named Moses. *The Gemstone Affair* (1978) and *The Scoop* (1978) are addressed to older children.

Kimenye's two collections of short stories, *Kalasanda* (1965) and *Kalasanda Revisited* (1966), which contain humorous glimpses of life in a Buganda village, were criticized by F. B. Welbourn for exhibiting a 'kizungu [European] imagination', but they have remained popular, as evidenced by their regular reprinting. One of the stories, 'The Battle of the Sacred Tree', has recently been made into a feature film.

KISWAHILI [See SWAHILI LITERATURE]

KONADU, (Samuel) Asare (1932-94), Ghanaian novelist, was born in Asamang in the Ashanti Region of Ghana and attended local schools and Abuakwa State College in eastern Ghana. He worked as a reporter and for radio before joining the Ghana Information Service in 1951 and later studied journalism in Europe on a Ghana government scholarship. Among the first generation of writers who stormed the Ghanaian market with their own brand of *popular literature known in neighbouring Nigeria as *Onitsha market literature, Konadu wrote about life in rural Ghana.

The title of his first novel, *The Wizard of Asamang* (1964), reveals his interest in traditional values and his obsession with superstition. A number of popular novels followed, including *Come Back Dora!* (1966), *Shadow of Wealth* (1966), *Night Watchers of Korlebu* (1967), *A Woman in Her Prime* (1967), *Ordained by the Oracle* (1969), and *The Coup Makers* (1994), often incorporating details of the traditional customs and practices of the Akan people of Ghana. He also published popular fiction under the pseudonym Kwabena Asare Bediako, most notably *Don't Leave Me Mercy* (1966) and *A Husband for Esi Ellua* (1967).

Kongi's Harvest (1965) A play by Wole *Soyinka. Though not as complex a play as *The *Road* or *Madmen and Specialists*, like these, *Kongi's Harvest* provides fierce insight into the political and social disorder that led Nigeria into the 1967-70 *Nigeria-Biafra war. The play parodies the neo-colonial one-party state through its depiction of the regime of the dictator Kongi; the plot revolves around attempts to contest the regime made by the traditional paramount chief, Danlola, and, more effectively, by the chief's heir, Daodu, the head of a farming commune, and the nightclub hostess Sigi. The play employs quasi-Brechtian satirical devices and elements of festival drama, especially in its spectacular denouement. Soyinka himself played Kongi in the 1970 film version.

KOUROUMA, Ahmadou (1927-), Côte d'Ivoirean novelist, was born in Ivory Coast (now Côte d'Ivoire), expelled from secondary school for leading a student strike and inducted in the 'tirailleurs' in 1945. Refusing to suppress a mutiny he was sent to Indochina where he became a broadcaster for the French military radio network.

After leaving the army, he studied engineering and became an actuary for insurance companies. He worked briefly in Ivory Coast at the beginning of the 1960s, then in Algeria. His first novel, *Les Soleils des indépendances*, was turned down by publishers in Paris in 1964. The Africanized French and the criticism of the new regimes had sounded reactionary at the time. It was published in Montreal in 1968 following an award from the journal *Études françaises*. Unfortunately the English translation *The Suns of Independence* (1981) as it stands is unable to convey the quality of the original. The novel was published in Paris in 1970 and got some scholarly attention for the linguistic creativity in Kourouma's Malinke syntax and the lack of neological restraint. In 1970 Ahmadou Kourouma went back to the Ivory Coast and his play *Tougnantigui, le diseur de vérité* (1973) was not liked by the authorities. Unable to find a job, Kourouma went into exile and became head of the African Insurance School in Yaoundé, Cameroon. In the 1980s he became head of the Reinsurance Company of the Franc Zone, a major economic position qualifying him as one of the leading experts of the insurance business in Africa. Few of his colleagues know he is the author of such a novel which is now very well-known and has become a standard part of school curricula. Meanwhile many regimes such as that of Guinée show their dark side, and more and more African writers express the desire to 'africanize' the French language. His second novel, *Monnè, outrages et défis* (1990) is an epic of 'collaboration' over a century of colonial rule. His third novel, *En attendant le vote des bêtes sauvages* (1998) was shortlisted for literary prizes in France and is the result of his observations of tyranny in Togo, where he lived for several years. Ahmadou Kourouma has now retired and lives in Abidjan; he is also the president of Africréation, a French based non-governmental organization aimed at African artistic promotion.

KRIO is one of the seventeen languages spoken in Sierra Leone, West Africa. It is the native language of the Krio people, some two per cent of a population of 4.5 million, the majority of whom are in Freetown and the Western Area. It is also a lingua franca, second language, and language of wider communication for a significant proportion of the population (anything from 50 to 80 per cent) in a stable multilingual situation.

Krio belongs to the language family called Pidgins and Creoles by linguists because it developed in language contact situations through the processes of pidginization and creolization. Important events related to the origins of Krio include Portuguese and English exploration in West Africa, the founding of Freetown in 1787, its settlement by waves of freed slaves including those released there by the British navy beginning in 1808, and the emergence of Krio society by the mid-nineteenth century in the then British colony of Sierra Leone. The rise of local Pidgins and their stabilization, expansion, and later creolization and development into what is now Krio were the social and linguistic consequences of those forces.

The origins of Krio have determined its synchronic characteristics; the language can be described as an English-related Creole, since its lexicon derives largely from English, which was the superstrate language of high prestige during its formation. But Krio also has an extensive African-language substrate, and perhaps a third of its lexicon came from African languages, principally *Yoruba and other languages along the west coast. Thus, because of this substrate and its impact during pidginization, Krio is more of an African language than its superficial resemblance to English might suggest.

Like most dynamic languages, Krio has different dialects and varieties that are a consequence of its geographical spread and use by native and non-native speakers at all points on the social spectrum, the patterns of its acquisition, and its co-existence with the other

Sierra Leonean languages and English, all of which allows code mixing, code switching and interference, and other forms of language behaviour. All dialects and varieties can be identified and marked on the levels of grammar, vocabulary and phonology, resulting in for example a native-speaker mainstream dialect, a non-native/non-mainstream dialect, and a sociolect.

From a sociolinguistic perspective, the Krio language now occupies an important place in Sierra Leone multilingualism. It is a major language and one of the four being promoted as national languages, the others being Mende, Temne, and Limba, because of its patterns of function, distribution, and use. In formal domains of language use such as the media, education, and the civil service, where English is the official language, Krio has infiltrated and appropriated to itself a variety of roles, for example as medium of instruction in the very early years in primary schools and for oral communication in the civil service. In informal domains it also has an extensive role, where its choice and use in different locations and specific situations within the country are determined by sociolinguistic variables.

Although Krio does not have a strong or long literary tradition, it is becoming a medium for literary creativity and expression in popular theatre and culture. In spite of difficulties with the acceptance of its discreteness from English and its intrinsic linguistic integrity and autonomy (a problem of many Creoles), with the development and broad acceptance of an orthography, and with issues of standardization, there is nevertheless a strong and growing body of literature in Krio not limited to translations of the Bible or of Shakespeare.

KUNENE, Daniel P. (1923-), South African critic and poet. Born at Edenville in the Orange Free State, Kunene took his BA at the University of South Africa and both his MA and Ph.D. at the University of Cape Town, where he lectured in the department of Bantu languages until 1964, when he left South Africa permanently. In 1976, he became professor of African languages and literature at the University of Wisconsin-Madison. A passionate advocate of African-language literatures, Kunene has spoken out in favour of African writers writing in the vernacular rather than in English. His research has focused on *Sesotho literature, especially on Thomas *Mofolo, whose *Chaka he translated, and on developing a new methodology for the study of African language literatures. His scholarly works include *The Works of Thomas Mofolo: Summaries and Critiques* (1967) and *Thomas Mofolo and the Emergence of Written Sesotho Prose* (1989). His creative writings comprise two collections of poetry, *Pirates Have Become Our Kings* (1978) and *A Seed Must Seem to Die* (1981), and a collection of stories entitled *From the Pit of Hell to the Spring of Life* (1986). In *A Seed Must Seem to Die*, born in the aftermath of the Soweto uprising of 1976, the poet mourns the loss of childhood and the deaths of children, but finally suggests that the 'seed that must seem to die' – the dead of Soweto – will reappear 'Sprouting/Rising/Living!' in celebration of coming liberation. The stories evoke the South Africa of *apartheid in portrayals of rural life and childhood experience and of the resourcefulness with which blacks counter the apparatus of white control and articulate the hope of freedom.

KUNENE, Mazisi (KaMdabuli) (1930–), South African poet, was born in Durban and educated at the University of Natal. He left South Africa in 1959 to pursue studies in England. Politically active in the African National Congress and South African National Front, he lived in Lesotho and taught at what is now the National University. He was later a professor of African literature and languages at the University of California, Los Angeles; in 1993, he returned to South Africa to assume a similar position at the University of Natal, Durban.

For *Zulu Poems* (1970), Kunene collected and translated into English his early poetry. Evolving from traditional *Zulu literature, the poems reflect the importance of his social and cultural inheritance. With the publication of *Emperor Shaka the Great* (1979), an epic poem inspired by the rise of the Zulu empire, followed by *Anthem of the Decades* (1981), a Zulu epic dedicated to the women of Africa, Kunene earned critical as well as popular recognition. His reputation was further enhanced by the lyrical and elegiacal poems collected in *The Ancestors and the Sacred Mountain* (1982). His most recent publications are *Isibusiso sikamhawu* (1994), *Indiba yamancasakazi* (1995) and *Umzwilili wama-Africa* (1996). Acknowledged for his commitment to the language and history of his Zulu heritage and for his persistence in the struggle for liberation in South Africa, Kunene is a major voice in African literature and an author of international significance. His poetic vision has enabled him, despite his living many years in exile, to assist in the creation of a new South African society.

Kurunmi (1969) A play by Ola *Rotimi. Along with two other plays (the first, *The *Gods Are Not to Blame*, 1968, and the third *Ovonrameme Nogbaise*, 1971), the play forms part of a trilogy that examines the nature of leadership, especially the qualities that are required and the limitations that individual character and historical circumstances place upon it. In *Kurunmi* Rotimi places his examination in the context of the 1858 war between the two Yoruba communities of Iyaye and Oyo. The context for the third play in the group is the British punitive expedition of 1898 against the Kingdom of Benin led by Sir Ralph Moore.

KUZWAYO, Ellen (1914–), South African autobiographer and short-story writer, grew up on the farm of her maternal grandparents near Thaba'Nchu in the Orange Free State. After her secondary schooling at Mariannhill in Natal, she went to Adams College in Durban and Lovedale in the Eastern Cape for teacher training. After the publication of her autobiography *Call Me Woman* (1985), with its story of community activism and dedication to improving women's lives, she became a spokesperson and role model for black women. The book is testimony to her ability to survive familial rejection and displacement and to recover from a disastrous marriage and enforced separation from her two young sons. Her own narrative is, however, subsumed in a larger narrative of the struggle of black women not only to survive but also to break free from traditionally ascribed roles and pursue their own life choices. She places on record the achievements of women who have forged their own paths and rendered valuable service to their communities. *Sit Down and Listen* (1990) is a collection of stories in which Kuzwayo assumes the role of the oral storyteller in order to keep alive a cultural heritage in danger of dying out. By juxtaposing past and present, she highlights the impact of dislocations and the move to the cities. Several stories demonstrate the value of traditional customs and attitudes, while others examine the plight of women caught between the old and the new or struggling to survive in the city.

L

LA GUMA, Alex(ander) (1925-85), South African short-story writer and novelist, was born in District Six, Cape Town, and graduated in 1945 from the Cape Technical College. At the time he was an active member of the Plant Workers Union of the Metal Box Company and was dismissed after organizing a strike for higher wages. He became politically active as a result of his dismissal, joining the Young Communist League in 1947 and the South African Communist party in 1948. Employed by *New Age* as a reporter in 1955, he began to write short stories critical of the government's policy of racial discrimination.

La Guma's strength lies in the short story form. His curiosity about the poverty, despair, oppression, and hopes of humanity combines with a deep concern about their suffering and affliction that inhabits the minutest detail of the fictional environment: the physical state of buildings, the smells that emanate from them, and the lives caught up in this environment. His first short story, 'Nocturne' (1957), reveals his ability to capture atmosphere, speech, and surface meaning. The straightforward narrative of a young man planning a robbery who is disturbed by classical music streaming in from outside blends event, scene, effective inner dialogue, and moral aim, making a point about social environment, status, transcendence, and South Africa's racist ugliness. La Guma saw his task, in a way, as similar to an African storyteller's, namely to record events as told to him and fashion a narrative both moral and entertaining. An example is the short story 'Coffee for the Road' (1965). Although some critics have seen the story as a demonstration of the spectacular mode of South African writing, it reminds the reader that a social practice such as racial discrimination is effective only in so far as it is willingly supported by those victimized by it. The Indian woman who is the protagonist represents the quintessential South African resister, for whom 'no' is not a word but a form of action.

In addition to many short stories, La Guma's novels include *A *Walk in the Night* (1962), *And a Threefold Cord* (1964), *The *Stone Country* (1967), **In the Fog of the Seasons' End* (1972), and **Time of the Butcherbird* (1979). At the time of his death, he was writing another novel, 'Zone of Fire'. Though each novel has its faults, such as an occasional slackening of pace and control, the prose is evocative, strong, and vivid. Each focuses on something specific, beginning with the unfolding of consciousness about social, economic, and political issues in the 'coloured' (mixed race) community in *A Walk in the Night*. *And a Threefold Cord* examines the poverty, misery, and loneliness of slum existence that engenders inertia and resignation, while *The Stone Country* portrays humanity imprisoned. *In the Fog of the Seasons' End* demonstrates the determination to overthrow the state nurtured by that imprisonment. *Time of the Butcherbird* reflects his conviction that only conscious resistance will rid South Africa of the scourge of racism and oppression. 'Zone of Fire' imagines the final phase of the protracted struggle for a democratic South Africa. Occasional accusations that La Guma is a mere propagandist are nullified by craftsmanship, and his grasp of the variety of human character and experience transcends narrow political interests.

He also wrote a travel book, *A Soviet Journey* (1978), and a biography of his father, *Jimmy La Guma* (1997). His early journalistic writings and cartoons have been collected in *Liberation Chabalala: The World of Alex La Guma*, ed. André Odendaal and Roger Field (1993).

Labyrinths (1971) Poems by Christopher *Okigbo. Published jointly with *Path of Thunder*, with which they must be read, the poems evoke themes and concerns typical of Okigbo's poetry, specifically how personal concerns are inextricably implicated in public issues. Okigbo's complex poetic is nowhere more fully revealed than in these sister volumes, in which the poet demonstrates how tribalism and public corruption compromise and threaten to destroy personal integrity. Okigbo is never more pessimistic about the possibilities for an independent Nigeria than in these poems.

LADIPO, Duro (1931-78), Nigerian dramatist, came into prominence as a composer of *Yoruba folk opera when he wrote a cantata for the 1961 Christmas season that incorporated such traditional instruments as the *bata* drum. It attracted the attention of the German promoter of Nigerian cultures, Ulli Beier, with whose encouragement and guidance he developed a distinctive and highly successful folk opera style. Hubert Ogunde had earlier popularized folk opera in Nigeria, a theatrical form that combines dialogue, singing, lively popular music, and choreographed dancing. But while Ogunde's plots were either biblical or folkloric in inspiration, Ladipo took his materials from Yoruba history. Furthermore, while Ogunde's general practice was inspired by the American minstrel tradition, Ladipo strove for fidelity to Yoruba traditional practice in all respects. As a base for his operations he founded the *Mbari Mbayo Club at Oshogbo in 1962, to inaugurate which he premiered *Oba M'Oro* [Ghost-catcher king]. His most popular achievement by far, however, was *Oba Ko So* [The king did not hang], with which he marked the club's first anniversary, following a year later with *Oba W'Aja* [The king is dead] (both published in *Three Yoruba Plays*, 1964). He collaborated with Ulli Beier on several adaptations, which they published using the pseudonym Obotunde Ijimere.

LAING, B(ernard) Kojo (1946-), Ghanaian novelist and poet, was born in Kumasi, the capital of the Ashanti Region of Ghana, and gained a master's degree at Glasgow University in 1968. He is the writer of three novels and one volume of poetry.

Search Sweet Country (1986), the first novel, is set in the Ghana of the 1970s and focuses on, among other things, the inability of Ghanaian intellectuals to envision a future for Ghana beyond the corrupt and inept dictatorship of Kutu Acheampong. Laing draws freely from both traditional *orature and contemporary world literature to represent his idea of the infinite complexity of perspectives. The second novel, *Woman of the Aeroplanes* (1988), and the third, *Major Gentl and the Achimota Wars* (1992), are similarly critical of the power-seekers who corrupt all efforts at human progress. *Woman of the Aeroplanes* is, in one way, a sequel to *Search Sweet Country*, blending the real and the supernatural in an international setting. *Major Gentl and the Achimota Wars* is the partly surreal account of the Wars of Existence, which take place in the year 2020 between Major Gentl of Africa and Torro the Terrible, a hybrid of Europe and Africa. Laing's linguistically innovative poetry is collected in *Godhorse* (1989).

As a poet and novelist Laing approaches language inventively: he pushes English to its limits and beyond by fusing Oxbridge with West African Pidgin, elements from African languages, and his own coinings, aiming to create one gigantic living and truly cosmopolitan language.

Lament for an African Pol (1985) A novel by Mongo *Beti, translated from the French (*Ruine presque cocasse d'un polichinelle*, 1979). Continuing the adventures of two of the characters from *Remember Ruben* (1974), the novelist moves further away from the realist model he had used previously, either by artistic choice or in order to avoid censorship, or both. The story begins realistically enough during an uprising resembling those that disturbed African city life in the 1960s and 70s, but soon the protagonists set out on an imaginary journey that brings them to a village where an immoral chief reigns supported by white missionaries.

The text then proposes an image of neo-colonialism and of the revolution necessary to overturn the regime: a new society can emerge only when the whites lose their position of power, the chief is replaced by the rightful heir, everyone participates in the struggle, science and technology become the tools of the revolution, and justice replaces vengeance.

Landlocked (1965) A novel by Doris *Lessing. The fourth and final novel of the *Children of Violence* series finds the hero, Martha Quest, disillusioned with her small communist group in the capital of a British colony in Africa modelled on Rhodesia at the end of the Second World War. As she withdraws from her affair with the leader of the communists, Martha becomes passionately involved with a Jewish refugee from Europe, Thomas Stern. But he is so consumed with anger following the war that his plans lead him away from her towards self-destruction. As the children of violence, they are the victims of the culture of war. Having lost her hope for progressive political change in southern Africa, Martha finally leaves the colony to go to England. Through her successive escapes and entrapments in marriage, radical politics, and sexual relationships, Martha Quest has become too intensely charged to endure the frustrating pace of change in post-war Africa.

Langbodo (1979) A play by Wale *Ogunyemi. A successful production in London in 1984 confirmed this as Ogunyemi's best-known play internationally. Based on a novel by the veteran Yoruba writer D.O. *Fagunwa (translated by Wole *Soyinka as *The *Forest of a Thousand Daemons*, 1968), *Langbodo* is a quest tale employing fantastic elements (all differences considered, somewhat in the manner of Amos *Tutuola) in order to comment powerfully and pessimistically on the social and political realities of the contemporary Nigerian state. An ambitious play with a large cast *Langbodo* shows Ogunyemi's mastery of stage craft at its strongest and marks an important contribution to the development of a total theatre that integrates dialogue with music and dance.

Last Harmattan of Alusine Dunbar, The (1990) A novel by Syl *Cheney-Coker. With tone and content reminiscent of Gabriel García Márquez's *One Hundred Years of Solitude*, the lyrical first novel by the poet Syl Cheney-Coker narrates the history of the fictional West African community of Malagueta. Among the founders of Malagueta are Sebastian Cromantine and his wife Jeanette, who escape enslavement in North America towards the end of the eighteenth century. Other characters include Malagueta's military leader Thomas Bookerman and Isatu, who returns to her home village to rediscover her African magic lore and defeat her sterility. Their fight against the colonial forces continues through generations until the present time, as predicted centuries earlier by the desert magician Alusine Dunbar, whose spirit constantly reappears to support the Malaguetans' cause. A Commonwealth Writers Prize awarded to the novel acknowledged the emergence of West African magic realism.

LAUNKO, Okinba, pseud. of Femi *Osofisan.

LAYE, Camara [See CAMARA LAYE]

LESSING, Doris (1919-), novelist and short-story writer, was born in Persia but moved with her parents in 1925 to the English colony of Rhodesia (now Zimbabwe), where her father had a farm in Banket, northwest of the capital of Salisbury (now Harare). After moving to Salisbury in 1938, Lessing became involved in the radical political opposition to the racial 'colour bar' in the colony and eventually left for London in 1949 with the manuscript of her first novel *The *Grass Is Singing* (1950).

Lessing's early writing shows the influence of Olive *Schreiner, the late-nineteenth-century South African novelist who dealt with similar themes concerning isolated women in colonial culture. In her first novel and her early short stories, collected in *African Stories* (1964), Lessing goes beyond Schreiner in dealing with the political and racial problems of colonialism. She also displays a great feeling for the loneliness, failure, and madness of colonial families. In *The Grass Is Singing*, an English couple descends into physical and mental illness as their farm fails, and the wife's erratic treatment of her African 'houseboy', alternating abuse with dependence, sets the stage for her murder.

Lessing's major work of African fiction is the series of novels *The Children of Violence*, which appeared in the 1950s and 60s and traces the development of a rebellious young English colonial woman named Martha Quest, whose life parallels Lessing's. Through the course of several rebellions, beginning in opposition to her mother, Martha Quest ends up in a series of traps and escapes that Lessing treats realistically yet ironically (*Martha Quest*, 1952). Successfully merging personal and political narratives, Lessing traces Martha Quest's progress through a brief loveless marriage to a colonial civil servant (*A *Proper Marriage*, 1954), a tortured affair with the authoritarian head of a small communist group (*A *Ripple from the Storm*, 1958), and a passionate love affair with a Jewish refugee from Poland who is so haunted by the war that he drives himself to destruction (*Landlocked*, 1965). With her naive idealism spent, Martha leaves for London after the war with little hope for an end to white colonial domination.

In her major feminist novel *The Golden Notebook* (1962), Lessing compresses part of the Martha Quest story. The protagonist, Anna Wulf, is an English

writer who had earlier lived in an African colony, shared some of the experience of communism, and written a novel about colonial relationships between blacks and whites. The character of Martha Quest returns in the apocalyptic novel *The Four Gated City* (1969), which ends with massive nerve gas leaks that decimate western Europe and North America and bring about the end of Martha Quest's world.

Though Lessing has gone on to explore madness, science fiction, and political terrorism in more recent novels, her major themes of personal, social, and political disintegration clearly began in her powerful African fiction.

Letters to Martha (1968) Poems by Dennis *Brutus. The title of Brutus' second volume of poems, written while he was imprisoned on Robben Island, refers to the banning order under South African *censorship laws which prevented him from publishing anything judged to be in any way inflammatory. The 'letters' are really a series of occasional poems written down as they randomly occur. They convey the wide range of emotions that are evoked in the *prison setting: the fear of torture juxtaposed with the sense of camaraderie that develops among prisoners and warders; the need for human contact experienced by the prisoner in solitary confinement; the continuing recognition of the loss in prison of commonplace things – the sight of the sea and sky, the faces of loved ones, the thrill of the song of a bird. Taken together they convey a rounded sense of the physical and spiritual life of the poet in prison.

Life & Times of Michael K (1983) A novel by J.M. *Coetzee and winner of the Booker Prize. Set in Cape Town, the novel shows the city in the grip of an imagined civil war. A heterodiegetic narrator tells the story of a harelipped gardener, Michael K, who attempts to realize his dying mother's wish to return to her birthplace in the country. She dies en route; having buried her ashes on a deserted farm, he constructs a burrow for his dwelling place and begins to cultivate pumpkins. Under suspicion of having supplied food to guerilla bands, he is taken to a military camp, where he refuses to eat and resists the attempts of the medical officer to save him. The section narrated by the medical officer becomes a self-reflexive commentary on the relationship between the writer and the inarticulate victim whose story he wishes to tell. The allegorical nature of the entire novel is made explicit in this section, and it becomes clear that Michael K has affinities with Kafka's protagonists from *The Trial*, *The Castle*, and 'The Hunger Artist'. Michael K's escape from the camp functions as an allegory for the ability to escape time, history, and ideology and establishes his status as 'a great escape artist, one of the great escapees'. The ending shows him with a new passenger, planning another journey into the countryside in search of a 'pocket outside time'.

LIKIMANI, Muthoni (*c*.1940-), novelist and poet, was born and brought up at Kahuhia Mission, Marang'a District, Kenya, and is the daughter of Levi Gachanja, one of the first ministers of the Kenyan Anglican church. She has worked as a teacher, a nutritionist, a social worker, a broadcaster, and a journalist. She lives in Nairobi, where she owns an advertising and promotion business.

Likimani is the author of the novels *They Shall Be Chastised* (1974) and *Passbook Number F.47927: Women and Mau Mau in Kenya* (1985), the narrative poem *What Does a Man Want?* (1974), and a Swahili storybook about children in Kenya called *Shangazi na Watoto*. She has written non-fiction on the subject of women in Kenya, and she has represented Kenya at several conferences including the United Nations Decade for Women Conference in 1985. In 1994 she received the National Council of Women of Kenya (NCWK) award in recognition of exemplary service to women's advancement in Kenya.

Likimani regards *Passbook Number F.47927*, the latter her own identity number during the Mau Mau struggle, as her most important work. The novel, which focuses on the crucial role played by Kenyan women in the Mau Mau insurgency, is a series of self-contained episodes that deal with such injustices as the lack of personal liberty for both men and women forced under penalty of incarceration to carry a passbook, the forced-labour gangs of women used for road building and trench digging, the oppressive detention camps, and the displacement of peasants from their land. *They Shall Be Chastised* deals with the early missionary schools and highlights the problems faced by the indigenous peoples caught between two very different cultures. *What Does a Man Want?* is a satirical view of the contradictions of married life in an African context, including a husband's infidelities, domestic violence, polygamy, prostitution, and the generation gap.

Limits (1962) Poems by Christopher *Okigbo. Following on from *Heavensgate*, the volume falls into two parts. The first identifies the poet's quest to find an authentic poetic voice and records his desire to establish a reputation as poet. Having found his voice in the first half, Okigbo goes on to comment on the consequences of colonial rule in Africa. Here as in *Heavensgate* he explores the duality of his African religious inheritance and his Christian training and seeks reconciliation. As the volume closes he affirms the rebirth of his traditional gods, at the same time recognizing the incivility of human behaviour.

Lion and the Jewel, The (1963) A play by Wole *Soyinka. Soyinka's earliest published full-length play remains one of his best known. A comedy, the play employs a far more genial species of satire than do later pieces such as *Opera Wonyosi* (1981) in order to puncture the pretensions of a superficially Westernized young schoolmaster who cherishes unrealistic dreams of modernizing the village of Ilujinle. The central action of the play deals with the competition between the schoolmaster, Lakunle, and the old chief, Baroka, for the hand of the village beauty, Sidi. Sometimes described as a 'festival drama', *The Lion and the Jewel* is impressively eloquent and graceful; critical discussion has focused on its thematic treatment of notions of tradition and Westernization.

LIPENGA, Ken (1954-), Malawian short-story writer, was born in the Mulanje district of southern Malawi and educated at Nazombe Primary and Mulanje Secondary schools, the University of Malawi (BA), the University of Leeds (MA), and the University of New Brunswick, Canada (Ph.D.). He taught at the University of Malawi and later became editor of Malawi's *Daily Times*, the national newspaper. His short-story collection *Waiting for a Turn* (1981) was praised for its accomplished style, humour, and lively intelligence. The title story pressed his comic style into service against the Banda regime: a potential suicide who plans to throw himself off Malawi's highest mountain finds a crowd already waiting with the same idea. As a busy journalist and editor, Lipenga seems to have little time for creative writing.

LITERARY CRITICISM The development of modern African literary criticism can be traced to the period immediately before and after the Second World War, when African French-language writers such as L.S. *Senghor, Birago *Diop, and their West Indian colleagues such as Aimé Césaire developed the theory of *negritude. The negritudinist critics drew the attention of fashionable European critics and thinkers such as Jean-Paul Sartre, who wrote an introduction entitled 'Black Orpheus' to the first anthology of black African writing published in France, Senghor's *Anthologie de la nouvelle poésie nègre et malgache de langue française* (1948). These critics insisted that African cultures and the literatures they produced had aesthetic and critical standards of their own and needed to be judged in the light of their differences and their specific concerns rather than as a mere offspring of the parental European cultures. The establishment of the critical magazine *Présence africaine*, founded by Alioune *Diop in Paris in 1947, had initiated a new critical interest in the French-language writing of Africa and the Caribbean, and this important magazine became the location for a number of crucial critical statements over the next twenty years or so, including Cheikh Anta *Diop's influential essay 'Nations, nègres et culture' and 'Of the Marvellous Realism of the Haitians' by Jacques Stephen Aléxis. With the decision to publish this magazine in both French and English from 1957 onwards, it also became an important location for critical consideration of African writing in English. Negritude and the work it developed took as its territory not only Africa but the whole of diasporic African culture, since negritude, as Senghor defined it, encompassed 'the sum total of the values of the civilization of the African world'. For this reason it was the earliest and most important movement in establishing a wider awareness of Africa's claim to cultural distinctiveness.

Despite the work of the negritudinist critics and that of a few pioneer European critics such as Ulli Beier, Janheinz Jahn, and Albert Gérard, who offered a broad comparativist basis for the development of European criticism of African literatures in the late 1950s and early 1960s, most early European and American critical responses to African literatures in this period continued to emphasize either their exotic quality – for example the famous review of Amos *Tutuola's The *Palm-wine Drinkard by Dylan Thomas in the Observer, which referred to it as 'a brief, thronged, grisly and bewitching story' – or, conversely, emphasized their legitimizing continuities with European forms and sources, as for example in essays such as A.G. Stock's 'Yeats and Achebe'. There was in both approaches a patronizing focus on the work's significance for its European readers and a simplistic concern with the presence or absence of universal values in the text under discussion. This over-simple opposition of the universal and the local by European and American critics led Chinua *Achebe in the 1970s to take to task the Euro–American assumption that the values of their own cultures coincided with these so-called universal values. As Achebe pithily put it, universality was perceived as a condition that was intrinsic to Euro-American art and only achievable by Africans with a conscious and sustained imitative effort, an effort that implied a proper concern with the themes and structures of European aesthetics. It was an important theoretical statement then and remains so in the light of the ill-informed and reactionary criticism that surfaced in the early 1990s, especially in America. Such criticism assumes that the emphasis on local and specific readings in criticism from post-colonial societies such as Africa denies the possibility of describing general human values and concerns. Achebe's comments make it clear that, in fact, it is precisely the denial of these values in their African manifestation which colonialist universalist criticism effects.

Although European and American criticism that sought to identify the European borrowings in African texts was frequently suspect, the same recognition of the hybridity of contemporary African writing in Eng-lish was also capable of identifying a much more complex process of exchange between the cultures of the colonizer and colonized. Emmanuel Obiechina, an influential early West African critic, strove to identify the parallels between the development of African writing in colonial languages and the development of the vernacular languages of Europe after the collapse of Latin as a universal language of empire, and emphasized the appropriative nature of the development of various local forms of African English. Obiechina was also the first African critic to draw attention to the existence of a rich *popular literature that had emerged in the market centres of West Africa and that used both indigenous languages and appropriated forms of colonial languages to communicate with the masses in a series of local self-published texts. This so-called 'market literature' drew on both the oral traditions of African societies and on the forms of western pulp fiction and self-help pamphlets. Obiechina's work demonstrates the demand, which remains a constant of African criticism, that the local nature of African texts be acknowledged and that they be seen in relation to both the power of oral and written production in the local languages and the local popular culture in English.

During the late 1960s, the 1970s, and the early 1980s European and American *literary theorists attempted to develop a critical methodology to deal with the new writing emerging from Africa. Their work reflected the dangers ironically implicit in the very recognition of the new writing, involving as it did the unequal relations of power between African and non-African scholars and critics of African literature. There is little doubt, however, that this criticism established African literature as a subject of critical attention overseas. The theoretical models that emerged included comparative studies of the writing of the black diaspora as a whole (Mercer Cook and Stephen E. Henderson, The Militant Black Writer in Africa and the United States, 1969); of African and Caribbean writing (Gareth Griffiths, A Double Exile, 1978, and Gerald Moore, The Chosen Tongue, 1969); continental surveys (Wilfred Cartey, Whispers from a Continent, 1969, Judith Gleason, This Africa, 1965, and David Cook, African Literature, 1977); studies of specific regional configurations within African writing (Stephen Gray, Southern African Literature, 1979, Andrew Gurr and Angus Calder, eds., Writers in East Africa, 1971, Margaret Laurence, Long Drums and Cannons, 1968, and Bernth Lindfors, ed., Critical Perspectives on Nigerian Literature, 1976); studies of individual authors (G.D. Killam, The Novels of Chinua Achebe, 1969 and David Carroll, Chinua Achebe, 1970); and one or two pioneer studies of African women writers (Maryse Condé, 'Three female writers in modern Africa', Présence africaine 82.2, 1972 and Lloyd W. Brown, Women Writers in Black Africa, 1981). There were also a number of collections of essays by and interviews with African writers and critics edited by European or North American critics (for example, G.D. Killam, *African Writers on African Writing*, 1973). This body of work clearly reflected a growing overseas interest in and attention to African writing in the ex-colonial languages. More significant, perhaps, was the growth in the same period of an equally wide-ranging set of studies by African critics (Oladele Taiwo, *An Introduction to West African Literature*, 1967, Eustace Palmer, *Introduction to the African Novel*, 1972, Gideon-Cyrus M. Mutiso, *Socio-Political Thought in African Literature*, 1974, Ernest Emenyonu, *The Rise of the Igbo Novel*, 1978, F. Abiola Irele, *The African Experience in Literature and Ideology*, 1981, and others). These included many works by creative writers who explored the critical significance of the context of African writing in monographs, in collections of essays, and in semi-autobiographical accounts. These include Lewis *Nkosi's *Home and Exile* (1965), *Ngugi wa Thiong'o's *Homecoming* (1972), Es'kia *Mphahlele's *Down Second Avenue* (1959), Richard *Rive's *Writing Black* (1981), Kofi *Awoonor's *The Breast of the Earth* (1975), Wole *Soyinka's *Myth, Literature and the African World* (1976), and others. More recently, the Kenyan critic Simon Gikandi, working within conventional critical frameworks but with an awareness of contemporary theoretical modes, has produced a general account of the African novel (*Reading the African Novel*, 1987) that is the most useful and up-to-date survey of the field and a study of the work of Chinua Achebe (*Reading Chinua Achebe*, 1991) that brings recent theories of discourse and ideology to bear on the close reading of texts in a fruitful way.

This body of local criticism is significant because it insists on the value of an African perspective and the existence of a distinctive African aesthetic while also addressing the issues of the relationship of these to the changing nature of African society and the complex influences at work on the texts produced in modern Africa. Thus a foundational African critical text like Soyinka's *Myth, Literature and the African World* sought to embrace the ongoing importance and independent significance of the Yoruba belief system in contemporary writing while simultaneously acknowledging the powerful effect of modernization processes on the African reality. This balanced assessment produced a reaction from critics who wanted to assert the complete independence of African texts from the effect of the long symbiosis with European forms and aesthetic ideas. To this school of thought writers like Soyinka were over-complex and too influenced by Euro-American models and forms. The three leading critics of this school, popularly known as the 'combat critics' (from the Nigerian term *bolekaja*, literally meaning to come down and fight), *Chinweizu, Onwuchekwa

Jemie, and Ihechukwu Madubuike, published a critical book designed to illustrate their principles of what constituted authentic African writing (*Towards the Decolonization of African Literature*, 1980). Their work reflected the increasing sense among many African writers and critics of the need for a period of active decolonization, in which writers would seek the precolonial roots of their culture and employ their forms and themes in contemporary work. There was also an accompanying demand that writers should return to indigenous languages to express African reality, since it was argued, the ex-colonial languages carried with them a baggage of Eurocentric ideas that would prevent the development of an independent African expression. The Kenyan writer and critic Ngugi wa Thiong'o was prominent in the group who advocated the return to the use of local languages in a process he referred to as a decolonization of the mind (*Decolonising the Mind*, 1986), though many others flirted with the idea. Even Soyinka, at one point, suggested the possibility of developing *Swahili into a pan-African lingua franca. Few writers so far, however, have followed Ngugi to the point of rejecting English entirely in favour of indigenous languages, as in the plays he devised before his political expulsion and in such novels as *Devil on the Cross* (1982) and *Matigari* (1986; trans. 1989), which he wrote in *Gikuyu. On the other hand there was the response of the writer *Okot p'Bitek, who advocated both the need to return to a local concept of culture and the need to employ a variety of languages in which to express this reality. Ngugi has argued that the use of the colonial languages restricts the audience to the elite who, he further argues, constitute a Fanonesque neo-colonial comprador class alienated from the people. On the other hand, others such as the South African writer and critic Lewis Nkosi have contended that the use of English allows a pan-African communication that is essential to contemporary international linkages and linkages between the different African cultures.

The development of a local criticism was not entirely preoccupied with the search for distinctive African aesthetics or with the recuperation of African traditional forms and themes. A number of African critics enthusiastically embraced the critical ideas of structuralism and post-structuralism. In *Structural Models and African Poetics* (1981), Sunday Anozie attempts to apply the ideas of structuralist criticism and semiotic analysis to African texts. However, formalist criticism has not been taken up strongly in Africa despite Anozie's lead. The collection edited by Emmanuel Ngara, *Stylistic Criticism and the African Novel* (1982), brings together some significant formalist essays. Criticism with a marxist basis seems to many to provide a programme for active political commitment by African writers in line with the traditional role of the African artist as a socially involved being whose work reflects and critiques community values and actions (Biodun Jeyifo, *The Truthful Lie*, 1980, Emmanuel Ngara, *Art and Ideology in the African Novel*, 1985, and George Gugelberger, ed., *Marxism and African Literature*, 1985). Writers as diverse as Femi *Osofisan and Kole *Omotoso in Nigeria, *Sembene Ousmane in Senegal, Jared *Angira and Meja *Mwangi in Kenya, Dambudzo *Marechera in Zimbabwe, Jack *Mapanje in Malawi, Can *Themba and Maishe Maponya in South Africa, and many others have been influenced by marxist ideas of direct communication with the popular audience despite the oppressive censorship of many contemporary African regimes. But very few of these writers have been doctrinaire marxists, and most even of those appear to have been moved by a more general anti-authoritarianism rather than a specific ideological commitment. There has been little or no 'party literature' produced in Africa, despite the enthusiasm with which many writers have adopted elements of the socialist programme for literature and art.

In an article entitled 'The Nature of Things' (*Research in African Literatures* 21.1, 1990) Biodun Jeyifo develops a significant leftist critique of the effect of the dominance of European Africanist criticism on the development of an African literary criticism. The sophisticated neo-marxian argument rejects the position of such critics as Chinweizu, which valorize the idea of an authentic 'insider' claim to exclusivity in African criticism, focusing instead on the institutional power that privileges European and American Africanist criticism over that produced by Africans within African institutions. The purpose of this essay is strongly polemical, but it does raise powerfully the question of how far African literary criticism can be perceived outside the institutional practice that brings it into being and that supports its development.

East Africa: The development of literary criticism in East Africa was closely linked to the rise of English-language literature and the development of a regional literary scene in the 1960s and 70s. A number of influential critics (*Okot p'Bitek, *Taban lo Liyong, and *Ngugi wa Thiong'o) were in fact major writers themselves who also contributed to the creation of a literary infrastructure by editing literary journals, organizing cultural festivals, or reorganizing literature studies at university and school levels.

Literary magazines contributed significantly to the unfolding of regional critical activity. Besides the internationally oriented *Transition*, originally edited from Uganda, and the more regionally oriented *East Africa Journal*, which took a lively interest in literary affairs, a number of university-supported magazines such as *Busara* (Nairobi), *Umma* (Dar es Salaam), and *Dhana* (Kampala) featured critiques of literary activities in the region as well as more general debates on

the political, social, and aesthetic dimensions of African literature.

One of the earliest centres of these critical debates was the campus of Makerere University in Kampala, where many budding East African writers and critics met in the early 1960s. Soon many of them, however, became disenchanted with 'Makerere aesthetics', which became a synonym for social and political aloofness, and began to explore new critical directions, focusing on a more active involvement of literature in post-colonial society. While East African criticism of the 1960s and 70s on the whole showed a remarkable pluralism of approaches, three broad currents of literary critique became particularly important.

Okot p'Bitek's *Africa's Cultural Revolution* (1973) initiated a cultural-nationalist criticism that became particularly interested in the relationship between traditional orality and written literature and explored the normative and aesthetic potential of traditional art for modern culture. A provocatively avant-garde, modernist tone was brought into the debate by Taban lo Liyong, who became something of an *enfant terrible* of the East African literary world and published several volumes of (often highly polemical) critical interventions, among them *The Last Word* (1969) and *Thirteen Offensives against Our Enemies* (1973). While Taban's critique of *negritude was shared by many East African critics, his iconoclastic insistence on the necessarily fragmentary character of literature sparked fierce controversies. A third grouping of critics rallied round the radical marxist-nationalist perspectives set out by Ngugi wa Thiong'o in his *Homecoming* (1972) and *Writers in Politics* (1981, rev. 1997), focusing on the political role of literature in colonial and post-colonial society, the class alignments of writers, and the critique of authorial ideology. Ngugi himself developed this approach further by introducing the issue of language use into the debate and eventually calling (as writer and critic) for an 'Afrocentric' literature written in African languages rather than in former colonial languages such as English. From the late 1970s onwards, the heated debate on the language issue to which Ngugi contributed with works such as *Barrel of a Pen* (1983), *Decolonising the Mind* (1986), *Moving the Centre* (1993), and *Penpoints, Gunpoints and Dreams* (1998) has been taken up in other parts of Africa and the postcolonial world.

Apart from a number of studies of individual authors and collections of critical essays, during the 1970s and 80s more general studies on East Africa as a literary region were published, including Adrian Roscoe's *Uhuru's Fire* (1977), Chris Wanjala's *For Home and Freedom* (1980), and *The Writing of East and Central Africa* (1984), edited by G.D. Killam. Some of the best-known East African critics include Micere *Mugo (*Visions of Africa*, 1978) Peter *Nazareth (*Literature and Society in Modern Africa*, 1972), and Chris

Wanjala (ed., *Standpoints on African Literature*, 1973; *The Season of Harvest*, 1978).

Following the break-up of the East African community in 1976, the vibrant critical debate in East Africa became increasingly muted. The eventual result was the destruction of much of the literary infrastructure (virtually all East African literary magazines folded in the late 1970s), a certain aridity induced by the preponderance of orthodox marxism in critical circles, and the growing political authoritarianism in Kenya, which forced many critical intellectuals into exile.

As in other areas of Africa, the gap created by the shift away from critical activities in the region has been filled by academic criticism originating from Western universities. In the wake of recent developments in post-colonial theory, this academic criticism has tended to focus on the writing strategies of individual well-known writers such as Ngugi or Okot rather than on East Africa as a literary region.

Southern Africa: Literary criticism in Southern Africa has been, until relatively recently, a white, masculine, middle-class enterprise and as such embeds the tensions and conflicts that characterize the literary culture of the region. The questions of the existence of an indigenous literature or literatures, the forms and possible purposes of such literatutes, and the inclusion and exclusion of various voices based on their race, class, gender, or language have shaped the body of texts that represent ideas about literature in the sub-continent.

English-language literary criticism in Southern Africa began, as it did in white settler colonies in North America and Australasia, with assumptions about the value and transferability of English literary traditions. Journals such as the *Cape of Good Hope Literary Gazette* (1830-5) and the *Cape Town Mirror* (1848-9) published book reviews and essays that debated the uses of imaginative writing, and lecturers at the South African College incorporated commentary on Shakespeare in their missionary work. The inclusion in the latter half of the nineteenth century of English literature as a subject for civil service examination influenced education in Southern Africa, since teachers destined for the colonies were required to master a body of facts about the lives of English writers.

Focused almost exclusively on literary production from the metropolitan centres, English-language literary criticism until the 1970s followed conservative European trends of practical criticism, for the most part resisting attempts to place literature within its social and political contexts. Exceptions included an essay by Sol T. *Plaatje entitled 'A South African's Homage', the first by a black South African, published in a tercentenary celebration of Shakespeare edited by Israel Gollancz. Manfred Nathan's *South African*

Literature (1925) and Sidney Mendelssohn's *South African Bibliogrpahy* (1910) were the first full-length treatments of a South African literature. Journals publishing conservative literary criticism such as *The State* (1909-12), *The Critic* (1932-9), and later the the academic journals – *English Studies in Africa* and *Unisa English Studies* – and full-length academic literary-critical studies of English canonical texts and authors were challenged by the journal *The Bluestocking*, aimed, as its title suggests, at university-educated women, and by *The South African Outlook*, which published black critics H.I.E. *Dhlomo and B.W. *Vilakazi, as well as by book reviewers in anti-*apartheid magazines like *New Age* and *The Torch*. Es'kia *Mphahlele's *The *African Image* (1962) initiated critical discussion of indigenous African literatures and European representation of Africans in literature.

The convergence in the closing decades of the twentieth century of interest in post-structuralist, feminist, and other politicized approaches to literary criticsm, in the emergence of 'national' literatures in the former colonial empires of Europe, and in the study of the post-colonial as a mode of literary production has produced a concomitant change in the critical climate of Southern Africa. Critics such as Mike Kirkwood, whose essay 'The Colonizer: A Critique of the English South African Culture Theory' (published in *Poetry South Africa*, 1976, ed. James Polley and Peter *Wilhelm) issued a challenge to the colonized critical community, J.M. *Coetzee, Stephen *Gray, and Michael Chapman have been persistent in their efforts to expose the privileges and assumptions implicit in conventional institutional criticism. Journals such as *Critical Arts*, *South African Theatre Journal*, *Current Writing*, and *Pretexts*, as well as conferences inside and outside the academies and journals outside Africa with an interest in African literary-cultural studies (*Ariel*, *Kunapipi*, *Research in African Literatures*, to name a few) regularly document developments in the continuing debate about the state of play in Southern African literary criticism.

West Africa: The emergence of West African literary criticism is intrinsically linked with the rise and development of West African literature, both *oral and written. And while West African oral literature predates its written form, it was not until the colonization of the region by European powers in the nineteenth and early twentieth centuries – when they conquered people and places and established schools and churches – that the region's literature was taken into serious consideration. In other words, although the political and social structure of the West African region was defined by its kingdoms (Ghana, Mali, Songhai, for example), its artistic expression was not formally discussed until the advent of European colonization. In discussing West African literary criticism, therefore, the starting point must necessarily be the impact of colonialism on the region's body of literature and, by implication, its critical standards.

Among the early western critics of African literature were Gerald Moore, Janheinz Jahn, Ulli Beier, G.D. Killam, Bernth Lindfors, Bruce King, Adrian Roscoe, Charles R. Larson, D.J. Enright, Ronald Christ, Keith Waterhouse, and Anthony West. Although some western critics kept faith with the principle of objective criticism, others were not only generally negative but were also prejudiced in their criticism. The basis for this prejudice is the misconception, perpetuated by colonialist attitudes, that Africa had no history, no culture, and therefore no claim to its own imaginative literature. But as G.D. Killam explains (in his *African Writers on African Writing*, 1978), 'African literature is, like all literature, an end in itself: it reveals a human need to create.... Like all literature, then, it needs no special justification'.

The cynicism and scepticism with which African literature was viewed by some Western critics was both widespread and intense. These critics, employing critical standards that glorified Western at the expense of other cultural values, argued that African authors were ill-equipped to write, especially since English was a second language to them. In particular, they believed that African literature was devoid of substance because of its emphasis on the fundamental concerns of the people at the expense of plot structure, characterization, and 'the universal'. But as Chinua *Achebe makes clear (in his essay 'The Role of the Writer in a New Nation'): 'We must first set the scene which is authentically African; then what follows will be meaningful and deep...the writer should be concerned with the question of human values'.

One of the responses to negative Western criticism was the emergence of a number of indigenous West African critics, whose concern, apart from rendering an objective and meaningful criticism to aesthetic discourse, was to correct the inaccuracies and misrepresentations surrounding African literature. Eldred D. Jones (*Wole Soyinka*, 1973), Emmanuel Obiechina (*Culture, Tradition and Society in the West African Novel*, 1975), Donatus Nwoga (ed. *West African Verse*, 1967), Abiola Irele (*The African Experience in Literature and Ideology*, 1981), Romanus Egudu (*Modern African Poetry and the African Predicament*, 1981), Eustace Palmer (*The Growth of the African Novel*, 1979), and Sunday Anozie (*Structural Models and African Poetics*, 1981) are among the West African critics who met the critical challenge. In addition, a number of West African creative writers joined the critical debate, either to critique their own work or to defend African literature against spurious criticisms. These included Chinua Achebe in *Morning Yet on Creation Day* (1975) and *Hopes and Impediments: Selected Essays, 1965-1987* (1988); J.P. Clark *Bekederemo in *The Example of Shakespeare* (1970); Wole

*Soyinka in *Myth, Literature and the African World* (1976); Kofi *Awoonor in *The Breast of the Earth* (1975); and Isidore *Okpewho, who has strongly defined the corpus of oral literature in *The Epic in Africa* (1979) and *African Oral Literature* (1992). Almost unanimously, West African creative writers and critics called attention to the need to consider the African cultural consciousness in any literary configuration. For example, Emmanuel Obiechina states (in his essay 'Cultural Nationalism in Modern African Creative Literature') 'The challenge of culture cannot be met through the cosmopolitan culture of the departed colonial powers; it can only be met through the new African culture, which is a composite of African and European cultural elements'.

Thus, while recognizing the Western critical criteria of I.A. Richards, F.R. Leavis, and others and the place of such formalized critical theories and concepts as marxism, structuralism, formalism, *feminism, and even to a greater or lesser degree *negritude, these West African writers and critics argued that every effort must be made not only to praise traditional cultural values, but also to repudiate all racist Western theories about Africa and its people.

West African criticism, however, by no means reflects a critical consensus among indigenous writers and critics; there is much disagreement and cross-current among them. For example, Obi Wali's controversial article 'The Dead End of African Literature' (*Transition*, No. 11, 1963) sparked a critical debate among indigenous critics about the form of criticism and the effect of employing a foreign language in African literary discourse. Thus, while Eldred Durasimi Jones advocates formalism (as he explains in *African Literature Today* 1, 1968) and close analysis of individual works, as does Dan Izevbaye, Abiola Irele favours the sociological framework, Sunday Anozie believes in structuralism, and Omafume Onoge's approach is marxist. And there are the *bolekaja* critics (a satirical term that alludes to Yoruba bus conductors, known for their aggressiveness), *Chinweizu, Onwuchekwa Jemie, and Ihechukwu Madubuike, who in their book *Toward the Decolonization of African Literature* (1980) not only criticize African writers and critics for imitating Western literary models, but urge them to disavow all forms of Western literary consciousness.

One major impact of post-colonial West African criticism is the realization that African literature needs more indigenous publishing to make the work of African authors and critics readily available to the outside world and challenge the distortions and the negative criticisms perpetrated by some western critics. Consequently several indigenous publishers, such as the Fourth Dimension in Enugu, New Horn Press in Ibadan, and the Ghana Publishing Corporation, among others, have joined university presses at Ibadan,

Lagos, Ife, and Port Harcourt in promoting the development of West African literary production. Also contributing to the dynamics of West African criticism, especially since they are edited by West African indigenes, are such journals as *African Literature Today* (edited by Eldred Durosimi Jones and Marjorie Jones), *Okike* (founded by Chinua Achebe), *Nigeria Magazine*, *ANA Review*, and *Kiabàrà*. Outside Africa, a number of publishers and journals have made similar contributions, which are significantly transforming the African literary and critical tradition: they include Heinemann, James Currey, Three Continents Press, Hans Zell, Longman, and Africa World Press among the publishers and *Research in African Literatures*, *World Literature Written in English*, *Journal of Commonwealth Literature*, *Ariel*, *The Literary Half-Yearly*, and *Kunapipi* among the *literary magazines and journals.

LITERARY MAGAZINES

East Africa: Frequent attempts to develop literary magazines have been undermined in part by the economic conditions in East African countries and in part by inattention to an appropriate target audience. The result has been an over-reliance on foreign exchange earned from overseas subscriptions rather than encouragement for a strong readership within the community.

The most successful literary magazine in East Africa has been *Transition* (1961-75), founded in Uganda, initially edited by Rajat Neogy and inspired by the achievements of *Black Orpheus* in Nigeria. Rather than developing an imitation of *Black Orpheus*, Neogy sought to break away from the black mystique associated with it. *Transition* was aimed at cultural redefinition and social and political comment. The first issues challenged conventional sensibilities and dealt with issues such as the question of the proper language for African literature which pitted Obiajunwa Wali advocating indiginization against Chinua *Achebe. Although few of the early submissions met editorial expectations, *Ngugi wa Thiong'o's short story 'The Return' was an exception. By the third issue the magazine began to attract international attention but lacked adequate funds to keep it afloat. The arrival of Es'kia *Mphahlele, who pledged the support of the Congress for Cultural Freedom, guaranteed its finances but led to a controversy over the matter of CCF funding as a move by the US to break Europe's monopolistic hold on African markets. By 1963 the magazine began to wean itself away from creative writing towards literary criticism and the more dangerous waters of political debate. The magazine became embroiled in the questions of pan-Africanism and literary 'universalism'. It suffered persecution by the Ugandan government in 1968 and 1969, and relocated to Ghana. After 1975 the name was changed to *Ch'indaba* and Wole *Soyinka was briefly its editor,

but it ceased publication the following year. Recently, it was revived in the USA under the tutelage of Henry Louis Gates, Jr, Anthony Kwame Appiah, and Soyinka.

In the late 1960s and early 1970s a cluster of literary magazines flourished and quickly faded in the shadow of *Transition*. *Busara*, a semi-annual, started in 1968 but ceased publication with the collapse of the East African market. Others include *East African Journal of Literature and Society* (1973), *Darlight* (1966), *Mawazo* (1967), *Nexus* (1967), and *Mzalendo* (1981).

South Africa: Few literary journals in South Africa have lasted more than a decade or two, and the first of them, the *South African Journal* (1824), edited by Thomas *Pringle and John Fairbairn, had a briefer life than most. Only two numbers appeared before the journal fell victim to the enmity of the autocratic governor, Lord Charles Somerset. Several other early periodicals survived briefly, with only the monthly *Cape of Good Hope Literary Gazette* (1830-5) and W.L. Sammons's satirical weekly *Sam Sly's African Journal* (1843-51) lasting for any length of time. The *Literary Gazette*, edited by A.J. Jardine, carried articles and reviews, including material culled from overseas as well as local sources. It was followed later by the *Cape Monthly Magazine*, edited by Roderick and John Noble, which ran for an exceptional twenty-two years (1857-79). There was little incentive to launch local journals in the face of overseas competition and a readership nurtured on metropolitan culture and values. In fact, the next literary journal of note appeared only in 1926. This was the provocatively titled *Voorslag* [whiplash], aimed by its editors Roy *Campbell, William *Plomer, and subsequently Laurens *van der Post, at stinging the South African public out of provincial complacency. The controversy it aroused led to its demise after only a few numbers. (A facsimile reprint of Nos. 1-3, edited by Colin Gardner and Michael Chapman, appeared in 1985). *The Sjambok* [Bullwhip], a satirical journal edited by Stephen *Black, ran intermittently from 1929, but ceased in 1931 in the face of libel suits. Other short-lived journals such as *The Touleier* (edited by H.C. *Bosman and A.J. Blignaut), *Trek* (edited by Bernard Sachs), and *South African Forum* (founded by R.J.K. Russell) followed in the 1930s.

In the immediate post-war period Uys Krige published *Vandag* [Today] (1947), a bilingual literary journal, while *Jewish Affairs* (1945) and the Afrikaans journal *Standpunte* (1945-80) did much to promote an interest in South African literature. In the 1950s several new publications began, including the short-lived *Vista* (1950), the cultural journal *Lantern* (1950, and still going strong), and *Drum* magazine, which from the 1950s on fostered the literary talents of black journalists such as Nat *Nakasa, Es'kia *Mphahlele,

Casey 'Kid' *Motsisi, and Richard *Rive and did much to raise the social consciousness of its readers. The *South African PEN Year Book*, first issued in 1954, *The Purple Renoster* (founded in 1956 by Lionel *Abrahams), and *Africa South* (1956, edited by Ronald Segal) provided further outlets for creative and critical writing. Apart from *Standpunte*, the most important literary journal to emerge in the postwar years was *Contrast*, founded in 1961 by Jack *Cope and edited by him for the next twenty-five years. *Contrast* (now called *New Contrast*) has made a major contribution to the fostering of a literary culture in South Africa.

Several other magazines emerged during the 1960s and 70s. *The Classic* (1963), a Johannesburg quarterly edited by Nat Nakasa and devoted to the publication of 'African writing of merit' was short-lived but is well-remembered: it briefly resurfaced in 1975 as *New Classic* before finally disappearing. A curious case was the Cape Town journal *The New African* (1962), which survived for over fifty issues. Although chiefly a political forum, it saw literature as an intrinsic part of political change. It always had literary contributions with some of the earliest work by writers such as Bessie *Head, *Ngugi wa Thiong'o, Alex *La Guma, and Dennis *Brutus. It saw the work of the new writers emerging to the north as giving heart to South Africans. After some twenty issues in Cape Town it was found guilty in court of the use of the obscene word 'bloody' in a short story by Can *Themba. Randolph Vigne and James Currey, having fled the country as the police closed in on the ARM resistance group, kept the journal going in London. For part of that period Lewis *Nkosi was its literary editor. Like *The Classic* in Johannesburg, *Transition* in Kampala and *Encounter* in London the journal had grants from the Congress for Cultural Freedom in Paris, where Ezekiel *Mphaphlele was director of its African programme. (It later turned out that the CCF was covertly funded by the CIA.) This meant that every issue could be sent free to the list of subscribers in South Africa. The name of the South African edition was changed at a faster and faster rate as the Bureau of State Security (BOSS) made sure it was banned; in the end each issue came out under a new journal title. The only index to the journal turned up in the BOSS files. *New Coin*, *Ophir*, and *Izwi* were devoted exclusively to poetry. *New Coin* (1965), a quarterly published from Grahamstown, marked its twenty-fifth anniversary with a commemorative anthology (*25/25*, 1989); *Ophir* (1967) and *Izwi* (1971) also did much to foster creative writing, but neither of these journals has survived. *Bolt,* produced in Durban in the early 1970s, was fitful, iconoclastic and oppositional; it combined powerful stories, essays by the political philosopher Rick Turner (later assassinated by the regime), poems by Douglas Livingstone and new black writing into a heady brew; two of its contributors plotted the

magazine that would become *Staffrider*. Other meteoric journals included the monthly review *New Nation* (which also published creative work) and *The Bloody Horse*, a stylish venture edited by Patrick *Cullinan.

The late 1970s were marked by the launching of the magazine *Staffrider*, founded in 1978 by Ravan Press, which aimed to speak directly to the experience of township black life after the repressive atmosphere of the 1960s and to restore a tradition of resistance literature in South Africa. It played an important sociopolitical role during a period of increasing governmental pressure.

Very different in character and aim are the various academic journals put out by university departments or associations. Among the former are *Theoria* (University of Natal, 1947), *English Studies in Africa* (University of the Witwatersrand, 1958), *Unisa English Studies* (University of South Africa, 1963), and *English in Africa* (Rhodes University, 1974), all of which are still going strong, as well as *Current Writing: Text and Reception in South Africa* (University of Natal, 1989) and *Pre/Texts: Studies in Literature and Language* (University of Cape Town, 1989). Literary journals put out by associations include the annual *English Academy Review* (1983) and the bilingual *Journal of Literary Studies* (1985, organ of the South African Society for General Literary Studies). More specialized in scope are *Critical Arts: A Journal for Media Studies* (1980), the *South African Theatre Journal* (1987), and *Crux* (1967), which focuses on the teaching of language and literature in secondary schools. Since 1987 the quarterly *Southern African Review of Books* has featured articles and reviews covering a wide range of publications relating to the subcontinent. Relative newcomers to the local literary scene are *Imprint* (1993), a magazine of the arts and *Alternations* (1995). Despite financial constraints and a limited readership, it is clear that there is an abundance of literary talent seeking suitable outlets.

West Africa: The use of periodicals as outlets for literary discourse in West Africa can be traced to the establishment in 1917 of London-based *West Africa*, which covered regional sociopolitical events, and its occasional literary reviews. Though the colonial government-established *Nigeria Magazine* (1934) had a literary supplement, and Dr. Azikiwe's *West African Pilot* (1937) provided 'poet's corners', it was in the 1950s and 60s that initiatives from governments, cultural organizations, educational institutions, and writers' workshops led to the flourishing of cultural journals that added creative writing, criticism, and book reviews to their standard essays on politics, anthropology, linguistics, painting, music, and dance. By 1953, a Senegalese news magazine, *Bingo*, carried short stories and book reviews.

In this development, as in the rise of African

nationalism, African-Americans and Antilleans such as Langston Hughes, Richard Wright, and Aimé Césaire played important roles. It was francophone West Africans, however, who pioneered the literary projection of Africa onto the world stage. One explanation for this was France's cultural assimilation policy, designed to transform Africans into French men and women. Nationalism among francophone West Africans therefore combined artistic, political, and intellectual protest into one rather than separate roles, as in anglophone territories. Senegalese intellectual Alioune *Diop inaugurated the trend by founding the journal Présence africaine in Paris in 1947 to foster dialogue with Europe and 'to help define African originality and to hasten its introduction into the modern world'. The journal received support from several French and African-American intellectuals and two of the founders of *negritude, L.S. *Senghor and Aimé Césaire. Within a decade, many prominent intellectuals from Africa and beyond were among its contributors, and it went bilingual (English-French) in 1965. Anglophone West Africa had nothing comparable to Présence africaine until Black Orpheus was founded in 1957 by German scholars Ulli Beier and Janheinz Jahn as 'a platform for creative writing'. The first issue featured the early poetry of Senghor (in English translation) and Gabriel *Okara. Financially supported by the Congress for Cultural Freedom and Nigeria's Ministry of Education, it soon rivalled Présence africaine in spread and prestige. But its editorial board also experienced considerable instability. Es'kia *Mphahlele and Wole *Soyinka, who joined Beier and Jahn as co-editors with number 7, quit in 1964 and 1966 respectively, Soyinka dissatisfied with the journal's Eurocentric name. The board's composition changed again in 1968.

In 1968, the Bulletin of the Association for African Literature in English grew into African Literature Today under the editorship of Eldred Durosimi Jones of the University of Sierra Leone and Eustace Palmer. Jones described the journal as 'a forum for the examination of the literature of Africa' and urged critics to take seriously their role of demonstrating the qualities of a work so as 'to make it accessible to a larger readership than the absence of criticism might have opened it to, and by an accumulation of such examinations to help establish literary standards'. The journal has become one of the most influential publications on African literature, with special numbers on topical issues such as African women's writing.

Writers' workshops are sometimes sponsored by universities or culture ministries, and this relationship has been crucial in the history of literary magazines. Whereas University Herald (1948), The Horn, and Ibadan (1957) were founded by University College, Ibadan, Okyeame [Spokesman] was founded (1964) by Ghana Writers' Workshop and the Institute of African

Studies, University of Ghana, Legon; the Cameroonian bilingual (English-French) Abbia (1964) by Centre de Littérature évangélique, supported by the Ministry of National Education, Ife Writing (1968) by the Writers' Circle of the University of Ife, and Ozila: Forum littéraire camérounais (1970) by the Cameroon Literary Workshop. In 1968, Journal of the Nigerian English Studies Association was founded under the auspices of the British Council.

During the 1970s and early 1980s, Nigeria's petroleum-driven economic boom led to the establishment of new universities whose English departments promptly launched literary magazines. The older universities had publications such as Opon Ifa and Review of English and Literary Studies at Ibadan, Nsukka Studies in African Literature at the University of Nigeria, Nsukka, Ife Studies in African Literature and the Arts at Ife, Positive Review by the leftist Ibadan-Ife axis, and Work in Progress at Ahmadu Bello University, Zaria. Publications from new universities included the University of Port Harcourt's Kiabàrà and the University of Benin's Benin Review, while student publications included The Muse (after the Igbo maiden spirit) at the University of Nigeria and Kuka [Baobab] and Saiwa at Ahmadu Bello. Occupying a special place is Okike: Journal of African New Writing, founded by Chinua Achebe in 1971.

All the publications have had troubled histories, and the failure rate has been high owing to shrinking national economies. All that survive have become annuals, including Nigeria Magazine, Okike, and African Literature Today. Some lie dormant for several years before they are revived: Transition, which became Ch'indaba from number 50, Black Orpheus, resuscitated at the University of Lagos (1981), and Nsukka Studies in African Literature, which has emerged from its late-1980s inactivity, are examples. Yet Okike has also grown into Okike Publications and Arts Centre, active in the 1990s, additionally publishing Okike Educational Supplement (launched 1982) for literature students and the literary-cultural bilingual (English-Igbo) Uwa Ndi Igbo: A Journal of Igbo Life and Culture (launched 1986), and the Association of Nigerian Authors (ANA) has launched its own ANA Review. The current prospect, therefore, is that, faced with extreme adversity, magazines lapse into dormancy, to re-emerge, leaner, years later, like mudfish after long hibernation.

LITERARY THEORY During the period since the mid-1980s critics of African literatures have responded in various ways to the development of contemporary literary theory. Work by *literary critics of colonialist discourse such as Edward Said, Gayatri Spivak, and Homi Bhabha, as well as commentaries by other critics responding to them from a materialist viewpoint such as Fredric Jameson and Leila Ahmed, have had an increasing influence on the theorizing of African writing. The most notable intervention into this discussion by an African critic is probably that of Abdul JanMohamed. In a major critical text, *Manichaean Aesthetics: The Politics of Literature in Colonial Africa* (1983), and subsequently in a number of essays he outlined a theory of the complex relationship between the hegemonic control of Eurocentric literary forms and the appropriation of these forms for the construction of a counter-hegemonic discourse. For JanMohamed the escape from the colonialist past involves a recognition of the continuing force of that past and its race-based binary divisiveness on the construction of alternative anti-racist readings and counter-discourses. Thus he is able to analyse the relationship of the work of a writer like Chinua *Achebe to texts of the colonial period not as a matter of simple literary influence in the classic humanist mode of an early European critic such as Molly Mahood but as an appropriative and counter-hegemonic rewriting of those texts, a 'writing back' that wrests control from the source and uses its modes and themes to establish an independent and invigorated rereading of that 'encounter', freeing it for employment in new ways and to new ends.

The Ghanaian/English critic Kwame Appiah has produced a controversial reading of contemporary African culture and its history in *In My Father's House* (1992), which draws heavily on post-modernist cultural theory. The reading is controversial in so far as it posits a disabling transference into African cultural theories of racist concepts generated by slavery in the New World. It argues that the 'invention of Africa' and of African 'nativist' cultural formations by figures as diverse as Alexander Crummell, Edward Blyden, and George Padmore are the product of an attempt to reverse the race-based categories created by slavery and its opposition in nineteenth-century America. So the fathers of pan-*Africanist discourse are trapped in the essentialist racist epistemology whose negative effects they sought to oppose, with profoundly limiting results for the discourses of Africanness they are able to promote. The result is a stress on the dependence of African cultural formations on outside influences, the political implications of which others have found difficult to accept. The strength of Appiah's work, however, is that it problematizes the idea of a pure and authentic cultural formation above the corrigibility and struggle of cultural interactions. As with other post-colonial texts influenced by post-modern theories of the power of discourse in the formation of social representations, it postulates a more complex idea of the process of cultural relationships in both the colonial and post-independence periods of African history and questions the construction of this relationship in terms of a simple model of opposition and recovery.

An earlier and more critical exploration of these same themes can be found in the work of the Zaïrean critic and philosopher V.Y. Mudimbe, *The Invention of Africa* (1988) and *The Idea of Africa* (1995). His careful tracing of the impact of contemporary structuralist and post-structuralist theories of subjectivity and of the structuring power of discursive systems challenges the certainty and simplicity with which such theory has sometimes been employed to analyse cross-cultural encounters and practices. He argues that external discourses such as those of anthropology and the missions clearly influenced the ways in which both western and African thinkers structured their identities. He provides a compelling portrait of how these discourses interacted with the local knowledges to shape contemporary African subjectivities and social models. Less pessimistic than Appiah, perhaps, he remains convinced of the possibility of constructing a distinctive, independent modern African identity.

Recent demands for the more strenuous application of 'local knowledges' to the explication of African cultures, including the literary texts written in colonial languages, echo this political shift in favour of the local. They have led to a call for interpretations based on a careful study of the values and forms of the societies that produced these texts rather than the exploitation of the texts as fodder for some pre-existent European theory or discourse. Of course, it is necessary to be aware of the possible dangers here too, since, as Mudimbe and Appiah have clearly shown, the 'local' is neither historically nor ontologically distinct. The long and complex involvement of African societies with European forms and institutions simply cannot be wished away. Contemporary theories are forced to contend with and account for the inevitable inscriptions these interactions have left on African subjectivity and on cultural practices. As a result of this conflict some critics have expressed concern that the emergence and application of post-modernist and post-colonial theories of culture may have had a negative effect on the project of resistance and decolonization. It is certainly true that the stress in such theories on the inevitable interconnectedness of colonizer and colonized creates an impression of the continuing dependence on colonialism in modern post-independence cultural formations, and that the stress on subversion and subversive strategies rather than direct opposition appears to deny the abrogative possibility of the decolonizing confrontation. Nevertheless the arguments of contemporary discourse theorists that opposition and resistance involve a mere inversion of the binary oppositions of colonial discourse, trapping the oppositionist discourse in the same epistemological condition it seeks to oppose, is a powerful one. Against this argument Florence Stratton has argued that, despite this danger, inversion is a necessary stage of resistance, quoting Jonathan Dollimore's view that to ignore the need for a stage that inverts or overturns the hierarchy of the dominant discourse is to 'leave it unchanged'. The necessity for an abrogative stage of this kind to precede the possibility of an appropriative moment of subversion has not always been sufficiently stressed in accounts that embrace the idea of a post-colonial syncretism or that emphasize the inter-dependencies of colonizer/colonized relations. Nevertheless, recent colonial discourse theory does problematize in a valuable way earlier notions of post-colonial resistance that postulate colonial relations as a system of irreducible and essentialist oppositions. Instead, they move theories of resistance towards a model that includes the process of a cultural exchange, albeit an unequal one, as an inescapable effect of the colonizing process.

Among the more significant recent developments in the application of literary theory to African texts has been the emergence of a number of Euro-American and African *feminist critics who have questioned the patriarchal bias in the evaluation of African literatures, citing the neglect of writers such as Efua *Sutherland, Ama Ata *Aidoo, and Flora *Nwapa in the early period of African writing. More recently, they argue, the higher profile of writers such as Mariama *Bâ, Bessie *Head, and Buchi *Emecheta has restored this balance, but they too have been subject to very negative critiques by some European and African male critics. Feminist critics have also criticized the degree to which discourses of post-colonialism and of decolonization can speak effectively across the gender divide. They argue that male critics have assumed falsely that the struggle against colonization is identical across the genders. In place of this view they argue for an understanding of the process of the double colonization of women. This formulation argues that women are subject to colonization both directly by the structures of the colonizers (themselves profoundly patriarchal in their assumptions) and indirectly by the patriarchal nature of the indigenous societies. In some cases critics argue that the patriarchal structures of the indigenous societies are created, or at least encouraged, by the colonizing power, in whose interest it is to support the internal controls implicit in patriarchal social structures. These issues have also been the subject of an increasing number of articles that critique both the inadequate coverage of women and the theorization of the role of gender within colonial and post-colonial literary critical formulations as well as the structuring bias of male literary discourse in its representation of African women and their role. That these representations by male novelists and historians contradict the historical evidence is also the burden of a number of feminist revisionary histories of colonization, such as that written by Nina Mba. Such feminist revisions offer an influential rereading of African literary texts and of the critical history of their reception.

Despite the work of European scholars of oral culture such as Ruth Finnegan, who argued for the study of African oral literatures in a context more literary than anthropological and initiated the study of such traditions, it was left to such African critics as Isidore *Okpewho to question the need to view these traditions through European taxonomies and as sub-categories of European classic models such as Homer or Aesop. More recently, a range of specialist and individual studies by critics such as Daniel P. *Kunene, Richard Taylor, Karin Barber, Elizabeth Gunner, and many others has established the importance of relating the study of oral culture to the practices of literate culture and not assuming a precedence or a lineage between the two that promotes the written above the oral or which consigns the oral to a 'fixed and dead' traditional/past position. Karin Barber's work on orality and discourse pioneered a new way of thinking about the inter-relationship of the oral and the written in cultures such as that of the Yoruba people of Nigeria. Following on from this, scholars such as Isabel Hofmeyr have argued that written and oral cultures exist within unified social situations and are mutually interactive. Such theories stress the need to avoid assuming that the oral is restricted to the past and that it is somehow subaltern to the written, and emphasize the continuing inter-relationships between oral and written structures in African societies. Such work also challenges the simplistic and culture-specific assumptions of the structural precedence of the written over the oral (logocentrism) developed by influential European critics such as Jacques Derrida. Recent African and Afro-American theory has emphasized that both oral and literary texts were important sites of articulations of difference and local resistance and that the writers, performers, and critics were often one and the same people and spoke a language comprehensible beyond the narrow boundaries of contemporary academic theoreticism, since it involved an awareness of cultural traditions in which art was a shared experience and not a realm of an inevitable, endless, and disabling absence.

Nevertheless, despite these developments there have been and continue to be misgivings with regard to the effect of literary theory on African cultural and literature studies. In an important essay Biodun Jeyifo suggests that from the point of view of African cultures contemporary literary theory can arguably be seen to have acted as a monolithic and suppressive Western phenomenon. An implicit view of theory as quintessentially Eurocentric, he suggests, is in danger of overriding the attempts either to bring into play existing local critical and aesthetic modes or to generate such modes within the dominated cultures. He further argues that this view is accompanied by a reification of theory, 'so that we now know theory as theory only when we see it in the garb of theoreticism'. Yet theory conceived as the articulation of the specific issues and practices of African cultures within their own worlds and in reaction to and interaction with colonial incursions is clearly much more broadly based than this. Barbara Christian's earlier assertion that theorizing by people of colour has often been in narrative forms and in a dynamic play with language raises powerful questions that deserve to be answered. As Jeyifo's work shows, such questions do not necessarily have to take the form of regressive assertions of reductive cultural essentialisms. It remains to be seen whether positions more mutual and uses more fruitful can be negotiated between African critics and the tools offered by contemporary theory.

Little Karoo, The (1925) Short stories by Pauline ★Smith. The Little Karoo is a region of South Africa's southwestern Cape; these stories are set there at the turn of the century. With austere economy, a quality perfectly commensurate with the frugal, self-denying lives of the rural Dutch settlers who are her characters, Smith explores the timeless themes of thwarted love, familial conflict, betrayal, and the harsh role of fate in human affairs. The community she portrays is isolated and backward, but Smith is aware of its strengths as well as its weaknesses: it is austere and repressed, but it is also capable of great warmth and humanity. Outstanding stories include 'The Pain', 'The Schoolmaster', and 'The Miller'.

LIVINGSTONE, Douglas (1932-96), South African poet, was born of Scottish parents in Kuala Lumpur. During the Japanese invasion of Malaysia in 1941 his father was taken prisoner, but the rest of the family managed to find its way to KwaZulu-Natal, South Africa, where he completed his schooling. After working in laboratories, he trained at the Pasteur Institute in Zimbabwe and from 1964 worked as a marine bacteriologist in Durban. He gained two doctorates from the University of Natal: one for his scientific work and an honorary one for his poetry. He produced five major volumes of verse: ★*Sjambok and Other Poems from Africa* (1964), *Eyes Closed against the Sun* (1970), *A Rosary of Bone* (1975, rev. 1983), *The Anvil's Undertone* (1978), and *A Littoral Zone* (1991). He also published *Selected Poems* (1984), three plays, and various translations.

Livingstone was a lyrical poet of considerable range. He wrote many striking poems about animals and birds ('Gentling a Wildcat' is one of his best-known pieces), and the 1991 collection focuses on the seacoast. His studies of creatures are also (as with D.H. Lawrence and Ted Hughes) implicitly about various aspects of life as it is lived or faced by human beings. His poems cover many other topics and themes: people, especially individuals who are lonely or frustrated; places; incidents and stories, at times handled in

mythic or phantasmagoric ways; and a wide range of seemingly more directly personal subjects (but one often senses the presence of a persona), including a fair number of poems about love. *A Rosary of Bone* consists mainly of love poems. Since the mid-1970s a few of his poems have touched on political themes. Livingstone's poetry – energetic, remarkably varied and inventive in texture and form – reveals a careful and cunning craftsman. Every poem has its own style, pace, and music; some poems are very dense and knotty, while a few are limpid and almost colloquial. The poems usually make some use of rhyme, often in unexpected ways; and a few poems exhibit, very successfully, surprisingly elaborate patternings of rhymes, half-rhymes, assonances, and alliteration: for example, 'The grindstone's rasped pyrotechnic/threatens the stopped-dead angled tip/of a stripped Cape cart that waits on/the return of its motivation' ('Mpondo's Smithy, Transkei').

The exuberance of the verbal life within the poetry is exhilarating, but the attitude embodied in many of the poems is astringent, disenchanted, anti-romantic. Some critics have supposed that Livingstone enjoyed his cynical stance. Though this may be true at some levels – there must obviously be pleasure, for the poet and for the reader (whether victim or not), in the dashing of conventional optimisms – the reader becomes aware that the romantic illusions so relentlessly undermined are to some extent his own. The poems demonstrate an ironic awareness of the harsh evolutionary context in which all life plays itself out, and the heat and occasional violence of Africa seem to intensify or underline some of the cruelties of life's processes. Human beings are subject to compulsions that they can neither understand nor tame: 'Sometimes we claim autonomy/ yet a ruthless fidelity/ – to what self? – lies coiled at the heart/ of our needy faithlessness' ('Cells at Station 11'). Human ambitions, whether largely noble or largely ignoble, are mostly doomed to failure.

Yet his picture of the world is not one of unrelieved gloom, the response is never defeatist, is always in some way strenuous. Though biological and psychic processes may seem usually to deny the value of human generosity and the possibility of humane meaning, the poet clearly, though perhaps with a willing suspension of total rationality, accepts and at times manages to assert those positives. Some of his poems are indeed bleak, though they are almost always moving in their verbal precision and vivid imaginativeness, but many others express varying degrees of grief, enthusiasm, tenderness, and wry, wistful, or even warm humour. Religious motifs appear occasionally; sometimes there is a faint suggestion of a possibility of transcendence. At times, in an altogether more relaxed mode, the persona of Giovanni Jacopo, a wily Renaissance man of the world, comments in a satirical and sometimes very funny way on contemporary mores.

Livingstone's lyrical style, for all its flexibility, did not take easily to political themes, though he himself was always opposed to *apartheid and to the totalitarianism that went with it. (Occasionally his irreverent and unillusioned view of human possibilities may have given the impression, wrongly, that he was politically conservative, as in the disconcerting Jacopo quatrain 'on the Egalitarian Society': 'All Men are Brothers/ – So runs the Fable,/ & the First of these/ Were Cain and Abel.') But in the 1970s, with the advent of black poets such as Mbuyiseni *Mtshali, Mongane Wally *Serote, and Sipho *Sepamla and the escalation of the anti-apartheid struggle, a healthy debate arose in literary circles about what kind of poetry could or should be written under conditions of political crisis. To some readers, Livingstone's lonely dedicated crafting came to seem inappropriate. He himself, while quietly defending his position, reacted warmly and sympathetically to much of the new poetry expressing the anger and the aspirations of the oppressed, though (as he pointed out in a 1976 article) he saw the new poets as often deficient in the kind of verbal skills that he believed in.

LIYONG, Taban lo [See TABAN LO LIYONG]

Looking on Darkness (1974) A novel by André *Brink. The openly oppositional character of the novel is signalled immediately by its male 'Cape coloured' (mixed race) narrator, Joseph Malan, whose first-person prison narrative chronicles the tortuous route by which he comes to be accused of the murder of his white lover, Jessica. Banned by the censors for being 'pornographic, blasphemous, and communistic', this novel is described by Brink as being 'one of the first Afrikaans novels openly to confront the *apartheid system'. It deals with such issues as the struggle for identity of a 'non-white' South African, love across the colour bar, both illegal and dangerous in apartheid South Africa, and the difficulty of direct political action in a repressive regime.

The Looming Shadow (1968) A novel by Legson *Kayira. This is the second Malawian novel in English to be published and the first of four to come from this sensitive writer, who has lived outside Malawi virtually all his writing life. Its graceful style casts a pastoral glow over Malawian rural life and governance before the intrusion of modern central government. It contrasts sharply with Kayira's later novel, *The Detainee* (1974), which is a frontal assault on the evils of the Banda regime.

LUBEGA, Bonnie (1929-), fiction writer and lexicographer, was born in Buganda province of Uganda, where he received his early education and qualified as

a teacher. As a journalist in the mid- 1950s he worked for several newspapers in Kampala and published his own pictorial magazine, *Ssanyu*. After gaining a diploma in journalism in Germany, he returned to Kampala and worked as a script writer and radio producer. His first book, *The Burning Bush* (1970), presents synchronic postcard shots of a herdsboy, Nakamwa-Ntette, whose witty, youthful narrative voice projects the authority of close observation. The major tension in the narrative arises from the challenge posed for Nakamwa-Ntette by the educated son of the village head and landlord, whose luxurious way of life contrasts with the deprivation of the rest of the villager-tenants. Lubega's narrative technique circumvents the stock plots of rural-urban clash and indigene-foreigner encounter. In *The Outcasts* (1971), he presents the marginalized migrant *balaalo*, despised by the dominant Bugandans, for whom they herd cattle. But the hero, Karekyesi, penetrates his exploiters' psychology and outwits them. *The Great Animal Land* (1971) and *Cry, Jungle Children* (1974), although strongly didactic, underscore Lubega's humanism as he refamiliarizes a youthful audience with Africa's threatened ecosystems. His Lugandan semantic dictionary, *Olulimi Oluganda Amakula* (1995), an original work, reflects an abiding cultural concern.

LUBWA P'CHONG, (1946-), playwright and poet, was born in Gulu, Uganda, had his early education there and in Kyambogo, taught for several years, and then later studied literature and linguistics at Makerere University. He founded and edited *Nanga*, the magazine of the National Teachers College, Kampala and edited *Dhana*, the Makerere *literary magazine. His poetry has appeared in East African magazines and anthologies. He is known mainly as a playwright and his work is concerned with tradition, much as is that of *Okot p'Bitek and Okello *Oculi, who is his father-in-law. His plays *Generosity Kills* and *The Last Safari* (1975) were followed by *Words of My Groaning* (1976), a painful portrait of life in independent Africa. His other plays are *The Minister's Wife* (1982), *The Bishop's Daughter* (1988), *Do Not Uproot the Pumpkin* (1987), *Kinsmen and Kinswomen* (1988), and *The Madman* (1989).

LUSOPHONE LITERATURE

Lusophone African writing from the five countries below has attracted sizeable audiences in Portugal and Brazil as well as Portuguese-speaking readers elsewhere in Europe and the Americas. Moreover, translations in several European languages, including English, continue to increase as proof of lusophone African literature's growing international recognition.

Cape Verde: For a number of social, economic, and political factors Cape Verde was the first of Portugal's

African colonies in which an indigenous middle class emerged. Its port city of Mindelo on São Vicente Island became important as the chief coaling station between Europe and the Americas. Cape Verdean literature had already taken off in the mid-nineteenth century. One of the earliest poets was a woman, Antónia Gertrudes Pusich, who was also a musician. Lasting popularity was achieved at the beginning of the twentieth century by Eugénio Tavares, from small Brava Island, mainly as the writer of *mornas*, slow, often sad songs, many of them composed in the Portuguese-based Creole of the islands. By the 1930s members of an educated elite of native sons and daughters, of mixed-race origin, had begun to proclaim their islands' social and cultural uniqueness, which, many of these intellectuals proclaimed, was a mixture of European and African elements, albeit more European than African.

Chief among the writers for *Claridade* (the title of a landmark literary journal begun in 1936) who sprang from this elite are poets Jorge Barbosa (1902-71), Osvaldo Alcântara, pen name of Baltasar Lopes (1907-89), and Manuel Lopes (1907-). Their poetry predates by at least a decade comparable initiatives by francophone and anglophone African writers. Moreover, as early as the mid-1930s Baltasar Lopes had published chapters from his novel *Chiquinho* [Frankie] (1947), one of the first novels of its kind to be published in all of sub-Saharan Africa. He also wrote moving poems in defence of the exploited poor labourers, as in the *Romanceiro de S. Tomé* [The Ballad Cycle of São Tomé]. Manuel Lopes, who wrote two major novels including the classic *Chuva Braba* [Torrential Rain] (1956), and António Aurélio Gonçalves (1901-84), with his several novellas, one of the best known being *Noite de Vento* [Windy Night] (1970), also wrote on the typically Cape Verdean subjects of drought, emigration, and homesickness.

Subsequent generations of more radical writers protested at what they saw as the *Claridade* generation's political escapism. A pivotal poem by Ovídio Martins (1928-) is entitled 'Anti-Evasão' (1962) ('Anti-Evasion', the English version, appears in D. Burness's 1989 anthology *A Horse of White Clouds: Poems from Lusophone Africa*). In that same year Onésimo Silveira (1935-) called for 'Um Poema Diferente', the English translation of which, 'A Different Poem,' is in Gerald Moore and Ulli Beier's *Modern African Poetry* (3rd edn., 1984). These two poems and others like them appeal for a more engaged Cape Verdean literary expression. Still, even the most militant writers, members of the African Independence party of Guinea and Cape Verde (PAIGC), respected and followed the cultural lead of their elders of the *Claridade* and *Certeza* [Certainty], (also the title of an important cultural/literary journal) movements.

The archipelago's Creole as the language of 'high', as opposed to popular, literature has long been debated among Cape Verdean intellectuals. Wherever individual writers stand on the subject, the reality has been an acceptance of both Portuguese and Creole as the vehicle of serious poetry.

In the 1990s Corsino Fortes (1933-), Oswaldo Osório (1937-), Arménio Vieira (1941-), Vera Duarte (1952-), and José Hopffer Almada (1960-) stand out among contemporary Cape Verdean poets. Among novelists of comparable talent are the experienced and prolific writer Henrique Teixeira de Sousa (1919-), Arménio Vieira, Manuel Veiga (1948-), whose *Oju d'Agu* [The Wellspring] (1987) is the first attempt at a prose work in Creole, and Germano Almeida (1945-), author of four novels, including the enormously popular *O Testamento do Sr. Napumoceno da Silva Araújo* [Mr. Napumoceno da Silva Araújo's last will and testament] (1989), on which a film has been based. Also in the realm of fiction are the stories of Orlanda Amarílis's (1924-) *Cais de Sodré té Salamansa* [From the dock of Sodré to the port of Salamansa] (1974) and two volumes of Cape Verdean stories set in Lisbon.

Angola: In Angola two precursors stand out. José da Silva Maia Ferreira (1827–1867), a widely travelled merchant, published a book of poetry already in 1850 as *Espontaneidades da minha Alma*, following Portuguese and Brazilian models. The other early writer was Joaquim Cordeiro da Mata (1857–1894), an African, whose verse in *Deírios* [Ravings] (1888) owes much to his mentor, the Swiss missionary Héli Chatelain, who pioneered as a collector of oral Angolan lore. His *Folk-Tales of Angola* became the first volume published by the American Folklore Society in 1894. A forceful pro-native author of realistic stories and novels of the Angolan hinterland appeared in the late 1930s, Fernando Castro Soromenho. His first works were the stories of *Nhari, Dramas da Gente negra* [The Black People's Drama] (1938), followed by *Noite de Angústia* [Night of Anguish] (1939). His novel *Terra morta* [Dead Land] (1945) was widely published and translated. In the early 1950s, under the banner of cultural revindication and a growing anti-colonialist militancy fanned by the Popular Movement of the Liberation of Angola (MPLA), the Luanda-based Young Intellectuals' movement got under way. This movement encompassed black, white, and mixed-race writers such as poets Aires de Almeida Santos (1922-), António Jacinto (1924-91), Viriato da Cruz (1928-73), Alda Lara (1930-62), António Cardoso (1933-), Mário António (Fernandes de Oliveira) (1934-89), (Fernando) Costa Andrade (1936-), and Arnaldo Santos (1937-). Among them, Mário António and Alda Lara stand out. During this period in Portugal, Agostinho *Neto (1922-79), who would become Angola's first president, wrote poems and was involved in clandestine political activities along with other

African intellectuals and writers who were members of the Lisbon-based House of Students from the Empire. This generation set a standard for such well-known poets as Arlindo Barbeitos (1940-), Manuel Rui (1941-), Rui Duarte de Carvalho, (1941-), and David Mestre (1948-98). They would be joined by post-independence poets Paula Tavares (1952-), E. Bonavena (1955-), José Luís Mendonça (1955-), Rui Augusto (1958-), Ana de Santana (1960-), and Lopito Feijóo (1963-).

Although most of these poets have come to grips, in one way or another, with the tensions between Portuguese, whether standard or an Angolan dialect, no writer has dealt more effectively with the dynamic relationships among the languages of Angola than José Luandino Vieira (1935-). Born José Mateus Vieira da Graça in rural Portugal, he grew up near Luanda's African shanty towns and learned the vocabulary and cadences of the black Portuguese mixed with Kimbundu that would influence the discourse of his eight collections of stories and two novels, most of which he wrote during his years as a political prisoner. Six of his works have been translated into at least nine languages. There are English translations of *A Vida Verdadeira de Domingos Xavier* (1974; *The Real Life of Domingos Xavier*, 1978) and *Luuanda* (1964; *Luuanda: Short Stories of Angola*, 1980); both volumes were published in the prestigious Heinemann African Writers Series. A translation of *João Vêncio: Os seus Amores* (1979; *The Loves of João Vêncio*, 1991) was published in the US by Harcourt Brace Jovanovich.

Pepetela (pseudonym of Artur Carlos Maurício Pestana dos Santos) (1941-) is another Angolan writer who has gained international recognition. Also of Portuguese extraction, Pepetela was born and raised in the southern Angolan town of Benguela. Unlike Luandino, all of whose stories are set in the city from which his name derives, Pepetela sets his eight novels, several stories, and two plays either in and around his native Benguela or in the northern enclave of Cabinda, as well as in Luanda. Of two of Pepetela's novels, *Mayombe* (1980; trans. 1983) and *A Geração da Utopia* [The Generation from Utopia] (1992), the first deals with conflicting views of the guerilla warfare in the north and the second expresses utter disillusionment about the condition of Angola since independence. And *O Desejo de Kianda* [The Goddess Kianda's Desire] (1995), set in Luanda, is a mythical fantasy with elements of humour and social satire. Pepetela is also the author of a fascinating novel dealing with famous African rulers of the past, *Lueji: O Nascimento dum Império* [Queen Lueji: The Birth of an Empire] (1990) and the play *A Revolta da Casa dos Idolos* [The Revolt of the Fetish House] (1980), about the King of the Congo who welcomed the Portuguese.

Among several other contemporary Angolan writers who also have captured the attention of the broader Portuguese-speaking world is Uanhenga Xitu, the Kimbundu name of Agostinho A. Mendes de Carvalho (1924-), author of several volumes of short stories and novels, one of which, a satire about an ignorant and pretentious man, has been translated into English: *Os Discursos do 'Mestre' Tamoda* (1985; *The World of 'Mestre' Tamoda*, 1988). Xitu, who once served as Angola's minister of health, used this experience to write the critical novel titled *O Ministro* [The Minister] (1990). In the same category of post-colonial works with a measure of social satire is *Crónica de um Mujimbo* [Chronicle of a Rumour] (1989) and *1 Morto & os Vivos* [One Dead Man and the Living] (1993), a novella and short stories by Manuel Rui. *Yes, Comrade!* (1993) is the translation of Rui's *Sim Camarada!* (1977), stories set in Luanda during the transitional period of Angolan independence.

Another recent Angolan novel written by Arnaldo Santos (1935-) is *A Boneca de Quilengues* [The Doll of the Quilengues] (1992) . It presents a man's puzzled analysis of the character and feelings of an unconventional, independent and seductive Mulatta from Benguela, whose confidant he is. The man uses a language replete with African expressions. Finally, in the expanding pantheon of post-colonial Angolan texts is José E. Agualusa's (1960-) *D. Nicolau Água-Rosada e Outras Histórias Verdadeiras e Inverossímeis* [Prince Nicolau Água-Rosada and other true and improbable tales] (1990).

Mozambique: Native Mozambican lore was first published by the Swiss missionary Henri Alexandre Junod from 1896 on, while José Pedro Campos Oliviera had gained a name in Mozambique with his poems since 1865. By the early 1950s literary activity was under way in Mozambique. In the capital Lourenço Marques (Maputo) and the city of Beira literary groups and journals sprang up, and a poetry of cultural revindication, racial identity, and incipient protest began to appear. Foremost among a number of socially committed poets were José Craveirinha (1922-), Mozambique's unofficial poet laureate, and Noémia de Sousa (1926-), who is lusophone Africa's first important female writer of colour. Also during the 1950s and 60s short stories dealing with characteristically Mozambican topics began to appear in print. *Nós Matámos o Cáo Tinhoso* (1964; *We Killed Mangy Dog and Other Mozambican Stories*, 1969) by Luís Bernardo Honwana (1942-) has set an enduring standard for Mozambican writers. The translation was the first lusophone African work to be published in the ★African Writers Series. Honwana never published another story. Some doubted the authorship of the book.

Among several outstanding post-independence Mozambican poets, Luís Carlos Patraquim (1953-) and Eduardo White (1963-) are especially noteworthy.

Among contemporary fiction writers, (Bernardo) Mia *Couto (1955-), of European extraction, two of whose books have been translated into English, and Ungulani Ba Ka Khosa (1957-), from the *Tsonga ethnic group, have both written unique works in a Portuguese that reflects oral tradition and indigenous Mozambican languages. So far, Couto's novel *Terra sonâmbula* [Sleepwalking Land] (1992) has remained his masterpiece, a hallucinating story of an old man and a boy wandering through the interior of Mozambique, a wasteland of the dead, mined and devastated during the past civil war. He used the technique of magical realism to do justice to the theme. Another writer whose experiences of the war have influenced her short stories and novels is Lina *Magaia.

Before independence, the country could boast of outstanding writers of European parentage. Rui Knopfli (1932-) has been greatly admired for his thoughtful, masterfully crafted poetry, published in books, such as *Mangas verde com sal* [Green Mangos with Salt] (1977) and *A Ilha de Moçambique. Roteiro poético* [Moçambique Island: A Lyrical Guide] (enlarged ed. 1989), down to the nostalgic *O Monhé das Cobras* [The Indian Snake Charmer] (1997). He was seconded by Glória de Sant 'Anna (1925-), a poet of much richer feminine artistry than Noémi de Sousa. Her poems appeared with the title *Amaranto* [Amaranth] (1988). Abundant and original poetry was created by António Quadros, using often the pen name J. P. Grabato Dias (1933-), in works like *As Quybyrycas. Poema ethyco* (1972), exaggerating Camões's epic style to sing the tragic battle of Alcacer Quibir, which cost young King Sebastian's life, or *Uma Meditação. 21 Laurentinas e dois fabulários* [A Meditation, 21 Odes of Lourenço Marques and two unsuccessful Lyrico-fables] (1971).

São Tomé e Príncipe: Although there were a few predecessors from São Tomé e Príncipe, notably the poet Caetano Costa Alegre (1864–96) who wrote poems from 1862 on, the geographer Francisco José Tenreiro (1921-63) easily qualifies as that former colony's first important poet. In fact, Tenreiro, who lived most of his short life in Portugal, as did Costa Alegre, is lusophone Africa's premier *negritude poet. The posthumous edition of his *Obra poética* (1967) contains *Ilha de Nome santo* [Islands with a Saintly Name] and the complete text of *Coração em Africa* [Heart of Africa]. He is also, along with Mário Pinto de Andrade (1928-90), the influential Angolan intellectual and literary critic, the first anthologizer of African poetry of Portuguese expression.

Maria Manuela Margarido (1925-), from Príncipe, the fiery Alda (do) Espírito Santo (1926-), and Tomás Medeiros (1931-), both from São Tomé, joined Tenreiro as their islands' standard-bearers of cultural resistance and social protest during colonial times. Since independence about a dozen poets have made their mark, four of the best being Marcelo da Veiga (1893-1976), whose poems were edited posthumously as *O Canto do Ossobó* [The Ossobó's Song] (1989), Francisco Costa Alegre (1953-), Frederico G. dos Anjos (1954-), and Conceição Lima (1962-). Dos Anjos is also one of very few writers of prose fiction from the islands. His *Bandeira para um Cadáver* [Flag for a cadaver] (1984) is very short but powerful. Another work of prose fiction, *Rosa do Riboque e Outros Contos* [Rosa from Riboque and other stories] (1985) was written by by Albertino Bragança (1942-). The Portuguese official Fausto Duarte (1903-53), who spent more than twenty years in the country, wrote well-observed stories and novels about native life, including his novel *Auá* (1934).

Guinea-Bissau: The oral lore of Guinea-Bissau began to be written down by the Catholic missionary Marcelino Marques de Barros (1844-1928) in the second half of the nineteenth century. He published most of it in *Literatura dos Negros* (1900). Later collections were made by Viriato Augusto Tadeu in *Contos o Caramó. Lendas e Fábulas dos Mandingas* [Stories of Caramó: Legends and Fables of the Mandings] (1945) and Benjamin Pinto Bull in *O Crioulo da Guiné-Bissau. Filosofia e Sabedoria* [The Creole of Guinea-Bissau: Philosophy and Wisdom] (1989). Guinea-Bissau is unique in never having attracted European settlers. A characteristic literature only began to appear after independence. Poems by Amílcar Cabral (1924-73), a Cape Verdean living in Guinea Bissau, the father of Guinean and Cape Verdean independence, and Vasco Cabral (1926-), both of whom might be considered precursors, appear in *Antologia Poética da Guiné-Bissau* [Poetry anthology from Guinea-Bissau] (1990). The other twelve poets represented, including Hélder Proença (1956-), a militant poet and a poet of love in *Não posso adiar a Palavra* [I cannot postpone speaking out] (1992). But José Carlos Schwartz (1949-77) became by far the most popular poet and musician. His Creole songs and poems were collected by Moema Parente Augel in *Ora di kantá tchiga* [The Hour of Singing is arriving] (1997).

Literary activities and publishing in Guinea-Bissau blossomed in the 1990s. Domingas Samy (1955-) became Guinea-Bissau's first post-colonial writer of prose fiction with the publication of *A Escola* [The school] (1993), a collection of three short stories. Another revelation is Abdulai Sila (1958-), Guinea-Bissau's first post-colonial novelist, with *Eterna Paixão* [Endless Passion] (1994), which tells of the disillusions and enduring sense of duty of an American black in post-independence Guinea-Bissau, and *A última Tragédia* [The Final Tragedy] (1995).

M

MACLENNAN, Donald (Alasdair Calum) (1929-), South African poet. Born in London, Maclennan came to South Africa in 1938; he was educated at the universities of the Witwatersrand and Edinburgh.

His first collection, *Life Songs*, was published by Bateleur in 1977. This collection of personal lyrics was followed by *In Memoriam Oskar Wolberheim* (1981), a collaboration combining Maclennan's poetry and the music of Norbert Nowotny. In *Reckonings* (1983), Maclennan engages with the subject matter and themes that reappear in his subsequent collections: the nature of being, the limits of human understanding, and the rhythms and cycles of the natural world. *Collecting Darkness* (1988) and *The Poetry Lesson* (1995) return to these preoccupations; with each collection he hones his wry, personal voice more sharply. *Letters* (1992) employs the device of an address to absent parties: family members, friends, lovers, and the poet himself. *Solstice* (1997), which won South Africa's 1997 Sanlam Literary Award, was praised for its simplicity of diction. The same qualities are evident in *Of Women and Some Men* (1998). In the most recent collections he finds a mature poetic voice, the relative obscurity of his earliest poems giving way to a poetic style that is limpid and terse.

MADAGASCAR [See MALAGASY]

MADANHIRE, Nevanji (1961-), novelist, was born in Fort Victoria, now Masvingo, in Southern Rhodesia, now Zimbabwe, and was educated at the University of Zimbabwe. Before becoming a full-time journalist he taught for some years; he is editor-in-chief of *The Financial Gazette*, an important weekly that offers an alternative to the interpretation of national issues provided by the publications of Zimbabwe Newspapers, which dominates Zimbabwe's media. In Madanhire's first novel, *Goatsmell* (1992), the doomed romance between two students, a Shona and an Ndebele, critiques politicians who exploit ethnic, regional, and racial differences in order to consolidate power. The authorities have in the past regarded writing on such subjects as subversive, and Madanhire's willingness to address such a sensitive issue is a significant development. The novel anticipates that a new generation will allow a sense of nation to transcend local loyalties. *Goatsmell*'s bold use of metaphorical language adds a new dimension to the already stylistically ambitious Zimbabwean novel in English.

Madanhire's second novel is *If the Wind Blew* (1996).

MADDY, Yulisa Amadu (formerly Pat Yulisa or Pat Maddy) (1936-), playwright and-novelist, was born in Freetown, Sierra Leone and educated in Sierra Leone and in the UK at Rose Bruford College and London University. He has worked as an actor and director and as a lecturer, instructor, and professor in Zambia, Nigeria, the UK, and the USA. His first play was *Obasai and Other Plays* (1971), which was followed by a novel, *No Past, No Present, No Future* (1973). He received the Sierra Leone National Arts Festival Award in 1973, the Gulbenkian Grant in 1978, and the Edinburgh Festival Award in 1979. His other plays are *Big Breeze Blow* (1984), *Take Tem Draw Di Rope* (1975), *Naw We Yone Dehn See* (1975), *Big Berrin* (1984), *A Journey into Christmas* (1980), *Drums, Voices and Worlds* (1985), *If Wishes Were Horses* (1963), a radio play, and *Saturday Night Out* (1980), a play for television. *Yon Kon* (1982) examines money and its control of society and provides a microcosm of his more developed plays. Its theme is developed further in *No Past, No Present, No Future*, in which three men's friendship is called into question in a foreign land as they attempt to escape the intricate social system of their native Sierra Leone. Like Ugandan playwright John *Ruganda, he has been influenced by European theatre, from absurdist comedy to political allusion to Brechtian theatrical technique. He writes mainly for an African audience, which he reaches by using Pidgin in combination with African proverbs and ritualistic theatre. In 1996 he co-authored with Donnarae MacCann *African Images in Juvenile Fiction: Commentaries on Neocolonialist Fiction*.

Madmen and Specialists (1971) A play by Wole *Soyinka. In common with the novel *Season of Anomy* (1973) and the prison journal *The Man Died* (1972), this play expresses Soyinka's outrage at the *Nigeria-Biafra war. Central to the plot is the conflict between Dr. Bero, a medic whom the war has transformed into an intelligence officer, and his father (Old Man), whose means of articulating the horror of the war is to propose the army convert to cannibalism. Old Man's savage irony is bolstered by a group of four Mendicants who perform throughout the play a series of satiric sketches that parody the vicious regime Dr. Bero serves: all this is predicated on the cynical mock-philosophy Old Man has taught them, the cult of 'As'. Some hope that older values may survive emerges through the actions of Bero's sister and two elderly

Earth Mothers, who guard a store of traditional medicines.

Mafeking Diary of Sol T. Plaatje, The (1999) Centenary edition of *The Boer War Diary*, Sol T. ★Plaatje (1973, 1990) *Mafeking Diary* is unique as the only known account of the ★Anglo-Boer war from the perspective of a black man. A highly personal document, it charts the development of the siege of Mafeking during 1900. Plaatje concerns himself largely with the effect of the emergency regulations on the African population. As court interpreter for Robert Baden-Powell, Plaatje gathered many snippets of conversation and recorded them in his diary; they offer details absent in other diaries of the siege. His concern with the plight of the African masses foreshadows the themes that would dominate his writing for the next thirty years. The multilingual approach linking specific activities to different groups of people in the siege prefigures a technique used with great virtuosity in ★*Mhudi*. The diary is rich in African idiom transposed into English.

Mafeking Road (1947) Short stories by H.C. ★Bosman. In the only collection of Bosman's stories to have appeared in his own lifetime, all but one of the twenty-one stories feature the wily backveld raconteur Oom Schalk Lourens, through whom Bosman is able to reflect ironically on the prejudices and weaknesses of the Marico community, a community he nonetheless evokes with great sympathy and understanding. Memorable stories include 'In the Withaak's Shade', 'The Music-Maker', 'Mafeking Road', 'Makapan's Caves', and 'The Rooinek'. It is clear, despite the regional setting and localized humour, that Bosman's concerns in these stories are not confined to the 'Groot Marico' but touch upon wider issues that extend to the entire South African population and beyond.

MAGAIA, Lina (1940s-), Mozambican short-story writer and novelist writing in Portuguese, was born in Maputo, Mozambique to parents who moved north in search of secondary educational opportunities for their children. Although her education in the Portuguese colonial school system, designed like French colonial education to reproduce European manners and sensibilities in Africans, might have turned her into an *assimilado*, she rebelled and joined the Mozambican Liberation Front (Frelimo) while still in high school, and she suffered a jail term of three months for her political activism. She graduated with a B.Sc. in economics from the University of Lisbon in 1975 and works as an agricultural administrator in the Mozambique public service.

During the war of independence, she served in the Mozambican Liberation Army, witnessing the atrocities of war and of the post-war period. Her first book,

Dumba nengue: histórias trágicas do banditismo (1987; *Dumba Nengue, Run For Your Life: Peasant Tales of Tragedy in Mozambique*, 1988), is based on interviews with survivors of atrocities committed by the counter-revolutionary terrorist organization Renamo on 22 July 1987, when 380 persons were massacred in a region of southern Mozambique known as Dumba nengue. *Dumba nengue* is also a local proverb that means 'Run for your life' or 'You have to trust your feet'. The simple, journalistic style of her stories can be gleaned from their titles ('Their Heads Were Crushed like Peanuts', 'Pieces of Human Flesh Fell on Belinda's Yard', etc.) and from passages like the following from 'The Pregnant Well': 'When she had looked into the well she had seen the heads of dead people staring at her as if pleading for help.... And the well had seemed pregnant to her'. Magaia has since published another collection of stories of war atrocities, *Duplo massacre em Moçambique: histórias trágicas do banditismo* (1989), and a novel, *Delehta: Pulos na vida* (1994).

MAGHREBI LITERATURE At the turn of the present century the greater part of the Maghreb was under French rule. Algeria was first settled by the French in 1830, and eventually made a French colony. It did not gain independence until 1962, after a national war that lasted more than seven years (1954-62). Tunisia and Morocco were declared French Protectorates in 1881 and 1912 respectively. Both countries became independent in 1956. The French colonial powers had direct rule over the secular life of people in the Maghreb, but did not interfere with their religious practices. Theological treatises and works of Muslim jurisprudence continued to be written in all three Maghreb countries under French occupation. There was little creative writing, however, apart from poetry which has been esteemed by Arabs since pre-Islamic times. Poetry during the colonial period was usually composed in keeping with classical Arabic rhyme and metres. Modern Arabic poetry did not appear in the Maghreb until the Tunisian Abu al-Qasim al-Shabbi (1909-34) began to write innovative verse, typical of the Romantic movement that was taking place in the rest of the Arabic-speaking world.

Fictional writing first began at the turn of the century with didactic narratives which in time developed into the short story genre. The novel did not emerge in the Maghreb until the 1940s and 50s with names like those of Bashir Khurayyif (1917-83) in Tunisia, Abdelmajid Benjelloun (1919-81) and Abd al-Karim Ghallab (1917-) in Morocco. In Algeria the novel appeared considerably later. *Rih al-Janub* (1971) by Abdelhamid Benhadouga (1925-97) and *Al-Laz* (1974) and *Al-Zilzal* (1974) by Tahar Wattar (1936-) are considered to be among the first examples of

Arabic novel-writing in Algeria. Modern Arabic creative writing in the form of poetry, the novel, the short story, and more recently drama also, has developed throughout the Maghreb in a relatively short time. Eclipsed for decades by the literary production of the Mashreq (the Middle East), it is now reaching a wide readership throughout the Arabic-speaking world.

It is the francophone literature of the Maghreb that has gained global recognition, having first emerged in Algeria in the 1920s. Algeria, being a *département* of France, attracted a number of writers from metropolitan France. It also became the home of two important French literary schools, *Les Algérianistes* and *L'École d'Alger*. The former was established at the turn of the century and continued until the mid-1930s, giving place to the latter which lasted until the 1950s, and included Albert Camus among its members. The first works of francophone fiction by indigenous writers, published in the 1920s and 30s, are negligible in number and are now mostly out of print. These early narrative works are a far cry from the francophone novels which began to appear in the 1940s and 50s, reaching peaks of excellence with the works of Mouloud Feraoun (1913-62), Mouloud Mammeri (1917-89) and Mohammed *Dib (1920-) in Algeria, Driss *Chraïbi (1926-) in Morocco, and Albert *Memmi (1920-) in Tunisia. These five writers are better known for their novels, although they wrote poetry and occasionally plays and non-fictional works also. They set an example for later generations of francophone writers who also seem to have opted for the novel more than any other literary genre. The first generation of writers, with the exception of Chraïbi, were relatively mild in their criticism of colonial rule. Yet they paved the way for the more virulent attacks of younger writers.

It was in 1956, with the publication of his highly controversial novel, *Nedjma*, that the Algerian Kateb Yacine (1929-89) added his name to a growing list of francophone authors. Drawing on autobiographical recollections, factual events and Algerian mythology, Kateb broke away completely from the socio-realistic mould that had characterized his predecessors' works. *Nedjma* is a collage of narrative prose and poetry in which the author presents the history of Algeria by concentrating on the story of the eponymous heroine who symbolizes Algeria. Nedjma, born of an Algerian father and a French mother, like Algeria, has a Franco-Arab heritage. And like Algeria too, she is pursued by a number of men who all want to possess her. Kateb had initially prepared over 400 pages of manuscript which he hoped to turn into a novel. *Nedjma* was eventually published in 256 pages. The rest of the material Kateb used in a play, *Le Cercle de représailles* (1959) and his second novel, *Le Polygone étoilé* (1966), in which he also explores the same themes.

A year after *Nedjma* was published, Assia *Djebar's first novel appeared. Djebar is to date the leading franco-phone woman writer in the Maghreb. One of the better-known women writers who predates Djebar is Taos Amrouche (1913-76) whose first novel, *Jacinthe noire*, appeared in 1947. Born in Algeria of a Berber family, she grew up in Tunisia before eventually moving to France. She was the sister of the well-known poet Jean Amrouche (1906-62) and the daughter of Fadhma Ait Amrouche (1882-1967) whose auto-biographical work, *Histoire de ma vie* (1968), published posthumously and prefaced by Kateb Yacine, is considered to be a minor classic. Another woman writer who rose to prominence in the eighties and nineties is Algerian Leïla Sebbar (1941-) who in her first two novels *Fatima ou les Algériennes au square* (1981) and *Shérazade, 17 ans, brune, frisée, les yeux verts* (1982; *Shérazade, Aged 17, Dark Curly Hair, Green Eyes, Missing*, 1991), sets out to describe the world of Maghrebi immigrant women and their rebellious daughters in France.

In the 1960s and early 70s francophone writing became a sensitive issue, particularly in Algeria where it was felt that there was a pressing need for a national literature in Arabic. A few francophone authors stopped writing altogether, while others, like Kateb and Djebar, turned to writing plays and film-scripts in colloquial Arabic. There was a relative lull in francophone literary production for almost a decade, although some major voices emerged during this period, among them that of Mohammed Khaïreddine (1941-95) in Morocco and Rachid Boudjedra (1941-) in Algeria. Both made a forceful impact on franco-phone literature with their first novels, *Agadir* (1967) and *La Répudiation* (1969; *The Repudiation*, 1995) respectively, in which they openly condemn the religious and sexual hypocrisy prevalent in their societies. Apart from criticizing religious fanaticism and gender inequality, some writers, foremost among them the Algerians Rachid Mimouni (1945-95) and Tahar Djaout (1954-93), began to denounce the social and political malaise which their countries were experiencing. Djaout was one of the first writers to be killed by religious fundamentalists when they began to target intellectuals and artists. In his last two novels, *L'Invention du désert* (1987) and *Les Vigiles* (1991) Djaout condemns religious fanaticism and the lack of freedom of the individual. Mimouni's penultimate novel, *Une Peine à vivre* (1992), hailed as a masterpiece, tries to analyse the thought processes of a ruthless despot who rises to power through devious means and becomes the undisputed leader of his country. In two earlier novels, *Le Fleuve détourné* (1982) and *Tombéza* (1984) Mimouni bemoans the fact that Algeria, bogged down by bureaucracy, hypocrisy and injustice, failed to keep the promises made to its people on the eve of independence. In *L'Honneur de la tribu* (1989;

The Honour of the Tribe, 1992) he advocates a gradual transition to modernity without abandoning completely one's culture and heritage.

Awarding the most coveted French literary prize to the Moroccan Tahar ★Ben Jelloun for his novel *La Nuit sacrée* (1987; *Sacred Night*, 1989) made Maghrebi francophone literature better known internationally. In both this novel and its prequel *L'Enfant de sable* (1985; *Sand Child*, 1987), Ben Jelloun deals with sexual ambiguity where his central character, a young girl, is brought up as a boy by her father because he has no male heirs. This theme gave Ben Jelloun the opportunity to explore other themes, namely alienation and dispossession, both on a personal as well as a national level. Ben Jelloun's works are inspired by the oral culture of Morocco, rich in proverbs, legends and fables. A psychiatrist by training, he has published collections of poetry and plays, although he is better known for his novels. Ben Jelloun has tackled a number of pressing issues in his works, relevant not only to the Maghreb, but to contemporary society in general. He is one of the best known and most prolific of a galaxy of Moroccan francophone writers, among them Abdelkébir Khatibi (1938), the author of *L'Amour bilingue* (1983; *Love in Two Languages*, 1990), dealing with decolonization mainly from a linguistic perspective, and Abdelhak Serhane (1950-) whose first novel *Messaouda* (1983; *Messaouda*, 1986) denounces traditional societies where individuals are at the mercy of the clan and young people are denied freedom.

Few Moroccan women have become as well known as men writers. One writer in Arabic, Leila Abouzeid (1950-), became known for her novel *'Am al-Fil* (1983; *Year of the Elephant*, 1989), translated into several languages. Abouzeid here introduces assertive women who take charge of their own lives. Contemporary Arabic writing in Morocco is reaching a far wider readership than before. Among novelists writing in Arabic are Mohamed Zafzaf (1945-) and Mohamed Berrada (1938-). The latter's award-winning novel, *Lu'bat al-Nisyan* (1986; *The Game of Forgetting*, 1997), relates, in episodic sequences, Morocco's modern history. There are several well-known poets who write in Arabic including Hasan al-Turaybiq (1945-) who also writes plays in verse, and Mohammed Bannis (1948-). The name that towers above the rest, however, is that of the francophone poet Abdellatif Laâbi (1942-) who has published several volumes of poetry and essays. Laâbi helped to promote experimental writing in Morocco by founding the review *Souffles* (1966) as a forum for innovative creative writing. He was imprisoned (1972-80) for his views which did not toe the party line. Apart from his poetry, Laâbi's other major contribution is the dialogue he established among writers, and particularly between those who write in Arabic and French. He himself has translated Arabic works into French and French works into Arabic. While Laâbi brought bilingualism to poetry, Tayeb Saddiki (1938-) introduced it into Moroccan theatre. A prolific playwright, catering for different tastes, Saddiki presents each play in the language that is best suited to a specific audience, whether French, literary Arabic or colloquial Moroccan Arabic.

Several Maghrebi bilingual writers have become well known outside their own countries. As well as the Moroccan writers already mentioned, the name that stands out in Algeria is that of Boudjedra, who in 1981, after publishing six novels in French, began to write Arabic novels. In Tunisia the poet Tahar Bekri (1951-) has published several volumes of poetry in both Arabic and French. Tunisia, unlike Algeria and Morocco, was for a long time better known for its Arabic rather than francophone creative writing. It was only recently that Tunisians writing in French came to add their name to the distinguished list of Maghrebi francophone writers. A leading Tunisian francophone novelist is Abdelwahab Meddeb (1946-) whose complex narrative style was first encountered in *Talismano* (1979), his debut novel in which he explores the themes of childhood memories and the task of the writer. Besides Bekri, the other important name in Tunisian francophone poetry is that of Hédi Bouraoui (1932-) who began publishing volumes of poetry in the mid-sixties. Bouraoui's style is highly innovative and he frequently experiments with language, coining his own words where necessary. Women francophone poets are represented by Sophie El Goulli (1932-) and Amina Saïd (1950-). There are a number of novelists, poets and dramatists writing in Arabic whose works are not available outside Tunisia, but whose names have become known to a French-reading public through the works of Father Jean Fontaine, the director of the Institut des Belles Lettres Arabes (IBLA) in Tunis and the leading authority on Tunisian literature.

A number of Maghrebi writers now live abroad, mainly in France. It was in France that a highly dynamic literary movement by young people of Maghrebian origin erupted on the French literary scene in the early eighties. Popularly referred to as Beur literature, it began with the novel, but came to include also poetry, drama, songs and film. Despite the variety of genres, the novel predominates, and to date it is only novelists who have made this literature internationally known. It was in 1983 that Mehdi Charef (1952-), using French street jargon, published his first novel *Le Thé au Harem d'Archi Ahmed* (1983; *Tea in the Harem*, 1989) which became an immediate success and was made into a film by Costa-Gavras. The novel, based on autobiographical incidents, evokes the life of children of Maghrebi immigrants, living in shantytowns, amid squalor, deprivation and racist insults. The title Charef chose is a rewording of

Archimedes' theorem (*Le Théorème d'Archimède*). In his next novel *Le Harki de Meriem* (1989) he describes the events leading to the murder of a young Maghrebi living in France who is the son of Algerian Harkis (those who sided with the French during the war of independence). A small part of the novel is set in Algeria where the young man's sister takes his body for burial. In the Algerian scenes Charef uses short extracts of dialogue in spoken Arabic which he reproduces in Latin script. Using word-play and introducing Arabic words and expressions seems to have become the hallmark of Beur writing. Sometimes the titles of Beur novels are either in another language or in a mixture of Arabic and French, as, for example, *Beur's Story* (1989) by Ferrudja Kessas (1958-), one of the few women writers among the group, and *Dis Oualla* (1997) by Azouz Begag (1957-), where a French word is followed by an Arabic one. Begag is perhaps the best known of Beur writers. He made his name with his first novel *Le gone du Chaâba* (1986) a humorous, autobiographical work, which was made into a film in 1998. The novel describes the world of a *gone*, the local term for 'lad' in Lyons, living in a large shantytown called *Chaâba* by its inhabitants, since the term means 'of the people' in Arabic. Begag and Charef represent the two main strands of Beur writing, the one funny and lighthearted, the other sombre and serious, despite the sardonic humour.

Children of Moroccan immigrants in the Netherlands began to write in Dutch from 1989. There have been several outstanding works which have won Dutch literary prizes, among them *De weg naar het noorden* (1995) by Naima El Bezaz (1974-), which charts the journey of a young Moroccan who leaves Meknes, El Bezaz's home town in Morocco, and travels through Europe in search of work. He arrives in the Netherlands illegally and is set upon and killed by a group of jeering Dutch thugs. Another award-winning novel is *Hoezo bloedmooi* (1995) by Hans Sahar (1974-) describing in Dutch street jargon the world of drug-pushers and others living on the margin of society. Several Moroccans in the Netherlands have written fiction and poetry in Tarifit, the Berber variety of northern Morocco. These works normally appear in bilingual text format, with their Dutch translations on facing pages. Works in the Kabyle Berber of Algeria started to appear in the 1980s in France, but have to date reached only a limited readership.

MAGONA, Sindiwe (1942-) South African autobiographer and short-story writer, grew up in a village in the Transkei and later in Guguletu, Cape Town. She has degrees from the University of South Africa and Columbia University and works for the United Nations in New York. Between the two parts of her autobiography, *To My Children's Children* (1990) and *Forced to Grow* (1992), she produced a collection of short stories, *Living, Loving, and Lying Awake at Night* (1991). Another collection, *Push-Push and Other Stories*, appeared in 1996.

Magona's autobiography is framed by an address to an imaginary great-granddaughter, who would otherwise have received her grandmother's story via oral tradition. The narrative itself shows little influence of oral tradition; it is the story of individual triumph against the ★apartheid system told with a foreign audience strongly in mind. Her most startling and interesting work is to be found in the series of humorous and satirical short stories under the subtitle 'Women at Work' in her 1991 collection.

MAHFOUZ, Naguib, (1911-), Egyptian novelist, generally regarded as the creator of the modern Arabic novel, also author of many short stories and film scripts; awarded the Nobel Prize for Literature in 1988. He was born in Cairo and received his early education in a Koranic primary school. In his teens he suffered a religious crisis brought on by the reading of Darwin. After taking a degree in philosophy in Cairo, he opted for a literary career, earning his living as a civil servant, first in the Ministry of Religious Endowments, later as a film censor in the Ministry of Culture.

Mahfouz's literary career falls into a series of clearly marked periods, separated by long silences provoked by personal or political crises. After three historical novels set in ancient Egypt, conceived as the beginning of a whole series, he changed course and wrote five novels concerned with the social problems of ordinary people in contemporary Cairo, including *Midaq Alley* (1947; trans. 1966) and *The Beginning and the End* (1949; trans. 1985). Then, in *The ★Cairo Trilogy*, which he called 'a history of my country and of myself', he follows the fortunes of a family through three generations: *Palace Walk* (1956; trans. 1990), *Palace of Desire* (1957; trans. 1991) and *Sugar Street* (1957; trans. 1992).

The trilogy was completed in 1952. Following the revolution of that year and a personal crisis, he wrote virtually nothing for several years, then took a new direction with his religious allegory ★*Children of Gebelawi* (1959; trans 1981), which was serialized in the newspaper *Al-Ahram* but never published as a book in Egypt because Muslim leaders attacked it as atheistic, although Mahfouz regarded it as re-affirming the transcendancy of true religion. The furore caused by this work provoked another silence, followed by six short novels, including *The Thief and the Dogs* (1961; trans. 1984), *Adrift on the Nile* (1966; trans. 1993) and *Miramar* (1967; 1978); these use stream-of-consciousness technique and are full of existential problems.

Egypt's defeat in the Six Days War of 1967 caused a further long silence, after which Mahfouz re-emerged writing works such as *Mirrors* (1972; trans.

1977) and *Fountain and Tomb* (1975: trans. 1988), in which the fragments are barely connected into a novel at all. His final period of activity shows a virtuostic variety. In *The Harafish* (1977; trans. 1994), he returns one last time to his epic mode, following a Cairo family through more than ten generations and reaffirming his faith in the possibility of a revolution that is both political and spiritual. In *Arabian Nights and Days* (1979; trans. 1995) and *The Journey of Ibn Fattouma* (1983; trans. 1992) he is inspired by classical Arabic models, and in *Al-A'ish fi'l-Haqiqa* (1985) he returns to the ancient Egypt with which he began his career.

Controversy was revived by the Nobel Prize and Mahfouz became the target of certain extreme Islamic groups, surviving an assassination attempt in October 1994. This only reinforced the popularity of an author who is felt by most Egyptians to be the embodiment of all that is best in their country, champion of the poor, of women and of the oppressed, advocate of tolerance and social solidarity.

MAINA wa Kinyatti [see ORAL TRADITION AND FOLKLORE, East Africa]

MALAGASY 'The Big Island', Madagascar, which is almost as big as France, was a rarity among French colonies being a kingdom with a single written language. Throughout the nineteenth century Malagasy – a Malay language – had been studied and written by Protestant Mission and Catholic Jesuit schools. At the same time there was a body of texts written in the Arabic script, since Islam had long been in the Indian Ocean.

Under French colonial policy, at the beginning of the twentieth century, a key decision was made to promote the intensive teaching of French, while paying lip service to Malagasy by the creation of a Malagasy Academy. Among the first teachers of French in Malagasy was Jean Paulhan, who was to become one of the key figures of French literary life in France and who started the teaching of Malagasy at the School of Oriental languages in Paris. He produced an edition with translation (1913) of one of the most important genres of oral poetry in Malagasy, the *hain teny*, short gnomic poems, not unlike the haiku. The tradition of study of oral literature was continued by Bakoly Domenichini Ramiaramanana (*Du Ohabolana au hain teny*, 1983) while written literature in the language was not developed.

The poems of Jean-Joseph *Rabéarivelo, who wrote in his language as well as in French marked the beginnings of contemporary Malagasy literature. Despite his inclusion in *Senghor's *Anthologie de la nouvelle poésie nègre et malgache de langue française* (1948) he was certainly not a negritude poet if this meant a commitment to Black African culture; nonetheless his

life, and suicide in 1937, were emblematic of the situation of the colonial intellectual. Jacques *Rabémananjara, his disciple, produced an important body of lyrical poetry as well as important essays putting Malagasy culture in an African perspective. Flavien Ranaivo (1914-) was the third Malagasy poet to be anthologized by Senghor and his work shows influence from traditional forms.

Literary production in French came to a standstill with the 'marxoid' revolution of 1972 which decided to promote the national language. Since there was heavy censorship the result of this policy was silence and exile. Novelist and playwright Michèle Rakotoson (1950-) chronicles the disillusion of a generation in French in her novel (*Dadabe*, 1984, *Le Bain des reliques*, 1988) . The return to democracy after the civil rights movement of 1992 produced a new surge of writing in French, among them playwright and short-story writer David Jaomanoro (1954-).

Man of the People, A (1966) A novel by Chinua *Achebe. Published on the eve of the first military coup d'etat in Nigeria, the novel presents a post-independence country resembling Nigeria, where unrestrained acquisitiveness, unchecked political corruption, and simple self-interest have taken the place of responsible leadership. Achebe suggests what qualities responsible leadership should possess through a depiction of its opposite in Chief Nanga, the charismatic 'man of the people' of the novel's title. So corrupt has the regime Achebe depicts become that military intervention is seen as the only possible redemption for a society in which traditional and imported constitutional methods are ineffective.

Man Who Lost his Shadow, The (1966) A novel by Fathy *Ghanem translated from the Arabic by Desmond Stewart, is the story of an ambitious young Cairo journalist, Yusif Hamid, told in turn by the novel's four main characters, a young peasant girl who becomes his father's second wife, a film starlet with whom Yusif lives and rejects, a senior journalist and editor who marries the rejected starlet and who loses his job to Yusif and, finally, Yusif himself. The novel exposes the jungle of the Cairo newspaper world exploited by the ruthless hero.

MANAKA, Matsemela (1956-98), South African poet and playwright. Born at Alexandra, in the Johannesburg area, Manaka was active in the grassroots black theatre movement that emerged after the Soweto riots of 1976, following the closure of opportunities for black artists and performers in mainstream South African theatres. Originally trained as a teacher, his original inspiration came from the heroism of the young schoolchildren who pitted themselves against the firepower of the *apartheid regime. He founded the Soyikwa African Theatre group, whose members performed unscripted, workshop-generated plays in quick response to the events of the day, turning acts of repression into provocatively satirical farces. Manaka's own plays grew out of the same kind of workshop context. They include *Egoli: City of Gold* (1979), *Blues Afrika Café* (1980), *Vuka* (1981), *Mbumba* (1984), *Children of Asazi* (published in *Woza Africa! An Anthology of South African Plays*, ed. Duma Ndlovu, 1986), *Domba, the Last Prince* (1986) and *Pula* [Rain] (published in *Market Plays*, ed. Stephen *Gray, 1986 and separately in 1990), *Size* (1987), *Toro* (1987), *Koma* (1988), *Gorée*, a musical (with Motsumi Makhene and Peter Boroto, 1989), *Ekhaya: Coming Home* (1991), *Ekhaya: Museum over Soweto* (1991), and *Yamina* (1993). Powerful instruments for promoting black consciousness among the black township audiences to which they are primarily addressed, these plays were also successfully performed at overseas theatre festivals in London, Edinburgh, Berlin, and Copenhagen, with *Pula* and *Mbumba* winning a Fringe Award at the Edinburgh Festival. Manaka also produced screenplays, including *Two Rivers* (co-authored with Ratshaka Ratshitanga, Mark Newman, and Eddie Wes) and *Kiba: The Beat Between*. Between 1979 and 1982, he was a member of the editorial collective of the literary magazine *Staffrider*. In 1987, he won the PEN International Freedom-to-Write Award.

MANGUA, Charles (*ca*. 1940-), Kenyan novelist born in Nyeri, Kenya and educated at the universities of Makerere and Oxford, worked as an economist with the African Development Bank in Abidjan before returning to Kenya after the publication of his best-known novel *Son of Woman*. His later work includes *A Tail in the Mouth* and short stories.

MAPANJE, Jack (1944-), Malawian poet, was born of Yao and Nyanja parents in Kadango village, Malawi. After attending Roman Catholic schools and training as a teacher, he taught before undertaking a BA at Chancellor College, where he was a member of a group of aspiring writers that met regularly to discuss one another's work. He gained M.Litt. and Ph.D. degrees at London University and worked as a university lecturer in Malawi before his detention in 1987-91 by the repressive Banda regime. After his release he moved to York, UK, where he has held a variety of teaching posts. Brief visits to Malawi since Banda's election defeat of 1994 have enabled him to contribute to the vigorous debate about the future of the country.

Although he has published a number of academic essays, co-edited two collections of poetry, and contributed poetry in Chichewa to a collection edited by Enoch Timpunza-Mvula, it is as a poet writing in English that Mapanje is of greatest significance. His two collections bring together the verses by which he should currently be judged. *Of Chameleons and Gods* (1981) includes work presented to the writers' group in the early 1970s, poems composed in London when he was doing his first postgraduate degree, and verses written on 'Re-entering Chingwe's Hole' on his return to Malawi with his M. Litt. *The Chattering Wagtails of Mikuyu Prison* (1993) includes material that was more or less ready for the press before his detention, together with poems written in prison and following his release.

All the elements of Mapanje the public poet are visible in his poetry: the excited undergraduate responding to the encouragement to use myths and taking up the burden of responsibility that literature in Africa was beginning to carry in the 1960s; the scholar studying the oral traditions; and, particularly insistent, a maturing individuality suggested by the emergence of a distinctive speaking voice. Throughout, the social commentator, anxious to express opinions but aware of the presence of the censor and so forced to be devious, to use images and codes, to 'speak in riddles'.

For readers unfamiliar with Malawian cultural traditions and politics, the poems of the early period can be somewhat hermeneutic, and a case can be made for starting at the stage when the state has done its worst, when Mapanje is in detention and 'released' to write. The lines that describe his arrest and locking up, that chart his feelings in prison, are better points from which to embark on his work. In them the values of home and humanity, of history and honest dealing, to which he has always been committed are clear. Recent work includes poems that follow up the trails begun in Mikuyu and responses to events in South Africa and Rwanda. As an academic he has shown continued concern with oral traditions and has embarked on an attempt to establish a theoretical basis for the critical examination of prison literature.

Marabi Dance, The (1973), a novel by Modikwe *Dikobe. Set in Doornfontein, one of the inner-city slumyards, in the 1930s, the novel deals with the predicament of Martha, who is caught between the Marabi culture of the mainly working-class slumyards and her more middle-class aspirations. Notable for its inner view of a culture and way of life that disappeared with the clearing of the slumyards in the 1930s and 40s, it depicts the processes of urbanization and acculturation and reveals how people were able to adapt and survive in their new surroundings. It reflects a mainly working-class perspective (that of the newly urbanized black proletariat). Its reception has been mixed: it was criticized initially for its supposedly 'clumsy construction' and 'wooden characterization'; later critics, often applying a class-based analysis, have been more willing to value it for its historical and sociological interest. The novel was workshopped as a play, *Marabi*, in 1981 and performed in 1982; a 1995 production is evidence of continuing interest.

MARECHERA, Dambudzo (1952-87), Zimbabwean novelist and poet, was born in Rusape and grew up amid racial discrimination, poverty, and violence. He attended St. Augustine's Mission, Penhalonga, where he clashed with his teachers over the colonial teaching syllabus, the University of Rhodesia, from which he was expelled during student unrest, and New College, Oxford, where his unsociable behaviour and academic dereliction led to another expulsion. In his short career he published a book of stories, two novels (one posthumously), a book of plays, prose, and poetry, and a collection of poetry (also posthumous).

His first book, ★*The House of Hunger* (1978), is the product of a period of despair following his time at Oxford. Among the nine stories the long title story describes the narrator's brutalized childhood and youth in colonial Rhodesia in a style that is emotionally compelling and verbally pyrotechnic. The narrative is characterized by shifts in time and place and a blurring of fantasy and reality. Regarded as signalling a new trend of incisive and visionary African writing, the book was awarded the 1979 *Guardian* fiction prize. *Black Sunlight* (1980), although it has been compared with the writing of James Joyce and Henry Miller, did not achieve the critical success of *House of Hunger*. Loosely structured and stylistically hallucinatory, with erudite digressions on various literary and philosophical points of discussion, it explores the idea of anarchism as a formal intellectual position. *The Black Insider* (1990) is set in a faculty of arts building that offers refuge for a group of intellectuals and artists from an unspecified war outside, which subsequently engulfs them as well. The conversation of the characters centres around African identity and the nature of art, with the protagonist arguing that the African image is merely another chauvinistic figure of authority.

Marechera returned to the newly liberated Zimbabwe in 1982 to assist in shooting the film of *House of Hunger* but fell out with the director and remained behind in Zimbabwe when the crew left, leading to a homeless existence in Harare before his death five years later. *Mindblast; or, The Definitive Buddy* (1984) was written the year after his return home and comprises three plays, a prose narrative, a collection of poems, and a park-bench diary. The book criticizes the materialism, intolerance, opportunism, and corruption of post-independence Zimbabwe, extending the political debate beyond the question of nationalism to embrace genuine social regeneration. The combination of intense self-scrutiny, cogent social criticism, and open, experimental form appealed to a young generation of Zimbabweans, the so-called mindblast generation, who were seeking new ways of perceiving their roles within the emergent nation.

Marechera's poetry was published posthumously under the title *Cemetery of Mind* (1992). Like his stories, his poems show the influence of modernist writers from Arthur Rimbaud and T.S. Eliot to Allen Ginsberg and Christopher ★Okigbo, and confirm his proclivity for perceptive social critique, intense self-exploration, and verbal daring.

In an interview Marechera said of himself, 'I think I am the doppelganger whom, until I appeared, African literature had not yet met'. This is an accurate assessment of Marechera's role in shocking the reader into looking at himself anew through the eyes of the other. His individualism, literary experimentation, and iconoclasm ensure that his work resists narrow definitions; it is constantly shifting and crossing boundaries.

Marriage of Anansewa, The (1975) A play by Efua ★Sutherland. Although the play was not published until 1975, a portion had appeared in print in 1969, and the play had a long gestation period. The published text comes with an important foreword in which Sutherland writes about the origin of the story-based theatre she was creating (*anansegoro*), the significance of Ananse ('a kind of Everyman, artistically exaggerated and distorted to serve society as a medium for self-examination'), the function of the musical interludes (*mboguo*), and the problems encountered in attempting to evoke the 'element of community participation'. The roots of the play lie in the Ananse storytelling tradition and its use by generations of teachers as the basis for individual dramas.

The plot is quickly outlined: impoverished Ananse, father of Anansewa, encourages each of four chiefs to believe he is the favoured suitor for the hand of his beautiful daughter; he expects and receives gifts from each of them. When the suitors all decide to visit their 'fiancée', Ananse extricates himself from embarrassment by announcing that his daughter has just died. This announcement brings a further batch of gifts and one suitor in person. Chief-Who-Is-Chief, who as luck would have it is the man Anansewa has fallen in love with, arrives. Resourceful and unscrupulous, Ananse pretends that, through the strength of her suitor's love, Anansewa has been brought back to life. As the drama moves to a close, the marriage of Anansewa to Chief-Who-Is-Chief is anticipated. A collaborator with the tradition, Sutherland simply makes available in a topical, highly theatrical manner the community's perception of the trickster hero and expects self-examination to follow. *The Marriage of Anansewa* is a substantial *anansegoro* text and represents Sutherland's major contribution to the debate about the form of African drama.

MARSHALL, Bill Okyere (1936-), Ghanaian

dramatist and novelist. Family traditions as to the origin of the surname vary, but the roots of the Marshalls are to be found in Larteh, Akuapem. Like many privileged children from that part of Ghana, Marshall was educated at Presbyterian schools; later he attended the Guildhall School of Music and Drama in London. After further studies in television, he spent a period in the USA, during which he composed the play *The Son of Umbele* (1973). On his return home, he wrote regularly for the press and from 1966 worked in the drama department of Ghana Television. In the 1970s he worked in advertising and subsequently set up his own media business, Studio Africain. During the early 1990s, he was both head of the National Film and Television Institute in Accra and lecturer at Legon's School of Performing Arts.

In addition to writing for the theatre Marshall has written radio and television plays, and his novels include *Bukom* (1979) and *Permit for Survival* (1981). His stage plays show the influence of such writers as Ibsen and Chekhov and an awareness of the discipline advocated by William Archer. His work challenges the notion that all can be explained, all actions accounted for, hinting at the legacy of the African past. Both large-scale plays such as *Umbele* and 'sitting-room dramas' such as *The Crows* (collected with *The Queue* and *Ali Dondo* in *The Crows and Other Plays*, 1998) display his discipline, control, and awareness of the significance of colour and sound.

In *Son of Umbele*, a drama of strong passions, burdened souls, unquiet questers, and those who have been labelled 'cursed' is played out before a fisherman's home. In *The Crows*, Marshall infuses a sense of authentic tragedy into a domestic drama involving those affected by the return from exile of a minister of religion. Not only does the play demonstrate that tragedy is not dead, it also shows that it can live in that most inhospitable environment, the sitting room. For too long, it seems, his 'European' surname has distracted attention from the work of a man who should be taken seriously as an African dramatist.

Martha Quest (1952) A novel by Doris *Lessing. The first in the series of four novels known as *The Children of Violence*, *Martha Quest* traces the personal development of the eponymous hero from a rebellious, intellectual, politically progressive teenager in a British African colony based on Rhodesia. She first escapes from her parents' farm to a large town modelled on Salisbury (now Harare) just before the Second World War and throws herself into the social whirl of the white colonial youth culture. Though she soon learns how irresponsibly escapist it is, Martha lets herself marry a conventional young man and become pregnant. Lessing develops her as a complex character divided between a deeper self and more superficial, social self. She establishes a pattern for the novels in which Martha escapes from one trap, life with her parents, only to find herself trapped in marriage and motherhood, from which she is soon determined to escape.

Master of Petersburg, The (1994) A novel by J. M. *Coetzee. The present-tense narrative relates the return of the protagonist, Dostoevsky, the Russian novelist, to St. Petersburg from Dresden to investigate the death of his stepson, Pavel Isaev. As in his first novel, *Dusklands* (1974), Coetzee blurs the boundaries between fiction and history: the novel is based on historical events involving Sergei Nechaev, a nihilist agitator who in 1869 organized the murder of his fellow revolutionary, Ivanov. Dostoevsky used this story in his novel *The Possessed*, and Coetzee introduces both historical and fictional characters into his novel while also fictionalizing Dostoevsky. In Coetzee's novel, Dostoevsky attempts to discover the truth about his stepson's death in interviews with the judicial investigator of the case and with Nechaev, whom he suspects has lured him to Petersburg by means of Pavel's death. The novel seems to function at one level as an allegory of Coetzee's attempt to tell the truth about the self – the soul – and it concludes with the character Dostoevsky's reflection that in being paid money for writing books 'he had to give up his soul in return'.

Matigari (1989) A novel by *Ngugi wa Thiong'o, translated from the Gikuyu (*Matigari*, 1986). Ngugi's sixth novel, the second written originally in Gikuyu, radically reconfigures the novel genre. Imaginatively fusing western realist and African oral narrative traditions, *Matigari* proposes a revolutionary concept of the novel as a form within which several genres coexist, not subordinately as in the past, and not merely equally, but equivalently, since there can be no recognizing one without the other. *Matigari* is simultaneously a traditional realist novel, an oral narrative performance, a hagiography, a myth, and a post-modern deconstructionist experiment.

MATTERA, Umaruiddin Don (1935-), South African poet, autobiographer, and short-story writer, was born in Western Native Township, Johannesburg, and was a founding member of the *Black Consciousness movement. His publications include *Azanian Love Song* (1983), a book of poems that won a PEN award in 1983; *Gone with the Twilight: A Story of Sophiatown* (1987; published in the USA as *Sophiatown: Coming of Age in South Africa*), an autobiography; *The Storyteller* (1989), a collection of stories; and *The Five Magic Pebbles* (1992), a children's book. He works as a journalist for the *Guardian/Weekly Mail*.

Mattera's work is focused firmly on the social and political world of South Africa. As a poet he has moved from indignation to empathy and compassion.

The spirit of reconciliation also characterizes his autobiography, where he talks about the disintegration of his immediate family, his time as the leader of the youth gang the Vultures and the gang's metamorphosis from a kind of defence unit for street kids into one of the most violent and feared gangs in Johannesburg, and about the destruction of his grandfather's house by the bulldozers that levelled Sophiatown.

MATTHEWS, James (1929-), South African poet and short-story writer. Born in Cape Town, the son of a dock labourer and a charwoman, Matthews has held a variety of jobs, including newspaper boy, messenger, reporter for the *Golden City Post* and *Drum, and night telephone operator. Of the generation of Es'kia *Mphahlele, Lewis *Nkosi, and Dennis *Brutus, he began writing short stories in the 1950s, was one of the leading poets in the black literary renaissance of the 1970s, founded Blac Publishing House, which published some of his own work, and was detained without trial in Victor Verster prison in 1976.

Undaunted by the banning of three of his collections of poetry, *Cry Rage!*, the anthology *Black Voices Shout!* (1974), and *Pass Me a Meatball, Jones* (1977), Matthews has gone on to publish *No Time for Dreams* (1981) and *Poisoned Wells and Other Delights* (1990). Early poems were passionate expressions of protest, full of pain and rage, attacking the inhumanity of *apartheid, criticizing whites' lack of concern, celebrating black survival. The verse is didactic and exhortatory, the language unadorned and direct, the influence of the ballad and the spiritual often apparent. In later work he meditates on the experience of solitary confinement, records the spread of violence post-Soweto, and finds sustenance in the struggle for freedom in the paradoxical image of 'poisoned wells' sustained through seventy-five poems. His short stories, twenty-four of which have been collected in *The Park and Other Stories* (1974), sensitively delineate the everyday sufferings of black peoples, making the reader aware of the wider context of social injustice, and in stories such as 'Azikwelwa' and 'The Park' depict incipient resistance. His novel *The Party Is Over* (1997), set in a 'coloured' (mixed race) area of Cape Town in the 1960s, deals with the frustration and despair of a writer trapped in a thwarting environment.

MAUNICK, Edouard (1931-) Mauritian poet, trained as a school teacher and a librarian. He published his first volume of poetry in Port Louis, *Ces Oiseaux de sang* (1954) . He moved to Paris in the early 1960s to work for the French overseas radio as producer . He started at that time to publish in *Présence africaine* and was closely associated with Alioune Diop. In 1964 *Les manèges de la mer* was published. It was the first demonstration of his warm and sensual lyricism, found in all his following works: *Mascaret ou le livre de la mer et de la mort* (1966), or in a more sombre tone, influenced by the Nigeria-Biafra war, *Fusillez moi* (1970). His career continued in the 1970s in association with international francophone organizations until he was appointed to UNESCO. After his retirement he had the distinction of becoming Mauritian ambassador to the new South Africa (1994). One of his most important works is his own personal anthology: *Anthologie personnelle* (1989).

MAURITIUS The former Ile de France became Mauritius after being taken by the British in 1814. The main language remained French as well as Creole, spoken by a population which today is mostly of Indian origin. The issue of Africanity of the island has been a major cultural and political issue, especially since the 1960s; before then, Mauritian literature was in French and revolved around the figures of poet, painter and thinker Malcolm de Chazal (1902-81). His most famous book *Sens plastique* is a collection of essays constantly reissued (last edition 1985). Robert Edward Hardt (1891-1954), a librarian, distinguished poet and translator of the *Bhagavad Ghita* (1936) was also an important figure of literary life.

In the 1960s Marcel Cabon (1912-72), a white Creole Mauritian, well-known journalist and literary critic, made the common people of Indian origin characters of his stories and novel (*Namaste*, 1965) and this signalled a populist turn in Mauritian literature which had an impact in all genres.

The poetry of Edouard *Maunick (1931-), his warm lyricism, his enthusiastic endorsement of Africanity, put Mauritius on the map of African literature. Today the issue is to find an original voice, neither dependent on European nor African circles to express the cultural diversity of this island where English, French but also several Indian languages are spoken and written. Of the new generation, novelist Carl de Sousa and Ananda Devi stand out. Many Mauritian writers made a life and a career in exile, such as the poet and novelist Loys Masson and novelist Marie Thérèse Humbert.

MAZRUI, Ali A. (1933-), Kenyan political scientist and essayist, was educated in Great Britain and has taught at Makerere College (Uganda) and the University of Michigan in the USA. He holds the Albert Schweitzer Chair in the Humanities at Binghamton University, New York. Three of his many books are *Towards a Pax Africana* (1967), *A World Federation of Cultures* (1976), and *Cultural Forces in World Politics* (1990), but he is also well-known for his novel, *The *Trial of Christopher Okigbo* (1971).

MBARI CLUB was founded in Ibadan, Nigeria, in March 1961. The foundation members were Wole *Soyinka and Ulli Beier (conveners), Ezekiel

*Mphahlele (first Chairman), Chinua *Achebe, Christopher *Okigbo, J. P. *Clark, Frances Ademola, the artists Demas Nwoko and Uche Okeke and Begum Hendrickse (Secretary). Later Amos *Tutuola, D. O. *Fagunwa and the Guyanese artist Denis Williams were co-opted. Its pivotal role in fostering writing, painting, sculpture and theatre has no other equivalent in English-speaking Africa.

The premises were an old Lebanese nightclub that was converted into an open-air performance venue, an art gallery, a library and an office. Food and drinks could be ordered from the adjoining Lebanese restaurant. Situated in the midst of a throbbing *Yoruba market it attracted all sections of society: students, academics, the Peace Corps, market people, passers-by and visitors from Lagos or up country. The performance space was used for Yoruba travelling theatres and dance groups. The great highlights were the premieres of Soyinka's *Brother Jero* with Yemi Lijadu in the title role and J. P. Clark's *Song of a Goat* with Wole Soyinka, Segun Olusola and Francesca Pereira.

The Mbari Art Gallery showed paintings by Demas Nwoko and Uche Okeke (Nigeria), Malangatana (Mozambique), drawings by Ibrahim el Salahi (Sudan), sculpture by Kofi Vincent (Ghana) and many others.

Mbari published seventeen books in three years, including Christopher Okigbo's first two volumes of poetry, J. P. Clark's *Poems* and *Song of a Goat, Three Plays* by Wole Soyinka and Alex La *Guma's novel *A Walk in the Night*.

The *Nigeria-Biafra war brought about the demise of Mbari – with Soyinka in jail and Christopher Okigbo killed in battle.

The Mbari Club in Ibadan inspired several other artists' clubs, like Mbari Enugu (run by John Ekwere), Mbari Mbayo Oshogbo (Duro *Ladipo and Ulli Beier), Mbari Mbayo Lagos (Tayo Aiyegbusi), Olokun in Benin City (Chief Ovia Idah), and the Chemchemi Centre in Nairobi created by Ezekiel Mphahlele. The imaginative role of Ulli Beier in introducing the emerging talent of Africa to Europe and North America was crucial.

MBULI, Mzwakhe (1959-), South African poet, was born in Sophiatown not long before its destruction in accordance with *apartheid policy and became acquainted with performance poetry as a child when he visited migrant workers' hostels with his father, a traditional harmonic singer. During the 1970s he was involved in a number of dramatic and musical groups that sought to promote black creativity under the aegis of *Black Consciousness. Mzwakhe, as he is known, has produced a book of poems, *Before Dawn* (1989), and four albums, *Change is Pain* (1986), *Unbroken Spirit* (1989), *Resistance and Defence* (1992), and *Africa*

(1993). His poems, mainly in English, seek to mobilize and console in the face of political oppression, drawing on a variety of influences including praise poetry, Soweto poetry, rap music, dub, and the rhetoric of the political speech or pamphlet. Among his best-known poems are 'Change is Pain', an apocalyptic vision of oppression and revolution, 'Triple-M', which satirizes Homeland leaders, and 'Alone', which he composed while in solitary confinement. He performed at the funeral of slain South African Communist party secretary Chris Hani and at the inauguration of Nelson Mandela as state president.

McLOUGHLIN, Timothy O. (1937-), Zimbabwean novelist, poet, and editor born of Irish parentage, was educated at St. George's School, Salisbury (now Harare) and obtained his BA and Ph.D. degrees at Trinity College, Dublin. Exiled during the liberation war after refusing his call-up to combat the so-called terrorists, he was recalled to Zimbabwe at independence to occupy the chair of English literature in Harare.

Apart from a considerable body of academic criticism on English and Anglo-Irish eighteenth-century and post-colonial literature, McLoughlin stands out for two main achievements in the creative field: his novel *Karima* (1985) and his encouragement of Zimbabwean poets. *Karima*, based on an incident at Karima village during the war, demonstrates with great psychological insight the feelings and commitments of those on both sides of the struggle; in particular it tries to render Shona customs and thought patterns. McLoughlin's contribution to the founding and editing of the literary magazine *Moto* has given young or new African writers the possibility to express a forward-looking liberated culture in both poetry and short stories.

MDA, Zakes (Zanemvula Kizito Gatyeni) (1948-), a prolific South African writer of plays, novels, poems, and articles for academic journals and newspapers. His creative work also includes paintings and theatre and film productions.

He was born in the Eastern Cape, spent his early childhood in Soweto, and finished his school education in Lesotho, where he had joined his father in exile. As a poet, he published in magazines such as *Staffrider, The Voice,* and *Oduma,* and in the anthologies *New South African Writing* (1977), *Summer Fires* (1982) and *Soho Square* (1992). His first volume of poems, *Bits of Debris,* came out in 1986.

In 1978 Mda's play *We Shall Sing for the Fatherland,* written in 1973, won the first Amstel Playwright of the Year Award. The following year he won this award again with *The Hill,* a play written in 1978. The publication of *We Shall Sing for the Fatherland and Other Plays* in 1980 enabled him to gain admission to Ohio

University for a three-year Master's degree in theatre. His play *The Road,* written in 1982, won the Christina Crawford Award of American Theatre Association in 1984, by which time his plays were being performed in the USSR, the USA, and Scotland as well as in various parts of southern Africa.

Mda returned from the USA in 1984, joining the University of Lesotho as lecturer in the Department of English in 1985. In 1989 he was awarded a Ph.D. by the University of Cape Town and his dissertation was later published as *When People Play People* in 1993, the same year as a collection of four plays, *And the Girls in Their Sunday Dresses.*

In 1991 Mda was writer-in-residence at the University of Durham, where he wrote *The Nun's Romantic Story;* in 1992 as research fellow at Yale University he wrote *The Dying Screams of the Moon,* another play, and his first novel, *Ways of Dying* (1995). By 1994 he was back in South Africa as visiting professor at the University of the Witwatersrand.

Mda's plays are distinguished by the combination of a close scrutiny of social values with elements of magic realism that is even more pronounced in his novels, *Ways of Dying* and *She Plays with the Darkness* (1995), and in his novella *Melville 67* (1998). His latest novel, *Ululants,* was due for release in 1999.

MEMMI, Albert (1920-), professor of sociology, novelist and essayist in French, was born in the Jewish ghetto of Tunis, Tunisia. He was educated in Tunis and at the University of Algiers before his studies were interrupted by the Second World War. During the German occupation of Tunisia, he was interned in a labour camp from which he later escaped. After the war, he completed his education in France before returning to Tunis, where he taught philosophy, worked as a journalist, and practised as a psychologist. When Tunisia gained independence in 1956, he re-settled in France, where he continues to reside.

For Memmi, the art of writing is a process of self-discovery as well as reconciliation with the past. As a Tunisian Jew, he explores the predicament of his dual heritage in both his fiction and his philosophical studies. His autobiographical first novel, *La Statue de sel* (1953; *The Pillar of Salt,* 1955), followed by *Agar* (1955; *Strangers,* 1960), established his early reputation as a provocative and controversial author. In both novels, he draws on his own experience to provide insight into the plight of the dominated and oppressed within Tunisian society. Torn between two cultures, the protagonist of his first novel is forced to confront the bitter reality of his divided existence and finds no other alternative than to submit to exile. The second novel focuses on the relationship of a couple, a Tunisian husband and his French wife, who return from France to live in Tunisia. As the female protagonist becomes increasingly alienated from her husband's

family and cultural milieu, the marriage eventually dissolves and the woman leaves her husband and returns to France. The complexities of cultural division within his fiction also provided Memmi with the impetus for his study on colonialism and decolonization, *Portrait du colonisé* (1957; *The Colonizer and the Colonized,* 1965), which focused on the destructive elements of oppression. A study of the Jewish condition, *Portrait d'un juif* (1962; *Portrait of a Jew,* 1962), was followed by *La Libération du juif* (1966; *The Liberation of the Jew,* 1966). After the publication of *L'Homme dominé* (1968; *Dominated Man,* 1968), he returned to fiction with *Le Scorpion* (1969; *The Scorpion,* 1971), a convoluted novel in which the protagonist becomes immersed in a metaphysical journey both to rediscover his past and to redefine his identity. His controversial study *Juifs et arabes* (1974; *Jews and Arabs,* 1975), was followed by *Le Désert* (1977), a novel set in the fifteenth century that provides Memmi with an imaginary venue to continue his quest for self-discovery. Two more studies, *La Dépendance* (1979; *Dependence,* 1984) and *Le Racisme* (1982), were followed by *Le Pharaon* (1988), a novel similar in context to his early fiction in which the conflicted protagonist is forced to choose between the two cultures of his inheritance.

Throughout his literary career, Memmi has maintained a unique commitment to his Tunisian heritage and his Jewish identity. He is the most prominent Tunisian novelist writing in French and one of the major theoreticians of ★Maghrebi literature.

MENIRU, Theresa Ekwutosi (1931-), Nigerian children's writer, trained as a teacher in Nigeria and Britain, and after her return to Nigeria taught in schools and colleges in Nigeria, served as principal of St. Theresa's Training College, and worked for the Nigerian federal and state ministries of education before her retirement in 1984. Her three publications, *The Bad Fairy and the Caterpillar* (1970), *The Carver and The Leopard* (1971), and *The Melting Girl and Other Stories* (1971), are informed by popular ★Igbo folktales. She co-authored *Omalinze* (1971), another reconstructed Igbo tale. Her later works, including *Unoma* (1976), *Unoma at College* (1981), *Footsteps in the Dark* (1982), and *Drums of Joy* (1982), are adventure stories of brave and courageous boys and girls, as are *Ibe the Cannon Boy* (1987) and *The Last Card.*

MEZU, S(ebastian) Okechukwu (1941-), Nigerian novelist, poet, and literary critic, was born in Owerri, Nigeria, and studied in Nigeria before continuing his education at Georgetown, La Salle, and Johns Hopkins universities in the USA, where he earned a doctorate. He was a UNESCO fellow at the Sorbonne and director of the African studies and research programme at the State University of New York, Buffalo.

He established the Black Academy Press, through which he published several books. His book of poems, *The Tropical Dawn* (1970), which includes an elaborate essay entitled 'Poetry and Revolution in Modern Africa', makes conscious use of elements from his cultural environment to create poetry with human concerns. His novel *Behind the Rising Sun* (1970) is about the *Nigeria-Biafra war. The plot, which centres on the protagonist Freddy Onuoha, examines the tribulations of a group of people desperate for survival and the subsequent effects of their interactions with dubious foreigners as well as dishonest compatriots. His critical works include *Léopold Sédar Senghor et la défense et illustration de la civilisation noire* (1968), *The Poetry of Léopold Sédar Senghor* (1973), and *The Philosophy of Pan-Africanism*. Mezu returned to Nigeria in the late 1970s and became involved in politics. When the military intervened he returned to publishing, and he has also become a successful businessman, now based in the USA, where he edits the revived *Black Academy Review*.

MHLOPHE, Gcina (1958-), South African children's writer, poet, and short-story writer, was born in Natal of a Xhosa mother and Zulu father and raised by her grandmother; she relates experiences of an eventful childhood in her autobiographical play, *Have You Seen Zandile?* (1988). After matriculating in the Eastern Cape and working for a year as a domestic in Johannesburg, she completed a journalism course and became a radio newsreader and writer for *Learn and Teach* magazine. Since 1983 she has been an actor, playwright, and director for the Market Theatre in Johannesburg.

Mhlophe's commitment to promoting and preserving oral tradition led her to found the Zanendaba Storytellers. A dynamic narrator who captivates audiences with her stories, movement, and music, she translates that talent in her written stories, with which she breaks down cultural barriers, creates a new awareness of history, and emphasizes the universality of experience within the framework of her tradition. Her short stories and poetry are regularly published in journals and anthologies, but she is primarily known for her folktales and children's stories: *The Snake with Seven Heads* (1989), *Queen of the Tortoises* (1990), *The Singing Dog* (1992), and *Hi, Zoleka!* (1994).

Mhudi (1930) A novel by Sol T. *Plaatje. Written between 1917 and 1920, *Mhudi* draws on the precolonial history of the Barolong people and charts their subsequent encounters with European colonizers. Plaatje's major concern is the effect of the interaction on the political future of the African people, and the book is a scathing attack on racial segregation and the Land Act of 1913. Stylistically, Plaatje draws on Shakespeare and Bunyan as well as on the African

oral tradition and attempts to reveal the common humanity underlying all nations by using several languages in the course of the narrative. He seeks to overthrow racial and gender stereotypes by casting Mhudi, a strong, courageous female character, as the central figure and by portraying pre-colonial Africa as a highly structured and moral society. Peter *Abrahams uses the same historical material in his novel *Wild Conquest* (1950), although he treats it as black-white struggle between tragic Matabele and unsympathetic Boers.

MILLER, Ruth (1919-69), South African poet, was born at Uitenhage in Cape Province, grew up in Pietersberg in the northern Transvaal, and spent her adult life in Belleville, Johannesburg, where she worked for many years as a clerk-typist and later as an English teacher. Her affection for the land account for the sense of awe in her poems; the loss of a fourteen-year-old son by electrocution may account for the pain that is often close to the surface.

Miller wrote poetry, short stories, and radio plays but is best remembered for her poetry, which was collected first as *Floating Island* (1965) and later in *Selected Poems* (1968). A selection of uncollected poems and other writing was published in *Ruth Miller: Poems Prose, Plays* (1991), edited by Lionel *Abrahams. Her poems, highly personal, are shaped by a wide reading of contemporary poets, a literary correspondence with Guy *Butler, and a profound sense and experience of the violence to the individual body and psyche of Verwoerd's *apartheid policies.

MILLIN, Sarah Gertrude (1888-1968), South African novelist. Millin was barely a year old when her family moved from Lithuania to where she was born, to the Vaal River.

Millin's career as a writer is characterized by contradiction. She was a friend of Jan Smuts and in many ways a liberal, yet her fiction reveals an obsession with racial purity. The social commentaries intended for readers outside South Africa were perceived internationally as overtly racist but were popular at home; her best-known novel, *God's Step-Children* (1924) was acclaimed in the USA on the basis of what proved to be a misreading of its racist theme, but did not find an audience in South Africa. Two historical novels *King of Bastards* (1949) and *The Burning Man* (1952) finally gained her the readership in South Africa she sought with *God's Step-Children*.

Critical debate about Millin continues. J.M. *Coetzee argues that, like many serious writers, she was influenced by the scientific and social theories of her time, which were racist and sexist. Her reputation as a writer who attempted to use her novels to justify white South African society's institutionalized racism should be 'tempered by a view of her as a practising novelist adapting whatever models and theories lie to hand to make writing possible'.

Mine Boy (1946) A novel by Peter *Abrahams. Portraying life in terms of class struggle, Abrahams displays the nature of progressive urban development as it affects the lives of a group of representative though highly individualized people who congregate in the shebeen of Leah. Wise to the ways of the city, Leah is both tough and compassionate. She looks after Daddy, an alcoholic who is broken by a fruitless fight for social justice. She understands Eliza, a schoolteacher who, Leah knows, deserves the products of the white world which will always be denied to her. She understands Johannes, a gentle giant when sober, an aggressive combatant when his angst is released through drink. Best of all she understands Xuma, the mine boy of the book's title, whose experience of the city and the mine is the main vehicle of the author's delineation of working-class life.

Mission to Kala (1958) A novel by Mongo *Beti, translated from the French (*Mission terminée*, 1957) and originally published in English as *Mission Accomplished*. This early and classic francophone African book is set in colonial French Cameroon in the early 1950s. The young protagonist, Jean-Marie Medza, is returning to his town from the larger district town, where he has just failed the prestigious baccalauréat exam. Expecting trouble from his father, he is instead immediately sent to the up-country village of Kala to retrieve his cousin Niam's runaway wife. When he arrives in unsophisticated, backward Kala, his relatives greatly overestimate Jean-Marie's learning and status, and he is greeted with three full weeks of honours and celebrations. He learns to drink, spends much time frustratedly chasing young women, observes village life, and to his great surprise gets married. He then returns to his home town, fights fiercely with his father, and leaves the region entirely. The story is told in the first person, past tense, with several years of distance. Its style and language are sophisticated, ironic, distanced, and cynical and serve as a critique of the terrible effects of colonialism on Cameroonian self-image and strength. Critics have written much on *Mission to Kala*, focusing mainly on its irony, humour, portrait of the effects of French colonial values, theme of alienation, and role in Beti's larger work.

MNTHALI, Felix (1933-), Malawian poet, novelist, and playwright, was born at Shurugwi in the midlands of Zimbabwe (where his maternal grandfather had worked for Cecil Rhodes) and educated at Pius XII University College (now the University of Lesotho) and the University of Alberta (MA, Ph.D.). Like many colleagues at the University of Malawi, he was jailed without charge in the 1970s. He is a professor of English at the University of Botswana.

Mnthali's publications include the poetry collection *When Sunset Comes to Sapitwa* (1980), a novel, *My Dear Anniversary* (1992), and several plays. His writing is 'a lifeline to sanity... the one way left for me to feel and appreciate my existence. In Cartesian parlance, I write, therefore I am!'

Diverse in its subjects and range of cultural reference, often triggered by human contact, and marked by religious symbolism and lexis, Mnthali's verse is carefully crafted and has strong audial qualities. Its typical mode formal and its tone one of mature serenity, it is also reverently humanist in a traditional way that affirms life and diversity. In no other African poet is the praise and citation of fellow writers so substantial a part of the writing, a practice at once consistent with modernism and indicative of his particularly African Christianity, with its strong sense of connectedness. The voices of *Okot p'Bitek, *Ngugi wa Thiong'o, Jack *Mapanje, Christopher *Okigbo, Chinua *Achebe, and Ken *Lipenga echo throughout verse that envisions a world beyond the ruin of youthful hopes for Malawi's indepencence. Personal diminishment within a renascent continent, blighted promise, and the Banda regime's contempt for hard-won skills and professional expertise are among Mnthali's chief themes.

MODISANE, William 'Bloke' (1923-86), South African autobiographer and short-story writer, grew up in Sophiatown, a black township in Johannesburg, where he saw one sister die of malnutrition and where his mother, called Ma-Bloke, ran a shebeen in order to support the family. He worked at Vanguard, a bookshop owned by a former trade unionist with radical sympathies, before becoming a journalist at *Drum, during that magazine's glory years in the 1950s, as part of a team of writers that included Henry Nxumalo, Can *Themba, Es'kia *Mphahlele, and Lewis *Nkosi. He also worked as jazz critic for the *Golden City Post*, the Johannesburg weekly tabloid and *Drum*'s sister publication. Inspired by American cinema, he cultivated a debonair style that suited Sophiatown, home to jazz singers, shebeen queens, and tsotsis (gangsters). His nickname, Bloke, was inspired by the Leslie Charteris thriller novels featuring the Saint.

Drum published his short stories 'The Dignity of Begging' (1951), about a beggar who prefers begging to working and who dreams of organizing a beggars' union, and 'The Respectable Pickpocket' (1954), about a thief who pits his wits against society and the legal system. The title of another story, 'The Situation', published in *Black Orpheus*, refers to the street slang for an educated African, like Modisane himself, who is 'situated' above his fellows and finds he does not belong anywhere. Modisane was part of the African

Theatre Workshop and played Shark in the first production of Athol *Fugard's play *No-Good Friday.

In 1959 he left South Africa for England. There in 1963 he published *Blame Me on History, his only book, which is remembered for its frankness and power. The book is at once a hymn to Sophiatown, destroyed in the late 1950s, and an analysis of what *apartheid does to the soul of the educated black man. The volume was banned in South Africa in 1966. In exile, he worked as a writer, actor, and broadcaster and had a leading part in the London production of Jean Genet's The Blacks at the Royal Court Theatre. He died in Dortmund, West Germany.

MOFOLO, Thomas (Mopoku) (1876-1948), novelist writing in Sesotho, was born at Khojane in the Mafeteng region of Lesotho. He was schooled at Morija mission and graduated as a teacher in 1888. He gained international recognition through the publication, in translation, of his third novel, *Chaka, in 1931.

His first novel, Moeti oa Bochabela [Traveller to the east] (1907) is an allegorical tale reminiscent of Bunyan's The Pilgrim's Progress. Despite its apparent simplicity, the novel shows the merging of traditional beliefs and Christian thought, thus pointing to a theme Mofolo develops more fully in his other novels. Another Sotho novel, Pitseng (1910), deals with the life of Katse and depicts the contrast between the ideal and the actual behaviour of Christians as well as the conflict between traditional beliefs and Christian values. While still busy writing Pitseng, Mofolo started collecting historical data on the life of the Zulu conqueror *Shaka. The results of his study were eventually published in 1925 as Chaka, a tragedy that describes the rise and subsequent fall of a hero whose pact with evil forces brings about one of the most brutal acts of destruction humankind has ever witnessed. The strength of the novel lies primarily in its characterization of the hero, portrayed as a man with noble possibilities that have gone tragically wrong. Mofolo's psychological and philosophical insight into a remarkably complex personality is virtually unparalleled in contemporary South African fiction.

MOORE, Bai T(amia) J(ohnson) (1916-), Liberian poet, novelist, folklorist, and essayist, was born in Dimeh, northwest of Monrovia, and originally trained as an agriculturist at the Virginia Union University, USA, from where he returned in 1941 as an administrator in the Liberian civil service. After a brief secondment to UNESCO, during which he served in the organization's education programme within Liberia itself, he joined the government of President William S. Tubman as an under-secretary of state for cultural affairs.

Moore's poetry first appeared in Echoes from the Valley: Being Odes and Other Poems, which he co-

edited with Ronald T. Dempster and T. H. Carey (1947). His main work includes a volume of poetry Ebony Dust (1962), a novella, Murder in the Cassava Patch (1963), which concerns a man betrayed by lover (reproduced in Liberian Writing, 1970), with an introduction by President Tubman, and a popular novel, The Money Doubler (1976). He also contributed a story to Four Stories by Liberian Writers, edited by Wilton Sankawulo (1980). With Jangaba Johnson he published a collection of Liberian folktales, Chips from the African Story Tree.

MOPELI-PAULUS, A(twell) S(idwell) (1913-60), poet and novelist, was resident in South Africa but born in Lesotho, a direct descendant of King Moshoeshoe's half-brother, Mopeli. He wrote both in Sesotho and in English, his Sesotho poetry being reflected best in Ho tamaea ke ho bona [To travel is to learn] (1945) which contains accounts of his experience as a soldier in the Cape Corps during the Second World War. He is known for his novel *Blanket Boy's Moon (1953) written in collaboration with Peter Lanham. Although his second English-language novel, Turn to the Dark (1956, written in collaboration with Miriam Basner) did not enjoy the same popular success as Blanket Boy Moon, his writing set the trend for many similar stories by black writers in the 1950s and 60s.

MOTSISI, (Karobo Moses) Casey 'Kid' (1932-77), South African journalist and short-story writer, was born in Western Native Township (Johannesburg) and was trained as a teacher in Pretoria, where he edited the school magazine. He worked as a journalist at *Drum magazine until 1962 and returned in 1974, having worked for The World in between. He first attracted attention with his 'Bugs' columns, short satirical sketches featuring dialogue between two bedbugs. His first column, 'If Bugs Were Men', reports on a conversation between two bugs in the 'House of Discussion' and satirizes parliamentary debate. He is best known for his 'On the Beat' column, which ran continuously from 1958 to 1962 and resumed in 1974. His style is a lively blend of American idiom and tsotsitaal (township slang); his literary models were Langston Hughes (Simple Speaks His Mind) and Damon Runyon. His sketches draw freely on the Sophiatown shebeen culture with which he was thoroughly familiar, depicting a gallery of such township types as Aunt Peggy, the shebeen queen, and a variety of rogues such as 'Kid Playboy' and 'Kid Hangover'. He also wrote a few stories for The Classic, a journal edited by Nat *Nakasa. Of these, 'Mita' (1963) is the most interesting: the story deftly evokes the Sophiatown milieu that inspired much of the black writing of the 1950s. A posthumous collection of his writings Casey and Co.: Selected Writings of Casey 'Kid' Motsisi was published in 1978.

MPHAHLELE, Es'kia (Ezekiel) (1919-), South African novelist, short-story writer, and critic, was born in Pretoria. After a late start at school he qualified as a teacher, and in 1945 joined the staff of Orlando High School. Dismissed from teaching for his opposition to 'Bantu education' in 1952, he joined the magazine ★*Drum* as political reporter and fiction editor. He gained a master's degree at the University of South Africa in 1956 and the following year began a period of exile that did not end until his return to South Africa in 1977. During his exile he taught at universities in Africa and the USA, gained a Ph.D. at the University of Denver, and served as director of the Congress for Cultural Freedom in Paris. He retired in 1987 as professor of African literature at the University of the Witwatersrand.

Mphahlele's reputation as a writer will probably rest on his autobiography, ★*Down Second Avenue* (1959). The prevalence of the autobiography in Africa has been attributed to a search for identity within the new world created by colonialism. Written in the mode of social realism interspersed with reflective passages, the book describes his childhood and the years leading up to his exile and is dominated by powerful female characters. The sequel to his autobiography, *Afrika My Music* (1984), was written and published on his return from exile and brings the story of his life up to date, recording in stream of consciousness fashion his reactions to the changing political face of Africa.

The autobiographical novel *The Wanderers* (1968), which earned Mphahlele his doctorate and a nomination for the Nobel Prize for Literature, is set in countries modelled on Nigeria and Kenya and deals with the experience of exile. It has narrative features in common with his other novel, *Chirundu* (1979), which chronicles the downfall of a Zambian cabinet minister after his bigamy is exposed and is thus typical of the post-colonial novel in its condemnation of the corrupt politician in the tradition of works by Chinua ★Achebe and Cyprian ★Ekwensi. But, as with his other work that does not deal with his own country, it lacks the immediacy and dynamism so characteristic of *Down Second Avenue* and his best short stories. Like the autobiography, the short story is a genre particularly favoured by black South African writers, and Mphahlele began his writing career with the collection *Man Must Live* (1946). Some of the stories that first appeared in *Drum* were included in his later collections, *The Living and Dead* (1961), *In Corner B* (1967), *The Unbroken Song* (1981), and *Renewal Time* (1988). All except for two set in Nigeria deal with human relationships and attitudes under the oppressive regime in South Africa but show that black life, through recourse to humour and a common humanity, constantly renews its own initiatives, much as do the short stories of Njabulo ★Ndebele, his younger compatriot and successor to his critical mantle. He also wrote a novella for young readers, *Father Come Home* (1984).

Mphahlele's wanderings over three continents figure his life-long search for a personal, intellectual, and cultural identity and its concomitant, the definition of a black aesthetic. His life and writing reveal a great compassion for humanity and celebrate that indomitable human spirit which refuses to buckle under restrictive and diminishing circumstances. His yearning to teach and write in a context that would not circumscribe his identity drove him away from ancestral ground into exile, but his realization of the accountability of the teacher and writer to their community, the tyranny of place, brought him home in the face of opposition from both the South African regime and other writers in exile. His encounters with the aesthetic of ★negritude and African-American writing compelled him continually to assess the role of culture in the political struggle, and his rigorous intellectual honesty has ensured that he has come closer than any other South African writer to defining a role for the intellectual within that struggle.

His development as a writer parallels that of many black South Africans in that he initially wrote for a white audience, but later identified with ★Black Consciousness and realized the need to harness culture to the liberation struggle. He has expressed his thoughts and experiences in numerous critical articles and two seminal volumes, *The African Image* (1962, rev. 1974) and *Voices in the Whirlwind* (1972), which have been called his intellectual autobiographies. Both books have had a far-reaching effect on African writing, since Mphahlele was one of the earliest critics to question the applicability of value judgements to the emerging African canon and to argue for a new way of reading African literature.

Mphahlele achieved notoriety with his criticism of negritude, which he argued failed to address the political needs of the African people and dismissed their revolutionary potential, thereby expressing a viewpoint shared by other African writers in English, including Wole ★Soyinka and Christopher ★Okigbo. Moreover he believes that only when black people can find their identity in the sum total of their experience of both traditional and western society will the process of cultural and political decolonization begin. Like ★Ngugi wa Thiong'o, he has voiced doubts about the effectiveness of writing in English for an African audience, given his belief in literature's role in raising the political consciousness of people. It is this realization that forms the basis for the black aesthetic he has spent his life seeking to define. The testimony of Mphahlele's life and work is that it is only in relation to people and their social context that art has any validity.

MPINA, Edison (1942-), Malawian poet and novelist. A Lomwe from Malawi's Mulanje district and a banker by profession, Mpina was educated at Zomba Catholic Secondary School but, untypically, missed tertiary studies and thus remains relatively uninfluenced by the University of Malawi's Writers' Workshop, which contributed to the development of fellow Malawian poets such as Ken *Lipenga and Jack *Mapanje. Indeed he did not begin to write until he reached middle age, after having experienced imprisonment without charge and personal tragedy. In 1981 his poem 'Summer Fires of Mulanje Mountain' won a BBC award over literally thousands of others. He regards as influential a visit to the Iowa International Workshop in 1982. His collection *Raw Pieces and his long poem Malawi Poetry Today (both 1986) appeared after his time there. With the fall of the Banda regime, his writing output increased and he set up a Malawian branch of PEN.

Deliberately distancing his work from the more theoretically informed poetry of his Malawian contemporaries, he writes about the land and the people of Malawi. Malawi Poetry Today wryly interrogates the context of most modern Malawian poetry, asserting that it should not be 'a poetry that's given birth in a workshop. Like a coffin'. He moves from withdrawn diffidence to confident assertiveness, from individualism to solidarity with the rural majority and with struggling younger poets; hence, his founding of Lingadzi Writers' Workshop in Lilongwe. In the early 1990s he turned to prose, his novels The Low Road to Death and Freedom Avenue appearing in 1990 and 1991 respectively. The first attacks materialism, the second deals with the forced labour system on the tea estates of colonial Nyasaland.

MTSHALI, (Oswald) Mbuyiseni (1940-), South African poet, was born and went to school in the north of KwaZulu-Natal. He moved to Johannesburg, but was prevented by *apartheid legislation from studying at the University of the Witwatersrand. He later went to the USA and completed master's degrees in creative writing and in education at Columbia University.

His first volume of poems, Sounds of a Cowhide Drum (1971), was a significant landmark in South African literature. His strikingly vivid, often ironical style, which he used for eloquent and pointed analyses of the everyday experiences of black people living in an oppressive society, made an impact on readers, white and black, who were not used to reading works by black authors. 'An Old Man in Church', for example, is a devastating yet sympathetic account of an exhausted worker whose prayer suits his employer's purposes: 'productivity would stall,/spoil the master's high profit estimate,/if on Sunday he did not go to church/ to recharge his spiritual batteries./...He falls on raw knees/ that smudge the bare floor with his piety./ He hits God's heart with screams as hard as stones/ flung from the slingshot of his soul'. The book

sold far better than any other book of South African verse had done. (The works of the previous generation of black writers, most of whom were now in exile, had been banned by the government in 1966.) Liberal whites, who were now suddenly receptive to poetry of this kind, began to become more acutely interested in local literature and its possibilities, both aesthetic and sociopolitical. More important, a number of black writers were inspired by Mtshali's example, which coincided with and partly provided an expression for the first strong stirrings of the *Black Consciousness movement: the next few years produced a remarkable number of volumes of verse by talented writers.

Many of the poets who followed Mtshali were more direct – more angry and/or more lyrical – than he had been. And as black politics became more militant in the next few years, Mtshali was often criticized for being too negative, for not offering vigorous resistance and a distinct alternative to apartheid oppression. With hindsight the limitedness of this vision may seem obvious, but in 1980, when Mtshali brought out Fireflames, his second volume of poems (it was also the year in which he returned to South Africa from the USA), he had changed his tune and his tone. Its strongest poems express a militancy that is immediate but that also looks back to the values of traditional African societies: 'A warrior drinks the goat's blood for bravery/as a willow in a swamp sucks water/to grow stalwart and stay evergreen' ('Weep not for a warrior'). Fireflames was banned by the government, but unbanned in 1986. After his return to South Africa Mtshali was active in education but published little. He once again lives in the USA.

MUGO, Micere Githae (1942-), Kenyan poet, playwright, and literary critic, was born in Baricho, in Kirinyaga district. After primary and secondary education in Kenya, she gained university degrees at Makerere University in Kampala, Uganda (BA) and the University of New Brunswick, Canada (MA, Ph.D.). She accepted a teaching position at the University of Nairobi in 1973, and in 1978 became the first female dean of the Faculty of Arts.

The Mau Mau struggle of the 1950s had impressed upon the adolescent Mugo notions of self-liberation, but an anglocentric colonial education disparaged that history and the local culture. Her intuitions about the Mau Mau were rekindled by the anti-*apartheid and American civil rights movements of the 1960s, which, along with her embrace of socialism, have left a lasting impact on her poetry. Because of her political views, Mugo suffered arbitrary arrests by the Kenyan police and with the confiscation of her passport in 1982 had to go into exile. Since 1984 she has been a Zimbabwean citizen.

Mugo's first collection of poems, Daughter of My

People, Sing! (1976), reflects an incisive questioning of the received ideas that constitute personal and cultural identities and a re-appreciation of values, including 'singing', that have made it possible for her people to confront various hostile forces. Mugo's heightened sense of her people's history comes out in the play she co-authored with *Ngugi wa Thiong'o in 1976, *The Trial of Dedan Kimathi*, while the vitality that she finds in oral forms radiates in the lyrical flourish of *My Mother's Song and Other Poems* (1994). In one telling poem in this collection, she salutes Africa's 'matriots', her ingenious coinage for women whose dynamism and transformative energies have advanced humankind. Mugo has written and with the Zimbabwean writer Shimmer *Chinodya edited plays and stories in Shona for an adolescent audience.

MULAISHO, Dominic (1933-) Zambian novelist, was born in Feira, Zambia. After attending Canisius College, Chalimbana, he graduated from the University College of Rhodesia and Nyasaland. He entered public service in various ministries, including Education, and by 1965 was Permanent Secretary in the office of the President, Kenneth Kaunda. Later, he became chairman of the Mining Industry, general manager of the National Agricultural Marketing Board and the managing director of Indeco, as well as economic adviser to the Zambian government. When there was a world shortage of copper in the late 1970s, and Zambian mines were booming, he and his opposite numbers in Chile and Zaïre were able to combine for a period to extract good prices from the rich countries of the north. His novel *The Tongue of the Dumb* (1971) was launched as the first Zambian novel by President Kaunda. The book is about a power struggle between a councillor and Chief; however, the book clearly drew on Mulaisho's experiences of the Zambian establishment. His next novel *The Smoke that Thunders* (1979) drew more obviously on his experience of public life. It is set in the period of power struggles between the colonialists and the African nationalists in the period leading to the independence of the British colony of Musi-o-Tunya near the Victoria Falls.

MUNGOSHI, Charles (1947-), Zimbabwean poet, short-story writer, and children's writer, is best known for his novels in both English and *Shona. Born in Manyene tribal trust land near Chivu, he attended the nearby Daramombe primary school, then St. Augustine's High School near Mutare. He worked before Zimbabwe's independence for the forestry commission, as a clerk in a book-shop, and as an editor for the Literature Bureau. After independence he moved to the Zimbabwe Publishing House and in 1985 spent a year as writer-in-residence at the University of Zimbabwe.

Mungoshi's first novel, the prize-winning *Makunun'unu maodzamwoyo* (1970), its title taken from the Shona proverb 'Brooding breeds despair', was followed by his short-story collection, *Coming of the Dry Season* (1972), which was banned in Rhodesia. *Waiting for the Rain* (1975), a novel set in his home region, centres on young Lucifer, educated, cynical about his roots, who visits his rural family home before leaving the country to take up a scholarship overseas. The novel depicts the disintegration of the Madengu family, trapped as Lucifer sees them by their ancestors and the settlers, while all around them the liberation war draws them to an uncertain future.

Conflict between younger and older generations and between rural and urban loyalties permeates much of Mungoshi's writing, as is evident in *Some Kinds of Wounds and Other Short Stories* (1980). His children's stories, largely adaptations from Shona, *Stories from a Shona Childhood* (1989) and *One Day Long Ago: More Stories from a Shona Childhood* (1991), are reminders of his grandmother's influence on him as a storyteller and his love for Shona oral traditions of narrative.

Mungoshi has won many awards for both his Shona and English works, including Commonwealth Writers Prizes (1988, 1998) and the Noma Award (1992). Versatile in the two languages, he explores the strengths of each as alternative modes of a Shona person's perception of the cultural complexities of Zimbabwe. His Shona novel of 1975, *Ndiko kupindana kwamazuva* [How time passes], introduces new techniques to Shona narrative, while his fictional writing in English, sharpened by his spare and gently ironic poetry, collected in *The Milkman Doesn't Only Deliver Milk* (1981), achieves a remarkable poise and sensitivity to the inner worlds, particularly of his younger characters. His translation of *Ngugi wa Thiong'o's *A *Grain of Wheat* (1987) is further evidence of this curiosity in language across cultures.

The stories in *Coming of the Dry Season* and *Some Kinds of Wounds* were reissued together as *The Setting Sun and the Rolling World* (1987). A new collection of stories, *Walking Still* (1997), won the 1998 Commonwealth Writers Prize (Africa Region) for fiction.

MUNONYE, John (1929-), Nigerian novelist, is a graduate of English at University College, Ibadan and an educationist of many years' standing. Born in Akokwa, Imo State, Nigeria, he is the author of six novels: *The *Only Son* (1966), *Obi* (1969), *Oil Man of Obange* (1971), *A Wreath for the Maidens* (1973), *A Dancer of Fortune* (1974), and *Bridge to a Wedding* (1978). Not even Chinua *Achebe, a contemporary with the same cultural background and a similar folkloric imagination, paints rural characters with as much sympathy as does Munonye. His work reminds the reader that the novel as a genre deals with the particular in characters, locale, and sociocultural environment. His focus is usually on the fortunes of particular individuals, and he seems to pay only marginal attention to the issues of racial, political, and economic ideology that have occupied the attention of so many African novelists as he explores the environment and responses of his characters with depth and empathy. His fidelity to the Igbo cultural and social background contributes to the legitimacy of the actions and aspirations of his characters. Such themes as ancestral continuity, conflicting indigenous and western religious sensibilities, the marriage institution as the bedrock of a stable and sane society, rural subsistence survival, and well-tested filial relationships recur in all his novels. It is also arguable that very few African novelists reveal as deep an understanding of children's psychology as Munonye. His unpretentious handling of the English language enables him to operate with ease at various levels of discourse involving character portraiture, descriptive narratology, and socio-anthropological information. His third novel, *Oil Man of Obange*, is a classic in the vivid depiction of the tragedy of the common person.

Muntu (1975) A play by Joe ★de Graft. Commissioned for the 1975 Nairobi assembly of the World Council of Churches, *Muntu* is, in de Graft's words, his 'first attempt to write for a really adult audience'. The play makes a series of serious points about some of the shared experiences of sub-Saharan Africa, addressing its audience on issues affecting the African continent through the general rather than the particular. As might be expected, the sweep of history is presented in a manner that recalls a pageant and with an honesty that does not spare the Water-People (Europeans), the Arab invaders, the Either-Neither-Man, nor the new breed of repressive dictators. De Graft, a resourceful dramatist, well read in world theatre, and a devoted teacher, spoke to a particular audience with a text that tried to find common denominators.

MURAGURI, Nicholas [See RUHENI, Mwangi]

Muriel at Metropolitan (1975) A novel by Miriam ★Tlali. The first novel to be published by a black woman in South Africa is episodic and autobiographical. Muriel, a young black woman, works as a clerk at a furniture company (Metropolitan) staffed by blacks and whites. Metropolitan functions as something of a microcosm of South African society, and Muriel finds herself 'caught between two fires: my own people on the one hand, and the white staff on the other'. These tensions are only finally resolved by her decision to resign. Throughout there is a clear didactic intention: the narrator wishes to open the eyes of readers to the indignities and injustices suffered by black workers in South Africa. The novel is notable for its convincing representation of Muriel's situation and for its lively,

humorous style, and has been translated into a number of European languages.

MUTLOATSE, Mothobi (1952-), South African anthologist and short-story writer. Born in Western Native Township, Johannesburg, Mutloatse gained experience in journalism with the *Golden City Post*, *Weekend World*, and *The Voice* before founding the only South African publishing house exclusively devoted to black writing, Skotaville. Deeply interested in largely forgotten black literary and historical traditions, Mutloatse has channelled much of his energy into the documentation of black literature and historiography. He has compiled four anthologies of black writing: the first, *Casey and Co.: Selected Writings of Casey 'Kid' Motsisi* (1978), a collection of articles for ★*Drum* and *The Classic*, celebrates the work of one of the older generation of black journalists. The others, which he refers to as his 'Azanian trilogy', he provides with important introductions. The first, entitled *Forced Landing: Africa South-Contemporary Writing* (1980) (banned on publication), he saw as 'cultural history penned down by the black man himself', arguing that the self-discovery of a people should find expression in new literary forms. *Reconstruction: Ninety Years of Black Historical Literature* (1981) focuses on hitherto ignored historical and journalistic texts by such writers as Tiyo Soga, Hope Dube, Noni ★Jabavu, and Sol T. ★Plaatje to give contemporary readers some sense of how earlier generations viewed their own history. The third, *Umhlaba Wethu* (1987), which encompasses African music, autobiography, and women and the struggle, for example, he presents as an exercise in nation-building, an alternative people's history.

Mutloatse's own creative writing comprises short fiction and a work for the stage. The short story 'The Truth, Mama', for example, portrays the torment of a mother forced to explain to her children that their father has been imprisoned for political activities, while the novella *Mama Ndiyalila* (1982) is a thinly disguised account of events in Soweto in 1976 that depicts their transformative effect on the conflicting loyalties of the black middle class. His tribute to the jazz musician Ntemi Piliso, *Baby, Come Duze*, performed at the Market Theatre Warehouse in 1990, reconstructs the vibrant literary and musical scene of the 1950s. He has also written a children's book, *The Boy Who Could Fly* (1990).

MUTSWAIRO, Solomon (1924-), Zimbabwean storyteller and poet, was born in Zawu, Mosowe district, central Zimbabwe, to Salvation Army missionaries and educated at Adams College, South Africa, Fort Hare University College, the University of Ottawa, Canada, and Howard University, Washington, DC. He won a Fulbright scholarship in 1960 and was the first ever writer-in-residence at the University of

Zimbabwe. His Shona-language fiction includes several novels, of which the first, *Feso* (1956; trans. 1974), prophetically describes a revolutionary war against white settler domination. His English-language novels, including *Mapondera, Soldier of Zimbabwe* (1978) and *Chaminuka, Prophet of Zimbabwe* (1983), also incorporate political protest. His intensely elegiac and pastoral poems not only exemplify the poetic nuances of the Shona language in which they are written but also celebrate the beauty of the rural environment of the author's childhood, which has been destroyed by white settler domination, colonialism, and the war of independence.

MWAMBUNGU, Osija, [See PRINCE KAGWEMA]

MWANGI, Meja (1948-), Kenyan novelist. Born in Nanyuki, Kenya, Mwangi studied up to A level at Kenyatta College. He worked as a sound technician with the French Broadcasting Corporation in Nairobi and as a visual aids officer with the British Council before devoting his time solely to writing. He has twice won the Kenyatta Prize for Literature and has received the Afro-Asian Writers Award and the Adolf Lotus Grimme Award.

Mwangi's work, more than any other Kenyan writer's, provides a representative view of the literature of the country as a whole, reflecting its main concerns and the direction of its evolution. He was the first to deal with the themes of the underworld in the post-colonial Kenyan city. *Kill Me Quick* (1973) exposes a hidden world of back streets and wretched humanity, revealing the relentless logic that brings people to such a fate. Two other novels belong to the same tradition of social engagement. *Going Down River Road* (1976) introduces the theme of the working class in Kenyan literature. A destitute crowd, assembled to work for a time on a building site, struggles for survival under conditions of near slavery with no prospects for improvement. Beneath the layer of apathy, a few workers retain some capacity for human compassion and a trace of will for resistance, perhaps a source for the eventual rehabilitation of the hostile world. *The Cockroach Dance* (1979) centres on the city slums as one more citadel of human degradation and on the strangely carefree subordination of the slum-dwellers to their surroundings. Two other novels, *Carcase for Hounds* (1974) and *Taste of Death* (1975), add to the corpus of literature dedicated to the Mau Mau anti-colonial struggle in Kenya. Mwangi's approach to the subject is marked by an emphasis on the actual military story. In *The Bushtrackers* (1979), a thriller about game poaching, he sets aside his social and historical concerns and joins the general movement in Kenyan literature away from social commitment. *Bread of Sorrow* (1987) continues in the thriller genre. The story of a decent, kind man who becomes

a criminal provides material for observations on psychology, human behaviour, and relationships. *The Return of Shaka* (1989), set in contemporary Southern Africa, is a mythical tale of armed resistance, and *Weapon of Hunger* (1989), which has an American rock star turned philanthropist as its central character, tells of relief efforts during a famine in a drought-stricken area of Africa. In *Striving for the Wind* (1990) Mwangi once again turns to look at his society, this time focusing on the village. Without identifying a cardinal disorder, he depicts life as a series of absurdities caused by individual human failings. The humorous tone of the narrative helps to advance this view. The outcome of the story suggests that people are capable of suddenly realizing and rising above some of their major weaknesses, but it is an ambiguous hope, since the general level of inadequacy of life remains unchanged. If this novel is an indication of a new direction in Mwangi's writing, then the distinctness of its outlines and the forcefulness typical of the style of this writer are yet to be achieved.

Myth, Literature, and the African World (1976) Essays by Wole ★Soyinka. In part a work of literary criticism that discusses African literary texts in relation to their ideological context, the book derives from a series of lectures given while Soyinka was visiting fellow at Cambridge University in 1973. Especially notable are the discussions of Chinua ★Achebe and of Ayi Kwei ★Armah's controversial novel ★*Two Thousand Seasons*. The book also offers an exploration of Yoruba intellectual and religious culture, in part as necessary background to an understanding of Soyinka's own poetry and drama. In that regard, the essay entitled 'The Fourth Stage' is particularly significant. The critical preferences and theoretical insights of *Myth, Literature, and the African World* are complemented by the essay collection *Art, Dialogue, and Outrage: Essays on Literature and Culture* (1988).

MZAMANE, Mbulelo (Vizikhungo) (1948-), South African fiction writer, was born in Brakpan and grew up in townships on the Witwatersrand. He attended secondary school in Swaziland, where he was taught by Can ★Themba, received his tertiary education at what was then the University of Botswana, Lesotho, and Swaziland, and taught at the Botswana and Lesotho campuses of the university. In 1979 he went to Sheffield, UK for his doctoral studies, and from there to the USA, where he held posts at the universities of Georgia and Vermont. He returned to South Africa to take up an appointment at the University of Fort Hare in the Eastern Cape, where he is Vice-Chancellor.

Mzamane has described himself as 'a teacher first, an aspiring literary critic next, and only very incidentally a writer'. His early exposure to the writings of black South Africans helps to explain why he turned naturally to the short story form. Many of the stories in *Mzala* (1980, published outside South Africa as *My Cousin Comes to Jo'burg and Other Stories*, 1981) were written some years earlier and first published in magazines such as *Contrast, Izwi,* and ★*Staffrider*. He was the joint recipient (along with Achmat ★Dangor) of the Mofolo-Plomer Prize for his stories in 1976. He acknowledges his debt in his fiction to his friends and relatives: many of the liveliest portraits in his stories are drawn directly from life. The stories in the first part of *Mzala* reverse the usual Jim-comes-to-Jo'burg stereotype in their celebration of the ability of the narrator's country cousin Jola to survive and even thrive in the city. Other stories deal humorously with various township types and situations, and suggest the resilience and adaptability of the ordinary people from whom Mzamane derives his inspiration. Although written in the politically charged atmosphere of the 1970s, the stories are unusual in their avoidance of explicit protest or attempts to conscientize.

Mzamane's most extended work of fiction is *The Children of Soweto* (1982), a thinly fictionalized account in three parts of the Soweto uprising of 1976. Readers with conventional novelistic expectations are likely to be disappointed: characters do not develop, and there is little exploration of interiority. The response of the community to the unfolding events and the attempts of the activists to assert some kind of control are foregrounded, although at times Mzamane's own fascination with township life and characters displaces the strict narrative of events. *The Children of Soweto* was banned shortly after its publication in 1982 and unbanned in 1987.

Mzamane's latest collection, *The Children of the Diaspora and Other Stories of Exile* (1996), builds upon his experience with South Africans abroad, most of whom, like Mzamane himself, have now returned home.

N

NAGENDA, John (1938-), poet and novelist, was born in Gahini, Rwanda. He graduated in English from Makerere University, where he also edited *Penpoint* magazine. He has worked with Oxford University Press and as a radio and TV producer in New York, London, and Kampala. His poems, short stories, and articles have appeared in various journals. Nagenda has recorded his experiences with the Uganda Human Rights Commission and written a children's book entitled *Mukasa* (1973).

The *★Seasons of Thomas Tebo* (1986) is concerned with an individual's involvement in the post-colonial struggle for political power in an African country. The story of the protagonist demonstrates that opposition to a repressive and corrupt regime may not necessarily be motivated by lofty ideals nor by a clear vision of an alternative; rather, it may be an impulsive rejection of inhumanity and an unconscious search for personal fulfilment.

NAKASA, Nat(haniel Ndazana) (1937-65), South African journalist, was born in Durban and settled in Johannesburg to pursue a career in journalism. He was a regular contributor to *★Drum* and *Golden City Post* and became the first black journalist on the *Rand Daily Mail*, for which he wrote a regular column. In 1963 he founded and edited the literary magazine *The Classic*, which sought to provide a publishing outlet for emerging black writers while promoting the principles of artistic freedom and multiracialism. He collaborated with white writers (including Nadine *★Gordimer) in his work on the magazine and for newspapers, and his writing insistently rejected the hardening racial attitudes in the South Africa of the late 1950s and early 1960s. In 1964 he was awarded a Niemann Fellowship to study journalism at Harvard College in the USA. When his application for a passport was rejected he was forced to leave South Africa on an exit permit. He recorded his experiences of America in 'Mr. Nakasa Goes to Harlem', commissioned by the *New York Times* in 1965. Here he wryly describes the mixed reception he was accorded as an African in black American society. He died after a fall from a highrise building in New York. A selection of his writings has been posthumously collected by Essop Patel as *The World of Nat Nakasa* (1975).

Naked Needle, A (1976) A novel by Nuruddin *★Farah. An experimental second novel, *A Naked Needle* foregrounds a Somali-English love story against a panorama of revolutionary Somali society. Its outstanding feature is a stylistic tour de force in which the mercurial, ideologically confused narrator Koschin combines satiric sketches of the new power elites with a geographical tour of the city and a summary of Somalia's post-war history, all the while turning a blind eye to the gathering forces of political repression.

Napolo Poems (1987) Poems by Steve *★Chimombo. The best introduction to the work of this highly productive Malawian writer, these poems are an impressive example of how a poet working under a repressive regime can marshall the resources of indirection and irony to retain inner equilibrium and attack injustice. They are also an example of how an African writer wanting to comment trenchantly on the modern order can effectively use a system of symbol and myth taken from tradition, in this case the Malawian oral texts surrounding a legendary figure called Mbona.

NAZARETH, Peter (1940-), critic and writer of fiction and drama, was born in Uganda of Goan and Malaysian ancestry and educated at Makerere University, Kampala, Uganda and at the universities of London and Leeds. Returning to Uganda after postgraduate study, he served as senior finance officer in Idi Amin's finance ministry until he was able to get out in 1973 to accept a fellowship at Yale University. As professor of English and African-American world studies at the University of Iowa, he has made important contributions to the fields of African and comparative literature through published criticism as well as through university teaching, appearances at conferences, and interviews with writers. In his work with the International Writing Program at Iowa, he has welcomed and encouraged writers from all over the world. Determined to bring the literature of his ancestral Goa to international attention, he has, for example, praised and publicized the work of Goan-Kenyan Violet Lannoy, whose writing was never published during her lifetime.

Nazareth's first novel, *In a Brown Mantle* (1972), forecast Idi Amin's coup and the subsequent expulsion of Asians from Uganda. *The General Is Up* (1991), his second novel, also deals with the Amin regime. He has written *Two Radio Plays* (1976) (*The Hospital* and *X* were produced for the BBC) as well as short stories. His critical writing includes *Literature and Society in Modern Africa* (1974; published in the USA as *An African View of Literature*); *The Third World*

Writer: His Social Responsibility (1978); *In the Trickster Tradition* (1994), a study of Andrew Salkey, Francis Ebejer, and Ishmael Reed; and studies of single authors such as *Taban lo Liyong, *Ngugi wa Thiong'o, and Joseph Conrad. He has also edited an anthology of East African fiction and one of Goan literature. His articles have appeared in journals in the USA and abroad.

NAZOMBE, Anthony (1955-), Malawian poet, was born in Nguludi, Malawi and was educated at Pius XII Minor Seminary, the University of Malawi, and Sheffield University, where he completed MA and Ph.D. degrees in English. Among the second wave of writers who emerged in Malawi during the 1970s, he is deeply spiritual and writes 'in response to an inner urge to co-create with God'. He edited *The Haunting Wind: New Poetry from Malawi* (1990), Malawi's second national anthology, in which only his attention to detail and his diplomacy prevented his running foul of Malawi's then notorious censorship laws. Nazombe's early association with the University of Malawi Writers' Workshop influenced his development as a poet. His work has been anthologized and has appeared in such journals as *Denga, Odi, Kunapipi, Marang, The Literary Half-Yearly, Caracoa,* and *Matatu.* His 'In Memoriam' and 'For a Singer' interrogate twin symptoms of life under the Banda regime: suicide as an escape for the poor and the raw vulnerability even of the professional class. 'The Racket' (*The Haunting Wind*) indicts the West's show of aid and its literary establishment's contempt for African literature. In the post-Banda era he is preparing another anthology, *Referendum Verse,* and acting as secretary for foreign affairs in the political group AFORD.

NDEBELE, Njabulo (Simakahle) (1948-), South African short-story writer and essayist, was born in Western Native Township near Johannesburg, educated at the University of Botswana, Lesotho and Swaziland (BOLESWA), Cambridge University, and the University of Denver, and since 1975 has been an academic and an administrator in Southern African universities.

Ndebele's relatively small body of published work has had a disproportionate influence on South African literature. *Fools and Other Stories* (1983), a collection of stories, won the Noma Award, and *Rediscovery of the Ordinary* (1991; published in the UK and the USA as *South African Literature and Culture: Rediscovery of the Ordinary*) collects his essays. Many of his most influential postulations are contained in the essay 'Turkish Tales and Some Thoughts on South African Fiction', first published in *Staffrider* in 1984. Rejecting protest fiction as an impoverishment of South African writing, Ndebele calls for 'storytelling' in the place of 'case-making' and praises writers who 'give African

readers the opportunity to experience themselves as makers of culture'. He uses the example of the figure of the oral storyteller on the buses or trains who tells stories of a largely 'apolitical' nature as tacit support for his own style of 'rediscovering the ordinary'.

Fools and Other Stories shows Ndebele attempting to put his theories into fictional form. In the story 'Uncle', the character Uncle, the rebel of the narrator's family, in effect redraws the white map of South Africa and charges it with the significance that rises out of a uniquely African perspective. His young nephew will begin to experience himself, his family, and his people (the black majority at large) as, to use Ndebele's own phrase, 'makers of culture'. Similarly, 'Fools' incorporates its politics in a layered narrative that explores character and relationship. In Ndebele's stories, people are capable of appropriating the landscape for their own social and political ends.

Ndebele has published two children's books, *Bonolo and the Peach Tree* (1992) and *Sarah, Rings and I* (1993), and his stories *The Prophetess* (1992) and *Death of a Son* (1996) have been reissued as pamphlets.

NDEBELE LITERATURE Ndebele or Sindebele is the second major indigenous language of Zimbabwe, after *Shona or ChiShona. Minor indigenous languages are *Tsonga, Nambya, Khalanga, Venda, *Sotho, and Shangane. More than 20 per cent of the indigenous Zimbabwean population speak Ndebele, of whom the bulk live in the provinces of Matabeleland South and Matabeleland North. Midlands Province has a substantial Ndebele-speaking population, and there are pockets of Ndebele speakers in the remaining five provinces, for example Chief Gwebu's people in Bhuhera in Manicaland.

The Ndebele language belongs to the Nguni group of languages, which includes *Zulu, spoken in Zululand in South Africa; *Xhosa, spoken in the Eastern Cape of South Africa, i.e. in Transkei and Ciskei, and in a few communities in Zimbabwe east of the city of Bulawayo; and Swazi, spoken in Swaziland and in the Mpumalanga region of South Africa. The fourth Nguni language is Ndebele, spoken in Zimbabwe and in two areas in South Africa, Southern Ndebele or KwaNdebele and Northern Ndebele in Transvaal. The three distinct varieties of Ndebele are a result of the influence of other indigenous languages located in their geographical surroundings and the length of time they have been separated from the other Nguni languages. The three varieties are Midlands Ndebele, largely influenced by the Karanga dialect of Shona; Plumtree Ndebele, influenced by Khalanga; and Gwanda Ndebele, influenced by the Sotho and Venda languages. Of the three varieties the Ndebele of Zimbabwe was the last to separate from the other Nguni groups and is closer to Zulu than is the Ndebele spoken in South Africa.

Historically the development of the Ndebele language is closely linked to the period of great upheaval in southern Africa beginning early in the nineteenth century. The Khumalo clan, a small group of Nguni speakers living under the protection of the Zulu emperor *Shaka, broke away in the 1820s and by the early 1830s had settled across the Vaal River. The original group of between 300 and 500 individuals incorporated followers from Sotho and Tswana tribes, and in this early period became known as Ndebele, a term that is believed to have been derived from a Sesotho phrase meaning 'people with long shields'. To avoid attacks by Griquas and Boers looking for grazing land, the Ndebele moved still further inland, eventually crossing the Limpopo River and settling in present-day Zimbabwe. As the Ndebele people – now numbering in the thousands – spread throughout the southwest, northwest, and central regions of Zimbabwe, so did their language, developing the varieties that are currently recognized.

Missionaries who established the Inyathi Mission among the Ndebele in Zimbabwe in 1859 were the first outsiders to make the link between the language of the Ndebele of Zimbabwe and that of the Zulus of South Africa. Having lived among the Zulus, they recognized a similarity between Zulu and Ndebele, and when they wrote Ndebele they wrote it as they had written Zulu. Later, when the white settler government introduced education for blacks, many of the teachers were Zulus from South Africa, who encouraged the use of Zulu reading materials on the grounds that Zulu was the same as Ndebele. Education authorities, not certain whether the two languages were separate, allowed Zulu to be taught in secondary schools and Zulu literature to be imported for school reading materials. In 1965 authorities agreed that Ndebele and Zulu were not the same language and that Ndebele language structure, literature, and culture would be taught separately as Ndebele/Zulu.

However, indigenous languages are taught as subjects rather than as the medium of instruction. Although they are treated as official languages they are not regarded as languages of business transaction nor, with very few exceptions, are those seeking employment required to speak them. As a result both Ndebele and Shona lag behind in developing appropriate terms to deal with the fast-changing technological environment.

NDHLALA, Geoffrey (1949-), Zimbabwean novelist, was born at St. Mary's Mission, Harare and educated at St. Augustine Mission, Mutare and at the University of Keele, UK. Since his return to Zimbabwe after graduating in 1973, he has worked as an advertising copywriter and a civil servant. His first novel, *Jikinya* (1979), is one of the few Zimbabwean novels known for its portrayal of an idyllic rural African life in pre-

colonial Zimbabwe. A beautiful but fragile existence imbued with humanistic values is shattered when white settlers invade the country and introduce materialistic values. His second novel, *The Southern Circle* (1984), explores the same theme but is more ambitious in scope, tracing three generations of an African family that becomes marginalized and dispossessed during the colonial period. Ndhlala's handling of the form of the novel is uneven, but his attempt to fuse nineteenth-century realism with elements of fantasy associated with African folktales is unique.

N'DJEHOYA, Blaise (1953-), novelist, born in Bangui, Central African Republic, of Cameroonian parents, went to France as a university student in 1973 and has remained there since. He is the author of *Bwanaland*, one section of *Un Regard noir* (1984), conceived as an anthropological study of Europe as seen by Africans. While the other section examines French beliefs in divination and magic, N'Djehoya's contribution, like his rather surrealistic novel, *Le Nègre Potemkine* (1988), is marked by an extremely vigorous use of word play, in which standard French, slang, various African languages, and English, are mixed with puns and allusions ranging from 'François Méritand', president of France, through 'grouchomarxisme', to a character named J.C. who is happy to be identified with Jesus Christ and John Coltrane. N'Djehoya uses the hybrid language of the expatriate African intellectual, whose world of references is wide but without a clear centre. His alter ego in *Un Regard noir* is Ed Makossa wa Makossa, who lives on Chester Himes Avenue and observes the strange behaviour and mating habits of the French. In *Le Nègre Potemkine* a group of research students go in search of the *tirailleurs sénégalais* who fought for France in two world wars and who have never received proper reward for their services to 'DiGol' and 'Zan Moulin' (Jean Moulin). Beyond the witty use of language, which N'Djehoya sees as the basis of his work, his theme is the mistreatment of the African in Europe and the lack of knowledge of African culture by those who claim cultural superiority.

NDU, Pol Nnamuzikam (1940-76), Nigerian poet, was born in Eastern Nigeria and graduated from the University of Nsukka. After the *Nigeria-Biafra war, which had a profound influence on him, he gained a Ph.D. in Afro-American literature from the State University of New York, USA and lectured in the US for two years before returning to Nigeria in 1976. His first poetry appeared in *Black Orpheus*. In his short life, he produced two collections of poetry, *Golgotha* (1971) and *Songs for Seers* (1974), on the strength of which he was described as the heir apparent of the poetic mantle of Christopher *Okigbo. The title poem of *Songs for Seers* is an elegy for Okigbo as Ndu's creative muse. Like his mentor, Ndu was a mythmaker.

NEGRITUDE Commentaries on negritude are often based on an attempt to find some synoptic consensus by means of an investigation of negritude's 'origins', particularly in the texts of Aimé Césaire and L.S. *Senghor. But as with any neologism first articulated within a difficult, even obscure poetics that is then taken up in a wide range of different discourses, in early critical texts in which the term is central (Jean-Paul Sartre's famous essay 'Orphée noir', for example), the term cannot be understood independently from these. Analyses, explanations, and extensions to which the term has given rise are all part of its meaning. The history of the term, then, bears witness to the fact that there is no stable, original base doctrine to be unproblematically discovered and in relation to which all others can be seen as extensions, subversions, even perversions. Its very instability, its free-floating meaning, guaranteed its survival and invited new and varied re-articulations in a wide range of discourses, principally poetic and political. All, however, are associated with a desire to express new ideas – hence the appeal of a new word – about blackness, black identity, black consciousness.

Negritude belongs to a particular historical period, in terms of its status as an ideology, one now passed. Negritude as a political programme is widely regarded as not having freed itself fully from a neo-colonial perspective. This is particularly true of Senghor's political position, which although it shifted and changed over the long period in which he was president of Senegal, was one he articulated by means of the term negritude.

The word 'négritude' first appeared in Aimé Césaire's long and difficult poem *Cahier d'un retour au pays natal* (1939 in the Parisian journal *Volontés*, 1947 in book form) in the famous section which begins 'Ma négritude n'est pas une pierre...'. What is proposed is a black ontology, and it was introduced at a moment when, internationally, a *prise de conscience nègre* was taking place. This *prise de conscience* of the 1930s and 40s was part of wider and fundamental changes in consciousness that occurred after the devastation of the First World War, the movement of peoples associated with it, the rise of new social sciences, psychology for example, and of new political ideologies, most particularly communism.

The birthplace of negritude as an ideology, rather than a poetics, was Paris, a meeting place for black intellectuals from Africa, America, and the Caribbean. Black Americans brought with them the ideas and convictions of what was later to be known as the New Negro movement or the Negro Renaissance, and a number of important texts by black intellectuals were published in the journal *La Revue du monde noir*, first published in 1931 in Paris and founded by Dr. Sajous from Liberia and two Martinican women, Paulette and Andrée Nardal. This was the first of a series of journals which are generally cited as the locus of negritude as an ideology. There were, however, a number of antecedents which are little known but which were also influential: *Le Paria: organe de l'Union intercontinentale* (1922-6), *Le Libéré* (1923-4), and *Les Continents*, founded in 1924 by René Maran and Kojo Tovalou Houénou. The last was significant in reproducing texts by Langston Hughes and Countee Cullen. Another influential little-known journal was *La Race nègre*, published irregularly between 1927 and 1936. Well-known journals more central to the development of negritude as a rallying ideology were *Légitime défense* (first published in 1932), which was explicitly concerned to align black political needs with communist objectives, and *L'Étudiant noir* (one issue in 1935). *La Revue* was moderate in its politics, advocating something closer to colonial reform rather than independence, but it sought to revise colonial history, to restore pride in black cultures, to restore black dignity. The intellectual climate in Paris, and the black contribution to it, fostered ideas to which young blacks arriving in Paris were drawn in part because of the utter sense of disappointment they experienced arriving as assimilated students of the French colonial empire. The experience of discrimination and of non-belonging was overwhelming despite their academic success and place within French educational structures.

There have been numerous attacks on negritude, particularly from anglophone black intellectuals, who almost unanimously regarded it as a spurious abstraction imitative of French intellectual movements. Black francophone critics of negritude as a movement or ideology include Frantz Fanon and Aimé Césaire himself. Other cogent attacks have been made by Marcien Towa in *Léopold Sédar Senghor: négritude ou servitude* (1971), Stanislas Adotevi, *Négritude ou négrologues* (1972), and René Depestre, *Bonjour et adieu ... la négritude* (1980). With hindsight it is clear that negritude as a pretext for political programmes was of limited use. Culturally and in the literary critical field it provided a focus for complex and important debates about black identity and the literary manifestation and exploration of these in language, particularly French, the colonial language.

Nervous Conditions (1988) A novel by Tsitsi *Dangarembga. The novel charts the educational odyssey of Tambu out of provincial poverty into the more affluent world of the anglophile professional elite, the co-opted middle class of school teachers and headmasters who occupy a fragile 'honorary space' between the white authorities and their own powerless poor relations. It is, as Tambu says on the last page, a story of women: in one scene mother, daughter, and niece stop eating in unanimous protest against the patriarch's force-fed diet of neo-colonial values. The novel makes a powerful plea for a less divisive, more composite African female identity, for a social order in which women of different generations, classes, and educational levels will have both individual and collective roles to play.

NETO, Agostinho (1922-79), Angolan poet, was born in Kaxikane, Angola. Trained as a physician in Portugal, he became involved in politics as a student and on his return to Angola in 1959 became involved in anti-colonial movements. In 1975, he became the first president of the Republic of Angola.

Neto's works can be found in *Sagrada esperança* (1974) and *A Renúncia impossível* (1983). A short story entitled 'Naúsea' was published in *Mensagem* in 1952, and various political writings have appeared posthumously. His poetry is often described as protest poetry because of its portayal of the struggle for independence and national identity. It also captures urban and rural scenes and often employs the motif of mother as earth, as Mother Africa or Mother Angola. Critical response to Neto's work ranges from analysis of its place in the context of Angolan history and *lusophone literature to individual close readings.

NGARA, Emmanuel (1947-), literary theorist and poet, was born in Mhondoro, Southern Rhodesia, now Zimbabwe, and educated at St. Ignatius College, Chishawasha, University College of Rhodesia, and the University of London, where he gained a Ph.D. He was senior lecturer in English at the University of Lesotho until 1980, and after a short spell as Zimbabwe's deputy ambassador to Ethiopia and ambassador to the OAU, he joined the University of Zimbabwe, where be became professor of English and pro-vice-chancellor. He is pro-vice-chancellor at the University of Natal in Durban, South Africa.

In his theoretical works Ngara brings to the study of African literature a critical practice alert to the formal expression in fiction and poetry of the interactions between ideology and material reality. His first book, *Stylistic Criticism and the African Novel* (1982), explores the way in which African novelists have used English to express attitudes and ideas they produce from African experiences. *Art and Ideology in the African Novel* (1985) develops an explicitly marxist theory, as does *Ideology and Form in African Poetry* (1990). In other theoretical and critical writing such as *Teaching Literature in Africa* (1984) he has been concerned with the practical issues involved in literacy training, bilingualism, and teaching literature. His volume of poems, *Songs from the Temple* (1992), shows an energetic commitment to the pan-African past of Cheikh Anta Diop's historical research, Zimbabwe's liberation war, and the recovery of Great Zimbabwe, the temple of the title, which becomes a metonymic extension of the monuments of pharaonic Egypt. Ngara's study of bilingualism allows his poetry confidently to appro-

priate – sometimes explicitly and sometimes as an echo – lines from T.S. Eliot, W.B. Yeats, Karl Marx and the Christian scriptures in order to enhance his poetic vision of Africa.

Ngara has also edited collections of criticism on African writing: *Literature, Language and the Nation* (co-edited with Andrew Morrison, 1989) and *New Writing from Southern Africa: Authors Who Have Become Prominent since 1980* (1996).

NGCOBO, Lauretta (1931-), South African novelist and essayist, was raised by her Zulu mother and educated in the Ixopo district of southern Natal and at Fort Hare University College (BA 1953). Her husband's detention in the aftermath of the Sharpeville massacre in 1960 led eventually to her escape into exile in 1963. After thirty-one years in exile she returned to Natal in 1994.

Ngcobo's rural background and her deep-seated rejection of the oppression of black South Africans under *apartheid are primary sources of her creativity. In her first novel, *Cross of Gold* (1981), Ngcobo laments the lack of options open to young black South Africans. Set in the 1960s, the narrative traces the progress of a young Zulu man, Mandla, through a chilling catalogue of institutionalized oppression towards his violent end as a freedom-fighter. The sequence of prisons, labour farms, and resettlement areas is relieved only by a brief, sensual glimpse of traditional rural life; Mandla's courtship of Nozipo is a pastoral idyll, a faint glimmer of life in rural South Africa. *And They Didn't Die* (1990) focuses on country women. At the time of the women's rebellion in Natal in the late 1950s, apartheid and tradition cause Jezile unbearable physical and psychological suffering as she fends for herself and her children in rural Natal in the absence of her migrant labourer husband. Her survival is made possible only by the solidarity of the women around her. The novel records the sacrifice made by countless black country women, for so long the stoic, unheard, unseen victims of apartheid's migrant labour system and the pass laws.

In exile, Ngcobo published articles and spoke at conferences. She also edited *Let It Be Told* (1988), an anthology of writing by black women living in Great Britain, and more recently has written a book for children, *Fiki Learns to Like Other People* (1994).

NGEMA, Mbongeni (1955-), South African playwright, musician, choreographer, and director, was born in Verulam, South Africa. He started his career as a theatre backing guitarist; he later worked with Gibson *Kente and discovered Stanislavsky, Brook, and Growtowski.

In 1979 he and fellow actor Percy Mtwa broke away from Kente's company to workshop *Woza Albert!* (1981), an episodic treatment of the gospels from a South African black theological perspective. Directed by Barney Simon for the Market Theatre (1980), the play toured the world, won more than twenty international awards, and was edited and recorded for the BBC. Ngema's award-winning *Asinamali!* (1984), a musical exploration of township rent strikes, was devised and directed for the Committed Artists, which he had started in 1982. *Sarafina* (1987), which celebrates the indomitable spirit of South African youth, was nominated for five Tony Awards and a Grammy after its successful transfer to New York. For the film version, which starred Whoopi Goldberg and Miriam Makeba, Ngema wrote and produced the soundtrack, co-wrote the screenplay with William Nicholson, and co-choreographed alongside Michael Peters. *Township Fever!* (1990) was based on a railway strike in which scab workers were killed. The musical *Magic at 4 am!* (1993), inspired by Muhammad Ali's 1974 fight against George Foreman in Zaire, premiered at Johannesburg's Civic Centre and toured the world in 1994. *Sarafina 2!* (1996), a musical commissioned by South Africa's Ministry of Health to combat the spread of AIDS, was criticized as ineffectual and as exorbitantly expensive to produce. Four of Ngema's scripts have been published in *The Best of Mbongeni Ngema: The Man and His Music* (1995).

NGUBIAH, Stephen N. (1936-), Kenyan novelist, was born in the Gikuyu area north of Nairobi and worked as a teacher in the years preceding Kenyan independence before gaining a BA at what was then University College, Nairobi. His only novel, *A Curse from God* (1970), emerged from the ambitious Students' Book-writing Scheme at University College Nairobi. The book fires some of the most incendiary salvoes of the post-independence debate over the viability and relevance of traditional Gikuyu culture. Eschewing nostalgic notions about the Edenic life that some Gikuyu believed their ancestors had led before the impact of British imperial rule and culture, he paints a picture of almost unrelenting affliction in his tribal society. Turmoil in polygamous marriages, spousal abuse, immoderate consumption of alcohol, painful clitoridectomies and circumcisions, and a stultifying generation gap are hallmarks of rural Gikuyu society. This perception squarely contradicted the position that the renowned Kenyan advocate of independence and prime minister Jomo *Kenyatta had taken in his well-known *Facing Mount Kenya* (1938) and is arguably Ngubiah's principal claim to a niche in Kenyan literary history.

During his years of study in Nairobi Ngubiah also wrote poetry and short stories and contributed an article to an anthology of literary criticism, but his promising career as an author never came to the fruition that *A Curse from God* suggested it might.

Eventually he entered local politics in his home district.

NGUGI wa Mirii [See CENSORSHIP, East Africa]

NGUGI wa Thiong'o (1938-), Kenyan novelist, playwright, and essayist (formerly known as James Ngugi), was born in Kamiriithu village near Limuru in Kenya. He had his early schooling at the Church of Scotland mission primary school, studied English at Makerere University College, Kampala, where he graduated in 1964, and later did graduate work in West Indian literature at Leeds, UK. He has taught at University College, Nairobi and at Northwestern University, USA and was the first African chair of the department of literature at the University of Nairobi. At the end of 1977 he was imprisoned for a year without trial for his outspoken criticism of the national government. Since the unsuccessful coup in Kenya in 1984, he has lived in exile in the UK, Sweden, and the USA, where he has taught at Yale University and New York University.

Ngugi's creative talent blossomed at Makerere: the first draft of his novel The *River Between (1965) was completed in 1961 under the title 'The Black Messiah'. *Weep Not, Child (1964) was written in 1962, as was the play *The Black Hermit* (1968). At Makerere Ngugi also emerged as a journalist and commentator on social and political affairs. He wrote his novel A *Grain of Wheat (1967) at Leeds.

The novel *Petals of Blood (1977) and the play *Ngaahika Ndeenda* (1977; *I Will Marry When I Want, 1982) constituted a frontal attack on the Kenyatta regime and resulted in his detention, an experience that led to the publication of *Detained (1981), which interprets the entire history of Kenya in terms of the marxist dialectic. Following the publication of a novel in *Gikuyu, *Caitaani Mutharaba-ini* (1980; *Devil on the Cross*, 1982), an allegory using Ngugi's favourite motif of the journey, he developed another Gikuyu play, *Maitu Njugira* (1982; *Mother, Sing for Me*), and with the active collaboration of the peasants; it was banned by the government and the people's open-air theatre dismantled. *Matigari (1986; trans. 1989), written in Gikuyu, is his most recent major creative work.

Ngugi's development as an artist and thinker has evolved through three stages. The first extends from 1960 to 1964, the year he graduated from Makerere, and was marked by the formative influences of Gikuyu social and cultural tradition, Christianity, and Western liberal thought. The second stage, from his arrival at Leeds in 1964 to his involvement in the Kamiriithu festival at Limuru in 1976, was influenced decisively by his introduction to marxism, Frantz Fanon, pan-Africanism, and the cause of black solidarity through his study of West Indian writing and awareness of the Black Power movement in the US. This period was characterized by his increasing disillusionment with bourgeois nationalism. In the third period, which extends from 1976 onward, the disillusionment is complete and Ngugi loses all hope of improving things in Kenya and in Africa except through total revolution brought about by the peasant masses. The turning point in his intellectual and emotional life was joining the Kamiriithu Cultural Centre in 1976. His theoretical leftism now assumes a concrete shape, and the change is nothing less than a spiritual conversion. His realization that he has nothing to teach and everything to learn from the Kenyan peasant he calls a 'homecoming' that marks the end of the alienating influence of colonial education. One result of this change is his resolution to write only in the language of his people; another is an increasing reliance on the theatre rather than the novel for creating revolutionary awareness.

The River Between, Weep Not, Child, and A Grain of Wheat, along with the play The Black Hermit and the collection of stories Secret Lives (1975), are the work of a liberal and Christian humanist who believes in the virtues of conciliation, compromise and love. There are militant characters such as Kabonyi and Boro, but they are not held up as models. Authorial approval goes to the conciliators like Waiyaki who, though he physically resembles Kenyatta, is a Christ figure. But I Will Marry When I Want, Mother Sing for Me, Devil on the Cross, and Matigari describe a different though familiar world. Ngugi's decision to write only in his mother tongue, which really meant writing primarily for his own people, necessitated a corresponding change in technique that led to a renunciation of realism and a greater recourse to allegory and fantasy. The dominant theme overall is the usurpation of power and wealth by the traitors and the people's persistent struggle to make them disgorge their ill-gotten gains.

Whether or not Ngugi has succeeded in winning the approval of the critics who had hailed his earlier work, there is no question that he has had tremendous success in winning the attention and adulation of his own people. These texts have acquired the status of folk epics and ballads and are read and heard in homes, taverns, and community centres.

Ngugi has also been an influential literary critic and cultural commentator, producing such works as Homecoming: Essays on African and Caribbean Literature, Culture and Politics (1972), Writers in Politics (1981; rev.1997), Barrel of a Pen: Resistance to Repression in Neo-Colonial Kenya (1983), Writing against Neocolonialism (1986), Decolonising the Mind: The Politics and Language of African Literature (1986), Moving the Centre: The Struggle for Cultural Freedoms (1993), and Penpoints, Gunpoints and Dreams (1998).

Ngugi's new novel, Murogi wa Kagoogo, written in Gikuyu, was due to be published in 1999.

NICOL, Abioseh (1924–94), Sierra Leonean poet, short-story writer, and critic. Nicol was born Davidson Sylvester Hector Willoughby Nicol in Bathurst village, Sierra Leone, had his early education in Nigeria, and gained a degree in science at Cambridge University in 1946. In the early 1950s he worked as a physician in the UK and by 1958 had received his Ph.D. He taught at the University of Ibadan, was the first Sierra Leonean principal of Fourah Bay College, and was vice-chancellor of the University of Sierra Leone; he was an economic director of UNITAR from 1972 to 1982; he was the first black to be elected a fellow at Cambridge; and he represented Sierra Leone as its ambassador in the United Kingdom.

Nicol was encouraged to write by Langston Hughes, who published one of his first stories in An African Treasury (1960). His two collections of stories, The Truly Married Woman (1965) and Two African Tales (1965), are reminiscent of Hughes's literary style. The Devil at Yolahun Bridge and The Leopard Hunt (published together as Two African Tales) show his fine handling of irony, wit and dialogue. His stories, most of which draw on traditional sources, provide insights into the customs of the Creole people of Sierra Leone. His other publications are Africa: A Subjective View (1965), Three Crowns (1965), Africanus Horton and Black Nationalism (1969), New and Modern Roles for Commonwealth and Empire (1976), and Nigeria and the Future of Africa (1980). He also wrote scholarly and medical essays.

NICOL, Mike (1951–), South African novelist and poet, was born in Cape Town and educated at the University of the Witwatersrand in Johannesburg. He has worked as a journalist on The Star, African Wildlife Magazine, and Leadership and has published two volumes of poetry, Among the Souvenirs (1978), which won the Ingrid Jonker Prize, and This Sad Place (1993), but he is best known for his novels, The Powers That Be (1989), This Day and Age (1992), and Horseman (1994). His fiction, often described as magic realist, seeks to combine fact and fantasy, myth and history; in rejecting the evocation of a known reality, its narratives become allegorical. The setting for all three novels is an unspecified time and place, an obscurity that is also a feature of his poetry. He draws on South African history as his source for an actuality that is apocalyptic and bloody. A Good-Looking Corpse (1991), a non-fiction account of the *Drum generation of black writers, contains anecdotes, stories written by the writers themselves, and photographs. The Waiting Country (1995), a meditation on the months surrounding the first democratic elections in South Africa, is a lyrical memoir that highlights random acts of violence and attempts to confront the question of the possibility of forgiveness. Africana Animals (1982) is a children's book about African fauna, with illustrations from the work of early artists and travellers.

NIGERIA-BIAFRA WAR The July 1967 to January 1970 civil war in Nigeria, often referred to as the Nigeria-Biafra war, has generated so impressive a body of literature that literary critics have come to regard that historical event as important in both the periodization and the aesthetic development of Nigerian literature. Sometimes called Nigerian civil war literature, this body of work is known as Biafran war literature mainly because more than three-quarters of its authors came from eastern Nigeria, which seceded as Biafra, where they were involved in the war effort as soldiers, civil defenders, bureaucrats, journalists, military technologists, and state propagandists.

Whereas much of Nigeria's pre-war literature emphasizes the bond between literature and history, the literature arising from the war details in six genres – oral and written poetry, the novel, the short story, the memoir, and dramatic literature – the strands of the large body of facts with which history is constructed. While the oral poems were composed and performed by soldiers, civil defenders, and folk artists, the written genres, composed during and after the war, were published in their final versions after the crisis. A checklist reveals thirteen volumes of poetry, numerous individual poems, twenty-six novels, many short stories, six plays and twenty-nine memoirs all by different writers. The themes include marital infidelity, strain in family relationships, the emergence of a refugee culture, the canonization of the survival instinct and its attendant materialism, corruption and immorality, the massive destruction of life and property, the tragedy of a disillusioned present built on a mythical past and foretelling a fragile future, and, ultimately, the recourse to heroic excesses as the possible panacea for despair.

The status of the texts that come out of the war as 'literature' is inevitably affected by the factuality of many of the events and experiences that inform it. For example, Pol *Ndu's poem 'July '66' is a powerful evocation of the mass killings of Igbo people in some parts of Nigeria, but a reader's knowledge of the event as it is narrated in Alexander Madiebo's memoir, *The Nigerian Revolution and the Nigerian Civil War* (1976), renders Ndu's poem too topical and somewhat partisan. Similarly, any reader of Elechi *Amadi's memoir *Sunset in Biafra* (1973) is likely to react less aesthetically to Chukwuemeka *Ike's *Sunset at Dawn* (1976), a fictional account of the same war experience. Even Isidore *Okpewho's *The Last Duty* (1976), which in technique and style is a masterpiece, reveals some themes susceptible to factual verifiability. Thus, many fictional texts about the war are quite reminiscent, even in particular details, of the experiences of particular individuals on both sides of the conflict. Biafran war literature is therefore striking in its revelation of the fluid interplay between fact and fiction.

Night of Darkness (1976) Short stories by Paul Tiyambe *Zeleza. The first book of Malawian short stories to be published is thus a milestone in the local development of the genre. Written and published while Zeleza was still an undergraduate, it reveals the early promise of the writer's work: his range of themes and situations and his historian's fascination with oral narrative as a source for modern written literature.

Nightwatcher, Nightsong (1986) Poems by Frank *Chipasula. Malawian poetry from the Banda years can be usefully classified as either internal or external. Chipasula became virulently outspoken in exile, his verse attacking the Banda regime with an openness and directness impossible for writers working inside the country. *Nightwatchers* best typifies this mode and contrasts sharply with the manner of his first (and internal) volume, *Visions and Reflections. The verse shows the poet in the role of watchman over a nation's dark night and employs imagery of extraordinary intensity as he transmutes the facts of contemporary history into the stuff of fantasy and nightmare.

NJAMI, Simon (1962-), Cameroonian novelist, was born in Lausanne, Switzerland of Cameroonian parents but has lived mainly in Europe. He studied in Switzerland and France and received a doctorate in law and also wrote a doctoral thesis on Boris Vian. He is editor of *La Revue noire*, a quarterly bilingual magazine devoted to black arts and literature. Njami has written two novels, *Cercueil et Cie* (1985; *Coffin and Company*, 1987) and *African Gigolo* (1989), as well as two books in Gallimard's Folio Junior collection for young people and a biography of James Baldwin. His two novels are set primarily in France. *Cercueil et Cie* is a *mise en abyme* involving the black detectives created by American novelist Chester Himes. *African Gigolo* is a story of the rootless life of a bright, handsome, but spoiled young African who wastes his time in Paris until, after traumatic experiences, he realizes he must return to Cameroon. A major theme of Njami's writing is the search for identity.

NJAU, Rebeka (1932-), pseud. Marina Gashe, novelist, short-story writer, and playwright, was born in Kanyariri, Kenya and educated in Kenya and at Makerere University, Uganda, where she gained a diploma in education. She has been a teacher, textile artist, researcher, and editor, writing only in her spare time. She has lived mostly in Kenya.

The Scar (1965), a poetic one-act play first performed at a Ugandan drama festival in 1960, marked Njau's debut as a writer. The play's heroine leads a movement of young women in a poverty-stricken Kenyan village against the traditional initiation ritual entailing genital laceration. She fails, not because of the opposition of the village's tradition-bound women, but because of a disclosure from her past by her erstwhile lover. Njau's second play, *In the Round*, first performed in 1964, represents some ambiguities about the Mau Mau political movement. She developed 'Alone with the Fig Tree', which won first prize in an East African novel competition in 1964, into *Ripples in the Pool* (1975), in which the anthropomorphic pool exercises a destructive influence on most of the characters, its principle of selection unclear. The ambiguous character Selina may reflect Njau's careful projection of a subjective fate and a neurosis that is symptomatic of Kenya's post-colonial condition. In *The Hypocrite and Other Stories* (1977), Njau re-tells a number of Kenyan folktales, and in *Kenyan Women Heroes and Their Mystical Power* (1984) she tells the stories of women who have been neglected in conventional historical records. Kenya's first female playwright, Njau is a pioneer in the literary representation of women.

NKOSI, Lewis (1936-), South African literary critic and novelist. Nkosi's move from *Ilanga lase Natal* [The Natal Sun] to *★Drum* magazine in 1956 introduced him into that remarkable group of writers who began to articulate a contemporary black South African literary discourse within the ★apartheid state, a discourse that has run parallel with South Africa's white colonial discourse to this day. However, his acceptance of a Nieman Fellowship at Harvard University in 1961 obliged him to leave South Africa on a one-way exit permit. After a year at Harvard, where he wrote a play, *The Rhythm of Violence* (1964), he moved to London and worked as a journalist and literary critic. He is professor of English at the University of Wyoming, USA.

In *Home and Exile* (1965) Nkosi criticized from exile black writers who paid excessive lip service to European literary aesthetics. His readings in this vein of well-known South African texts render his carefully argued, skilfully crafted essays controversial. In *The Transplanted Heart* (1975), for example, Nkosi sees Athol ★Fugard's *The ★Blood Knot* (1963) as subversively extolling white supremacy over black people, while in *Masks and Tasks: Themes and Styles of African Literature* (1981) he draws a distinction between black writers who invoke traditional African society (*masks*) and those who strive for new African orders (*tasks*). Such premises are developed further in 'Constructing the Cross-Border Reader' (in *Altered State? Writing and South Africa*, 1994, edited by E. ★Boehmer *et al.*), in which he suggests that a template of political, linguistic, and cultural boundaries obfuscates South African literary discourse.

The deeply embedded irony of his first novel, *Mating Birds* (1986), reinforces Nkosi's critical standpoint by revealing the sad state of European spirituality. In his own land, Sibya is accused of raping a white woman and condemned to death by a white court that safeguards those same European values that sanctioned the colonization of Africa. The novel *Underground People* (1993) focuses on the people oppressed by apartheid and the freedom fighter's accountability to his commitment in the armed struggle.

No Bride Price (1967) A novel by David ★Rubadiri. Malawi's first novel in English, *No Bride Price* appeared one year before Legson ★Kayira's novel *The ★Looming Shadow*. It was also the first piece of prose fiction to reflect disenchantment with the Banda regime's stewardship of independence. Rubadiri, whose career has been divided between academe and diplomacy, was a key figure in Banda's first administration and was ambassador to the UN until he went into exile in Uganda, at about the time his novel was published. After Banda fell from power, Rubadiri was reappointed as Malawi's amabassador at the UN.

No Longer at Ease (1960) A novel by Chinua ★Achebe. Set in the period just before Nigeria's independence from colonial rule in 1960, the novel tells the story of the failure of a well-educated young man to come to terms with his rapidly changing society. Obi Okonkwo is aware of the historical traditions of his Igbo society, the ways in which these are dealt with by his Christianized family, and the constraints that are placed on him in a modern and westernized present. His failure to resolve the conflicts that his awareness creates, together with a distanced, smug, and supercilious attitude engendered by his overseas education, results in public humiliation and personal tragedy for a young man of intelligence and promise. Achebe offers an implicit warning of the problems – social, political, and economic – Nigeria will face as the country attains independence.

No Sweetness Here (1970) Short stories by Ama Ata ★Aidoo. In these eleven stories Aidoo tackles some of the most pressing issues of contemporary Africa from a wide range of perspectives and stylistic approaches. Manifestations of neo-colonial mentality pervade the first two stories. In 'Everything Counts' the widespread scramble for material wealth and European fashion bitterly frustrates the protagonist's ideals, while in 'For Whom Things Did Not Change' the old servant Zirigu can hardly tell the difference between his former European and his present Ghanaian masters. Such a topic is poignantly interwoven with the African woman's condition, especially in 'No Sweetness Here', 'Certain Winds from the South', and 'Something to Talk About on the Way to the Funeral'. In the latter story several voices comment on the deceased Araba's past trials, exemplifying Aidoo's efforts to recover the strategies of orality in written literature. Her oral techniques also include the shifting point of view typical of the storyteller ('A Gift from Somewhere'), the empathic authorial voice ('Two

Sisters') and the narrator recounting his adventures to a responsive audience. ('In the Cutting of a Drink').

No-Good Friday (1958) A play by Athol ★Fugard. One of Fugard's early plays, it had its first performance at the Bantu Men's Social Centre in Johannesburg. The action takes place over one week, and all the scenes are set in a back yard in Sophiatown. Various stories involving Willie, the main character, Rebecca, the woman he lives with, Shark, a thug, and a host of others finally interlock at the full realization that for black people in ★apartheid South Africa there can be no progress in spite of hard work, and no bodily protection from either thugs or the police. As Friday comes around, the play ends with Willie waiting for certain death at the hands of Shark, representing the end of ideals and hope. The play's strength lies in its interesting characters and in the various ways each tries to make sense of his or her life, but overall it is repetitive and has rarely been performed since its first two stagings.

None to Accompany Me (1994), a novel by Nadine ★Gordimer. Published in the same year as South Africa's first democratic elections, *None to Accompany Me* represents the period of the transition of power to the majority. As often in Gordimer's fiction, family relationships, sexuality, and personal history provide the context for an examination of South Africa's politics. Here Vera Stark, a lawyer in late middle age, has been recruited to the committee that will draft the country's new constitution. As South Africa moves into an unknowable future so does Vera, leaving the predictable comforts of marriage and family ties for an uncertain independence.

NORTJE, Arthur (1942-70), South African poet, was born in Oudtshoorn and educated at Paterson High School, Port Elizabeth, where he was taught by the writer Dennis ★Brutus (Nortje and Brutus were both prize-winners of the Mbari poetry competition in 1962), University College of the Western Cape, and Oxford University, where he received a scholarship. In 1967 he emigrated to Canada but returned to Oxford in 1970, where he died shortly afterwards under mysterious circumstances. His poems were published posthumously in the collections *Dead Roots* (1973) and *Lonely Against the Light* (1973).

Failure of relationships, an inability to establish enduring attachments, form the basis of much of Nortje's poetry, which is preoccupied with experiences of alienation and fragmentation. Classification as 'coloured' (mixed race) in ★apartheid South Africa eroded Nortje's selfhood. His exploration of the experience of alienation, though informed by his experiences of rejection and racial discrimination, leads him to the more disturbing insight that the con-struction of the psyche as such is an effect of difference.

Exile is frequently cited as an important factor in explaining Nortje's sense of alienation. In his poetry, exile becomes the guiding metaphor of the themes of homelessness and marginality. In the poem 'Waiting' the speaker avers that exile has brought knowledge, but such 'knowledge is / a tale of disillusion merely, / a parody of self in shattered mirrors'. The metaphor of exile comes to stand for both an external eventuality and an inner condition, disturbing the dualistic relation between world and self, showing how that which is commonly understood to reside outside, that is, the other, inhabits the self in the form of an inner division. His poetry shows a facility for inventive image making and passionate and elegant phrasing, revealing an introspective poet who lived intensely and questioned deeply the conditions and circumstances of his existence.

THE NOVEL

East Africa: Although such European settlers as Karen Blixen and Elspeth Huxley had written semi-fictional accounts of their fascination with Kenya earlier in the twentieth century, the novel really began in that part of East Africa with independence and the deliberate publishing policies that included subsidized presses. ★Ngugi wa Thiong'o, the best-known writer of the area, has had an obvious influence on prose and drama, but a fertile literary life in the area has been the nourishing ground for his novels, and his themes and narrative modes are in permanent dialogue with regional production.

In an explosion of talent during the 1960s and 70s young East African novelists expressed an angry dissatisfaction at the world they found at independence. The Tanzanian Peter ★Palangyo in *Dying in the Sun* (1968) reproaches the generation of fathers and their blend of external submission and authoritarianism in the home. Leonard ★Kibera's *Voices in the Dark* (1970) is a sombre satirical picture of a new and arrogant middle class. The novelists are often represented by figures of artists or intellectuals, who are never in a very favourable light; they are unable to act to stem the rise of violence in Peter ★Nazareth's *In a Brown Mantle* (1972), Robert ★Serumaga's *Return to the Shadows* (1969), or Ali ★Mazrui's *The ★Trial of Christopher Okigbo* (1971). These early texts experiment with the blending of modes, merging the techniques of drama and poetry in the prose narrative.

Several themes soon established themselves as characteristic of this part of East Africa. Rural life is represented, but without nostalgia or idealization. The plots about traditional communities integrate a realistic description of hardships and a vision of spiritual unbalance, often revolving around a story of transgression and curse: *The Promised Land* (1966) by Grace

*Ogot or *Ripples in the Pool* (1975) by Rebeka *Njau. Very early, however, East African novelists chose the city as their image of contemporary life, a city described in a moralizing, sometimes apocalyptic mode. The evils of urban life are catalogued with a tone of prophetic imprecation and an allegorical dimension in *Prostitute* (1968) by Okello *Oculi, typical in its use of the 'fallen woman' as an image of modern society. In the same blend of near-journalistic documentary and cautionary parable are *The Slums* (1981) by Thomas Akare and the urban novels of Meja *Mwangi. In their gloomy vision of an anomic society and their imagery of sterility and decay, such texts are close to the mood of the popular literature of the time, where even Charles *Mangua's flippant style has undertones of despair.

The Mau Mau guerilla war and the ten years of emergency provided subjects for a whole range of novels, historical accounts such as Godwin *Wachira's *Ordeal in the Forest* (1967) or Charles Mangua's *A Tail in the Mouth* (1972). In all of his novels Ngugi wa Thiong'o is mostly concerned with the role played in contemporary Kenya by the divisions and guilt of the past, whereas Meja Mwangi uses the romantic appeal of a doomed fight and solitary heroes in *Carcase for Hounds* (1974), for instance.

These three major themes express a collective vision, a preoccupation with the future as well as with the past in a period of swift social change. The books rarely suggest an intimate tone, an interest in the personal life of protagonists. Ngugi wa Thiong'o, in his four novels in English, is alone in focusing on the doubts and dreams of his heroes. Samuel *Kahiga's *The Girl from Abroad* (1974) is an interesting portrait of a modern couple.

From the 1980s onwards, the overall picture has changed greatly. The publishing situation is not so favourable to novels of an experimental nature or on potentially controversial political subjects. Ngugi's two novels in Gikuyu have a certain polemic verve but none of the complexity and human richness of his first books. Meja Mwangi, Samuel Kahiga, and Mwangi *Ruheni have turned out formula-based fiction in popular collections. Some writers also return to well-tried topics: Samuel Kahiga reveals yet another vision of Mau Mau in *Dedan Kimathi: The Real Story* (1990), Meja Mwangi resurrects one more mythical figure in *The Return of Chaka* (1989), indicts again the exploitation of the peasantry by the bourgeoisie in *Striving for the Wind* (1990). John *Nagenda gives another tragico-burlesque account of the violent transition between Obote and Amin in Uganda in *The *Seasons of Thomas Tebo* (1986). The generation that came to power in the 1960s is represented in Peter Katuliiba's *Muhoyo's Crusade* (1987): the portrait of an older politician out of touch with modern mores is more compassionate than satirical.

Some new themes take prominence, one of them being the renewed interest in regional identities: Timothy *Wangusa in *Upon this Mountain* (1989) looks back to the 1940s to contrast again mission education and the traditional training for manhood. On this topic, Henry Ole Kulet goes on exploring the contradiction of a Masai identity in contemporary society in sober and moving narratives that never sentimentalize the issues. After Rebeka Njau and Grace Ogot, particularly influential with the female character of *The Graduate* (1980), several women novelists explored the condition of modern women. Popular novels with conventional plots yet finely analysed situations create a new imaginary space and appeal to a new range of readers. Marjorie Oludhe Macgoye's is an original voice, particularly in her successful *Coming to Birth* (1986), which narrates Kenya's social history from the perspective of ordinary wives and mothers. In this period, whatever political comment there is occurs in the thrillers, which comment on the police, corruption linked to smuggling, the repression of journalists, and international aid. Under the stereotyped situations and characters of novels by such writers as Wahome Mutahi, for instance, can be read a powerful indictment of arbitrary power.

It is significant that the major novels of the 1990s are published in Great Britain or North America, where the writers live. Peter Nazareth's *The General Is Up* (1991) narrates the oppression and eviction of Asians in Uganda in a distanced narrative mode that is meant to give a universal relevance to the subject. M. G. *Vassanji re-creates from Canada the long saga of southeast Asians on the east coast of Africa in *The *Gunny Sack* (1989), a book with both comedy and nostalgia that places the complex coastal societies on the fictional map. Abdulrazak *Gurnah also evokes this area in a narrative of many Muslim groups – Swahili, Arabs, Somalis, Indians – a world of traders and adventurers that lends itself to poetic re-creation in *Paradise* (1994). Perhaps these arresting novelists represent a modernized version of the exotic, dwelling as they do on lost communities in a land now distant for foreign readers. The evolution of serious novels in East Africa itself depends on economic and political factors which would allow once more a real dialogue between ambitious texts and readers outside the narrow institutional market.

Francophone: The first francophone African novels appeared in the 1920s. *Force Bonte* (1926), by Babari Diallo and *L'Esclave* (1929), by Felix *Couchoro had supported the colonial system while asking for full assimilation. Not until the 1960s was the body of work large enough to declare its independence from the French novel while sharing common aesthetic concerns. By the mid-1990s about 800 titles had been published.

Although there are a few French-language publishers in Africa, such as the Centre de Littérature Évangélique in Yaoundé (Cameroon) and Nouvelles Éditions Africaines du Sénégal, Dakar, most books are published in France. The consequences of foreign publication are not limited to high costs; it also allows governments to stop the sale of imported books if they wish to censor a particular work or author. In addition, overseas publication undoubtedly alters the evolution of the literature overall, since the decision to publish a text is taken in a foreign country and at times by non-Africans. The commitment of both writers and readers to this body of work is, in the circumstances, remarkable.

The following description relies on English translations for examples of general trends and essential facts about this literature. Although these translations are perhaps too few to show its complexities, they are sufficient to hint at a sense of its variety.

Before 1960, the year most French-speaking countries achieved independence, the forty or so published novels mainly critiqued colonialism and a disparaging colonialist discourse that misrepresented Africa. In *Doguicimi* (1935; trans. 1989), for example, Paul Hazoumé describes nineteenth-century courtly life in Benin complete with the horrors of human sacrifice, but the distinguished female protagonist expresses dignity and courage by demanding to be buried alive with the remains of her husband. The novel does not idealize African life, nor does it advocate the preservation of outdated customs, as had the work of poet, essayist, and former president of Senegal, Léopold S. *Senghor, who originated the concept of *negritude. Indeed, Mongo *Beti was not alone in his disapproval of *Camara Laye's novel *L'Enfant noir* (1953; *The *African Child*, 1954), which represents African life without conflicts and without a sense of the restrictions imposed by old customs. Novelists who wanted to demonstrate that black Africa had a history, albeit not written, cultures, and dignified peoples began working in the realist mode, rejecting facile exoticism, folklorism, and nostalgia for a non-existent past.

As the colonial period advanced, opposition to it intensified and was expressed in novels. Paul Hazoumé had already criticized Europeans for destroying the balance of power in Africa and for enriching themselves at the expense of local populations. In *Le Docker noir* (1956; *Black Docker*, 1987) and *Les Bouts de bois de Dieu* (1960; *God's Bits of Wood*, 1962) *Sembene Ousmane denounced white racists who employed black workers without proper compensation or who used force against them to break strikes. While Sembene decries exploitative working conditions, in *Le Pauvre Christ de Bomba* (1956; *The *Poor Christ of Bomba*, 1971) Beti emphasizes the similarities in the schools and churches, the domain of Catholic missionaries whom he denounces for their greed, their hypocrisy, and their disregard for local customs. Although he did not believe traditional Africa should remain unchanged, he could see that the priests lacked moral integrity and that they supported the colonialist enterprise. In *L'Aventure ambiguë* (1961; *Ambiguous Adventure*, 1969), Cheikh Hamidou *Kane introduces the difficult problem of identity. Men who were educated in the French system or who fought as soldiers for France in Algeria or Vietnam had lost their pride in their cultural heritage. Cut off from their past, they lived in France or in their own countries as exiles. Without the clear purpose of immigrants, some could not adapt to the new situation, with tragic results.

Even after independence, anti-colonialist novels continued to appear for a number of reasons. First, the time elapsed between a novel's composition and the date of its publication was often long. Second, those who wrote about the suffering of the colonialist period helped their compatriots regain their dignity. Third, because in too many cases the new authorities behaved at least as badly as the French or the Belgians, a few post-independence novels with anti-colonialist themes refer to current regimes.

Eventually, writers began to turn to new themes, but the question of power remains at the centre of their preoccupations. In *Le Bel Immonde* (1976; *Before the Birth of the Moon*, 1989), V.Y. Mudimbe describes the relationship of a government minister with a prostitute to expose the workings of clientelism, a system that flourishes where money and jobs are scarce. A patron offers a position, a car, a house, or any material benefit to a client, who in return owes him obedience. Job opportunities, promotions, pay rises have little to do with accomplishment. Although the system offers some protection, it deprives everyone involved of moral principles: for example, the minister must allow the president to mistreat a colleague to avoid losing his own portfolio. It makes any love relationship a business arrangement: the minister offers his mistress an apartment, but with no employment she cannot live independently. Similarly, the minister depends on the president. The latter, when he suspects the former of sympathizing with the rebellion, simply arranges a fatal car accident to get rid of him. If a president enforces obedience through fear, the marabout − a religious leader, sometimes a sorcerer − has God's power to impose his will. In *La Grève des Bàttu* (1979; *The Beggar's Strike*, 1981) by Aminata Sow Fall, the marabout opposes the government, which wants to clear the city of unsightly beggars. He wins because he threatens the authorities with God's wrath. Even those who do not have the marabout's hidden powers or who do not have money, thugs, or policemen at their disposal can wield power if they know how to influence public opinion or play with others' reputations. In Mariama *Bâ's *Un chant écarlate* (1981; *Scarlet Song*,

1986), a mother declares that her son has lost his 'Africanity' by marrying a white woman. She works on the family and on his friends until he takes a black woman as a second wife.

Whether power is exercised in the private sphere of the family or in public, it demands that people conform, thus encroaching on freedom. Characters may revolt against it, but rarely triumph. At the end of Tierno Monénembo's *Les Crapauds-brousse* (1979; *The Bush-Toads*, 1983), the protagonists reject tyranny when they leave the city and plan to start an uprising. However, the reader is left with a sense of incompleteness, since the protagonists have no other plans for their future except to rebel.

A general malaise related to unfulfilled hopes for independence pervades the novels. Protagonists who do not plan, who do not organize their lives, who exist day to day, are manipulated by anyone with power: a mother over a son, an uncle over a nephew, a boss over an employee, a priest over a parishoner, a marabout or a sorcerer over everybody. These passive protagonists may be influenced by traditional beliefs, by Islamic fatalism, by clientelism, or by a widespread feeling that citizens have no control over their governments. In *Le Cercle des tropiques* (1972; *Tropical Circle*, 1980) by Alioum Fantouré, for example, a character finds himself caught incomprehensibly in a political struggle. The power others wield over the characters explains all action; rather than describing the thoughts or the psychology of the characters, the writers simply recount what happens to them.

In the 1970s two Muslim writers from the Sahelian belt produced novels of epic quality: the picaresque *L'Etrange destin de Wangrin* (1973, trans., the Fortunes of Wangrin 1999) by Amadou Hampâté ★Ba and *Les Soleil des indépendances* (1970) by Ahmadou ★Kourouma.

Three broad categories of subgenres provide an idea of the general range of themes novelists employ: revolution, everyday life, and historical events. For fear of upsetting the authorities, few writers work in the first category. When they do deal with revolution, as in *The Bush-Toads* or *Tropical Circle*, they insist on their characters' lack of mastery over their fate, on their inability to improve their lot, and on the haphazard development of historical events. Most novels fall into the second category, describing everyday life. Francis Bebey's *La Poupée ashanti* (1973; *Ashanti Doll*, 1977) and *Le Roi Albert d'Effidi* (1976; *King Albert*, 1981) are good examples of this subgenre. They tell the stories of ordinary people trying to find their way between the traditional values of the village and modern city life. The themes revolve around love, money, power, and adaptation to new situations.

The third category includes some distinctive novels. During colonialist times, novelists declared their desire to give Africa back its history. Yet few wrote historical novels, and those who did wrote mostly about the period just preceding the arrival of whites or during colonialism. Yambo Ouologuem, exceptionally, begins his novel *Le Devoir de violence* (1968; *Bound to Violence*, 1971) in the fifteenth century, ending it in the twentieth. He distinguishes himself from his colleagues by underlining the violence Africans have used against each other rather than describing a glorious past. He registers his discontent with negritude by dwelling on violent acts and sexual perversions. The accumulation of these descriptions creates a powerful but distorted image that has little to do with an 'objective' realism. In *Wirriyamu* (1976; trans. 1980), a novel about a revolution against Portuguese colonialists, Williams ★Sassine uses the same tactic. The novel contains so many deaths and blood flows so freely that hope resides only in the birth of a child and in some poems written by one of the characters.

The tendency to magnify and revel in violence sometimes reaches such extremes that the text loses any connection with realistic representation. But African novelists had already taken liberties with realism when they experimented with the marvellous in the 1930s. In *Doguicimi*, for example, Hazoumé interrupts his authentic description of a character's life to reproduce a conversation between birds; in *Le Regard du roi* (1954; *The Radiance of the King*, 1956) by Camara Laye, Clarence cannot distinguish between reality and hallucinations. More recently, Nafissatou Diallo, in the posthumously published *La Princess de Tiali* (1987; *Princess of Tiali*, 1988), tells the story of a dwarf king who falls in love with a beautiful low-class girl whom he marries thanks to the magic intervention of a sorcerer. For these novelists and others, reference to illogical worlds or irrational powers represents their continuity with traditional African storytelling and keeps them in touch with their readers, many of whom believe in the influence of hidden powers over their lives. Moreover, such literary tactics offer the advantage of masking messages unapproved by the authorities.

If the input of the marvellous and of exaggeration alter the realist model, so do moralism and idealism. In *Les Méduses, ou, les Orties de mer* (1982; *The Madman and the Medusa*, 1989) Tchicaya U Tam'si uses the visions of a madman and temporal distortion to express his dissatisfaction with his compatriots for their lack of responsibility, motivation, and aspiration. Behind the text and its moral lessons is an idealism that cannot accept the weaknesses of humanity. Similarly, novelists like Tchicaya also modify the language. To pepper a French rather academic at times, they incorporate African words, riddles, proverbs, songs, local idioms, and names.

As the number of African novels in French increases, more subgenres appear: detective stories, science fiction, political fiction. More writers from different backgrounds publish their work. Women add their own contributions, finding inspiration in everyday events (Bâ's *Scarlet Song*) or in traditional tales (Diallo's *Princess of Tiali*) for fiction that insists on the improvement of women's lives. For example, Bâ's *Une si longue lettre* (1979; *So Long a Letter*, 1981) demonstrates the importance for women of developing working skills so they will not have to depend so much on men for their livelihood or for the care of their children.

Lusophone [See LUSOPHONE LITERATURE]

South Africa: The South African novel in English is usually dated from the publication of Olive *Schreiner's The *Story of an African Farm* in 1883. In the century since then writers such as Sol T. *Plaatje, Pauline *Smith, Alan *Paton and Alex *La Guma have produced important work in this genre, and several well-known English writers have written major 'South African' novels (William *Plomer's *Turbott Wolfe, 1926, Dan *Jacobson's *The Beginners*, 1966, Christopher *Hope's *Kruger's Alp*, 1984). Nadine *Gordimer and J.M. *Coetzee, both of whom are continuing to add to already substantial bodies of work, are uncontestably the major upholders and renewers of Schreiner's tradition.

The Story of an African Farm brought instant fame to its 28-year-old author, largely because of its bold criticism of the treatment of women in the Cape colony, its exposé of the general mindlessness and anti-intellectualism there, and its unusual multi-generic form. Schreiner's other works have not enjoyed the ongoing republication and attention enjoyed by this novel, but she did continue in her later fiction to raise serious and frequently unpopular political, economic, and gender issues.

Other novels in English from the turn of the nineteenth century have survived the passage of time only in the investigations of academics. Between 1899 and 1908, Douglas *Blackburn published his 'Sarel Erasmus trilogy', *Prinsloo of Prinsloosdorp*, *A Burgher Quixote*, and *I Came and Saw*. These novels have a naturalist picaresque style and deal comically yet sympathetically with Boer characters. In *Leaven: A Black and White Story* (1908), Blackburn turned his attention to the plight of a black man leaving his village for work in the city, a theme pursued later by such writers as Peter *Abrahams in *Mine Boy* (1946), Alan *Paton in his classic novel, *Cry, the Beloved Country* (1948), Hans Hofmeyr in *The Skin Is Deep* (1958), and Athol *Fugard in *Tsotsi* (1984.

The 1920s and 1930s saw the emergence of the first generation of black writers, many educated at mission schools. Thomas *Mofolo's *Chaka* (1925), a work that mythologized the once-powerful Zulu king, enjoyed a wide readership and was translated

from Sotho into English, German, Italian, French, Afrikaans, and Yoruba. About the same time, Sol *Plaatje's *Mhudi* appeared. The date of its original publication is recorded variously as 1922 and 1930. What is clear from a comparison of the original manuscript with the Lovedale Press's publication of 1930 is that the mission-controlled publishers removed passages that they considered inflammatory or offensive. Plaatje's novel centred on the collision between the Matabele nation and the Voortrekkers moving into the interior, and the plight of the helpless tribes caught in the conflict. While he credits the religious fervour of the missionaries, Plaatje also points to the ways in which Christianity has undermined the life of the tribes. Blackburn's theme of the country boy embattled in the city is taken up in a fictionalized pamphlet written by R.R.R. *Dhlomo and published by the Lovedale Press as *An *African Tragedy* (1928).

Pauline *Smith and Sarah Gertrude *Millin also published accomplished early work in the 1920s. Although their ideologies, techniques, and personal loyalties diverged, their work had some things in common. Both, like Schreiner, set their fiction in rural landscapes; unlike Schreiner, neither challenged the fact of colonialism nor critiqued its patriarchal, racist, and anti-intellectual qualities. The Afrikaners in Smith's *The *Little Karoo* (1925) and *The *Beadle* (1926) are an emergent and wandering nation, self-styled Israelites, chosen by God to fulfil a divine purpose and tested by a series of hardships, not least of which were the English. The covert political implications of Smith's agenda are troubling, although the power of her characterizations, the stark tragedies of many of the stories, and her understanding of how those who have been oppressed easily become oppressors has encouraged readers to return to her work.

Although Sarah Gertrude Millin was an important English language writer of the period between Olive Schreiner and Nadine Gordimer, her treatment of race and her insistence on the distinguishing qualities of 'blood' have, since 1945 at least, become morally objectionable. She was, however, a prolific writer. Her first novel, *The Dark River*, appeared in 1920; her last, *The Wizard Bird*, in 1962. In between these dates she wrote seven major works of fiction, the best-known being *God's Step-Children* (1924) and *King of the Bastards* (1950).

Alan Paton's *Cry, the Beloved Country* and *Too Late the Phalarope* (1953) evoke South Africa's human and physical landscapes with a spare and unsparing realism, Hemingwayesque but earnestly moral, biblical in some of its cadences and epiphanies. So close is the fit between the country he depicts and the moral frame through which he views it that South Africa became for many readers inside and outside the country a unique object lesson, an infamous twentieth-century dilemma. The fiction of his immediate successors,

Dan Jacobson (whose *A *Dance in the Sun* would appear in 1956) and Nadine Gordimer, would bring to bear an equally intense realist scrutiny, but only to highlight existential uncertainty and a fringing darkness.

As these writers were producing their early novels to wide acclaim, black writers from townships like Sophiatown were reflecting the physical conditions of their lives, and the remorseless deadlines of magazines like *Drum, Zonk!, Afrika,* and *Bona,* in a racy, agitated impressionism that quivered with nervous energy and caustic wit. The harsh realities of their lives included police surveillance and brutality, violence, and criminality. As Es'kia *Mphahlele points out, poetry was almost entirely absent in the 1950s. Narrative prose and essays became the handiest and most accessible modes of expression to deal with personal anger and a sense of urgency. Among the fiction writers and journalists working at the time were Mphahlele (whose novels, written later, are *The Wanderers,* 1968, and *Chirundu,* 1979), Peter Abrahams (*Song of the City,* 1945, *Mine Boy,* 1946, *The *Path of Thunder,* 1948, *Wild Conquest,* 1950, *A Wreath for Udomo,* 1956, *A Night of Their Own,* 1965, *This Island Now,* 1966, *The View from Coyoba,* 1985), Can *Themba, Bloke *Modisane, Lewis *Nkosi (*Mating Birds,* 1986, *Underground People,* 1993), Casey *Motsisi, Nat *Nakasa, and Alex La Guma (*A *Walk in the Night,* 1965, *And a Threefold Cord,* 1964, *The *Stone Country,* 1967, *In the Fog of the Seasons' End,* 1972, *Time of the Butcherbird,* 1979). All these writers went into exile; all their work was banned in South Africa until the relaxation of censorship in the 1980s. Following the same route in the 1960s (and also into exile, in her case in Botswana) was Bessie *Head (*When Rain Clouds Gather,* 1968, *Maru,* 1971, *A Question of Power,* 1973, *A Bewitched Crossroad,* 1984).

The black contributors to *Drum, Bona,* and *Zonk* would be the forebears of a generation of *Black Consciousness novelists such as Mongane Wally *Serote, predominantly a poet but also the author of a very powerful novel, *To Every Birth Its Blood* (1981), Sipho *Sepamla, another poet-novelist, the writer of two technically experimental novels, *The Root Is One* (1979) and *A Ride on the Whirlwind* (1981), Lauretta *Ngcobo (*Cross of Gold,* 1981), Mbulelo *Mzamane (*The Children of Soweto,* 1982) and Miriam *Tlali (*Muriel at Metropolitan,* 1975, *Amandla,* 1980).

Nadine Gordimer, winner of the Nobel Prize for Literature in 1991, began her writing career aged twenty-six when her first collection of short stories, *Face to Face* (1949), was published. To date she has published twelve novels. Apart from the Nobel Prize, she has won The James Tait Black Memorial Prize for her novel *A *Guest of Honour* (1970), the Booker Prize for *The *Conservationist* (1974), the South African CNA (Central News Agency) Award for *The Conser-*

vationist, *July's People* (1981) and *My Son's Story* (1990), and the French Grand Aigle d'Or.

While Gordimer has kept each novel locked into its own moment of political oppression and subversion while allowing the present time of the narrative to look towards an imminent future, J.M. *Coetzee has explored questions of colonialism (and its underpinnings in greed and racism) from a broader temporal and geographic setting in the seven novels he has published since 1974 (*Dusklands,* 1974, *In the Heart of the Country,* 1977, *Waiting for the Barbarians,* 1980, *Life & Times of Michael K,* 1983, *Foe,* 1986, *Age of Iron,* 1990, *The *Master of Petersburg,* 1994). Nearly all these novels have won major prizes, including the Booker Prize (*Life & Times of Michael K*) in 1983. Landscapes range from a familiar South Africa to an unidentifiable outpost of empire, and time ranges from the eighteenth century to an uncertain future.

Since the late 1970s, when novel writing seemed to gain fresh impetus from intimations of political change, on one hand, and late-modernist and postmodernist experimentation on the other, a number of other South African novelists have come to the fore (among them Stephen *Gray, Ahmed *Essop, Sheila *Roberts, Peter *Wilhelm, Achmat *Dangor and Rose Zwi) and many new voices have been heard. Those from whom interesting work may be expected in the future include Ivan *Vladislavić (*The Folly,* 1993), Zoë *Wicomb (*You Can't Get Lost in Cape Town,* 1987), Mike *Nicol (*The Powers That Be,* 1989, *This Day and Age,* 1992, *Horseman,* 1994), Menán *du Plessis (*A State of Fear,* 1983, *Longlive!,* 1989), Zakes *Mda (*Ways of Dying,* 1995), and Elleke *Boehmer (*Screens Against the Sky,* 1990).

West Africa: In 1958, Chinua *Achebe published the first standard West African novel in English, *Things Fall Apart.* Since that time hundreds of other titles have appeared: more than five hundred from Nigeria and some fifty from Ghana, Sierra Leone, and Gambia. (Novels written in French are discussed under the francophone *novel.) Some critics regard Olaudah *Equiano's *The Interesting Narrative of the Life of Olaudah Equiano, or Gustavus Vassa, the African, Written by Himself* (1789), which appeared in two abridgements in 1967 and 1968 and a facsimile reprint in 1969 (all edited by Paul Edwards), as the ancestor of the West African novel in English. Others think that the story should begin with Cyprian *Ekwensi's *People of the City* (1952). But these works exhibit certain characteristics of style, treatment, and organization that might deny them the status of novel proper. For example, critic Bernth Lindfors detects in Ekwensi's work an absence of what he calls 'artistic discretion'.

Since Nigeria has made the largest contribution to the growth of the West African novel in English at least in sheer numbers, the history of this growth is largely the history of the Nigerian novel. The earlier writers such as Achebe and his followers were pre-occupied in their early works with cultural nationalism, a term that relates to the novels dealing with the colonial encounter, those re-creating life in the past with its imperfections, or those merely retreating into the serenity of rural life. Achebe's *Things Fall Apart* and *Arrow of God* (1964) encouraged other writers to exploit the literary potential of West Africa's cultural past. Elechi *Amadi, re-creating the past in his first two novels, The *Concubine* (1966) and The Great Ponds* (1969), took his cue from Achebe. Flora *Nwapa's first two novels, *Efuru* (1966) and *Idu* (1969), set in the past, examine the condition of women in a traditional society. In his first two novels, *Toads for Supper* (1965) and *The Naked Gods* (1970), Chukwuemeka *Ike makes ample use of proverbs in the manner of Achebe as the 'palm oil with which words are eaten'.

Following political independence in Nigeria, writers turned their attention to the immediate realities of their society. The new political elite that had abused and misused power became the focus of their anger. Novels written in Nigeria shortly after independence and portraying political corruption and social decadence have come to be known as novels of post-independence disillusionment. Wole *Soyinka's The *Interpreters* (1965) is the first to reflect this disenchantment with the new political regime. Achebe's *A Man of the People* (1966) flays the antics of such leaders as Chief Nanga.

For most of the time since 1966 the army has been in power in Nigeria, a development foreshadowed at the end of *A Man of the People*. Under the military, corruption has become institutionalized. Twenty years after the publication of *A Man of the People* Achebe wrote *Anthills of the Savannah* (1987), severely criticizing military rule in Nigeria. In the novel, Ikem Osodi, an abrasive marxist intellectual and editor of the official newspaper, resists official pressure on him to compromise his professional integrity by using the paper to sing his master's praise. Instead, his crusading editorials excoriate the failures of government.

The oil boom of the early 1980s sensitized Nigerian writers. The scandals associated with that boom underlie such novels as Kole *Omotoso's *Memories of Our Recent Boom* (1982) and Ifeoma *Okoye's *Men Without Ears* (1984), in which unscrupulous men enrich themselves by wheeling and dealing. Ken *Saro-Wiwa is even more direct in addressing the issue of public corruption in *Prisoners of Jebs* (1988) and *Pita Dumbrok's Prison* (1991). In the former, all of the country's leaders, both civilian and military, as well as the social elite meet their nemesis when they are imprisoned in a gigantic hothouse.

Festus *Iyayi, who is equally outraged by the spec-

tacle of corruption in Nigerian public life, is unique in exposing it from a class perspective. He identifies fully with the dilemma of the working class, responding to *Ngugi wa Thiong'o's call for African writers to adopt socialist realism – a critique of social decadence from a class perspective – in their evaluation of society. Soyinka's *Season of Anomy* (1973) is a half-hearted attempt at the socialist-realist mode; the Dentist, who stands for socialist revolutionary principles in the novel, is undermined by Ofeyi's cautious approach to reform, and the novel presents the Dentist as a caricature of those marxist ideologues whom Soyinka mocks as 'patriots of ideology'. Socialist realism sits well with the radical dramatists who held sway on the Nigerian stage in the 1980s, but in fiction, only Iyayi has written convincingly in this mode. His novel *Violence* (1979) is unambiguous in its commitment to a socialist world view. It exposes the widening gap between rich and poor in the characters of the prostitute Queen and her husband Obofun, who has made his fortune from government contracts secured with bribes, and in the characters of the labourer Idemudia and his wife. Iyayi's next novel, *Heroes* (1986), reappraises the *Nigeria-Biafra war from a class perspective.

The civil war (1967-70), as an event that traumatized the national psyche, stimulated *war literature, including fiction. Novels about the civil war portray it in terms of betrayal and intrigue, rape, murder, and violence, but never in terms of bravery. The writers affirm that the war brought out the most hideous instincts in human nature. 'There is a sadist, a rapist, a fascist and a murderer in men who wait for war and army uniforms to give them expression', says the narrator of *Heroes*, winner of a Commonwealth Writers Prize. Iyayi analyses the causes of the war from a class perspective, seeing it primarily as a business enterprise prosecuted for profit at the expense of the poor. Like George Bernard Shaw, Iyayi examines the concept of military heroism and finds the officer class to be cowardly. He calls for the formation of a third army, a people's army made up of recruits from both sides, to face the common enemy, the generals and the politicians. But not only the military is shown to be callous. In Isidore *Okpewho's novel *The Last Duty* (1976), a businessman sees the war as an occasion to get even with his business rival, whom he has had imprisoned on trumped-up charges and whose wife he seduces. In *Sozaboy: A Novel in Rotten English* (1985), Ken Saro-Wiwa tries to demythologize army life. Buchi *Emecheta's novel *Destination Biafra* (1982) draws heavily on history, although her characterization of the Igbos as ambitious and greedy is untenable, in both the context of the pre-war years and in contemporary Nigeria, where the Igbos have been marginalized.

Nigerian women writers have played a part in the

development of the Nigerian novel. There are four important female novelists: Flora Nwapa, Buchi Emecheta, Ifeoma *Okoye, and Zaynab *Alkali. Marriage and the problems of motherhood feature as the focus of the narrative conflict in their work. Nwapa's novels *Efuru* and *Idu* situate their protagonists in traditional roles, presenting them as ideal house-wives but unfulfilled because childless. The ideal is problematic: both Efuru and Idu are too tender, too loving, and too forgiving to be credible: they are wor-shipful servant-wives to erring husbands. Idu even takes her life and the life of her unborn baby after her husband's death to make the point that a woman 'dies' when her husband dies. In Nwapa's later novel, *Women Are Different* (1986), the husbands of three educated women are as unfaithful and unreliable as Efuru's runaway husbands, but because the women are educated, their condition is not as hopeless as Idu's. The novel suggests that women are superior to men in their ability to forgive and to love. In Emecheta's *The *Joys of Motherhood* (1979), Nnu Ego, abandoned by her first husband when she fails to become pregnant, is finally able to have children by her second husband. By then, however, she has come to see herself as mere property belonging to her hus-band. In her autobiography, *Head Above Water* (1986), Emecheta characterizes the joy of mother-hood as 'a beautiful funeral'. In Ifeoma Okoye's *Behind the Clouds* (1982), the wife, Ije, maintains her composure in the face of provocations from her ill-tempered mother-in-law and the shameless Virginia. In Zaynab Alkali's *The Stillborn* (1984), the young woman, Li, marries a young man, Habu Adams, who soon runs away from her. But when Li is at the peak of her career as a college teacher, she returns to Habu, now crippled and broken. Li's explanation of her strange behaviour is that age, experience, and educa-tion have made her wiser and more forgiving. Although in *Double Yoke* (1982) Emecheta rebels against this kind of submissiveness with a protagonist, Nko, who defies tradition to act as an individual, the general trend in the novels written by Nigerian women demonstrates that in marital relationships women suffer greatly.

Two writers that stand apart in the sense that their work is not consciously oriented towards the critical socialist-realist outlook of many other writers are Ben *Okri and Ibrahim *Tahir. Okri is the most significant talent among the younger generation of Nigerian writers, distinguished by a commitment to his art that is revealed in the intensity of his literary style. The exploration of the magic of language, with himself, the artist, enchanted by its beauty, is the major pre-occupation of his early novels. His cosmopolitan background (he lives in London) tends to dispose him towards writing pure fiction, in which individuals pursue their private visions and dreams. *Flowers and Shadows* (1980) and *The Landscapes Within* (1981) are expressionistic earlier works sounding out the nuances and implications of symbols and images. *Flowers and Shadows* plumbs the significance of 'flower' and 'shadow' in the life of the members of Jonan's family. The influence of James Joyce is evident in *Landscapes Within*, both in the aesthetic purity of the language and in the exploration of the psychic unease of a young artist, Omovo, seen against the background of a sordid domestic environment and the tyranny of a bankrupt father. *The *Famished Road* (1991), for which Okri received the Booker Prize, is structured by magic, fantasy, and dream and re-writes Amos *Tutuola's bush of ghosts stories in standard English. Okri's fantasy embraces endless itineraries and meta-morphoses on a road that has no beginning and no end.

Ibrahim Tahir's *The Last Imam* (1984) is a religious novel that affirms the values of Islam. Tahir mourns the passing of the teaching of the true Islamic principles among the imams, who have become increasingly worldly, greedy, and materialistic. The novel has a dynamic and heightened style reminiscent of Soyinka's.

The novel in English has not developed as rapidly or with as much success in Ghana, Sierra Leone, or Gambia as it has in Nigeria. Some critics have attri-buted the literary silence in Ghana to the country's economic difficulties and to the suppression of free-dom of expression in the Nkrumah years. Some Ghanaian scholars suggest that Joseph Ephraïm *Casely-Hayford's *Ethiopia Unbound* (1911) is the first West African novel, a claim disputed by critic Emmanuel Obiechina, who characterizes the work as a fable that lacks the formal structure of the novel; Obiechina also suggests that R.E. Obeng's *Eighteen-pence* (1943) is a moral tale rather than a novel. Ghana-ian novels of the 1960s include Joseph *Abruquah's *The Catechist* (1965), Francis *Selormey's *The Narrow Path* (1966), and Asare *Konadu's *A Woman in Her Prime* (1967). The first two are largely autobiographi-cal, describing the disruptive effect of western culture on the lives of two men who, as employees of the church, are condemned to move from place to place as a catechist or as a headmaster (*The Narrow Path*). Both novels reflect the cultural nationalism of the time in their covert satire on Christianity.

The Ghanaian novel came to maturity in the work of Ayi Kwei *Armah and Kofi *Awoonor. Armah's first two novels, *The *Beautyful Ones Are Not Yet Born* (1968) and *Fragments* (1970), and Awoonor's *This Earth, My Brother* (1971) re-enact the drama of post-independence disillusionment in the manner of the Nigerian novel of the 1960s and 70s. In *The Beautyful Ones* and *Fragments*, the imagery of scatology and of cargo cults signifies the excessive corruption and acquisitive materialism of post-independence Ghana. The man in *The Beautyful Ones*, Baako in *Fragments*, and Amamu in *This Earth, My Brother* are sensitive to the situation but are rendered powerless by a deeply entrenched system of corruption and oppression. Awoonor's *Comes the Voyager at Last* (1992) is the tale of the mythic return of a questing black American hero, Sheik Lumumba Mandela (the collocation is significant), to his ancestral roots in Africa. His quest terminates in a festival of universal reconciliation in which injustice, oppression, and racial differences disappear and human and god, animal and vegetable nature live in harmony.

Kojo *Laing, a much younger writer than Armah and Awoonor, injects new energy into the Ghanaian novel by his bold experimentation with language and his use of magic in *Search Sweet Country* (1986). The world of the witch Adwoa Adde defies space and time. Doors and windows open on their own in her presence and she cruises over Accra at night. But these magical feats are perhaps less exciting than Laing's original and concrete metaphors, which stand out as fresh and innovative in their context. The novel is not as overtly political as those of his predecessors, but it is the more intensely satirical, since the author exposes the folly of public life as well as that of private lives.

Critic Eustace Palmer has noted that Sierra Leoneans have shown greater flair for poetry than fiction. But the principal reason for the literary silence in Sierra Leone, he argues, is the cultural complacency of the country's educated class, the Krios, the descendants of the freed slaves who settled along the coast of Freetown towards the end of the eighteenth century. They were detribalized and alienated, Palmer argues, from 'the rich source of African creative writing'. The few Sierra Leonean novels in English that filtered through, such as William *Conton's *The African* (1960) and R.S. *Easmon's *The Burnt-Out Marriage* (1967), are not concerned with those cultural questions that interested other African novelists. Sierra Leonean literature begins to enter the mainstream of African literature only with the works of such writers (mostly poets) as Syl *Cheyney-Coker, with his magic realist novel *The *Last Harmattan of Alusine Dunbar* (1990), Lemuel *Johnson, and Muktarr Mustapha.

The only significant novelist in English in Gambia is Lenrie *Peters, who, since the publication of *The Second Round* (1965), has turned to poetry.

For a variety of political, cultural, and social reasons, the novel in English has not developed in Cameroon as it has in other parts of West Africa. Creative writers have published poetry and short fiction in journals and on radio, but outlets for longer fiction have always been scarce; while potential novelists realize that publishers in Europe and North America could provide wide dissemination for their work, they seldom offer manuscripts, fearing that they will not meet foreign standards. Fortunately, local printing houses have been publishing novelists in the anglophone provinces.

Among the anglophone novelists of the 1960s are Sankie Maimo and Mbella Sonne Dipoko. Maimo's novel is *Adventuring with Jaja* (1962), a children's adventure story set in Lagos, Nigeria, where it was published. It concerns Jaja, a self-assured youth who engages in duels and battles sea monsters. Dipoko set his first novel in France, where he was a law student and staff member of *Présence africaine*. *A Few Nights and Days* (1966) deals with the theme of inter-racial marriage. A later novel, *Because of Women* (1968), is set in Cameroon and considers sexuality and society. Both novels were published abroad.

An increase during the 1970s in English-language creative writing of all kinds extended to prose fiction. Notable are Kenjo Jumbam's two novellas, published together, *Lukong and the Leopard* and *The White Man of Cattle* (1975). The former is a story of youthful courage in the traditional African world, the latter is about the early stages of western influence in that world. *The White Man of God* (1980), a sequel to *The White Man of Cattle*, portrays the advanced stage of implantation of western culture in Nso, Jumbam's birthplace in Cameroon, and the conflicts that result from the encounter between the Roman Catholic missionary effort and indigenous cultural belief. Peter Eba's novel *The Good Foot* (1977) describes the painful experiences of a serious youth, Mbamu, as he is confronted with the changes imposed by colonialism, particularly rural exodus and formal education.

The number of published novels continued to increase in the 1980s, with a noticeable emphasis on plots involving education. Talla Ngarka's novel *The Herbalist* (1988) focuses on school girls in an urban setting; Comfort Achu traces boyhood experiences in anglophone schools from primary to secondary level in *Ayamoh's Days at School* (1985); and *He Would Have Made Himself* (1988) by Zacceus Ntumngia describes the bitter experiences of a youth as he attempts to overcome the obstacles to education in contemporary Cameroon. A few writers explore politics, corruption, and power: Albert Mukong, a political dissident, describes his encounters with Cameroonian government and prisons during the pre-independence movement in *Prisoner without a Crime* (1985); Ndeley Mokosso's collection of stories entitled *Man Pass Man and Other Stories* (1987) deals with such issues as political manipulation, patronage appointments, and life in plantation camps; three novels by Maurice Sotabinda, *Dangerous Waters* (1980), *Life Is a Lottery* (1984), and *The Money Doublers* (1985), deal mainly with the power of money. The fiction of Joseph Ngongwikuo deals in general with Kom traditional culture and the challenge of Westernization. *The Lost Child* (1985) and *The Village School Girl* (1985) are novellas; *Taboo Love* (1985), which examines the expectations of the traditional world and the demands of modernity, and *Taboo Kingdom* (1985) are novels. *The Last of the Virgins* (1985) by Atanga George Che describes a young woman's experiences, especially in love, as she reaches maturity. Relatively fewer novels have been published in the first half of the 1990s. John Menget's novel *The Arrow of My Love* (1995) considers juvenile love in modern Africa. *Born to Rule* (1993) by Tah Asongwed is a political novel that satirizes presidential power in contemporary Africa. Linus Asong's novels *A Stranger in His Homeland* and *The Crown of Thorns* (both 1990) and *A Legend of the Dead* (1993) deal with the political life and intrigues of the chieftaincy system in contact with modernity. *No Way to Die* (1993) is a psychological novel that depicts the resistance of the African old order to integration with and replacement by the modern order.

NTIRU, Richard Carl (1946-), Ugandan poet, was born in Kigezi, Uganda and attended Makerere University College, Kampala, where he graduated with an honours degree, edited *The Makererean* and *Penpoint*, and managed the Makerere Travelling Theatre. He works as an editor for the International Centre for Research in Agro-Forestry in Nairobi. His only collection is *Tensions* (1971), which is rich in imagery reminiscent of the poetry of Christopher *Okigbo and Pol *Ndu. Unlike his fellow Ugandan poets Grace *Ogot and *Okot p'Bitek, he deals with issues of contemporary East Africa. Acknowledging other poets in other literatures, he consciously explores the divisions within human society and critiques his society's attitudes towards the unfortunate. His strongest work is in shorter forms. Apart from poetry he has also written a radio play and short stories.

NWABUEZE, Emeka (1952-), dramatist, was born at Awka, Nigeria and studied at the University of Nigeria and Eastern Michigan and Bowling Green state universities in the USA, gaining a Ph.D. in theatre. Nwabueze has taught in several universities and has received many fellowships and academic honours around the globe. Nwabueze's published plays include *Spokesman for the Oracle* (1986), a parable of the erosion of moral values; *Guardian of the Cosmos* (1990), a terse, rhythmic, and idiomatic commentary on the predicament of the social reformer in a corrupt and materialistic society; *A Dance of the Dead* (1991), which examines the moral crisis inflicted on society by conscienceless wealthy citizens; and *When the Arrow Rebounds* (1991), a dramatized recreation of Chinua *Achebe's *Arrow of God. The plays interweave humour with bitter truth and incorporate a wealth of folklore to represent Africa's cosmic experience.

NWAKOBY, Martina Awele (1937-), Nigerian writer of children's fiction and novelist, was born in Ogwashi-Uku, Nigeria and educated at schools in Nigeria and Birmingham, at the University of Pittsburgh, and at the University of Ibadan, where she gained a Ph.D. in library studies. She is a lecturer at the Abia State University, Uturu, Nigeria. Nwakoby is the author of the children's books *Ten in the Family* (1975) and *A Lucky Chance* (1980) and the adult novel *A House Divided* (1985); she won the 1978 Macmillan children's book competition. *Quiz Time* (1980) is part of her efforts to encourage children to read and write. *Ten in the Family*, *A Lucky Chance*, and *A House Divided* are rooted in Nigerian social life and reflect the vices and virtues of both contemporary and traditional Nigerian life. *A House Divided* explores ethnic conflicts, love, and prejudice and seeks to project social ideals.

NWANKWO, Nkem (1936-), Nigerian novelist, was born in Nawfia, Nigeria and educated in schools and colleges in Lagos and at University College, Ibadan. After graduation he taught briefly and worked for *Drum magazine before he started work for the Nigerian Broadcasting Corporation. Winning an *Encounter* prize in 1960 for a play encouraged him to produce more creative writing, and he published two books for teenagers, *Tales Out of School* (1963) and *More Tales Out of School* (1965), that chronicle the adventures of two boys, Bayo and Ike. Nwankwo's best-known novel, *Danda* (1964), with its picaresque hero and loose narrative structure, enhanced his reputation as one of the major first-generation African literary voices. In Biafra he worked as a member of the Arts Council between 1967 and 1970, and after the *Nigeria-Biafra war he worked as an editor of the *Daily Times* (Lagos). In 1973 he was appointed writer-in-residence at the African Studies Center at Michigan State University. His second novel, *My Mercedes Is Bigger than Yours* (1975), is a political satire in which wit and humour contribute to the narrative strategy. In the 1970s Nwankwo embarked on further academic studies and obtained the master's and Ph.D. degrees from the University of Indiana. His third novel, *The Scapegoat* (1984), explores the underside of contemporary Nigerian society.

NWAPA, Flora (1931-93), Nigerian novelist, was the first Nigerian woman to write novels; she also wrote short stories and stories for children, and she was a publisher, again the first Nigerian woman. She was born at Oguta in Imo State of eastern Nigeria. With a BA degree (1957) and a diploma in education (1958) she began her professional career as a civil servant and subsequently served her community as a commissioner in various ministries in the then East Central State post-Nigeria-Biafra war government. She established the Tana Press and Flora Nwapa Books in Enugu and received the Merit Award for

Authorship/Publishing of the University of Ife Book Fair in 1985.

Nwapa is known as a writer mainly for two novels, *Efuru* (1966) and *Idu* (1970), set in the early colonial period in the Oguta area of Igboland. The novels examine from different perspectives the problems of women in traditional society, particularly in relation to their ability to bear children. Here, as in the later novels, she reverses the usual positions of men and women, making women central. A short semi-autobiographical novel, *Never Again* (1975), is based on her experiences during the civil war. Her last two novels, *One is Enough* (1981) and *Women Are Different* (1986), have a modern urban setting; the former explores the themes of childlessness and women's economic independence, and the latter insists that women have options other than marriage and motherhood. As a short-story writer, Nwapa maintains her focus on women's experience: her first collection, *This Is Lagos and Other Stories* (1971), focuses on societal ills such as sexual exploitation of women, criminality, and violence; in *Wives at War and Other Stories* (1980), women defend their rights to freedom from oppression. She began writing for children to satisfy her own children's needs for stories with which they could identify. The dual purpose of teaching and entertainment runs through the stories beginning with *Emeka-Driver's Guard* (1979) through *The Miracle Kittens* (1980), *Adventures of Deke* (1980), and *Journey to Space* (1980).

Nwapa's prose writing is evidence of her mastery of the art of storytelling. She adapts her style to the content and mood of her characters. In *Efuru* and *Idu*, the high frequency of proverbs and imagery reflects the traditional African's use of language. In *Never Again*, the recurrence of very short sentences creates a broken rhythm that corresponds to the staccato rhythm of life in the war zone and accentuates tension. Although she did not consider herself a feminist, her vision emphasizes the need to liberate women from all forms of fetters.

NYAMFUKUDZA, Stanley (1951-), Zimbabwean novelist and short-story writer, was born in Wedza, Zimbabwe and educated in Zimbabwe and at Oxford University, where he gained a BA in 1977. Like Dambudzo *Marechera, Nyamfukudza belongs to an angry generation that grew up politically alienated in a period when African nationalists remained divided and weak. His first novel, *The Non-Believer's Journey* (1980) is notable for its protagonist, who both affirms and interrogates the viability of African nationalism, its scathingly ironic tone, and the despair and disillusionment associated with African writing of the post-independence era. The same questioning attitude is apparent in *Aftermaths* (1983), a collection of eleven short stories that is mercilessly critical of male charac-

ters and somewhat positively inclined towards the female characters. The ten stories in *If God Was a Woman* (1991) focus on ordinary characters and their relationships with the opposite sex. Nyamfukudza's complex, paradoxical vision shuns the easy affirmation of principle or value.

NYAMUBAYA, Freedom (1958-), poet and prose writer, was born in Murehwa, Zimbabwe and educated at primary and secondary schools. She abandoned her school career to join Zimbabwe's liberation struggle in 1975 and achieved the rank of field operational commander and secretary for education for the political party ZANU. From 1982 to 1984 she studied social science at Ruskin College, Oxford, and has since then become director of a non-governmental organization she founded to assist rural farmers in Zaïre. Her first publication, *On the Road Again* (1986) suggests that her forte lies in her harnessing of Shona proverbial expressions, folktale elements, myths, and traditional sayings, which she transforms into a unique poetic voice that expresses the tragedies of war and the resilience of the human spirit. The influence of African orature is also noticeable in her second collection of poems, *Dusk of Dawn* (1995), in which the anger and bitterness of the first collection gives way to a more reflective and sombre tone. The writer's love for life, for Zimbabwe, and for Mozambique, which sheltered the fighters during the war, finds expression in her poetry, but her love is at the same time qualified by her recognition of the harsh and brutal side of life and history. In the same collection are two prose pieces notable for their exquisitely painful memory of those fighters who dedicated their lives to the liberation struggle. Nyamubaya's writing is accessible, unique in texture and in orientation.

NZEKWU, Onuora (1928-), Nigerian novelist, was born in Kafanchan, Nigeria of Igbo parents and was educated in several schools including St. Anthony's School and St. Charles Higher Elementary Teacher Training College, Makurdi. His nine years of teaching in Oturkpo, Onitsha, and Lagos provided much of the material that was to serve him in his writing career, and later he received Rockefeller Foundation and UNESCO fellowships that enabled him to travel widely. He became editorial assistant of *Nigeria Magazine* in 1956, rising to the position of editor in 1962, and his working relationship with historian Michael Crowder helped him to publish his first novel, *Wand of Noble Wood* (1961). His second novel, *Blade among the Boys* (1962), appeared the next year. In these novels of cultural conflict, Nzekwu was perceived as a sociological novelist whose desire to explain his culture to a foreign audience stultified the narratives. Crowder and Nzekwu co-authored a novel for children entitled *Eze Goes to School* (1963), which made a tremendous impact on both school children and their teachers. Nzekwu's third novel, *Highlife for Lizards* (1965), examines polygamy. His career was interrupted by the *Nigeria-Biafra war, and at its end he returned to public service. A sequel to *Eze Goes to School*, entitled *Eze Goes to College* (1988), also co-authored with Crowder, continues the story of the trials of Eze. Nzekwu, as one of the first generation of African writers in English, helped pioneer a new vision in African literature.

OBAFEMI, Olu (1948-), Nigerian dramatist, was born in Akutupa, a small town in Kiriland, Nigeria and had his university education in Zaria, Nigeria and in Sheffield and Leeds, UK. His published plays include *Nights of a Mystical Beast* and *The New Dawn* (1986), *Suicide Syndrome*, and *Naira Has No Gender* (1993), and he has had plays produced both in Britain, while he was on a fellowship at the School of Drama, University of Leeds, and in Nigeria. His novel, *Wheels* (1997), was serialized in the *Nigerian Herald*. He is a professor of English and the founder of the Ajon Players, an active drama society in Ilorin, Nigeria.

Nigerian writers in the academy are often located in the Ibadan-Ife-Ilorin triad. Obafemi, who is the chair of the Kwara State branch of the Association of Nigerian Authors, is one of the most accomplished writers of the Ilorin axis. He belongs to the generation of Femi ★Osofisan, Niyi ★Osundare, Kole ★Omotoso, Tanure ★Ojaide and Biodun Jeyifo, who brought politics into literature.

Nights of a Mystical Beast uses folkloric and mythic images and icons to explore the primeval chaos that typifies the pre-colonial social form and the violence of colonialism. In *The New Dawn*, he envisions a new political consciousness emerging from the struggle to negate the history of colonialism and its attendant exploitation and fragmentation. The dominant voice in *Suicide Syndrome* is that of an ideologue-artist who manoeuvres character and actions, songs and dance to amplify his class sympathy.

Obafemi has also published two scholarly studies, *Nigerian Writers on the Nigerian Civil War* (1992) and *Contemporary Nigerian Theatre: Cultural Heritage and Social Vision* (1996), and has edited *New Introduction to Literature* (1994).

OCULI, Okello (1942-), Ugandan novelist and poet, was born in Dokolo in northern Uganda and educated at Soroti College and St. Peter's College, Tororo, St. Mary's College, Kisubu, and Makerere University, Kampala, where he studied political science and worked as news editor of *The Makererean* and as a tutorial fellow. His poetry, like that of ★Okot p'Bitek and Joseph Buruga, seeks to re-assert the cultural heritage of Africa with a critique of foreign influences in East Africa. His first publication, *Orphan* (1968), is an allegory in verse and prose in which an orphan symbolizes Africans who either do not know or have forgotten their heritage. Its several monologues lament the abandonment of African values for colonial ones. In *Prosti-*

tute (1968), a novel, the central thread is the continuous deterioration of the slums, where the prostitutes live and operate. The nameless protagonist is a prostitute-victim; like Cyprian ★Ekwensi's Jagua Nana she is portrayed as someone trying to make the best of her life with the chances she has left. The novel's close observations of East African society, sometimes in shocking detail, argues that complacency in the face of foreign values, particularly among the powerful, contributes to the destruction of tradition and the permanent loss of an African past. His other publications include *Koolokem* (1978), an episodic account of a victimized woman and her husband; *Malak* (1976), a long verse essay inspired by the regime of Idi Amin, and *Kanti Riti* (1974). Oculi speaks with a communal voice invoking the collective symbols of Africa. Some commentators criticize his work as excessively abstract and unwilling to acknowledge the positive contributions of Western influences.

Of Chameleons and Gods (1981) Poems by Jack ★Mapanje. Of the poems in this collection, Mapanje says they span 'ten turbulent years in which I have been attempting to find a voice or voices as a way of preserving some sanity. Obviously where personal voices are too easily muffled, this is a difficult task.' The poems, like those of Mapanje's contemporaries, Malawian poets Steve ★Chimombo, Frank ★Chipasula, and Felix ★Mnthali, draw on the oral traditons and beliefs of Malawian society as a means of addressing pressing social and political problems. Mapanje, like his contemporaries, believes in the healing power of poetry.

OFEIMUN, Odia (1950-), Nigerian poet, was born in Irhukpen, Nigeria and read political science at the University of Ibadan. He was private secretary to the late Chief Obafemi Awolowo, one of Nigeria's foremost politicians, and a culture-page editor for the Lagos *Guardian*, where he helped to develop the vibrant tradition of art through the newspaper medium. As president of the Association of Nigerian Authors, he occupies an important position in the struggle to sustain a viable literary culture in Nigeria.

Ofeimun's major poetry collections are *The Poet Lied* (1980), *A Handle for the Flutist and Other Poems* (1986), and *Under African Skies* (1990). The publication of *The Poet Lied* generated literary and legal debate when Nigerian poet J.P. Clark ★Bekederemo threatened court action against the book's publisher, alleging that the title poem referred to him and injured his reputation. Eventually the libel case halted the circulation of the book, and although the case was finally settled out of court, the controversy lingers on.

Many critics see Ofeimun's *The Poet Lied* as a metatext that confronts certain aesthetic traditions and viewpoints expressed by a particular writer on the *Nigeria-Biafra war. The speaker, irrepressible and political, berates a fellow poet for abandoning truth, the very grain of art. In rejecting the aloofness and abstractions of apolitical art and arguing for a literature of social and political relevance, Ofeimun's poetry reveals the essence of a new aesthetic tradition that finds expression in the works of such Nigerian writers as Niyi *Osundare, Femi *Osofisan, and Tanure *Ojaide.

OGOT, Grace (Emily) (1930-), Kenyan short-story writer and novelist. Educated at Ng'iya Girls' School and Butere High School and trained as a nurse and midwife, Ogot later served as an announcer and script writer for the BBC, a community development officer, a public relations specialist, a member of parliament, and a representative to the United Nations for Kenya. Considered by some critics to be the leading short-story writer in East Africa, she has published two novels, *The Promised Land* (1966) and *The Island of Tears* (1980); two story collections, *Land without Thunder* (1968) and *The Other Woman* (1976); a novella, *The Graduate* (1980); and a retelling of Luo village myth, *Miaha* (1983). She often draws on her childhood and her work as a nurse as well as African folktales and traditional practice for her plots and characters. An interesting though not always successful blending of ordinary African settings with violent and macabre action characterizes some of her work.

The Promised Land, though at one level a melodramatic tale of tribal hatreds, is often more complex than that. A young farmer and his wife who have migrated to Tanzania from Kenya become embroiled in issues of personal jealousy and materialism. Clearly presented here is Ogot's conception of the ideal African wife: she is obedient and submissive to her husband at all times, oriented to family and community, not to goals of material well-being and acquisition. Although short stories in the two collections draw on both urban and rural Kenyan experience, 'The White Veil', from *Land without Thunder*, is in some ways representative of the sorts of conflicts and resolutions in Ogot's fiction. Elizabeth is a young female office worker, vulnerable because of her age, her sex, and the prevailing attitudes about male-female relationships. She is raped by her employer, becomes pregnant, discovers she has no recourse and will be held to blame for the circumstances, and finally commits suicide as her only way out. Nothing happens to her boss, and life goes on much as before. Even though the employer has broken

the rules of society, he will not be punished in this life. Some critics have judged Elizabeth's fate as impossibly one-dimensional and simple-minded; others have seen it as a realistic portrayal of social conditions in Kenya.

Praise for Ogot's fiction is generally qualified by concerns about her writing style, characterization, and narrative technique. Her writing is sometimes called uninspired and pedestrian and her characters criticized as wooden and underdeveloped by those who feel her writing does not possess sufficient subtlety or political commitment. Others, though, have discovered a prevailing irony in her fiction which gives her stories power and relevance.

OGUIBE, Olu (1964-), Nigerian poet, was born in Aba, Nigeria and educated at the University of Nsukka, Nigeria, where he was expelled in 1989 for political activism, and the University of London, where he gained a Ph.D. in art history. In 1995 he became an assistant professor of art history at the University of Illinois. His first book of poetry, the lyrical long poem *A Song from Exile* (1990), explores the pain of exile. The poet's feelings of anger and despair at his powerlessness and separation from his country progressively merge with the greater sorrow of his community. He establishes his commitment to Nigeria and, without being prescriptive, the artist's role within his society and his relevance to it. *A Gathering Fear* (1992) was highly acclaimed in Africa, where it won the 1992 All-Africa Okigbo Prize and a mention by the 1993 Noma Award jury. A sense of loss and collective pain dominates these eloquent poems, whose elegiac and proclamatory mode locate them within the minstrel tradition. A later collection, *Songs for Catalina* (1994), contains ten love poems. He also edited *Sojourners: New Writing by Africans in Britain* (1994). Chinua *Achebe has compared Oguibe's poetry to Christopher *Okigbo's. His work has been translated into Spanish and Catalan and has been published in Nigeria, Germany, Mexico, and Spain. Pitika Ntuli's interview with him has been published as a pamphlet entitled *The Battle for South Africa's Mind: Towards a Post-Apartheid Culture* (1995).

OGUNDE, Hubert [See DRAMA, West Africa; FRANCOPHONE-ANGLOPHONE LITERARY RELATIONS]

OGUNDIPE-LESLIE, Molara (1949-), Nigerian literary critic and poet, was born in Lagos. She received her early schooling and university education in Nigeria, then went on to further study at London, Oxford, Cambridge, Columbia, and Harvard. The recipient of many awards and academic honours, she has taught at universities in Canada and the US and has initiated new courses in criticism, in African poetry and fiction, and in women's writing at several Nigerian universities. Her critical writing includes *Re-creat-*

ing *Ourselves: Women and Critical Transformations in Africa* (1994). She is a founding member of several women's organizations, national and international, and in Nigeria has frequently been consulted by government ministries regarding women's issues.

Ogundipe-Leslie's extensive training in the field of English and comparative literatures enables her to read anglophone American literature as a component of contemporary world literature, not to patronize it as a minor, lesser field. As a feminist critic and a strong believer in the creative power of women, she avoids applying rigid or doctrinaire criteria to women's writing, acknowledging that there are many feminisms and also various talents and perceptions among the writers of Africa and the Caribbean. As a creative writer she is the author of a volume of poetry, *Sew the Old Days* (1985), which is often highly ironic; she reveals the unconscious but ludicrous snobbery of the colonizer in a poem about her British landlady, and she contrives a witty verse in which each line is the title of an African novel. She is also an accomplished speaker, has been an actress and producer of plays, and appears frequently on radio. The diversity of her work contributes to the force of her activism and the quality of her writing, both critical and creative.

OGUNYEMI, Wale (1939-), Nigerian playwright, was born in Igbajo, about 150 miles northwest of Lagos. Although he had no formal training in theatre arts – he learned his craft through employment, from 1962, as an actor with the then Western Nigerian Television station, with the touring mini-troupe Theatre Express, and with Wole *Soyinka's Orisun theatre group – in 1967 he joined the Institute of African Studies at the University of Ibadan, where his focus is on research and writing.

Ogunyemi is one of the most familiar of Nigerian playwrights working in English. He has been exceptionally prolific, his fifteen published plays (to 1991) representing only a fraction of his total output for stage, television, and radio. His most frequently performed play, *The *Divorce* (1977), is a domestic comedy that has been criticized for its chauvinistic treatment of a wife's responsibilities. *Business Headache* (1966) is a comedy in Nigerian *Pidgin, sharply observant of the economic realities most Nigerians confront in their daily lives. *Partners in Business* (1991), like *The Divorce*, deals with a marital crisis in a modern setting, but works through high melodrama rather than comedy. The bulk of Ogunyemi's plays, however, are treatments of Yoruba myth, of relations between the Yoruba gods, and of Yoruba history. Plays such as *Eshu Elegbara* (1970) and *Obaluaye* (1972) deal with the problematic relationship between the gods and humankind. In these plays, as elsewhere, he works in a mode that comes close to total theatre, with *gestus* and (especially) music playing as vital a part of the perfor-

mance as does dialogue. *Eniyan*, Ogunyemi's adaptation of *Everyman* (1987; first performed 1969), is significant for the harshness with which the playwright, here as elsewhere, deals with impiety and social transgression. His plays have made a considerable impact on younger dramatists, despite reservations concerning his conservative vision of Nigeria's social and political history and his unmediated treatment of Yoruba myth and religious belief.

Oil Man of Obange (1971) A novel by John *Munonye. This tightly structured tragedy of everyday life is the story of Jeri, abjectly poor but blessed with brilliant children. Determined to give them the best education, Jeri opts for the tedious palm oil trade in preference to farming on scarce and unproductive farmland. But a catalogue of disasters obstructs Jeri's attempt to raise enough funds to train his children and leads to his death by suicide. While members of the community praise his heroic resilience, they wonder whether it is worthwhile for a man to sacrifice everything for the sake of his children.

OJAIDE, Tanure (1948-), Nigerian poet, was educated at the University of Ibadan, Nigeria (BA) and at Syracuse University, USA (MA, Ph.D.). He is a productive poet and has won several awards; collections include *Children of Iroko* (1973), *Labyrinths of the Delta* (1986), which won a Commonwealth Poetry Prize, and *The Eagle's Vision* (1987), which won the Christopher Okigbo Prize. *The Endless Song* (1989) was specially mentioned by the Noma Award committee, *The Fate of Vultures and Other Poems* (1990) won the Association of Nigerian Authors' (ANA) Poetry Award, and the title poem of the latter volume received a BBC Arts and Africa Poetry Award. Other collections are *The Blood of Peace* (1991), *Invoking the Warrior God* (1995), which won the ANA's Poetry Award, *Cannons for the Brave* (1995), and *Daydream of Ants* (1995). He has been a fellow of the Headlands Center for the Arts in Sausalito, California, and he teaches at the University of North Carolina at Charlotte. His scholarly publishing includes *The Poetry of Wole Soyinka* (1994) and *Poetic Imagination in Black Africa: Essays on African Poetry* (1996).

The frequent appearance of traditional African imagery, rhythm, and music and the use of Nigerian English to express Nigerian/African experience characterize Ojaide's poetry, as they do that of his countrymen Niyi *Osundare and Odia *Ofeimun, with whom he has much in common as a poet. With its sociopolitical themes and its distinctive imagery and diction, the poetry is relatively accessible and often politically committed. In 1998 he published a personal memoir, *Great Boys: An African Childhood*.

OKAI, Atukwei (1941-), Ghanaian poet, was born in

Accra, Ghana and educated at the Gorky Literary Institute, Moscow (MA, 1967) and the University of London. Having taught Russian literature at the University of Ghana, he is a faculty member of the Institute of African Studies, Legon and an executive of the Pan-African Writers' Association. He has published four volumes of poems, including one for children: *Flowerfall* (1969), *The Oath of the Fontomfrom and Other Poems* (1971), *Lorgorligi Logarithms* (1974), and *The Anthill in the Sea* (1988), subtitled 'Verses and Chants for Children'. In poems that are strongly aural and prophetic he explores the plight of post-independence Africa, but a sense of cosmic balance tempers the gravity inherent in such reflections. *The Anthill in the Sea*, with its strong graphics, marks a singular departure in publishing for children in Ghana.

OKARA, Gabriel (Imomotimi Gbaingbain)

(1921-), Nigerian poet, was born in Bumoundi, Western Nigeria. He received his secondary schooling in Umuahia and Lagos and worked as a book binder and a journalist after the Second World War. During the ★Nigeria-Biafra war (1967-70), Okara, then head of information services for the Eastern region, helped foster relief efforts by going on poetry recital tours in the USA. After the war, he took on the management of the Rivers State Broadcasting Corporation, which ran the first and only FM station in black Africa. He also edited a newspaper, *Nigerian Tide*. Upon retirement in 1975, he was appointed writer-in-residence of the Rivers State Council for Arts and Culture.

His widely anthologized poems, which first appeared in the magazine *Black Orpheus*, borrow imagery from his Ijo birthplace and from Dylan Thomas, William Blake, W.B. Yeats and G.M. Hopkins to reflect on the tribulations of nation-building and the traumas that befall the self. Often torn between the 'jungle drums and the concerto', he is hesitant to embrace a syncretic, neo-African culture. The title poem of his slim but dense collection, *The ★Fisherman's Invocation* (1978), is his most ambitious; the collection shared a Commonwealth Poetry Prize.

In his poetic novel *The ★Voice* (1964), Okolo's hallucinatory quest through Sologa ends in self-sacrifice and death. In its parabolic approach, *The Voice* resembles later Ghanaian novels by Kofi ★Awoonor or Ayi Kwei ★Armah (and possibly those of Canada's A.M. Klein or Guyana's Wilson Harris), but it also shares with Chinua ★Achebe's more realistic oeuvre a disillusionment with post-independence moral bankruptcy. The novel's pseudo-naive tone is the result of a self-conscious linguistic experiment sustained by the metaphorical opposition between Okolo's 'straight words' in Ijo – that is, an English informed with Ijo word order – and the 'crooked [English] words' of political propaganda.

Okara has written children's books: *Little Snake and Little Frog* (1981) and *An Adventure to Juju Island* (1981). His contribution to Nigerian literary culture has also established him as a teaching voice. Whether during a storytelling session in the village or on television, his voice has carried well beyond the waves of radio, television and the Niger Delta.

OKIGBO, (Ifeanyichukwu) Christopher (1932-67), Nigerian poet, was born in Ojoto village in the former Eastern Region of Nigeria, baptized in the Roman Catholic religion, and educated at the prestigious Government College, Umuahia and University College, Ibadan, where he obtained a degree in classics in 1956. As an undergraduate at Ibadan, he edited the *University Weekly*, joined the ★Mbari Club, the literary society that published *Black Orpheus*, played jazz clarinet, and demonstrated talent as an athlete.

In the ten years following graduation in 1956, he held brief appointments with the Nigerian Tobacco Company, the United African Company, and the federal Ministry of Research and Information in Lagos; was vice-principal at Fiditi Grammar School; was appointed acting registrar of the new University of Nigeria at Nsukka; and represented Cambridge University Press in West Africa. The ★Nigeria-Biafra war (1967-70) forced him back to Eastern Nigeria, where he died at Nsukka while fighting as a major in the Biafran army. Although his life was brief, he exerted a profound influence on the African literary canon. For example, as Cambridge University Press representative in West Africa, he travelled widely in Africa and Europe, and he was an editor of *Transition*. In 1962 he attended the First African Writers Conference at Makerere University in Kampala, Uganda, where he made a controversial presentation entitled 'What Is African Literature?' In 1965 he read his poetry at the Commonwealth Arts Festival in Edinburgh and in 1966 he declined to accept the Negro Festival Arts Prize for his poem ★*Limits* on the grounds that the award had 'colour' or ★negritude connotations. In 1966, he co-founded with Chinua ★Achebe the short-lived Citadel Publishing Company.

Okigbo's major accomplishment as an artist is his poetry, which he described as 'a necessary part of my being alive'. His poetic works are ★*Heavensgate* (1962), which is organized into five sections that highlight the protagonist's religious experience; *Limits* (1964), which consists of two lyrics ('Siren Limits' and 'Fragments out of the Deluge', both organized into twelve segments) that deal with the themes of art, religion, and culture; *Silences* (1965), which embodies two protest poems ('Lament of the Silent Sisters', first published in *Transition*, 1963, and 'Lament of the Drums') that treat national and international issues including the death of Patrice Lumumba and the imprisonment of Chief Awolowo; *Distances* (first published in *Transition*, 1964), which continues the themes of personal concerns – religion, art, and nature – explored in his earlier poetry; and the posthumous volumes *Labyrinths, with Path of Thunder* (1971) and *Collected Poems* (1986). His earlier verse (for example, *Heavensgate*) celebrates private and personal quests such as love and religion; his later work (for example *Path of Thunder*) addresses public issues such as nationalism and communal responsibility as well. The influences on his work of Igbo mythology and folklore and classical and modernist aesthetic practices, including those of Dante, Stéphane Mallarmé, G.M. Hopkins, T.S. Eliot, and Ezra Pound, lead some readers to describe it as impenetrable. Although he did not set out to be obscure, his insatiable intellectual curiosity, huge capacity for effort, and frequent revisions produced an abstruse lyricism. Despite his reputation as a difficult poet, however, he remains widely popular with other poets and critics as well as readers. His strengths as an artist are complemented by the fact that he also inspired the lyric poets of his generation, including Okogbule Wonodi and Michael *Echeruo.

OKO, Akomaye (1943-), Nigerian poet and playwright, is a member of the generation of writers inspired by the *Nigeria-Biafra war (1967-70). Born at Ibong, near Obudu, Cross River State, he enrolled at Ahmadu Bello University, Zaria, after his secondary education at Maryknoll College, Ogoja but fled to the University of Nigeria, Nsukka in the wake of the massacre of easterners in northern Nigeria in September 1966. During the war he was a member of a student delegation that toured Europe and America to promote the Biafran case among overseas student colleagues. His poetry, first published in *Nsukka Harvest* (1972), edited by Chukwuma Azuonye, and in the wartime German anthology *Gedichte aus Biafra* (1968), is mainly a record of his personal experience of war from the 1966 massacres to the end of the war in 1970. In his first collection, *Clouds* (1992), memories of war blossom into a celebration of life in the midst of death. His play *The Cynic* (1992), an allegorical conflict between the forces of light and the forces of evil with clear allusions to post-civil war Nigeria, was first produced at the University of Benin (1978). He published a critical book, *The Tragic Paradox: A Study of Wole Soyinka and His Works*, in 1992.

OKOME, Onookome (1960-), Nigerian poet, was born on Nigeria's independence day, 1 October 1960, in Sapele, in present day Delta State. He holds a BA in English from the University of Nigeria, Nsukka and master's and Ph.D. degrees from the University of Ibadan. He is a member of the faculty of the department of theatre arts at the University of Calabar. His poems first appeared on the pages of the *Guardian* (Lagos), a newspaper to which he regularly contributes articles on literature, culture, film, and politics. A selection from his unpublished collection of poems, 'Chapters of Pain', features in the Association of Nigerian Authors (ANA) anthology of Nigerian poetry, *Voices from the Fringe* (1988), edited by Harry *Garuba. His first collection of poems, *Pendants* (1993), is informed by disillusionment and outrage over the confused politics and pervasive moral bankruptcy in contemporary Nigeria. With Jonathan Haynes he has written a scholarly book, *Cinema and Social Change in West Africa* (1995).

OKOT P'BITEK (1931-82), Ugandan poet, was born in Gulu, Uganda and attended Gulu High School and King's College, Budo. He studied law at Aberystwyth, Wales and social anthropology at Oxford, completing a B.Litt. thesis on the traditional songs of the Acoli and Lango. In 1966 he returned to Uganda as director of the Uganda Cultural Centre and later founded arts festivals at Gulu and Kisumu. Dismissed from his position for writing critically of the Amin government, he lived in exile in Kenya, where he was a faculty member of the literature department in the University of Nairobi. He was a fellow in the International Writing Program at the University of Iowa in 1969-70 and a visiting professor at the University of Texas at Austin and the University of Ife in Nigeria in 1978. In 1979, after Idi Amin was overthrown, he returned to Uganda, where he was appointed a professor of creative writing in the department of literature at Makerere University.

Okot p'Bitek's early Acoli-language novel *Lak Tar Miyo Kinyero Wi Lobo* (1953; *White Teeth*, 1989) was followed by the long poem *Song of Lawino*, first composed in Acoli rhyming couplets in 1956 and published in English in 1966. Described by some observers as the most influential African poem of the 1960s, not only in Uganda but throughout Africa, *Song of Lawino* is comprised of a series of complaints by Lawino, an Acoli wife whose husband Ocol has rejected her for a younger, more Westernized woman. *Song of Ocol* (1970) is the sophisticated, self-serving response of the unrepentant Ocol, who has embraced the new culture as fervently as he has his new spouse. Ocol sees nothing worth preserving in the old ways and has few reservations in saying so. The future, he asserts, is with Western culture and the technology that makes it dominant. Commentary on the *Song of Ocol*, decidedly less enthusiastic than critical opinion on its predecessor, points out that the poem is dated, since by 1970 the sorts of political and cultural positions espoused by Ocol were no longer tenable for an African politician. However, the two make a fascinating and revealing pair of contrasting philosophies.

Another set of paired poems, *Two Songs*, was published in 1971: 'Song of Prisoner' and 'Song of Malaya', are dedicated to the memory of Patrice Lumumba, the prime minister of Congo who was murdered in 1961. The hypocrisy with which the politically and economically powerful exploit and condemn the prisoner and prostitute is revealed in these intense 'songs'. The poems, in the voices of a murderer and a street prostitute respectively, reassert Okot's position as a leading poet of his time and an uncompromising social critic. *Africa's Cultural Revolution* (1973) and *Artist, the Ruler: Essays on Art, Culture and Values* (1986) are collections of essays, *Horn of My Love* (1974) a collection of oral verse translated from Acoli, *Hare and Hornbill* (1978) a collection of folktales, and *Acholi Proverbs* (1985) a collection of sayings. He also produced two scholarly works: *African Religions in Western Scholarship* (1971) and *Religion of the Central Luo* (1971).

With his interest and training in African *oral traditions, it is not surprising to find that Okot hoped to redefine literature in order to reposition traditional expression at the centre of poetic and narrative expression. He was concerned that written literature was too elitist and saw oral performance as the authentic expressive mode. His own perspective derived from the cultural expressions of his Acoli society, particularly its response to modern, western intrusions. It is fair to say that he influenced a generation of poets and novelists throughout Africa and that he awakened western readers to the power and intensity of African poetic expression.

OKOYE, Ifeoma, who does not give her date of birth, is the most important Nigerian female novelist after Flora *Nwapa and Buchi *Emecheta, the pioneer writers who are her predecessors. She was born in Anambra State in the former Eastern Nigeria and was educated at the University of Nigeria, Nsukka (1974-7), where she read English, and at Aston University in the UK (1986-7), where she gained a post-graduate degree in English. She teaches English at Nnamdi Azikiwe University, Nigeria.

Okoye has written three major novels, *Behind the Clouds* (1982), *Men without Ears* (1984), and *Chimere* (1992), and a number of children's books. *Behind the Clouds* questions from a feminist perspective the certainty in African culture that women are to blame for childlessness, a myth to which Flora Nwapa subscribes in *Efuru* (1966) and *Idu* (1970). *Men without Ears* depicts the human greed of the Nigerian oil boom of the 1980s through the story of Uloko Adaba, who lives above his means and supports his expensive habits by borrowing and stealing. In *Chimere*, a detective novel, a young woman who is mocked by fellow students for being fatherless sets out in search of her father against the will of her mother. Okoye is the best prose stylist among Nigerian female writers: her language has a delicacy, vigour, and confidence and her style a precision and clarity that make them classical. Her stories are compelling, their conflicts convincingly resolved.

Men without Ears was declared the best fiction of the year in 1984 by the Association of Nigerian Authors.

OKPEWHO, Isidore (1941-), novelist and critic. Born in Abraka, Nigeria, Okpewho was educated at St. Patrick's College, Asaba, University of Ibadan, and University of Denver. Besides editing a poetry anthology, *The Heritage of African Poetry: An Anthology of Oral and Written Poetry* (1985), Okpewho has published three novels: *The Victims* (1970), *The Last Duty* (1976), and *Tides* (1993); three scholarly studies: *The Epic in Africa* (1979), *Myth in Africa* (1983), and *African Oral Literature* (1992); and a large body of criticism.

Rejecting what he sees as an inartistic straining after anthropological exactitude in conventional African fiction, Okpewho concentrates instead on interactions between individual personalities and social forces in modern Africa's tragedy. *The Victims* takes the traditional literary archetype of a wife plotting against her rival and transforms it into a tragedy of individual failures occasioned by cultural resistance to change. Despite the onset of modernization, the Ozala people cling to beliefs rooted in their vanishing agrarian culture, attributing personal misfortunes to enemies' malevolence and stigmatizing infertility in a woman as a cosmic threat. Having borne only one child in thirteen years of marriage to the drink-besotted Obanua, Nwabunor blames her misfortune on Obanua's more fortunate second wife, Ogugua, and thus renders herself easy prey to unscrupulous medicine men. The catastrophic denouement effectively integrates a moral tale into Okpewho's social criticism, as Nwabunor's poisoning of Ogugua's children also destroys her own child and brings ruin upon herself and her contemptible husband. *The Last Duty* is an allegory of the atavistic ethnic nationalisms and dysfunctional leadership that prevent the creation of viable nation states from unwieldy multi-ethnic federations created by European colonialists to serve their interests. The events take place during the *Nigeria-Biafra civil war (fictionalized as the Igabo-Simbi war) in an Igabo village where the presence of a Simbi woman married to an Igabo man unleashes a maelstrom of intrigues motivated by base opportunism and ethnic hatred. It is here that Major Idris valiantly but unsuccessfully undertakes his 'last duty': to administer justice and repel Simbi attacks. *Tides* addresses the problem of environmental pollution in the oil-producing areas of Nigeria. Ebika Harrison, a member of the otherwise peaceful Committee of Concerned Citizens, resorts to acts of violence in order to force the government to act on behalf of communities whose livelihood is threatened by the devastating effects of a big dam.

Though he offers no ideological formula for social reconstruction, Okpewho has contributed to the development of modern African literature with his combination of an accomplished prose style and a sensitive probing of the forces that undermine post-colonial Africa's quest for nationhood.

OKRI, Ben (1959-), Nigerian poet, novelist, and short-story writer. Born in Minna, Nigeria, Okri studied at Children's Home School, Sapele, Christ School, Ibadan, Urhobo College, Warri, and University of Essex, UK. Apart from writing, Okri has been poetry editor for *West Africa*, broadcaster for the BBC, and Visiting Fellow Commoner in Creative Arts, Trinity College, Cambridge. His novels include *Flowers and Shadows* (1980), *The Landscapes Within* (1981), *The *Famished Road* (1991), which won the 1991 Booker Prize, *Songs of Enchantment* (1993), and *Dangerous Love* (1996), a re-working of *The Landscapes Within*. His collections of short stories are *Incidents at the Shrine* (1986) and *Stars of the New Curfew* (1988), and his poetry collection is *An African Elegy* (1992). His essays have been published as *Birds of Heaven* (1996) and A *Way of Being Free* (1997). He is the first African since Nadine Gordimer to win the highly influential Booker Prize. He has also won a Commonwealth Writers Prize and the *Paris Review* Aga Khan Prize for fiction.

Okri, one of the most important new voices in contemporary African literature in English, is very conscious of the post-independence realities of African societies; hence his works are often satirical and critical of the various political and economic crises that have plagued African countries since the end of the colonial period. His first novel, *Flowers and Shadows*, examines the issue of corruption and its devastating effects on a family and a society. The short story 'Laughter Beneath the Bridge', in *Incidents at the Shrine*, focuses on the disastrous consequences of the *Nigeria-Biafra war of 1967-70 on ordinary people. The soldiers' brutality shows that they are victims as much as the people they violate and exploit.

Okri translates his remarkable knowledge of African cultures into a rich array of images and symbols. His interest in the relationship between the natural and supernatural worlds leads to a negotiation between the two paradigms that characterizes his approach to the discussion of human existence. For example, the image of the *abiku*, the spirit child of Yoruba myth who dies soon after birth only to be reborn again and again, recurs in Okri's work, particularly in *The Famished Road* and *An African Elegy*. Although the *abiku* image has been used by Wole *Soyinka and J.P. Clark *Bekederemo, Okri subverts its ordinary connotations to posit contemporary meanings and an extension of its semantic implications. In *The Famished Road*, Azaro is the *abiku* child who, continually aware of spirit companions demanding his return to the spirit world, shifts among worlds of the living, the dead, and the unborn, a trinity that is unique in the African world view. In 'Political Abiku', in *An African Elegy*, the *abiku* image represents Nigeria's attempts to fashion a sustainable political tradition: from the time of independence in 1960, Nigerian governments have died in their early stages, to be reborn in other guises time after time.

Okri's English is simple, lucid, and image-laden, ensuring easy communication. *The Famished Road* especially is generally poetic, incantatory, and descriptive, evoking the book of John in the New Testament in the first paragraphs. Nigerian English – words and expressions that communicate a unique Nigerian world-view such as 'peppersoup', 'ogogoro', and 'bukka' for example – help situate the text closely within the culture that produces it. Though rendered in their original Nigerian languages because of the lack of one-to-one equivalents in English, these loan words are understandable contextually.

OLAFIOYE, Tayo Peter (1948-), Nigerian poet and novelist, was born in Igbotako and educated at the University of Lagos in Nigeria and later at universities in the USA, where he gained a Ph.D. He has taught at the University of Ilorin in Nigeria and at universities in California. He has won prizes for his poetry in the US and in Europe.

The combination in Olafioye's poetry and fiction of rural imagery and cosmopolitan themes reflects life in the riverine area of Ondo State and in Nigerian and American cities, a duality that graphically represents the universal and the human. His poetry and fiction incorporate myth, symbols, festival rites, and African gods, as well as proverbs and idioms, to express his despair over Africa's current condition. The poems of *Sorrows of a Town Crier* (1988) tell in elegiac tones of the abuse of power in Africa, continental disillusionment, and the devaluation of human values. In *Bush Girl Comes to Town* (1988), the characters forget their African background as they embrace the pleasures of life in California, a life that leaves them undefined and unfulfilled. His other publications include *The Excellence of Silence*, a book of poems; *The Saga of Sego* (1982), a novel; and two books of literary criticism: *Response to Creativity* (1988) and *Critic as Terrorist: Views on New African Writings* (1989).

Old Man and the Medal, The (1969) A novel by Ferdinand *Oyono, translated from the French (*Le Vieux nègre et la médaille*, 1956). Published the same year as *Houseboy*, this novel differs from it in two major respects. First, it is not specifically anti-colonial; rather it resembles a novel of manners criticizing the folly of an old man, and by extension his society, to whom the appearance of power, symbolized here by the medal, is more important than real authority. Second, its humour gives it a light tone rarely seen today in writing in French from Africa. However, like Toundi in *Houseboy*, Meka undergoes a painful initiation. During the award ceremony, the heat of the sun, his narrow shoes, and the need to relieve himself test his endurance to the limit. At the end he can appreciate the foolishness of his behaviour and laugh at himself, in that way regaining his dignity.

OLUDHE MACGOYE, Marjorie [See WAR LITERATURE, East Africa]

OMOTOSO, Kole (1943-), Nigerian novelist, playwright, and critic, was born in Akure, Nigeria and studied in Ibadan and in Edinburgh, where he gained a Ph.D. He has been actively involved in African writers' organizations, has taught at universities in Nigeria, and is professor of African languages and literatures at the University of the Western Cape, South Africa. His substantial body of work includes several novels, a number of plays, and books and articles on political and social issues.

Together with Femi *Osofisan, Biodun Jeyifo, and Niyi *Osundare, Omotoso belongs to a group of writers who have been critical of the first-generation African writers: Wole *Soyinka, Chinua *Achebe, Christopher *Okigbo, and others. While paying the elders their due respect, they claim that African literature should be about contemporary social reality in Africa and that rather than trying to explain Africa to Europeans it should explain Africa to Africans. Omotoso has experimented widely with literary styles and techniques to achieve his aim of reaching ordinary African people. He has written in the form of the allegory (his novel *The Combat*, 1972) and the detective novel (the first ever in Nigerian literature, *Fella's Choice*, 1974) and combines fact and fiction in *Just before Dawn* (1988) and in his autobiographical novel *Memories of Our Recent Boom* (1990). His two plays, *The Curse* (1976) and *Shadows in the Horizon* (1977), reflect a radical vision of equality. *The Curse* critiques the perpetuation of corruption from one military coup to the next; in *Shadows in the Horizon* the conflagration that ends the play is the instrument for the redistribution of the wealth and property accumulated by the rich. Most remarkable is his work in journalism: his column in *West Africa* during the 1980s was a respected literary forum. He has also written a critical study, *Achebe or Soyinka? A Study in Contrasts* (1996), and a book of commentary on Africa's crises, *Season of Migration to the South* (1994).

One Man One Wife (1959) A novel by Timothy *Aluko. A humorous attack on the 'civilization' that missionaries brought into Africa in the late nineteenth century, the novel reveals, especially in the figures of Pastor David and Royasin as co-believers, the unhealthy influence of the new faith on rural farmers in Western Nigeria, whose traditions, including polygamy and heathenism, clash with militant Christianity. The satiric humour in Aluko's narrative negatively

affects characterization, structure, and language as defined by his compatriot Chinua *Achebe, but Aluko endeavours to expose the hypocrisy that troubles his newly urbanized society.

ONITSHA POPULAR MARKET LITERATURE In the years after the end of the Second World War, the town of Onitsha on the eastern bank of the Niger ferry-crossing became the centre of what Dr E. N. Obiechina describes as 'a spate of popular pamphleteering' akin in many ways to chapbook publishing in eighteenth-century England. Onitsha attracted people from all over Nigeria, rich and poor, as a haven for adventurous traders, entrepreneurs of all kinds in the rapidly-expanding market, young rebels, social and political, an increasing number of literate school-leavers from the villages drifting to the towns as well as thieves, swindlers, pimps, prostitutes and beggars. The town also contained several distinguished secondary schools, a new Anglican cathedral and intense commercial, industrial and technological activity.

Out of this dynamic mixture of diverse talent, young and old, devout and decadent, emerged *popular pamphlets such as *Veronica Makes Up Her Own Mind*, *Man Works Hard for Money*, *The Game of Love*, *Mabel and the Sweet Honey that Flowed Away*, *Election Rigging*, *Money-Monger Girls*, *Escape*, *Arrest and Martyrdom of Lumumba*, *Sayings of the Wise*, *Vagabond versus Princess* and hundreds of others. This was all made possible through the enterprising cheap purchase of WW2-surplus printing presses from the government and the army. A full bibliography is given in E.N. Obiechina's *Onitsha Market Literature* (African Writers Series No. 109) and an extended discussion of this literary, cultural and social phenomenon in his *Literature for the Masses* (1971).

Only Son, The (1966) A novel by John *Munonye. With *Obi* (1969) and *Bridge to a Wedding* (1978), *The Only Son* forms a trilogy. The hero of *The Only Son*, Nnanna, becomes Joe in *Obi* and Mr. Kafo in *Bridge to a Wedding*. The thematic preoccupation is the family and the Igbo concept of *ahamefule* [may my ancestral identity be preserved], which is fulfilled in children and a family house. In *The Only Son*, a fatherless Nnanna [father's father] is painstakingly brought up by his widowed mother, Chiaku, to be a model young man and the incarnation of his father. His conversion to Christianity towards the end of the novel appears threatening to Chiaku, who sees that Christian ethics are insensitive to indigenous cultural institutions. Joe's refusal in *Obi* (*obi* is the architectural symbol of *ahamefule*) to marry another wife when the first is apparently barren confirms Chiaku's fears. At the end of the novel, Joe is exiled from the family house he has been erecting in his father's compound in their ancestral home of Umudiobia, and the search for an *obi* therefore remains unsuccessful. But *Bridge to a Wedding* resolves the network of conflicts generated by this search. In this novel, the prosperous, city-dwelling Mr. and Mrs. Kafo have six children, and the wedding of one of their daughters becomes an opportunity for Mr. Kafo to reconcile with his ancestral village and complete the family house begun in *Obi*.

ONWUEME, Tess Akaeke (1955-), Nigerian playwright, was born in Ogwashi-Ukwu, Delta State, Nigeria. She holds degrees in literature and drama and is a university teacher. She won the 1986 Association of Nigerian Authors Award in drama and the 1988 Distinguished Author Award from Obafemi Awolowo University, her alma mater. Her published plays include *A Hen Too Soon* (1983), *The Broken Calabash* (1984), *A Scent of Onions* (1985), *The Desert Encroaches* (1985), *Ban Empty Barn and Other Plays* (1986), *Mirror for Campus* (1987), *The ★Reign of Wazobia* (1988), *Legacies* (1989), *Parable for a Season* (1991), *Riot in Heaven* (1991), and *Go Tell It to the Women* (1992). Although her plays explore a wide range of themes such as poverty, elitism, corruption, hypocrisy, and cultural conflict, the unfulfilled potential of women in a patriarchal culture is the strand that runs through them all; *The Reign of Wazobia* is perhaps her most pointedly feminist challenge to that culture. Onwueme's plays often draw on Igbo mythology, operatic structures, folklore, and Brechtian techniques to argue that the positive aspects of women's role in society were seriously eroded by the influences of cross-cultural patriarchal legacies characteristic of modern society. Her most important plays, particularly the very polemical *Go Tell It to the Women*, argue that a universal feminist awareness must acknowledge and accommodate African gender sensibilities, values, and needs. *The Broken Calabash*, *Parables for a Season*, and *The Reign of Wazobia* have been collected in *Three Plays* (1993).

ONYEAMA, Dillibe (1951-), autobiographer, biographer, and novelist, was born in Enugu, Nigeria but educated mainly in England, where he lived between 1959 and 1981. His first book, *Nigger at Eton* (1972), deals with his experiences as a black student at the famous public school. His *The Return: Homecoming of a Negro from Eton* (1978) and *Notes of So-called Afro-Saxon* (1988), sequels to the first book, focus on the problems that he encountered as he tried to adjust to Nigeria. In *Chief Onyeama: The Story of an African God* (1982) he writes of the life and times of his late grandfather, a man who was reputed to be one of the most feared traditional rulers of his time. A foray into the supernatural produced *Juju* (1976) and *Godfathers of Voodoo* (1985), a book described by a commentator as 'a supernatural thriller of love and African magic'. His other books include *John Bull's Nigger* (1974), *The Book of Black*

Man's Humour (1975), *Sex Is a Nigger's Game* (1976), *Secret Society* (1978), *Revenge of the Medicine Man* (1980), and the biographies *Modern Messiah: The Jim Nwobodo Story* (1983) and *African Legend: The Incredible Story of Francis Arthur Nzeribe* (1984).

ORAL TRADITION AND FOLKLORE

East Africa: Understood from two perspectives, literary and anthropological, folklore in East Africa flourishes mainly as oral literature text books with a bias towards school syllabi and as an authentic record of the ways of the forebears. The centrality of folk culture has made it a source for modern East African creative writers such as Okoiti Omtatah, whose *Lwanda Magere* (1991) is a play fashioned after the Luo legend about the hero by the same name, and ★Okot p'Bitek, whose two long poems, ★*Song of Lawino* (1960) and *Song of Ocol* (1972), are cast in the oral literary tradition of the Acoli people.

The collection and study of East African folklore began at the turn of the twentieth century with European explorers, missionaries, travellers, and administrators. They were guided partly by their perception of prehistoric people as an object of fancy and partly by the search for what they saw as the raw material that would help them understand African culture, a knowledge that would in turn enhance the subjugation of the continent. Writers in this period were influenced by Bishop E. Steer, who put together *Stories from Zanzibar* (1910), and A.C. Hollis's two books, *The Maasai: Their Language and Folklore* (1905) and *The Nandi: Their Language and Folklore* (1909). Closely resembling these works is M.W. Beech's *The Suk: Their Language and Folklore* (1911). Read together with C. Cagnolo's *The Agikuyu: Their Customs, Traditions and Folklore* (1933), these collections are essentially amateurish. K. G. Lindblom's *Akamba Folklore* (1940) is somewhat more refined.

With the advent of colonialism, Africans created and employed folklore as a reaction to the new oppressive reality. Jomo Kenyatta's anthropological treatise *Facing Mount Kenya* (1938) is the classic representation. Maina wa Kinyatti's *Thunder from the Mountain: Mau Mau Patriotic Songs* (1980) is a more recent example of the anti-colonial resistance spirit.

In the 1960s the Oxford Library of African Literature, edited by E.E. Evans-Pritchard, G. Lienhardt and W. H. Whiteley, provided an avenue for the scholarly study of folklore, and in the 1970s Frantz Boas's widely accepted view that a people's folklore is a repository of their culture and history led to the introduction of oral literature into school and university syllabi. This more scientific approach resulted in the proliferation of folklore texts in the region. In Uganda, among the Ankole, H.F. Morris collected and edited *Bahima Praise Poetry* (1964), which was followed by J.S. Mbiti's *Akamba Stories* (1966). In *Horn of My Love*

(1974), Okot p'Bitek records in both English and Acoli the oral poetry of the Acoli of northern Uganda, capturing the Acoli moral values manifest in love songs, satirical verses, and funeral dirges and discussing dance as well as occasions on which it is performed. The Luo legacy has been recorded by Onyango Ogutu and Adrian Roscoe in Keep My Words: Luo Oral Literature (1974), which, while documenting African oral literature, manages to leave intact the essence of the tales. A scholarly introduction provides concise and useful information on Luo culture and customs as a background against which the folklore material is to be understood.

Of all the folklore genres, folktales have been most widely documented. Rose Kimani Gecau's The Gikuyu Folk Tales (1970) was followed by H.M. Kabulya's collection Tales of Bwamba (1976) from the Bwamba people of western Uganda. Okot p'Bitek published Hare and Hornbill (1978), while his contemporary *Taban lo Liyong wrote Eating Chiefs (1974). From the stories of the Wairaqw, who live in the Arusha region of Tanzania, W.D. Kamera has published Tales of Wairaqw of Tanzania (1976). Most of the characters in these collections are ordinary human beings, and in one story, entitled 'Honey Gatherers', a little boy manages to outwit a superhuman being with the aid of a dog, demonstrating humanity's power to determine its own destiny.

Naomi Kipury's collection Oral Literature of the Maasai (1983) and C. Chesaina's compilation Kalenjin Oral Literature (1991) are both useful as texts for scholarly analysis but also include edited data that at times defy the ethics of collection. Kavetsa Adagala and Wanjiku Kabira's Kenyan Oral Narratives: A Selection (1981) moves away from the work of Kipury and Chesaina: whereas the first two books attempt to cover all genres of oral literature, the third restricts itself to folktale, although it attempts to include most Kenyan ethnic communities.

Wanjiku Kabira's The Oral Artist (1983) is a departure from the mere recording of the artifacts of a whole community, entering the realm of individual artistry. Kabira criticizes scholarship that lumps all oral artists together as if they were creations of the same society. In a study of one oral artist with whose individual creativity she felt a strong connection, she attempts to identify the features that make Kabebe an accomplished oral artist by focusing on his narrative style. In Oral Literature: A School Certificate Course (1982) S.K. Akivaga and Bole Odaga seek to introduce oral literature as an everyday living experience. Adapted for the classroom, the book prepares students for the crucial methods of collecting oral material.

East African folklore also flourishes in folk music. The burgeoning music and dance culture in the region has been glaringly neglected by scholars. Paul Kavyu's An Introduction to Kamba Music (1977) attempts to fill this gap by examining the dance, circumcision songs, instrumental melody, and the rhythm of his own native Kamba people.

South Africa: A. C. *Jordan's Tales from Southern Africa (1973) is the clearest evidence of the strong interest in folklore and legend demonstrated in his own The Wrath of the Ancestors (1980) and in the work of many pioneering black South African writers like Sol T. *Plaatje, who used the oral tradition and referred to numerous African legends in an attempt to preserve what he felt was a dying culture. Legends and myths are carefully interposed in his texts and are often set against European equivalents. Legendary African heroes feature in much of the writing of H.I.E. *Dhlomo, his brother R.R.R. *Dhlomo, and Thomas *Mofolo. Mofolo's Sotho novel *Chaka (1925; trans. 1931) is a tour de force in the use of South African legends, weaving traditional material with the story of Shaka's life. Among white writers, South African novelist Jack *Cope collected various tales about the Tokoloshe, or Trickster Boy, and has used this metaphor successfully in some of his fiction. Penny Miller's Myths and Legends of Southern Africa (1979) provides a comprehensive overview of the legends of Southern Africa.

There is some irony in the assiduous use of traditional African legends in *Afrikaans writing. Many of the legends imbedded in the Afrikaans language itself are drawn from the oral traditions of Malay slaves. Afrikaans and Malay legends are full of humour and lend themselves more to the oral than to the written tradition. Monsters, Heroes and Sultan's Daughters (1989) and Pieter W. Brobbelaar's Famous South African Folk Tales (1985) are examples of these legends. The work of Wilma Stockenström is firmly rooted in African prehistory, while both André *Brink and Antjie Krog exploit the African continent as part of their search for identity in Africa.

In addition to folkloric oral prose narratives, oral poetry has been an important feature of South African society since the development of the first human communities in the subcontinent, from the lyric songs of the Khoikhoi and *Bushmen, expressing complex mythological and social understandings, to the praise poems (izibongo, lithoko) of African societies, which serve to negotiate relations of power between ruler and ruled. In addition to the public forms of the panegyric to the chief, other forms of oral poetry flourished within African society: songs to the clan or family, love lyrics, children's verse, work songs, lullabies, personal praises, religious songs, songs to animals, and songs of divination. The influence of missionaries on the tradition of oral poetry gave rise to forms influenced by the harmonies and poetics of the Christian hymn. In approximately 1815 the Xhosa convert Ntsikana, for example, composed his 'Great Hymn' in the style of praise poetry, and the Zulu evangelist Isaiah Shembe was to achieve enormous influence in Natal in the early part of the twentieth century by hybridizing Zulu oral poetry with the textual Christian tradition in order to articulate religious and political resistance to colonization. With the processes of urbanization following rapidly on colonial occupation, oral forms were adapted to industrialized, politicized contexts. Migrant workers in mine compounds have used forms of praise poetry for most of this century to praise or criticize those in authority over them. ★Sotho miners have developed a new genre of oral poetry called *sefela* that aesthetically encodes their experiences as migrant workers, while Sotho women perform poetic narratives (*seoeleoele*) through song and dance in shebeens and bars. Within the former ethnically devised 'Bantustans', particularly the Transkei, praise poets played an important role in orchestrating resistance to corrupt and despotic rulers. A number of poets had also adapted oral forms to the printed page, among them S.E.K Mqhayi, H.I.E. Dhlomo, Mazisi ★Kunene, B.W. ★Vilakazi, and A.C. Jordan. During the political upheaval of the 1970s, such Soweto poets as Ingoapele Madingoane experimented with oral performance as a means of disseminating poems that avoided the gatekeeping of white-controlled literary magazines. Oral poetry has also been linked to trade union activity for many years in South Africa, with reports of praise poets performing at worker gatherings from as early as the 1930s. During the 1980s, poets such as Alfred ★Qabula, Mi S'dumo Hlatshwayo, and Nise Malange used the form of *izibongo* in mobilizing support for the union movement, while Mzwakhe ★Mbuli achieved enormous acclaim for his poetry performances at mass meetings and political funerals. A number of white poets have also experimented with oral performance, particularly Christopher Mann, Jeremy Cronin and Peter Horn. British and American music has recently influenced oral poetry, with poets like Lesego ★Rampolokeng and Sandile Dikeni using rap and dub rhythms in delivering their poems. Praise poets performed at the inauguration of Nelson Mandela as state president and at the opening of South Africa's first democratic parliament.

Despite an abundance and diversity of oral forms, many of which still live in the daily experiences of South African people, there has been a profound lack of critical debate about oral poetry in South African literary studies. Some research has been conducted on oral literature in African languages (see for example the work of H.I.E. Dhlomo, B.W. Vilakazi, Mazisi Kunene, David Rycroft and others), and several important collections of oral poems have appeared, but the oral tradition has largely been written out of literary history. It is only now being recovered, both through the work of sociologists and anthropologists, and through a revisionist awareness of the processes of exclusion, occlusion, and effacement in the construction of South African cultural history.

The study of oral poetry in South Africa has received impetus recently from the far-reaching political changes in the country, which have emphasized the need for the creation of inclusive cultural histories, the broadening of the scope and methodology of literary studies to include 'popular', non-canonical forms, and developments in oral theory and critical practice. Areas which have received particular attention recently include orality and history, oral forms and conceptions of gender, oral poetry and political power, and the adaptation of performance genres to contexts of modernity.

West Africa: As in other parts of Africa, folklore in West Africa comprises a variety of texts, some in verse and some in prose, some quite massive (the ★Yoruba Ifa corpus), and some extremely brief (the deep sigh which the Yoruba pose as a riddle, and whose solution is a private insight). Some scholars now prefer the term 'oral literature' or '★orature' to 'folklore' as a means of calling attention to the creative dimension of folkloric texts. The practice is also a reminder that, like 'literature', 'folklore' encompasses religious, medical, educational, diversionary, and other subjects. Representative genres include myth and folktale in prose and divination texts, epic, praise or panegyric, proverbs, and riddles in verse.

Myths record the founding charters and accounts of the primordial activities of a society's gods. They also contain information about the people's beliefs regarding the nature and purpose of human existence and the principles underlying relationships among humans, the divinities, and other creatures. Usually the preserve of priests and initiates of the cults to which they are attached, myths are performed typically on cultic occasions. They are in prose, and without a fixed form. Undoubtedly the most elaborate and best developed example is the Dogon cosmology that Marcel Griaule recorded from his conversations with the sage Ogotemmeli and published as *Dieu d'Eau: entretiens avec Ogotemmeli* (1948; *Conversations with Ogotemmeli: An Introduction to Dogon Religious Ideas*, 1965).

Folktales serve as family or communal entertainment during hours of leisure, typically after the day's last meal and before retirement for the night. The featured characters may be all human, all animal, or a mixture of both. Whatever the case, they are anthropomorphic and use human languages, so that when a tale includes both humans and animals communication among them poses no difficulty. These characters are types, since the emphasis in the tales is on their responses to certain circumstances and the lessons to be learned about the appropriateness of a particular response in a particular circumstance. Because each tale thus purveys a moral, some scholars have suggested that they are equivalent in traditional societies to formal schooling in modern ones. They are, however, unquestionably intended for entertainment and the display of creativity. This latter function is especially significant in Mende *domeisia* performances, where rivals vie to concoct the most elaborate twists for well-known story plots.

Important subgenres of the folktale are the trickster and dilemma tales. The trickster is usually an animal with a very highly developed imagination and underdeveloped scruples. The animal differs from one society to another; in Ghana, Ivory Coast, and Sierra Leone he is the spider, known as Ananse among the Akan of Ghana, while in Benin, Nigeria, and Cameroon he is the tortoise, the Yoruba japa and the Kalabari Ikaki, for example. Usually male, he is ever seeking advantages for himself over larger and more powerful animals, or busy extricating himself from scrapes his ill-considered antics get him into. Other characteristic traits are greed, laziness, selfishness, and nosiness, although occasionally he does employ his wiles to benefit others. Dilemma tales are open-ended tales that pose a problem for which different, equally plausible solutions are available. Their point, undoubtedly, is to demonstrate that life offers few clear-cut choices. They also provide opportunities for people to hone their skills of argumentation in proving the preferability of their chosen solution.

Texts that require some degree of stability in their preservation or exactness in their performance tend to be couched in verse form. An example is the divinatory text, the most remarkable in West Africa being Ifa, which, although most closely associated with the Yoruba, is also found among the Ewe and the Fon to the west and the Edo to the east. The Yoruba corpus comprises 256 major chapters each containing 600 verses. Each verse is a case history that records a supplicant's particular problem in the distant past, the prescription received as a solution for the problem, and the outcome of the supplicant's observing or ignoring the prescription. The diviner matches each new supplicant with an appropriate Ifa verse, which he recites from memory, and offers the indicated prescription with the assumption that the outcome in this instance will be as in the original consultation.

Closely related to Ifa is Erindinlogun. It is simpler than the former and exclusive to the Yoruba; it is also the version that is more popular among the descendants of the Yoruba in the Americas, mainly in Cuba. Since Ifa's knowledge is comprehensive, encompassing even the first things and the secrets of the gods, its corpus is a valuable source for scholars interested in a deep knowledge of the people's cosmology.

Following Ruth Finnegan's assertion in *Oral Literature in Africa* (1970) that the epic, as it exists in Europe, is absent from Africa, some scholars have published evidence that shows that in fact extensive heroic narratives in verse do exist in Africa, and certainly in West Africa. One such scholar is Isidore *Okpewho, who has amply demonstrated in *The Epic in Africa* (1979) that these narratives do share significant features with the epics of Europe, although they do not exactly replicate all the characteristic features. The argument arises because of the adoption of the term 'epic' for the African texts, with the inevitable suggestion of essential correspondence. The best-known West African texts in this genre are those in praise of Sun-Jata (Sundiata), the legendary king of Mali; *Kambili*, in praise of a Malian hunter hero, and *Ozidi*, belonging to the Ijo of the Niger Delta area.

Praises or panegyrics are elaborate poems that catalogue the noteworthy qualities or accomplishments of their subject, which may be a person, his or her lineage, a god, a natural phenomenon, an animal, a plant, or a disease. Contrary to the implication of their designation, praises or panegyrics, which are usually associated with the courts of kings or the households of famous members of the community, may focus on actions or qualities that are awesome rather than praiseworthy. They are typically composed by professional praise singers who commit them to memory and perform them on appropriate, usually public, occasions. These professionals may attach themselves permanently to the court of a king or the household of an illustrious patron. They are also sometimes itinerant mendicants who seek out appropriate occasions for their services and subsist on the largese of the subjects. Among the Bambara, the Malinke, and the Wolof of the Western Sudan the *griot* is one such professional.

The *ijala* of the Yoruba is a specialized type of panegyric that belongs to the hunting profession. It originated as a celebration of Ogun, the god of metals and patron of hunters, but there are *ijala* verses in praise of famous hunters, assorted animals, and even plants. The Hausa praises in honour of their medium spirits belong in this classification, as does the Yoruba bride's song the new bride sings on the occasion of her removal to her groom's home. Funeral dirges such as those of the Akan would also fit in this category.

Proverbs are brief sayings that, although they occur as part of regular, everyday discourse as well as within other longer genres (both verse and prose), belong among verse forms principally by virtue of their pithiness and symmetrical structure. Basically, they are sagacious deductions from observations of life, couched in refreshing imagery and language. In folk transactions they might function as authority to bolster a point or view, or as justification for a recommended course of action, or as a discreet corrective to errant behaviour. In some societies adeptness in their use is indispensable for effectiveness in conversation.

Riddles are a test of people's capacity for recognizing common qualities between different objects and situations. The underlying analogical feature makes them comparable to proverbs, and indeed some proverbs can be rephrased as riddles and vice versa. Audiences for a storytelling session often pose and solve riddles before the storytelling begins, a custom that suggests that the activity is a device for sharpening the perception of the group.

ORATURE An interest in their oral heritage is abundantly evident in the works of modern and contemporary African writers throughout the continent and testifies to the power and aesthetic pleasure to be found in traditional African orature. These writers' combination of traditional inculturation and colonial, Western education, and their incorporation of aspects of their oral traditions into their writing is significant evidence of orature's vitality. The burgeoning scholarly interest in both traditional and modern-day, urban forms – ★Yoruba folk theatre, South African township ★drama, or the music of popular groups like Sunny Ade in Nigeria or Manu Dibango in Cameroon – is another example.

According to European classification systems, African orature, similar to many others, consists of panegyric, elegiac, lyric, epic, ¬ligious, children's, political, and 'special purpose' ★poetry, songs, and chants; mythic, legendary, and historical prose narratives; and drama, oratory, riddles, puns, and proverbs. Clearly such tidy categories, while convenient for scholarly analysis, convey very little of the pleasure, power, or purpose of this art either in Africa or elsewhere. Contemporary African scholars have revolutionized the study of African orature through transcriptions, translations, and analyses of traditional art; as insiders, they are acquainted with the occasions of such performances and keenly sensitive to the intricacies of African languages.

One prominent area of current academic interest in African orature is the public/private nature of its composition and performance. In the past, scholars posited the communal composition of hunting chants, such as the Yoruba *ijala*, for instance, or even children's animal tales; current work, however, reveals the formal and informal training of individual artists, however communal the performance of this material. The formal aspects of the genres are also being studied with the understanding that their purpose is to affect performance and audience interaction. For instance, stylistic qualities of orature such as repetition, vocables, formulas, semantic and structural parallelism, coupling or linking images, tonal counterpoint, ideophones, digression, and imagery are now examined as elements that create certain moods, aid in movement transitions, and attempt to evoke particular audience responses and active participation during performances, not primarily as methods to convey ideas, as they might be employed in literary texts. Repetition,

in particular, in its varied artistic forms, is valued for the atmosphere it creates during the acting out of a secular narrative or religious chant and its symbiosis with dance and music.

Writers as diverse as Uganda's ★Okot p'Bitek, Ghana's Ama Ata ★Aidoo, Kenya's ★Ngugi wa Thiong'o, and Nigeria's Wole ★Soyinka incorporate in their texts the diverse forms of their orature, with its grounding in performance and the sound of language, spoken, chanted, or sung. As importantly, these writers and many others are attempting to recapture the multiple social purposes of orature and to re-create the important aesthetic, political, religious, and psychological links it forces between artists and their communities and African communities and their histories.

Ordeal in the Forest (1968) A novel by Godwin ★Wachira. In a narrative about the resistance of the Kikuyu people of Kenya against colonialism, this historical novel exposes the multifarious ills of foreign domination, tracing the mounting discontent of the oppressed, the growth of anti-colonial consciousness, and the organization and carrying out of the military and political struggle for liberation. Wachira handles this theme, which lends itself easily to heroic interpretation, with objectivity, revealing the complexity of a collective endeavour in which nobility co-exists with pettiness, selflessness with egotism, and courage with frailty to make immediate victory difficult and to plant the seeds of future social disillusionment.

OSADEBAY, Dennis (Chukude) (1911-95), Nigerian poet, was born in Asaba and was a journalist, a jurist, and a politician generally credited as one of the founders of the National Council of Nigeria and the Cameroon (NCNC) party. He had his early education at the Hope Waddell Institute in Calabar before he travelled to England to study law. As a nationalist of the First Republic of Nigeria whose contemporaries included Nnamdi Azikiwe, Abubakar Tafawa Balewa, Obafemi Awolowo, Ahmadu Bello, Samuel Ladoke Akintola, and Anthony Enahoro, he along with these leaders inspired the London Constitutional Conference that led to Nigeria's independence in 1960. He held several important positions in his country: for instance, he was president of the senate during the First Republic; he also served as the first premier of the defunct Mid-West Region of Nigeria.

As a poet Osadebay is generally grouped, along with Gladys ★Casely-Hayford, Raphael E.G. ★Armattoe, and Michael ★Dei-Anang, among the 'pioneer poets' of West Africa who, while generally extolling African traditional values, vigorously assail European colonialism. *Africa Sings* (1952), published while he was in England, explores three major themes: the celebration of indigenous African cultural values and black pride (as in 'Rise of Africa'); the ironic glorification of Great Britain as a colonizing power (as in 'Africa Speaks to England'); and the celebration of nature (as in 'Ode to the Palm Tree'). The poems show his knack for translation (some of his verse was translated from his native Igbo to English), and his diction is characterized by Pidgin and dialect. *Africa Sings* was reissued with later verse in *Poems of a Nationalist*.

OSAHON, Naiwu (1937-), Nigerian cultural critic and children's writer, was born in Benin, Nigeria. He obtained a master's degree in marketing and worked for the United African Company, but when his union activities led to his dismissal he established a publishing company, Di Nigro Press (known later as Third World First Publications and later still as Heritage Books), and started publishing his own writing. His first book, *The Climate of Darkness* (1971), was followed by *A Nation in Custody* (1973), *Black Power: The African Predicament* (1976), *Victim of UAC* (1977), and *Fires of Africa* (1973); these books expound his views on racism and the need for the assertion of an African identity. Ironically, the book for which Osahon is best known is *Sex Is a Nigger* (1971), which details sexual escapades in Sweden; *Mr. Sugar Daddy* and *Lagos Na Waa, I Swear* are in a similar vein. However he is also the author of creative and critical works that include *No Answer from the Oracle* (1974) and *Poems for Young Lovers* (1974). In 1981 he published twenty-five books for children including five colouring books, five adventure stories, and fifteen storybooks. The variety of the stories indicates the influence of oral traditions, a didactic purpose, and a philosophical objective.

Osahon has earned a reputation as a critic of corruption, demonstrated in *The Colour of Anger* (1991). His racial view of reality apparently informs *God Is Black* (1993), in which he argues that internalized racial issues associated with religion must be eliminated. He has been a consistent and dedicated exponent of the virtues of the black race.

Osiris Rising (1995) A novel by Ayi Kwei ★Armah. Ast, the African-American protagonist of Armah's long-awaited sixth novel, is an Egyptologist who moves to a fictional West African state – representing Ghana – in search of her true home. There she rejoins her colleague and former partner Asar, the leader of the secret society of the Ankh, which is inspired by the namesake companionship that centuries earlier worked to preserve life-affirming values and fight slave traders. Together with other educational reformers, Asar intends to reinstate ancient Egypt as the matrix of African history and culture and begin long-term changes capable of breaking the contemporary neo-colonial deadlock. Their efforts are thwarted by the ambitious Seth, state security chief. Pregnant by Asar, Ast will have to witness the assassination of her beloved, who is violently dismembered in a re-creation of the Osiris myth, further evidence of Armah's deep interest in ancient Egyptian culture.

OSOFISAN, Femi (1946-), a prolific Nigerian critic, poet, novelist, and playwright whose work attacks political corruption and injustice, was born in Erunwon village in the old Western Region of Nigeria and educated at the universities of Ibadan, Dakar, and Paris; he is a professor of drama at the University of Ibadan. Among the literary awards and commendations he has won are prizes from the Association of Nigerian Authors (ANA) for both drama (1980) and poetry (1989). He is the only Nigerian author to be honoured with that award twice.

A radical who writes from the ideological left, he has generated some controversy not only because he asserts that his work departs from the literary traditions of his contemporaries, particularly J.P. Clark ★Bekederemo and Wole ★Soyinka (his mentor), who, he claims, are too rooted in the past and to a celebration of imitative classical models, but because, unlike them, he primarily seeks new aesthetic forms. His only novel, *Kolera Kolej* (1975), written while he was a student in Paris, deals with corruption among students and faculty at a university. Under the pseudonym Okinba Launko, he has published two volumes of poetry, *Minted Coins* (1987), which explores topical themes as they relate to inequities, and *Dream Seeker on Divining Chain* (1993), which invokes traditional metaphors from Ifa, an oracle significant to the Yoruba people of southwestern Nigeria. As a journalist and critic he has contributed insightful essays to several magazines and newspapers, including *West Africa*, *Daily Times*, *Newswatch*, and the Lagos *Guardian*. His forte as a writer, however, is drama, and he has written more than a dozen plays, including *A Restless Run of Locusts* (1975), which deals with political corruption and violence; *Once Upon Four Robbers* (1978), which examines the morality of armed robbery and public executions in Nigeria; *Morountodun* (1982), which effectively employs myth, folklore, and history to address institutional oppression and armed revolt; and *Aringindin and the Nightwatchmen* (1991), which calls attention to the levels of despotism in the Nigerian polity. Several of his plays are collected in *Birthdays Are Not for Dying and Other Plays* (1990) and *The Oriki of a Grasshopper and Other Plays* (1995). His writing employs a range of humour, irony, song, dance, folktale, and fable.

OSUNDARE, Niyi (1946-), poet, was born in Ikere-Ekiti, Nigeria and gained degrees at the University of Ibadan (BA), the University of Leeds (MA) and York University, Canada (Ph.D.). A prolific poet, he published *Songs of the Marketplace*, his first book, in 1983. Some of his other collections include *Village Voices* (1984), *The Eye of the Earth* (1986), *Moonsongs* (1988), *Midlife* (1993), ★*Waiting Laughters* (1990), and

Selected Poems (1992). He has struggled for a space for poetry in Nigerian newspapers, particularly the *Sunday Tribune*, where his poems began to appear in 1985 under the title 'Songs of the Season'. He has won prestigious international literary prizes: *The Eye of the Earth* won a Commonwealth Poetry Prize and *Waiting Laughters* won the Noma Award. He is professor and head of English at the University of Ibadan.

Most of the poems in *Songs of the Marketplace* are concerned with the decay of social life in the poet's society. In poem after poem the contrasting images of poverty and affluence expose the absurdities of class contradictions. *Songs of the Marketplace*, however, ends with the optimistic vision of a harmonic social order in a new world, a theme Osundare later explores more intensely in *Waiting Laughters*. *Village Voices* enriches bucolic tradition with local songs, myths, and panegyric verses. His intention is not to idealize or romanticize tradition but to contrast it with the so-called modern social formation that now suppresses it.

More than any of Osundare's books of poetry, *The Eye of the Earth* accommodates textual materials that lend themselves to materialist investigation. Its appeal lies in the poet's materialist interpretation of the shift in the mode of production from agrarian to capitalist and his protest at the rupture of a communal society by individualism and plunder.

OTI, Sonny (1941-), Nigerian playwright and songwriter. Born in Arochukwu, Abia State, Nigeria, Oti was a teacher in mission primary schools before he enrolled in the Department of English at the University of Ibadan at a time when the Theatre Arts Department was evolving from the travelling theatre group organized by Geoffrey Axworthy. Under Axworthy's tutelage, Oti emerged as a nationally celebrated comic actor, playing Falstaff in episodes adapted from Shakespeare and more colourfully the picaresque hero of Nkem *Nwankwo's novel *Danda* (1964). Fleeing in the wake of the massacre of easterners in Northern and Western Nigeria in 1966, he was among the zero-hour graduates of what for the brief moment between the Biafra declaration of independence on 30 May 1967 and the outbreak of the *Nigeria-Biafra war on 6 June 1967 was the University of Biafra. In Biafra, he was quick to organize the Armed Forces Theatre Group, modelled on the Ibadan travelling threatre, which toured military camps and war zones with a revue of songs, skits, and morale-boosting enactments often based on the events of the day. Shortly after the war, he enrolled in the Leeds University School of Theatre Arts, where he obtained an MA in 1972. Returning to Nigeria, he joined the faculty of the Department of Theatre Arts at the University of Jos, where he is a professor. He is the author of the farcical plays *The Carvers, The Drummers, Return Home and Roost Awhile*, and *Dreams and Realities* (1979) as well as *The Old*

Masters (1977), *The Return of Jerome* (1981), and *Evangelist Jeremiah* (1982). Recordings of his songs have been available since the early 1970s.

Our Sister Killjoy (1977) A novel by Ama Ata *Aidoo. In some ways the most representative as well as the most innovative of Aidoo's work, her first novel follows Sissie, our sister, from Ghana to Europe on a scholarship. Touching on the African diaspora, the history of slavery and underdevelopment, and on exploitation and post-independence failure, it centres on the need to recover and remember a forgotten archive of African values as a first step towards forging a subjectivity for African men and women. The novel identifies the pressing need to bring the old values of Africa into a meaningful relationship with the present and future.

OUSMANE SEMBENE [See SEMBENE OUSMANE]

OVBIAGELE, Helen (1940s-), Nigerian novelist. Born in Benin City, Ovbiagele was educated at schools in Nigeria and at the University of Lagos, where she received a degree in education. She later studied in London, after which she taught at the Lagos City College, Yaba, and Corona School, Ikoyi. She is the women's page editor of the *Nigerian Vanguard*. Her novels, all in Macmillan's Pacesetter series, exploit the romance formula of the kind associated with Denise Robins and Barbara Cartland, but her heroines are frequently older, independent women, including divorcees and country-women-come-to-town who may yield even to prostitution, as in *Evbu My Love* (1980), in order to liberate themselves through better education. Her other novels are *A Fresh Start* (1982), *You Never Know* (1982), *Forever Yours* (1985), and *Who Really Cares* (1986).

OWUSU, Martin (Okyere) (1943-), Ghanaian dramatist. Born in Agona Kwaman, Ghana, the son of a catechist, Martin Owusu received his secondary schooling at Mfantsipim School, Cape Coast, where he was influenced by his teacher Joe *de Graft; trained as a teacher at the Presbyterian Training College, Akropong-Akuapem; and completed the diploma in theatre studies at the School of Music and Drama in Legon. He has two postgraduate degrees: an M.Litt. from Bristol (1973) and a Ph.D. from Brandeis (1979), both concerned with the classical influences on West African playwrights. He has held appointments at universities in Ghana and the USA and is a senior lecturer the School of Performing Arts at Legon.

Although he is a significant figure on a national level as an actor, academic, teacher, and director, Owusu's reputation rests on his published stage plays. The first of these were *Adventures of Sasa and Esi* (1968), playlets based on short stories about children encountering a giant and a witch. *The Story Ananse Told* (1970), originally prepared for the annual staff production at Mfantsipim, makes use of material from the body of stories known as *Anansesem* and links Owusu with those, like Efua *Sutherland and de Graft, who have contributed to a national theatrical tradition linked with Ananse. From *The Sudden Return and Other Plays* (1973), which brings together experiments with various kinds of narrative drama, Owusu emerges as a journeyman playwright, adept at dramatizing an Ananse tale (*A Bird Called 'Go-back-for-the-answer'*), or 'a story we were told when we were young' (*Anane*), at adapting a foreign model, 'The Pot of Broth' by W. B. Yeats, for example (*The Pot of Okro Soup*), or at making a play out of a sensational superstition (*The Sudden Return*). These succeed as fragments rather than as wholes, providing glimpses of Owusu's awareness of what works on the stage but not asking difficult questions or undertaking thoroughgoing investigations. His most important play is a historical drama, *The Mightier Sword*, also published in *The Sudden Return and Other Plays*, based on events that occurred during the first Ashanti-Denkyira war. Though more ambitious and providing evidence of a theatrical imagination that can encompass both the comic and the courtly, it too remains superficial. Lapses in diction, looseness in dramatic structure, and a reluctance to come to grips with issues mean that the promise is greater than the achievement. Owusu's plays have been popular with student groups, but as time passes it becomes clear that his major contribution to the Ghanaian theatre is as a director rather than as a playwright. His doctoral dissertation was published as *Drama of the Gods: A Study of Seven African Plays* (1983).

OYEBODE, Femi (1954-), Nigerian poet, was born in Lagos and trained in medicine and psychiatry in Nigeria and Britain. His first poetry collection, entitled *Naked to Your Softness and Other Dreams* (1989), explores the varieties of the poet's experience in both his personal and public life. In spite of the erotic implications of the title the poet weaves in a concern for humanity. In the second collection of poems, *Wednesday Is a Colour* (1990), his personal experience of life in Britain is adroitly made to reflect his impressions of the society and the people. *Forest of Transformations* (1991) draws upon the mythical and legendary world of the Yoruba.

OYEKUNLE, Segun (1944-), Nigerian playwright, was born in Kwara State, Nigeria and is a graduate of Ahmadu Bello University, Zaria, whose drama unit was especially active and innovatory in the 1970s. During the 1980s, resident in Los Angeles, Oyekunle turned increasingly to filmscript writing. His best known work is, however, the stage play *Katakata for*

Sofahead (1983; first produced 1978). Written in (a somewhat simplified) Pidgin, *Katakata* is set in a prison cell and explores the 'working' relationship among six prisoners as they establish a hierarchy among themselves and as they investigate the case history of Lateef, the newest arrival. Frequent role-playing episodes and the emphasis on direction, as the cell boss, Jangidi, insists on an effective telling of Lateef's story, make *Katakata* a powerful exploration of the processes by which individuals confront their own experience. Vivid and funny, the play has been produced successfully outside Nigeria (Johannesburg 1994, for example), vindicating the Pidgin medium's ability to travel.

OYONO, Ferdinand (1929-), Cameroonian novelist. After obtaining his high school diploma in Yaoundé, Oyono went to the *lycée* of Provins (France), where he received his *baccalauréat*, and studied law in Paris while attending the École Nationale d'Administration. After his return to Cameroon he worked in the Ministry of Foreign Affairs, became an ambassador, represented Cameroon at the United Nations, and eventually became Minister of Foreign Affairs.

Of his three novels, *Une vie de boy* (1956; *Houseboy* 1966), *Le Vieux Nègre et la médaille* (1956; *The Old Man and the Medal* 1969), and *Chemin d'Europe* (1960; *Road to Europe*, 1989), the first has become a classic. In the form of a diary, it tells the story of Joseph Toundi, a teenager who leaves his family to work for a white missionary, and his experiences among the colonizers. The novel, which had a strong impact when it appeared, was considered an excellent representation of the wrongs brought by colonialism, but Oyono criticizes the system's morality more than its economic or cultural impact. No white character shows any moral rectitude: one character treats black workers as inferiors, another orders them to perform undignified duties, and the missionaries are hypocrites who find sadistic pleasure in watching naked black women flogged. Violence makes the system work; worse yet, it is applied without justice. In addition to its anti-colonialist views, the novel evokes the Old Testament tale of Joseph and Potiphar's wife, the structure of a *Bildungsroman* in its narrative treatment of Joseph's experience, and the scheme of a *Sô* initiation in some of its ethnographic detail. The latter pattern suggests that Oyono was not writing just for a white audience but also for other Cameroonians. The book encouraged other Africans to write and to experiment with a realism marked by African idiosyncrasies: a passive hero, characters that resemble caricatures, an exacerbated violence, ethnographical information, the use of local names and vocabulary, and allusions to folklore.

The Old Man and the Medal ridicules Meka who, because the French administration offers him a medal, believes he has become a friend of the whites, and who ends up in jail instead. In *Road to Europe*, Aki Barnabas hopes to go to France, but only when he joins a religious group can he fulfil his dream. Both novels use humour to show how easily people can be fooled. Comedy in situation, in characters, and in language lightens the stories, a feature Oyono's texts share with the early texts of Mongo *Beti but that appears rarely in later Francophone African *novels.

OYONO-MBIA, Guillaume (1939–), Cameroonian dramatist writing in English and French, was born in Mvoutessi, Cameroon and educated locally and then at the Collège Évangélique in Libamba. His first play, *Trois prétendants, un mari* (1964; *Three Suitors, One Husband*, 1968), was immensely successful when it was first performed and continued to be popular in Cameroon for many years. The play explores the consequences and complications of the practice in marriage of the dowry. He founded his first troupe in Libamba, where he held his first teaching post. He was awarded a British Council scholarship, which he held at the University of Keele in the UK, and won first

prize in the BBC Africa Service's theatre competition for his play *Until Further Notice* (1968), which was performed at the Edinburgh Festival in 1967. In this play the expectations of a village are raised by the return of a young couple from Europe. *His Excellency's Special Train*, a radio play, was first broadcast by the BBC in 1969. On his return to Africa he was appointed to a post in the English department of the University of Yaoundé, and in the 1970s he worked for a period as head of cultural affairs in the Ministry of Information and Culture. His later work includes three collections of tales, *Chroniques de Mvoutessi* (1971–2), first begun in 1964.

Oyono-Mbia's plays inaugurated and inspired a tradition of Cameroonian theatre in which the confrontation between tradition and modernity is explored with humour and to great comic effect. He has translated most of his writing, which is thus available in both French and English versions, making it accessible and widely known in both the anglophone and francophone regions of Cameroon.

P

PALANGYO, Peter (1939-93), Tanzanian novelist, was born in Nkoaranga, Tanzania and educated at St. Olaf College, Minnesota, USA (BA), Makerere University College, Uganda (Dip.Ed.), Iowa State University (MA), and the State University of New York at Buffalo (Ph.D). He has been Tanzania's ambassador to Canada.

Palangyo's novel *Dying in the Sun* (1968) was the first Tanzanian novel in English. It tells the story of Ntanya, a symbol of Africa caught between the past and the future, uncertain whether to retreat into a world of traditional cultural values undiluted by the advent of the white man or to meet the modern world directly. In the end Ntanya achieves peace, sensing that Africa should first be proud of itself and then seek to achieve things for the people.

Palm-wine Drinkard, The (1952) A novel by Amos *Tutuola. Among the earliest of the so-called first generation of West African *novels in English, Tutuola's first published novel is the tale of a journey undertaken by an incurable 'drinkard' from the world of the 'alives' to 'the Deads' Town' in search of his tapster, who has fallen to his death while tapping palm-wine. Aided by the juju inherited from his father, the hero survives numerous tests before reaching his destination, one test being the successful capture of Death. When he eventually finds his dead tapster he learns that the dead cannot return to live again among the living, and the tapster gives the drinkard a magic egg that will supply his palm-wine needs.

The book owed its success in large measure to Dylan Thomas's glowing review, in which he described the work as a 'brief, thronged, grisly, and bewitching story...written in young English...about the journey of an expert and devoted palm-wine drinkard through a nightmare of indescribable adventures, all simply and carefully described in the spirit-bristling bush'. Tutuola's poor English necessitated some editorial intervention to render him intelligible to his readers without quite eliminating his stylistic idiosyncrasies. With regard to the plot structure, Tutuola later told an interviewer that he set down episodes in the order in which they occurred to him.

Paradise Farm (1993) A novel by Samuel *Kahiga. The winding story line and the complexity of the plot, operating as it does on the plane of illusion and reality, the supernatural and the actual, the anomalous and the acceptedly normal, serve one primary purpose: to provide a diversity of challenges and tests in the face of which the true meaning and the durability of love, as well as the worth of other fundamental qualities of the human species, can be revealed. The book was selected for Special Honourable Mention in the 1995 Jomo Kenyatta Prize for Literature.

Path of Thunder, The (1948) A novel by Peter *Abrahams. The third of Abrahams' politically charged novels conveys the disastrous consequence of any attempt at bridging the gap between people of different colours in South Africa. The setting is the harsh land of the Karoo, and the novel tells the story of Lennie Swartz, a black man, and Sarie Villiers, an Afrikaans woman. Their love denied, both die in a gun battle with white racists, but not before Lennie has killed three of their oppressors. *The Path of Thunder* is implicitly a plea for liberal beliefs and action.

PATON, Alan (Stewart) (1903-88), South African novelist, poet, and biographer, was born in Pietermaritzburg and had a distinguished academic career before beginning work as a teacher at Ixopo, where in later years he would set much of the action of *Cry, the Beloved Country* (1948). He made a momentous career change in 1935, taking on the post of director of a turbulent borstal for black youths, Diepkloof, near Johannesburg. Here he formed most of the important political ideas that were to shape his writing and his life.

Shortly after the Second World War Paton was sent on a tour of similar borstals in Scandinavia, Britain, and North America, during which he wrote *Cry, the Beloved Country*. He finished it in the USA, and it was immediately accepted by Scribner's. Its success was immediate and lasting; it is widely recognized today as one of the great novels of the twentieth century. With its hauntingly beautiful biblical style, its message of hope and compassion, and its evocation of a world that was startlingly exotic to most readers, but that the author obviously knew thoroughly, *Cry, the Beloved Country* conveyed a message of passionate protest at the treatment of blacks in terms that had a tremendous impact, not only in South Africa, but in countries such as the USA, where the civil rights movement was taking shape. The book's sales rapidly went into the millions, and it still sells more than fifty thousand copies a year.

Cry, the Beloved Country changed Paton's life, as the experience at Diepkloof had done. When the Nationalist government, which had come to power in the year of the novel's publication, decided that the director of Diepkloof was 'soft on blacks' and removed him from his post, closing the institution shortly thereafter, he became a full-time writer, turning out a stream of poems and a succession of biographies and novels. *Too Late the Phalarope* (1953), his second novel, focuses on the tragedy of the Afrikaner, imprisoned and consumed by the *apartheid he had created. Its protagonist, a white policeman in a country town, sleeps with a black woman, is arrested and tried for the offence, and suffers the destruction of his reputation, his position in society, and much of his family as a result. Modelled on a Greek tragedy, it is better constructed than *Cry, the Beloved Country*, but it made less international impact, in spite of sales that almost any other writer would have envied.

In pursuit of his non-racial ideals, Paton helped to found the South Africa Liberal party and became its president. From then on his career became increasingly political and dedicated to helping all racial groups in South Africa. Accordingly he was harassed by the Nationalist government, and only his international eminence saved him from imprisonment. He produced a steady stream of fine poems, many of them unpublished in his own lifetime, most of them having a political message and a satirical edge; these were published posthumously as *Songs of Africa: Collected Poems* (1995). He also produced two important political biographies, of his political mentor J. H. Hofmeyr (*Hofmeyr*, 1964), and of the Anglican bishop Geoffrey Clayton (*Apartheid and the Archbishop*, 1973). He saw these two very different men as representative of the roots of South African liberalism, and his biographies, like his novels, poems, and other writings, are part of a consistent moral and political concern that actuated him all his life. The same is true of his two volumes of autobiography, *Toward the Mountain* (1980) and *Journey Continued* (1988), in which he articulates his view of human life as a moral and spiritual pilgrimage. In his later years he found himself criticized both from the left and from the right as political polarization produced greater extremism. He stubbornly stood his ground, arguing that violence and repression were wrong no matter who was practising them. He died in Durban.

People of the City (1954) A novel by Cyprian *Ekwensi. Using the form of the realistic novel, Ekwensi describes in a series of related episodes the complexities of life in a modern African city. Through the activities of Amusa Sango, crime reporter for a Lagos newspaper and part-time bandleader in a Lagos night club, Ekwensi explores the formlessness and chaos, the uncertainties and fears and temporary joyousness of a variety of characters who live on the fringes of success and stability. He offers comment on

public, political, social, and national issues and, as with all social realists, attempts to make implicit criticism of the quality of contemporary Lagostian life.

PEPETELA, pseud. of Artur Carlos Maurício Pestana dos Santos [see LUSOPHONE LITERATURE; POLITICS AND LITERATURE, Angola].

Perpetua and the Habit of Unhappiness (1978) A novel by Mongo *Beti, translated from the French (*Perpétue, ou l'habitude du malheur*, 1974). Beti's fifth novel is a novel of manners with a touch of African culture (proverbs, vocabulary, a ritual killing), although it is more metaphoric than realist. It describes the life of city dwellers with factual details, but the story of Perpetua becomes representative of all Cameroonians who do not exercise power. She is not just a character, but a sacrificial victim expiating the sins of her society: alcoholism, laziness, lack of education, love, and compassion, and lack of freedom to develop into a mature, self-supporting adult.

Petals of Blood (1977) Ngugi wa Thiongo's novel, is an exposure of the post-independence betrayal of the majority of the Kenyan people by a comprador bourgeois class of Kenyans in collaboration with international finance capitalism. Church and government are also presented in league with financial institutions to exploit the peasantry and extort the wealth they produce.

This is Ngugi's message and he conveys it, suitably enough, within the framework of a novel about murder and detection.

Three directors of a local brewery in Ilmorog, the principal setting of the novel, have been burned to death in a fire in a brothel. The principal characters in the novel, Munira, Abdulla, Karega and Wanja (who owns the brothel) are arrested as suspects. As Inspector Godfrey, whose support for the Kenyan establishment is unambiguous, conducts his examination for discovery of the guilty party, the intersecting lives of these four characters (and the victims of the fire) are revealed and through them the developing nature of Kenya, principally from the time of independence.

But Ngugi also moves backwards and forwards in time to construct his vision of the evolution of Kenyan society since the beginnings of time, through the advent of Europeans to time present. We see Old Ilmorog transformed from a dusty, out-of-the-way village into a gleaming and corrupt modern city, a mataphor for the transformation of modern Kenya under capitalist sway. We see traditional villagers alienated from their land and converted to a condition of serfdom or simply cast aside. We see wealth accumulate in the hands of the few. And we see political coercive methods put in place to assure a continuance of the exploitative methods.

Ngugi weaves a complex web of experience and coincidence in the lives of the four main characters as these touch and are affected by the three directors burned in the fire – Chui, Kimeria and Nderi wa Rieri. Munira, the main character, victim of a failed marriage, son of an apostate Christian minister who collaborated with the colonial regime during the independence struggle (and ironically handsomely rewarded in the independence period), escapes to Ilmorog to become a teacher in a village school. There he comes in contact with (and contracts a failing love for) Wanja, an abused 'bar girl' who having failed to found a successful business with Abdulla, becomes a ruthless and self-serving madam, determined to have her share and possibly form a useful life and profit from the spoils of development. Abdulla, a freedom fighter who lost a leg in the struggle for independence is himself repudiated and cast on the dung heap of modern Ilmorog. Karega is also a teacher, who finds no consolations in the lessons of literature or history, but does find solace in his work as a union organiser.

It is Munira, now an alcoholic and confused Christian, who has torched Wanja's brothel, seeking to save Karega from her evil. Unintentionally and ironically he destroys three of the principal agents of exploitation.

Ngugi finds no consolation here (unlike his earlier work) in the proscriptions of Christian teaching and religious education. His solutions to current political and economic problems are found in the possibilities of modified marxism. The novel is close to a political tract, its rhetoric redeemed by the sensitive feeling he displays for the victims of a system they are, in the context the novel evokes, unable to alter.

PETERS, Lenrie (Leopold Wilfred) (1932-), Gambian poet and novelist, was born in Bathurst (now Banjul) and educated at the universities of Cambridge and London, UK. He qualified as a surgeon in 1959 and has practised in England, Sierra Leone, and since 1969 in his native Gambia.

Peters' poetry, first published as *Poems* (1964), owes little to the oral tradition and, with the rare exception of the forsaken fertility god in the title poem of *Katchikali* (1971), makes no use of indigenous mythology. He is a cosmopolitan poet whose densely packed, minimalist stanzaic structures accommodate the broad universal spectrum of human experience: ageing and death, the risks of love, the loneliness of exile. In the earlier *Satellites* (1967), the poet-doctor's surgical detachment is a metaphor for the uprooted individual's painful existential isolation, his scalpel's probing 'at the cutting chaotic edge of things' an image for the imaginative piercing and spiritual penetration which are the real goals of the poet's quest.

He is generally regarded as one of the most intellectual poets of his generation. Ideas – about politics,

evolution, science, and music – orchestrate his images in the form of debates. Though he rages at the frustrations of Africa's underdevelopment, he reflects on blind, ill-considered modes of 'progress' that have no continuity with the past and destroy more than they preserve. In his only novel, *The Second Round* (1965), a British-trained African physician, a victim of the 'massacre of the soul' wrought by Westernization, returns to the capital city of his native land full of 'noble ideas about progress in Africa' but ends by taking a post in a remote bush hospital, thus immersing himself deeper in the traditional experience. The new poems in *Selected Poetry* (1981) castigate the corrupt greed of tribalized leadership elites and balance nostalgia for a pastoral past with cautious assertions of hope for a future built on that past.

PIDGIN LITERATURE The formation of West African Pidgins was a result of the exigencies of communication among Africans in pre-colonial times, and later between West Africans and Europeans. The first speech form to have arisen from the latter encounter was a kind of Pidgin Portuguese, the Portuguese having first landed in Nigeria around 1469. When Portuguese interests were not sustained in Nigeria, this contact language failed to develop further, as did Crioulo in Guinea-Bissau or Sotavento and Barlavento in the islands of São Tomé and Príncipe. The Portuguese substratum was soon ousted by the English one, since the chief European participants in the slave trade from roughly 1650 onwards were the English.

The Calabar area on the Nigerian coast registers the oldest records of Nigerian Pidgin English or NP(E) (also EnPi). The diary of Antera Duke, an eighteenth-century Efik slave trader, bears witness to an earlier state of NP. As a makeshift idiom, however, it may not be a Pidgin at all, since a Pidgin tends to borrow its wordstock but not its grammar from European languages.

NP now thrives in Warri, Sapele and Port Harcourt, and other parts of the Niger Delta as well as the *Sabongari* [stranger-settlements] in the cities around the country. From an auxiliary jargon, it has expanded into a Creole, now boasting a community of native speakers. It is used unofficially in primary education, informally in religion, and now officially in news broadcasting in Anambra, Bendel, and Rivers States.

Many efforts have been deployed by Nigerian linguists to identify NP, to disentangle it from the web of false linguistic affinities such as Freetown *Krio, 'broken' English, 'minimal' English, or simply 'bad' English. In an effort to ascertain what is real NP, B.O. Elugbe and Augusta Omamor, in the first book-length study of NP, have dissected the language of the allegedly NP characters of Zebudaya, the hero of the popular drama series *Masquerade*, and of 'Walkabout' in *The Lagos Weekend*. Their analysis reveals that arbitrariness in spelling was used for comic effect in a kind of free-for-all linguistic stew. In their quest for a stable orthography, linguists have favoured the Delta variety over other NP interlanguages – from the Lagos variety to that spoken in Enugu or Onitsha – because it already enjoys wide recognition.

One way of securing official viability for a Pidgin is to develop a literature in it. But the potential language gatekeepers, that is, the writers themselves, either use an anglicized writing or use spelling inconsistently. While Frank *Aig-Imoukhuede's *Pidgin Stew and Sufferhead* (1982) is considered the closest a work can come to NP, his celebrated poem 'One Wife for One Man' is not up to NP standards. Short of waiting for the translation of the Bible in NP, the obscene publication *Ikebe* (Urhobo: 'buttocks') has been diagnosed as being true NP.

With the exception of some of the poets featured in the 'Poetiri' corner of the weekly *Lagos Life*, most writers such as Chinua *Achebe, Vincent *Ike, Ezenwa-Ohaeto, Femi *Osofisan, and Adaora *Ulasi use a convergent form of interbreeding between NP and standard English. Wole *Soyinka's NP in *The *Road* has been translated as *Français Populaire d'Abidjan*. Scripting NP for use in literature thus remains a compromise between a desire for linguistic realism and a desire for maximal intelligibility. As such, it is part of the larger post-colonial theory of the Creole continuum, which takes linguistic variation as the substance rather than the periphery of language study.

Ken *Saro-Wiwa's novel *Sozaboy* (1985) is 'rotten English', as its subtitle observes, a lawless mixture of 'broken' English, Kana, standard Nigerian English and NP concocted to suit the peregrinations of a naive recruit thrust into the atrocities of the *Nigeria-Biafra war. As the most conscious linguistic experiment with non-standard speech among West African first-person narratives, the novel demonstrates NP's potential to be released from its decorative confinement to jocular dialogues and be carried to book length.

Despite such experiments, NP is still stigmatized as baby talk and bush talk, as the language of marginally literate characters put in the mouths of houseboys, messengers, village layabouts, thugs, or detribalized characters who, like Cyprian *Ekwensi's Lagos prostitute in *Jagua Nana*, wish to avoid 'too many embarrassing reminders of clan or custom'. This pseudo-Pidgin is used as a class denominator and indicator of humour in popular pamphleteering such as *Onitsha market literature as well as in canonical novels such as Achebe's *Anthills of the Savannah* (1987). The legendary 'levity of Pidgin', to use Achebe's phrase in A *Man of the People*, is confirmed in its neo-comic use by the mass media, in popular entertainment, and in advertising.

The very orality of the medium, combined with its secular origins, may explain the dominance of theatre in NP. Younger dramatists such as Segun *Oyekunle in *Katakata for Sofahead* (1983) and Tunde *Fatunde in *No Food No Country* (1985), *Oga Na Tief-Man* (1986), and *Water No Get Enemy* (1989) use NP not to depict the lower classes but to address them directly. Yet Fatunde, who is the foremost representative of agitprop art in Nigeria, has been taken to task by linguists for his view that Pidgin is the language of the lower classes only. Indeed a sizeable percentage of NP speakers are uneducated, but NP does extend solidarity even among the educated.

Matters have come to a head or, in NP, 'wota don pas gari', since NP has now become the first language of some eight million habitual locutors, mainly from urban mixed families. It might develop into some sort of Nigerian Krio, to judge by Robert Hall's definition that a Creole language arises when a Pidgin becomes the native language of a speech community. NP is as widely used as any of the three major languages – *Yoruba, *Igbo, and *Hausa, the other true lingua franca in Nigeria. As such, it is not only a major Nigerian language but, because it is not associated with any linguistic or ethnic group, a potential official language as well. The failure to impose Tok Pisin in Papua New Guinea may act as a deterrent for the promotion of NP as a national language, but the success story of Bislama, the national language of Vanuatu (formerly the New Hebrides) named after the sea slug, is encouraging.

PLAATJE, Solomon T(shekisho) (1876-1932), South African journalist and novelist. Born on a Lutheran mission in the Orange Free State, Plaatje had no more than an elementary education. At the age of seventeen, after a number of years as a student teacher, he moved to Kimberley, where he was employed as a messenger in the colonial postal service. A talented linguist, Plaatje could speak at least nine languages fluently. In 1899, he moved to Mafeking, where he worked as court interpreter during the *Anglo-Boer war (1899-1903). His diary of the siege of Mafeking was his first extended piece of writing. After the war, he edited the first Setswana newspaper, *Koranta ea Bechuana* [The friend of the Bechuana], soon becoming known as a campaigner for the rights of his people. A political activist as well as a journalist, he was one of the founding members of the South African Natives National Congress (later the ANC) and headed two unsuccessful deputations to Britain to appeal for direct intervention on behalf of South Africa's native population against the Land Act of 1913. The effects of the Land Act on Africans are recorded in *Native Life in South Africa* (1916). Although by the time he died his political career had ended, he remained a respected figure among Africans and Europeans alike. His other achievements include translating Shakespeare into

Setswana; research into Setswana proverbs and phonetics, including the publication of the *Sechuana Reader* (1916), the first phonetic transcription of any African language; and the publication of the first anglophone novel, ★*Mhudi* (1930), by a black South African.

The Mafeking diary, written in 1900 but published posthumously as *The Boer War Diary of Sol T. Plaatje* (1973) and, in a new edition as The ★*Mafeking Diary of Sol. T. Plaatje* (1999), is a personal document reflecting on the role played by Africans during the siege and the only record of the Anglo-Boer war from the perspective of a black man. Plaatje focuses on the effect of emergency regulations on the African population, foreshadowing major themes in his later work. The multilingual approach that denotes tasks associated specifically with one group of people reflects his ability to interpret accurately the mood and feelings of the different language groups, a technique later refined in *Mhudi*. Plaatje's reputation as a writer was established by *Native Life in South Africa*, a bitter indictment of segregation and dispossession based on his observations during 1913 of the distribution of land in relation to the Land Act. The book is a political treatise on African opinion of the period and symbolizes the initial resistance of Africans to a policy of racial segregation. *Mhudi* was generally favourably received, but critics failed to see its importance as an epic, commenting on its shortcomings as a realistic narrative. Modern scholars treat *Mhudi* as a major literary achievement that incorporates both the English written and the African oral traditions. The novel tries to reveal the underlying humanity of all nations while simultaneously providing a political allegory for modern South Africa. As a political document, *Mhudi* is an indictment of racial policies, a theme central to all of Plaatje's writing.

PLOMER, William (Charles Franklyn) (1903–73), South African poet, novelist, and autobiographer, was born in Pietersburg, in the Transvaal, but spent much of his youth, including the period of the First World War, at school in England. In the early 1920s he tried farming in the Eastern Cape, without much success, and trading in Zululand, but before the end of 1926 he had left South Africa permanently. His career as a writer falls into three distinct periods: in an early and precocious stage, primarily in South Africa, he attacked narrowness and complacency with creative passion; in the 1930s his writing was marked by tentativeness and dissatisfaction; and during and after the Second World War, increasing self-acceptance led to three productive decades of poetry.

If Plomer had written nothing more after the age of thirty, he would still be assured of a central place in South African literary history. His first novel, *Turbott Wolfe* (1926), published by Leonard and Virginia

Woolf, grew out of his experience in Zululand. Its treatment of race and sexuality aroused hostility in South Africa and anticipated an enduring preoccupation of literature in that country. Similarly his story 'Ula Masondo', in which a young black man experiences racial discrimination and insensitivity, prefigures cultural conflict as a stock literary theme. During his last year in South Africa, Plomer collaborated with the meteoric and truculent poet Roy ★Campbell on the ★literary magazine *Voorslag*. Plomer, Campbell, and Laurens ★van der Post produced most of what was published during the journal's short life. When *Voorslag* drew the same hostile responses as *Turbott Wolfe*, Plomer was persuaded that there was no place for him in South Africa.

Before settling finally in England in 1929, Plomer lived and taught in Japan. The writing from this period, *Paper Houses* (1929) and *Sado* (1931), stories and a novel respectively, suggest that his life-long sense of alienation was beginning to surface in his work, perhaps in connection with his acknowledgement of his homosexuality. Following his move to England, where he came increasingly in contact with well-known writers and publishers, he published two novels, *The Case Is Altered* (1929), in which a young woman is murderd by her husband, and *The Invaders* (1934), in which the two characters must adjust to life as outsiders, and two biographies, *Cecil Rhodes* (1933) and *Ali the Lion* (1936). His own dissatisfaction with the novels and their lukewarm critical reception eventually led him away from prose. Although he had written poetry from the beginning, he concentrated his efforts in that direction from the 1940s on. The fifteen volumes of poetry he produced over his career range widely in time and subject, starting in 1927 with *Notes for Poems* and continuing throughout the period during and after the Second World War, when he wrote the accomplished, lyrical verse for which he is best known, including *In a Bombed House* (1942), *Borderline Ballads* (1955), *Taste and Remember* (1966), and a number of collections and selections. During this last period, he also collaborated with the composer Benjamin Britten, for whom he wrote the libretti for *Gloriana* (1952) and three 'church' operas: *Curlew River*, *The Burning Fiery Furnace*, and *The Prodigal Son*. The two volumes of his autobiography, which are often characterized as reserved, are entitled *Double Lives* (1943) and *At Home* (1958).

POETRY

East Africa: Oral poetry is undeniably a nourishing ground for most East African poetry. Two major practitioners anchored their inspiration in the wealth of this heritage as they wrote English versions, poetic texts in their own right, of traditional ★orature: ★Okot p'Bitek with *Horn of My Love* (1974) from the Acoli and ★Taban lo Liyong with his free rendering of Luo songs and poems in *Eating Chiefs* (1970). The most influential single text is Okot p'Bitek's ★*Song of Lawino*, adapted by the poet from his own Acoli version in 1966.

Living in a world where praise poems, dirges, political comments, and love songs are still invented or performed at social gatherings, writers effortlessly adapt in written English some of the features of such collectively received texts. They tend to communicate directly with an implied readership that is almost an audience. Oral delivery is never far from these poems, which often address topical issues. The modes of address are varied, including invective and eulogy, dialogue, conversation, or solemn rhetoric. Comic verse is to be found alongside meditations or ironical monologues in most collections. The poems by Micere Githae ★Mugo in *Daughter of My People, Sing!* (1976) owe much of their inspiration to the songs of women at the time of the Mau Mau.

The system of blank verse adopted by Okot p'Bitek for his long 'songs' – *Song of Lawino* (1966), *Song of Ocol* (1970), and *Two Songs: Song of Prisoner, Song of Malaya* (1971) – can be said to have started a tradition, sometimes called the Ugandan school of song poetry, with many long narrative texts that are part drama, part poetry, or part novel. Okello ★Oculi's *Orphan* (1968), about 'orphaned' Africa, is like a long oratorio, and Joseph Buruga's *The Abandoned Hut* (1969) is a dramatized lament on a similar theme. Free verse was the preferred mode for many writers, for example Muthoni ★Likimani in *What Does a Man Want?* (1974), where the voices of several women reflect on love and unfaithfulness, and even in some popular books, such as the three volumes of David Maillu's *The Kommon Man* (1975-6).

From the start, poetry has also been very much alive in student ★literary magazines, from which early anthologies were collected: *Drum Beat* (1967) by Lennard Okola, *Origin East Africa* (1965) by David Cook, *Poems from East Africa* (1971) by David Cook and David ★Rubadiri, *Pulsations: An East African Anthology of Poetry* (1971) by Arthur Kemoli, and *Singing with the Night* (1974) by Chris Wanjala. Some representative poems are also selected in Wole ★Soyinka's *Poems of Black Africa* (1975). The contributions often came from writers who have since made their names in other fields, such as novelists Timothy ★Wangusa and Bahadur ★Tejani or playwrights Francis ★Imbuga, John ★Ruganda, or Micere Githae Mugo.

In the lively scene of the 1960s and 70s, some distinctive voices can be identified. The most accomplished poet, Jared ★Angira, has a recognizable style, intimate and musical, with a particular attention to rhythm. His five books mark an evolution from a preoccupation with social change to a more dreamy, meditative tone. A similar process can be found in the volumes of verse by Taban lo Liyong. Moving from

sarcastic comments on the ills of the world to a marked ironical distance particularly apparent in the haiku-like poems of *Another Nigger Dead* (1972), his work becomes less polemical, more introspective, expressing a kind of ontological malaise in *Ballads of Underdevelopment* (1976).

The influence of Jared Angira can be seen in Richard ★Ntiru's *Tensions* (1971), reflexive poems showing an original talent. Grace Akello's *My Barren Song* (1979) has a similarly sombre inspiration but is a less polished collection. Gerald Kithinji in *Whispers at Dawn* (1976) displays a variety of voices to express anxiety in the face of a fast-changing modern world. A similar pastoral nostalgia pervades *Sunset on Navaisha* (1973) by Khadambi ★Asalache, poems about exile or a lost rural past.

After the promise of the early years, Angira remains unchallenged as the only poet with a consistent body of work, in spite of interesting developments from such often anthologized writers as Amin Kassam, for example. That the art is still very much alive can be seen in anthologies like A. D. Ameteshe's *An Anthology of East African Poetry* (1988) or in national collections such as *Boundless Voices: Poems from Kenya* (1988), edited by Arthur Luvai, or *Summons: Poems from Tanzania* (1980), edited by R. S. Mabala. Observers note a new interest in the genre in Tanzania, where for a long time most of the written poetry was in ★Swahili, along the line of the well-known writer Shaaban Robert. In *Tales to Tell* (1991) and *A Chequered Serenade to Mother Africa* (1996) Mutu wa Gethoi once more establishes a link with oral modes, but his dense short pieces are the product of a man of the first generation of writers rather than a new development.

South Africa: South African poetry in English began with the arrival at the Cape of the British settlers of 1820, among them the Scotsman Thomas ★Pringle who would become the 'father' of South African poetry in English. In the manner of colonial poets throughout the British empire, he grafted his African experience on to the traditional forms of British verse, in the process creating a poetic convention against which future poets would rebel. 'Afar in the Desert', one of Pringle's best-known poems, echoes the earnest romantic vein of Wordsworth in its construction of the poet as a hunter-explorer alienated by colonial politics and identifying with the timeless African landscape, a 'wilderness' unknown alike to indigene and white settler, empty, awaiting settlement. Pringle draws on the Eden myth in order to contrast it with a hellish South Africa, a dusty desert hospitable only to snakes, lizards, and bats. But this hardy pioneer is also a man of conscience, and Pringle is among the first to articulate concern over the treatment of indigenous people.

Adventurers seeking their fortunes in the 1870s and 80s in the diamond mines of Kimberley and the goldfields of the Witwatersrand also contributed to a South African poetic melting pot. 'Digger' ballads and poetry emerged from the diamond fields, while Albert Brodrick was dubbed the 'poet laureate' of the Transvaal. The *Anglo-Boer war elicited its share of poetry, including some by Rudyard Kipling and Thomas Hardy. With the formation of the Union of South Africa after the war, the Johannesburg-based group known as the Veldsingers [Singers of the veld], including Denys Lefebvre, Francis Emley Walrond, and Alice Mabel Alder, attempted to formulate a recognizably South African poetic tradition. Although their collective name implied that their attention was fixed on the pastoral, they also demonstrated an interest in modernism, producing poems that exploited imagism and symbolism.

Modernism was more consistently represented in South Africa by William *Plomer and Roy *Campbell, two native-born poets. In 1925 they established the literary journal Voorslag, which, as its name [Whiplash] suggests, they used to goad their conservative colonial compatriots. Both soon left South Africa to find a more favourable climate for their poetry and ideas, but their early work remains an important part of South African literary tradition. Campbell's sharp, energetic, accomplished images of Africa and sympathetic awareness of racial injustice emerge in such poems as 'The Zebras' and 'The Zulu Girl'. Plomer's interest in the ballad form, with its local historical resonances, was a way of exploring social and political issues.

In the years that followed the departure of Plomer and Campbell, the conservative voice of Francis Carey *Slater, poet and editor of two landmark *anthologies, The Centenary Book of South African Verse (1925) and The New Centenary Book of South African Verse (1945), influenced South African readers and writers for more than twenty years. Carey's passion for a poetry that was true to South Africa, rather than an imitation of English forms, also marked the work of Guy *Butler, likewise an anthologist (the Oxford Book of South African Verse, 1959). Butler was among a group of liberal humanist poets, including Alan *Paton, David Wright, Anthony Delius, Roy McNab, and N.H. *Brettell, who witnessed the post-war ascendancy of Afrikaner nationalism and the advent of the *apartheid period. At a time that many of the black contributors to *Drum magazine were having their work banned and planning to leave the country, individuals such as Delius and Wright exiled themselves as well; others remained to try to make sense of life in South Africa.

The Sharpeville massacre of 1960 and South Africa's expulsion from the British Commonwealth in 1961 enforced a separation of English-speaking South African poets from one of their principal sources of tradition and identification. As liberal values faltered

and Jack *Cope's Contrast struggled to keep the craft of poetry alive, Ruth *Miller and Sidney *Clouts explored the possibilities of a modernist poetry in which a lonely, more obsessive and image-led vision registered the moral issues raised by apartheid more obliquely. At the end of the decade the return of Douglas *Livingstone from newly independent Zambia to the Natal province of his boyhood provided this late-colonial lyricist with the emotional range and technical virtuosity of a major poet. Over the next three decades his increasingly impressive oeuvre would counterpoint the other major development in South African poetry: the emergence of a black South African poetic tradition.

The *Black Consciousness movement was a major source of this development within South Africa, while censorship and exile inhibited contact with poets like Dennis *Brutus, Keorapetse *Kgositsile, Mazisi *Kunene and Daniel P. *Kunene, who were all publishing abroad as the pivotal decade of the 1970s opened. In time the Black Consciousness poets would include exiles, too, and this intermittent dialogue between poets inside and outside the country would only be resolved with the defeat of apartheid in the 1990s. As a seminal theoretician of Black Consciousness who was also a very considerable poet, Mafika *Gwala became and would remain a central voice, intellectual and streetwise by turns. By the end of the decade the mesmeric, stalking, steely voice of Mongane *Serote had made the most unmistakable impression, while Sipho *Sepamla was the most prolific of the 'big three', a fluent poet with witty and inventive strategies. Of these three, Serote has been especially productive in the post-liberation 1990s, publishing three long poems as separate volumes and winning the Noma Award for Third World Express in 1992.

Simultaneously Adam Small and Oswald Mbuyiseni *Mtshali were approaching the moment of Black Consciousness on trajectories outside the central philosophical and political thrust of the movement. In the 1960s Small, an academic whose other passion was philosophy, had written poetry in an Afrikaans 'coloured' (mixed race) dialect, peppered with English and its own idioms, but in 1975 his Black, Bronze, Beautiful consisted of poems written entirely in English. If Small had a readership among the book-buying (and mainly white) liberal public, the poet who had made this breakthrough first was undeniably Mtshali with Sounds of a Cowhide Drum, a collection that offered vivid cameos of black urban life and a measure of protest, but stopped short of suggesting the redefinition of South African reality proposed by Black Consciousness.

Whether they aimed at a cultural revolution or simply at protest, the black poets of the early 1970s appeared under the auspices of avant-garde *literary magazines and small publishing houses run by whites, though attempts to launch publishing ventures such as Blac, the creation of another prominent poet, James *Matthews, were to be a feature of the 1970s. White poets who made small reputations while the new black poetry was claiming the stage included Wopko Jensma, Patrick *Cullinan, Don *Maclennan, Christopher *Hope, Christopher Mann and perhaps a dozen more of comparable interest and merit. As South African society moved from repression into crisis, however, the role of poetry was undergoing a metamorphosis. The new poetry was a fiery breath as well as a textual performance. Clandestine readings were being held in townships up and down the country and a generation of poets–cum–activists and (rather more numerous) activists–cum–poets was stepping forward. By the end of a decade marked by the Durban strikes and the rise of the labour movement, the martyrdom of Steve Biko, the Soweto uprising and the banning of the Black Consciousness organizations, new poets were appearing by the score in each issue of *Staffrider magazine. Most of the poems were ephemeral but they were ardent and widely read where it counted most – in the black townships rather than the white suburbs. Though the first-wave Black Consciousness poets were by now iconic figures for this readership, the performance poetry of Ingoapele Madingoane and his imitators – in long, incanted poems such as 'Black Trial', 'Africa My Beginning' and 'Behold, My Son' – was taking poetry to the streets, at least in Soweto and the other Transvaal townships. A second wave of younger black poets who made literary as well as platform reputations at this time included Chris *van Wyk, Achmat *Dangor and Donald Parenzee.

By the mid-1980s Black Consciousness was a spent force as a political movement. The poetic momentum it had created, however, extended into a period dominated by the revival of internal political resistance around the United Democratic Front, the rise of worker organizations around the Congress of South African Trade Unions, and the growing 'ungovernability' of the black townships, where open support for the ANC-led liberation movement was well displayed. Performance poetry, particularly, flourished in this new context, with Alfred *Qabula, Mi Hlatshwayo and Nise Malange inspiring worker audiences and Mzwakhe *Mbuli becoming the poet laureate of the political meeting. Published at this time, Jeremy Cronin's Inside (1983) combined the many disparate elements in the mix of South African poetry: prison poems from the heart of the struggle, written by a technically sophisticated poet obsessed by the sheer physical presence of the words that are his go-betweens. If Cronin's interest in performance poetry is a journey from the text to the platform, Lesego *Rampolokeng (Horns for Hondo, 1990, Talking Rain, 1993) meets him coming the other way, while Stephen

*Watson has drawn on oral tradition more indirectly in his 'versions from the /Xam' (Return of the Moon, 1991).

South African poetry, beginning as a masculinist, colonial project, has been subverted and remade by black poets; its next remaking may be a feminizing movement. Cecily Lockett's anthology, Breaking the Silence: a Century of South African Women's Poetry (1990) has provided the retrospect that anthologies like The Return of the Amasi Bird and Voices From Within (both 1982) applied to black poetry. Poets like Ingrid de Kok, Karen Press, Sue Clark and Jennifer Davids are important voices in the post-liberation 1990s.

West Africa: Among the West Africans generally credited with having first experimented with lyric poetry as genre are Juan Latino (1516-94), Phillis *Wheatley (1753?-84), and Olaudah *Equiano. However, because these poets were former slaves who wrote outside Africa, with little or no deep commitment to the homeland (Latino was kidnapped aged seven and taken to Spain, where he wrote praise poetry, albeit in Latin, in honour of Philip II; Phillis Wheatley was captured aged seven or eight and sent to America, where she wrote lyric poetry; and Equiano was kidnapped aged twelve and taken to several places including America, the West Indies, and England, where he wrote poetry), they cannot be characterized as the true architects of West African verse.

The origin of West African poetry in English can be traced to the pioneering efforts of the first generation of West African nationalists, who, although they had no credo or collective literary manifesto, employed their verse in extolling the tenets of the Christian religion or in arousing political awareness, especially in the aftermath of the Second World War. These nationalists – Dennis *Osadebay and Nnamdi Azikiwe of Nigeria; R.E.G. *Armattoe, Gladys *Casely-Hayford, and Michael *Dei-Anang of Ghana; Roland Dempster of Liberia; and Crispin George of Sierra Leone – unlike the *oral poet who frequently used narrative verse in promoting cultural values within the clan or the immediate neighbourhood, also employed their poetry in propagating pride of race and cultural nationalism, especially since by virtue of their western education they had better contacts with the outside world.

Generally known as the 'pioneer poets' of West Africa, these nationalists initially found outlets for their work on the pages of regional newspapers such as the Sierra Leone Weekly News and the West African Pilot. The first individual volumes of poetry among them are those by Armattoe in his cyclostyled Between the Forest and the Sea (1950), Osadebay's Africa Sings (1952), and Crispin George's Precious Gems Unearthed by an Africa (1952). Later, however, their verse was to be found in general anthologies, including Olumbe Bassir's Antho *ogy of West African Verse* (1957), Henry Swanzy's *Voices of Ghana: Literary Contributions to the Ghana Broadcasting System, 1955-57* (1958), Langston Hughes's *An African Treasury* (1960), and Frances Ademola's *Reflections: Nigerian Prose and Verse* (1962).

In addition to poetry that celebrated Christian orthodoxy, pride of race, and the dignity of humanity, the pioneer poets also glorified pre-colonial African civilization with lofty themes. However, much of their verse is characterized by romanticization, cliché and stereotype, often using biblical or hymnal diction (for example 'deep down', 'thou'); sometimes its structure degenerates into sing-song and melodrama, even apology (for example Osadebay's poem 'Africa Speaks to England').

The tenor of West African poetry changed during the 1950s and 60s, the period of independence movements throughout the continent. Consequently, the poetry of this period, in contrast to oral poetry or that of the pioneer poets, was more focused, energetic, and defiant in character. The major poets who emerged during this period include Gabriel *Okara, Kofi *Awoonor, Christopher *Okigbo, J.P. Clark *Bekederemo, Kwesi *Brew, Wole *Soyinka, and Lenrie *Peters. Although the poets of the independence era addressed many of the same themes as their predecessors, their tone was militant and their craftsmanship accomplished. Some of the difference in content and form can be attributed to education. For example, Awoonor, Okigbo, Bekederemo, and Soyinka not only studied humanities but taught literature in college, unlike most of the pioneer poets, who studied in disciplines outside the arts and consequently were not as versed in the nuances of language and in the principles of literary discourse: Osadebay studied law, Azikiwe read political science, Armattoe was a physician. Moreover, the poets of the independence era were more politically sensitive and more alert to the concept of the ideological basis of literature and the idea of imaginative writing as a viable tool for self-definition and determination and for addressing Western cultural and *political hegemony. Furthermore, being fully influenced by the prosody of such modern poets as G.M. Hopkins, W.B. Yeats, Ezra Pound, T.S. Eliot, and W.H. Auden, who broke rank with traditional poetic structures, these West African poets of the independence era are remarkable for their ability to match content with form, especially in their use of images and symbols from both Western and indigenous cultures.

In treating the theme of Western colonialism, for instance, Okara, generally regarded as the first modern West African poet to be published (his poems first appeared in *Black Orpheus* in 1957), sees colonialism in his 'Piano and Drums' as promoting confusion; the piano, which to him symbolizes Western civilization, leaves the protagonist perpetually 'lost'. Without mincing words, Okigbo in 'Heavensgate', Brew in 'A Plea for Mercy', Bekederemo in 'Ivbie', Peters in *Satellites* (1967), and Awoonor in 'The Cathedral' similarly depict the negative impact of Western colonialism through images and symbols that fascinate by their authenticity.

Since independence, however, the thematic emphasis of West African poetry has shifted dramatically to matters affecting the nation, the state, tribe, and clan. Issues of corruption, tribalism, nepotism, discrimination, and social and political justice have taken centre stage in modern West African poetry. The *Nigeria-Biafra war (1967-70) provides an example of how poets have responded with a multiplicity of voices in a country whose moral fibre is threatened by distrust and corruption. For example, Chinua *Achebe in *Beware, Soul Brother* (1971) laments the irony of humanity's inhumanity, Soyinka in *A Shuttle in the Crypt* (1972) recounts the personal and collective agonies that violence engenders, while Clark Bekederemo in *Casualties* (1970) castigates the futility of resorting to *war as a means of resolving human problems.

There is also a growing feminist voice in modern West African verse. Molara *Ogundipe-Leslie in *Sew the Old Days* (1985), Mabel *Segun in *Conflict and Other Poems* (1986), Ama Ata *Aidoo in *Someone Talking to Sometime* (1985) and *An Angry Letter in January* (1992), Catherine *Acholonu in *The Spring's Last Drop* (1985) and *Nigeria in the Year 1999* (1985), and Ebele Eko in *Wings of the Morning* (1987) and *Bridges of Gold* (1990) display a sensitivity that is remarkable for its exploration of universal themes focusing on love, social inequity, and humanity's relationship with the divine.

Contemporary West African poetry is characterized by a rich variety of form and structure. From the Pidgin of Frank *Aig-Imoukhuede (*Pidgin Stew and Sufferhead*, 1982) and Mamman J. *Vatsa (*Tori For Geti Bow Leg*, 1981) to the oral resonance of Atukwei *Okai (*The Oath of the Fontomfrom*, 1971), Pol *Ndu (*Song for Seers*, 1974) and Kofi *Anyidoho (*Elegy for the Revolution*, 1978); from the threnodic lyricism of Ken *Saro-Wiwa (*Songs in a Time of Civil War*, 1985), Tanure *Ojaide (*Children of Iroko*, 1973), and Funso *Aiyejina (*A Letter to Lynda*, 1988) to the satirical tone of Odia *Ofeimun (*The Poet Lied*, 1980), *Chinweizu (*Energy Crisis*, 1978), Niyi *Osundare (*Songs of the Marketplace*, 1983, *Songs of the Season*, 1990), and Syl *Cheney-Coker (*The Graveyard Also Has Teeth*, 1980, *The Blood in the Desert's Eyes*, 1990), we can say that the future of West African poetry has limitless possibilities. For example: Kalu *Uka, Harry *Garuba, Femi *Fatoba, Onwuchekwa Jemie, Ossie *Enekwe, Obiora *Udechukwu, Duben Okafor, Ezenwa-Ohaeto, Esiaba Irobi, Uche Nduka, Olu *Oguibe, Ada *Ugah, and Nduka Otiono (Nigeria), Kojo

*Laing, Kobena Eyi *Acquah, and Asieudu Aboagye (Ghana), Abioseh *Nicol, and Mukhtarr Mustapha (Sierra Leone) and others have become increasingly experimental, employing dramatic contrast, irony, wry humour, ambiguity, sarcasm, and other poetic and rhetorical subtleties to articulate their disillusionment with the post-independence period (characterized by human suffering, corruption, greed, and violence), and consequently have enriched the structure of the West African poetic canon.

POLITICS AND LITERATURE

Angola and Mozambique: Most of what the Western world knows about the literatures of Angola and Mozambique consists of Portuguese-language texts and some translations from Portuguese into English. However, even texts in these two languages often fail to be recognized or circulated in the West. Accordingly, indigenous-language literatures from the two countries appear to be nonexistent. Furthermore, the insistence by many critics, translators, editors, compilers of anthologies, Africanists, and *lusophonists on treating Angolan and Mozambican literatures as loosely connected pieces of a self-evident *lusofonia* has had the effect of, among other things, deflecting attention from the particularities of these national literatures beyond the vulgar bond of their Portuguese composition or the mulatto origins of many of their authors.

The English-reading world is apparently most familiar with translations of resistance poetry in anthologies such as Margaret Dickinson's *When Bullets Begin to Flower* (1972), Michael Wolfers' *Poems from Angola* (1979), Frank *Chipasula's *When My Brothers Come Home* (1985), and Don Burness's poorly translated *A Horse of White Clouds* (1989). Among the foreign-produced texts claiming the task of illuminating African-language literatures is Albert Gérard's *African Language Literatures* (1981), which hardly mentions then-extant literary texts in Angolan or Mozambican indigenous languages. The introduction to American scholar Russell Hamilton's *Voices from an Empire* (1975; re-published in Portuguese as *Literatura africana, literatura necessária*, 1981), announces the book's purpose as being 'to elucidate the modern cultural history of *Portuguese* Africa'. While lamenting the fact that 'Most anthologies of modern African literature written in European languages include a sampling of poetry and prose fiction from *Portuguese* Africa', he is even more troubled that 'very few critical studies have been devoted to *Lusophone* writing' (emphasis added). Gérard's and Hamilton's books form a likely trio with Janheiz Jahn's *Bibliography of Creative African Writing* (1971), subsequently enlarged to accommodate more texts in English at the expense of African languages. In 1975 Manuel Ferreira, Cape Verdean novelist and short story writer, began an anthology of Portuguese-language poetry called *No Reino de Caliban* [In

Caliban's kingdom] in three volumes: Cabo Verde an Guiné-Bissau; Angola, São Tomé and Príncipe; an Mozambique. *Caliban* emphasizes the African rath than the Portuguese ethos of the poetries of the thre regions, as its subtitle, *Antologia panôramica da poes africana de expressão portuguesa*, demonstrates.

Before independence in 1975, the peoples of Angola and Mozambique experienced bloodshe poverty, and the sabotage of the infrastructure as th colonizer prepared to depart. The natural resources of both countries (Angola in particular) and their geo political positions relative to *apartheid South Afric and the USA made them vulnerable to foreign inter vention and so-called low-intensity warfare. Civil w and foreign intervention channelled mainly throug South Africa have devastated Angolan and Mozambica efforts to devise the means for national unification fo their respective societies or to build functional infra structures for economic, cultural, and political rehabili tation. Little has changed since the 1970s, and the post independence literatures of both countries mirror panorama still bloodied by traces of colonialism, supe power politics, ethnic rivalry, and ideological rifts.

Like that of other European powers, Portugues colonial policy was premised on racial hierarchy. Th colonial ploy of *assimilação* was instrumental to th ascent of a loosely defined *mestizo* 'class' whose writin often expressed the existential double consciousness of the neither-nor, even as this 'class' subtly or overtl criticized political and social conditions under colonia rule and claimed its place in the sun. This phenome non is well dramatized in the works of two Mozambi cans: Raul Honwana's autobiographical *Historias ouv das e vividas dos homens e da terra* (1985; *The Life Histor of Raul Honwana*, 1988) and his son Luís Bernard Honwana's *Nós matámos o cao-Tinhoso* (1969; *We Kille Mangy Dog and Other Stories*, 1986). Both demonstrat not only divided self-image but also the impulse t construct a self distinct from the colonial-forged on through a process of self-affirmation and political affil iation. As colonial repression accelerated, however the assimilated *mestizos* would increasingly join th ranks of their black compatriots and dissident whites Hierarchy also characterized the relative status of citie vis-à-vis rural towns and villages. Whatever 'cultural life existed in the colonies – libraries, printing presses theatres – tended to centre around cities. The devel opment of cities in the former colonies only amplifie the divide between the centres of power (and com merce) and outlying areas, so that Luanda, Benguela and Huambo in Angola, and Beira, Quelimane, and Maputo in Mozambique provided most of the rare opportunities available to colonial subjects in the area of education and training. Consequently, most indige nous books and periodicals of the early period have their genesis in urban settings.

There is evidence of writing by Angolan African

dating back to the letters of the Kongo princes and kings, such as those of King Afonso I (Mbemba-a-Nzinga) to the Portuguese royalty in the period 1510–53, and other writings between 1500 and the second half of the nineteenth century. In his *Essays in Portuguese-African Literature* (1969), Gerald M. Moser discusses the formation in Luanda of a black and *mestizo* middle class during the last quarter of the nineteenth century, a number of periodicals of the same period published both in Kimbundu and Portuguese, and several African writers including Joaquim Dias Cordeiro da Matta (1857-94), author of *Delirios* [Raptures] (1887), a book of poems. Da Matta published a collection of more than seven hundred Kimbundu proverbs and riddles from the Luanda district dedicated to his fellow countrymen (1891), a Kimbundu grammar (1892), and a dictionary (1893). He enjoyed the friendship and support of Héli Chatelain, a Swiss missionary and collector of African folklore. Two literary journals edited by black and *mestizo* Angolans, Francisco Castelbranco's *Ensaios Litterarios* [Literary essays] and Pedro da Paixão Francisco's *Luz e Crença* [Light and belief], appeared in 1901-02.

A global upsurge of anti-colonial sentiment and political activism in the 1930s and 40s gained momentum in the 1950s and 60s. 'Vamos descobrir Angola!' [Let's discover Angola!] became the rallying cry of African students studying in Lisbon, self-consciously naming themselves Estudantes do Império [Students from the empire] and mobilizing around an Angolan core. They established the journal *Mesagem* [Message] and related outlets for the poetic expression of young writers from the colonies. Though *Mesagem* would soon be banned because it was a vehicle for a socialist politics and advocated Angolan independence, it published some poets whose anti-colonial voices were central in the decolonization process: Agostinho *Neto, António Jacinto, Alda Lara, and Mário António. Meanwhile the review *Cultura* featured the poetry of Arnaldo Santos and the short fiction of José Luandino Vieira. Luandino Vieira's sketches of working-class and *lumpen* existence in the *musseques* of Luanda, written in a mixture of Kimbundu and Portuguese, was published as *Luuanda* (1964); it led to his imprisonment on charges of distributing 'subversive' pamphlets and was banned a second time in 1972. Luandino Vieira's other work of the same transitional period, *A vida verdadeira de Domingos Xavier* (1974; *The Real Life of Domingos Xavier*, 1978) demonstrates the urgent need for solidarity among the oppressed, the emergence of a conscientized working class, and the clandestine but vital collaboration of whites, blacks, and *mestizos* in the anti-colonial resistance.

Two other exemplary texts of emergent Angolan literature, besides the relatively well anthologized poetry, are the novel *Mayombe* (1971; trans. 1984) by Pepetela and the short-story collection *Sim Camarada!*

(1977; *Yes, Comrade*, 1993) by Manuel Rui. The narrative structure of *Mayombe*, signalled by the formulaic 'I, the narrator...' that repeatedly introduces the stories and reflections of individual guerillas and pre-empts an omniscient narrator, underscores the varieties of experience within the struggle for national independence. These experiences epitomize the interrelation of personal identity and the struggle for national identity, as the narratives of Theory, Fearless, Muatianvua, Miracle, Struggle, New World, the Political Commissar, Ondine, and others demonstrate. What Pepetela emphasizes most is the necessity for human beings to change themselves first if they are to transform the world. In an Angola setting out on a marxist-leninist path, Pepetela, through his character Fearless, enunciates the urgency to renounce the kind of philosophical certainty and ideological purity that could lead to dogmatism and political repression. The Mayombe of the novel's setting has an African diasporic ring to it, as certainly does the symbolic figure of Ogun, *Yoruba god of iron, whom Pepetela calls the African Prometheus. Mayombe is as much the terrain of the war as it is an ally of, and an agent in, Angola's liberation struggle. The armed resistance of the MPLA (Popular Movement of the Liberation of Angola) guerillas parallels Prometheus' challenge to Zeus, to wrest fire from the 'gods' for the use of the masses of Angola.

The original Portuguese edition of Manuel Rui's *Yes, Comrade!* was published not in Angola but in Portugal by Ediçoes 70 for the Union of Angolan Writers because at the time all operative printing presses in Angola were being mobilized in the revolutionary effort. Rui's manuscript was printed in Lisbon and then returned to Angola, paralleling in the process the route taken by the timepiece in the short story 'The Watch', manufactured in Europe (with materials readily available in Angola) and then imported as a finished product. 'The Watch' thus projects Angola's future against a backdrop of possible dependency on the outgoing colonial power. Like Pepetela, Rui makes extensive use of *orature. The story of the watch involves a project that allows Angolans of all ages to construct themselves in the future through narratives that must accommodate dialectical change and the creative input of all. Both 'The Watch' and 'Five Days after Independence' advance on a momentum provided by the framework of orature. The story-within-a-story rubric, a particular feature of the oral tradition, is indeed the very dynamic that propels the history of Angola, in particular the 'new' stories that must be recounted in the form of a collective countermemory and as oppositional cultural practice. Indigenous languages and a vocabulary born in a multilinguistic milieu have increasingly become a feature in the writings of Angolan writers, including Manuel Rui, Pepetela, and Uanhenga Xitu.

The history of indigenous Mozambican writing

resembles that of Angolan writing, except that the former seems to have fared far worse than the latter. Although coastal Mozambique was part of the Zenj empire, there is little, if any, mention of indigenous-language Mozambican texts from the nineteenth or early twentieth century, for instance those written in Arabic script. Gérard makes oblique reference to *Sasavona*, the 'first creative work of Tsonga authorship ever to reach print', a short novel by Daniel Cornel Marivate, published in 1938 by the Swiss Mission Press in Johannesburg. While this makes *Sasavona* a South African text, it is possible that it could have motivated Tonga speakers across the border in Mozambique. It is likely that the Swiss missionary H. A. Junod's collection of Tonga poetry, published in 1940, had indigenous input. In 1908 the black journalist João Albasini and his brother José established *O Africano*, a bilingual weekly (in Ronga and Portuguese) which became *O Brado Africano* [The African call] in 1918.

In the 1950s and 60s a heightened national consciousness drew together black and *mestizo* writers, journalists, and activists. A poetry collection called *Msaho* was first published in 1952; it featured the works of, among others, Reinaldo Ferreira, Ruy Guerra, and Virgílio de Lemos. The *Msaho* movement sought to assert 'Africanness' while offering a cultural nationalist challenge to colonialism. *O Brado Literario*, an offshoot of *O Brado Africano*, circulated between 1955 and 1957, publishing the poetry of José Craveirinha, Gualter Soares, Marcelino dos Santos, and Rui Nogar. Between 1957 and 1961 *Paralelo 20* circulated from Beira, featuring the works of Rui Knopfli, Nuno Bermudes, Francisco de Sousa Neves, Fernando Couto, and Carlos Monteiro dos Santos. Between 1960 and 1976, literary and cultural expression also found an outlet in *A Voz de Moçambique*. Armando Guebuza and Jorge Rebelo surged forward as the independence struggle intensified in the 1960s and into the 1970s, as did Mia ★Couto, Luís Carlos Patraquim, Maria Manuela de Sousa Lobo, Lina ★Magaia, and Mutimati Bernabé João in the post-independence period.

As in the case of Angola, Mozambican writing, and especially the poetry of protest, combat, and self-affirmation (Noemia de Sousa, José Craveirinha, Armando Guebuza, Marcelino dos Santos, and the Frelimo-published *Poemas de Combate* of 1971) resounds with such themes as the plight of migrant workers, the *contratado* or forced labour system, ★negritude, the suppression of African culture, colonial alienation, the fragmentation of family life, racism, revolutionary sacrifice in the armed struggle, and the search for dignity and hope. Much post-independence Mozambican literature explores individual efforts at self-constitution, collective striving towards a national polity based on indigenously cultivated ideals, as well

as the political instability engendered by internal and external forces. The short fiction of Mia Couto, in *Vozes anoitecidas* (1986; *Voices Made Night*, 1990) and *Cada homen e uma raca* (1990; *Every Man Is a Race*, 1994) explores the complexity of human existence beyond the confines of race or geography, the tragedy of civil war with its extreme violence, the absurd legacy of colonialism, and the enduring search for total national liberation.

East Africa: There is hardly an aspect of national life in East Africa that has been treated more critically by writers of drama, poetry, and particularly fiction than politics. Creative writers have focused their critique mainly on politics in the post-independence period; however, contrary to the expectations of readers trained on the trend in historical fiction to glorify the mass struggle for independence, even novels that deal with the politics of the national liberation movement exhibit a predominantly negative disposition.

Several novels represent the processes leading to political independence. Peter ★Nazareth's *In a Brown Mantle* (1972) portrays the politically guided opposition to colonialism in the imaginary East African country of Damibia, from the people's first awareness of foreign domination to independence. Throughout, the seemingly noble crusade is characterized by demagogy, opportunism, selfishness, and lack of vision that lead to compromise in the name of 'practical politics' and the erosion of ideals. *The Half-brothers* (1974) by Davis Sebukima, another Ugandan, entwines a story of fraternal envy with that of an unnamed African country's evolution from 'the first vague shakings of nationalist political agitation' through self-government to independence. The United Freedom Movement is the party of 'tea-time politics', and Kigere, one of the half-brothers, is a mediocre and malicious young man whose casual encounter with the movement becomes accomplished political opportunism. *The Serpent-hearted Politician* (1982), a satirical novel by Tanzanian E.J.E. Makaidi exposes as a sham the political process leading to independence in the fictitious African country of Sanya. Through the trickery of a paid stooge of British colonial interests, the people are hoodwinked into supporting a deal with their betrayers. ★Ngugi's *The ★River Between* (1965) portrays as an ambiguous venture the first attempt of the Gikuyu people to give political expression to their growing awareness of oppression and of the need for resistance. While the Kiama, the nascent quasi-political party, is true to its objectives, to 'rid the country of the influence of the white man' and to 'restore the purity of the tribe and its wisdom', its leadership stumbles into the pitfall of obsession with power and the ruthlessness that often accompanies it.

Novels that deal with the politics of the postndependence period are in the majority. Even in the novels that describe the period leading up to independence, linear plots trace the passage from pre-independence to independence, suggesting that the roots of present-day political malaise go deep into a tainted political past. The message of all political novels is that the basic principle on which political leadership and political activism should rest, i.e. service to the public, has been replaced by its direct opposite, the quest for personal material gain. Authors elucidate this phenomenon from various angles, concentrating on concrete political distortions. Corruption becomes the cardinal evil since, by its malignant nature, it never affects the domain of politics alone but spreads into all other spheres of life. *In a Brown Mantle* is perhaps the most explicit illustration: Nazareth shows how, having eaten into politics, corruption then erodes the civil service, the economy, the army, public morality, and intellectual integrity. Kenyan O. Wambakha's *The Closed Road to Wapi* (1978) unfolds as a monumental story of corruption perpetrated by both the government and the opposition. Dishonesty and hypocrisy are the common tools corrupt regimes use in their pseudo-communication with the public, as a number of authors demonstrate. For the protagonist of *The Serpent-hearted Politician*, hypocrisy is actually the mainstay of power. In an absurd kingdom, the naive population takes a lifetime to decode its president's utterances and actions. Their unveiled meanings inevitably turn out to be a mockery of what they express at face value. In *The Final Blasphemy* (1978) by Ugandan Felix Okoboi the media sing 'hosannas ... to the so-called revolutionary government of the day' and draw 'a false image of a country that was far from being stable...'. In Gabriel *Ruhumbika's *Village in Uhuru* (1969), political double-dealers of TANU (the Tanganyika African National Union) drown themselves in rhetoric, oblivious to the people's doubts, fears, and rejection. Father Mateba tells the protagonist Balinde: 'You men all know how to talk. I have never seen any of your men of *siasa* [politics] speak few words', but the irony is all but lost on the party official. In *The Gathering Storm* (1977) by Hamza Sokko, the political evolution of TANU functionaries ends in rejection and cynicism. Sengene, one of the stalwarts of the party, resigns his post in TANU soon after independence and starts a business, feeling that 'it is his time to see whether the *uhuru* he had been fighting for so hard is of some value or not'.

Political repression, as an alternative means employed by anti-popular regimes to sustain power, is a recurrent theme in East African political fiction. In Kenyan Wahome Mutahi's *Three Days on the Cross* (1991) the Special Police obtain impossible confessions in their torture chambers in the service of a president who is gripped by a maniacal fear of dissent. Similar episodes characterize *The Half-brothers*, Ugandan

Grace Ibingira's *Bitter Harvest* (1980), Godfrey Kalimugogo's *Sandu the Prince* (1982), and *The Serpent-hearted Politician*. Some novels emphasize the extension of political repression to wanton brutality unleashed on the entire population. Two novels by Ugandan writers, *The Rape of the Pearl* (1985) by Magala-Nyago and *The *Seasons of Thomas Tebo* (1986) by John *Nagenda, are the most striking examples. Other novels show specific interest in the aspect of political repression related to the intelligence system that serves it. The Triple Service in *The Final Blasphemy* and the members of the State Research Bureau (SRB) in *The Rape of the Pearl* are puppets inebriated with a power they can only grossly mishandle. By way of contrast to these representations of illegal political repression, the head of state in Ugandan Cyprian Karamagi's *Bulemu the Bastard* (1980) organizes the detention camp in the Nile Republic according to the law of 'civilized men'. He condemns all forms of physical punishment and declares, 'Keeping your influential enemy in an uninfluential corner is enough torture. We placed [dissidents] in isolation to realize our point of view'.

Writers have also examined the possibility of political reform. As a rule, change in such novels comes abruptly, either through a coup, as in Ugandan Robert *Serumaga's *Return to the Shadows* (1969), in *Bitter Harvest*, and in *The Seasons of Thomas Tebo*, or as a result of a popular revolt, as in *The Serpent-hearted Politician*. At best, it produces uncertainty about the new day; most typically, it leaves an uneasy feeling of wasted effort and false hope. Joe, the protagonist of Serumaga's novels, reminisces about the several coups in his country and acknowledges that 'each one [has been] more futile and destructive than the last'. And the eponymous hero of Nagenda's novel, having himself played a crucial role in the liquidation of a dictator, wonders from his ambiguous exile 'what had it all been worth ... seeing his own part as more minuscule and meaningless than ever before'.

These examinations of political reality most often represent the people as victims. Even when the point of view is the ultimate triumph of the masses, as in Ngugi's *Petals of Blood* (1977), the victory is projected in the indefinite future, while in the present political power rests firmly in the hands of oppressors like Nderi wa Riera. However, a group of novels does raise the question of the people's political responsibility, even their guilt. Joe, in *Return to the Shadows*, wrestles with an obtrusive self-accusation: 'If more of us had done our duty before, there would not be so much room for so many stupid imbeciles to become politicians'. Mike, in *The Seasons of Thomas Tebo*, bemoans the plight of decent folk at the hands of politicians and at the same time suggests the former's own complicity: 'how did we ever allow it to happen?' Although such observations are largely limited to the educated elite, Ambayisi Namale's *Honourable Criminals* (1994), a novel that focuses on electoral politics in Kenya, suggests that the whole populace deserves the inadequate leaders they help to put in power. The humorous tone, which implies the electorate's levity towards their own well-being, enhances rather than weakens the criticism. The stereotypical gullibility of the masses here metamorphoses into a proclivity for corruption and opportunism.

Student politics, in which high school and university students demonstrate their stand on issues of national significance as well as on local matters of the organization and functioning of their institutions, constitutes another sub-theme in political writing. The idealism and commitment that mark this kind of student self-expression set it, for East African writers, a world apart from professional politics. Juma, the protagonist of M.G. *Vassanji's *The *Gunny Sack* (1989), captures the attitude of his colleagues at the university in newly independent Tanzania as they form SNAFU, Students for a New Africa: 'We thought the country was listening, Africa needed us'. Self-respect, a quest for active self-assertion, and a clear sense of direction motivate the student strikes at Siriana School in *Petals of Blood* and the student revolt and subsequent strike in *In a Brown Mantle*. But there is also the suggestion that there are darker sides to this overall picture of revolutionary fervour. Chui, the popular student leader at Siriana, later becomes a merciless exploiter, a transformation that moves the reader to reassess the ambitious nature that propels him into student leadership. The executive of the student guild in *In a Brown Mantle* are suspected of misuse of collective funds.

A few novels follow politics into settings otherwise largely unexplored in East African fiction. Civic politics is the subject of Karuga Wandai's autobiographical *Mayor in Prison* (1993), set in Thika Municipal Council, Kenya. *Sunrise at Midnight* (1996), by Kenyan Ongoro wa Munga, belongs in the category of political thrillers, rare for East Africa.

The image of the politician that emerges from the East African political novel reflects all the characteristics of the 'trade'. Whatever his personal peculiarities, the politician is above all a recognizable type, embodying by choice and with determination the very essence of the political game, never attempting to change its rules or mould it according to an ideal. The politician is thus easily the most negative corporate hero in East African prose fiction. However, the portrayal of exceptional and exemplary politicians has allowed East African writers to express what little hope they have for the political kingdom. Perhaps the most notable of these is Pius Cota of *In a Brown Mantle*, a combination of honesty, selflessness, intelligence, inexhaustible energy, genuine love for the people, and sober pragmatism. Another is the prime minister in *Sandu the Prince*, an unusual case of political success

based on a capacity for introspection and a preoccupation with justice, duty, and action. Nevertheless, F Cota is assassinated by his political adversaries with tacit consent of the head of state, his former close as ciate, and the protagonist strives unsuccessfully build his political career on the model provided by t leader. The prime minister in *Sandu*, on the oth hand, is a highly speculative character in a humoro novel whose setting is a nameless, exotically utop country, a never-never land. The political optimism East African writers is indeed minimal.

The attention of East African playwrights has be captured by the worst failings and the most negati excesses of political performance. The murdero brutality of degenerate political regimes is at the cen of *The Floods* (1980) by John *Ruganda and t Luganda-language play *Olusozi lwa Batulege* [The H of the chequered zebra] (1986) by another Ugandа Andrew Kibuuka. *The Burdens* (1972) by Ruganda a *Betrayal in the City* (1976) and *Game of Silence* (197 by Kenyan Francis *Imbuga deal with the issue political repression on a broader scale. *The Succes* (1979) by Imbuga and *Olusozi lwa Batulege* expe blind ambition for power as a dangerous vie Ugandan Byron Kawaddwa's Luganda-langua musical drama *Olyimba lwa Wankoko* (1971; *Song Wankoko*, 1976) satirizes self-seeking politicians. In similar vein, two other Ugandan playwrights, Elvar Namukwaya Zirimu in *When the Hunchback Made Ra* (1974) and Nuwa Sentongo in *The Invisible Bo* (1975), illustrate how individuals exploit politica bankrupt systems for personal ends. Robert Seruma and Alex Mukulu, in *Majangwa* (1974) and *Thirty Yea of Bananas* (1993) respectively, recreate episodes Uganda's political history. Penina Muhando's Swahil language plays *Harakati za Ukombozi* [Liberatic struggles] (1980) and *Lena Ubani* [There is an antido for rot] (1985) deal in part with the major politic problems of Tanzania, especially the distortion of t *Ujamaa* [socialist] policies.

East African poets such as Jared *Angira, Gera Kithinji, and Sam Mbure of Kenya; *Okot p'Bite Richard *Ntiru, and Okello *Oculi of Uganda; ar Kundi Faraja, Kajibu, Isaac Mruma, and Jwa Mwaikusa of Tanzania have been concerned with suc political issues as the alienation of the political eli from the people, the social injustice engendered b political systems, and the hypocrisy that permeate political activity. Oculi's long poem *Malak* (1977) an some of Kithinji's poems in *Whispers at Dawn* (197(represent Africa as the victim of an oppressive interna tional political order. A number of the poems fror Tanzania gathered in *Summons* (1980) call for revolu tionary action against tyrannical rule. In Mwaikusa 'Chaos in the Palace', 'chaos' and 'fear' give way t 'the forces of justice'.

Relating literature to politics provides a context i

which the validity of ascribing a social function to the former can be judged. East African creative writing has played an important role in sensitizing its local readers to the political problems that beset them and creating the condition for corrective social action.

South Africa: South Africa's long tradition of politically committed literature includes such landmarks as Sol T. *Plaatje's creative and historical work early in the century, which prompted an angry attack in the South African parliament; the oppositional work of R.R.R. and particularly H.I.E. *Dhlomo in the 1930s and 40s; Alan *Paton's *Cry, the Beloved Country, published in 1948, the year the Nationalist party came to power and instituted *apartheid as official state policy; and the racier, but also more radical work of the *Drum writers of the 1950s.

Two things distinguish the period after 1960 from what went before. First, the South African government, through *censorship legislation and other means, began to act more aggressively against writers who opposed it. Secondly, a gap began to open between writers who sought to relate their writing to political ends and those who preferred to keep literature largely free of politics. Both sides had adherents among academics and intellectuals, who polemicized in support of one position or the other.

Before 1960, censorship in South Africa was ad hoc and piecemeal. With the Publications and Entertainments Act of 1963 a new phase began in which censorship was rigidly codified and enforced. A revamped act in 1974 imposed even harsher censorship regulations, among other things ending the right of appeal to the courts against censorship decisions and making the possession of books banned for political reasons a criminal offence. In the same year the first banning of a literary work in Afrikaans occurred, André *Brink's novel Kennis van die Aand (1973; *Looking on Darkness, 1975). Two years earlier, James *Matthews' Cry Rage (1972) had been the first volume of poetry to be banned.

Government action against writers went far beyond censorship legislation. Under the notorious Suppression of Communism Act of 1950 and its various successors, the government, especially during the 1970s and 80s, repeatedly held writers in *prison without trial. More frequently, the authorities 'banned' writers, which meant, among many other things, that their work could not be legally read or distributed in South Africa, nor could they be quoted by others, including literary critics and reviewers. In 1966 the government invoked the act to ban a dozen or so writers who were living in exile, among them writers of such international stature as Es'kia *Mphahlele, Lewis *Nkosi, and Mazisi *Kunene. By this action, an entire generation of black writers who had come into prominence in the late 1950s and early 1960s and who had

already been driven into exile were forcibly cut off from their audience. Two other noted writers and activists of the same generation, the novelist and short story writer Alex *La Guma and the poet Dennis *Brutus, were banned several years before the others.

As the political crisis deepened in the 1970s and again in the 1980s, a rift grew between those writers and intellectuals, mainly but by no means exclusively black, who produced or espoused writing as a part of political struggle for full political rights, and those, mainly but not exclusively white, who saw politics as largely inimical to the creative imagination. This is a familiar battle, fought out in virtually every society that has passed through periods of upheaval and repression from the French Revolution to the present day, between those who believe in the autonomy of literature and the untrammelled individual creativity of the artist and those who emphasize the context in which literature arises and the social responsibility of the artist. For the latter, not only is literature unavoidably political and social, no matter how apolitical it seeks to be, but it should be made directly and explicitly so.

Politically committed writing and the debates surrounding it went through two fairly distinct phases. The rise of the *Black Consciousness movement in the early 1970s was accompanied by a vibrant literary and cultural initiative. Inspired by the movement, and despite all the censorship and banning of earlier writers, a new generation of writers emerged. One interesting feature of the period was that in several centres writers formed collectives that published or, in the case of playwrights, staged the work of their members. At the same time as Black Consciousness writing was emerging, the work of certain white writers, notably Nadine *Gordimer, Athol *Fugard, and André Brink, was also becoming increasingly politicized.

During the brutal political repression that followed the student uprising in Soweto in June 1976 and the countrywide unrest that followed it, writing and other cultural activities associated with the Black Consciousness movement quickly took on greater urgency and became increasingly politically radicalized. *Staffrider magazine, founded in 1978, became the most prominent vehicle for the political poetry and fiction that flourished at the time. Its publisher, Ravan Press, founded a couple of years earlier, also issued many of the novels and volumes of poetry, short stories, and plays produced by these writers.

The period stretching from the years just before the Soweto uprising through the years of repression that followed it produced a considerable body of important political literature, including, among the more notable or influential, volumes of poetry by Mongane *Serote, Mafika *Gwala and Ingoapele Madingoane, Serote's novel *To Every Birth Its Blood (1981), Gordimer's *Burger's Daughter (1979), Brink's A *Dry White Season (1979), Mtutuzeli Matshoba's story collection *Call Men Not a Man* (1979), Mbulelo *Mzamane's *The Children of Soweto* (1982), Sipho *Sepamla's *A Ride on the Whirlwind* (1981), and the plays of Fugard and Zakes *Mda. Not only were many of the works published during the period banned, but within a few years several of the writers who contributed to the cultural ferment of the 1970s were, like their predecessors of the 1950s and 60s, living in exile. Among those who remained in South Africa, several were regularly harassed by the authorities and in some cases detained without trial.

The repression of the late 1970s and early 1980s to a large extent succeeded in temporarily stifling anti-apartheid political activity, or at least driving it further underground. With the founding of the United Democratic Front in 1983, energies again turned to direct political engagement, and again overflowed into cultural activities. Organizations such as COSAW (the Congress of South African Writers), which was affiliated with the United Democratic Front, emerged to encourage and channel the new cultural activism. The period was marked by the emergence of such things as 'worker' poetry and drama – that is, texts written (sometimes collectively) by workers and performed at labour union meetings and the like. Similarly, it was a regular feature of anti-apartheid political gatherings at the time to have politically involved poets read, or, in the case of oral poets such as Mzwakhe *Mbuli and Mi Hlatshwayo, whose popularity grew rapidly during the period, perform their work for enthusiastic audiences. Such practices led to the adoption of the term 'cultural worker' to describe the relation of politically radical writers and artists to the anti-apartheid struggle.

This second phase of political and cultural ferment, brutally repressed with the declaration of a nationwide state of emergency in 1986, produced, as did the earlier one, an important body of politically radical literature. Among the many interesting and valuable works are Njabulo *Ndebele's *Fools* (1983), Gordimer's *A *Sport of Nature* (1987) and *My Son's Story* (1990), Richard *Rive's *Emergency Continued* (1990), and Menán *du Plessis's *A State of Fear* (1983) and *Longlive!* (1989). Jeremy Cronin's *Inside* (1983; the title refers to his years as a political prisoner) is one of the finest volumes of radical political poetry in English produced anywhere in this century, and he was just one of several fine poets publishing radical verse during the period. More ambiguously related to the anti-apartheid politics of the period are J. M. *Coetzee's *Life & Times of Michael K* (1983) and *Age of Iron* (1990) and Fugard's *My Children! My Africa!* (1990).

The award of the Nobel Prize in literature to Nadine Gordimer in 1991 may be thought of as the apogee of political literature in South Africa. The award marked the international acknowledgment of the role that Gordimer, along with many other writers, had played under apartheid, and to that extent she

was the representative of all those who had devoted their creative energies to fashioning a literature of opposition to apartheid. At the same time, the award marked something like a terminal point in that cultural project. With the dramatic transformation of the country in the 1990s, oppositional literature no longer had the mission that had long sustained it. Almost overnight, it seems in retrospect, writers whose work had been shaped by the long political crisis have had to begin seeking a new enabling stance from which to write. As writers begin to explore new possibilities, the once heated debates over the proper relation of literature to politics in South Africa have, for the time being at least, abated.

West Africa: African literature in English, like other African literatures in colonial languages, is a direct result of a political act, that is, colonialism. Consequently the literature itself is often a political act. Chinua *Achebe rightly argues in 'The African Writer and the Biafran Cause' that 'an African creative writer who tries to avoid the big social and political issues of contemporary Africa will end up being completely irrelevant – like the absurd man in the proverb who leaves his burning house to pursue a rat fleeing from the flame'. So prevalent have politics and the political been in African literature in colonial languages that some critics have described the bulk of it as protest or propaganda literature. The implication is that writers disregard form and style in favour of the politically appropriate or correct within their contexts as subject people in search of political, cultural, and economic liberation. This may be a correct view with reference to some of the early writing from West Africa, especially the poets of the early 1950s, but it cannot be an accurate description of the highly complex intermarriage of form and subject matter in the work of such politically conscious West African writers as Achebe, Kofi *Awoonor, Christopher *Okigbo, and Wole *Soyinka.

By the time of the birth of West African literature in English in the 1950s, colonialism had become a fact of life. During this period, the ongoing resistance to the colonial system had coalesced around the anti-colonial movement that opposed colonialism on several fronts: the political, the cultural, and the artistic. Opposition on the artistic front was led by poet-politicians who sought to articulate the plight of their people and to celebrate the indigenous culture that colonialism had conspired to destroy. These were time- and event-specific poems designed to make certain points relevant to a particular political moment, not to survive beyond their immediate context and historical period. Those that have survived into the present have done so more for their historical relevance than for their artistic excellence. One writer from this period whose work has survived for both its political relevance and its artistic qualities is the Ghanaian Joseph Ephraïm *Casely-Hayford, whose *Ethiopia Unbound* (1911) concerns itself with the notion that no people can despise itself and its culture and expect to survive – a reference to the aptitude of educated Africans for abandoning their own culture for Arab-Muslim or Euro-Christian values. The pan-African design in Casely-Hayford's work is to be found also in the novels of Cyprian *Ekwensi and William *Conton, and the poetry of *Chinweizu.

The relationship between literature and politics in West African literature in English can be viewed from a number of perspectives: the treatment of politics in the literature; the influence of political issues such as censorship and political oppression on the writers' choice and treatment of themes; and the influence of literature on the political culture of the region. The last is the easiest to dispose of: for literature to have any influence on politics, the politician would first have to read the literary works. Judging by the behaviour of African politicians, observers might conclude that they do not read their writers, or that if they do, they do not learn anything from them. The failure of the political elite to read creative writing is satirized in the book-launch scene in Achebe's A *Man of the People (1966), where Chief Nanga fails to distinguish between a Dudley Stamp, a Michael West, and a novelist. On the other hand, however, given the degree of persecution of writers and the official and unofficial banning of books that take place in Africa, especially in Central, East, and pre-liberation South Africa, it is obvious that African politicians are aware of the power of literature. *Censorship has not been very blatant in West Africa, but since writers have also been in the vanguard of political opposition to governments, it is never clear whether harassment is a result of their writing or their politics. Achebe narrowly escaped summary execution after the revenge coup of July 1966 when some of the soldiers behind it reasoned that he must have been a conspirator in the January 1966 coup since A Man of the People, whose publication coincided with the coup, predicted a similar event. The logic of their position, however, breaks down in light of the rest of the novel's plot and also in the light of the length of time it takes for a novel to be written, edited and published – a point rather scornfully made by Achebe himself. Soyinka's prison memoir, *The Man Died* (1972), suffered an unofficial ban when it was first published because it castigated Gowon and his cronies.

The range of political themes in West African literature covers traditional politics as it existed before colonialism and as it operated during and after the colonial experience; modern Africa's flirtation with multi-party democracy, the one-party system, and military dictatorship; and the struggle to devise alternative political cultures in Africa. Achebe's oeuvre

perhaps best illustrates this range. *Things Fall Apart* (1958) and *Arrow of God* (1964) portray the complex traditional governance of a republican Igbo people who value both authority and consensus, and the tragic demise of this indigenous system as a result of colonialism on the one hand and the failure of the system to undertake timely reforms on the other. In *No Longer at Ease* (1960), the days of the colonial overlords are numbered and independence is on the horizon. In *A Man of the People*, set in the post-independence period, he examines the endemic corruption that has become the bane of African nations as many people fight for a share of a limited national cake. The deep suspicion of the military alternative to chaotic civilian rule in A Man of the People also characterizes Ayi Kwei *Armah's first novel, The *Beautyful Ones Are Not Yet Born (1968), which ends with a policeman taking a bribe from a lorry driver at a checkpoint soon after a coup that has been touted as a panacea for the corruption in the society.

Corruption in public life is the most common political theme in West African literature in English, from Achebe's A Man of the People through Armah's The Beautyful Ones and Nkem *Nwankwo's My Mercedes Is Bigger Than Yours (1975) to the novels of Ben *Okri, in which politics and its repercussions are always hovering. One of the consequences of the corruption in public life and the immorality and materialism of politicians is the people's disillusionment. Most of the heroes of West African novels about post-independence disillusionment are, however, hardly moved to initiate the necessary steps to change their condition. They lack the will to act; they are variants of the man in The Beautyful Ones, watchers and witnesses unwilling to move against those who have robbed them of their dignity. Even when they are educated, as with Soyinka's interpreters or Achebe's aspiring new-generation politicians, the sum total of their action is often tantamount to collusion by default. Gabriel *Okara's Okolo (in The *Voice, 1964) is one of the few with the courage to challenge members of the corrupt political elite. For daring, he is promptly eliminated. In Isidore *Okpewho's Tides (1993) the hero adopts an extremist and anarchical reaction to oppression.

Anglophone West African writers have always been suspicious of the political philosophies propounded by their leaders, viewing such philosophies as tools for the re-enslavement of the people and as devices to divert attention from the failure of those leaders to use independence to improve the lot of the people. It is against this background that Soyinka's treatment of the leader who mouths a philosophy that seems to be an amalgam of *negritude, African personality, and African socialism in the satirical *Kongi's Harvest* (1967) is to be understood. This play also highlights the conflict between divine traditional authority and contemporary political leadership, which is often cornered by a manipulative, educated wealthy class.

If West African writers have been vocal in their condemnation of the political class, they have been even more insistent that the military class that presents itself across Africa as the solution to corruption and political instability is worse than the political class they are always so quick to replace. If there were any doubt that the military were not the 'beautiful ones' expected by the people and desired by the writers, their performance in government has put an end to it. Of West African novels that examine military government, Achebe's ★*Anthills of the Savannah* (1987) is the most incisive and the most fully realized. In the person of Sam, the general, Achebe captures the lack of vision, the insatiable appetite for power, and the viciousness of African military leaders. Sam is a self-centred individual whose personality is rooted solely in his *generalness*, as is evidenced by his lack of history (he has no surname) and community (he has no family). His lack of vision and his obscene materialism, both of which have been the hallmark of Africa's political elite, whether military or civilian, also inform Kole ★Omotoso's *Memories of Our Recent Boom* (1982), Ifeoma ★Okoye's *Men Without Ears* (1984), Festus ★Iyayi's *Violence* (1979), and Ken ★Saro-Wiwa's ★*Prisoners of Jebs* (1988). Sam is the quintessential contemporary African leader: he is the general in Nuruddin ★Farah's many novels about dictatorship, the reincarnation of Wole Soyinka's Kongi, and a confirmation of Dr. Bero of Soyinka's ★*Madmen and Specialists* (1971) and the bizarre collection of real-life sinister military buffoons in *A Play of Giants* (1984).

Ola ★Rotimi is another West African playwright who has considered the political evolution of Africa. His plays cover the various political phases of the continent, using the example of Nigeria. In *Ovonramwen Nogbaisi* (1974), which is set in the Kingdom of Benin on the eve of its destruction and plunder by the British, Rotimi presents the political structure that kept the Oba of Benin on the throne as an absolute monarch and the excesses and challenges which helped to undermine him and lay the groundwork for his conquest by the British. Similarly, *Kurunmi* (1971) documents the politics of suspicion and antagonism among the Yoruba nation states that facilitated their individual conquests by the British. *If* (1983) is concerned with the nature of the exploitation of Africans by Africans in independent African states, while *Our Husband Has Gone Mad Again* (1977) examines political corruption in Africa, locating the arena of conflict within a domestic context. The theme of political corruption continues to preoccupy West Africa's new generation of playwrights, from Femi ★Osofisan and Kole Omotoso through Yulissa Amadu ★Maddy, Akanji Nasiru, Bode ★Sowande, Olu ★Obafemi, and Tunde ★Fatunde to Tess ★Onwueme.

The treatment of political themes has also been central to African poetry. In many traditional African societies, a culture of satirical and praise poetry includes political comment. Modern African poets have continued this tradition of employing poetry for the articulation of their political visions. Gabriel Okara's poetry in the late 1950s signalled the birth of a poetry that was both politically relevant and accomplished in technique. Since then, West Africa has produced a large number of political poets who have mastered their craft while remaining committed to the political liberation of the African continent and imagination. Christopher Okigbo is, perhaps, the most outstanding of this crop of poets. His poetry is suffused with references to political events in Nigeria as well as the rest of Africa. Every major historical phase and its political implications for Africa are represented in his poetry. The colonial experience looms large in his early poetry and is concretized in the image of eagles with destructive talons; the political chaos that dogged independence in Africa, as in the case of Lumumba in the Congo and Awolowo in Nigeria, dictates the threnodic tone of 'Silences', and the final collapse of Nigerian society is articulated in 'Path of Thunder', which anticipated the ★Nigeria-Biafra ★war in which Okigbo was to die. His awareness of the sociopolitical landscape of Africa and his ability to convey it in lyrical lines and refreshing images are perhaps his most significant contribution to the development of political poetry in West Africa.

In addition to such other obviously political poets from the Okigbo generation as Kofi Awoonor, Chinua Achebe, J.P. Clark ★Bekederemo, and Wole Soyinka, a body of younger political poets, including Syl ★Cheney-Coker (Sierra Leone), Kofi ★Anyidoho and Atukwei ★Okai (Ghana), and ★Chinweizu, Okinba Launko, Odia ★Ofeimun, Olu ★Oguibe, Tanure ★Ojaide, and Niyi ★Osundare (Nigeria), has emerged to produce some exciting political poetry and to advance the frontiers of poetry beyond the limit to which Okigbo had taken them. Most of these newer poets, like traditional African poets who acted as the social conscience of their people and the purifiers of their language, are socially anchored and technically confident.

Obi Wali was the first to draw attention to the politics of language in African literature in graphic terms when he claimed that writing in colonial languages would only lead such writers to a dead end. But the debate on the politics of language has not been as intense in West Africa as it has been in East Africa, where it has led ★Ngugi wa Thiong'o to abandon English for Gikuyu, his mother tongue. Because of the vibrant tradition of indigenous literatures in West Africa, especially Nigeria, the writer in English has not felt as much pressure to abandon English for his or her mother tongue. Instead of abandoning English, those who have adopted it have evolved a number of ways to deal with their choice, ranging from the grammatically incorrect but enchanting prose of Amos *Tutuola, through Gabriel Okara's capturing of the rhythm and linguistic structure of Ijaw in his English, to Achebe's style, which obeys the grammatical rules of standard English while maintaining the world view and logic of the Igbo culture. Ken Saro-Wiwa, later executed by the Nigerian military regime, cheekily made a political point by calling *Sozaboy 'a novel in rotten English'.

The politics of race, which is at the root of the francophone West African concept of *negritude, is absent in anglophone West African writing. This is not to deny that there are individual anglophone West African writers, Okara and Armah for example, with negritude or near-negritude sentiments. The politics of gender has also not found adequate expression in anglophone West African writing. In most of the works by the leading writers, the politics of gender is only indirectly, possibly unintentionally, expressed through the absence of vibrant female voices. For example, the women in most of Achebe's novels are silent until Anthills of the Savannah, in which the woman's role is larger than that of 'fire fighter' and she is the bearer of the ultimate vision of salvation. Also, although Soyinka and Armah have included female characters, the dominant voices have always been male. Even in writing by the earlier generation of female writers such as Flora *Nwapa and Mabel *Segun, there is no concerted grappling with the politics of gender. Not until Buchi *Emecheta's The Joy of Motherhood (1979) exposes the abuse of African women and Molara *Ogundipe-Leslie's poetry insists on a socialist analysis of Africa do West African literature directly and rigorously confront gender issues.

Poor Christ of Bomba, The (1971) A novel by Mongo *Beti, translated from the French (Le Pauvre Christ de Bomba, 1956). Beti's second novel is the story of a white missionary and his black attendant, Denis, told through the latter's naive eyes. During a trip in the Nyong and Sanaga regions of Cameroon, both undergo a symbolic initiation, the first spiritual, the second sexual and mental. By the end of their adventures, Father Drumont has doubts about his ability to evangelize, and Denis has begun to enjoy sex while learning not to mistake appearance for substance. Despite its irreverence and its humour, the book raises serious questions about religious sincerity, about the materialistic interest of an institution devoted to charity, about the unchecked use of power, about the character of those who should set an example, and about the right of one people to impose its rules on another.

POPULAR LITERATURE

East Africa: *Ngugi wa Thiong'o, a leading writer and critic of African literature, has addressed the issue of popular writing, calling on African creative writers to seek aggressively the integration and communication with the majority of people in their societies that writing in vernacular languages can provide.

Popular fiction has undergone an important development, especially in Kenya, although it is not always easy to classify particular texts or writers: publishing difficulties after the 1980s have compelled some novelists to evoke major issues in the form of thrillers and adventure books. The first and earlier group of popular novels represents a very earnest literature, often in government-subsidized presses. Titles like John Karoki's The Land is Ours (1970) and Stephen *Ngubiah's A Curse from God (1970) describe the sufferings of rural communities from a traditional perspective. Others that resemble *Ngugi wa Thiong'o's novels aim at analysing the difficult conditions of the peasantry: Struggling for Survival (1983) by Sam Githinji is an example. Urban life is described in moralizing tones: recurrent tales of incest represent a deep-seated anguish in the face of the anonymity and anomy of the cities. In a less sombre mood, the novels of G. Kalimugogo or Yusuf K. Dawood introduce readers to the workings of modern institutions and professions. In a more recent development women writers aim at a middle-class female readership: they are romantic in their description of the new codes of love, but also very matter-of-fact in the assessment of the conflict between the desire for personal achievement and the necessity of upholding family values. The construction of most such books is loosely episodic, the plots contrived, yet their detailed, realistic description of contemporary life is part of their appeal.

The second group, of which Charles *Mangua's Son of Woman (1971) is an early example, was a reaction to prevailing edifying modes. The hero is amoral, the Americanized style inspired by films and magazines. All the characters pursue unashamedly the pleasures of sex, drink, and money so relentlessly that such books were banned in Tanzania. In the 1970s writers like Mwangi *Ruheni exalted the new individual freedom and social ascension of the middle class. The prolific David Maillu started his own press and published a wide range of novels in which he is both the moralizing columnist and the purveyor of simple thrills and romance. Some of his sexy romances were designedly published in tiny formats so that they could discreetly slip into a secretary's handbag to be read illicitly in the office. After 4.30 was about what happened after the office doors were locked at the Nairobi closing time. The Flesh (Part 1) and The Flesh (Part 2) were several hundred pages in 'verse' based on the style of *Okot p'Bitek's *Song of Lawino; the short lines took readers through the pages with exciting speed. After the 1980s, the excitement gave way to a more anguished evocation of the social descent of incautious heroes;

low life, prostitution, even drug use and violence provide a kind of raw energy balanced by a pattern of harsh retribution.

A third category includes formula-based novels, many of them issued by international popular collections aimed at the whole African market. The writing is uneven, sometimes very competent, with racy dialogue and skilled handling of plot and suspense. Under the conventional patterns of romance, crime, or international thrillers some recurrent themes reflect properly East African preoccupations. The many tales about smuggling, particularly at the Uganda–Kenya border, question the morality and the very existence of the nation-state. Investigation stories that feature journalists expose the workings of corruption and arbitrary power at the highest level, and the many titles about prison life project a bleak vision of society. Even stories describing juvenile romance aimed at adolescent readers, such as the titles in the Macmillan Pacesetter series and Heinemann Kenya's Spear Books, are anchored in a recognizable social reality in which personal emotions compete for recognition in a context of unemployment, family division, and a general uncertainty about the future. According to convention love triumphs and crime is punished, but the picture of the difficulties of daily life is so convincing that these texts cannot be classified as purely escapist fiction. Altogether, the vitality of this popular literature can be said to represent a testing ground for new topics and new writers in the region.

South Africa: Some literary critics define popular literature on the basis of best-selling books. In the South African case the unproblematized application of this criterion gives rise to a misnomer. While the South African writer Wilbur Smith, for example, is without doubt a 'popular' writer, in South Africa his novels appeal mainly, although perhaps not exclusively, to white South African readers. Historically this minority, privileged by education and earning power in a racially stratified economy, has dominated the book marketplace. Popular prose writing for the country's black majority, on the other hand, has favoured the story form over the novel, accessing its readership through low-priced magazines and newspapers. This is not the only reason for the popularity of the story, however: this genre also draws directly on the story-telling tradition in oral literature – as does the popular performance poetry of the late *apartheid period.

Some critics also attempt to characterize the popular literature published in such magazines as *Drum and *Staffrider, or performed before mass audiences, as 'protest literature', aimed at a 'politicized' audience and therefore not truly 'popular'. This approach makes light of at least two significant factors. In the first place it neglects the role of writers like Casey *Motsisi and Can *Themba, to name only two, in defining a black

urban popular culture; similarly, it fails to register the deliberate emphasis on everyday life in highly politicized but also very popular writers like Njabulo *Ndebele. Secondly, it underestimates the capacity of genres like the story and the praise poem to popularize (or 'conscientize') political themes which, in the South African case, were embedded in the everyday experience of the majority of the population.

It is an intriguing irony, therefore, that the material most obviously constituting 'popular literature' in the South African case is treated under numerous headings elsewhere in this companion (Apartheid, Biography and Autobiography, Black Consciousness, Drama, *Drum*, Humour and Satire, Literary Magazines, Literature and Politics, Novel, Oral Tradition and Folklore, Poetry, Prison Literature, Short Story, *Staffrider* and Women Writers) while here we focus, in the main, on the recreational literature consumed by the market-privileged white elite. It is a further irony, perhaps, that this latter literature, in the past, shared a history of exclusion from conventional canonical studies of South African English literature. Both, however, are now the focus of serious scrutiny by academics working in postmodern frameworks.

Within the field proposed by this limited definition of South African 'popular literature', the adventure story emerges as the most enduring genre. Building on the tradition established by colonial birds of passage such as Rider Haggard and John Buchan, Stuart *Cloete fashioned fifteen or so adventure novels, of which *Turning Wheels* (1937), set during the Great Trek of 1836, and *Rags of Glory* (1963), set in the *Anglo-Boer war, were the most successful. Among current South African writers of the genre, Wilbur Smith is far and away the most prolific and widely recognized. His well-stirred recipe of action, sex, and generally African settings, as in *When the Lion Feeds* (1964), *The Sunbird* (1972), and *Rage* (1987), random examples from his twenty-five (and rising) novels, are now translated into at least fourteen languages. Offshoot of the adventure story, two of the novels of Sir Laurens *van der Post, *Venture to the Interior* (1952) and *The Hunter and the Whale* (1967), feature quests of a more philosophical and spiritual nature. Antony Trew's *Smoke Island* (1964) and *Running Wild* (1982) are also action tales set against a politically charged canvas. The masculinist tenor of the adventure story genre is attested to by the dearth of woman writers in this category.

South Africa has a number of successful crime writers of considerable accomplishment, some of whom during the apartheid era subverted the genre's formulaic conservatism in order to throw doubt on the desirability of the political order and its laws. Foremost of South Africa's crime writers is the Pietermaritzburg-born James McClure, with his fictional detective-plus-sidekick Afrikaner lieutenant Tromp Kramer and the Zulu detective sergeant Michael Zondi of the Trekkersburg (Pietermaritzburg) murder and robbery squad. Much of the dynamic tension in their relationship arises from Kramer's racism and Zondi's refusal to fill a subservient black role. In his first novel, *The Steam Pig* (1971), which won a Golden Dagger award, Kramer and Zondi must solve a murder committed as an indirect consequence of South Africa's racial classification system and the Immorality Act. In *The Gooseberry Fool* (1974), the murder victim is an agent of the notorious Bureau of State Security (BOSS). It is interesting to conjecture why McClure is so much better known abroad than in South Africa. Another thriller which uses the Immorality Act against interracial sex as its crime motivator is Herman Charles *Bosman's last novel *Willemsdorp* (1977), written just before his death in 1951. This novel was the first in South Africa to use the thriller story to subvert the status quo rather than to support it. June Drummond has written nearly twenty-five novels, many of which are thrillers, since her first, *The Black Unicorn* (1960). Several of her books have been adapted for radio serialization in South Africa. Though many do not have a South African setting, the thriller by which she is best known, *The Farewell Party* (1971), is set near Durban. *Junta* (1989) is set against South African politics and carries a progressive, liberal hope for stability and change. Wessel Ebersohn is a South African thriller writer who has used the form to challenge the South African state. He achieved commercial success with *A Lonely Place to Die* (1979), the first in a series featuring the South African Jewish prison psychologist Yudel Gordon. Others in the series are *Divide the Night* (1981) and *Closed Circle* (1990). *Store Up the Anger* (1980) uses the mystery novel form to investigate the death of a *Black Consciousness leader clearly based on Steve Biko (it was banned as a result).

An interesting sign of the redefinition of market-defined popular literature in post-apartheid South Africa is the emergence in the 1990s of a number of thriller writers who are targeting a predominantly black readership. Foremost among them is Gomolemo Mokae, whose novel *The Secret in My Bosom* (1996) features Colonel Makena, a Sherlock Holmes-style detective living in Soweto. Nandi D'lovu is the pseudonym of a white woman journalist whose *Murder by Magic* (1995) stars sex detective Jon Zulu. In this thriller, the Manhattan-based Zulu interrupts a holiday in his native South Africa to rescue an orphaned girl in danger.

Less commercially successful in South Africa than the adventure and thriller genres is the popular historical romance. Among the leading exponents are Joy Packer (*Valley of the Vines*, 1955, *The Man in the Mews*, 1964, and *Blind Spot*, 1967), whose novels are mainly set in the Cape, and June Drummond (*The Blue Stocking*, 1985, and *The Impostor*, 1993). More intellectually highbrow are Daphne Rooke's *A Lover for Estelle* (1961), *The Greyling* (1962), and *Diamond Jo* (1965), set in the early days of Kimberley. Rooke's first novel, *A Grove of Fever Trees* (1950) won a major South African literary prize. It is interesting to compare popular literature in this vein with the work of Miriam *Tlali, who uses elements of the romance genre but combines them with political critique and a message of women's solidarity in *Muriel at Metropolitan* (1975) and a collection of short stories, *Footprints in the Quag* (1989).

West Africa: Creative writing geared toward the masses in West Africa, written either in vernacular African or in European languages, most often takes the form of novellas, dramas, guides to life, essays about history, politics, or culture, or collections of folktales, proverbs, and anecdotes. Its general strategy is to reach the vast majority of people to amuse, entertain, and educate about adapting to a changing world. It is mostly written by amateurs rather than by professional or intellectual writers, costs very little, and does not demand much intellectual concentration from the readers.

The pamphlet literature of the *Onitsha market in Nigeria is an example of such popular forms. It is a literature about the common people by some of their peers for everyone's enjoyment. It is brief and communicates its interests instantly in small rather than large doses of experience. It was born out of the growth in literacy that followed the Second World War, the rapid growth in the urban population at about the same time, the spread of locally owned and operated printing presses, the diversion of much of the energy and money previously devoted to the war effort to commercial, industrial, and technological development, and the flourishing of what might be called the democratic spirit, which led to a highly developed sense of human awareness and the acute insistence of individuals on their human relevance.

The audience for pamphlet literature comprises grammar and elementary school students, office workers, journalists, primary school teachers, traders, mechanics, taxi drivers, farmers, and the new literates who attend adult education classes and night school. Its authors are amateurs (school teachers, local printing press owners, journalists, railwaymen, traders, clerks, artisans, farmers, and even grammar-school students) who have some full-time occupation from which they earn their living and take up writing as a pastime.

PORTUGUESE LITERATURE [See LUSOPHONE LITERATURE]

PRINCE KAGWEMA (pseud. of Osija Mwam-bungu) (1931-), novelist, was born east of Tukuyu, Tanzania and studied at Makerere University College, Uganda, where he obtained a BA, and at Cambridge University, UK. He worked in the civil service until his retirement in 1976. The characters of his novels *Married Love Is a Plant* (1983), *Chausiku's Dozen* (1983), and *Society in the Dock* (1984) discuss love, sex, and politics, his uninhibited approach to which caused the temporary banning of his novel *Veneer of Love* (1975) in Tanzania. He confesses that a didactic intent governs all his writing.

PRINGLE, Thomas (1789-1834), Scottish poet, journalist and non-fiction writer. Regarded as the first published South African poet, Pringle was born on a farm near Kelso, Scotland and educated at Edinburgh University. His early verse epistle, 'The Autumnal Excursion', was adapted by James Hogg for inclusion in *The Poetic Mirror* and received praise from Sir Walter Scott. In 1820 Pringle and his family took advantage of the government's emigration scheme to settle British farmers in the Eastern Cape. Later he took up an appointment as sub-librarian of the Government (later South African) Library in Cape Town; he also opened a small private school. In 1824 he started the monthly *South African Journal*, and soon he was also co-editing a newspaper, *The Commercial Advertiser*, founded by Robert Greig. When Pringle published an article in the *Journal* critical of the government's handling of the grievances of the settlers, the governor used his influence to bring about Pringle's financial ruin, and he was forced to sell up and return to England, where he arrived after just six years in South Africa. His travels and experiences in the colony had impressed on him the plight of the indigenous peoples, and his article on slavery at the Cape in the *New Monthly Magazine* (October 1826) led to his appointment as secretary of the Anti-Slavery Society soon after his arrival in London. Greig continued, and ultimately won, the campaign launched by Pringle to ensure freedom of the press in South Africa.

Whereas Pringle's earlier verse had been competent but largely conventional, the poems he wrote in South Africa, or that were prompted by his residence there, reveal both the impact on him of a new world of experience and his attempts to render that experience as vitally and truthfully as possible. This is well illustrated in *Ephemerides: or Occasional Poems, Written in Scotland and South Africa* (1928) as well as the later *Poems Illustrative of South Africa*, which formed part one of *African Sketches* (1834). Poems such as 'The Bechuana Boy', 'Afar in the Desert' (highly praised by Coleridge and one of the most frequently reprinted poems in nineteenth-century Britain), 'Makanna's Gathering' and 'The Forester of the Neutral Ground' (the first South African poem to deal with miscegena-tion) illustrate Pringle's empathy with Africans, victims of Boer oppression and British imperialism. Apart from pamphlets produced for the Anti-Slavery Society, Pringle edited George Thompson's *Travels and Adventures in Southern Africa* (1828), as well as a successful annual, *Friendship's Offering*, and completed his prose *Narrative of a Residence in South Africa*, published as part two of *African Sketches*. His achievement is that he produced without models some of the first truly South African — as opposed to British-humanist — *poetry. Most South Africans, however, remember him for his role in securing freedom of the press.

PRISON LITERATURE IN SOUTH AFRICA

In the turbulent South African society imprisonment of political opponents has until recently been a characteristic punitive measure. It has led to the development of literature dealing with the experience of solitary confinement, torture, detention, and long-term imprisonment. The concentration of prison writings between 1960 and 1995 points to the intensification of political polarization under *apartheid (1948-94). In this literature Robben Island features as a central symbol of political oppression and incarceration, and Robben Island texts form a subgenre, in some ways comparable to Holocaust writings.

The roots of contemporary prison writing lie in the pre-colonial and colonial period (1652-1910). Autshumato (or Harry die Strandloper), an indigenous Khoikhoi agent of English navigators using the Cape as a refreshment station, was banished to Robben Island as early as 1632 (until 1640). He was followed by Xhosa chiefs Maqoma (1857-69, 1871-3) and Makhanda, also known as Makanna or Nxele (1819-20). Langalibalele, a Hlubi chief from Zululand, spent 1874-5 on the island. Reference is made to these banishments in the oral tradition in Zulu or Xhosa praise poems such as 'Maqoma son of Ngqika', although there are no written records by these prisoners. Prison writings from before 1870 probably exist, but these have not yet become part of literary consciousness.

The written record of South African prison literature commences with the translated /Xam narrative '//Kabbo's Capture and Journey to Cape Town - 1871' (in *Specimens of Bushmen Folklore*, 1911). //Kabbo, a member of the extinct /Xam, orally narrated his memoir to Wilhelm Bleek, who recorded it in both /Xam and English. This heavily mediated written record of an oral prison memoir is remarkable for the indigenous perspective it offers on colonial times and for the reflection of oral narrative style (repetition, cyclic narration, etc.).

Similarly the German missionary Nachtigal in 1875 recorded the oral testimony of 'Rooizak', a Swazi prisoner, published by Peter Delius as *The Conversion: Death Cell Conversations of 'Rooizak' and the*

Missionaries – Lydenburg 1875 (1984). After seven months in solitary confinement Rooizak attempts suicide, without success; the endless ministering that follows sometimes borders on psychological torture. In spite of its heavy mediation this text is a striking testimony of a prisoner's trauma and of intercultural conflict.

The British military designed the concept of concentration camps during the *Anglo-Boer War (1899-1902) to house women, children, and indigenous 'others' as part of their scorched-earth policy. Of the 118,000 people incarcerated roughly 27,000 died of malnutrition, disease, or other causes. Experiences in the camps gave rise to numerous diaries, memoirs, and journals published in *Afrikaans, Dutch, and English. (Many appeared in the 1930s and 40s, probably as a result of rising Afrikaner nationalism). Important examples are *Het Concentratie-Kamp van Irène* [The concentration camp at Irené] (1905), a diary kept by Johanna Brandt-Van Warmeloo, who served as a nurse with the Red Cross in this camp in 1901; *Woman's Endurance* (1904), a diary by A.D.L., a chaplain in the camp at Bethulie in 1901; and Napier Devitt's factual discussion of *The Concentration Camps in South Africa during the Anglo-Boer War of 1899-1902* (1941). Devitt's text was an attempt to counteract what he called the 'propaganda' about the camps being disseminated during the 1930s and 40s. Other texts emanating from the Anglo-Boer war dealt with the conditions in exile camps in St. Helena, Ceylon, Bermuda, and India, where 26,000 Boer prisoners-of-war were sent. Memorable texts are Joubert Reitz's poem 'The Seachlight', dealing with his longing for his lost fatherland, and G.S. Preller's *Ons parool: dae uit die dagboek van 'n krygsgevangene* [Our parole: days from the diary of a prisoner-of-war] (1938).

The earliest text dealing with conditions in South African prisons under apartheid is Henry Nxumalo's account in 'Mr. Drum Goes to Gaol' (published in *Drum in 1954). Prison writing stemming from this era appears in many genres and languages.

In the category of autobiography, Ruth First (assassinated in 1982) published *117 Days: An Account of Confinement and Interrogation under the South African Ninety-Day Detention Law* (1965). Albie Sachs also used the diary form in *The Jail Diary of Albie Sachs* (1966). Michael Dingake's *My Fight against Apartheid* (1982) describes his fifteen years as political prisoner on Robben Island. Hugh Lewin's *Bandiet: Seven Years in a South African Prison* (1974) was followed by Moses Dlamini's *Hell-Hole Robben Island: Prisoner 872/63* (no date), Molefe Pheto's *And Night Fell: Memoirs of a Political Prisoner in South Africa* (1983), and Indres Naidoo's account as told to Albie Sachs, *Prisoner 885/63: Island in Chains* (1982). Arguably the two most important autobiographical texts are widely divergent: Breyten *Breytenbach's *The True Confessions of an Albino

Terrorist* (1984) and Nelson Mandela's *Long Walk to Freedom* (1994). Breytenbach was incarcerated as an established Afrikaans writer, somewhat peripherally involved in the political struggle (disavowed by the ANC when imprisoned), whereas Mandela was sentenced to life as a pivotally important political leader of the ANC. *The True Confessions of an Albino Terrorist* is a complex literary text focused on an individual's psychological struggle for survival. *Long Walk to Freedom* (partially written by Richard Stengel) expresses throughout a sense of communal striving towards the goal of political freedom. It follows a straightforward narrative line, unlike the post-modernist fragmentary structure of Breytenbach's text. Mandela's observation that no one truly knows a nation without having been inside its jails and that imprisoned African citizens were treated 'like animals' is a damning reflection of South Africa under apartheid.

There are many examples of fiction concerned with prison experience. Herman Charles *Bosman's *Cold Stone Jug* (1949) was inspired by Bosman's jail sentence on a charge of murder. Alex *La Guma's *The *Stone Country* (1967) is dedicated to 'the daily average of 70,351 prisoners in South African gaols in 1964'. This was followed by D.M. Zwelonke's *Robben Island* (1973) and Mtutuzeli *Matshoba's 'A Pilgrimage to the Isle of Makanna' (in *Call Me Not a Man*, 1979). Steve Biko's last ten days and eventual death at the hands of the security police are fictionalized in Wessel Ebersohn's memorable *Store Up the Anger* (1980), Lewis *Nkosi describes imprisonment as the result of a loving relationship between a black man and a white woman in *Mating Birds* (1986), and Breyten Breytenbach fictionalizes his experience as political prisoner in a section of *Memory of Snow and of Dust* (1988).

Single poems about prison were anthologized in *One Day in June* (1986) and *The Return of the Amasi Bird* (1982). English collections include those by James *Matthews (*Pass Me a Meatball, Jones*, 1977; *No Time for Dreams*, 1981), Dennis *Brutus (*Letters to Martha: Poems from a South African Prison*, 1968; *A Simple Lust*, 1973), and Jeremy Cronin (*Inside*, 1983). Frank Anthony published a heavily annotated Afrikaans collection *Robbeneiland my kruis my huis* [Robben Island my cross my house] (1983), while Dikobe wa Mogale's *Prison Poems* (1992) are strangely unpolitical verses, mostly about love and longing. Breyten Breytenbach published 400 Afrikaans prison poems in five volumes: *Voetskrif* [Footscript] (1976), *Eklips* [Eclipse] (1983), ('YK') ['Ache'] (1983), *Buffalo Bill* (1984), and *Lewendood* [Life and death] (1985). *Judas Eye and Self Portrait/Deathwatch* (1988) contains a few translations of these poems into English. The shifting forms of address used in the poems (the poet wavers between 'us', where he includes himself as a South African, and 'you', where he distances himself), suggest uncertainty about Breytenbach's sense of belonging.

Among examples of dramatic literature Athol ★Fugard's *The Island* (1973), Jon Blai and Norman Fenton's *The Biko Inquest* (1978), and Strini Moodley's *Prison Walls* (1985) are some of the central texts.

Other forms have also been explored. Govan Mbeki's *Learning from Robben Island: The Prison Writings of Govan Mbeki* (1991) is didactic, having its origin in the forum for political education that developed on Robben Island. Mosiuoa Patrick (Terror) Lekota's teachings in epistolary form about South African history, *Prison Letters to my Daughter* (1991), was written to his daughter, Tjhabi, while he was incarcerated on Robben Island.

Prisoners of Jebs (1988) A collection of columns by Ken ★Saro-Wiwa. This collection, along with its companion *Pita Dumbrok's Prison* (1991), are an integral part of the Saro-Wiwa story and repay close reading. The points of reference are sometimes local and topical, very obviously related to specific moments in Nigeria's public self-scrutiny. Certain passages deliberately recall Jonathan Swift's *Gulliver's Travels*, prompting the reader to extend to the books an awareness that they belong to a time and place when literary giants were resolutely engaged in writing about the Lilliputians and Yahoos around them.

Saro-Wiwa's achievement lies in the elaboration of his initial conceit, the eloquence of his style, and the evidence of a mischievous, passionate, concerned imagination at work. The conceit centres on the proposition that an artificial prison island has been established off the coast of Nigeria, which becomes a parade ground for follies and vices. Saro-Wiwa uses it and the adventures of some of those connected with it to comment on specific scandals, including 'disappearing millions', and national weaknesses, including unwillingness to take responsibility for actions. With dozens of delightful turns of phrase and through the generation of bizarre, moving, and absurd situations, he provides entertainment and comment.

Given the ferocity that has characterized politics in Nigeria, the courage of the writing is remarkable. Saro-Wiwa dared to be a satirist in a state where criticism was sometimes taken as insult and where dissent was often met with violence. Within the generous embrace of his work, he finds occasion to raise provocatively the question of his own identity and to interrogate the position of the satirist. A protagonist, Pita Dumbrok, replies to the question 'Who is Saro-Wiwa?' with 'He is a mean, spiteful little wretch, and so small you wouldn't find him among a colony of soldier ants. He is learning to be a satirist'.

Saro-Wiwa was hanged at Port Harcourt on 10 November 1995. The military regime used his support of Ogoni autonomy to eliminate a troublesome voice. They underestimated the international outcry at this extraordinary injustice. His ability to frighten and disturb the sleep of chiefs, governors, customs officers, professors, journalists, and members of the armed forces had made him a marked man long before – when he started writing about Jebs Prison for Nigerian newspapers.

Proper Marriage, A (1954) A novel by Doris ★Lessing. The second novel in the *Children of Violence* series finds the hero, Martha Quest, at the start of the Second World War feeling trapped at the age of twenty-one in a loveless marriage in a British colonial town modelled on Salisbury, Rhodesia (now Harare, Zimbabwe). When her husband is sent off to the war, Martha renews her political idealism and becomes involved with a group of white leftists in the colony, some of whom are European refugees and others working-class Royal Air Force men from Britain. When Russia suddenly becomes Britain's ally during the battle of Stalingrad, Martha dedicates herself to communism. For the first time, Lessing develops her character's obsession with the idea of revolution as a means of utterly breaking with colonial culture and the bourgeois family in which she is caught.

PUBLISHING IN SUB-SAHARAN AFRICA
During the past three decades indigenous publishing in Africa has made great strides, and despite the continuing domination by the British and French multinational firms, with their ready access to capital and expertise, independent, autonomous publishing has established itself quite firmly since the late 1960s and early 1970s. The industry still faces enormous obstacles, but over the past few years a number of significant developments have included a range of initiatives designed to find collective solutions to different aspects of African publishers' common problems.

The International Conference on Publishing and Book Development in Africa held at the University of Ife in Nigeria in 1973 was a milestone in the development of autonomous publishing capacity in Africa. By that time indigenous publishing in many African countries was poised to challenge the monopoly of foreign publishers. An awareness was growing in all African nations of the need for a home-grown style of publishing geared to the requirements and experiences of the local people. Until Kenyan independence, the only locally owned publishing house was the East African Literature Bureau (EALB), operating under the auspices of the East African High Commission and, with only a few exceptions, employing English expatriates. The EALB published books such as Stephen ★Ngubiah's *A Curse from God* (1970), Kenneth ★Watene's *My Son for My Freedom* (1973), and Barnabas Katigula's *Groping in the Dark* (1974), and Muthoni ★Likimani's *They Shall be Chastised* (1974).

However, while the 1970s might have been a decade of relative boom and expansion for the African book industries, the 1980s was a decade of crisis, and the crisis has intensified through the 1990s. The constantly deepening economic recession and chronic balance of payments problems in most African countries have taken a severe toll on publishing and book development. Government funds for textbooks and library purchases have dramatically declined, and many publishing operations have become dormant or have ceased trading altogether. Currencies in most African countries have collapsed: for example in 1983 it took less than one Nigerian naira to purchase one US dollar; fourteen years later it takes almost sixty times that amount. In the same period the Tanzanian shilling went from twelve to the dollar to 538. Since many of the materials for book production still need to be imported, including paper and printing equipment, it is not surprising that many publishers have gone out of business. In the meanwhile foreign exchange has become so scarce that many university and public libraries in Africa have been unable to purchase new books over the past ten years, much less maintain their serials collections, and the majority of them are now dependent on donations of books and journals from abroad. Although the situation varies from country to country, and in Zimbabwe or Kenya, for example, it is significantly better than in some other parts of the continent, many bookshops in Africa are empty, schools are without books, and teachers and scholars lack material to pursue their studies, to maintain their understanding of developments taking place in their disciplines elsewhere in the world, and to keep their teaching and research up to date. African academics have become more and more marginalized, many unable to participate in contemporary academic debates or conferences. In the late 1980s and early 1990s Africa increasingly became a bookless society. The term 'book famine' was coined and has been the subject of much concern among librarians, academics, and the international book community in their attempts to alleviate the distressing picture of book starvation in Africa.

Few African governments have taken decisive action to support their book industries, certainly not in the private sector, and in many countries the book industries, as well as library services, have had to take a back seat in the pursuit of national development. Although there have been a few instances of positive government support, government participation in book publishing in Africa has been generally ill conceived. State-aided companies were either hampered by bureaucracy or inefficiency, or have led to publishing monopolies, a development that has stifled the growth of independent publishing.

The development of the book industries in Africa today has been and will continue to be affected by problems of infrastructure and by the unfavourable economic conditions in most parts of the continent. Furthermore, many social and cultural issues compound the problem: a multiplicity of languages together with high illiteracy, poor transportation and communications, and lack of training and expertise have all hindered the development of the reading habit and the growth of a healthy book industry, quite apart from the fact that the majority of people in Africa have very limited amounts of money at their disposal to spend on books. Effective distribution is still a serious problem, although some publishers have explored new methods of getting books to the marketplace and to rural communities.

One of the most fundamental issues for publishers and writers alike is the question of language. The question of whether to write in an African or in a European language has been vigorously argued, and debates about new norms, new ways for writers to reach the people, continue. An increasing number of African writers try to reach a national audience through an indigenous language, perhaps most prominent among them the Kenyan writer *Ngugi wa Thiong'o, who has repeatedly stated that only through writing in an African language can an African sensibility truly develop, and that writing in an African language might compel African writers to become more relevant, more meaningful, and closer to the realities of African life. However, dissenting voices have argued that to write in any of the African languages restricts the number of readers for a given text, and that to select an international language provides a medium of communication that allows African books to be published and read in many countries. While this debate will no doubt continue, the language issue also greatly affects publishing developments: on the one hand the vast number of languages creates special problems for African publishers, and on the other hand African governments' decisions on language policy will significantly influence publishing developments in general, and the success and viability of publishing in the African languages in particular. African writers have repeatedly called on African publishers to devote more time and resources to publishing material in African languages for the general reader, and on books intended for enjoyment rather than achievement reading. Some publishers have bravely experimented in this area, but despite some modest successes, publishing in the African languages has often been commercially disappointing, certainly for titles for the general markets. At the same time publishers are unwilling to experiment unless the books are subsidized or they can carry such innovation on the back of mainstream publishing and the more lucrative educational book markets.

Journals and magazines have been the victims of the very difficult economic conditions in Africa. From the mid-1960s to the late 1970s there was a plethora of fine *literary and cultural magazines, including *Abbia*, *Asemka*, *Black Orpheus*, *Busara*, *Joliso*, *Kiabàrà*, *Marang*,

New Culture, Okike, Okyeame, the famous *Transition* (later *Ch'indaba*), and several others. Although one or two have resurfaced from time to time (for example *Black Orpheus* and *Transition*, which is now published from New York and bears little resemblance to the earlier publication), the rest ceased to publish long ago. A few new literary and cultural magazines have emerged periodically, but they have either been of poor quality or have not survived beyond volume 1, number 1.

The demise of literary journals has resulted in a dearth of publishing outlets for writers in general and for young and as yet unknown or inexperienced writers in particular, an outcome that has probably also led to a stifling of creative writing. Much of the early work of the best-known names in African literature was first published in a number of (then) flourishing literary magazines, but today there are very few publishing outlets of this sort. There are occasional promising newcomers to the scene, for example the impressive *Glendora Review* (Lagos), which published its first two issues in 1995, but their survival, especially in the present very difficult market conditions and with the markets within Africa virtually collapsed, is by no means guaranteed.

Despite the very difficult economic conditions, the lack of government encouragement, and the many obstacles facing the indigenous book industries, innovative new publishing ventures are getting started in many places. A wide range of books of the highest quality have emerged from some African countries, there is evidence of great intellectual vigour, and a number of privately owned firms in particular have demonstrated imaginative entrepreneurial skill in the midst of adversity. Although the mortality rate has been high over the past decade, there are today about 200 active indigenous firms with fairly sizeable publishing programmes, plus several hundred more small imprints, though most of these live a somewhat precarious existence.

Although many indigenous publishers still have difficulty competing with the multinationals on real terms, there are some especially dynamic autonomous publishing companies in Zimbabwe, Kenya, Nigeria, Ghana, and South Africa. In the latter, the end of *apartheid has brought about dramatic changes in the country's educational structures and its publishing industry. A number of South African publishers who hitherto faithfully served the repressive apartheid regime and its 'Bantu education' policy of segregated and unequal learning seem to have undergone a remarkably smooth transition and are now proudly proclaiming a new-found social responsibility, publishing socially committed books and literature for the 'new' South Africa. Meantime the field of educational and textbook publishing has become a fiercely contested terrain, with some publishers attempting to

secure privileged access to the state educational structures in post-apartheid South Africa. Changes in ownership, mergers, regroupings, and restructuring have accompanied the search for new alliances within the book industry or through partnerships with overseas publishers.

Leading publishers in English-speaking Africa with strong literary lists include Baobab Books (Harare), College Press (Harare), East African Educational Publishers (Nairobi; formerly Heinemann East Africa, thereafter Heinemann Kenya); Fountain Publishers (Kampala), Fourth Dimension Publishers (Enugu), Heinemann Educational Books Nigeria (Ibadan), Malthouse Press (Lagos), Mambo Press (Gweru), Saros International Publishers (Port Harcourt), Sedco Publishing (Accra), Spectrum Books (Ibadan), University Press plc (Ibadan, formerly OUP Nigeria), and the Zimbabwe Publishing House (Harare). A number of small imprints such as Woeli Publishing Services and Afram Publications (both Accra), Lake Publishers (Kisumu, Kenya), New Namibia Books (Windhoek), or Fountain Publications and New Horn Press (both Ibadan) also publish fiction, drama, and poetry. In South Africa, publishers with literary publishing programmes are too numerous to list but include David Philip, Ravan Press, and Skotaville Publishers, who were all in the forefront of oppositional publishing during the apartheid days; small imprints such as Buchu Books, COSAW Publishing, Mayibuye Books, Hippogriff Press, Queillerie Press, and Snail Press; and major companies such as Tafelberg, Maskew Miller Longman, and Heinemann South Africa.

Publishing in francophone Africa has been in sharp decline in recent years, although French publishers and their allies remain a strong force in Africa. French-language publishing was dominated until recently by Les Nouvelles Éditions Africaines (NEA), a joint undertaking by the governments of Senegal, Côte d'Ivoire, and Togo together with French publishing interests, and NEA developed a massive and impressive list including many titles of belles-lettres. However, their dominance, and near monopoly, arguably stifled the growth of small independent publishers. NEA-Dakar has since split with their former branches in Lomé and Abidjan, and all three have gone their separate ways. In addition to well-established firms such as Éditions CEDA in Abidjan, a number of new autonomous imprints have emerged in Senegal and Côte d'Ivoire; the devalued CFA franc may also provide a stimulus for increased indigenous publishing and a reduction in the traffic of books imported from France, which have now become much more expensive as a result of the devaluation. New publishing companies include Aminata Sow Fall's Édition Khoudia in Dakar and Les Éditions du Livre du Sud/ EDILIS in Abidjan, a dynamic new autonomous publisher in francophone West Africa headed by Mical-

Dréhi Lorougnon. A leading force in francophone African publishing in the 1970s and 80s, Éditions CLE in Yaoundé has dramatically cut back its publishing programme in recent years, although it continues to publish occasional works of fiction and drama.

Publishing in the lusophone African countries has been confined to Mozambique, where it has been characterized by a high degree of central control under a single state monopoly. However, the political transformation in Mozambique has been followed by the emergence of a number of private sector independent publishers.

A good indicator of the intellectual vigour and enterprise of African publishers is the diverse range of books that have been submitted for the Noma Award competition over the past sixteen years. Established in 1979 by the late Shoichi Noma (formerly president of Kodansha Ltd., the Japanese publishing giant), the Noma Award is open to African writers and scholars whose work is published in Africa and is now well established as Africa's leading annual book award. The US$5,000 prize (administered by the journal *African Book Publishing Record*) has been won in all three of the fairly wide categories of books eligible for the award, namely academic or scholarly, children's books, and literature and creative writing. Books are admissible in any of the languages of Africa, both indigenous and European. The first award was won in 1980 by Mariama ★Bâ for her novel *Une si longue lettre* (1979; ★*So Long a Letter*, 1981), which has since acquired the status of a classic in modern African literature and has been translated into sixteen languages. The 1995 winner was Marlene van Niekerk, whose novel *Triomf* [Triumph] was the first novel in Afrikaans to receive the prize. By 1996, the main prize had been won twice each for works of fiction in English and in French and once in Afrikaans; on three occasions the prize was awarded for volumes of poetry, two in English and one in Portuguese; two winners were children's books in English; and the remaining seven winners (or joint winners) were for scholarly works. Although a title in ★Gikuyu by Gakaara wa Wanjau, *Mwandiki wa Mau Mau Ithaamirio-ini*, described by the jury as 'the single most significant historical document of the entire resistance literature from Kenya', was the joint winner in 1993, no work of fiction, poetry, or drama in an African language has thus far won the prize outright, although books in Gikuyu, ★Hausa, ★Swahili, ★Ndebele, ★Shona, and ★Yoruba have been cited for honourable mention on eight occasions.

Among new initiatives that have helped to strengthen autonomous publishing in Africa and to increase the visibility of African books overseas is the Oxford-based African Books Collective Ltd. (ABC), a self-help initiative set up by a group of African publishers in 1989 to promote and distribute their books in Europe, North America, and other parts of the world. From an initial seventeen founder members in 1989, ABC has grown to include forty-eight African publishers in fourteen African countries.

James Currey Publishers, also in Oxford, have specialized in co-publishing academic paperbacks with publishers in Africa. Their informal publishing network with EAEP (Nairobi), Baobab (Harare), Fountain Publishers (Kampala), Mkuki na Nyota (Tanzania), David Philip (Cape Town) and others has helped circulate African books throughout the continent and in Europe, America and the rest of the world.

Another initiative, a seminar on publishing in the third world held in 1991 in Bellagio, Italy, brought together a group of publishers from Africa and Asia, as well as representatives of donor agencies, and led to the establishment of the Bellagio Group, an informal association of donors and other organizations dedicated to strengthening indigenous publishing in the third world. The group has productively interacted with African publishers and book trade organizations and has provided a forum for discussion and a collaborative network for assisting publishing and book development. The Research and Information Centre of the Bellagio Group (now based at Boston College) assists the network by sponsoring research related to book development and publishing and produces the quarterly *Bellagio Publishing Network Newsletter*.

A third initiative is APNET, begun in 1992 and based in Harare, Zimbabwe. APNET indicates a growing trend towards collective approaches to the issues of African book publishing: it seeks to promote co-ordinated strategies among its members, and one of its primary objectives is to strengthen national publishers' associations. Training for the book industries is also high on its agenda, as is the promotion of an intra-African book trade. It publishes the bimonthly *African Publishing Review*. Harare is also the venue for the annual Zimbabwe International Book Fair, a shop window on African publishing output and an important trading crossroads for African publishers.

Within Africa one of the biggest challenges facing African publishers is effective marketing and distribution of African books, both within individual African countries and across borders. Outside Africa, in the countries of the north, the publication and promotion of African literature, both in the original language of publication and in translation, still face many obstacles that seem to prevent a wide acceptance of African writing; apart from a few notable exceptions (such as Chinua ★Achebe, Nadine ★Gordimer, Ben ★Okri, Ngugi wa Thiong'o, Wole ★Soyinka, and a few lonely women's voices such as Bessie ★Head, Ama Ata ★Aidoo or Tsitsi ★Dangarembga), African literature has yet to gain significant international recognition. Despite several Noma Award winners distinguished for works of fiction and poetry, and despite three African winners of the Nobel Prize (Wole Soyinka,

Naguib *Mahfouz and Nadine Gordimer) and two winners of the Booker Prize (Nadine Gordimer and Ben Okri), much of the great canon of African literature is still marginalized and difficult to buy. African publishers and the African Books Collective, despite its UK base, have difficulty placing African books and African literature in leading bookshops and retail outlets, and even the larger companies, with their launch parties and professional sales force, have similar problems. What, then, are the major obstacles to African literatures being accepted as world literature? What are the problems of genre and theme? Are the contexts of some African novels so foreign to general readers that they cannot relate or understand? What are the realistic chances of translation into the major European languages? What are the problems of translation in relation to language, style, and literary form? What are the publishing realities and the problems of achieving publishing viability for works of African literature? These are just some of the issues that will need to be addressed among publishers both in Africa and in Europe and North America who have published, with varying degrees of success, a range of African literature.

A body of opinion maintains that there is a considerable corpus of literature in the African languages that remains largely undiscovered, certainly untranslated, because colonial powers of the past always treated indigenous or so-called vernacular languages or literatures as second rate and because European languages as the medium of instruction and culture have suppressed indigenous languages as a vehicle for creative literary output. African writers and scholars of African literature have urged publishers both in the UK and in Africa to publish more of this material, but British publishers tend to focus on the difficulty of selling African literature in English, let alone in translation, and the extra costs of translation. Some African publishers might argue that they have tried and failed; that being adventurous is risky and costs money, because

unless the runs are very large prices are too high; and that for the most part the general public will not buy the books because the emphasis is still on achievement reading rather than reading for pleasure, and many people will buy textbooks to help them pass examinations before spending money on general books.

While African publishers have a major role to play in developing and reinforcing literacy, they cannot do it on their own, and in any event publishing and providing books does not necessarily create literacy or cultivate the reading habit. The initiatives for significant change must come from government-sponsored programmes. Although some African governments actively promoted literacy in the 1960s and 70s, governments in most African countries cannot now be relied upon to play a major part in developing a reading culture and sustainable literacy. In fact in some countries, Ghana for example, literacy is actually going down because parents are now required to pay for their children's primary education and many are unable to afford it. In some African countries NGOs or donor organizations are stepping in where governments have failed. One positive aspect of this otherwise unhappy picture is the possibility for new alliances between commercial publishers and people's education movements or publishing co-operatives. Commercial publishers would do well to learn what makes people want to buy books and to read them from the grassroots experiences of community publishing initiatives such as the Mzumbe Book Project in Tanzania and the remarkable Community Publishing Process in Zimbabwe. Innovative and experimental approaches will be needed to identify the audience and elicit responses, and new methods will have to be found for book distribution. Ultimately, the publishing industries must meet the challenge of a potentially vast readership in order to bring books to the 'non-literary' marketplace and into the economic reach of the rural poor and the disadvantaged.

Q

QABULA, Alfred Temba (1942-), South African poet, was born at Flagstaff, in what was then the Transkei, and experienced the hardships of migrancy and the homeland system at first hand. As part of the trade unions' mobilization of cultural forms to bolster opposition to capital and the *apartheid state, Qabula began in 1983 to compose and perform poems influenced by the praise poetry or *izibongo* he had heard in the Transkei and in urban hostels. His poems are concerned mainly with issues of union organization and seek to adapt traditional Zulu and Xhosa poetic forms to new urbanized and politicized contexts (though black workers have used a variety of oral forms in industrialized contexts for most of this century). He constantly emphasizes that poetry is not the preserve of an educated elite. His best-known composition is 'Praise Poem to FOSATU', in which he uses the form of *izibongo* (which mediates between ruler and subjects) to negotiate relations of power between workers and union. Among his other poems of note is 'Tears of a Creator', which he performed with Mi S'dumo Hlatswayo at the Durban launch of the Congress of South African Trade Unions in 1985. His more recent poems, such as 'Africa's Black Buffalo' or 'Dear', are increasingly narrative and reveal a greater concern with national issues than those of the shop floor. Recent criticism has emphasized the value of Qabula's work and that of other worker poets by placing it within the broader history of oral poetry in South Africa. Qabula has published poems in *Black Mamba Rising: South African Worker Poets in Struggle* (1986) and in magazines, and has written his autobiography, *A Working Life: Cruel Beyond Belief* (1989).

Question of Power, A (1973) A novel by Bessie *Head. Semi-autobiographical in nature, Head's most challenging and unusual novel explores the process of mental breakdown and recovery in the protagonist, Elizabeth. The novel employs an interiorized narrative style and is characterized chiefly by vertiginous passages detailing the terror of a descent into madness. These are juxtaposed with passages dealing with a recognizable social world of co-operative gardening, human interaction, and everyday events in a Botswanan village. The novel is significant in that it shifts attention away from the social-political arena favoured by the African novel and turns inwards on the consciousness of a central protagonist.

R

RABÉARIVELO, Jean-Joseph (1903-37) Malagasy poet and novelist. Born into a noble but poor family, an illegitimate child, he was a self-taught literature student who dared compete with the masters of French Symbolist poetry. He became associated with literary and poetic circles in Malagasy working as a proofreader and was soon known for the variety of his talents. Writing in Malagasy, translating his own works into French, corresponding with literary figures all over the world, he was also writing a novel, as well as keeping a diary. In his poetry collections (*La coupes des cendres*, 1924; *Sylves*, 1927; *Volumes*, 1928) he expresses his longing for the old Malagasy ethos of the nobility as well as his aspiration to know the rest of the world. He writes a fluid free verse which conveys the volatility and subtlety of his feelings, being in the words of Wole ★Soyinka, 'doomed to remain in the threshold of reality'. He also attempted to translate his own work and published poems in both French and Malagasy (*Presque-songes*, 1934; *Traduit de la nuit*, 1935) using 'translation as a creative principle', to use the apt description of his approach given by M. Adejunmobi. Unable to get a passage to France, suffering from the subaltern condition of the indigenous intellectual, he committed suicide. His mastery of language and his linguistic consciousness made his work one of the most remarkable achievements of French writing outside France. Two posthumous novels (*L'Interférence*, 1988; *L'Aube rouge*, 1998) have been published which add to his stature as a writer. A diary remains to see the light of day. He was one of the first francophone poets to be translated in the ★Mbari publications (*24 Poems*, 1962) in Ibadan in the early 1960s.

RABÉMANAJARA, Jacques (1913-) Malagasy poet, dramatist and politician. Born in Maroantsetra he became a well-known figure of Malagasy cultural life in the 1930s, to the extent that Jean-Joseph ★Rabéarivelo made him, in one of his last letters, his spiritual heir. Rabémanajara published poetry volumes and was also involved in colonial administration. During the war he was in France and wrote literary dramas (*Les Dieux malgaches*, 1942). In 1945 he started to be involved in Malagasy nationalist politics, and became a *deputé* of Madagascar to the French National Assembly. In 1947 after the insurrection that was savagely put down by the French colonial army he was prosecuted and sentenced to death. This sentence was commuted to a term in jail; while in prison he wrote several poetry collections, notably *Antsa* (1948, reissued in 1956 with

a preface – dedicated 'to his brother in Christ, unjustly jailed' – by well-known novelist and Nobel Prize winner François Mauriac). Liberated in 1955 he was associated with the First Congress of Black Writers and Artists gathered at the Sorbonne in 1956 by Alioune Diop, and published several books (*Les Boutriers de l'aurore*, drama, 1957; *Nationalisme et problèmes malgaches*, 1958). He re-entered Malagasy politics at the time of independence, eventually rising to Vice-President of the Republic, until the 1972 revolution sent him back into exile; he lives in Paris and is still closely associated with *Présence africaine*.

Rainmaker, The (1975) A play by Steve ★Chimombo. First performed at the inauguration of the University of Malawi's open air theatre and using the myth of the legendary figure Mbona as its plot, this play became a national classic virtually overnight. It can be seen as marking the beginnings of a modern homegrown tradition of Malawian drama in English.

RAMMITLOA, Marks [See DIKOBE, Modikwe]

RAMPOLOKENG, Lesego (1965-), South African poet, was born in Orlando West, Soweto, and as a poet and performer he is outstanding among an innovative group of younger South Africans. Early sources of his poetry were his grandmother, who taught him the art of *dithoko*, the recitations of the se★Sotho of South Africa, and the ★Black Consciousness poets, including Ingoapele Madingoane, Maishe Maponya, and others; later he incorporated elements of rap from poets such as Linton Kwesi Johnson and Mutabaruka, blending these elements into an urban performance poetry acidly critical of contemporary South Africa both before and since the 1994 elections. He confronts the most tabooed subjects of South African reality: misuse of religion, sexuality, the violence that comes out of suppressed anxiety, the corruption of politicians old and new. He understands his role in society as that of a critical observer who speaks his truths in order to clear the path for renewal. The Congress of South African Writers (COSAW) has published two volumes of his poetry: *Horns for Hondo* (1990) and *Talking Rain* (1993).

Raw Pieces (1986) Poems by Edison ★Mpina. Mpina did not receive a university education and thus was not influenced by the Writers' Workshop, which has played so central a part in the growth of modern

Malawian verse. Mpina suffered grievously during the Banda regime (including prison without trial). The collection strives for a distinctly demotic voice and posture celebrating material Malawi, its villages and gardens, its fishing communities, its seasons and harvests.

Rediscovery (1964) Poems by Kofi *Awoonor (then George Awoonor-Williams). The poems draw on both indigenous Ewe beliefs and customs, incorporated to show their strength and sustaining power, and the generally deleterious effects of colonial/Western culture on a subject people. Awoonor's verse has much in common with the so-called first wave of writing out of black Africa as African writers responded to and reacted against the imposed values of an alien culture. The poems in *Rediscovery* not only evoke the dilemmas created by those contending forces but show what, as the title of the volume implies, can be retrieved from the past to make the present amenable.

The Reign of Wazobia (1988) A play by Tess Akaeke *Onwueme (1988). Some African *feminists argue that indigenous political, social, and economic structures can sustain a non-Eurocentric feminist posture. *The Reign of Wazobia* could be used to illustrate such a position. The Kingdom of Ilaa in the play provides a political arrangement which allows a woman to be a king-regent for three months before a new king can succeed to the throne. But the hero of the play, Wazobia – her name, meaning 'Come', derives from three major Nigerian languages – uses her opportunity as king-regent to rally the women in the kingdom to dismantle the structures of patriarchal hegemony. With an array of operatic resources, Onwueme ingeniously re-interprets *Igbo mythology from a feminist perspective.

RELIGION AND LITERATURE Although religion and literature are not necessarily consubstantial, it is hard to think of a culture in which religious activities do not involve poetry or parables and in which literary expression does not draw upon religious icons and idioms to enhance meaning. This contiguity is particularly pronounced in the case of Africa, where religion is an all-inclusive philosophy and cannot be separated from the political, the cultural, the social, or the creative realms of society. Any literary attempt to convey the character of the African society, therefore, will necessarily involve an acknowledgement of religion's central role.

While monotheism insists on the recognition of only one supreme divinity, African religion upholds the totality of existence as a religious phenomenon and the individual as existing within a universe governed by religious forces that can be placated, employed, and

deployed in the service of humanity. In the African world view, God is the originator, preserver, and sustainer of life; the divinities and spirits are charged with the task of overseeing life, especially human life, modulating human destiny, and interceding with God on humanity's behalf; and animals, plants, and natural phenomena and objects constitute the environment in which humanity, the centre of this ontology, lives. Because nature provides the means of existence and sustenance within the context of this cosmic totality, humanity, in gratitude and awe, establishes a mystical relationship with such utilitarian phenomena in nature as rain, mountains, and trees.

This context of traditional African religions was interrupted by the eruption of Islam and Christianity (see below) on the continent during the periods of the trans-Saharan and trans-Atlantic slave trades. Both of these monotheistic religions systematically waged open and subtle wars of attrition on traditional African belief systems and bribed Africans away from them with the lure of education, jobs, and political power. In essence, nowhere has the battle been more aggressive than on the religious front. Although the stated aim of both Islam and Christianity has always been the salvation of the soul from eternal damnation, the truth is that both religions had, and still have, designs to control the souls of Africans as a necessary first step towards the control of their political and economic life. This reading of the colonial encounter is at the heart of many anglophone novels about colonialism, with Ayi Kwei *Armah's *Two Thousand Seasons* (1973) looking at both the Arab-Islamic and Euro-Christian agendas.

Traditional Religions and Literature: Because of the centrality of religion in Africa and the active contribution of foreign religions to colonization, it has remained one of the inevitable subject matters in African literature. The divisive impact of Christianity has been documented by Chinua *Achebe in his novels which are a conscious attempt to remedy that injustice, to show Africans that, as he says in 'The Novelist as Teacher' (*New Statesman*, 29 January 1965), contrary to Euro-Christian propaganda, their 'past – with all its imperfections – was not one long night of savagery from which the first Europeans acting on God's behalf delivered them'. Achebe has continued to articulate the Igbo world view and the religious and ethical belief system that holds that world together as evidence of the existence of an authentic African philosophy before, during, and after the colonial experience. Achebe and other novelists convey the intimate and religious relationship between Africans and their landscape through references to nature gods who dominate the agricultural and professional calendar of Africa. Among Igbo writers there are references to Ani/Ala (the earth goddess), Idemili (the god of water), and Amadioha (the god of thunder), to name the three most frequently recurring and Yoruba writers invoke Ogun (the god of war and creativity), Sango (the god of thunder and lightning and, in contemporary application, of electricity), and Orunmila/Ifa (the divinity of mysteries and wisdom), to name a few. When in Wole *Soyinka's *The *Interpreters* (1965) the interpreters castigate educated Africans for embracing plastic flowers and plants instead of the vitality and vibrancy of nature, they are indirectly condemning their abandonment of African tradition and religion. Similarly, the twilight world of Amos *Tutuola's *The *Palm-wine Drinkard* (1952), in which spirit forces, the dead, and the living commingle, makes abundant sense within the context of Yoruba metaphysics.

Among West African playwrights, Wole Soyinka and Ola *Rotimi have been at the forefront of the exposition of traditional African religious concepts in their dramaturgy. The strength of Rotimi's plays is to be found both in his use of an English that approximates the Yoruba language and in his integrated use of African rituals, both social and metaphysical. Soyinka's most complex play, A *Dance of the Forests (1963), although it examines the nature and meaning of political independence, takes its structure and internal dynamics from the rites of passage associated with the dead among African peoples, particularly the complex rituals of communication with the dead overseen by members of the masquerade cults. The masquerade idiom is at the centre of three plays by Soyinka: A Dance of the Forests, in which traditional masquerade ritual expectations are subverted to produce a cautionary tale about uncritical glorification of the past as a warning that not all who have died deserve to be treated as heroes; The *Road (1965), in which the meaning of death, and therefore life, is sought from a man in a state of suspended animation because he had been knocked over and made mute by a truck while acting as a medium of the dead; and *Death and the King's Horseman (1975), in which Mr. and Mrs. Pilkings display their smug and ignorant attitude towards Africans and their world view by donning masquerade outfits as their disguises for a ball. Soyinka's use of the masquerade idiom is similar to Achebe's preoccupation with the principle of the ancestor cult in *Things Fall Apart, *Arrow of God, and A *Man of the People (1966). In the first two novels the principles and morality of the cult of ancestors are supreme, but by the time of the post-independence era, which is the setting for A Man of the People, the cult has lost its mystique, retaining only its entertainment value, in the face of the onslaught from Euro-Christian doctrines. The ways in which some Africans use these Euro-Christian doctrines to exploit other Africans are dramatically rendered in Soyinka's The *Trials of Brother Jero (1963), a play about a charlatan beach prophet.

Poetry and religion have always been intricately intertwined in Africa. African rituals are realized through the medium of poetry and music. Court poetry combines political and spiritual elements in its validation of the authority of the king and praise poetry often employs the poetic transfer of qualities from nature to humankind in its attempt ritualistically to invoke such qualities in the person being praised. But the most ritual-based poetry in Africa can be said to be cult poetry. In traditional Africa, most guilds are run at their highest levels as cults with rituals and ceremonies, which in turn have accompanying poetry, accessible only to initiated members and closely guarded as guild secrets. Such poems often embody the philosophy and world views that dictate the day-to-day behaviour of the members of the cults. Among the Yoruba people of Nigeria, the Babalawo [father of all cults] is the diviner and the poet of Ifa, a complex body of pharmacological, metaphysical, and religious doctrines.

A number of modern African poets have elected to draw their inspiration from traditional African poetry and to appropriate elements of cult poetry into their writing in order properly to reflect the nature of poetry in Africa and to create an authentic African aesthetic [See Christopher *Okigbo, Wole Soyinka, Kofi *Awoonor, Kofi *Anyidoho, and Okinba Launko]

Christianity and Literature: Christianity has played an extensive and important role in the history of African literatures.

The Christian heritage
Under Roman rule, much of North Africa was Christian. After the seventh century, when Islam and Arab culture gradually eroded this Christian presence, only Ethiopian Christianity and Coptic minorities in Egypt and elsewhere successfully resisted them. In the fifteenth century, however, Spain and Portugal extended Christian Reconquista with garrisons in North and West Africa. By the Treaty of Tordessillas (1494), the Spanish agreed to Portuguese dominance in Africa, though French, British, and Dutch competition quickly challenged this monopoly. A massive resurgence of missionary activity occurred in the late eighteenth and early nineteenth centuries, and by the end of the nineteenth century, various Roman Catholic, protestant, and lay missionary organizations were established features of the European colonization of Africa, which now included Belgian, German, and some Danish interests. Independence movements developed all over Africa in the 1950s and began to achieve their goals up to and during the 1960s. Today, independent and prophetic native churches compete with Christian and Islamic institutions for the hearts and souls of Africans.

Early Christian writings from Egypt, Ethiopia, Nubia, and Roman North Africa constitute Africa's first literatures. From Egypt came the second-century

240

gnostic treatises of Valentinus and Basilides and the second-, third-, and fourth-century theological work of Alexandrian church fathers Clement, Origen, Didymus the Blind, Athanasius, and Cyril the Great. The early third-century desert ascetics, Anthony and Pachomius, knew the Gospels and the Psalter in Coptic. The *Rule of Pachomius* and Athanasius' colourful *Life of Anthony* made their way westward to inspire the monastic movement of early medieval Europe. In the sixth century, the Nubian kingdoms converted to Christianity, and written records of their religion include fragments of scripture, liturgical texts, and lives of saints. Third- and fourth-century North Africa left a strong Christian literary heritage, including the *Passion of Saints Perpetua and Felicitas* (ca. 203) and the theological writings of Tertullian, Cyprian, and Augustine, the father of Western Christianity and author of a classic spiritual autobiography, the *Confessions* (397), and of the *City of God* (411-26), an epic vindication of the Christian church. In the seventh century, Islam and Arab culture spread through Egypt across North Africa, and by the eleventh century, Christianity had all but disappeared from the Maghreb. In 1317, Nubia's Dongola Cathedral officially became a mosque. Coptic Christians form a minority in today's Muslim Egypt. The Ethiopian church began with Athanasius' consecration of Frumentius, Bishop of Aksum. By the end of the sixth century, it possessed vernacular Old and New Testaments, liturgical texts, the *Rule of Pachomius*, and the *Life of Anthony*, as well as the *Qerellos*, an anthology of writings by Athanasius and Cyril the Great. Most importantly, this period also produced the first version of the *Kebra Nagast* [The glory of kings], Ethiopia's national religious epic. Rewritten and expanded in the fourteenth century, this mythic account of Ethiopian Christianity's origins in the union of King Solomon and the Queen of Sheba and of their son Menelik I's removal of the Ark of the Covenant from Jerusalem to Aksum established Ethiopians as God's new chosen people and their land as Siyon. Increasingly isolated among Muslim neighbours, later Ethiopian Christians sometimes assumed a militant posture in their efforts to maintain such certainties. A collection of readings for Saturday and Sunday sabbaths, Zara Ya'iqob's *Mashafa Berhan* [The book of light] (ca. 1450) exhorts Christians to brand themselves with marks of faith as a safeguard against lapsing into non-Christian ways. Two sixteenth-century works, Galawdewos' *Confession of Faith* and Enbaqom's *Anqasa Amim* [Door of the faith], indicate that Portuguese Jesuit efforts to romanize Ethiopian Christianity succeeded only in strengthening its unique identity. In its isolation, Ethiopian Christianity never developed a missionary agenda. Joseph Ephraïm *Casely-Hayford's *Ethiopia Unbound* (1911) mixes a black God and a Christ born of an Ethiopian woman with indigenous Fanti traditions, but this Gold Coast epic is equally a reaction against the European Christianity of modern colonial missionaries. Less apologetic, Daniachew Worku's contemporary Amharic novel *The Thirteenth Sun* (1973) depicts local superstitions and Ethiopian Christianity existing side by side against the unifying backdrop of a harsh Ethiopian landscape.

The European missions and slavery

No account of Christianity and African literatures should ignore the involvement of the missionaries in the slave trade. The Portuguese Angolan see derived its main income from instructing and baptizing slaves. Many slaves were recruited as catechists, and some received further education in Europe. A slave student at the cathedral school in Granada, Juan Latino, composed several Latin poems praising Christian Spain as the new Ethiopia, including the *Austriad* (1571), an epic celebrating Don Juan and the Holy League's victory over the Turks at the battle of Lepanto. Educated slaves returned to Africa to proselytize among their own people. Jacobus Eliza Capitan (1717-47), a freed Dutch slave, went as an ordained missionary to Ghana, where he translated the Lord's Prayer, the Twelve Articles of Belief and the Ten Commandments into Fanti. But the fact that only Christian slaves could be traded, and these only to Christians, remains the most astonishing aspect of missionary complicity in this traffic of human beings. Africa's first Anglican missionary, the Rev. Thomas Thompson, who worked with slaves in North America, sought and, in 1752, gained appointment to the Gold Coast, yet saw no contradiction in writing *The African Trade for Negro Slaves Shown to be Consistent with the Principles of Humanity and with the Laws of Revealed Religion* (1758).

Ironically, however, British control of the slave trade also produced several eloquent condemnations of slavery by slaves. Published posthumously, the *Letters* (1782) of Ignatius *Sancho, who was born on a slave ship, orphaned, and taken to England, censor English Christians for drinking on Sundays at home and for acting like barbarians abroad. In *Thoughts and Sentiments on the Evil of Slavery* (1787), Ottobah *Cuguano invokes Christian charity to condemn English slave traders: 'the destroyers and enslavers of men can be no Christians'. *The Interesting Narrative of the Life of Olaudah *Equiano, or Gustavus Vassa, the African, Written by Himself* (1789) also campaigns to abolish slavery by stressing the hypocrisy of Christian Great Britain's involvement in the trading of human beings. In 1791, John Wesley, the founder of Methodism, had *The Interesting Narrative* read to him on his deathbed. Partly in response to such testimonies, Westminster outlawed the African slave trade in 1807 and banished slavery itself from the British empire in 1833.

The European missions and the spread of Christianity

But the influence of Christian missionaries in Africa

extends beyond their involvement in the slave trade. In the sixteenth and seventeenth centuries, Jesuit, Capuchin, Augustinian, and Dominican missionary priests served the Portuguese crown in West Africa and Mozambique. Published as *Correspondence de Dom Afonso, 1506-43* (1974), the life writings of Mvemba Nzinga, the baptized King Afonso I of Kongo, offers numerous insights into the early indigenizing of Christianity in Africa. In the Cape Verde islands, a *lusophone-African Christian elite developed, with their own Crioulo language, a blend of Portuguese and African vernacular elements. Portuguese colonial writing often betrays European racism in Africa. In *Princesa negra: O presça da civilizaçao em Africa (Black Princess: The Price of Civilization in Africa*, 1932), Luiz Figueira portrays native Africans as marginalized, sometimes romanticized savages. Perhaps for this reason, Portuguese missionary efforts have left an ambiguous heritage. Angolan poet Mario Antonio and other luso-African writers focus on reclaiming their native heritage from colonial occupation in different ways. In *Os noivos, ou conferência dramática sobre o nobolo* [The newlyweds; or, dramatic consultation on the bride price] (1971), Martiniquan playwright Lindo Longho dramatizes cultural tensions between Christian and native traditions, also a pervasive theme in *Auto de natal* [A Christmas play] (1972), by Angolan Domingos Van-Dúnem. Both dramatists were educated at mission schools. In a short story, 'Dina', collected in *Vidas novas* (1976), by another Angolan writer, José Luandino, the prostitute Dina recalls how colonial troops killed her parents even as they sought sanction in the Mission of São Paulo. Ironically, Christian scriptures become a source for such protests against missionary complicity in the colonial project. Mozambiquan Rui de Noronha's poem 'Suge e ambula' [Get up and walk] invokes one of Jesus' miracles to awaken Africans from their colonial slumber. Portuguese power declined in the sixteenth and seventeenth centuries. Great Britain and France in particular were only too keen to occupy the resulting vacuum. At the same time, eighteenth- and nineteenth-century evangelical revivals in Europe and America reinvigorated non-African Christians with fresh proselytizing fervour. New missionary organizations with their eyes on Africa were founded, including the British Baptist Missionary Society (1792), the London Missionary Society (1795), the Church Missionary Society (1799), the British and Foreign Bible Society (1804), the American Board of Commissioners for Foreign Missions (1810), the Leeds Methodist Society (1813), the Wesleyan Methodist Society (1817), the Basel Mission (1815), the Societé des Missions Evangéliques (1822), the Berlin Mission (1824), the Bremen Mission (1836), the Plymouth Brethren (1830s), the Sudan United Mission (1870s), the Sudan Interior Mission, the Africa Inland Mission,

the Heart of Africa Mission, the Gospel Missionary Union, and the Christian and Missionary Alliance. Some of these faith missions found themselves competing for African souls with evangelising high Anglicans; the Oxford Movement of the 1830s had induced missionary zeal in the Society for the Propagation of the Gospel, and in 1859 the Universities' Mission to Central Africa was founded. For the Roman Catholic church the Vatican reconstituted the Society of Jesus in 1814 and Propaganda Fide in 1816 and approved the founding in France of a powerful fundraising organization, Work for the Propagation of the Faith (1822). The English Society of St. Joseph, or Mill Hill Fathers (1866), the Oblates of Mary Immaculate (1816), the Society of the Sacred Heart of Mary (1840), the Society of African Missions (1854), and the Society of Missionaries of Africa, or White Fathers (1868) also pursued Roman Catholic interests in Africa, and the Holy Ghost Fathers gained new life by joining forces with the Society of the Sacred Heart of Mary in 1848.

The European missions and education

The European powers used missionary educational policy and cultural influence to further their economic and political interests in the name of progress. Nevertheless, missionaries played a key role in education and in developing orthographies for native languages. As early as 1815 there is a record of the *Xhosa prophet Ntsikana converting to Christianity and replacing red ochre and the ways of the ancestors with God's sovereignty, the holiness of Sunday, river baptism, monogamy, and prayer. His 'Great Hymn' opens the African Wesleyan *Book of Songs* (1835). European and native African missionaries translated Christian literature into indigenous languages for use as educational textbooks. Tiyo and John H. Soga, followers of Ntsikana, rendered the Bible, *Pilgrim's Progress*, and several Christian hymns into Xhosa. By 1895, others had repeated the work in Sotho and Zulu. In West Africa, Christian literature became available in Twi, *Yoruba, *Hausa, Ewe, Fanti, and Ga. Samuel Ajayi Crowther, yet another freed slave who became a missionary, developed Yoruba orthography and translated the Bible and *Pilgrim's Progress*. Christian missionaries have also helped to perpetuate African oral traditions, though sometimes in odd ways. In *The Black Mind: A History of African Literature* (1974), O.R. Dathorne repeats a Nigerian Efik riddle: 'What is it that God our Father made but which we cannot sit on? Answer: A palm fruit with thorns'. Christianized, the traditional riddle has become a parable. Oral traditions are also preserved in literary collections. The work of the missionary Paul M.B. Mushindo, *Imilumbe ne ishimi: Shintu bashimika ku lubemba* [Stories (with and without songs): The ones they tell in the Bemba region] (1957) gathers Bemba folk tales from Northern Rhodesia, now Zambia.

The missions and vernacular writing

Christian missionaries also encouraged the writing and distribution of original poetry and fiction in indigenous languages. In Southern Africa, missionaries set up a Xhosa press in Lovedale, a *Zulu press in Mariannhill, and a *Sotho press in Morija in Basutoland, and there were missionary presses in other colonial possessions as well. Inevitably, the first literatures in indigenous languages ring with biblical overtones and Christian didacticism. *Pilgrim's Progress* inspired many imitators, of which Thomas *Mofolo's *Moeti oa bochabela* [Traveller to the east] (1907) is probably the most celebrated. Serialized in *Leselinyana*, the newspaper of the Morija Book Depot, where Mofolo worked, his Sotho story tells how kindly whites lead a despairing native African to Christianity. The first original Xhosa novel, Henry Masila Ndawa's *U-Hambo luka Gqoboka* [The journey of Gqoboka the Christian] (1909), depicts the hero's spiritual trials in a quest for Christian truth. Likewise, Nigerian Pita Nwana's *Igbo novel, *Omenuko* (1933), reflects Bunyan's influence. A more adventurous emulation of *Pilgrim's Progress*, D.O. *Fagunwa's *Ogboju-Ode Ninu Igbo Irunmale* (1938; The *Forest of a Thousand Daemons*, 1968) pitches traditional spirit beings against the providential power of the Christian God. In this Yoruba novel, each magical adventure of the hero, Akara-Ogun, results in increased Christian insight and faith.

Not all Christian influences on African literatures in indigenous languages are inspired by Bunyan's allegorical masterpiece. In Nigeria, the Bethel African Church, which seceded from the Breadfruit Church, and St. Jude's Church, Ebute Metta, which seceded from the Lagos Pastorate Circuit, jointly formed Egbe Ife, a dramatic club, and produced *King Eljigbo* (1904). J. Sobowale Sowande's poems, the first published in Yoruba, introduce Christian themes into traditional chants (1905, 1906). Edward Motsamai's *Mehla ea malimo* [The times of the cannibals] (1912), a collection of eighteen stories about providential escapes from capture, exercises Christian judgement on traditional culture, as do the works of fellow Lesotho writers E.L. Segoete and Z.D. Mangoela. Mofolo's third novel, *Pitseng* (1910), infuses Sotho traditions with Christian ethics. Malawian S.A. Paliani's Nyanja novel, *1930 kunadza mchape* [In 1930 came a witchdoctor] (1930), celebrates the triumph of Christianity over native superstition. Marriage appears as the principal theme in several novels. In the Xhosa story *U-Nomalizo* (1918), Enoch S. Guma rewards the Christian heroine's trials of faith with marriage to her sweetheart. B.W. *Vilakazi's novel *Noma nini* [For ever and ever] (1935) portrays the tribulations of the Zulu hero and his mission station girlfriend in their efforts to find true love and marry. Albert Nqueku's Sotho novel *Lilahloane* (1951) shows what happens when Roman

Catholic teachings convince a woman to disobey her father's marriage wishes. Similarly, Zimbabwean Paul Chidyansiku's Shona novel *Nhoroondo dzukuwanana* [Getting married] (1958) reveals a didactic concern with Christian salvation and ethics.

Christian influences also pervade more self-conscious vernacular celebrations of African identity. Ghanaian Joseph Ghartey celebrates the New Year in the Fanti poem 'Nde ye ehurusi da' ['This is the day of rejoicing'] (1950) with biblical diction. On a far grander scale, the Roman Catholic cleric and poet Abbé Alexis *Kagame transforms a traditional Kinyarwanda praise song to the Rwandan king into a Christian pastoral epic addressed to God. Adopting a triumphalist Tutsi perspective, Kagame's *Umulirimbyi wa nyili-ibiremwa* [The song of the land of creation] (1952) Christianizes every detail of Rwandan life, celebrating the cows so central to Tutsi economy and society as God's creatures and locating Rwandan history within the Christian mythic cycle, from creation to the world's end, purgatory, heaven, and hell. Less ambitious but equally convinced of the truth of Christianity, Zaïrean Stephen A. Mpashi's historical fiction *Abapatili bafika ku babemba* [The Catholic priests arrive among the Bemba] (1956) and M.K. Chifwaila's Bemba novel *Ululumbi lwa mulanda kukakaata* [The fate of the stubborn poor person] (1956) both glorify the Roman Catholic church for saving native Africans from tribal superstitions and even from the ravages of slavery. Several pre-independence Zimbabwean novels reveal similar convictions, notably *Karikoga gumiremisere* [Karikoga and his ten arrows] (1958), by the Roman Catholic priest Patrick Chakaipa, and David Ndoda's Ndebele novel *Uvusezindala* [In days gone by] (1958).

But missionary attitudes towards African vernacular literatures have not always been positive. Although Mofolo's Morija masters were delighted with *Moeti oa bochabela*, they stalled the publication of his second novel for more than fifteen years. *Chaka* (1925; English trans. 1931), whose publication had been delayed since 1908, displeased them not only because Mofolo makes a hero of an unrepentant Zulu warrior, but also because he describes the ritual practices of natural witchcraft with uncritical relish. The missionaries never doubted Mofolo's personal faith, but like John Milton, he painted too attractive a portrait of their spiritual adversaries. Associated with Lovedale and sometimes regarded as the father of Xhosa literature, Samuel Edward Krune Loliwe Mqhayi created waves with a poem celebrating the visit to South Africa in 1925 of the Prince of Wales and the Duke of Kent that mentions the Bible and barrels of brandy in the same breath. This ambivalence about the role of Christianity in the colonial project informs A.C. *Jordan's *Ingqumbo yeminyanya* (1940; *The Wrath of the Ancestors*, 1980) too. This Xhosa novel portrays Christianity as the means by which African pride is awakened and sustained, only to suggest that such pride is a masked revival of pre-colonial tribal identity. Ambivalence may lead to religious nihilism, an idea that Zimbabwean Charles *Mungoshi captures in his Shona novel *Ndiko KupindanaKwama* [The passing days] (1975).

The missions and contemporary literature

This ambivalence towards Christianity characterizes a good deal of contemporary African literature. By the beginning of the twentieth century, the British and the French were the dominant colonial powers in Africa. The British often ruled indirectly, through a native bureaucracy, while the French pursued a policy of assimilation and centralization. British strategy kept education at the minimum needed for administrative purposes, while French cultural assimilation of natives often meant higher education in Europe for those Africans who could achieve the required entrance standards. The French policy of complete assimilation created *évolués*, an African upper class that was inevitably alienated from their own people. But in British and other colonial territories, educated African elites also arose, sometimes becoming conduits for the neo-colonial exploitation of their own people. Whatever the differences in administrative policy, however, missionaries in the territories of both colonial powers generally supported bans on tribal naming, traditional initiation, marriage, and burial rites, dancing, drumming, and singing, African dress, and storytelling sessions.

The relationship between Christianity and colonialism in Africa therefore became very ambiguous. The need to be free of European missionary triumphalism created both native African churches with looser affiliations to established denominations, such as Dr. Mojola Agbebi's Native Baptist Church in Nigeria, or the South African Zionist churches, now more than 2,000 in number, and such new prophetic churches as the Harrisites on the Gold Coast. Education produced literate and articulate Africans capable of mounting successful independence movements against colonial and neo-colonial exploitation, sometimes with contradictory results. In the case of the Kenyan Mau Mau, for example, some Gikuyu Christians associated freedom from colonial oppression with freedom from missionary authority, a position that aligned them with marxist political revolutionaries, whilst other Christians were martyred.

Out of the ambiguities of Christianity and colonialism, two major African literary traditions have evolved, one in French, the other in English.

Certainly early *drama in these languages reflects a variety of Christian influences. English- and French-language African theatre developed out of mission school dramatizations of biblical stories. In the 1880s, such dramatizations excluded all things African. Often secessionist native churches reintroduced African

instruments, dance, and song. Some early English-language theatre in West and South Africa, for example, blends Christian ethics with traditional arts. In *The *Girl Who Killed to Save* (1935), South African Zulu dramatist Herbert I.E. *Dhlomo mounts a Christian attack on tribal superstition and magic. During the Second World War, Nigerian Herbert Ogunde began organizing 'concert party' performances of native song cycles to celebrate Easter and Christmas. A Christian morality play, Ogunde's *The Garden of Eden and the Throne of God* (1944) dramatizes the rebellion of Adam and Eve against God. As late as 1962, Chawanda Kutse, a South African radio dramatist, broadcast *The Creation*, *The Crucifixion*, and *The Resurrection*, introductions to western radio drama considered sufficiently respectable for an African audience.

For other playwrights, colonial issues problematize the staging of Christian themes. Tensions between indigenized and European Christian traditions permeate the work of Nigerian Nobel Prize laureate Wole *Soyinka, who often transforms Western church dogma into a kind of grace more appropriate to the African context. So ironically, in *The *Road* (1965), the Professor's profound rejection of Western Christian orthodoxy involves a self-transformation reminiscent of Pauline conversion, but without church dogma. Christian dogmatism also comes under attack in Patrick Ilboudo's *Le Procès du muet* (1987). In this darkly humorous play, Imam Samba, a Muslim zealot, offers Judas as the real victim of Christ's trial, arguing that different cultural perspectives suggest different offenders, different victims, and different verdicts. South African Lewis *Nkosi paints an even starker picture in *The Rhythm of Violence* (1964), in which a Zulu demands that Jesus choose a side in South Africa. Similarly, in *L'Europe inculpée* (1969), Congolese Antoine Letembet-Ambilly invokes the story of Noah and his sons to allegorize Europe's sins as colonizers of Africa, while Aimé Césaire's *Une saison au Congo* (1966) implicates missionaries in the processes of Zairean moral decline. Christianity also has its contemporary apologists. The All Africa Council of Churches commissioned a play from Ghanaian J.C *de Graft, whose *Muntu* (1977) imposes a Christian determinism on human affairs.

*Poetry in French and English ranges across a similar spectrum of attitudes towards Christianity. In the 1940s and early 1950s, 'pioneer poets' like Ghana's Gladys *Casely-Hayford, Michael *Dei-Anang, and R.E.G. *Armattoe, Nigeria's Dennis *Osadebay, and Sierra Leone's Crispin George published pieces replete with doctrinaire protestant principles. Osadebay's *Africa Sings* (1952), for example, disdains traditional religious practice, while George's *Precious Gems Unearthed by an African* (1952) proclaims self-deprecatory thanks to an almighty God. Though less moralistically than George, the Liberian poet Roland Dempster is also preoccupied with Christianity's place in Africa, notably in *A Song out of Midnight* (1959). Collected in *Beware, Soul Brother* (1972), Chinua *Achebe's 'Poems about War' incarnate several deeply moving images. 'Christmas in Biafra' contrasts an emaciated war-baby with a plump infant Jesus in the manger to capture the horrors of the Nigerian civil conflict.

The *Nigeria-Biafra war claimed one of Africa's most promising poets, Christopher *Okigbo, who was killed in the fighting. Okigbo draws eclectically upon several religious iconographies, including the Christian. Conceived as a mass, but offered to 'Mother Idoto', the stream that washes and sanctifies Okigbo's village, *Heavensgate's 'Easter Sequence' (1962) portrays ancestral gods purifying themselves by way of 'stations of the cross'. 'Silences' casts the Congolese freedom fighter Lumumba as a Christ figure, betrayed by the very people he would save from colonial oppression, who stand by powerless like nuns lamenting their saviour's death. In *Limits (1964), 'John the Baptist' deprecates Roman Catholic indoctrination as lifeless; and in 'Fireseed', a parody of the parable of the mustard seed, Christian missionaries sow not the seed of the kingdom of God, but fireseed, which consumes African culture. Ironically, in the last poem of *The Shuttle in the Crypt* (1971), fellow Nigerian Soyinka suggests to Okigbo's ghost that dying like Christ is better than enduring like Prometheus.

The work of L.S. *Senghor, father of the celebrated *negritude movement, embodies many of the ambiguities of the colonial situation. In *Hosties Noires* (1948), this Senegalese man of letters expresses gratitude to France for Christian faith, though later verses lament the wickedness of the imperial centre and French despoliation of Africa. 'Snow upon Paris' (1964), for example, identifies the suffering of slaves with the suffering of Christ, a theme Ivory Coast poet Bernard *Dadié reiterates in 'Thank You God' (1964). Other negritude poets are less sanguine about the Roman Catholic church. In 'Viaticum' (1960), Senegalese Bernard Diop invokes this Roman Catholic rite to venerate the ancestors and in so doing seems implicitly to condemn the *viaticum* as a hollow superstition. In 'Nigger Tramp' (1964), another Senegalese, David *Diop, portrays an African tramp as a Christ figure; in 'The Vultures' he censures missionary priests for failing to discourage forced labour.

Other African poets in French raise similar issues of injustice. Incorporating oral rhythms into *Feu de brousse* (1957; *Bush Fire*, 1964), Zaïrean Felix Tchicaya U'Tam'si condemns churches for serving colonial interests, while *À Triche-coeur* (1958) plays on the notion that the ecclesiastical keys that unlock heaven's gates for some, lock them for others. Some of his later poems resonate with liberation theology's preferential option for the poor. 'Bush Fire' likens Congolese, wretched on the banks of the River Congo, to

Israelites weeping by the waters of Babylon, while 'The Scorner' contrasts a bourgeois church with Christ's 'crown of thorns', which native Africans share. Nor is this sense of injustice peculiar to African poetry in French. Herbert Dhlomo's *Valley of a Thousand Hills* (1941) depicts whites satanically assuming divine powers and the native African as a Christ figure nailed to the cross. Ugandan *Okot p'Bitek's *Song of Lawino* (1966) mounts an equally indignant attack not only on missionaries, but on Christianity as a whole. The title character satirizes African converts, Christian names, holy communion as cannibalism, and priests as lechers. In a particularly bitter image, God becomes a 'hunchback', for in the Lwo language, *rubanga* signifies both the divine and the ghost who causes spinal tuberculosis. In his *African Religions and Western Scholarship* he takes issue with writers such as John Mbiti who attempt to reconcile Christianity and African religions. Similarly, 'Our aim our dreams our destinations', one of South African Dennis *Brutus's *China Poems* (1975), echoes Job's rebellion against God. Christianity successfully demystifies indigenous religious traditions, then betrays itself as the hypocritical handmaiden of Western imperialism. But once exhausted, righteous indignation over such hypocrisy may leave distrust not just of Christianity, but of all things spiritual. These ironies recur in several ways. In *A Reed in the Tide* (1965), the first single-authored African poetry collection to be published for an international audience, J.P. Clark *Bekederemo's epic poem, 'Ivbie' draws upon Christian images of redemption, hope, forgiveness, healing, and love to lament the loss of these values in traditional African culture. The verses of Ghanaian poet Kwesi *Brew abound in traditional tribal and Christian motifs. But scepticism overwhelms Brew's 'personal hopes' in *The Shadows of Laughter* (1968). Several poems in Ghanaian Kofi *Awoonor's collection *Night of My Blood* (1971) echo such sentiments. 'The Cathedral' portrays Christianity as a cathedral whose grand artificial structures stand in pretentious contrast to the natural landscape of traditional spirituality. 'The Weaver Bird' denounces the way in which missionaries have abused African hospitality and undermined native traditions, just like the weaver bird, whose excrement defiles ancient ancestral shrines. Kenyan Jared *Angira draws the inevitable conclusion in *Silent Voices* (1972). 'He Will Come' exposes Christian hubris: turning the virtue of charity against them, Angira accuses Christians of unfairly failing to take account of the circumstances of the Kenyans they try to convert.

Tragically, the desperate cry of Awoonor's 'Easter Dawn' for 'final ritual' for the traditional gods reverberates through much of contemporary African poetry. Occasionally, however, there are glimmers of hope. In *Another Nigger Dead* (1972), *Taban Lo Liyong defines the situation facing Africans who desire faith as a choice between beliefs. But then the satirical 'Bless the African Coups', which sees no difference between black totalitarian and white colonial tyranny, also expresses hope for a Christ-like resurrection of African culture. There is another kind of hope in Felix *Mnthali's 'Corpus Christi, 1977'. The Malawian poet wonders if Africanized Christian rituals are merely superficial or whether they represent a genuine human need for the eternal. Thus relativized, Christianity becomes another vehicle through which deeper African spiritual impulses seek to find passion in life and dignity in death. Perhaps the syncretistic aura of such themes brings us full circle to an African Christianity-in-the-making. In *The Blood in the Desert's Eye* (1990), Sierra Leone poet Syl *Cheney-Coker draws widely on biblical and Christian theological motifs. 'Apocalypse', 'The Outsider', and 'The Philosopher' invoke the feast of Passover, the Last Supper, and the crucifixion in calls for God to purge the African homeland of the suffering caused by white colonial and black neo-colonial oppressors alike. Bereft of the benefits of Christ's salvific sacrifice, Sierra Leone reeks of death and decay. But in images that figure hope Cheney-Coker calls upon Jeremiah to save Sierra Leone, as he did Israel.

In *novels, *short stories and auto*biographies Chistianity is a recurring theme. In his early autobiography, *The Story of an African Chief* (1935), the Ugandan prince Akiki K. Nyabongo details life among the Bugandan aristocracy but also criticizes the elitism of colonial administrators and Christian missionaries alike. Many early novels amounted to little more than Christian didacticism. Heavily influenced by biblical language and cadences, Ghanaian R.E. Obeng's *Eighteenpence* (1943) exemplifies this tendency. Less moralistic, but still exhibiting a strong missionary influence, the hero of *Le Fils du fétiche* (1955), by Togo novelist David Ananou, despairs of his village and converts to Christianity. But not all confessing Christians resort to didacticism. Influenced by D.O. Fagunwa's work, Nigerian Amos *Tutuola's *The *Palm-Wine Drinkard* (1953) is generally regarded as the first important modern African narrative in English. Tutuola submitted the book to the United Society for Christian Literature, but it was passed on to Faber and Faber. Fusing indigenous folklore and Christian beliefs, *The Palm-Wine Drinkard* relates the protagonist's magical quest to fetch his tapster from the land of the dead. Tutuola plays a variation on this formula in *Ajaiyi and His Inherited Wealth* (1967), in which the title character's friends make a Faustian bargain with the devil, while Ajaiyi uses an unexpected inheritance not for pleasure, but to build churches to bring people to Christ. Yet seldom does an African narrator even satirically advocate fanatical Christianity, as in Nigerian Chukwuemeka *Ike's *Toads for Supper* (1965). Nor are we much encouraged to take seriously the evangelical Simeon, as he brandishes his *Watchtower* magazine in Legson *Kayira's The *Looming Shadows* (1967). Millennial or not, Christian fervour in African literature usually translates into religious intolerance, as in Stanlake *Samkange's *The Year of the Uprising* (1978), a fictional reconstruction of the Mhondoro cult uprising of 1896.

Many commentators consider Cameroon's Mongo *Beti to be the first distinguished African novelist in French. Written in the form of an altar boy's journal, *Le Pauvre Christ de Bomba* (1956; *The *Poor Christ of Bomba*, 1971) satirizes the missionary efforts of Father Drumont, as well as those Africans who become Christians to get access to European power. Sermons about the sinfulness of drumming on Good Friday saturate traditional ways with feelings of guilt. As cruel as the colonial rulers, the church exacts huge tithes even from the poor, the old, and the infirm. Ostensibly to frustrate premarital sex, priests confine native girls in the *sixa* for three months, where catechists rape them, sowing seeds of syphilis among future African families. Drumont returns to Europe a failed and embittered man. Other French- and English-language novels depict missionaries as untrustworthy figures. Beti's *Le Roi miraculé* (1958; *King Lazarus*, 1960) portrays Father Le Guen as a spineless weakling, always at the beck and call of the colonial administration. In Nigerian Onuora *Nzekwu's *Blade among the Boys* (1962), Patrick Ikenga's mother tries to rear her son as a tribal leader, fearing the Roman Catholic church will emasculate him. Ikenga rejects his birthright, becomes a priest, and allows the family line to die. In *The Narrow Path* (1966), Ghanaian Francis *Selormey describes European mission society's superior attitudes towards native teachers. Unlikeable missionaries also appear in Nigerian John *Munonye's *The *Only Son* (1966) and Malawian Legson Kayira's *Jingala* (1969). In Munonye's novel, Christians are mad and evangelizing missionaries who dismiss African customs as unacceptable. In Kayira's novel, a Roman Catholic mission school alienates Gregory, an only son, from his father, Jingala, thus disrupting tribal ties. More recently, Kenjo Jumbam's *The White Man of God* (1980) depicts the divisive effects of Christian missionaries upon a Cameroonian village. Not all fictional representations of Christian missions convey this despair. Peter *Abrahams' *The View from Coyoba* (1985) admiringly portrays black American missionary Jacob Brown, a disciple of W.E.B. du Bois and later bishop in Liberia and in Uganda, before and after independence. But this perception is rare. The sort of missionary deception that makes a martyr of Ndatshan, the main character in Stanlake Samkange's *The Mourned One* (1975), still dominates African literature in English and French. A native teacher at the mission school, Ndatshan is falsely accused of rape and sentenced to death. The missionary testifies against him. Zaïrean novelist

Ngandu Nkashama perpetuates these negative impressions in *La Mort faite homme* (1986), which identifies the mission school Father Director as an abusive hypocrite.

The ritual of marriage sits at the centre of traditional and Christian African life, and thus matrimonial subjects preoccupy numerous writers. Beti's *Le Roi miraculé*, for example, also tells of a tribal chief becoming a Christian, disavowing polygamy, then refusing to reveal which wife he intends to keep. In Nigerian T.M. *Aluko's *One Man, One Wife* (1959), the devoutly Christian Joshua decides to take a second wife without telling the first. Gambian Lenrie *Peters offers a different perspective. Set in the Creole society of Freetown, Sierra Leone *The Second Round* (1965) contains a subplot in which Roman Catholic dogma prevents the protagonist's neighbour, Mr. Marshall, from obtaining a divorce from an unfaithful wife. In Nigerian Flora *Nwapa's *Efuru* (1966), the title character's marriage to a Christian brings disaster. Envious of her family's superior tribal status, Gilbert courts Efuru in a 'civilized' way, resisting the temptations of premarital sex. When she turns out to be infertile, he fathers a child by another woman. An uncompromising attack on polygamy from the Christian standpoint, Stephen *Ngubiah's *A Curse from God* (1970) reveals another attitude toward matrimony. Ngubiah's protagonist, Karagu, has to choose between Gikuyu polygamy and Christian monogamy, rejects the latter, but becomes an alcoholic wife-beater and commits suicide. Samkange's *The Mourned One* offers a more hopeful symbol of accommodation between indigenous and Christian tradition. Despite her cousin Ndatshan's fate, Chibinha marries a Roman Catholic schoolteacher, Mayikoro, in a wedding ceremony at once Bantu and Christian.

Clearly, African writers in both French and English conceive of Christianity as at best an ambiguous presence. On the one hand, missionaries provide education as a means of individual advancement in the new social order, as well as the promise of spiritual fulfilment, if not in this world, then in the next. On the other hand, missionaries sometimes foment a self-righteous sense of superiority towards traditional spirituality that inevitably disrupts and fragments inherited social and cultural structures. Numerous novelists play upon the implications of these conflicting influences in still other ways. In his autobiography, *Tell Freedom* (1954), Abrahams speaks warmly of Anglican teachers who were generous of spirit and not racist. Yet missionary education may be a mixed blessing. The experience of Michael Udomo, the protagonist in Abrahams' *A Wreath for Udomo* (1956), typifies a common pattern of native African alienation. The missionaries take the cleverest boy in the village to educate. Travelling abroad, Udomo returns home to fight for his country's freedom from colonial in-

fluences, including Christianity. Too ruthless in pursuit of his goals, he is murdered by the very people he tries to liberate. Ironically, in this novel missionary education cultivates hope, only to reap despair. Similarly, the narrator of Malawian Aubrey *Kachingwe's *No Easy Task* (1966) accepts missionary schooling to prepare himself as a member of the independence movement, only to become so tied to European ways that he is no longer at home among his own people. Subtitled *Dieu, un prête, la révolution*, V.Y. Mudimbe's *Entre les eaux* (1973) tells of a native Zaïrean priest, Pierre Landu, who attempts to domesticate Christianity by locating the gospel in Karl Marx's socialist teachings. But self-interested elites have appropriated both ideologies, leaving Landu resigned to a life of hollow monastic ceremony. In T. Obinkaram *Echewa's *The Land's Lord* (1976), Father Higler's servant, Philip, commits suicide, caught between Christianity and his abandoned vocation as Njoku, the acolyte of the yam god of his people. Some writers try to anticipate the future of Christian missions in Africa. Satirizing Dr. Christian Barnard's transplant of a black woman's heart into a white man, Ghanaian Ama Ata *Aidoo's *Our Sister Killjoy* (1977) wonders about the relevance of God represented with Western imagery and of missionaries who teach the necessity of a Christian name for salvation. But unresolved tensions continue. Reared in Christian ways, Mwambu, the main protagonist of Ugandan Timothy *Wangusa's *Upon this Mountain* (1989), finds himself torn between tribal traditions and the teachings of the church. In a humorous scene at the end of the novel, tribal members discover Mwambu has been circumcised in hospital and demands that he be circumcised again, properly. Confused, Mwambu remembers both the call to fight manfully under Christ's banner and the taunt that he is only half a man.

Other novelists take Christianity to task for confusing the material and spiritual worlds. Too often preoccupied with the things of this world, Christianity becomes 'churchianity', to use a term coined by Es'kia *Mphahlele in his autobiography, *Down Second Avenue* (1959). In *Le Vieux nègre et la médaille* (1956; *The *Old Man and the Medal*, 1969), another celebrated Cameroon novelist, Ferdinand *Oyono, casts the Roman Catholic church as a tool of colonial propaganda. A respected tribal elder, Meka strives for honour among the Europeans and receives a citizen's medal for donating land to the church. After the presentation ceremony, he is arrested for being drunk on palm-wine. Banned as sinful by the priest, Father Vandermayer, the wine alleviates the old man's rheumatic pain. Ostracized by the church, living in a hut on the edge of the Christian cemetery, Meka returns to traditional ways a broken man. A fictional biography of his father, J.W. *Abruquah's *The Catechist* (1965) recapitulates Meka's fate. A catechist in a

Ghanaian mission, the old man resists peer pressure to leave the church, which repays his loyalty with expulsion for minor indiscretions of one kind or another. In a different vein, Ghanaian Ayi Kwei *Armah's *Two Thousand Seasons (1973) mocks the Bible's 'fables' as insulting to adult intelligence, fit only for childish minds. In other texts, Christian hypocrisy assumes the explicit form of sexual immorality. In Oyono's Une vie de boy (1960; *Houseboy, 1966), Father Gilbert uses conversion to bring French civilization to Africa, but gonorrhoeal catechists reflect European Christianity's true decadence. Zaïrean Thomas Mpoyi-Buatu also frames Christian corruption in sexual terms. In Osija Mwambungu's (*Prince Kagwema) Veneer of Love (1975), sexual promiscuity invades the traditional game of wanya-kayusa. Tanzanian boys and girls used to pair off and hide together for fun; now Christian teenagers use the game for clandestine sex. Ranging from mid-nineteenth-century to contemporary Kinshasa, Mpoyi-Buata's La Réproduction (1986) attacks the Roman Catholic church for being a partner in the colonial exploitation of Africa, for racial prejudice, and for imposing a superficial veneer of ritual and theological abstraction upon African life. In this fictional prison journal, a black priest revels in scatological sex with a prostitute. Symbolic of African spiritual degradation, this motif resonates in Cannibale (1986), by fellow Zaïrean Thomas Bolya Baenga, in which a black priest indulges in necrophilia and masturbates over the Christian altar.

Many commentators especially celebrate the novels of Soyinka, Chinua Achebe and *Ngugi wa Thiong'o for unveiling more nuanced, though different, pictures of Christianity in Africa. Drawing upon the biblical stories of Lazarus and Barabbas, Soyinka's The *Interpreters (1965) tells of Sekoni, a Muslim from northern Nigeria, who marries a Christian girl. Sekoni is disinherited by his family, but the marriage remains a symbol of peaceful co-existence in a post-colonial Nigeria. In *Season of Anomy (1973), Taiila admires the serenity of Christian nuns, while Soyinka skilfully weaves together biblical images of Herod and the parable of the sower with Yoruba, Graeco-Roman, and even Hindu symbols. Achebe represents Christianity as a complex factor in the painful transformation of traditional African culture and society. In *Things Fall Apart (1958), Mr. Brown and Mr. Smith reflect the two faces of colonial Christianity, one benevolent, the other autocratic. For Achebe, African converts play a crucial role, too. Occasionally, Achebe seems to find beauty in these dynamics, as in Things Fall Apart, where Christianity attracts Nwoye with its poetry. But tragic consequences often result from the clash between Igbo and European Christian mores. From the Christian standpoint, Nwoye sees his fellow Africans as 'savages'. Similarly, Enoch's unmasking of the spirit at the Egwugwu ceremonies is cruelly over-

zealous. In *Arrow of God (1964), John Goodcountry, a native Christian missionary, and Ezeulu, the titular head of the priesthood of the traditional god Ulu, embody these conflicts. Ezeulu miscalculates the strength of his control over the tribe, which turns from the cult of Ulu to Christianity. In both novels, the symbol of the python captures this tension; the snake functions at one moment as a sacred native totem, at another as a Christian figure of original sin.

Ngugi's novels also embody the ambiguities of Christianity's presence in Africa. In *Weep Not, Child (1964), District Officer Howland's soldiers accuse Njoroge's teacher, Isaka, of terrorist sympathies, then cruelly murder him for denying he has exchanged Jesus for Mau Mau. Ngugi writes warmly of the missionaries who never patronized Africans and whose school seemed free of race consciousness. Elsewhere in the novel, this Kenyan nationalist mixes Christian Old Testament and ancestral Gikuyu myths of divine dispensation to justify native reappropriation of lands stolen by the colonial invader. In language reminiscent of liberation theology, Jomo Kenyatta becomes a black Moses, leading his people out of repression into the promised land. Ngugi's Gikuyu claim a divine right to their land, almost an ironic response, it seems, to the South African Boers of Abrahams' Wild Conquest (1950) or Jack *Cope's The *Fair House (1955). This motif recurs in Ngugi's The *River Between (1965). Like the Christian God of the Dutch Reformed Afrikaners, the Kameno deity Murungu echoes Yahweh's gift of Canaan to the Israelites. But the irony embodied in this figure reflects wider tensions within Ngugi's novel. The Rev. Mr. Livingston's efforts to ban female circumcision create conflict between the traditionalist Kameno and the Christian Makuyu. Dividing to conquer, the missionary misconceives the nature of Christian charity. Neither the Christian convert, Joshua, nor the traditionalist, Kabonyi, who both attend the mission school, shows compassion for Muthoni, who dies from a badly performed circumcision, as the river between the two communities carries the girl's body away. In A *Grain of Wheat (1967), Ngugi's portrayal of the Mau Mau rebel Kihika as a Gikuyu martyr, again blurs the lines between Christian religious and Kenyan nationalist ideologies. Ngugi describes himself as 'deeply Christian' when he wrote his first few novels, under the name James Ngugi, and he admits that he was attempting in those books to strip off the trappings of western culture from Christian doctrine in order to see how Christianity might be combined with the indigenous belief. When he dropped his 'Christian' name and began writing his novels in Gikuyu, Ngugi also rejected institutional Christianity for marxism, but in books such as *Matigari (1983; trans. 1989) and Caitaani Mutharabaini (1980; *Devil on the Cross, 1982), he still employs many biblical themes and allusions, the structure of biblical parable, and an allegorical tradition with huge debts to Bunyan. In *Decolonising the Mind*, Ngugi says that he incorporates such elements because literate Gikuyu would have read the Bible and his writing would then be rooted in a more familiar tradition than the linear Western *Bildungsroman*.

Christianity's association with European colonial oppression has earned the religion justified suspicion. Indeed, sometimes colonial settlement of Africa assumed a sense of divine destiny. Much modern and contemporary African literature at once expresses and embodies a moral condemnation of the so-called white man's burden to civilize the African savage. Ironically, this condemnation is frequently as deeply rooted in Christian convictions as the racist ideology it seeks to eradicate. Even as the nineteenth century was closing, Olive *Schreiner's *Trooper Peter Halket of Mashonaland* (1897) adopted a Christian moral stance to rebuke Cecil Rhodes's racism as sin. But nowhere is Christian hegemony more evident than in the sense of divine dispensation animating the Great Trek of the Afrikaner Boers in the 1830s. As we have seen, Abrahams' *Wild Conquest* and Cope's *The Fair House* vividly dramatize this extreme form of Christian white supremacism. In South Africa, European ascendancy has only recently yielded to the will of the majority. Unwittingly, nearly contemporary South African literature still exposes Christianity's complicity in the colonial project. Afrikaaner novels like Stuart *Cloete's *The Hill of Doves* (1941) and Herman Charles *Bosman's *Mafeking Road* (1947) piously appropriate such Christian sacred texts as the Lord's Prayer and Psalm 23 to glorify the God of the Dutch Reformed church. Neither native nor European South African writers have left this view unchallenged. Embodying a Christian concern for the brotherhood of races, Alan *Paton's *Cry, the Beloved Country* (1948) makes clear the hypocrisy of a Christianity that preaches equality but refuses it to South African blacks. In his autobiography, *Blame Me on History* (1963), Bloke *Modisane quite openly identifies the symbols, institutions, and authority of the Christian church in South Africa with the evils of *apartheid. Laurens *van der Post's *Heart of the Hunter* (1961) draws upon the biblical story of Jacob and Esau to dramatize the relationship between settler and bushman, who are brothers despite themselves. André *Brink writes *Kennis van die Aand* (1973; *Looking on Darkness*, 1974) in the 'sacred language of Afrikaans', then translates the novel into English, questioning the Afrikaner sense of a chosen people in a god-given land.

More probably, the Christian scriptures may still inspire visions of beauty and justice, though in ways that appear unconventional from a European Christian perspective. Playing upon the biblical trope of the Garden of Eden, for example, Elizabeth, the protagonist in Bessie *Head's *A *Question of Power* (1974),

suggests that the ideals of democracy, freedom of thought, human rights, and moral order all reflect Eden's perfection. The secularized biblical vision at the heart of these words also infuses Dambudzo *Marechera's *The *House of Hunger* (1978). Conniving with Ian Smith's racist Rhodesian regime compromises the ethical authority of the Anglican church in this Zimbabwean novel, but Marechera still expresses a transforming moment of youthful insight in Christian New Testament terms. In the end, perhaps Jean-Marie Adiaffi's allegorical novel *La Carte d'identité* (1980; *The Identity Card*, 1983) best expresses the key issue: not belief or lack of it, but respect. Maybe the literary subversion of colonial Christian ideology begins with the poetry and short stories of James J.R. Jolobe, who wrote in both Xhosa and English. But African writers certainly keep bringing new perspectives to the issues defining Christianity's place in Africa. In South African Farida *Karodia's *A Shattering of Silence* (1993), witnessing the brutal murder of her Canadian missionary parents turns the eight-year-old Faith into a mute. As a woman, she struggles with allegiances both to colonial and to native Africans in Mozambique's war of independence. In the preface to an anthology of new African drama, *Woza Afrika* (1986), Imamu Amiri Baraka once again wonders how Jesus Christ would have reacted to the situation in South Africa before Nelson Mandela became president – or we might add, to any other reigning instance of colonial oppression or neo-colonial tyranny.

Islam and Literature: Islam arrived in Africa during the seventh century, spreading quickly down the Nile into East Africa as far south as the coast of Mozambique and across the Sahara Desert into West Africa. Although it has contributed immensely to the literature of the continent, the study of Islam and literature in Africa has until recently been limited. The first important book on this subject for serious study is probably Albert Gérard's *African Language Literatures* (1981), which like most books that discuss the relationship between literature and Islam, suffers from two shortcomings: a failure to take into account African oral traditions, and an exclusive focus on contemporary literature.

Islam has been a significant factor in the African imagination but there has been a temptation to sideline its impact on anglophone literature which may derive from the fact that writers from Islamic areas have written more in Arabic and their indigenous languages than in English. Shehu Usman bn. Fodio, the architect of the *jihad* in Nigeria, for example, is reputed to have composed about 480 poems in Arabic, Fulfulde, and *Hausa, in addition to writing several books in Arabic. In addition, Islam has not received the same kind of scrutiny to which Christianity has been subjected at the hands of novelists. The role of

Islam has been better documented by francophone writers such as the Senegalese Cheikh Hamidou ★Kane (*L'Aventure ambiguë* (1961; *Ambiguous Adventure*, 1969) and Yambo Ouologuem of Mali (*Le Devoir de violence*, 1968; *Bound to Violence*, 1971). In the few cases where anglophone novelists have examined the role of Islam in West Africa, the efforts have been more celebratory than critical. Ibrahim ★Tahir's *The Last Imam* (1984), for example, merely extols the values of Islam and laments the corruption of Islamic principles and ideals by greedy and self-serving imams. The destruction of the traditional belief system by Islam is not at issue in this novel.

The variety of Islamic experience has thus been under-represented in the historical literature, especially in West Africa, and has been distorted by three main influences. First, the dominance of the orientalist approach has resulted in the neglect of the history of Islam in the colonial period; second, the study of Arabic literature and the concept of Islam as a monolith fails to reflect the multicultural society within Africa and, thus, denies the authenticity of an African-language tradition. Third, the colonial Islamicist tradition perceived Islam as a competitor with Europe for hegemonic control over Africa. That challenge relates to the *a'jami* script and a mode of poetry essentially derived from Islamic theology and the resulting barrier between European languages and Islamic tradition.

The first major African text to provide a defence against European ideology was Kane's *L'Aventure ambiguë*, which revolves around the struggle between the secular and religious establishments in Senegal over control of the representation of the word. In the end it vindicates Islam's essential role in the community. In the work of ★Camara Laye Islam is syncretized with traditional rites, although a muted tension between the two worlds reveals many of the elements of Sufism. In the Sahel countries of Africa Islam is a dominant theme in an indigenous film industry. The work of ★Sembene Ousmane projects Islam as an object barring the integration of the soul and society. Ghanaian novelist Ayi Kwei ★Armah and Senegalese poet Birago ★Diop view Islam as a colonizing force similar to the European Christian tradition. In the works of Tayeb ★Salih women in Islamic communities are portrayed as being both victim and devil. However, the general picture of Islam in the Sahel is of a unifying force against a European Christian tradition.

Return to Beirut, The (1989) A novel by Andrée ★Chedid, translated from the French (*La Maison sans racines*, 1985). Set in war-torn Lebanon in 1975, three stories told concurrently converge in a final tragic climax. A European grandmother, reminiscing, returns to Beirut, the city of her youth. There her twelve-year-old American granddaughter joins her and they come to love each other. Then two young women, one Muslim, one Christian, contrive to lead a women's peace demonstration to end in their meeting in Beirut's public square. But one is shot and the other hovers over her, indistinguishable. Chedid composed three endings for the novel, but ultimately felt forced to choose the one that most depicts the war's indiscriminate slaughter. The child, running heedlessly to the square to join her grandmother, is struck down by a sniper, and the hope for a truce is lost.

RÉUNION The former Ile Bourbon, now Réunion, is a French '*département*', and as such part of the EU and getting massive support from the 'colonial metropolis'. Situated less than one hour's flight from ★Mauritius it belongs to an entirely different economic and cultural universe. The population is mostly *métis*, black, white and Indian and reflects the inheritance of a slave and plantation society, not unlike South Africa. The whites dominated the colony until 1945, when the island became a *département* and was integrated into French politics, with a very important Communist party, mostly dedicated to defending support from the metropolis for an ailing economy. Totally unpopulated before French colonization its literature was started by French colonists. Evariste de Parny (1753-1814) claimed to have translated from ★Malagasy his *Chansons madécasses* (1787), thus inaugurating an interest for oral tradition, but the question of their authenticity is open. In the nineteenth century the French poet Leconte de Lisle (1818-94), master of Parnassian poetry, made no reference in his work to his island origins. This was not the case of Marius-Ary Leblond, a partnership formed by two cousins (Georges Athenas, 1877-1953, and Aimé Merlo, 1880-1958) who became the masters of colonial literature in French, and whose work was very influential, campaining for French imperialism while defending the dignity of the black population with a great deal of paternalism (*Ulysse, Cafre*, 1924). In the 1970s a new generation of writers started expressing itself in Creole following the example of Jean Albany (1917-84). Poets such as Boris Gamaleya (1930-) found followers. Axel Gauvin (1944-), for instance, a novelist chronicling contemporary life of the island in a language marked by Réunion French (*L'Aimé*, 1990), wrote novels in French and translated himself into Creole. Poets use the resources of Creole: Carpanin Marimotou (1945-), a university professor, is one of those who have been very influential in the making of an original Réunion voice, which will for long be constrained by the ambiguous luxury of dependence.

Ripple from the Storm, A (1958) A novel by Doris ★Lessing. In the third novel in the *Children of Violence* series Martha Quest is involved with a small band of communists in the capital of a British colony in Africa modelled on Rhodesia during the Second World War.

She learns that the strong political will of the communist leader Anton Hesse does not extend to his personal life when she is chosen to be his mistress. She finds him rigid and conservative, yet marries him to prevent his deportation as a European refugee. Her small group of leftists becomes involved in the less radical Social Democratic party, but they are eventually frustrated by the ingrained racism of the white working-class representatives. Ironically, Martha's desire to escape the stultifying colonial culture has only led her to be trapped and thwarted by her commitment to communism.

RIVE, Richard (1931-89), South African short-story writer and novelist, was born in District Six, the multiracial, working-class area of Cape Town. A distinguished academic career in South Africa and overseas included a Fulbright Fellowship in 1965 and a research fellowship at Oxford, where he wrote a doctorate on Olive *Schreiner, whose letters he would later edit.

Rive was an individualist amid the polarities of South African society. In an age of *Black Consciousness he believed firmly in non-racialism; in an age when many writers had been forced into exile, he stayed on in the country, staunchly defending the role of those who remained. Himself classified as 'coloured' (mixed race), he rejected the racial divisions of *apartheid; he refused to align himself with any literary or political organization, in order to avoid compromising his objectivity as a writer.

A wit and raconteur, Rive owed his early literary success to short stories depicting the brutalization and humiliations of apartheid such as 'Dagga-smoker's Dream' and 'The Bench', which won prizes; many of his stories appeared in magazines such as *Drum and Fighting Talk. Since publishers displayed little interest in writing by blacks, he had his first collection of stories, African Songs (1963), published in East Berlin. He also edited two anthologies, Quartet: New Voices from South Africa (1963), which introduced work by fellow Western Cape writers James *Matthews, Alex *La Guma, and Alf Wannenburgh, and Modern African Prose (1964), a pioneering collection of writing from across the continent.

His first novel, Emergency (1964), was set against the background of the unrest following upon the Sharpeville shootings of 1960 and the subsequent declaration of a state of emergency. It addresses important issues through the moral and political dilemma of a young school teacher, Andrew Dreyer, whose biography bears some resemblance to that of Rive himself. A disappointing autobiography, Writing Black (1981), was followed by his second novel, 'Buckingham Palace', District Six (1986), which celebrates the community life of District Six, bulldozed in the name of apartheid. Structured as a cycle of stories, the novel characterizes

District Six as 'an island in a sea of apartheid' and detects in its very destruction a flicker of resistance and reason to hope. His last novel, Emergency Continued (1990), published posthumously after Rive was brutally murdered at his home in Cape Town, is at once a realistic representation of political events in Cape Town during the state of emergency of 1985 and a metafictional meditation on the nature of the political novel and the relationship of truth to fiction.

River Between, The (1965) *Ngugi wa Thiong'o's second published novel in English (but the first written) is set in Kenya and deals with events of the 1930s and 40s on the ridges rising from the Honia river. Opposing religious factions occupy two ridges: Christian, led by Joshua, on one, and traditionalists led by Kabonyi on the other.

The action of the novel devolves around Waiyaki's attempt to resolve the differences between the groups. Thought by his father possibly to be the saviour predicted by the sage Mugo wa Kibero, Waiyaki seeks to bring about reconciliation by attending mission school while simultaneously honouring the traditions of the clan. The clan is suspicious of his Christian education, however, and thus of his motives; and he is expelled from the mission school because he undertakes traditional initiation.

Thus thwarted, Waiyaki founds his own school, assisted by two boyhood friends, Kamau and Kinuthia. Waiyaki falls in love with Joshua's daughter Nyambura, whose sister Mathoni also tries to reconcile the differences between the two factions by practising Christianity while undergoing the rites of female circumcision, and dying when the wound fails to heal. Kamau also loves Nyambura, and is jealous of Waiyaki.

The founding of the Kiama, an anti-Christian, anti-government movement led by Kabonyi, presents Waiyaki with further problems. Faced with the complex political and religious movements around him and unable to deny his love for Nyambura before the Kiama, Waiyaki is led away with Nyambura. The inference is that they are led to their deaths.

Waiyaki's personal difficulties and his inability to reconcile the opposites in his life adumbrate the concerns and actions of forces leading towards the violent confrontation in the lives of Kenyans in the Emergency period.

Road, The (1965) A play by Wole *Soyinka. Although arguably Soyinka's finest play and enthusiastically received in London (in 1965 and in 1993), The Road has been produced only infrequently in Nigeria, a fact that has led to some mythification of its difficulty. In reality much of its treatment of the lives of Nigeria's urban poor is highly accessible, in turn affectionate, disturbing, sharply humorous. Set in a motor park during the political crisis of the mid-1960s, the play depicts the working lives of a group of transport touts, mechanics, and petty criminals, in particular their relationship with a former lay preacher and document forger, the Professor. Through the latter's quest for 'the Word' and through the personal histories of other characters Soyinka explores a community's range of responses to death, as it touches on, and even defines, their lives; Yoruba myth forms the cardinal reference point for this exploration. *The Road* is remarkable especially for its virtuoso command of language.

ROBERT, Shaaban [See POETRY, East Africa; SWAHILI LITERATURE]

ROBERTS, Sheila (1937-), South African short-story writer, novelist, and poet, was born in Johannesburg. She left South Africa in the late 1970s to settle in the USA, where she is Professor of English at the University of Wisconsin in Milwaukee.

Roberts contributed much to South African literature in the 1970s and 80s. Her first volume of stories, *Outside Life's Feast* (1975), received the Olive Schreiner Prize and is remarkable for its insights into white working-class society in South Africa. Her first collection of poems, *Lou's Life and Other Poems* (1977), appeared in a volume jointly with three other South African poets. Her first novel, *He's My Brother* (1977; published in North America as *Johannesburg Requiem*, 1980), was banned at the time for sexual explicitness. It was followed by *The Weekenders* (1981), a second novel. A second collection of stories, *This Time of Year* (1983), again explores white working-class life in South Africa. She was awarded the Thomas Pringle Prize by the English Academy of South Africa for stories published in the literary periodical *Contrast*. Her critical study *Dan Jacobson* (1984) was followed by another collection of poems, *Dialogues and Divertimenti* (1985), the novel *Jacks in Corners* (1987), and more stories, *Coming In and Other Stories* (1993).

Roberts is best known for her masterly short stories, in which she portrays the lives of the white underclass in South Africa without prejudice. Her familiarity with the world of her characters gives her writing an immediacy and a refreshing freedom from guilt that is unusual in white South African fiction. In her later stories she moves away from the realist mode and experiments with a more reflexive narrative style, most conspicuous in her humorous and playful 'Carlotta's Vinyl Skin' (in *Coming In and Other Stories*).

ROTIMI, Ola (1938-), Nigerian dramatist, was born in Bendel State, Nigeria to a *Yoruba father and Ijo mother. After study in the USA, where some of his early plays were performed (including *Our Husband Has Gone Mad Again*, at Yale in 1966), he returned to Nigeria and in 1967 was appointed to the University of Ife (now Obafemi Awolowo University), where he

was a leading founder of the Ori Olokun Theatre. Rotimi's plays from this period – *The *Gods Are Not To Blame* (1971), *Kurunmi* (1971), *Ovonramwen Nogbaisi* (1974) – are among the best known of all Nigerian plays, frequently set as school texts and (especially *The Gods*) widely performed. In 1977 Rotimi left Ife and joined the University of Port Harcourt, where he remained until 1992, returning then to Ife to establish a professional company, African Cradle Theatre.

Although several radio plays, a large-scale historical play entitled *Akassa Youmi* (first performed 1977), and a popular short Pidgin comedy, *Grip 'Am* (adapted from a Yoruba play by Agedoke Durojaiye), remain unpublished, the seven published plays demonstrate Rotimi's versatility. *Our Husband Has Gone Mad Again* (1974) is a genial political satire (with a somewhat wavering aim); *Holding Talks* (1979) is much less genial, an often scathingly funny satire on the abuse of language in the interests of power relations. *The Gods Are Not To Blame*, one of many Nigerian adaptations of earlier stage plays, reworks Sophocles' *Oedipus* in the context of a pre-colonial Yoruba court. Although this play has provoked critical controversy (over its language, and its perceived cultural contradiction), it is undeniably a compelling experience when effectively staged. *Kurunmi* and *Ovonramwen Nogbaisi* are historical plays that deal with crises in nineteenth-century Yoruba and Benin history respectively. These plays have been criticized on ideological grounds, the suggestion being that here Rotimi becomes fixated with the trials of the tragic leader-figure and neglects to explore the conservative nature of the state and the conservative implications of so massively foregrounding the role of the governing elite. Two more recent plays have been highly successful in production: *If* (1983) and *Hopes of the Living Dead* (1988). The former deals with the lives of the inhabitants of a working-class city tenement. Here Rotimi focuses, with humour and with sharp sympathetic concern, on economic privation and political manipulation. *Hopes* dramatizes strategies for collaboration against oppression, drawing on an event from the 1920s when, under Ikoli Harcourt Whyte's guidance, a group of lepers resisted attempts by the colonial authorities to have them evicted from a Port Harcourt hospital. *If* and *Hopes* are Rotimi's most successful attempts to date to popularize literary drama.

RUBADIRI, David (1930-), Malawian poet and novelist, was born in Liule and educated at Makerere University College, Uganda and later at King's College, Cambridge. After serving as Malawi's first ambassador to the USA and the United Nations, he broke with the Banda regime and left the country to return to the academic world, where he remains. He served as Professor of Education at the University of Botswana until Banda fell from power, whereupon he was reappointed Malawi's ambassador to the United Nations.

Rubadiri's only novel, ★*No Bride Price* (1967), reflects early disenchantment with Banda's post-independence style. It was well received and, with Legson ★Kayira's work, was among the first Malawian novels to be published. He also wrote a play, *Come to Tea* (1965), which was published in *New African*. He is best known, however, as a poet, and his work appeared in international journals such as *Transition*, *Black Orpheus*, and *Présence africaine*, as well as Gerald Moore's and Ulli Beier's pioneering anthology *Modern Poetry from Africa* (1963, rev. 1968), at a time when much African verse in English was still imitating Western models. His poems pointed to a new development among African writers, a fruitful combination of African influences and an awareness of European poetic modes. Concerned passionately about the place of African literature in the continent's school and college syllabi, he emphasizes the importance of suitable teaching texts. Thus he edited *Poems from East Africa* (1971) with David Cook and *Growing Up With Poetry: An Anthology for Secondary Schools* (1989) for Botswanan students.

RUGANDA, John (1941-), Ugandan playwright and novelist, graduated from Makerere University, Kampala, was the senior fellow in creative writing at Makerere University, and later joined the Department of Literature at the University of Nairobi, and then the Department of English at the University of Swaziland. His literary reputation rests on his plays, for which he has won several playwriting competitions. Along with Robert ★Serumaga he is considered the main force behind the development of the theatre in Uganda in the 1970s and 80s. His first play, *The Burdens* (1972), which came second in the 1972 Kenyatta Prize for Literature competition, uses the microcosm of family life to explore the problems of a larger society. In *Black Mamba* (1973), a satire, the figure of the prostitute is symbolic of the oppressed people of Africa. *Covenant with Death* (1973) is an investigation of social and psychological alienation. Other published plays include *Music without Tears* (1982), *Echoes of Silence* (1986), and *The Floods* (1980), which revolves around power and the suffering of innocent victims at the hands of corrupt and incompetent governments while culpable elites fail to act.

RUHENI, Mwangi (pseud. of Nicholas Muraguri) (1934-), novelist, was born in Kenya. He holds B.Sc. and M.Sc. degrees from Makerere University College, Uganda, where he was also the editor of *St. Augustine's Newsletter*, produced by Catholic students. His second M.Sc. is from the University of Strathclyde, Scotland. He was the government chemist for Kenya for twenty-two years and retired in 1990.

Ruheni's first novel, *What a Life!* (1972), won him instant recognition and marked a new trend in Kenyan

literature, which his subsequent novels, *The Future Leaders* (1973), *What a Husband!* (1974), and *The Minister's Daughter* (1975), helped to consolidate. His novels are characterized by a combination of social criticism moderated by a happy ending or by the humorous attitude of the protagonists to the problems they encounter and the entertaining spirit of ★popular literature, without its pornographic or thrilling extremes. His chief preoccupation has been the difficult process of young people's maturing into adults and their integration in social life. With *The Mystery Smugglers* (1975) and *The Love Root* (1976) Ruheni crosses the border to popular writing. He has also written a children's book, *In Search of Their Parents* (1973). *Random Thoughts Book I* (1995) is a kind of diary arrangement of essays written around a variety of thoughts, ranging from religion and politics to publishing and soccer. No longer a public servant worried about prudence, Nicholas Muraguri has this time used his real name.

RUHUMBIKA, Gabriel (1938-), Tanzanian novelist and short-story writer, was born in Ukerewe Islands, Tanzania and studied at the University of Makerere, Uganda and the Sorbonne in Paris, where he gained a Ph.D. in African literature (1964). Since 1970 he has taught literature at universities in East Africa and the USA.

Ruhumbika's first novel, *Village in Uhuru* (1969), focuses on the problem of ethnic identities in the context of national unity; read politically, it reflects Tanzania's need to provide a homogenized society under socialism. Musilanga, the headman of Chamambo village, is pitted against his son, who recognizes the poverty of the people and determines to change their circumstances through political activism.

Ruhumbika, like ★Ngugi wa Thiong'o, abandoned English and published his subsequent books, a collection of stories and another novel, in ★Swahili. *Uwike Usiwike Kutakucha* [Whether the cock crows or not it dawns] (1978) examines the failures of Uhuru as promised by the elite. *Miradi Bubu ya Wazalendo* [Invisible enterprises of the patriots] (1991) is a historical novel about the plight of those who fought for Uhuru.

RUI, Manuel [See LUSOPHONE LITERATURE; POLITICS AND LITERATURE, Angola and Mozambique]

Rumours of Rain (1978). A novel by André ★Brink. On the eve of the Soweto riots, the narrator, a wealthy Afrikaner businessman, is travelling with his son to the family farm. During this weekend visit, his carefully controlled world collapses with the conviction of his best friend for 'terrorism', the revolt of his son, the loss of his mistress, and the sale of the farm. Brink's ironic first-person account is used to alienate the reader and to illustrate the moral bankruptcy of the Afrikaner apologist. The novel's structure reflects Mynhardt's attempt and ultimate failure to control and keep separate the various elements of his life in a personal equivalent of the *apartheid system. Despite his apparent self-examination, his narration is shown to be merely a 'striptease of the soul' designed to expiate his guilt, and he is shown in the end as a victim of his own paradoxes. Imagery of drought and rain is used throughout to suggest the impending apocalypse and the inevitability of political change.

RUNGANO, Kristina (1963-), poet and short-story writer, was born in Harare, Zimbabwe and grew up near Kuatama Mission. She attended Catholic-run boarding schools in Selous and Harare, studied management in Britain, and is working on a doctoral degree in computing and mathematics at South Bank University, London. She is Zimbabwe's first published female poet, and *A Storm Is Brewing* (1984) is her first collection. She has since contributed poems to the anthologies *Daughters of Africa* (1992) and *The Heinemann Book of African Women's Poetry* (1995) and written short stories. Although she views her poetry primarily as a means of self-release, her themes are resonant: self-exploration, aspects of womanhood, love, loneliness, alienation, and war are among her subjects. Her enduring strengths include her ability to capture inwardly felt experience using a variety of personae.

S

SAADAWI, Nawal el (1931-), Egyptian writer of fiction and non-fiction in Arabic, was born in the Egyptian village of Kafr Tahla and has worked in medicine, politics, government, literature, and cultural analysis for the equality of Muslim women in political, economic, and domestic life. Perhaps because of her reputation as a reformer, her accomplishments as a writer were long minimized, and her fictional works have only recently been available in English translation. She is the founder of the Arab Women's Solidarity Association, a founder of the Arab Organization for Human Rights, has been arrested and imprisoned, has lived under death threats by Muslim fundamentalists, and has had her books and appearances on radio and television banned in Egypt and other Middle Eastern countries. With all this, she has managed to write twenty-seven books, including many works of fiction. *Memoirs from the Women's Prison* (1981; trans. 1986) is a vivid account of her own jail experiences. In the novel *Woman at Point Zero* (1975; trans. 1983) a female inmate on death row says 'I was killed by revealing the truth, not in using the knife. They aren't afraid of the knife; it's the truth that terrifies them.' Her short stories are terse, specific, and objectively told, and have appeared in several journals as well as in four collections, including *Death of an Ex-Minister* (trans. 1987) and *She Has No Place in Paradise* (trans. 1987). She often treats of traumas women feel from sequestration, from the veil, from sexual mutilation. She also deals with the forces of tradition to suppress independent action for both men and women. Her seven novels depict both rural and urban life in contemporary Egypt and the abuses of power by a tyrannical government. Her novels include *God Dies by the Nile* (1975; trans. 1985), *The Circling Song* (trans. 1989), and *Searching* (trans. 1991). She was early recognized in France through translations of her works by the Algerian writer Assia *Djebar. Although Saadawi was known in the USA for her activism, her fiction did not appear in English translation until the 1980s. *A Daughter of Isis: The Autobiography of Nawal el Saadawi* (1999), covering the early years of her life, was translated from the Arabic by Sherif Hetata.

SALIH, Tayeb (1929-), novelist writing in Arabic, was born in the northern axis of central Sudan to an ethnic group reputed for the propagation of Islamic scholarship in the region. His primary education was religious, and it ignited his precocity to such an extent that by the time he entered secondary school in Khartoum he had already studied prominent Arab authors such as al Tahtawi, Muhammed Abdul, and Dr. Taha Husayn. After gaining an advanced degree in London, he worked for the BBC as the head of Arabic drama. On his return to Sudan, he became director of Sudanese National Radio; later he accepted a secondment as director general of the Ministry of Information of the Emirate of Qatar, where he makes his home.

Salih's writing, drawn from his experience of communal village life, centres on people and their complex relationships. At various levels and with varying degrees of psychoanalytic emphasis, he deals with themes of reality and illusion, the cultural dissonance between the West and the exotic orient, the harmony and conflict of brotherhood, and the individual's responsibility to find a fusion between his or her contradictions. These motifs and their contexts derive from both his Islamic cultural background and the experience of modern Africa, both pre- and postcolonial. In his novels, *Al-Rajul al Qubrosi* (*The Cypriot Man*, 1978), *Urs al Zayn* (*The Wedding of Zein*, 1969), *Mawsim al-Hijra ila al-Shamal* (*★Season of Migration to the North*, 1969), and *Daumat Wad Hamid* (*The Doum Tree of Wad Hamid*, 1985), he constructs an impervious unity of the social, religious, and political essence of the African or African Arab. He firmly holds that a harmony of existence is possible for individuals in a society of values and ethics. His books have been translated into several languages.

SALLAH, Tijan M(omodou) (1958-), poet, was born in Sere Kunda, Gambia. After attending St. Augustine's High School, he went to the USA, where he gained a BA from Berea College, Kentucky, and an MA and a Ph.D. from Virginia Polytechnic. He taught economics at Virginia Polytechnic, Kutztown University, and the University of North Carolina before going to work for the World Bank. His collections of poetry include *When Africa Was a Young Woman* (1980), *Kora Land* (1989), and *Dreams of Dusty Roads* (1993). His fourth publication, *Before the New Earth* (1988), is a collection of short stories. Africa's underdevelopment, its causative factors, and possible solutions constitute his central thematic preoccupations. He has strong faith in the positive elements of African communal values, a distrust of the decadent influence of Western modernity, and a strong metaphysical interest in the infinite. A progression towards excellence characterizes his poetic style. He has moved from epigrammatic poetry of simple diction, simple narration, and simple imagery, in which similes proliferate, to mature poetry of description, imaginatively mixed metaphors, and satirically humorous or tragically engaging poetic narratives that often imitate the traditional art of the *griot*. His short stories are poetically styled, and, like the poems, derive their imagery mostly from nature. The latter are positive, while images of modernity are often negative.

SAMKANGE, Stanlake (1922-88), Zimbabwean journalist, historian, and historical novelist, was born in Zvimba, Zimbabwe, then Southern Rhodesia, the son of the Rev. Thompson Samkange, Methodist minister and nationalist politician, and his wife, Grace Mano, a Methodist evangelist. Thompson Samkange worked in both Matabeleland and Mashonaland during Samkange's childhood, and a characteristic of Samkange's writing is his refusal to adopt regional and ethnic perspectives. He was educated at Adams College in Natal, University College of Fort Hare, and the University of Indiana, USA. After returning from Fort Hare to teach in Southern Rhodesia in 1948 he began to plan Nyatsime College, a secondary school to be controlled by blacks rather than government or missionaries, which was finally opened in 1962. Samkange was deeply involved in the liberal politics of Southern Rhodesia during the 1950s and 60s, but when it became clear that the white electorate would reject any multiracial option he moved to the USA, where his most important literary work was produced.

Samkange's first novel was *On Trial for My Country* (1966), in which both Cecil Rhodes and Lobengula, the Ndebele ruler, are tried by their ancestors for their respective parts in obtaining and granting the various concessions that gave an air of legality to Rhodes's occupation of Mashonaland. It was banned in Rhodesia. It was followed by the rather pedestrian *Origins of Rhodesia* (1968), a formal history covering the same ground as the novel had done. *The Mourned One* (1975), a novel, is partly autobiographical; *Year of the Uprising* (1978) is a fictional reconstruction of the 1896 rising. He returned to Rhodesia in 1978 but retired from active politics before the Lancaster House talks, concentrating instead on his writing. With his wife, Tommie Anderson, he wrote *Hunuism or Ubuntuism* (1980), an attempt to systematize an African epistemology, and *African Saga* (1971), a popular history of Africa. His last novels were *Among Them Yanks* (1985) and *On Trial for That UDI* (1986), which put rebel Rhodesian prime minister Ian Smith and British prime minister Harold Wilson on trial.

In his historical fiction Samkange draws heavily on published documents and has been criticized for a confusion of the historical and the imaginative. This criticism underestimates his achievement. In all his writings the texts of imperialism or Rhodesian official-

dom are refused the authority they claim for themselves and instead have the context a black writer allows them. The white voice is not silenced but is forced into a dialogue with a black voice, a narrative strategy with radical implications in the Rhodesia of the 1960s and 70s. In the three novels the black voice has access to rich mythic and spiritual sources whose authority is reproduced in a complex secular order, whether it is the Ndebele state in *On Trial for My Country* or village life in *The Mourned One*. A growing despair at white intransigence and a corresponding radicalism can be seen in the novels: in the first Rhodes and Lobengula both have a right to call the country theirs; the ending of *Year of the Uprising* suggests that compromise with whites is impossible.

SANCHO, Ignatius (1729-80), letter-writer, was born in a slave ship between Africa and South America and died in England. He was baptized Ignatius by a bishop in South America and was sold to three Englishwomen at Greenwich after being separated from his parents around the age of two. These sisters, whom he detested, gave him the second name, Sancho, for the resemblance they saw between him and Don Quixote's servant, Sancho Panza. Often the three sisters taunted him with the prospect of selling him back into slavery in the Americas. While in the household of the Duchess of Montagu, where he was employed as a butler, he cultivated the friendship of the English novelist Laurence Sterne. He was well acquainted with the theatre and made many friends as well among sculptors and painters, and a picture was made of him by Gainsborough. Among his other friends were Henry Fielding, David Garrick, and John Mortimer, who regularly consulted him on his views about painting.

Sancho is best known for his *Letters of the Late Ignatius Sancho, an African* (1782), which went into five editions. The letters, most often addressed to friends, contain lively details of domestic life and evidence of his affection for his six children, whom he calls the 'Sanchonets', as well as observations and comment on a range of topics relevant to eighteenth-century city life. He also wrote music and a *Theory of Music*, dedicated to the Princess Royal, which has not survived. Although his writing bears the styles and values of polite English society, the language of protest surfaces in discussions such as those focused on poverty and slavery.

SARO-WIWA, Ken(ule Beeson) (1941-95), Nigerian novelist, non-fiction writer and television and film producer, was educated at Government College, Umuahia and the University of Ibadan. He held the political and administrative positions of Commissioner of Works, Land, and Transport, of Education, and of Information and Home Affairs in Rivers State between 1968 and 1973. During the *Nigeria–Biafra war (1967–70) he served as administrator of the oil port of Bonny. In 1973 he published his first two books, *Tambari* and *Tambari in Dukana*, both intended for a youthful audience. Leaving government service the same year, he embarked on a successful business career in several fields, including publishing.

In 1985 he published a collection of his poetry, *Songs in a Time of War*, and the novel *Sozaboy: A Novel in Rotten English*. *Sozaboy* in particular received critical attention because of its creative mix of Pidgin, broken, and standard English. In the novel, Mene, the innocent and impoverished protagonist, joins the Biafran army for economic reasons and because of his romantic dream of being a 'soza', a soldier. The portrayal of Mene's disillusionment as he witnesses the brutalities of warfare and the hypocrisy of those who precipitated the conflict make *Sozaboy* a compelling anti-war novel. In the mid-1980s Saro-Wiwa turned to television production; his 'Basi & Co.' series was extremely popular, with more than 150 separate episodes finally being aired. Basi and his get-rich-quick schemes became the subject of *Basi and Company: A Modern African Folktale* (1987), a series of children's books featuring 'Mr. B', *Basi and Company: Four Television Plays* (1988), and *Four Farcical Plays* (1989).

With the publication of *On a Darkling Plain: An Account of the Nigerian Civil War* (1989), Saro-Wiwa's autobiographical description of the conflict, his social activism on behalf of his people, the Ogoni, emerges. He portrays the Ibo as oppressors of the ethnic minorities in eastern Nigeria, particularly the Ogoni, who are caught between the Yoruba, Ibo, and Hausa. Although he continued writing gentle satire and literature for children, his concerns about the injustice and corruption he saw in Nigeria came to dominate, with some of his most compelling and critical comments appearing in *Prisoners of Jebs* (1988), *Nigeria: The Brink of Disaster* (1991) and *Similia: Essays on Anomic Nigeria* (1991). The books, which collect newspaper columns and articles written over the previous two decades, cover a wide range of subjects and are perhaps the best source for an overview of Saro-Wiwa's concerns. Among those concerns was the fate of the Ogoni people and their mistreatment by multinational oil companies and collaborating Nigerian government officials. In *Genocide in Nigeria: The Ogoni Tragedy* (1992) he argues that the Ogoni are an exploited minority in Nigeria. Arrested and charged with treason, he was imprisoned briefly in 1993, an experience he describes in *A Month and a Day* (1995). Upon his release he continued his efforts on behalf of the Ogoni, and through the organization Movement for the Survival of the Ogoni People charged Shell Oil and the Nigerian federal government with creating an ecological disaster in Ogoni lands. In 1995 he was accused of incitement to murder when some village heads were killed at a rally, and after a controversial trial was hanged. Because of his civil rights activities and his violent death, he is now best remembered for his reform efforts and advocacy of Ogoni rights. However, his longer-term reputation rests with his novel *Sozaboy* and its creative use of language.

SASSINE, Williams (1944–96), Guinean novelist who wrote in French. Unlike *Camara Laye, his role model, who accommodated the animist, Islamic, and French backgrounds of an African child, Williams Sassine had to negotiate his sense of exclusion. He attributes his childhood stammering to his triple learning experience – catechism to please his Christian Lebanese father, the Koran to abide by his African mother's Islamic heritage, and the school system of a French colony. Mathematics served as an escape. Dissatisfied with Sékou Touré's stranglehold over Guinean youth, Sassine fled Guinea in 1961 and survived in France as a student and immigrant for five years. From 1966 to 1988, he wrote four novels while making a living for his family (five children) as a mathematics teacher and headmaster in West African countries from Ivory Coast to Mauritania, circling around Guinea until he finally returned to his native 'prison-homeland'. In his position as chief editor of the satirical newspaper *Le Lynx*, he comments on Guinea's slow recovery from ethnic rivalries and Sékou Touré's dictatorship.

In *Saint Monsieur Baly* (1973) and *Wirriyamu* (1976; trans. 1980) (the latter is the name of a village in an imaginary Portuguese colony) Sassine creates marginal characters whose fortitude is meant to give hope for survival after civil war. Both the holy schoolteacher (M. Baly) and the sacrificial albino of Wirriyamu could be considered as Christ-like figures. However, the sacrilegious 'young man made of sand' (*Le Jeune Homme de sable*, 1979) is probably more moving as an opposition figure in that his helplessness enhances his temerity. Symbolism and poetry alleviate this novel's finding that opponents to dictatorship are estranged even from those who should side with them. Sékou Touré's death in 1984 inspired Sassine with a renewed, humorous opposition style. *Le Zéhros n'est pas n'importe qui* (1985) is based on a pun about an exile who is called back to his country after the death of the PDG (Président-Directeur-Général) to serve as a 'hero', even though his failures have confirmed him a 'zero'. Written before his return to Guinea, this novel foresees the dereliction of a country that has stagnated in poverty for the past thirty years. Sassine is a talented writer who has experienced rather than speculated on the aftermath of a dictatorship.

SCHREINER, Olive (Emilie Albertina) (1855–1920). Born one of twelve children in South Africa's northeastern Cape, Olive Schreiner rejected her missionary parents' religion from an early age. Her father's bankruptcy forced her to leave home at twelve, initiating what became a lifetime of anxious wandering. First dependent upon various relatives, Schreiner began working as a governess at fifteen. She read widely (including works by Emerson, Herbert Spencer, J.S. Mill, Darwin, and Carl Vogt), kept a journal from childhood, and began writing seriously in late adolescence. The *Story of an African Farm (1883), Undine (1929), and From Man to Man (1926), her three novels, were all under way while she was in her twenties.

In England, where she had gone in 1881, she resumed her literary career when her asthma prevented her studying medicine. The commercial and critical success of African Farm provided the opportunity for acquaintance with Havelock Ellis, Karl Pearson, and Edward Carpenter, among others, but despite the intensity of her participation in the feminist and socialist intellectual activity of the time, she remained an outsider without conventional family or social ties. She returned to South Africa in 1889, married Samuel Cronwright, and hoped to realize her long-held desire for motherhood, but the baby born in 1895 died and she did not have another. She focused her writing from this period on allegory and political analysis, travelled again to England late in her life and there renewed her involvement in feminism and pacifism. She returned in 1920 to Cape Town, where she died.

Schreiner's fiction has often been mined for biographical detail. Undine, her first major work (but published posthumously), is, by her own account, 'exact autobiography', and all her novels describe children with tenuous family links whose unconventional behaviour brings further alienation and who turn to freethinking after an early loss of faith. Similarly her descriptions of the eastern Cape countryside and portrayals of the towns that emerged after the 1867 discovery of diamonds provide insight into the social context of her early life.

Traces of Schreiner's colonial location emerge in other ways too. The setting for much of Undine is an imaginary England, indicative both of Schreiner's isolation from the metropolitan centre and her inability to perceive local culture as sufficiently viable material for fiction. By the time of African Farm she is more able to 'paint what lies before her', as she instructs local artists in the preface to the second edition. African Farm further illustrates what critics have termed the 'discontinuities of colonial experience', with its mixture of genres, 'formless' plot and 'deficiencies' of character indicative of an uneasiness about the African environment.

Schreiner's novels also provide valuable insights into the position of women under colonialism. Like Schreiner herself, female characters are denied a formal education, branded 'odd' for their 'manly' behaviour, and hounded when they contravene the stifling sexual mores of parochial eastern Cape towns. Schreiner thus exposes how colonial society simultaneously afforded white women greater freedom and yet constrained them to uphold the family. The metaphor of seduction in From Man to Man represents the colonized land as feminized, anticipating the perspective of North American and Australian women writers, as well as her compatriot Pauline *Smith in The *Beadle (1926).

Schreiner's interest in allegory, clear in her novels as well as in the collections Dreams (1870) and Dream Life and Real Life (1893), combine with her passion for politics in Trooper Peter Halket of Mashonaland (1897), a critique of the 'civilizing' mission of the Chartered Company. Much of her non-fiction is didactic, directed against imperial policy and Rhodes's aggressive capitalism. Her idealization of rural Boer life in Thoughts on South Africa (1923) was intended as a strategic defence of the Afrikaner in the aftermath of the Jameson Raid. An English South African's View of the Situation (1899) aims to avert the impending *Anglo-Boer conflict. Schreiner similarly intended to shock an intended British audience with Trooper Peter Halket and force a parliamentary re-examination of the affairs of the Chartered Company. Closer Union (1909) continues the critique of monopoly capitalism and segregation and proposes federalism for South Africa.

Woman and Labour (1911), praised as the 'Bible of the women's movement', articulates Schreiner's theory that the exclusion of women from education and employment produces a condition of sex parasitism, which reduces women to the 'passive performance of sex functions alone'. The latter part of Woman and Labour addresses women's relation to war, reflecting her growing concern. 'The Dawn of Civilisation' (1921) is a final discussion of gender and sex.

Traditionally Schreiner's marginal position as a writer has been associated with a sense of her failure. Only recently, through re-readings of her work attentive to her position as a colonial woman writer in turn-of-the-century South Africa, has a more nuanced portrait of Schreiner emerged, one sensitive to her manifest achievements as well as her limitations.

SCULLY, William Charles (1855-1943), novelist, poet, and autobiographer, was born in Dublin, Ireland and came with his family to King Williamstown in the Eastern Cape in 1867. As his volumes of autobiographical reminiscences reveal, Scully had a rich and varied life – as a prospector for diamonds in Kimberley, for gold in Lydenberg and Pilgrim's Rest; as a Cape civil servant in 1876, rising through the ranks to become magistrate and civil commissioner in the Transkei, Namaqualand, and the Transvaal. As an imperialist he believed in and supported imperialism's aims and objectives while deploring the jingoistic excesses that, in his mind, not only precipitated the *Anglo–Boer war of 1899-1902 (he deals with this subject in *The Harrow*, 1921, a retrospective account of Boer suffering under siege), but that implicitly and overtly fostered racism through its paternalistic attitudes to African peoples.

Scully's writing shows a wide, varied, and sympathetic interest in and understanding of the South African landscape, its peoples, and the impact of imperial intruders on the former. His work includes *The Wreck of the Grosvenor and Other South African Poems*, published anonymously in 1886, *Poems* (1892), and *Between Sun and Sand* (1898), about the lives and experiences of nomadic peoples in Namaqualand, emphasizing the difficulty of human existence in this setting. *Lodges in the Wilderness* (1915), again about Namaqualand, suggests the spirituality of the desert places. *Daniel Vananda: The Life Story of a Human Being* (1923) conveys Scully's sympathetic understanding of African values and experiences in both rural and urban settings, viewed retrospectively over the period 1880 to 1920. He published three further collections of short stories, *Kafir Stories* (1895), *The White Hecatomb and Other Stories* (1897), *By Veldt and Kopje* (1907); *The Ridge of White Waters ('Witwatersrand'); or, Impressions of a Visit to Johannesburg* (1912); and the autobiographical *Reminiscences of a South African Pioneer* (1913) and *Further Reminiscences of a South African Pioneer* (1913).

Season of Anomy (1973) A novel by Wole *Soyinka. The legend of Orpheus and Euridice becomes the story of Ofeiyi and Iriyese in an allegorical comment on post-colonial Nigeria and by extension or implication on other post-colonial African states. Ofeiyi strives to create a society that is the opposite of the pragmatic and ruthless military-industrial 'Cartel', a self-seeking, manipulative and violent world that ultimately destroys the idealized world Ofeiyi seeks to create and protect. The novel has its origins in the 'anomy' of the pogroms that took place in Northern Nigeria in 1966 when law and order collapsed, and that ultimately resulted in the *Nigeria-Biafra war.

Season of Migration to the North (1969) A novel by Tayeb *Salih, translated from the Arabic. This is a complex and sometimes confusing novel produced, the author says, under the influence of Freud and with literary debts to Shakespeare's *Richard III* and *King Lear*, Conrad's *Heart of Darkness* and *Nostromo*, as well as the experiences of Lawrence of Arabia and the writings of Sir Richard Burton. It was described by *The Observer*, London, as 'An Arabian nights in reverse...'

It has two principal characters, an unnamed narrator (who is nevertheless sometimes called Muhaymid) and Mustafa Sa'id who tells his story in direct speech. The lives of these two characters are in many ways so curiously alike that their experiences may be seen as those of one personality.

Each has grown up in a native village in the Sudan; each has been to Europe for several years to gain advanced education; each has returned to Africa to find the 'warmth of the village' as a contrast with the coldness of Europe.

Mustafa says he will appease his race by liberating Africa with his penis, thus reversing and re-enacting the rape of Africa. He exploits three British women who fall in love with him and who eventually commit suicide. He meets his match in a woman who teases him, cajoles him into marriage and eventually coaxes him into killing her. For this he goes to prison for seven years.

On his return to Africa he tries to block out his past by participating in village life and by marrying a village woman who bears him two sons. But he cannot overcome his sense of disillusionment and guilt and at a time of flood drowns in a swollen river, either by accident or suicide.

After his death the unnamed narrator takes up the story. He is drawn into the life of Mustafa and his wife and sons. He refuses to marry the widow in order to save her from a loveless arranged marriage. The arranged marriage takes place and, failing to protect herself from the brutal advance of the new husband, the widow kills the second husband and herself.

The narrator realizes too late that he has in fact loved her. More than this he realises that ancient customs such as arranged marriages are out of step with the times. He realizes therefore that he cannot accept the customs, conventions and mentality of the village in which he first sought refuge, and contemplates, but rejects, suicide.

The village scenes are realistic in style. But Tayeb Salih adopts a contrasting style approaching parody for the London flashbacks.

Seasons of Thomas Tebo, The (1986) A novel by John *Nagenda. The novel concerns the calamities that befall an independent African country when successive regimes follow a brutal pattern of political leadership. Parallel to the misfortunes of the nation and under their decisive impact runs the life of the protagonist. The magnitude of the devastation and the impossibility of meaningful resistance on both levels generate a sense of futility and doom. But just as the people discover in their very suffering and in their repulsion for inhumanity the remnants of will and wisdom that enable them to attempt to raise from the near-ashes, so the individual, Thomas Tebo, submitting to the power of reason, transcends his cancerous frustration and resolves to resume his earthly journey. Herein lies the hope in whose glimmer the narrative ends.

SEGUN, Mabel (Dorothy) (1930-), poet and children's writer, was born in Ondo, Nigeria and studied at the University College of Ibadan. She has worked as an editor, broadcaster, teacher, and researcher at the University of Ibadan, and was founder and first president of the Children's Literature Association of Nigeria (CLAN).

Segun's focus on children's literature emerges from her conviction that humanity's struggle for equilibrium requires intellectual alertness, emotional balance, and loyalty to cultural roots. Her poems, stories, and cultural commentary promote ideals such as collectiveness, patriotism, and self-reliance and critique narrow ethnicity, the romanticizing of the past, and the political, social, and economic contradictions in present-day Nigeria. Her style is always direct, simple (not simplistic), and full of irony, sometimes employing an oral technique that makes her poems sound like tales in verse. Her publications include *My Father's Daughter* (1965), an autobiographical reader for children, *Youth Day Parade* (1983), *My Mother's Daughter* (1985), *Olu and the Broken Statue* (1985), *Sorry, No Vacancy* (1985), and *Conflict and Other Poems* (1986). *Friends, Nigerians, Countrymen* (1977) is a collection of her satirical radio broadcasts. Her short fiction has been collected in *The Surrender and Other Stories* (1995).

SEKYI (William Essuman-Gwira) Kobina (1892-1956), Ghanaian dramatist. Educated at Richmond College of West Africa, the University of London, and the Inns of Court, Sekyi became a member of the Inner Temple and the Aristotelian Society. In 1918 he returned to the then Cape Coast to embark on a legal career and became active in social and cultural clubs devoted to social reform and education.

Sekyi's concern with reform and development is evident in his many essays and addresses, published in the 1930s and 40s, and in poetry related to issues of nationalism, but his satirical play *The Blinkards* (not published until 1974) will arguably remain his greatest literary accomplishment. *The Blinkards*, first produced by the Cosmopolitan Club in Cape Coast in 1915, is an African comedy of manners written in two languages, Fante and English. The play satirizes middle-class, western-oriented Fantis who embrace everything that they think is western. Sekyi reserves his greatest scorn for the likes of Mrs. Brofusem, who, in her not-quite-complete assimilation into the colonizer's culture, consistently misappropriates its most unseemly aspects. Such mimic men and women, suggests Sekyi, are the ridiculous offspring of a colonial culture, unable to take pride in and retain the best of their own traditions while also engaging with the colonizer. If such aspects of the colonizer's culture as dress and religion impede the more tempered modernity that Sekyi seems to advocate, a retrospective reading of the play is bound to raise the issues of what Sekyi himself sees as inappropriate modernity; thus for instance a contemporary feminist reading may well observe the collusion of nationalism and patriarchy in Sekyi's insistence that Christianity and Westernization 'corrupt' the African woman. While such issues of interpretation remain open, it is clear that Sekyi and *The Blinkards* in particular are critical manifestations of an important era of West African history.

SELLASSIE, Sahle (1936-), Ethiopian novelist, was born in Wardena, Ethiopia and educated in Ethiopia and at the University of Aix-Marseilles, France and the University of California, USA.

His literary career began with *Shinega's Village: Scenes of Ethiopian Life* (1964), a fictionalized recollection of Ethiopian life during the 1940s, which was translated from Chaha, an Amharic dialect, into English. *The Afersata* (1969), his first novel in English, centres on an investigation by traditional collective means into the burning of a villager's hut. *Warrior King* (1974), a historical novel, is about Emperor Tewodros II, the nineteenth-century bandit who became an emperor, and in *Firebrands* (1979) a man struggles to resist the corruption all around him in a society slowly crumbling during the reign of Haile Sellassie Mariam. Sellassie's novels provide with considerable sociological detail a poignant description of the lives of the urban elite and the rural poor in Ethiopia.

SELORMEY, Francis (1927-88), Ghanaian novelist, was born in a seaside village near Keta in what was then Gold Coast and was educated at a Roman Catholic primary school in his home area, St. Augustine's College, Cape Coast, the University of Ghana, Legon, where he studied physical education, and in Germany. He was chief physical education instructor at St. Francis Teacher Training College and later became the senior sports administrator in the Volta Region. He turned to writing initially as an avocation. In his autobiographical first novel, *The Narrow Path* (1966), a boy grows up to learn that his Christian father's harsh behaviour towards him was a mark of his love. He also wrote two film scripts: 'Towards a United Africa' and 'The Great Lake', about Ghana's Volta Lake. His patriotism and deep interest in African unity also inform some of his poetry.

SEMBENE OUSMANE (1923-), pioneering Senegalese writer and filmmaker, was born in Ziguinchor, in the southern Casamance region of Senegal, then French West Africa. (Though he is frequently referred to as 'Sembene Ousmane,' Sembene is his family name, Ousmane his given name, and recently he requested a preference to be known simply as Sembene.) His family was of the coastal Lebou branch of the Wolof people, and of the Muslim faith. As a boy, he was influenced by his maternal uncle, an Islamic scholar, and attended koranic schools in the Casamance. At age twelve he travelled north to Dakar to attend French schools there, but dropped out after two years, turning to an apprenticeship in masonry, further Islamic engagements, immersion in traditional culture, fledgling union activity, and local theatre. In 1942 he joined the French colonial military and fought in both Europe and Africa during World War Two. Demobilized in 1946, he participated in the landmark 1947-8 Dakar–Niger railway workers' strike against the French. In 1948 he left again for Europe, not to return for some thirteen years. Though principally resident in France, he also travelled to Denmark, the USSR, China, North Vietnam, and elsewhere during this time.

Sembene's artistic career began in the early 1950s when he began writing poetry for French working-class periodicals. His first ★novel, Le Docker noir (The ★Black Docker, 1987), appeared in 1956: from an auto-biographical base, it tells of the difficult life of African workers in the large French port city of Marseilles. His next novel, O pays, mon beau peuple, followed a year later, telling a classic story of a young man who returns to Senegal after a stay in France and meets with great difficulty. Les Bouts de bois de Dieu (★God's Bits of Wood, 1962), appeared in 1960 and propelled him into international fame as one of Africa's most important writers. A sweeping realist historical novel with much resonance in Zola, Les Bouts de bois de Dieu offers a fictionalized heroic account of the railworkers' strike in which Sembene had taken part. He would return to Africa soon after its publication, but upon his return in 1961 it struck him how little impact the European-language literature he was writing could have on the broad African populace, only rarely literate in European languages. From that point forward he moved strongly into film. Following a year of study at the Gorky studios in Moscow, Sembene released his first two films – L'Empire Sonhrai and Borom Sarret [The cart driver] – in 1964, inaugurating a period of productivity in both literature and film that has continued for three decades. By 1997, Sembene had produced some ten novels or novella collections and eleven films, the most important of which include the novel Le Mandat (1965; The Money Order, 1972), which was made into the film Mandabi (1968); another novel, Xala (1974; trans. 1976), made into a film with the same name (1975); and the film Camp de Thiaroye (1989).

Sembene's writing and work in film show both range and focus. He shifts easily from epics of nineteenth-century Islamic intrigue (the film Ceddo, 1976) to brutal exposés of French colonial history (Camp de Thiaroye; the 1976 film Emitaï) to tragic or savage depictions of post-colonial life (Xala; the 1981 novel Le Dernier de l'empire; The Last of Empire, 1983). Despite this great thematic range his work never wavers in its commitment to justice and social critique. Most often ordinary men (and notably, throughout his work, women) are depicted as dignified or heroic,

while the neo-African bourgeoisie, the former French colonial administration, and religious hypocrites of all types are relentlessly attacked. Stylistically, Sembene prefers, in the main, straightforward narration and is not a literary experimentalist. His films are, importantly, shot most often in the Wolof or Diola languages, with subtitles in French.

Sembene's works have received much critical attention and are frequently taught in both English and French. Among his novels, God's Bits of Wood stands above the rest in the eyes of most critics, being widely regarded as one of the great rallying resistance novels of Africa's late colonial era. Here and in his other novels, he is seen very much as a narrator of the people, an inheritor of the griots, or traditional story-tellers, he strives explicitly to honour.

Perhaps along with Kenya's ★Ngugi wa Thiong'o, Sembene has become at once one of the most honoured and the most consistently, unwaveringly radical of Africa's major literary producers. His commitment to social justice, to resistance against both colonialism and neo-colonialism, and to African popular audiences has made him one of the most important figures in African culture of the latter half of the twentieth century. That he has produced novels and films with such commitment at the same time as he has maintained the highest artistic standards will ensure him an honoured place in African literature and culture for many generations to come.

SENGHOR, L(éopold) S(édar) (1906-), Senegalese poet, politician, and polemicist first of ★negritude and later la francophonie. Born in the coastal town of Joal, Senegal, he came from a relatively wealthy family, mercantile Christians belonging to the Serer tribe. He was educated at mission schools and later at the Sorbonne. He passed the agrégation in 1935 and taught until 1939, when he was called up. He was imprisoned by the Germans in 1940 but released two years later because of ill health. He entered Senegalese politics at the end of the war and in 1947 founded the Bloc démocratique sénégalais. In 1960 he was elected first president of Senegal, a position he held until 1980. He was the most powerful politician in francophone West Africa and has also been enormously influential within francophone associations worldwide.

Senghor is best known in literary terms for his early promotion of and theoretical reflection on negritude with the West Indian writer Aimé Césaire and other black students and émigrés whom he met in Paris as a young man. His poetry, as a manifestation of negritude as a poetics, was among the earliest francophone African poetry to be read and highly appreciated in France. His Anthologie de la nouvelle poésie nègre et malgache (1948) was one of the very early works to introduce black writing in French from the colonies to a wide audience. The collection was also highly influential because it was introduced by Jean-Paul Sartre's powerful essay 'Orphée noir'. Difficult and elliptically argued, the essay introduced a range of ideas that formed the foundations of diverse literary critical approaches to Senghor's own writings and the work of other francophone African writers. A member of the Académie française and a great francophile, Senghor has lived his life between two worlds, the French and the West African. This dualism and the possibility of finding synthesis at different levels – political, philosophical, linguistic – permeates all his writings, particularly and most obviously the several volumes of his essays, *Liberté*. These ideas are most directly manifest in his notion of *la civilisation de l'universel*. Within his poetry this dualism is a powerful source, occasionally of synthesis, but more often one that conveys the complexities and conflicts of his experience. The differences between the vision that emerges from his poetry and that of his more polemical essays is often greatly underestimated by commentators in an attempt to find a spurious coherence. It is in the dissonances, the ruptures, and the tensions of his *oeuvre* that Senghor emerges at his most subtle, powerful, and important as a writer.

The dominant tone of Senghor's first collection, *Chants d'ombre*, which he wrote before the war but which was published in 1945, is nostalgic. The Africa from which he was individually exiled is also the Africa from which all Africans have been exiled by the vicissitudes of colonialism. His more private, elegiac, and often lyrical voice, though it also speaks for his people, gives way to an angry, public poetry in *Hosties noires* (1948), in which the focus is no longer on a lost Africa but on the denunciation of much associated with the West. The experience of Senegalese soldiers, the *tirailleurs sénégalais*, is important in the later collection. *Nocturnes* (1961; *Nocturnes: Love Poems*, 1969) combines the personal and the public. Technically and formally Senghor's poetry invites comparison with the French poet Paul Claudel, particularly because of the former's use of the *verset*, but also with the West Indian poet Saint-John Perse. But relationships with poetry in French should not obscure others: his knowledge of Wolof, Serer, Bambara, and Peuhl, and stories and poems of the *oral traditions of these languages, for example. These origins are most important in *Éthiopiques* (1956). His later collections, *Lettres d'hivernage* (1973) and *Élégies majeures* (1979), are grander and more intellectual except where they touch on love, sexuality, and eroticism, where a richness and immediacy animate a more formulaic poetics. Many of the later poems are tributes to famous friends and are reminiscent of Charles Baudelaire's poetic voice.

It is Senghor's prose writings that have aroused the greatest hostility. Among his most vociferous critics are Marcien Towa (*Essai sur la promblématique philosophique dans l'Afrique actuelle*, 1971 and L.S. Senghor:

Négritude ou servitude? 1971), Stanilas Adotevi (*Négritude et négrologues*, 1972), and René Depestre (*Bonjour et adieu ... la négritude*, 1980). It is Senghor the theorist, polemicist, and politician of negritude who is attacked in these works, not the poet. Other commentators have sought to evaluate Senghor's negritude within a broader historical context (P. Hountondji, *Sur la philosophie africaine*, 1977) and argue that negritude was a necessary, if limited, counter-ideology at a moment when colonial structures needed to be challenged both intellectually and politically.

SEPAMLA, Sipho (Sydney) (1932-), South African poet and novelist, was born in West Rand Consolidated Mines Township outside Krugersdorp and trained as a teacher at Pretoria Normal College. He has published six collections of poetry, ending with *Selected Works* (1984) and *From Gorée to Soweto* (1988), and several novels, including *The Root Is One* (1979), *A Ride on the Whirlwind* (1981) and *Rainbow Journey* (1996). In 1976 he was co-recipient (with Lionel *Abrahams) of the Pringle Award and in 1985 received the Order of Arts and Literature from France. His achievement is not limited to his work as a writer; he has been an active encourager of art and culture for blacks in South Africa.

Sepamla's creative energies were awoken by the philosophy of *Black Consciousness. He published *Hurry Up to It!* (1975), a poetry collection, at about the same time as similar collections by Mongane *Serote and Mafika *Gwala. What sets his poetry apart is its often ironic and satirical register. His poems frequently include a combination of English, Afrikaans, and African languages to form a patois or *tsotsi-taal* (township slang). As a novelist, he has explored what it means to be black in South Africa in an iconoclastic fashion, increasingly articulating his regret at the loss of community and respect for elders that has occurred since 1976.

In 1978 Sepamla was instrumental in establishing the Federated Union of Black Artists (FUBA) Arts Centre, now known as the Fuba Academy of Arts. He briefly revived and edited the *literary magazine *The Classic* under the title *New Classic*, and was editor of the theatre magazine *S'ketsh'*. More recently he has served on the Arts and Culture Task Group, a think tank that advises government on artistic and cultural issues.

SEREMBA, George (1957-), playwright, was born in Kampala, Uganda and educated in Buganda Province and at Makerere University. Abducted and left for dead by soldiers loyal to Milton Obote, whose bloody bid for Uganda's presidency was being resisted by a body of students, Seremba miraculously survived his execution and escaped to Kenya. Since 1984 he has lived in Canada. His play *Come Good Rain* (1993), first produced in Toronto in 1992, re-enacts his virtual execution and survival, framing the story with that of Nsimb'egwire, the girl of Bugandan folktale who is buried alive by her jealous stepmother. Critical response to *Come Good Rain* has been generally positive. Seremba is also co-editor of *Beyond the Pale* (1996), an anthology of dramatic writing.

SEROTE, Mongane Wally (1944-), South African poet, was born in Sophiatown but brought up in Alexandra, a black township on the north side of Johannesburg. When he left school he worked as a journalist and became an active participant in the cultural and political struggle against *apartheid. In 1969 he was detained without trial for nine months. Four years later he won the Ingrid Jonker Prize for his first volume of poetry. In 1974 he went to the USA, where he gained a master's degree in creative writing at Columbia University. He then returned to southern Africa and became one of the leading members of the exile community in Botswana. By this time his work was well known and admired in progressive literary circles within South Africa; in 1983 he won the Ad. Donker Prize. In 1986 he moved to London, where he worked for the ANC's department of arts and culture; in this capacity he travelled fairly widely. He returned to South Africa in 1990, shortly after the unbanning of the liberation movements. In the first democratic election, in April 1994, he became an ANC member of parliament; he chairs the parliamentary committee on arts, culture, science, and technology.

Serote was one of a group of black poets who began to write and publish in the late 1960s and early 1970s, when apartheid was being applied fiercely, almost all opposition to it appeared to have crumbled, and most of the previous generation of black writers had been forced to leave the country. Serote was perhaps the most striking writer of this group: in many of his poems he succeeded in turning an acute sociopolitical awareness and an active commitment to the cause of justice and liberation into imaginative metaphors permeated by a wholly personal, passionate lyricism. He created a new tone, a new music in South African poetry: part anger, part grief and despair, part yearning, part quiet determination. While the apartheid regime lasted, Serote's poems were an inspiration to many South Africans, whites as well as blacks: they evoked and defined both the outrage and the way in which it might be confronted. In the post-apartheid period these poems have yielded new fruit: besides their continuing relevance to human and social possibilities, they give a sense of the mixture of strength and magnanimity that made a relatively peaceful political transition possible.

Serote's poems are not all of the same kind, however; their content evolved partly in response to the changing sociopolitical situation, and the verse forms changed too. His first two volumes, *Yakhal'inkomo* (1972) and *Tsetlo* (1974), consisted mainly of short lyrics. But *No Baby Must Weep* (1975) is a single poem of nearly sixty pages; it is a metaphoric personal and political autobiography, a quest poem, of almost epic proportions. The speaker seeks freedom from mental and social imprisonment and yearns for personal fulfilment within an experience of true community. This theme is elaborated in the long title poem of *Behold Mama, Flowers* (1978). His next two collections, *The Night Keeps Winking* (1982) and, another long poem, *A Tough Tale* (1987), were written during the period in which pressure on the South African regime was being intensified: while retaining the emotional richness of the earlier poetry, they have at times a more directly militant tone.

In 1981 Serote published a novel, *To Every Birth Its Blood*. Written over a period of six years, it seems to have changed in direction as it developed, and thus provides, self-consciously, a vivid insight not only into life in a revolutionary society but into the very processes through which personal and political commitments develop. He has also produced a *Selected Poems* (1982) and a book of essays, *On the Horizon* (1990). He is one of the few poets of his generation to have continued writing after the great watershed year 1990. He has produced three more long poems: *Third World Express* (1992), for which he won a Noma Award, *Come and Hope with Me* (1994), and *Freedom Lament and Song* (1997). In these poems he confronts, in his characteristically probing and impassioned way, some of the promises and dangers of a social order that is in a state of vigorous transition.

SERUMA, Eneriko (pseud. of Henry S. Kimbugwe) (1944-), Ugandan novelist and short-story writer. Born in Uganda and educated in the USA, Seruma was very active in the East African literary world in the late 1960s and the 1970s. He was a public relations officer for the East African Publishing House and wrote short stories and poems for *Ghala, Busara, Zuka,* and *Transition* *literary magazines. He is an award winner of the East African Literature Bureau's and Deutsche Welle's creative writing competitions.

Although the title of *The *Experience* (1970) refers to 'the impossible life of a black man in a white world' in America, the novel also depicts the unsatisfying condition that results from a plunge into a new mode of existence only superficially imagined. The short stories in *The Heart Seller* (1971) are an accurate observer's portrayal of human characters and situations in Africa and America.

SERUMAGA, Robert (1939-80), Ugandan playwright and novelist, attended Makerere University, Uganda and Trinity College, Dublin, where he received a master's degree in economics. He was involved in drama at the BBC before returning to Uganda in 1966 to set up his own semi-professional theatre company, Theatre Limited. His novel *Return to the Shadows* (1969) deals with political and social upheaval in an African state. The main character, an economist, returns home to Africa determined to play his part in the new nation but is caught in a military coup. However, Serumaga's reputation as a writer rests mainly on his plays, which include *The Elephants* (1971), *A Play* (1968), and *Majangwa* (1974). Most of his work shows his preoccupation with social and political change, whether at the national level, as in *Return to the Shadows*, or at the interpersonal level, as in *The Elephants*. Some of his plays incorporate music and dance, most notably *Renga Moi* (1972), which experiments with traditional African material. Serumaga was arrested in 1979 for allegedly attempting to overthrow the government of Idi Amin; he was later minister of commerce in Okello's government.

Shaihu Umar (1967), a novel by Abubakar Tafawa Balewa, translated from the ★Hausa (*Shaihu Umar*, 1934). Written by the first prime minister of Nigeria (1957-66), the novel is devoid of the conventional fantasy of its contemporaries and unambiguously set in a historical period of turmoil. By situating the hero's saintly character within the moral mainstream of the exemplar of traditional Islamic social values, Abubakar makes concrete *mutumin Kirki*, the Hausa concept of the good man. The novel's marked didacticism suggests that the author aimed to incorporate in a prose narrative the themes that characterize nineteenth-century Hausa poetry. It remains, and not only because of who its author was, a favourite Hausa novel. A stage version appeared in English (1975) and in Hausa (1974), which was subsequently filmed.

SHAKA IN AFRICAN LITERATURE Shaka, the legendary ★Zulu king (1787-1828), has been an important subject of African literature since the first praise poems in his honour were performed during his lifetime. Praise poems to Shaka, part of the great oral tradition of Zulu *izibongo* (praise poetry), are thought to mark a transition in the form from personal to national, which in turn reflected a transition in leadership from tribal to national.

Oral tradition influenced historical writing on Shaka, which started shortly after his death and continued until after the turn of the century, the borderline between fact and fiction in constant haze. The king's appearance in written literature most probably originates from historical accounts such as Nathaniel Isaacs' *Travels and Adventures in Eastern Africa* (1836), John C. Brown's 1852 English translation of T. Arbousset and F. Daumas's *Relation d'un voyage d'exploration au nord-est de la Colonie du Cap de Bonne Espérance* (1842), Holden's

The Past and Future of the Kaffir [*sic*] *Races* (1866), Gibson's *The Story of the Zulu* (1903), and Bryant's introduction to his *A Zulu-English Dictionary* (1905). Some of these authors also had access to manuscript versions of what was eventually (but too late) published under the title *The Diary of Henry Francis Fynn* (1951). Fynn, a medical doctor who was close to the king, recorded his personal experiences in the king's company. His testimonies refute claims about the king's habits and purported conduct in several respects.

In *Leselinyana la Lesotho*, the newspaper of the Paris Evangelical Mission Society, the Lesotho historian Sekese published two articles under the title 'Buka ea taba tsa Zult' [Book on the history of the Zulu] (15/2 and 1/3/1894). These articles must have had considerable influence on the ★Sotho author Thomas ★Mofolo, whose novel ★*Chaka* was ready by 1909, although its publication was delayed by the missionary authorities, who may have over-reacted to the role of the supernatural in the story. When the work eventually appeared in 1925 (with J.S. King's drawing of Shaka, which had appeared in Isaacs' book and later in Gibson's), it divided its readers into two camps, as it had the Morija missionaries before publication. During a period of just over two years, between 1926 and 1928, eight significant letters from readers appeared in the missionary journal. The letters make a fascinating study of the work's early reception: admiration, rejection, puzzlement.

Mofolo's work appeared in Sesotho and became the fountainhead for novel writing in the language. Through translation it also became the fountainhead for what has become a tradition of written texts on Shaka throughout Africa. *Chaka* was translated into English (1931 and 1981), French (1940), German (1952 and 1988), Italian (1959), and ★Afrikaans (1974). Francophone African authors L.S. ★Senghor (1955), Seydou Badian (*La Mort de Chaka*, 1961), Abdou Anta Ka (*Quatre pièces*, 1972), Nénékhaly-Camara (*Continent-Afrique* and *Amazoulou*, 1970), and Djibril Tamsir Niane (*Chaka*, 1971) drew their inspiration and documentation from Mofolo's work for some of ★negritude's finest dramatic writing and bolstered their ideals of Africanness. The Shaka figure looms large, together with the ★Yoruba deity of fire and warfare, in Wole ★Soyinka's *Ogun Abibiman* (1976), an epic poem dedicated to the fallen of Soweto.

Most of southern Africa's languages and genres include some text on Shaka. As the king's tongue, Zulu itself is strongly represented. The first Zulu novel, by John L. Dube, is *Insela kaShaka* (1930; *Jeqe, the Bodyservant of King Shaka*, 1951). R.R.R. ★Dhlomo's novel *UShaka* (1937) was translated into German. The king features in the Zulu poetry of B. W. ★Vilakazi (1935 and 1945) and Elliot Zondi's tragedy *Ukafu KukaShaka* [The death of Shaka] (1960). Mbuyiseni ★Mtshali's 'The Birth of Shaka' (*Sounds of a*

Cowhide Drum, 1971) addresses the birth and death of the king, and Mazisi ★Kunene's *Emperor Shaka the Great* (1977) is a long, broadly worked out epic, the Zulu original of which is still to appear. John Ross's historical *Tshaka* (1934) was written in ★Xhosa. E.A. Ritter's *Shaka Zulu* (1955) is probably the best originally researched romance on the king in English. Stephen ★Gray's vision of the king, *The Assassination of Shaka* (1974), is a large scale dramatic monologue with a narrative structure derived from tribal and Old Testament traditions.

As in West Africa, and almost simultaneously, a collection of dramatic works on Shaka developed in southern African languages. Baloyi's *Xaka* (1960) is in ★Tsonga, while Lesoro's *Tau ya ha Zulu* (1967) is in Sesotho and clearly inspired by Mofolo's work. Fourie's Afrikaans *Tsjaka* (1976) and Matlala's Northern Sotho *Tshaka* (1976) appeared in the same eventful year as the Soweto freedom uprising. In 1986 a ten-hour epic, *Shaka Zulu*, was aired on South African television. It was a spectacular contemporary tribute to the king.

SHONA LITERATURE   A southern African Bantu language related to the Nguni and ★Sotho clusters to the south, Shona is spoken by some 9,000,000 citizens of the Republic of Zimbabwe (1992 estimated population 10,400,000) in addition to small communities in Mozambique, Zambia, and Botswana. There are six dialects: Zezuru (centre), Manyika (northeast), Ndau (southeast), Karanga (south), Kalanga (west), and Korekore (north). The name 'Shona', used in the early nineteenth century by Sotho and Nguni neighbours to identify speakers of one of the dialects, subsequently adopted by Europeans for the whole Shona group. It was accepted by the people themselves only during the present century. Within Zimbabwe, the only two other significant language groups, both relative newcomers, are ★Ndebele and English.

The Shona language has existed as a distinct entity for more than a thousand years. By the beginning of the tenth century, state-like structures based on agricultural communities had been established, and soon thereafter, the gold trade was initiated with Muslim cities to the east. By the late eleventh century, the future Great Zimbabwe site had been occupied, and construction of the famous stone wall complex begun by the late thirteenth century. After reaching the zenith of its power during the following century, the Great Zimbabwe state was in decline by 1500. Contact with Portuguese traders and missionaries was established soon after. A brief revival of Shona power in the seventeenth century was followed by renewed decline. In 1890, Rhodes's British South Africa Company established bases in the area, which soon fell under colonial rule. Despite armed uprisings in 1896-97 (the first 'Chimurenga'), British authority prevailed

in the area until the Unilateral Declaration of Independence in 1965, when the local white minority replaced the colonial master. A long war of liberation followed, which led to the creation of the modern state in 1980.

Oral literature in Shona is both extensive and generically varied. Praise poems, histories, myths, legends, folktales, proverbs, riddles, and a great variety of songs for both adults and children make up the corpus. Since written literature in Shona is a recent phenomenon, links with oral tradition are still strong, influencing writing in English as well. These links are all the more significant in that the celebration of the heroic Shona past became part of the ideological basis for the long national liberation struggle.

As was the case elsewhere, English-speaking Protestant missionaries in the region played a vital role in the establishment of written Shona. A.M. Hartmann published a Shona grammar in Cape Town in 1893, followed by a dictionary and phrase book the following year. Translations of the gospels appeared in 1898, 1901, and 1903, and a complete New Testament was produced in 1907. School readers and religious texts in various dialects were published over the next two decades. Missionary authorities were aware of the need for a unified orthography and a standard written form for this cluster of dialects, and consequently, in 1927, the Native Commissioners Conference endorsed the creation of a unified language, which eventually became the basis for standard literary Shona. In order to supply books in African languages to the increasingly literate population (with the condition that they should be free of controversial political content), the Southern Rhodesia African Literature Bureau was created in 1953 to work closely with the Ministry of Education. As a result, the first original work in Shona, a short historical novel by S. M. Mutswairo (1924-) entitled *Feso*, was published in 1956. Formally innovative, the novel deals with an episode of the pre-colonial past. It appears translated in Mutswairo's *Zimbabwe: Prose and Poetry* (1974). Further, the first edition of M. Hannan's *Standard Shona Dictionary* appeared in 1959.

The first important work of modern Shona poetry appeared soon after *Feso*. *Soko Risina Musoro* ('Tale without a Head') by H. W. Chitepo (1923-75) was published (together with an English translation) in 1958. This 'symbolic-epic' poem tells of a time of drought (an allegory for the political situation) and of the resulting confusion of a thoughtful African symbolically named the Wanderer. Subsequently, the works of authors such as Mutswairo, W. B. Chivaura (1927-68), H. Pote (1939-), M. B. ★Zimunya (1949-), G. Mandishona, O. Munyaradzi, and R. Zhuwarara were published in poetry journals and anthologies of modern texts, often with English translation. In the area of traditional poetry, A. Hodza's studies are particularly worthy of note. During the war years, immediate political reality was reflected in the so-called 'Chimurenga songs', composed by both known authors and anonymous poets, and celebrating the national past while exhorting to heroic resistance.

Although Shona authors writing in their own language have shunned the short story, the novel has been practised by a large number of writers. Kahari perceives an evolution in the novel from traditionalism (with subjects drawn from oral history, legend, and the folk tale) to a latter-day modernist realism, a thematic evolution which is reflected in changing styles.

The formal and thematic conservatism of early novels is illustrated in the work of a number of writers born before 1939. B. T. G. Chidzero's (1927-) novel *Nzvenqamutsvairo* [Dodge the broom] (1957) favours a Christian synthesis of traditional and modern cultures. P. Chakaipa (1932-) evokes the whole range of Shona experience from rural tradition to urban modernism in a series of novels published between 1958 and 1968. The same breadth of vision characterizes the works of P. Chidyausiku (1927-); of special note is *Nvadzi dzinokunda rufu* [Death before dishonour] (1962), a forceful tableau of urban degradation. Other early authors include J. Marangwanda (*ca.* 1922-), S. Marimazhira, L. W. Chapavadza (1926-1964), K. S. Bepswa (1927-), E. F. Ribeiro (1935-), and G. Kuimba (1936-).

Members of the post-war generation of Shona novelists have largely chosen to write in English, although their work retains strong cultural, linguistic, and formal links with Shona culture. Members of this category include Chenjerai ★Hove (1956-), Dambudzo ★Marechera (1952-87), Shimmer ★Chinodya (1957-), and Tsitsi ★Dangarembga (1959-). A brilliant exception to the rule is Charles ★Mungoshi (1947-), who has in fact distinguished himself in both languages. He has written three novels in Shona in which problems of cultural adaptation are explored: *Makunun'unu maodzamwoyo* [Heartbreak] (1970), *Ndiko kupindana kwamazuva* [How time passes] (1975), and *Kunvarara hakusi kutaura?* [Is silence not a form of speech?] (1983). Other Shona novelists include women writers J. Chifamba, who transcribed folk tales, and J. Simango (1948-), who has proposed a Christian reaction to certain traditional practices.

In 1962, Chidyausiku inaugurated Shona theatre by publishing *Ndakambokuyambira* ['I warned you before'], a comedy on the theme of acculturation. Mungoshi has also written for the theatre; his *Inongova niakeniake* [Each does his own thing] (1980), pessimistically portrays the materialistic society to come. While didactic theatre in Shona was produced in the guerilla camps during the liberation war, most reflective theatre since 1980 has been written in English, because of the perceived need for unfettered intercultural communication in the modern state.

SHORT STORY

East Africa: The continuity between short story and traditional tales is apparent in the many English versions of folk narratives, among them Martha Mvungi's *Three Solid Stones* (1975) from Tanzania, ★Taban lo Liyong's *Eating Chiefs* (1970) from Uganda, and R.N. Gecau's *Kikiyu Folk Tales* (1966) and Njumbu Njururi's *Agikuyu Folk Tales* (1966) from Kenya. Some short pieces in modern settings use to great effect the features of such tales. Grace ★Ogot excels at rendering feelings of unrest and anguish in contemporary life, in a hospital background for instance, while suggesting a world where transgression or curse can lead to supernatural retribution in the stories in *Land without Thunder* (1968) and *The Other Woman* (1976). Eneriko ★Seruma also plays on anxiety in *The Heart Seller* (1971). In the more serene *The Island of Tears* (1980), Ogot's distinctive voice effortlessly blends traditional rhetoric and contemporary characters or situations, as in the title story. In a similar vein, the novelist Rebeka ★Njau mixes social comment and the atmosphere of the tale in *The Hypocrite* (1977).

In ★Ngugi wa Thiong'o's *Secret Lives* (1975), early stories such as 'The Fig Tree', 'The Black Bird', and 'Meeting in the Dark' rely similarly on a mysterious atmosphere and a sense of guilt and retribution, just as in traditional texts. He successfully renders the oppressive mood with fantastic undertones that the next novels do not explore. Other stories show the writer trying his hand at social satire with a verve that anticipates the later novels.

Potent Ash (1968) by the brothers Leonard ★Kibera and Samuel ★Kahiga deals, like *Secret Lives*, with the troubled Kikuyu communities at the time of the emergency and just after independence. The tone is more detached, sarcastic even, with the control of an ironical distance and anti-climactic endings. Muthoni ★Likimani in *Passport Number F.47927* (1985) provides fifteen fictional accounts of characters caught in the cycle of violence and repression. Its blend of fact and fiction is didactic and angry, with an effective brand of realism that resembles militant South African writing.

In a more relaxed mood, Barbara ★Kimenye's ★*Kalasanda* (1965) and *Kalasanda Revisited* (1966) present the comedy of village life, with its eccentrics, its moments of greed and romance under the watchful eyes of all. The presentation of ordinary humanity has qualities of tolerance and wisdom and a peaceful mood rare in Ugandan fiction. M.G. ★Vassanji's *Uhuru Street* (1992) also uses short stories to delineate characters in a small community – a street of Asian traders in Dar es Salaam before and after Uhuru (independence). The amused tone of the early stories takes on a new meaning in the second half of the collection, when the writer's retrospective glance from Canada suggests nostalgia for an African–Asian world forever lost and grief at an uprooting that might have been avoided.

The work of Taban lo Liyong defies classification. The richly inventive writer is at ease with experimental short texts that can be poems, transcribed folk tales, essays, or 'meditations', and the short texts in *Fixions and Other Stories* (1969) and *The Uniformed Man* (1971) merge with the other genres. Some are sarcastic political comments, others fables or monologues, still others open-ended philosophical parables with a cosmopolitan range of references. The result is uneven but stimulating, and the two books offer some of the most arresting prose in the region.

South Africa: South African literature has consistently excelled in the genre of short fiction: such prominent writers in English as H.C. *Bosman, Nadine *Gordimer, Es'kia *Mphahlele, and many others have used the short-story form extensively. Two of the earliest collections of South African tales are R. Hodges's *The Settler in South Africa and Other Tales* (1860) and A.W. Drayson's *Tales at the Outspan; or, Adventures in the Wild Regions of Southern Africa* (1862). Olive *Schreiner was the earliest female short-story writer of note with her *Dreams* (1891). In the late nineteenth century short-story collections proliferated, many of them demonstrating in their titles their affinity with an oral milieu, like Percy *Fitzpatrick's *The Outspan: Tales of South Africa* (1897). Among this early group of writers, W. C. *Scully and Fitzpatrick are the only two whose stories have been reissued.

Stories by Perceval *Gibbon, Pauline *Smith, R.R.R. *Dhlomo, and Herman Charles Bosman characterize the genre during the first half of the twentieth century. Gibbon's well-crafted collection *The Vrouw Grobelaar's Leading Cases* (1905) demonstrates greater technical skill and complexity of social vision than those of his predecessors. In some ways it anticipates Smith's *The *Little Karoo* (1925), probably the earliest South African collection of stories to achieve lasting international recognition. Each of the ten stories included in *The Little Karoo* (two were added to the original eight of the first edition) exemplifies Smith's remarkable ability to capture the stark, elemental quality of her rural Dutch characters and the oppressiveness of their lives. Stories by Dhlomo, whose work of the late 1920s and 1930s may be taken to represent the emergence of black South African short fiction, show traces of a residual orality, although these are masked by a heavy reliance on western literary models. Dhlomo's numerous stories and journalistic sketches of life on the mines in the 1920s and 30s appeared in the black newspapers of the time but have never been collected into volume form. William *Plomer's stories appeared in *I Speak of Africa* (1927) and *The Child of Queen Victoria and Other Stories* (1933). The title story of the second volume is one of his best known and, as its title suggests, concerns the dilemma of a traditional Englishman whose attraction to a young African woman in rural Natal threatens to disrupt his conceptual and moral universe. A selected edition of Plomer's stories appeared in 1984.

Herman Charles Bosman is probably South Africa's most popular short story writer, and his stories have appeared in numerous collections over the years, including a *Collected Works* (1981), edited by Bosman's pupil and literary executor Lionel *Abrahams, and a *Selected Stories* edited by Stephen *Gray. *Mafeking Road* (1947), however, is by far Bosman's best-known collection and was the only one to appear in his own lifetime. Bosman's storyteller figure, the wily backveld raconteur Oom Schalk Lourens, features in all but three of the stories in *Mafeking Road*. In Schalk Lourens, Bosman was to make use of his very distinctive brand of irony to undermine white assumptions of superiority, a technique that has not always been properly interpreted by all readers of the Schalk Lourens stories. Between 1930 and 1951 dozens of stories appeared in this sequence, most of which have been taken up in posthumous collections of his work. The later 'Voorkamer' stories, which feature a number of narrators in the format of a conversation forum, also testify to Bosman's skill as a storyteller.

The trajectory of the South African short story from the 1860s to the 1950s parallels the demographic shifts in South Africa from countryside to city occasioned by the mineral discoveries of the late nineteenth century and subsequent industrialization and urbanization. Stories with a predominantly rural setting and a close relationship to oral lore, legend, and smalltown gossip give way in the 1950s and after to stories urbanized, increasingly fragmented in nature, and predominantly social realist in mode. With apartheid, a clear divide between white and black perceptions of this new landscape became apparent. Among white story writers in the post-war period, the best-known are Alan *Paton, Nadine Gordimer, Dan *Jacobson, and Jack *Cope. Some of the biting social realism and pathos of Paton's novels is contained in the short stories in *Debbie Go Home* (1961). As is the case with her novels, Gordimer's stories from *Face to Face* (1949) onwards trace, in penetrating and often painful detail, the effects of South African politics and society on the individual. Dan Jacobson is a prolific story writer whose stories have appeared in several collections over the years, beginning with *A Long Way from London* (1958). Jack Cope's reputation was established in the 1960s with *The Tame Ox* (1960) and *The Man Who Doubted* (1967).

Meanwhile the pioneering work of R.R.R. Dhlomo had been followed in 1946 by the publication of Es'kia *Mphahlele's first collection of stories, *Man Must Live and Other Stories*, which heralded an era of unprecedented literary activity among black writers of the 1950s and 60s, mostly centred around the *literary magazine *Drum*. The short story, often taking the form of a magazine column or anecdote, was the dominant genre, and *Drum* published the bulk of them, including stories by Nat *Nakasa, Can *Themba, and Casey *Motsisi. Posthumous collections of stories and sketches by these writers have appeared under the titles *The World of Nat Nakasa* (1975), *The World of Can Themba* (1985), and *Casey and Co.: Selected Writings of Casey 'Kid' Motsisi* (1978). Mphahlele was the most prolific writer of the period; his classic 'Mrs. Plum', which appeared in his *In Corner B* (1967), explores the lives of black servants in relation to their privileged mistresses. His *The Unbroken Song: Selected Writings* appeared in 1981.

The magazine *Staffrider*, which first appeared in the late 1970s, was *Drum*'s more radical successor. Like *Drum* it spawned a wealth of talented black writers, many of them writers of short stories. Mtutuzeli Matshoba, Mbulelo *Mzamane, Mothobi *Mutloatse and Njabulo *Ndebele are among the writers whose work first appeared in *Staffrider* and whose collections of stories were later put out by the publishers of the magazine, Ravan Press. Matshoba's *Call Me Not a Man* (1979), Mzamane's *Mzala* (1980), and Mutloatse's *Mama Ndiyalila* (1982) share a concern with presenting the life of black people in a starkly realistic mode, and often incorporate elements of African oral culture in an attempt to shrug off western literary influence. Ndebele's *Fools and Other Stories* (1983) has enjoyed more sustained success than the collections of some of his contemporaries. His stories combine minute observation of township life, seen through the eyes of a young and sensitive protagonist.

Writing from exile after emerging as a writer at the end of the *Drum* period, Bessie *Head engages effectively with the issues that emerge in Botswanan village life: tribal history, the arrival of the missionaries, religious conflict, witchcraft, rising illegitimacy and, throughout, problems that the women in the society encounter. Her book *The *Collector of Treasures* (1977) employs many techniques and devices germane to the oral milieu of the village. Other story writers of the 1970s and 80s include *Staffrider* regulars Ahmed *Essop and Peter *Wilhelm, and Sheila *Roberts. Essop's *The Hajji and Other Stories* (1978) – comic, ironic, and often deeply moving – set a high standard for literary representations, surprisingly sparse to date, of South Africa's large Indian minority. Cape Town's cosmopolitan District Six, demolished in the 1960s, is the setting for a number of short stories, among them some by Alex *La Guma, Achmat *Dangor, James *Matthews and Richard *Rive. The richness of La Guma's work in exile, banned for so long in South Africa, is still 'coming home'. Rive's best work was done early, while Dangor's may be yet to come. Both he and Matthews are equally well-known as poets.

The contemporary South African short story manifests a fascinating diversity of techniques. The social realism so prominent in the 1970s and 80s has given way to metafictional experimentation in a variety of forms. Predictably, this development involves a further movement away from forms of story writing that draw on oral culture, the milieu in which the South African short story was spawned. The voices heard in Ivan *Vladislavić's *Missing Persons* (1989), for example, are those of alienated city-dwellers, cut off not only from forms of community embedded in the oral tale, but even from the communality of neighbours across the fence.

West Africa: The short story is the most popular form of literature in the region, patronized by amateurs and masters, young and old. Short stories are published everywhere all over the region: in secondary school and university student magazines and broadsides; in local, regional, and national newspapers, magazines, radio, and television; and in intra-continental and international literary and academic journals, anthologies, and single-author collections. A great many, if not most, of the short stories that are published never find their way into any systematized and permanent storage in book form or on library shelves. Perhaps as a result of this plenitude, literary critics have practically neglected the study of the genre. There are no bibliographies, and except for introductions to anthologies, a few scattered essays, and one pioneer critical study by F. Odun *Balogun entitled *Tradition and Modernity in the African Short Story: An Introduction to a Literature in Search of Critics* (1991), there are no helpful materials on which a scholar may rely to provide authoritative critical judgement on the West African practice of the genre.

The enormous popularity of the short story in West Africa has at least three related explanations. First, because of its brevity of form and the closeness of its language to the language of daily communication, the short story is not perceived by writers to be as intimidating as the allusive language of poetry or the complexity and time involved in producing a novel. This is the reason for its patronage by most novice writers. Second, with so many avenues for the publication of short stories throughout West Africa, almost any story, regardless of its level of accomplishment, is potentially publishable. Third, and most important, the form of the European short story in many respects resembles that of the indigenous African folktale, which remains very popular as an artistic form for community entertainment and social commentary. Except that the former is usually contemporary in thematic preoccupation and realistic in method, while the latter for diplomatic reasons prefers a remote temporal and thematic setting and a method that emphasizes the fabulous, they are alike in stressing brevity of form and narration, or the telling of what happens next. These similarities provide sufficient confidence for the West

African writer to try his or her hand at creating the imported genre, even though it has never been as entertaining as the highly performance-oriented local genre. In any case, the short story provides an avenue, if not for entertainment, then for quick, surreptitious participation in the national sociopolitical discourse, just as the folktale partook of the community discourse in the past.

West African short stories reflect the mixed character of the region's European and African origins. While most stories tend towards the European realistic form even as they are spiced with the fabulous plot and performance elements of the African folktale, the others dispense entirely with realism, preferring to imitate the parabolic or phantasmagoric and symbolic forms of traditional folk narratives. A third minority group take their cue from the rhythmic structure and the song and musical insertions of folktales, or from European poetry, to become, with varying degrees of success, prose poems. However, while specific stories may neatly fit into these separate categories, certain writers, especially the most accomplished, traverse the boundaries in their creative practice to broaden their aesthetic appeal. Furthermore, other perspectives with which to analyse West African short stories also exist, though these too lack iron-clad boundaries. There is, for instance, the class-audience dichotomy that separates stories predominantly addressed to the middle-class elites from those directed towards the working class. There is also the age classification of stories into those written either by first-generation or by younger writers.

Of the stories realistically written, the most successful are usually those spiced with humour and irony. 'The Truly Married Woman' by Abioseh *Nicol and Davie Owoyele's 'The Will of Allah' are typical examples by writers of the older generation. Among stories belonging to this class written by younger writers, 'The House Girl' by Oke Chigbo is a good example. This latter story, like the stories of *Sembene Ousmane and Kole *Omotoso, has the additional quality of drawing the reader's attention to the callous exploitation of the poor by the African elite, except that while Chigbo is humorous, Omotoso tends to be tragic in tone. Cyprian *Ekwensi also focuses attention on the plight of working people in his stories, though this plight is as much the result of exploitation by the elite as of the hidden dangers behind the lure of the modern cities to which youth become easy prey. Ama Ata *Aidoo, who excels in realistically reproducing the language of female characters to the extent of utilizing gossip as a narrative technique, shows in her stories that while the lure of the city may be powerful and often fatal, it is not always tragic. A village girl, turned prostitute in the city, may still regain virtue with a little help from loved ones. Aidoo's focus is mostly on the exploitation of

women caused either by obsolete African traditions or the harsh conditions of colonialism and modernization, which take men away from their mothers and wives. Chinua *Achebe's stories are at their best when he is ironically poetic, as in 'The Madman', or tragically humorous and dramatically performative, as in 'Civil Peace'. Tijan M. *Sallah's stories are often indistinguishable from poetry, being consciously wrought prose poems. Private and continental history is the subject of R. S. *Easmon's and F. Odun Balogun's stories. Younger writers such as Ben *Okri, Ba'bila Mutia, and Kojo *Laing explore with irony the mysterious, not in the realistic manner of I.N.C. *Aniebo, but in the fabulously marvellous mode of Amos *Tutuola.

SIBENKE, Ben (1945-), Zimbabwean playwright, was born in the midlands near Gweru in what was then Rhodesia and educated at Cyrene Mission School and Mutare Teacher Training College. Known also as a director and actor, he founded the Mashonaland Art, Drama, and Cultural Association in 1978 and the People's Theatre Company in 1982, and is deeply involved in the activities of the National Theatre Organization as a resource person on acting, writing, and directing. His first publication, *My Uncle Grey Bhonzo* (1982), originally written in *Shona in 1974, won a National Theatre Award for promising comedies, while the playwright himself won the Bell Award for both acting and directing the same play. Other plays have been produced on stage, on radio, and on Zimbabwe television, including *Dr. Manzuma and the Vipers* and a number of plays in Shona. Sibenke's comic vision is informed by traditional African values increasingly threatened by Western ones. Beneath the comedy, however, is a serious attempt to ascertain what, ultimately, the human character amounts to in life.

Simbi and the Satyr of the Dark Jungle (1955) A novel by Amos *Tutuola. Disconsolate over the kidnapping of her friends, young and beautiful Simbi leaves the home of her wealthy mother to seek poverty and punishment. With the aid of an Ifa priest she succeeds in getting herself kidnapped and is thus launched on her adventure. Among other perils, she is set adrift in a coffin, enslaved, nearly beheaded, loses the two children she bears her woodcutter husband, and repeatedly fights a satyr. Victorious at last she rescues her kidnapped friends and returns home to warn others to avoid adventures like hers.

Sirens Knuckles Boots (1963) Poems by Dennis *Brutus. The title indicates the general tone of Brutus' first collection. It suggests the fear of the South African black or, as with Brutus, 'coloured' (mixed race) person who lives in persistent fear of the police.

Images of pain and fear are modulated, occasionally, by moments of tenderness and by the recognition that there is in human beings, whatever the stress they are under, a capacity to survive 'somehow'. At the same time a nostalgic tone suggests the poet who writes and publishes in exile.

SITHOLE, Ndabaningi [See BIOGRAPHY AND AUTOBIOGRAPHY; CENSORSHIP]

Sixth Day, The (1960) A novel by Andrée *Chedid, translated from the French (*Le Sixième jour*, 1960). The novel tells the story of the struggle of a Cairo washerwoman who seeks to hide her grandson during a cholera epidemic in Egypt. Those stricken by the disease must by law be sent to hospitals, but the hospitals are so overcrowded that the patients who die are carted out to mass graves and buried without traditional rites. Om Hassam, terrified that the sick child will be taken from her, plans to tend and shelter him for the legendary six days while the fever mounts to a crisis and the patient either dies or survives. Om Hassam's progress from her village, to an apartment roof, through the streets of Cairo, to a felucca on the Nile gives a panoramic view of street life in a city stricken by plague. Her strength epitomizes the tragedy, but her devotion and faith ultimately evoke compassion in all those around her.

Sizwe Bansi Is Dead (1972) A play by Athol *Fugard. During one of the most repressive and censorious years of *apartheid, the play opened in Cape Town and then went on something like a fugitive tour, using private or lecture rooms without any theatre equipment of any kind. During a performance at the University of the Witwatersrand in Johannesburg, the police arrived and arrested students who were demonstrating outside the venue and then entered the theatre and disrupted performance and audience. Why the play should have been regarded as dangerously subversive is a question that has never been adequately addressed. The action opens with a long monologue by a one-time factory worker, Styles, who has opened his own small photographic studio. He speaks of how his photographs can provide those who have them taken with altered and more glamorous images of themselves. In a sense, Styles is a purveyor of dreams. His self-congratulatory speech is interrupted by a customer who says his name is Robert Zwelinzima asking for a new photograph for his passbook. What emerges through flashback and dialogue is that the customer, whose real name is Sizwe Banzi, has taken the passbook and assumed the identity of a man whom he and his friend Buntu found dead one night. Buntu also tries to explain to the illiterate Sizwe the complex ramifications of the need for a passbook and pass number in order to work and find lodgings; the matter of

permits and licences; and influx control. But what taking Zwelinzima's identity amounts to is the threat of the loss of Sizwe Banzi's own.

SLATER, Francis Carey (1876-1958), South African poet and anthologist. His first volume of poems, *Footpaths thro' the Veld* (1905), and a collection of stories, *The Sunburnt South* (1908), revealed little originality, and further collections showed little advance on the colonial verse characteristic of the period; however, *The Karroo and Other Poems* (1924) revealed a more individual voice and a less Eurocentric perspective, and in 1925 he published the first major anthology of South African poetry, *The Centenary Book of South African Verse*, an authoritative collection that drew attention to a body of poetry comparable with that produced in other Commonwealth countries.

Slater's successful long poem *Drought: A South African Parable* (1929) depicts not only physical desolation but the 'drought of the spirit' produced by hatred. A second collection of stories, *The Secret Veld* (1930), was followed by his best volume of verse, *Dark Folk and Other Poems* (1935), in which his evocations of African life are lyrical and vivid. An epic poem on the Dutch voortrekkers, *The Trek* (1938), contains some excellent vignettes of Boer leaders. In 1945 he published a revised, updated anthology, the *New Centenary Book of South African Verse*, and in 1949 his last volume of poems, *Veld Patriarch and Other Poems*. A selection of his poetry was published by Oxford University Press in 1947, and in 1954 he produced an autobiography, *Settler's Heritage*. He devoted his last years to a definitive edition, *The Collected Poems of Francis Carey Slater* (1957).

SMITH, Pauline (Janet) (1882-1959), South African short-story writer and novelist. Born in Oudtshoorn in the Little Karoo region of the Cape, Pauline Smith enjoyed a happy childhood, and the beauty of the Karoo landscape and the simple kindness of the Dutch-Afrikaans farmers made a deep impression on her. To console herself after the sudden death of her father, she began writing the sketches, stories, and poems based on her childhood memories that were later to be published as *Platkops Children* (1935). After settling with her mother and sister in Britain she began contributing stories and sketches of Scottish life to the *Evening Gazette* and *Aberdeen Free Press* under the name Janet Tamsen (1902-5) and started on a novel. During her first return visit to South Africa with her mother in 1905, she kept a diary recording the places they revisited, as well as local stories, customs, and idiom of the Little Karoo and its people.

After a chance meeting in 1909 the novelist Arnold Bennett, impressed by her 'Platkops' sketches, became her mentor, and for the next twenty-two years he encouraged and sometimes bullied her into drawing more deeply on her experience of and insight into the lives of the people of the Little Karoo. The success of *The ★Little Karoo* (1925) (it went into a fourth impression in the first year) encouraged her to complete a novel she had been working on, *The ★Beadle* (1926).

During the next five years Smith wrote several more stories, two of them included in a new edition of *The Little Karoo* published in 1930, paid return visits to South Africa, and signed a contract for a new novel, the never-to-be-completed 'Winter Sacrifice'. After Bennett's death in 1931 she set about writing a memoir, *A.B. … 'A Minor Marginal Note'* (1933), which not only pays tribute to Bennett but offers a surprisingly objective and often wryly amusing account of their friendship. His death, however, robbed her of a prime motivating force. She made little progress with her novel, and her last major publication was *Platkops Children*. Yet her work won increasing recognition, and in the year before her death William ★Plomer and Roy Macnab presented her with an illuminated scroll signed by twenty-five South African writers as a tribute to her art and the essential humanity of her vision. Although she produced only two major works, *The Beadle* and *The Little Karoo*, they have both remained in print as classics of South African prose.

So Long a Letter (1981) A novel by Mariama ★Bâ, translated from the French (*Une si longue lettre*, 1979). The novel, narrated in the first person by the recently widowed Ramatoulaye, is an account of married life addressed to her childhood friend Aissatou. Both women have suffered from neglect within polygamous marriages, Aissatou opting for divorce while Ramatoulaye remains emotionally bound to her husband until his death. The first person narration allows Bâ to render an extremely poignant insider account of the emotional anguish suffered by these women and, more broadly, of Ramatoulaye's appreciation of her role in her community. Bâ details the structuring principles of Senegalese Islamic society and of women's insertion in them, for example polygamy and inheritance law. She also demonstrates how women – young brides and mothers-in-law – are led to collaborate in the oppression of women in this society in the interests of their own material security. Despite its considerable insight, however, and its power to move, *So Long a Letter* has been criticized for its near idealization of the politics of Senegal's post-colonial elite and its highly restricted range of characterization.

SOFOLA, Zulu (1935-95), playwright, was born to Igbo/Edo parents in Delta State, Nigeria. She began primary school in Nigeria and completed high school and university in the USA. Her first degree in English was from the Virginia Union Baptist Seminary in Nashville, Tennessee; she later moved on to the Catholic University of America in Washington, DC,

where she studied drama. She returned to Nigeria to teach at the University of Ilorin. She appeared several times on television and radio in Nigeria as a critic and theatre practitioner with a deep commitment to Nigerian culture and values, and she published criticism and opinion on African society and drama in journals in Africa, Europe, and America.

Sofola's plays are widely read and discussed in Nigeria, and a few often make the list of texts for the West African Examinations Council. All her plays are accessible, and their thematic preoccupations and social criticisms engage contemporary Nigerian reality comprehensively. Although her plays suggest she was a cultural nationalist, they view the past not in idyllic terms but as a source of material for revamping the fabric of a colonially bruised present. Boldly experimental with fluid settings, their style is lucid, their diction often takes account of the relationship between language and class in Nigeria's culturally diverse society, and their dramaturgic resources are drawn from the traditional African roots of myth and ritual. Like most modern Nigerian playwrights she drew for some of her work on classical Western drama. Of the dozen or more published (and unpublished) plays, the following have received the most attention: *The Disturbed Peace of Christmas* (1971), *Wedlock of the Gods* (1972), *The Sweet Trap* (1977), *The Deer and the Hunter's Pearl* (1969), *King Emene* (1974), *The Wizard of Law* (1975), and *Old Wines Are Tasty* (1981).

Sofola was not a dramatist of the big theme or historical event or character. Her practice stayed with cultural conflict, human quirks, and social failings. Even in issues of gender, which animate many female African writers and critics, she is restrained and prefers to see such issues as part of a complex of temporary, transitional problems to be dealt with in Africa's contact with the West. Some critics find her work too derivative, especially when such plays as *King Emene* are compared with generic Western tragedies, which place a high premium on the calibrated development of character and action and the tidy resolution of tragic conflicts, but the kinder generality of criticism leaves her in the comfortable vanguard area of the development of Nigerian drama.

Son of Woman (1971) A novel by Charles ★Mangua. The son of woman is Dodge Kiunyu the son of a Nairobi prostitute who has made his way to Makerere, graduated successfully and entered the civil service. Bored, he embarks on a series of tax evasion schemes and lands up in gaol. On release, he marries his childhood girlfriend, also a criminal, and they set off for Mombasa, determined to reform and live happily and honestly.

Song of Lawino (1966) Long poem by ★Okot p'Bitek. Lawino laments the failings of her husband Ocol when he deserts her for a younger woman. The conflict between husband and wife poignantly and humorously seems to symbolize the conflict of African and western cultures, and the poem goes well beyond the plaints of a woman scorned when Lawino directs her sorrow and aggravation at new education, religious fashions (Christianity), and social behaviours dominating contemporary life in Uganda. Ocol, with his western education and lack of respect for tradition, comes in for especially scathing treatment as Lawino praises traditional Acoli ways that he has abandoned. As a representative of the African ruling class, Ocol is the subject of p'Bitek's biting satire, which exposes the greed and cultural poverty of these new leaders.

Sons and Daughters (1964) A play by Joe *de Graft. *Sons and Daughters* grew out of de Graft's work at Mfantsipim School, Cape Coast, where he established a vigorous tradition of productions involving both staff and pupils. It is a modest, conventional, well-structured play marked out by easy, flowing dialogue, sharp characterization, and neatly contrived dramatic moments. At the centre of the play, ready for a rather too easy resolution, are concerns with careers and a determination to challenge the prevailing conviction among Cape Coasters that only law, engineering, and medicine afford worthwhile prospects. De Graft's humane response was to draw attention to opportunities to work in the arts. In form and depth the play is of minor interest, but it has an important place in the evolution of a significant playwright and throws light on attitudes among the middle classes as Ghana became independent. Like de Graft, Prime Minister Kwame Nkrumah recognized the importance of artistic creativity in nation building and personal development.

SONY LABOU TANSI (1947-95), Congolese novelist and playwright, was born in Zaïre (now Democratic Republic of Congo), where he spent part of his childhood. Returning to the Congo, he studied at Brazzaville's École normale supérieure and taught English and French for some years before taking up employment with the Ministry of Culture. Made famous by the successes of the Rocado Zulu Théâtre, a theatre company he formed in 1979, he achieved critical and popular acclaim with numerous plays and novels influential particularly for their vivacious, fearless language. His plays include *Conscience de tracteur* (1979), *La Parenthèse de sang* (1981; *Parentheses of Blood*, 1986), *Je soussigné cardiaque* (1981), *Antoine m'a vendu son destin* (1986), *Moi, veuve de l'empire* (1987), *Qui a mangé Madame d'Avoine Berghota?* (1989) and *Une chouette petite vie bien osée* (1992). Based on universal themes yet going to the heart of the Congolese ambience, many of his plays were popular in Africa as well as Europe, where he often toured. He is also well known

for his novels, which are challenging in their narrative style and content and always critical of the 'barbaric attitude of man against man'. They include *La Vie et demie* (1979), *L'État honteux* (1981), *L'Antépeuple* (1983; *The Antipeople*, 1988), *Les Sept solitudes de Lorsa Lopez* (1985; *The Seven Solitudes of Lorsa Lopez*, 1995), and *Les Yeux du volcan* (1988). His work has earned many literary awards.

SOTHO LITERATURE
Northern: Northern Sotho is a southern Bantu language of the Sotho cluster (along with Tswana, Lozi, and Southern Sotho) spoken by more than a million people in the northeastern Transvaal region of South Africa. Although Northern Sotho is frequently equated with Pedi, the latter term is more properly limited to a subgroup of the former, associated with the Maroteng paramountcy. Although oral tradition traces the history of the Northern Sotho peoples back into the seventeenth and early eighteenth centuries, events can be traced with assurance only in more recent times. Like the rest of southern Africa, the area was profoundly changed by the disturbances and migrations unleashed during the *difaqane* wars occasioned by Zulu expansion in the southeast. Afrikaans-speaking trekkers reached the area in 1845, while Lutheran missionaries of the Berlin Missionary Society established a station in 1861. Maroteng power was definitively crushed by the British in 1879.

As elsewhere in southern Africa, Protestant missionaries played a vital role in the development of written Northern Sotho, publishing a book of folktales in 1893 and a Bible in 1904 or 1905. The first book written by a native speaker of Northern Sotho was a biography of an early minister and hymn writer, A. Serote (1865-1930), published in 1935. The author was E. P. Ramaila (1897-1962), who also served as editor of *Mogwara wad babaso* [Friend of the black people], a missionary periodical.

Ramaila later published two books of short stories and a novel. Other early writers include M. M. Sehlodimela, author of a novel and a book of poetry, M. J. S. Madiba, and A. Phalane, who treated the ubiquitous theme of the degradations suffered by migrant labour. Although the first play in Northern Sotho was written by a German missionary in 1940, E.K.K. Matlala's play *Tshukudu* [Rhinoceros], a tragedy written in verse incorporating traditional poetry, appeared the following year.

After the Second World War, writing in Northern Sotho was ironically encouraged by the repressive Bantu Education Act of 1953. By determining that the 'Bantu child' should be educated in his or her mother tongue, rather than English or Afrikaans, this act in fact created a great need for books in all African languages, both school texts and more general reading material. The best known and most influential Northern

Sotho writer of this period is Oliver K. Matsepe (1932-74), author of nine novels and six volumes of poetry. In his novels, Matsepe looks to tradition as a source of enduring and effective values to which modern society may look for guidance. Often complex in structure, they present revolutionary narrative techniques. Titles include *Sebata-kgome* [Spotted cow] (1962), *Kgorong ya Mosate* [At the chief's court] (1962), *Le sita-phiri* [Big problem] (1963), *Mecokqo ya bioko* [Harvest of thought] (1969), and *Letsofalela* [An unending problem] (1972). Other authors include M. Rammala (1924-), S.P.P. Mminele (1937), M. Fela, and H.M.L. Lentsoane (1946-).

Southern: Southern Sotho is a transnational language spoken by about 4,000,000 first-language speakers in the Kingdom of Lesotho and in the Free State, Eastern Cape, and Gauteng provinces of South Africa. The birthplace of the written literature is Morija in Lesotho, where Eugène Casalis and Thomas Arbousset settled in 1833 as the first missionaries of the Paris Evangelical Mission Society (PEMS). The Basotho have had a living tradition of oral art since time immemorial, and the first recordings of praise poems, folktales, riddles, and proverbs by Casalis were published in his *Études sur la langue Séchuana* (1841), which was, in fact, an introduction to the grammar and literature of Southern Sotho and not really of Setswana as the title suggests. The second half of the work contains fifty pages giving examples of annotated texts. Among these are three praise poems and 'Kammpa and Litaolane', the first recorded version of a tale that would be handed down later under the title 'Moshanyana Senkatana' [The boy Senkatana] and that would acquire considerable significance in modern literature and the Sesotho world view.

Arbousset's *Relation d'un voyage d'exploration au nord-est de la Colonie du Cap de Bonne Espérance* (1842) contains less material than Casalis' work but is equally useful. One of the tales of which only the French version appears in the work is 'Tselane le Dimo' (a Sesotho version of 'Little Red Riding Hood'). Arbousset ventures a modest attempt at literary criticism in his comments on style, originality, and beauty throughout the text.

In 1863 the PEMS in Lesotho started the publication of the missionary journal *Leselinyana la Lesotho* [The little light of Lesotho]. This step would have as great an influence on the growth of the literature as on the spread of Christianity, sometimes even conflicting with the latter. While continuing the recording of oral traditional literature with A. Sekese's numerous historical accounts, praise poems, and folktales and E. Segoete's collection of riddles, the journal also served as a forum for the first generation of writers, who made their debut in the journal: Sekese, Thomas *Mofolo, Segoete, E. Motsamai, and Z. Mangoaela.

During the 1880s Sekese wrote his *Pitso ya Dinonyana* [Gathering of the birds], which was not published until 1928. Superficially it is a harmless folkloristic dialogue, but close reading soon reveals its metaphorical implications and satirical topicality to the prevailing circumstances in Lesotho. Reminiscent of the medieval epic *Van den Vos Reynaerde* and George Orwell's *Animal Farm*, the play was a worthy forerunner of playwriting in Southern Sotho and shows a political involvement comparable to committed literature of the twentieth century.

The first novel to appear in Southern Sotho was Thomas Mofolo's *Moeti wa Botjhabela* [Traveller to the east] (1907; serialized beginning January 1906). The theme of light contrasted to darkness and the victory over darkness reappears in Mofolo's *Pitseng* (1910; serialized beginning January 1909). Virtue also surfaces as the central idea in Segoete's *Monono ke mohodi, ke mouwane* [Riches are a mist, a vapour] (1910; serialized that year). The religious awareness of these first novels was clearly inspired by the missionary zeal of pioneers such as Casalis and his family (who worked in Lesotho for several generations), Arbousset, and others who worked for the PEMS.

Segoete also produced *Raphepheng: Bophelo ba Basotho ba kgale* [Raphepheng and the life of the Basotho of old] (1915), a narrative about an idealized traditional Mosotho, which included his collection of riddles, already serialized in 1911. Motsamai and Mangoaela each produced a volume of short stories based on the experiences of their time: the former's *Mehla ya madimo* [In the time of the cannibals] (1912), on the age of cannibalism during the wars of destruction (1821-33), and the latter's *Hara dibatana le dinyamatsane* (1912), on strange encounters between humans and animals.

Mofolo's third and best work, *Chaka, which was widely advertised but not serialized in *Leselinyana*, appeared in 1925, but more recent research reveals that the manuscript was probably completed by 1909. This work shows connections with various oral and modern literary genres such as folktale, fable, saga, allegory, and even fantasy. Its stylistic grandeur and poetic prose combine with its historical and fictional elements, the appraisal of African military expertise and heroism, and the tragic outcome of the battle between man and monster.

Output during the middle period of the written literature (roughly 1930-60) doubled that of the first period, partly because of the addition of authors and publishers from South Africa. However, the foundation of the literature was firmly laid in Lesotho, where the Morija Sesotho Book Depot (Protestant) and the Mazenod Book Centre (Catholic) remained leaders for the greater part of the period. It was also at Morija that the first modern play, T.M. Mofokeng's well-made and delightful *Sekhona sa jwala* [The beer mug] was first seen in 1939. In 1942 Mazenod published Nqheku's *Arola naheng ya Maburu* [Arola in the country of the Boers], an outspoken work on racial tension in the eastern Free State.

K.E. Ntsane and B.M. Khaketla produced the best modern poetry of the period with their volumes *Mmusapelo* [Heart restorers] (1946) and *Lipshamathe* [Lively talk] (1954) respectively. As a satirist, Ntsane did not scruple to attack any of the fallacies of his time: lost freedom, colonialism, racial tension, divided religious roots, hypocrisy, the erosion of values in the big cities, insensitivity towards fellow citizens, prejudice, and social evils of various kinds. Khaketla's poetry includes poems on the nature and effects of the First World War. In his two most successful plays, *Tholwana tsa sethepu* [The fruits of polygamy] (1954) and *Bulane* (1958), Khaketla works with familiar material: conflicting views on marriage linked to the right of succession in the traditional kingdom. His novel *Mosadi a nkgola* [The woman lands me in trouble] (1960) is based on the same conflict, but with wider consequences for modern society. Set in the heyday of British colonial rule in Lesotho, the novel explores the consequences when a young ruler, who has had a wide education and who values the freedom of choice, has to face the prejudice of conservative traditionalists.

S.M. Mofokeng made crucial contributions to the literature with a play, a collection of short stories, and another of essays. His *Senkatana* (1952) is a dramatic reworking of the legend-cum-myth with the same title. Providing an alternative to the violence that often accompanies the maintenance of government, the play considers justice, patience, love, and the non-vialibity of retribution. *Leetong* [On the way] (1954) contains a story based on the life of the biblical Ruth. Set in the eastern Free State and portraying the lasting bond between two women, black and white, the story gives a worthwhile view of ideal race relations in southern Africa. He also wrote *Pelong ya ka* [Out of my heart] (1962). His essays on the transience of life are thoughtful and moving: he died at the age of thirty-four.

The modern period (1960-) began with several historical novels by Samson Guma and Simon Majara, E. Lesoro's modern poetry, and Maile's didactic township plays. Guma's (1923-91) first novel, *Morena Mohlomi, mora Monyane* [Chief Mohlomi, son of Monyane] (1960), is an imaginative reconstruction of the life and work of the legendary prophet and healer Mohlomi, who is said to have blessed King Moshoeshoe I before his rise to the leadership of the Basotho nation. Guma's *Tshehlana tseo tsa Basia* [Those Basia girls with the light complexion] (1962) is a reconstruction of the life of Mmanthatisi (1781-1836), the legendary female regent chief of the Batlokwa.

Lesoro produced several collections of modern poetry, often inspired by the English Romantic poets

on whom he fondly draws for mottos in his collections. Although criticized for devoting much creative energy to a somewhat forced end-rhyme structure, he also took considerable inspiration from African traditional poetry.

Maile's plays, *Boiphethetso* [Revenge] (1960) and *Ba ntena ba nteka* [They annoy and try me] (1962), are set in seedy townships and revolve around the social problems that arise from extra-marital relationships. N.M. Khaketla, wife of B.M. Khaketla and an influential personality in intellectual circles in Lesotho, dominated the scene during the 1970s with her realism and perspective on the role of women. She produced no fewer than six plays in less than a decade, three of which appeared during International Women's Year.

Several writers made their appearance during the 1980s, among them I.M. Moephuli, R.J.R. Masiea, and K.P.D. Maphalla. *Peo ena e jetswe ke wena!* [This seed has been sown by you] (1982), Moephuli's only novel, is one of the best thriller fictions in the literature. The story takes Soweto as its background, and describes how Samina, a woman of doubtful morals, blackmails four of her men. Masiea's most important work is a verse drama entitled *Mmualle* (1984), which deals with the first marriage between a Sotho princess and a Hlubi civilian and its complications for traditional Sotho aristocracy. His novel *Meriti ya bosiu* [Shadows of the night] (1985) deals with the evil of the migrant labour system, its disruption of family life, and the prostitution this encourages, thus continuing a thematic line which can be traced back through P.R.S. Maphike's *Dikenkeng tsa Tshepo* [Tshepo's adventures] (1976), J.J. Moiloa's play *Jaa, o siele moswalle* [Eat, but leave some for your friend] (1966), S.P. Lekeba's novel *Gautaen tjhapile* [Johannesburg has destroyed me] (1961), S. Matlosa's novel *Molahlehi* [The lost one] (1946), and Albert Nqheku's *Arola naheng ya Maburu* (1942, see above).

Maphalla's poetry is often introspective. Apart from expressing his own feelings, he also voices those of his people and laments the miseries of contemporary circumstances. His poetry is formulaic and song-like, as exemplified in the refrains at the close of stanzas. These techniques are already apparent in *Mahohodi* [Drift sand] (1983), *Kgapa tsa ka* [My tears] (1984), *Fuba tsa ka* [My feelings] (1984), and *Dikano* [Vows] (1985) and blossom in the equally introspective *Sentebale* [Forget me not] (1986).

Thabonyane Mafata is a young novelist who teaches at the Bensonvale Institution in the Herschel district of northern Transkei, where Thomas Mofolo himself taught for some time. His contribution to the literature since the late 1980s is two novels, *Mosikong wa lerato* [Upheaval of love] (1988) and *Mehaladitwe ha e eketheha* [When the daisies wave to and fro] (1991).

In 1991 J.J. Moiloa published what is probably his most ambitious work. Following a writing career of three decades and the publication of well over a dozen essays, plays, novels, poetry, and miscellaneous writings, *Thesele* (eulogy of King Moshoeshoe I of Lesotho) is an epic in the classical *dithoko* [praise poem] tradition. Moiloa follows history closely to celebrate the phases, feats, and fortunes of the life of the famous founder of the Basotho nation.

Two young writers from whom much is expected in years to come are Nhlanhla Maake, playwright and novelist, and Thapelo Selepe, essayist and poet. Both are from South Africa and they are looking at a new country, still in transition but free from the restrictions their predecessors had to cope with. They are applying their considerable academic backgrounds and general erudition to their already significant creative work. Things are looking up for kin and country.

SOWANDE, Bode (1948-), Nigerian playwright and novelist. Born to Egba parents, Sowande was educated at Government College, Ibadan, and the Universities of Ife, Nigeria and Sheffield, UK. A prolific author of novels, television and radio scripts, and newspaper articles as well as dramas, he has also kept alive a theatre company, Odu Themes. His work draws on elements in his Yoruba background but also reaches out in other directions; for example, he brings cultures together in a Yoruba version of Molière's *The Miser*, a drama about the mythological figure of Mammywater, and in *Ajantala-Pinocchio*, a study of two rebellious children, which opened in Italy in 1992. However, his reputation rests on two collections of plays, *Farewell to Babylon and Other Plays* (1979) and *Flamingo and Other Plays* (1986). Of the seven plays in the two collections, three – *The Night Before*, *Farewell to Babylon,* and *Flamingo* – comprise a trilogy that spans the period between Sowande's own undergraduate years and the late 1970s and scrutinizes the problems of living in Nigeria. Another, *Sanctus for Women*, written while he was a graduate student at Sheffield, represents a deliberate attempt to use Yoruba folklore and mythology as a source for drama. Although his writing is sometimes uneven, he has responded to the increasing politicization of his society by repeatedly examining the problems faced by those who attempt to uphold humane values and high principles in a hostile environment.

SOYINKA, Wole (1934-), Nigerian playwright, poet, novelist, and essayist. The first African to be awarded the Nobel Prize (1986), Soyinka is a prolific writer whose eclectic and syncretic work draws freely upon European models and is at the same time deeply rooted in ★Yoruba cultural practice, which itself derives from a thought system that is subtle and heterogeneous. Soyinka's reputation worldwide is sustained by the popularity of such works as the autobiographical ★*Aké: The Years of Childhood* (1981) and

by productions of such plays as ★*Death and the King's Horseman* (1975) and The ★*Lion and the Jewel* (1963). In Nigeria, he is both a household name and a protean figure of many professional and popular identities. His work has attracted sharp criticism, focused first on the charge that his use of language and form, in the novels and poetry especially, is needlessly complex, even obscurantist, and that this characteristic is symptomatic of an unhealthy Eurocentrism (the latter point is eccentric given the complexity and elusiveness found in Yoruba oral poetry). The second charge, that his writing is idealist and neglectful of Africa's harsh political realities, is often based on a selective reading of his work and a failure to acknowledge his demand that history be investigated at the level of (multiple) collective consciousness as well as through the dissection of specific social phenomena.

Born near Abeokuta, in southwestern Nigeria, Soyinka was educated at the universities of Ibadan and at Leeds in the UK. Several early plays, including *The Lion and the Jewel*, were written while he was still in Britain, where, between 1957 and 1959, he worked as playreader at the Royal Court Theatre, London. He returned to Nigeria in 1960, where he established two theatre groups in succession, the 1960 Masks and Orisun Theatre Company, and taught at the universities of Ibadan, Ife (now Obafemi Awolowo) and Lagos. With an increasingly turbulent political situation developing in the mid-1960s, Soyinka's work began to reflect the sociocultural complexity and political contradictions of his country: the anxieties expressed in his independence play A ★*Dance of the Forests* (1963) are further developed in The ★*Road* (1965) and ★*Kongi's Harvest* (1967), in the poems of ★*Idanre and Other Poems* (1967), and in a complex but also vividly documentary novel, The ★*Interpreters* (1965). He was imprisoned by Nigeria's military government for twenty-seven months between 1967 and 1969, during the ★Nigeria–Biafra war; the causes and traumas of the ★war are investigated in the novel ★*Season of Anomy* (1973), in the poems in A *Shuttle in the Crypt* (1971), and, perhaps the most painful and theatrically most audacious of all his plays, ★*Madmen and Specialists* (1971). This and his two subsequent full-length plays serve to demonstrate his versatility. *Death and the King's Horseman* is a reflective play based on an incident in Nigeria's colonial history but dealing with the individual and collective apprehension of death and with the structuring of cultural consciousness. Often highly successful in production (Chicago and Washington, 1979; Manchester, UK, 1990) and a work of spectacular beauty, this play has, however, served as a focal point for criticism of Soyinka's alleged idealism and view of history. By contrast, *Opera Wonyosi* (1981) is a musical satire, based on Brecht's *The Threepenny Opera*, and a vehement attack on Africa's military dictators. In 1978 he founded the

University of Ife Guerrilla Theatre Unit and in 1983 produced the satirical record *Unlimited Liability Company*, both examples of his use of theatre and music for specific political goals. Through the 1980s his high profile in Nigeria was augmented by his much-publicized chairship of a Road Safety Corps and by virulent attacks on his work by critics such as ★Chinweizu. Retiring from full-time academic life in 1985 he continued to work in virtually all literary genres. An active opponent of military dictatorship, in November 1994 he left Nigeria clandestinely after the seizure of his passport by the authorities.

Much of Soyinka's early life is described in three autobiographical works. *Aké* explores his childhood, with particular emphasis on the child's apprehension of the community around him. ★*Ibadan: The Penkelemes Years 1946-65* (1994) carries the story forward to events immediately preceding the civil war. In the preface he explicitly identifies his fears for the Nigerian state in the 1990s as a stimulus for writing the book. *The Man Died* (1972) is a highly polemical account of his war internment that retains a powerful impact. His essays on literature are also frequently disputatious, quarrels with other critics being extended to extraordinary lengths. The collection *Art, Dialogue and Outrage* (1988) provides alarming examples of such quarrels but is also packed with fresh insight. A formidably reflective work is ★*Myth, Literature and the African World* (1976), a theorizing of African aesthetics and, in particular, an investigation of performance in African theatre in relation to central aspects of Yoruba thought. Here he focuses especially on the god Ogun, whose perilous embodiment of contradiction provides a key reference point in his apprehension of creative energy, and on the Yoruba concept of liminality, of transition points in the life-death continuum, as a powerful touchstone for the African theatre practitioner.

Soyinka's novels have been relatively neglected. Both *The Interpreters* and *Season of Anomy* suffer from being thematically grounded in symbolic structures that are overloaded and, at worst, inchoate. Yet the first, paradoxically, also gives a startlingly concrete picture of life in southwestern Nigeria in the early 1960s. *Isarà: A Voyage Around 'Essay'* (1983), has been variously classified as novel and ★biography. Much more accessible than the first two novels, it is an affectionate account of the circle of friends that gathered around Soyinka's father from the 1920s to the 1940s.

Between 1967 and 1989 Soyinka published four volumes of poetry (his best-known poem, the wryly satirical 'Telephone Conversation', remains uncollected). The earlier poetry ranges in language and form from the jewel-like precision and clarity of 'Three Millet Stalks' (in *A Shuttle in the Crypt*) to the extreme complexity of the title poem of *Idanre and Other Poems*, in which he explores Yoruba myth, his

own absorption in it, and its bearing on Nigeria's contemporary sociopolitical realities. *Ogun Abibiman* (1976) is his longest single poem, a 500-line exploration of the nature and significance for contemporary Africa of two figures, the Yoruba god Ogun and the nineteenth-century ★Zulu emperor ★Shaka. The poem's ★political inspiration is stated in a prefatory note applauding Mozambican leader Samora Machel's declaration of hostilities towards white-ruled Rhodesia. The opening poems in *Mandela's Earth and Other Poems* (1988) address the condition of South Africa in what were to be the last years of ★apartheid; this wide-ranging collection also includes 'Cremation of a Wormy Caryatid', a dazzlingly beautiful meditation on the historical fortunes of Yoruba culture.

By the mid-1990s Soyinka had published seventeen individual plays as well as a collection of revue sketches, *Before the Blackout* (1971); later satirical sketches, collectively titled 'Priority Projects', remain unpublished. The most widely performed of the plays are those that are basically naturalistic in idiom: the comedies *The ★Trials of Brother Jero* and *The Lion and the Jewel* (both 1963). The first of these, like the later but less securely achieved *Requiem for a Futurologist* (1985), satirizes religious charlatanism; the second is a genially satirical treatment of the competition between a chief and an insecurely self-assured schoolteacher for the love of a village beauty. In other plays he has returned again and again to dissect the brutal tyrannies of dictatorship: as well as *Kongi's Harvest* and *Opera Wonyosi*, this group includes *A Play of Giants* (1984) and *From Zia, with Love* (1992). Some critics have found the satire in the later plays strained and shallow. These are terms that can hardly be applied to those plays that either examine or find new applications for Yoruba ritual. *The Bacchae of Euripides* (1973) has been neglected since a reputedly misconceived London premiere (National Theatre, 1973) but is a challenging, if ideologically uneven, rereading of the significance of Pentheus's catastrophe. *A Dance of the Forests* has remained virtually unstaged since its 1960 Lagos première but has a richly intriguing and resonant dramatic scenario, couched in gripping verbal imagery. *The ★Strong Breed* (1963) is a key text in understanding Soyinka's romantic projection of the isolated visionary hero. Most remarkable of all is *The Road*, premiered to enthusiastic recognition in London in 1965. In this play the willpower of a charlatan/visionary 'Professor' is pitched against the religious sensibilities of *egungun* (Yoruba masquerade) performers. Set in a period in which southwestern Nigeria was experiencing appalling political violence, the play explores how, locked between the Professor and the *egungun*, a group of touts and motor mechanics confront, or fail to confront, the oppression in their lives and their random deaths. In this play Soyinka achieves an extraordinary intensity.

Sozaboy: A Novel in Rotten English (1985) A novel by Ken *Saro-Wiwa. Sozaboy is a 'soldier-boy' volunteer for the Biafran army. His picaresque quest for his wife and mother, killed by a Federal bomb, takes him back to his native Kukana, where he is mistaken for a ghost and the harbinger of a cholera epidemic. The naive recruit speaks a lawless lingo Saro-Wiwa has wrought from scraps of his mother tongue, Kana, standard and 'broken' English, and Nigerian *Pidgin. This 'rotten English', the discordant voice of post-civil war Nigerian society, is thus far the most conscious linguistic experiment with non-standard speech in the West African first-person narrative.

Sport of Nature, A (1987) A novel by Nadine *Gordimer. Hillela, the renegade of a respectable white South African family, is linked through a transgressive sexuality with independence movements throughout black Africa. Gordimer often combines the sexual with the political; in this novel Hillela is not only disowned by her bourgeois family for radically inappropriate sexual behaviour, but she also goes on to marry a black South African liberationist in Ghana and later the president of the OAU, with whom she attends independence ceremonies in a free South Africa. The novel's mythical overtones and its narrative structure set it apart from many of Gordimer's other novels.

Staffrider Named for the commuters who ride illegally on the trains between the townships and the city centre, the magazine appeared for the first time in March 1978, nearly two years after the Soweto uprisings. The brainchild of Mike Kirkwood, manager of Ravan Press, and Mothobi *Mutloatse, a journalist, it was to speak directly to the experience of black township life after the repressive atmosphere of the 1960s. Featuring short stories, photographs, graphics, essays, popular history, and poems, it provided an outlet for young and inexperienced writers to publish their work alongside the more established writers of the time. *Staffrider* questioned and exerted pressure on the idea of 'good writing' and on the differences among genres. The content of the magazine was informed by the ideology of *Black Consciousness, which also influenced a self-editing policy partly derived from the concept of self-reliance it promulgated. At the same time, the magazine's open and democratic stance demonstrated a wider commitment to goals such as storytelling, worker autobiography, revisionist and popular history, documentary photography, popular education, and writing for children: it was a stalking horse for these and other features of Ravan's book publishing programme.

Staffrider tried to restore a tradition of resistance literature in South Africa by attempting to recover and re-insert the writings of earlier generations. Contributors came from the spectrum of South African society; regulars included such writers as Miriam *Tlali, Chris *van Wyk, Kelwyn Sole, Mongane Wally *Serote, Jaki Seroke, Jayapranga Reddy, Essop Patel, Andries Oliphant, Mike *Nicol, Njabulo *Ndebele, Mothobi *Mutloatse, Mtutuzeli Matshoba, Matsemela Cain *Manaka, Gcina *Mhlophe, Joel Matlou, *Mafika Pascal *Gwala, Ahmed *Essop, and Boitumelo, to name a few. The magazine also featured work by artists and illustrators such as Fikile, Mzwakhe Nhlabatsi, Thami Mnyele, Gerard Sekoto, Paul Stopforth, William Kentridge, and Bongiwe Dhlomo, and photographers such as Ralph Ndawo and Paul Weinberg. The first editorial declared that the magazine would try to address the surge of creativity and act as a forum to shape future writing. The self-editing policy was later terminated and Chris van Wyk, a black poet, was appointed editor. With the wane of Black Consciousness and the popularity of non-racial politics the magazine established links with other formations, such as the Congress of South African Writers (COSAW), which now publishes it, the Congress of South African Trade Unions, and the African Writers Association.

States of Emergency (1988) A novel by André *Brink. Reflecting Brink's enjoyment of experimentation, the novel uses metafictional devices to examine the intersections between the private and the political and the possibility of writing a love story in a political 'state of emergency' in which the state controls all representations. The project is complicated by the deliberate inclusion in the text of actual incidents, people, events, and parallels between Brink's own life and work and the textual references within the novel. The narrator, for example, is a writer and academic struggling with a novel entitled 'The Lives of Adamastor' (Brink's own *The First Life of Adamastor* was published in English in 1993) who has an affair with a young graduate student. (The novel has not been published in South Africa after being cited as part of Brink's divorce settlement). Whereas the writer in the novel decides against publishing his book, which does not appear to him an adequate response to the violent and overwhelming demands of his time, Brink's book is both written and published, providing a thought-provoking commentary on the links between 'word' and 'world'.

Stone Country, The (1967) A novel by Alex *La Guma. Much of the environment and the action of the stone country – the prison – is based on La Guma's personal experience of imprisonment for political activism. The prison is a microcosm of racist South African society, the hierarchies within the jail mirroring those of the *apartheid police state. Those with unquestioned power are the guards; below them are the cell bosses, who collude with the guards to victimize and terrorize weaker inmates. Around the cell bosses gather the toadies and henchmen who help make the lives of the ordinary inmates even more fearful and miserable. Below the guards and equal in power to the cell bosses are the 'coloured' (mixed race) guards. Sadly, even as the prisoners are brutalized and humiliated by the guards and the cell bosses, they expend their energy in personal hatreds and animosities instead of making common cause against the cruel power structure. Through all the violence and degradation, one prisoner, Adams, retains his humanity, sharing his food, listening to the miserable stories of the others, and wishing that they could all unite to fight the system.

Story of an African Farm, The (1883) A novel by Olive *Schreiner. Often cited as the book that initiated South African fiction written in English, Olive Schreiner's best known novel recounts the lives of three children growing up on a farm in the Karoo region of South Africa in the 1860s. The loosely structured narrative is interspersed with biblically inspired mystical allegories and lengthy polemical passages. Long criticized as diffuse and fragmentary, the novel has been recognized more recently for its innovations in narrative form. Most of the debate surrounding it, however, has been generated by its ideas. Its early audience celebrated the novel's agnosticism and resonance with contemporary politics and philosophy, while successive generations of readers have been drawn more to its feminist and colonial concerns.

Strong Breed, The (1963) A play by Wole *Soyinka. Eman, a school teacher, challenges the assumptions of the community he has travelled to work among, and sets those assumptions against the traditions of his home town. He is, it transpires, a man with a mission, whose death at the hands of atavistic villagers offers a faint possibility of change. When the play was published many hoped that it would be the first of a succession of plays in which Soyinka would explore general issues through precisely localized dramas. No such series has appeared and much of Soyinka's recent work has been aimed at very specific targets. *The Strong Breed*, with its economy, reverberations, and clarity, remains a very substantial but rather isolated achievement.

SUTHERLAND, Efua T(heodora) (1924–96), Ghanaian playwright. Born Efua Theodora Morgue at Cape Coast in the Central Region of Ghana, Sutherland received her early education at St. Monica's School and Training College and taught for five-and-a-half years before proceeding to Homerton College, Cambridge University, where she obtained her BA in education. She spent another year at the School of Oriental and African Studies, London, where she studied linguistics, African languages, and drama. She returned to Ghana, then the Gold Coast, where she

taught at her old school, St. Monica's, at Fijai Secondary School, Secondi, and later at Achimota School. In 1954, she married an African-American, William Sutherland, with whom she had three children. She was the organizing energy behind the establishment of the Ghana Society of Writers in 1957, the Ghana Experimental Theatre Company a year later, and *Okyeame*, a *literary magazine, in 1959. With funds from the Rockefeller Foundation and the Arts Council of Ghana, she founded the Ghana Drama Studio in 1960. The studio became part of the University of Ghana, where it was housed in the Institute of African Studies. She held a long-term research position in the Institute.

Sutherland's keen interest in the welfare of children translated into numerous schemes, including Children's Drama Development of Ghana. As a direct outcome of her efforts for children in Ghana, the government established the Ghana National Commission on Children, with Sutherland as its first chair.

In addition to essays, articles, short stories, and poems, she has published extensively in the genre of drama. Her best known plays include *Foriwa* (1967), *Edufa* (1967), a Ghanaian rendition of Euripides' *Alcestis*, and The *Marriage of Anansewa* (1975), a veiled satiric comment on the early post-independent leadership in Ghana under Kwame Nkrumah, and by extension Africa as a whole. Her other published work includes *You Swore an Oath* (1964), *Vulture! Vulture* (and *Tahinta*) (1968), *The Original Bob: The Story of Bob Johnson, Ghana's Ace Comedian* (1970), *Anansegoro: Story-telling Drama in Ghana* (1983), and *The Voice in the Forest* (1983). *The Roadmakers* (1961), a pictorial presentation of Ghanaian life with photographs by Willis Bell, is for children. She published another picture book for children, *Playtime in Africa*, the following year, also in conjunction with Willis Bell.

Although she studied widely in and outside of Africa, Sutherland's drama seeks an audience among children and adults in Ghana, both literate and non-literate. She was a visionary who created with her society in mind, sensing 'the goals...society is reaching for': that is, the vision of a better society. Trained in the folklore of the Akan people of Ghana, she acknowledged the oral roots of her art in her choice of drama as her medium of expression, operationalizing her understanding of cultural education as the best foundation on which to establish a better society. Her pioneering work in Ghanaian drama and theatre has undoubtedly been a major influence on other Ghanaian dramatists such as Ama Ata *Aidoo, Patience Henaku Addo, and Joe *de Graft.

SWAHILI LITERATURE Swahili is spoken by at least 40 million people in East Africa today, thus serving as the lingua franca of the region. Linguistically, it belongs to the Bantu family of languages which are spoken in the southern third of Africa, from Cameroon and Kenya to South Africa. Until the 1960s, Swahili was spoken as a mother-tongue on the east coast of Africa, from the southern part of Somalia to the northern areas of Msumbiji (Mozambique), including the islands of the Lamu archipelago off the coast of Kenya, Pemba, Zanzibar, Mafia, and Kilwa off the coast of Tanzania and the Comoro islands. The location of these places on the Indian Ocean basin encouraged trade with other peoples across the seas, most notably with the Arabs, who introduced *Islam in the region by at least the ninth century. With Islam came the desirability, if not the necessity, of having to read the Koran and hence the acquisition of the Arabic script by a significant segment of the population. The script, modified to express Swahili sounds, was used to produce works of literature, especially poetry.

The earliest phase of Swahili written literature - seventeenth century to the nineteenth century - is dominated by poetry whose themes are drawn from the formative period of Islam in Arabia of the seventh century. The life of Prophet Muhammad and that of his companions provided inspiration to Swahili poets who recreated for themselves the holy men's spiritual and even worldly experiences in the fashion and style accomplished by earlier Arab poets. In some cases, the latter's works were recast in Swahili in a poetic form that was both suitable to the theme and, perhaps more importantly, familiar to the literati of the East African coast. A significant example is the *Hamziyah* composed at Pate (in the Lamu archipelago) in 1652 by Idarus bin Othman; it is based on an Arabic poem of the same name composed in the thirteenth century by the famous Egyptian poet, al-Busiri (d.1296) in praise of the Prophet.

The Swahili *Hamziyah* is the oldest manuscript of a Swahili poem available today; yet its language and metre is developed to a degree which suggests the presence of a poetic tradition on the East African coast earlier than 1652. It prompts Jan Knappert in *Swahili Islamic Poetry* (1971) to remark that 'Swahili verse arrives in history ready-made and perfect'.

Although the *Hamziyah* has not been translated in its entirety, sections have been rendered into English in a way that enables an appreciation of its qualities. The following translation is given by Knappert in *Four Centuries of Swahili Verse* (1979: 105); the verses depict the vision of Muhammad by Khadija, a businesswoman in Makkah. The miraculous nature of the vision convinces her of Muhammad's position, and, indeed, of her own as someone chosen to share in that mission:

61. For this reason she proposed to him that he should marry her; it would be the most beautiful favour that came to the wise.

62. And the Angel Gabriel came to where Hadija lived, and the intelligent woman considered things, measuring them.

63. She removed her veil so that she might know whether that which came to her was a true revelation or a dream.

64. And she hid her head while the angel revealed [himself to her] lest he come back, and she covered herself [until he had gone].

65. Then it appeared to Hadija that this was the hidden treasure which she had wanted, the elixir, the blissful knowledge.

In the same vein as the *Hamziyah* are poems on the birth of the Prophet (the *maulidi*), on the celestial journey and his experiences in heaven (the *miiraji*), on his character and virtues, and on his companions and the relationship he had with them. Most of these have been extensively translated and their content explained by Knappert in many publications including his *Traditional Swahili Poetry* (1967).

Another poem which draws on this tradition, but whose content is expressed somewhat differently, is 'The Camel and the Gazelle' (*Utendi wa Ngamia na Paa*), translated in its entirety into English by J. W. T. Allen in *Tendi: Six Examples of a Swahili Classical Verse Form* (1971). It is an unusual poem in that the main characters – the camel and the gazelle – are made to interact with the Prophet and his companions in a way that brings out the compassion they feel for the animals because of the cruelty meted out to them by their owners.

A popular topic in religious literature is the ephemeral nature of life on earth, and, consequently, the necessity of ethical conduct towards God's creation, be it human, animal, vegetable or mineral. A classic poem on this topic in Swahili is *al-Inkishafi* by Sayyid Abdallah Nasir (d.1820). The poet laments the passing glory of the city of Pate (the birthplace of the *Hamziyah* mentioned above) which, by the nineteenth century, had fallen into decline, with its imperial palaces in ruins. The downfall of the city evokes in the poet reflections on the transitoriness of life, thus relating the impoverishment of the city to issues of morality.

Al-Inkishafi, literally meaning 'the uncovering', has been translated into English on three separate occasions by eminent scholars of Swahili. The first is by the Reverend W. E. Taylor in his introduction to Stigand's *A Grammar of Dialectic Change in the Kiswahili Language* (1915). It is a classicist translation by a scholar who considered the poem as 'a great, if not the greatest religious classic of the race'. The second is *al-Inkishafi: The Soul's Awakening* by William Hichens (1939; 1972). The third is by far the most culturally insightful: it is by James de Vere Allen (1977), not to be confused with John Allen, the translator of 'The camel and the gazelle' mentioned above. Allen's translation of *al-Inkishafi*, sub-titled *Catechism of a Soul*, is free-flowing as he transcends the verse structure of the original Swahili. It reads well, and the reader is helped to place it in context by an introduction provided by Swahili academic, Ali *Mazrui.

The content of *al-Inkishafi* is also noteworthy from another literary perspective. For, as Ohly points out in Andrzejewksi, *et al.*, *Literatures in African Languages* (1985) by the early nineteenth century Swahili poets were no longer drawing their topics from the Middle East but were 'using instead the social and historical realities of East Africa as a means of propagating the precepts of Islam'.

This is certainly true of another popular poem, *Utendi wa Mwana Kupona* translated into English by J.W.T. Allen (1971). It is advice by a mother – Mwana Kupona bt Msham (d.*c.*1860 in Pate) – to her daughter on wifely conduct and duties. The advice is, by today's standards, conservative and traditional as the wife is meant to devote herself entirely to her husband's comfort and well-being. A few verses will illustrate this point:

24. Please your husband all the days you live with him and on the day you receive your call, his approval will be clear.

25. If you die first, seek his blessing and go with it upon you, so you will find the way.

26. When you rise again the choice is your husband's; he will be asked his will and that will be done.

27. If he wishes you to go to Paradise, at once you will go; if he says to Hell, there must you be sent.

28. Live with him orderly, anger him not; if he rebuke you, do not argue; try to be silent.

29. Give him all your heart, do not refuse what he wants; listen to each other, for obstinacy is hurtful.

30. If he goes out, see him off; on his return welcome him and then make ready a place for him to rest.

Finally, three translations need to be mentioned in this section of poetry which reflect a change of content from the religious to the secular. The first is a volume by M.H. Abdulaziz (1979) of the poems of the celebrated Mombasa poet, Muyaka bin Haji (1776–1840), *Muyaka: Nineteenth-Century Swahili Popular Poetry*. In this work Abdulaziz discusses the life of Muyaka, the cultural and linguistic background to the poems, and categories of the poems themselves. Another is *A Choice of Flowers: An Anthology of Swahili Love Poetry*, edited and translated by Jan Knappert, whose stated purpose is to provide students of Swahili literature with 'a collection of modern lyrical verse in the "classical" tradition'. The volume presents a hundred poems, most of them with the contexts of their composition, dealing with various aspects of love: from the sweet ecstasy of furtive meetings to the pain of separation, recriminations and rejection. Two verses of the poem 'My heart' should suffice as an illustration:

I had made you my darling
and we loved one another with real love.
Then you did something stupid
thinking that love was unimportant.

You thought that I would not be able to
relinquish what there was between us,
and you were incited
by a worthless councillor [sic - counsellor];
you made love cheap,
the dear love we had.

The final example is from Tanzania's foremost poet, Shaaban Robert (d.1962). Robert was a prolific poet, novelist and essayist. He was also a nationalist: he had been a member of the African Association founded in 1926, and later, of its successor, Tanganyika African Nationalist Union (TANU) which won independence in 1961. The new nation honoured Robert after his death by having a street in the capital named after him; Robert would also have approved the adoption of his other passion, Swahili, as the national language of Tanganyika (and now of Tanzania). Not many of his poems have been translated into English - snippets occur in Harries, *Swahili Poetry* (1962) where one also finds his lecture on poetry - but Robert himself edited, and presumably translated into English, eleven of his poems in a slim volume entitled *Almasi za Afrika* ,'Diamonds of Africa' (1960). The collection opens with a poem in honour of Princess Margaret's visit to East Africa in October 1956. One verse reads:

I beg to welcome you, O younger sister of the Queen
We bid you welcome to Tanganyika;
Our people one and all come to greet you with joy -
Welcome, Your Royal Highness, Star of Freedom.

It is not paradoxical that Robert, a nationalist, should have dedicated a poem to the sister of the head of state of the colonial government. For, as the example below shows, Shaaban Robert had the capacity of transcending boundaries in his understanding of humanity. It was thus in character that he addressed himself to the important issue of his day, which, sadly, is still with us: the colour of a person's skin as the measure of his worth. Two verses from the poem are quoted below, though it has to be said that Robert's own translation does not do full justice to the original. All the same, it has been retained as it gives a flavour of his thoughts on the matter:

Colour is God's ornament, far from demerit,
All [people] are the same whether they eat millet- or wheat-bread,
Eaters of wheat and lentils, living and dead
Colour is God's ornament, far from a mark of demerit.

He [God] adorns the stars and the Heavens, roses and jasmines,
Colour is God's majesty, and on the [human] body it's not uncleanness
It is neither a mark of bitterness, nor sin nor blemish,
Colour is the beauty of the Perfect God Almighty.

It has been necessary to focus extensively on poetry so far as this is the genre which not only developed first in Swahili literature but also received most attention in

Western scholarship, and hence in its translation. The other two genres - prose and drama - are only scantily represented in other languages. It is surprising that, despite a steady output of Swahili novels since independence, particularly in the two decades from the late 1960s, not a single novel has yet been translated into English. Bertoncini has provided us with an excellent anthology of Swahili literature in his *Outline of Swahili Literature* (1989), with entry details in English and, recently, untranslated excerpts of prose works which reflect the status of women in Swahili literature, *Vamps and Victims: Women in Modern Swahili Literature* (1996). But these volumes, especially the latter, are for those who already know Swahili. English readers searching for translations of Swahili prose can only be referred to earlier travelogues and biographies. Most notable of these are Abakari's unique account of his travels to Russia and Siberia in 1896 in Harries' *Swahili Prose Texts* (1965), Mtoro Bakari's descriptions and observations on Swahili customs in *The Customs of the Swahili People* (ed. and trans. J.W.T. Allen, 1981), and Tippu Tib's biography recounting events which occurred on his caravan trips on the mainland of Tanganyika in the nineteenth century. *Marsha ya Hamed bin Muhammed el Murjebi yaani Tippu Tib* (1866, trans. 1958 W. H. Whiteley).

The other genre, drama, has not fared any better though Ebrahim Hussein's renowned play *Kinjeketile* has been translated into English by the playwright himself (1970). The original has the distinction of being the first full-length play in Swahili. Its theme – rebellion against German colonial occupation – is perceived as the artist's perception of the first 'national' struggle for freedom which actually took place in the region from 1905 to 1907. The plot revolves around a prophet, Kinjeketile, who, possessed by a spirit, delivers to the people anointed water thought to be invincible against German guns and bullets. He succeeds in uniting the tribes of southern Tanganyika to the cause. In his introduction to the play, Hussein makes it clear that although a prophet named Kinjeketile did exist, the hero of the play 'is not an historical evocation of the real man' but 'a creature of the imagination'.

It is interesting to note that Hussein's translation has had to shed some of the techniques integral to the original. For instance, the characters in the original play speak Swahili with dialectic variations; when Kinjeketile is possessed, the state of possession is signalled by a switch to standard Swahili. This could not of course be maintained in the English version; instead, the possessed Kinjeketile speaks in (English) verse to distinguish his utterances from his normal speech.

Another play whose English translation should be mentioned in passing is Topan's *Aliyeonja Pepo* (1973), translated as 'A Taste of Heaven' by M. Mkombo 1980). A critique of the play may be found in Kruisheer's article in *Research in African Literatures*, 30, 1 (1999).

Sweet and Sour Milk (1979) A novel by Nuruddin *Farah. The first in a trilogy entitled *Variations on the Theme of an African Dictatorship* that deals with the years of totalitarian terror, the novel ingeniously combines the techniques of the political thriller and the detective novel to present a deranged world, an Orwellian nightmare of disappearing 'unpersons', secret detentions, and rearranged history. In this novel and the next in the trilogy, *Sardines* (1981), traditional forms and values are not innocent but are implicated in the new terror. The oral culture lends itself to political abuse and the new military despotism is merely the patriarchal authoritarianism of the Somali family writ large: domestic and political tyranny are mutually reinforcing, invoking each other's authority and sanctioning each other's violence. The trilogy closes with a more benign portrait of patriarchy. Deeriye, the ailing asthmatic grandfather of *Close Sesame* (1983), is a devout Muslim and veteran hero of the anti-colonial struggle who lives harmoniously with children and grandchildren in a non-authoritarian household. Meanwhile, in post-emergency Somalia active opposition to an increasingly vicious regime is carried on, albeit ineffectually, by the sons. After his son's death in prison, Deeriye rejoins the struggle and dies in a futile attempt to assassinate the General, an ambiguously presented event that contains the rival options of revenge, religious martyrdom, and suicide.

T

TABAN LO LIYONG (*ca.*1939-), Ugandan poet, critic, novelist, and short-story writer, was born of Ugandan parents in southern Sudan. He received his early education at Gulu High School and the Sir Samuel Baker School, and subsequently studied at a teachers' college in Uganda, at Howard University, USA (BA), and at the University of Iowa, USA, where he was the first African to receive the MFA degree in creative writing and where he cultivated his unconventional writing style. He has taught at several universities, including the University of Papua New Guinea, the University of Nairobi in Kenya, where he co-founded the department of literature with *Ngugi wa Thiong'o, and Juba University in Khartoum, Sudan. A former cultural affairs director in southern Sudan, he teaches at the University of Venda in South Africa.

No single distinctive style or voice dominates Taban's aesthetic. His work assimilates *oral traditions, conscious and unconscious integration of heterogeneous sources, fragmented utterances, and a prosaic diction with little or no regard for a coherent logical sequence. *Fixions and Other Stories* (1969), filled with Luo mythology and folktales, is an example of his experimentation with the short story as genre, while *Meditations in Limbo* (1970), which creates a persona who acts antithetically with his father, is more or less a novel. Both, despite their structural flaws, demonstrate his strong sense of commitment to the indigenous culture and oral tradition as a viable source of literary imagery. The poems in *Frantz Fanon's Uneven Ribs* (1971), *Another Nigger Dead* (1972), *Thirteen Offensives against Our Enemies* (1973), and *Ballads of Underdevelopment)* (1976) employ contrast, paradox, irony, innuendo, repetition, humour, cradle song, gossip, and surprise. 'With Purity Hath Nothing Been Won' (in *Another Nigger Dead*), for example, argues that success is never achieved through honesty, contrasting 'purity' and 'impurity' to draw the moral that evil ultimately triumphs over good and surprising with the premise that evil predominates over good, which runs counter to traditional belief. Echoes of other writers reverberate in his work, especially in some of the title poems. For example, 'The Marriage of Black and White' recalls Blake's 'The Marriage of Heaven and Hell', while 'Telephone Conversation Number Two' echoes Wole *Soyinka's 'Telephone Conversation', demonstrating his affinity with other writers and his ability as an experimental poet to borrow and adapt and move with the times.

The Last Word (1969) is a critical study that centres on African traditional values, African literature, and such authors as *Okot p'Bitek and Amos *Tutuola to comment on what Taban characterizes as 'East African literary barrenness'. He envisions a vanishing literary landscape of 'mountains', 'valleys', 'lakes', and 'waterfalls' that he hopes to rebuild with authentic literary beauty. His symbolism is clear enough: African literary sterility is attributable to European colonialism, specifically Western authors who not only distorted African history and culture but painted a grim view of the continent for selfish considerations. For Taban, the true picture of Africa, its people, and its culture can best be rendered by Africans themselves. *Eating Chiefs: Luo Culture from Lolwe to Malkal* (1970), *Another Last Word* (1990), and *Culture Is Rustan* (1991) contain essays about culture, people, places, politics, and his personal philosophy about life, employing pun, irony, humour, and wit to elaborate his satirical perspectives. His recent *poetry has been collected in *The Cows of Shambat: Sudanese Poems* (1992), *Words That Melt a Mountain* (1996), which was inspired by a stay in Japan, and *Carrying Knowledge up a Palm Tree* (1997).

TAHIR, Ibrahim (1940-), Nigerian novelist, was born in Bauchi, Nigeria and educated at King's College, Cambridge University, where he obtained undergraduate and graduate degrees in social anthropology. As a student in England he contributed to the *Hausa programme of the BBC's Africa Service in London. When he returned to Nigeria he taught sociology and became head of department at Ahmadu Bello University, Zaria and later worked towards the formation of the National party of Nigeria. When the military intervened in 1983 he was among the politicians detained. While he was in detention the novel *The Last Imam* (1984), which he had drafted in the 1960s, was published. Through the story of Imam Usman, Tahir criticizes the conservatism of his Muslim society as well as the cultural heritage that emasculates individual development. The characters are appealing and the conflicts in the novel are part of the fascination of the story. Tahir has been engaged in business and political activities since his release from detention.

TEJANI, Bahadur (1942-), poet, novelist, and short-story writer. Of Gujarati origin and born in Kenya, Tejani is Ugandan by nationality. He studied at Makerere and Cambridge universities and gained a

Ph.D. in African literature from the University of Nairobi, and he is an associate professor at the State University of New York.

The Rape of Literature and Other Poems (1969) is a response to the poet's meeting with India, an ancestral home and a reality where inhumanity is 'so natural'. The novel *Day After Tomorrow* (1971) projects a picture of a harmonious East African society born out of a deliberate and voluntary attempt by the African and Asian communities at integration. Some of Tejani's short stories are oriented towards the American world and its materialism and technology, revealing a continuing preoccupation with multiculturalism and a humanist vision.

Tell Freedom (1954) Autobiography by Peter *Abrahams. Here Abrahams states the political beliefs that have animated his fiction. The writing is distinguished by its clarity of expression, and the book is essential reading for anyone who wants to understand the political developments and their social consequences in South Africa from the late 1930s to the book's date of publication.

THEATRE [See DRAMA]

THEMBA, (Daniel Canodoise) Can (1924-68), South African short-story writer, was born in Marabastad, outside Pretoria, but was to spend most of his productive literary life in Sophiatown, near Johannesburg, before it was bulldozed under the provisions of the Group Areas Act. He received a first-class degree in English and a teacher's diploma at Fort Hare University College. In the 1950s he wrote for *Drum* magazine after having won its first short-story contest; later he wrote for *The Classic* and *Africa South*, as well as the *Golden City Post*, also a *Drum* publication. In 1966, while he was working as a teacher in Swaziland, he was declared a 'statutory communist' and his work was banned in South Africa. Only in the 1980s did it become freely available with the publication of two collections, *The *Will to Die* (1972) and *The World of Can Themba* (1985).

To his writing Themba brought the contradictions of the 'new Africans', who had university education but were prevented from realizing their potential by a plethora of racist laws and regulations, and who were both attracted and repelled by white liberal society but felt no affinity for black tribal culture.

Most of his stories, modelled on the romance or thriller genres, reveal an acute understanding of how life for people of colour had been dominated by the *apartheid legislation of the 1950s. His style, both literary and streetwise, reflects a personal life in which he had friends among both intellectuals and gangsters. His writing of the 1960s reveals his despair and frustration over the difficulties of living life as an outcast in his

own country and his increasing reliance on alcohol: introspective pieces such as 'Crepuscle', 'The Will to Die', and 'The Bottom of the Bottle' are evidence of a growing darkness of sentiment and style. He died of alcoholic complications in Swaziland.

Things Fall Apart (1958) A novel by Chinua *Achebe. In his first novel, Achebe describes the subtle ways in which British Christian imperialism undermined traditional Igbo society in Eastern Nigeria in the period around the turn of the twentieth century. The tragic story of the disintegration of Igbo society is embodied in the story of Okonkwo, the novel's hero. Igbo society is portrayed as possessing a strong sense of communal purpose, shored up by strong religious beliefs, while at the same time recognizing and honouring individuality when it conforms to the mores of the clan. Achebe is able to show the resilience of tribal society when foreign values are imposed, indeed forced upon it. Okonkwo's refusal to betray the values of his own culture brings about his death. *Things Fall Apart* is one of the most widely read novels of the century.

THIONG'O, NGUGI WA [See NGUGI WA THIONG'O]

THOMAS, Gladys (1934-), South African poet and playwright, was born to a mixed-race family and has lived most of her life in Cape Town. She left school at fifteen to work in a clothing factory, but in 1983 she attended the International Writing Program in Iowa City. Since her work has been critical of *apartheid, much of it was banned; when a production of hers was praised by *The World* in 1979, her three plays were banned and she was detained. That year she received Kwanzaa honours for 'writing under oppressive conditions'. Her poems, stories, and plays are often sparked by incidents under apartheid law and recount her encounters with its victims. When the community of Crossroads was bulldozed in 1986 to make room for a white suburb, she interviewed the dispossessed children and told their stories in *Children of Crossroads* (1986). She based *The Wynberg Seven* (1987) on her interviews with parents who watched their teenagers being taken into Pollsmoor Prison. Her work – direct, forceful, terse – has been published in newspapers, journals, *anthologies, including *Cry Rage* (1972) and *Exile Within* (1986), and privately. She has also published *Spotty Dog and Other Stories: Stories for and of South African Township Children* (*ca.*1983) and a play, *Avalon Court (Vignettes of Life of the Coloured People on the Cape Flats of Cape Town)* (1992).

Thoughts and Sentiments on the Evil of Slavery (1787) Autobiography of Ottobah *Cugoano.

Through a Film Darkly (1970) A play by Joe *de

Graft. The title of de Graft's major examination of values in a Ghanaian context evokes a biblical quotation about modes of perception, with the significant alteration of 'glass' to 'film'. The text suggests that the film referred to is a film of sputum, the expectoration of hate. Subtle, intelligent, demanding, but not without loose ends that yet another revision might have eliminated, *Through a Film Darkly* has sometimes been seen as an examination of racial tensions, sometimes in terms of culture conflict. From the beginning, the play announces its intention to confront issues of perception. At its centre stands an urbane individual who comfortably bridges cultures and who, employed in a range of self-conscious theatrical devices, communicates easily with the audience. Gabriel Lorca is quoted, and Luigi Pirandello and J.B. Priestley seem to hover in the wings as the compelling, deeply felt drama moves to a melodramatic climax.

Time of the Butcherbird (1979) A novel by Alex ★La Guma. In the first of his novels conceived and written entirely outside of South Africa, La Guma turns his attention to the matter of the 'Homelands', the euphemism applied to the small pockets of infertile, undeveloped countryside into which black people dispossessed of their ancient tribal lands were forced. In South African farming mythology, the butcherbird serves as a cleanser, eating the ticks off the bodies of cattle and horses, thus saving them from illness. What South Africa now needs is a 'butcherbird' to cleanse the country of the illness of Afrikaner Nationalism and its inhumane policies against the indigenous populations. Shilling Murile, a man in search of revenge for the death of his brother Timi, becomes the butcherbird when he shoots both Timi's killer Hannes Meulen, whose ancestors took possession of land in the Karoo and considered it their own, and the Englishman Edgar Stopes, as an indication that the butcherbird will not ignore the English who have supported the ★apartheid regime.

TLALI, Miriam (1933-), South African novelist, was the first black woman writer to publish a novel in English inside South Africa. She was born in Doornfontein, grew up in Sophiatown, and lives in Soweto. Although she studied at the University of the Witwatersrand and then at Roma University in Lesotho, financial difficulties forced her to leave before taking a degree. Her experiences as a bookkeeper at a Johannesburg furniture store with a large African clientele prompted her to write her first, largely autobiographical novel, ★*Muriel at Metropolitan*. Although completed in 1969, it was only finally published (in expurgated form to circumvent censorship) by Ravan Press in 1975. When Longman published an international version in 1979 based on her original manuscript, both versions were banned.

Tlali has written eloquently of the enormous difficulties facing a black woman writer in South Africa; her own life has been a determined struggle to fulfil what she sees as her role as a writer: to 'conscientize the people and to tell the truth as she sees it, undeterred by ★censorship or the constraints of custom and tradition. She has played an active role in encouraging writing by women, was a regular contributor to ★*Staffrider*, and served on the board of Skotaville Press. Her frequent visits overseas brought her into contact with other writers and gave her a space for her own writing. She writes in English because it is a uniting factor and enables her to reach a wide audience.

Amandla (1980) was a great success by South African publishing standards: 5,000 copies were sold in a few weeks before it was banned. The novel is one of several by black South African writers reflecting the 1976 Soweto uprising. The central character, Pholoso, is a student leader who witnesses the shooting of a friend. He is arrested and tortured, but escapes and flees the country, leaving behind his girlfriend Felleng. Through the interweaving of a number of stories, the impact of events on the wider community is registered. Although Tlali has said that in the novel women are represented as 'mothers and militants at the same time', their role still seems largely supportive.

Beginning with its first issue in March 1978, Tlali contributed a regular column to *Staffrider* entitled 'Soweto Speaking', in which ordinary people spoke about their lives. Two of these pieces, as well as three travelogues and a short story, were reprinted in *Mihloti* (1984). Her most important contribution to date is collection of short stories, ★*Footprints in the Quag* (1989, published internationally as *Soweto Stories*). The stories are notable for their detailed, sympathetic representation of the predicament of black women as they struggle to survive in a society that is both racist and sexist. Her recent work increasingly foregrounds the experience of women and their struggle to determine their own lives.

TRADITIONAL AFRICAN RELIGIONS [See RELIGION AND LITERATURE]

Transition [See LITERARY MAGAZINES, East Africa]

Trial of Christopher Okigbo, The (1971) A novel by Ali ★Mazrui. The events of the novel take place in the afterworld, called After-Africa. Ostensibly the story is about the Nigerian poet Christopher ★Okigbo, who died in the ★Nigeria-Biafra war: he is being put on trial for having given more weight to his Biafran nationalism than to his art. The fact, however, is that we neither see nor hear directly from Okigbo, whose trial turns into that of his prosecutor, a Ghanaian, for the sin of impatience, and of his defence attorney, a Muslim Kenyan, for that of miscalculation. In the end

Okigbo benefits from the equivalent of a hung jury for lack of sufficient evidence; his prosecutor is set free to begin a 'normal' life in After-Africa, whereas his defence attorney is found guilty and sentenced to live in a baobab tree in Gabon, in 'regular' Africa. Love triumphs when he is joined there by the woman whose death he had caused indirectly by a miscalculation in his previous life. The novel depends for its clarity and power on some of the assumptions of the African cultural nationalism prevalent from the 1950s to the 1970s: Africa is one and the same and pan-Africanism such an influence that death itself becomes 'an exercise in Pan-Africanism'. The narrative is astutely interspersed with numerous and relevant quotations from Okigbo's poems.

Trials of Brother Jero, The (1963) A play by Wole *Soyinka. One of Soyinka's best-known plays, both as a set text in schools all over Africa and on stage, it is perhaps the most frequently performed English-language play in Nigeria. It satirizes the activities of Nigeria's popular charismatic preachers, exposing the fraudulent practices of Brother Jero, while at the same time celebrating his ingenuity. Much of the play's comedy turns on Jero's relationship with his hapless assistant Chume. Soyinka returned to his main character for a later and bleaker comedy, *Jero's Metamorphosis* (1973) .

TSODZO, T(hompson) K(umbirai) (1947-), playwright and novelist, was born in the Charter district of Southern Rhodesia, now Zimbabwe, and educated at the University of Zimbabwe and the University of Michigan, USA. After Zimbabwean independence he became a senior official in the Ministry of Youth, Sport, and Culture. He lectures in the Department of English at the University of Zimbabwe.

Tsodzo's novels and plays use satire to address pressing social and political concerns. Of the plays, *Babamunini Francis* (1977) deals with the lives of the wives of long-distance lorry drivers and has been criticized as sexist, *Rugare* (1982) examines the problems of urban migration, and *Tsano* (1982) the consequent crime among the cities' unemployed. In 1983 he turned his satire against the politicians of the newly independent state and in *Shanduko* exposes their failure to fulfil their promises. His first novel, *Pafunge* (1972), represents the failure of colonial education to relate to Zimbabwean experience, and *Tawanda, My Son* (1986) continues his critique of intellectual colonialism. The *Shona novel *Mudhuri Murefurefu* (1992) considers the problem of retaining a stable identity amid the rapid economic and social changes of Zimbabwe, adding a new dimension to Shona literature.

TSONGA LITERATURE The Tsonga group of languages includes Tsonga (with the largest number of speakers), Ronga, and Tshwa; its speakers live in the southeastern coastal areas of Mozambique and adjacent interior (approximately 3,000,000 speakers) and in South Africa (approximately 1,500,000). In Mozambique, speakers of Mozambican Tsonga, which is also known there as Changana, occupy the area south of the Limpopo River. Ronga is spoken mainly around Maputo, and speakers of Tshwa are clustered around Inhambane. In South Africa, Tsonga speakers are found mainly in the newly defined provinces of Northern Transvaal, Eastern Transvaal, and Gauteng (all previously included within the Transvaal province), and there are several thousand Tsonga-speaking miners in the goldfields of the Free State and a smaller group, largely labourers, in the sugarcane fields of northern KwaZulu/Natal.

For the Tsonga languages, the international border between South Africa and Mozambique represents more than a political or geographical fixture: it also reflects the African experience of two different colonial histories and colonial language policies. These two sets of changing political and social histories have marked the literary expression of the Tsonga languages in different ways.

Portuguese colonial policy defined the historical experience of Mozambicans from the time of the great maritime explorations of the sixteenth century until the end of the struggle for independence in 1974. The *lusophone language policy of the Portuguese rulers effectively stifled all indigenous literary expression, with the exception of the traditional oral genres. From 1929, all teaching was in Portuguese. Despite such policies, however, the 1980 census taken in Mozambique indicated that 76 per cent of the population did not speak Portuguese. For most of the nineteenth century the region's history – and its languages – bore the marks of a successful invasion by Soshangana, one of emperor *Shaka's lieutenants, who established the Nguni empire of KwaGaza after overrunning the area as far as the Limpopo River. The Portuguese colonists retreated to the Island of Mozambique. The empire lasted from 1826 to 1895, and as the speakers of the Tsonga languages learned the Zulu language of the conquerors, they also learned about their praise poetry. The result was an elaboration and enrichment of the Tsonga personal and clan praises under the influence of the long and elaborate Nguni praising style (of which the praises of Shaka are the prime example).

In the late nineteenth century Swiss and American protestant missionaries extended their mission field from South Africa into Mozambique, although their efforts were greatly facilitated by Mozambican men who had encountered literacy and Christianity through the rapidly growing demand for migrant labour in the expanding South African economy. Christianization led to deep penetration of the primary oral Mozambican culture by the influence of the

Western written literary tradition, cast in the missionary mould. It led first to the transcription and grammatical description of the indigenous languages, which was soon followed by publications of Christian literature, Bible translations, and hymn books. The establishment of formal education for protestant converts led to a demand for learning and teaching material for the mission-run schools in both Mozambique and South Africa. The secular education of Roman Catholic converts had been largely ignored by the priests, whose focus was almost exclusively on religious matters.

In South Africa, missionary dominance of education and publishing was brought to an abrupt end by the Bantu Education Act, one of the first pieces of legislation of the *apartheid era (1948-90). Early in the 1950s, the Tsonga Language Board was established by the state with the aim of standardizing and modernizing the language and promoting the production of educational material. The school market and the development of literary and educational material for students became the driving force for the many new Afrikaner-owned publishing houses established during this period. The effects of the installation of the government of national unity in 1994 on literary production in the Tsonga language remain to be evaluated.

During the closing years of the colonial period in Mozambique, protest literature existed largely underground and was better known by the outside world than by Mozambicans. The struggle for independence (1964-74) and later the civil war (1980-94) led to a hiatus in literary production in the indigenous languages, which in any event had never really flourished. Oral forms emerged: for instance, peasant productions of protest songs in the local languages were heard on the *prazos*. Before independence, revolutionary and guerilla poetry, lying on the border between battle reports and poetry, were published – but largely in Portuguese – in local newspapers such as *Herois*.

Within South Africa, literature in Tsonga began with the publication in 1883 in Lausanne, Switzerland of two books: a selection of translated biblical texts and the words of fifty-seven hymns, and a simple outline grammar, in French, of the 'Gwamba' language. In 1884, the first school reader was published and in 1907 the complete Tsonga Bible, the work of H. Berthoud, A. Jaques, T. Mandlati, J. Mawelele, and E. Thomas. A steady stream of religious publications appeared, as well as a growing number of scientific grammars, a dictionary, and educational works for the mission schools. The ethnographic writings – in French or English – of the Swiss pastors H.A. Junod and A. Jaques resulted in several published collections of Tsonga oral literature, mainly tales, proverbs, and riddles. Some seventy titles were published during the missionary era.

Tsonga creative writing began with the publication in 1938 of a short novel by the first Tsonga-speaking author, D.C. Marivate. Other novels, plays, and poetry followed, mainly for schoolchildren. During the period 1940-60 novels were published by S.J. Baloyi, E.P. Ndhambi, H.W.E. Ntsan'wisi, and H.E. Ntsan'wisi, while D.C. Marivate, C. Maphophe, F.M. Maboko, P.M. Shiluvana, and P.E. Ntsan'wisi published biographies. There were also two poetry collections by E.P. Ndhambi and P.E. Ntsan'wisi and one collection of folklore by H.-P. Junod. Between 1960 and 1980 there were novels by B.K. Mtombeni, J. Thuketane, E.M. Nkondo, T.H. Khosa, and I.N. Khosa. In Tsonga poetry W.Z. Nkondo and E.M. Nkondo broke the old formal boundaries, while G.J. Maphalakasi and M.M. Marhanele also made interesting contributions. The most significant work, however, was that of B.J. Masebenza, with a style rooted in praise poetry.

More recent novels are those by W.R. Chauke (1992), M.G. Magagane (1992), C.M. Lubisi (1991, 1992), and K.T.C. Manganyi (1987, 1992). Collections of short stories have been published by W.R. Chauke (1991) and G.S. Mayevu (1992), while a promising young poet is V.A. Mudau (1990). Among Tsonga plays – few of which are notable – are those by B.K. Mtombeni and E.M. Nkondo .

In the post-apartheid era, younger authors such as I.N. Khosa, I.S. Shabangu, C.M. Lubisi, K.T.C. Manganyi, and W.R. Chauke have shown maturity and a willingness to explore previously neglected social and ethical issues, as well as to begin to reflect in their writing some of the political and social turmoil that marked the years of revolt. Male writers have dominated Tsonga literary production; women's voices have not yet been heard. The efforts of publishing houses and literary competitions may encourage established and future writers to greater productivity. Language planning decisions yet to be taken by both the new government of national unity and the provincial legislatures may result in enhancement of the status of this minority language.

Early literary expression in Mozambican Tsonga languages was similarly dominated largely by the religious and educational writings of Swiss pastors such as H.A. Junod and A. Grandjean. J. A. Persson's dictionary (1928), his linguistic description (1932), and that of A. Helgesson (1950) remain the only linguistic sources. The first New Testament in Tshwa was not published until 1964; it was followed by the complete Bible in 1970. Early collections of oral literature in Tshwa were published by E. S. Mucambe (1935) and A. S. Mukhombo (1928). One of the few solid works on Tshwa culture and people was written by N. J. Mbanze (6th reprint, 1981). Most of the total output in Tshwa was published by the Central Mission Press in South Africa. Given the official language policy, it is not surprising that creative writing in the languages of

Mozambique lagged far behind that of its South African neighbour.

Because of the complete prohibition on the publication of books in Tshwa, the increasingly difficult conditions under which the Protestant missionary educational endeavours laboured after the Roman Catholic church became solely responsible for education in 1929, surveillance by the state security police after 1957, and the censorship of correspondence, many publications, produced ostensibly for literacy training, became channels for what has been called bootleg education. Even literacy materials had to be disguised as religious education, and the term 'religious' took on an increasingly secular component. Migrant Tshwa labourers working in the mines of South Africa bought literacy readers and exercise books there and brought them home clandestinely to Mozambique. Many of the leaders of the Mozambican liberation movement received part of their education in Protestant missionary schools.

Literary expression in Ronga is the most impoverished of the three Mozambican Tsonga languages. In the period between 1950 and 1970, publications in Tsonga/Changane and Ronga were mainly 'roneo' or 'multilith' copies, cardboard bound and undated, produced by the Igreja Presbiteriana de Moçambique. Their focus was still on religious matters, primary health care, and the Christian family. Some of the writers were G. Andrie, A. Beuchat, P. Loze, E. Morgenthaler, and G. Morier-Genoud; such indigenous authors as P. Sibane, A. A. Sidumo, and N. Sumbane wrote firmly within the dominant missionary ideology. No novels, poetry, plays, or other genres were published in Ronga during the colonial era.

After its installation in 1974, the transitional government of Mozambique built many new educational and literacy centres. The adult illiteracy rate dropped from 90 per cent to 73 per cent in five years, new reading material was prepared for school children, new teaching and learning materials were produced, and the future for literatures in the Tsonga languages of Mozambique appeared more hopeful. Seminars on a language policy for post-colonial Mozambique were held in 1975, on the policies to be adopted for the teaching of Portuguese in 1979, and on the standardization of the orthographies of Mozambican languages in 1987. The final report was published in 1989. The language policy decisions taken in 1983 recognized the four major Mozambican languages: Makua (spoken by an estimated 41 per cent of the population), Tsonga (including Ronga and Tshwa, 19 per cent), Nyanja (10 per cent) and *Shona (8 per cent), and heralded a new status for these languages. The status accorded to Portuguese as the main official language makes more sense than is apparent, since it is in the process of structural, lexical, and semantic nativization as a language of national unity. However, natural disasters, the drastic reduction in the number of migrant labour contracts in South Africa, and above all the systematic destruction of the newly founded infrastructure from 1980 by the Renamo rebels and the destabilization policies of the South African government, even after the signing of the Nkomati Accord in 1982, all contributed to ending early hopes for strengthening the position of indigenous languages. Academics in the Faculty of Arts of the Eduardo Mondlane University, those working within INDE, the National Institute for the Development of Education, and writers in the Association of Mozambican Authors have tried to stimulate indigenous language literatures and have called for the wider use of indigenous languages in the spheres of education, administration, official communications, courts, the media, and economic life. The poet G. Makavi and the novelists B. Sitoe and P. Manyisa have all contributed to a new surge in Tsonga/Changana literary activity since 1980. Several works circulate only in photocopied form, as lack of facilities for printing and publishing as well as financial constraints continue to impede the development of indigenous literature. Radio plays in Tsonga/Changana and in Ronga by F. Mafumu, A. Magaia, P. Manyisa, E. T. Mpfumo, M. Ndlate, F. Ntamele, B. Sitoe, and R. M. Sitoe, among others, have contributed to the enjoyment of literature.

Much of present Mozambican literary production, however, is still in Portuguese, raising the question of whether a break with the colonial dominance of the past is possible if writers do not turn to their own languages, or whether a nativized Portuguese can become a vehicle for literary expression on a national level. Literary production in Mozambique is further plagued by the continuing existence of non-standard versions of the indigenous languages, by a high rate of adult illiteracy, and by the lack of coherent language planning based on research into language distribution, usage, and attitudes. To the question 'Is there a national literature in Mozambique?' many would answer in the negative, especially since any perception of national unity is confined to the metropolitan capital of Maputo.

Imprisoned within the boundaries of inimical and unjust colonial language policies, stifled by missionary idealism, lured away by the promotion of false concepts of literature propagated by the apartheid world view, and agonized by the daily reality of a devastating civil war, Tsonga literatures have yet to find full freedom of expression.

Turbott Wolfe (1925) A novel by William *Plomer. The novel caused a near sensation at the time of its publication for dealing frankly with the question of colour, African aspirations, and inter-racial sex. It announces that miscegenation is the means for 'Africa to be secured for the Africans' and yet expresses alarm when a white woman in the novel proposes to marry an African man. Plomer includes a number of characters, near stereotypes, who advance opposing attitudes to his central theme: a missionary, Friston, who claims that 'the white man's day is over', Mabel van der Horst, who marries an African, and a racist trader, Bloodfield, who annexes Wolfe's trading post when the latter is driven from the land.

TUTUOLA, Amos (1920–97), Nigerian fiction writer, was born in Western Nigeria to Charles Tutuola, a cocoa farmer, and his wife Esther Aina. His brief education was limited to six years (from 1934 to 1939), after which he trained as a metalsmith. From 1944 until the end of the Second World War he worked as a coppersmith for the West African Air Corps of the Royal Air Force. Unable to establish himself in a trade or profession after the war, he joined the colonial service in 1948 as a messenger in the Labour Department. His career as a writer began while he was so employed. Despite his meagre education and a poor mastery of English (the language in which he writes), he has earned a remarkable international reputation. In 1979 he held a visiting research fellowship at the University of Ife (now Obafemi Owolowo University) at Ile-Ife, Nigeria, and in 1983 he was an associate of the International Writing Program at the University of Iowa. After he retired, he divided his time between residences at Ibadan and Ago-Odo.

Tutuola has published two collections of short stories, a volume of ★Yoruba folktales, and nine folkloric narratives, of which The ★Palm-wine Drinkard, a kind of quest tale that incorporates traditional Yoruba folk material, is the best known. In each he has repeated the structure and style of the first, sometimes even reintroducing whole episodes and characters from earlier narratives in later ones. Despite similarities in plot, structure, style, and theme, the later texts do indicate Tutuola's recourse to ★religion and mythology as new sources (such as John Bunyan's The Pilgrim's Progress, The Arabian Nights, and Edith Hamilton's Mythology). Occasional startlingly out-of-place words in them also testify to his use of dictionaries as quarries for new vocabulary.

★Simbi and the Satyr of the Dark Jungle (1955) and The Brave African Huntress (1958), Tutuola's third and fourth books, do depart somewhat from the general pattern, specifically in the choice of women as the principals. Indeed, it is to Tutuola's credit that unlike most highly educated male African writers of his generation he needed no urging from feminist activism before placing women at centre stage in his fiction. Adebisi, the brave huntress, is the more formidable of the two heroines. Having inherited her father's hunting profession along with all his powerful charms, she sets out to rescue her four older brothers, who had disappeared on a hunting trip into the fearful Jungle of the Pigmies. She emerges from the jungle after surviving the familiar string of perils, not only with her brothers, but also with thousands of other captives, as well as a large quantity of precious metals that made her 'at once' a very rich lady.

The critical reception abroad of Tutuola's work was initially enthusiastic, although it was mixed among fellow Nigerians put off by his incorrect English and haphazard plots. By the 1970s the enthusiasm had cooled, but Nigerian critical regard for his accomplishments has increased. For example, in a 1970 article Molara ★Ogundipe-Leslie commended his accurate representation of an African (especially Yoruba) consciousness, and Chinua ★Achebe devoted a 1987 lecture to praising him as 'the most moralistic of all Nigerian writers'.

Despite his successful career Tutuola has nevertheless remained marginal among African writers, excluded from forums where the latter discuss literary and other issues and from the international lecture circuit that has become a prerequisite for African European-language writers of comparable reputation. His other works are My Life in the Bush of Ghosts (1954), Feather Woman of the Jungle (1962), Ajaiyi and his Inherited Poverty (1967), The ★Witch-Herbalist of the Remote Town (1981), The Wild Hunter in the Bush of the Ghosts (1982; revised 1989), Pauper, Brawler, and Slanderer (1987), The Village Witch Doctor and Other Stories (1990), and the collection Yoruba Folktales (1986).

Two Thousand Seasons (1973) A novel by Ayi Kwei ★Armah. The novel's use of the first person plural embodies its communal vision. Sweeping through a mythical span, it narrates the loss of the original 'way' (a world view centred on the balance between giving and receiving), the coming of the 'predators' (ie. Arabs), the black diaspora southwards, and the slave trade introduced by the 'destroyers' (ie. whites). The protagonists, coaxed into a slave ship by their own king but managing to escape, organize a pan-African guerila war and conquer a slave castle. The novel, Armah's most controversial, has been both praised for its innovative style, which reproduces the lyrical eloquence of the oral bard as repository of a collective philosophy, and criticized for its acrimony against Africa's invaders.

U

UDECHUKWU, Obiora (1946-), Nigerian poet and playwright, is a professor of painting at the University of Nigeria, Nsukka, where he graduated in 1972. His book of poems, *What the Madman Said* (1990), won the Association of Nigerian Authors/ Cadbury poetry prize (1990). He started writing poetry seriously during the ★Nigeria-Biafra war in 1967, and his English and Igbo poems have appeared in journals and anthologies. His poetry, which in some ways recalls the lapidary quality of Christopher ★Okigbo, is marked by juxtaposition of African and European cultural elements, eclecticism, and oblique reference, and he employs the same satirical undertones in both painting and poetry. In *What the Madman Said*, artistic sensibility is sharpened by the sufferings of the war. The first section, 'Totem of Lament', written between 1967 and 1973, contains images of physical ravages, while the second section, 'What the Madman Said', continues the portrayal of distorted values. With members of Odunke Artists, he co-wrote two Igbo plays, *Ojadili* (1977) and *Onukwube* (1986). He makes remarkable use of vivid diction and images.

UGAH, Ada (1958-), novelist, essayist, and poet, was born in Iga-Okpoya, Nigeria. Educated in both Nigeria and France, he is a lecturer at the University of Calabar, Nigeria and an active member of the Association of Nigerian Authors (ANA). His collection *The Rainmaker's Daughter and Other Stories* (1992), which won an ANA prize in 1993, reveals his interest in tradition and in the plight of humanity in a rapidly changing world. But he is perhaps best known for his experimental 'novel in ballad', *The Ballads of the Unknown Soldier* (1989), which one critic described as 'a bold contribution to the restructuring of the African literary landscape'. He continues the experiment with the balladic narrative with even greater vigour in *Colours of the Rainbow* (1991), in which he employs aspects of Idoma mythology to bewail the failure of Africans to harness Africa's potential. Other works include *Naked Hearts* (1982), *Rêves interdits* (1983), and *Errance sans Frontières* (1996), poems; *Hanini's Paradise* (1985), a novel; *Anatomy of Nigerian Poetics* (1982) and *Reflections on a Republic* (1983), essays; and *In the Beginning: Chinua Achebe at Work* (1990), a biography.

UKA, Kalu (1938-), Nigerian poet, novelist, and theatre artist, was born at Akaanu Ohafia, Abia State. After schooling at Hope Waddell Training Institution, Calabar and Methodist College, Uzuakoli (1951-7) he graduated with a BA in English from University College, Ibadan, and an MA from the University of Toronto, Canada. He is a professor of theatre arts at the University of Calabar. Uka's only collection of poetry, *Earth to Earth* (1971) is comprised mainly of poems inspired by the Nigerian crisis and the ★Nigeria-Biafra war (1967-70). His attempt to write similar poetry in ★Igbo (see 'Ukpara Kititki' in *Aka Weta*, 1978, edited by Chinua ★Achebe and Obiora Udechukwu), was less successful. The textured language that characterizes the poetry does not seem to work well as a medium for prose narrative. Thus, his two published novels, also set in the Biafran war and its aftermath (*A Consummation of Fire*, 1978, and *Colonel Ben Brim*, 1985) test the reader's concentration without offering any compensatory sublimity of vision. More successful as a professor of theatre arts and theatre director, Uka founded the Oak Theatre at the University of Nigeria and produced a successful stage adaptation of Achebe's ★*Things Fall Apart* and ★*Arrow of God* under the title *A Harvest for Ants* (1979). He has also produced his own play, *Ikhamma* (1978).

ULASI, Adaora Lily (1932-), Nigerian novelist, has a BA in journalism, has been a newspaper and magazine editor, and has worked for Voice of America and the BBC. Her major contribution to African literature, however, is as the first Nigerian detective novelist writing in English. Her first novel, *Many Thing You No Understand* (1970), and its continuation, *Many Thing Begin for Change* (1971), take place in 1935 in England. The theme of both novels is the confrontation between traditional ★Igbo authority and British colonial authority. Her third novel, *The Night Harry Died* (1974), is set in the southern USA. Her most accomplished detective novel is *Who Is Jonah?*, set in southeastern Nigeria. Her incorporation of aspects of the African occult in the Nigerian novels reflects the pervasiveness of black magic in Africa and provide mystery and tension, especially in *The Man from Sagamu* (1978), the last of her novels set in western Nigeria.

UMELO, Rosina (1930-), writer of children's books, was born of British parents in Cheshire, UK, and educated at Bedford College, University of London. She married a Nigerian and in 1971 became a Nigerian citizen. In Nigeria she has worked in education as a school principal and author of curriculum material for study in English literature and in publishing as an editor. As a creative writer she has won awards including a BBC story prize in 1966, the Nigerian Broadcasting Corporation short-story competition prizes in 1972 and 1974, and the Cheltenham Literary Festival Prize in 1973. Her collection of stories *The Man Who Ate the Money* (1978) explores various aspects of Nigerian society, and the teenage novels *Felicia* (1978), *Finger of Suspicion* (1984), and *Something to Hide* (1986) address contemporary issues through effective narrative techniques.

V

Valley of a Thousand Hills, The (1941) A long poem by H.I.E. *Dhlomo. Contrasting the harmony of nature with the cruelty of humanity, the poem's visions of the past, present, and future attempt to plumb the African soul. The style is romantic-Victorian and displays varying degrees of competence. Contemporary African critics felt that the poem was not romantic enough, whereas later critics accuse Dhlomo of being a romantic escapist. All missed such militant lines as 'We'll strike and take! If others will not give', which signalled the hardening of the African consciousness.

VAMBE, Lawrence (1917-), autobiographer and journalist, was born in Chishawasha, Southern Rhodesia, now Zimbabwe, and educated at the Roman Catholic seminary at Chishawasha, although he chose to leave before ordination, and Francis College, Mariannhill, South Africa. In 1946 he joined Africa Newspapers and by 1953 was editor-in-chief of the group. He founded *African Parade*, one of the first publications to express in a popular form the life of the country's urban blacks and provide an opportunity for the publication of some of the first black-authored fiction, and the *Zimbabwean Review*, ZAPU's British newsletter. *An Ill-fated People* (1972), an ambitious autobiography, uses anecdotes of his own and his family's experiences to reconstruct Shona culture before the colonial occupation and to write the early history of Rhodesia from the point of view of the colonized. His account registers complex attitudes towards the missionaries who occupied his people's ancestral land. *From Rhodesia to Zimbabwe* (1976) followed, again registering national history partly through personal experience. In addition to his autobiographies, Vambe's importance for Zimbabwean literature lies in his journalism, which for more than forty years has sought to negotiate a middle ground between the various extremes of national life. Vambe edits *Southern African Encounter*.

VAN DER POST, (Sir) Laurens (Jan) (1906-97), South African novelist and travel writer, was born at Philippolis, Orange Free State, into a distinguished Afrikaans family. On his family's farms, van der Post got to know and admire the Khoisan people; he was subsequently to claim them as one of the dominant influences in his life. He was educated at local schools, including Grey College, Bloemfontein.

In the English-speaking, liberal atmosphere of the *Natal Advertiser*, where he began work as a reporter in 1925, he came into contact with a range of ideas alien to his deeply conservative upbringing; he also met the poet Roy *Campbell and the novelist William *Plomer, whom he joined in 1926 in editing the journal *Voorslag* [Whiplash], which was sharply critical of the 'colour bar', as *apartheid was then called. In 1928 he travelled to Europe, and in 1934 published his first novel, *In a Province*. The book's indebtedness to Plomer's writing, with its (for the time) radically unconventional ideas on race relations, is clear throughout: in its depiction of friendship between blacks and whites, in its study of the destructive effects of Western ways on a tribal African, and in its assertion that love is stronger than the extreme politics being offered by left and right in the 1930s.

During the Second World War he served with the British forces, and his experiences as a prisoner of the Japanese were to result in *A Bar of Shadow* (1952), and in the film *Merry Christmas Mr. Lawrence* (1983). From 1948 on he lived in England, travelled indefatigably, and turned out a stream of books, twenty-five in total by the time of his death.

Van der Post made a number of trips to Africa during the 1950s, several of which resulted in books, notably *Venture to the Interior* (1951), an account of an expedition to East Africa, and *The Lost World of the Kalahari* (1958), describing his encounter with the *Bushmen of what is now Botswana. These were the books that made his name, being widely acclaimed and winning several literary prizes. Other notable volumes among his large output include *The Heart of the Hunter* (1961), *A Story like the Wind* (1972), and *A Far-off Place* (1974). In 1951 he met Carl Jung and became a confirmed Jungian. This strand of his thought shows most obviously in *Jung and the Story of Our Time* (1975) and in a television documentary he made on Jung in 1971, but Jung's ideas are evident everywhere in his writing from the mid-1950s on, combined with a late-Romantic mysticism that is van der Post's own.

VAN WYK, Christopher (1957-), South African poet, novelist, editor, and children's writer, was born in Soweto and has worked as a clerk and for the independent South African Committee for Higher Education (SACHED) as an educational writer of accessible literature for new readers. He was editor of *Staffrider* from 1981 to 1986 and in 1980 started the short-lived *Wietie* magazine with Fhazel Johennesse. He lives in Johannesburg and works as a writer and freelance editor.

During the literary explosion among black writers that followed the Soweto uprising in 1976 van Wyk published a volume of poetry, *It Is Time to Go Home* (1979), that won the 1980 Olive Schreiner Prize. The book is characterized by the preoccupations of other Soweto poets such as Mongane *Serote, Sipho *Sepamla, and Mafika *Gwala and employs the language of defiance and assertion in poetry that reveals at all times the *Black Consciousness of the era. It shows also the particular wit and humour that is present in all van Wyk's writing. In 1981 he received the Maskew Miller Longman Award for black children's literature for *A Message in the Wind* (1982), the story of two boys who travel in their homemade time machine to their shared tribal past of 1679. Other children's stories include *Peppy 'n Them* (1991) and *Petroleum and the Orphaned Ostrich* (1988). He has written books for neo-literate adults, such as *The Murder of Mrs. Mohapi* (1995), *My Cousin Thabo* (1995), *Take a Chance* (1995), *My Name is Selina Mabiletsa* (1996), and *Sergeant Dlamini Falls in Love* (1996), biographies of Sol *Plaatje and Oliver Tambo for teenagers, and adaptations of works by Bessie *Head, Sol Plaatje, and Can *Themba. He won the 1996 Sanlam Literary Award for his short story 'Relatives', published in *Crossing Over* (1995). *The Year of the Tapeworm* (1996) is an adult novel and warns of government control of the media.

VASSANJI, M(oyez) G. (1950-), novelist and short-story writer, was born in Nairobi, Kenya, finished high school in Tanzania, and gained graduate degrees in physics at the Massachusetts Institute of Technology and the University of Pennsylvania, USA. He subsequently moved to Canada, and for ten years pursued his scientific career. When he turned to creative writing, it was to tell the full story of his people, the Indians of East Africa. His first novel, *The *Gunny Sack* (1989), which won a Commonwealth Writers Prize, is about a young Tanzanian Asian's search for identity. With his unusual inheritance, a gunny sack full of multifarious ambiguous mementoes, as guide, he seeks his community's past. Although he does not find an ultimate truth, the quest reveals that the legacy of the Asian population is today an interactive and evolving cultural and spiritual reality that invokes a sense of wholeness for its individual members. *The *Book of Secrets* (1994), winner of Canada's Giller Prize, views the history of the same Asian community from new perspectives. The narrative revolves around a British colonial administrator's 1913 diary, found in Dar es Salaam in 1988. The retired schoolteacher who attempts to explore its entries is overwhelmed by the way in which the past connects with the present. The same truth catches up with Nurdin of *No New Land* (1991). The setting of the novel is Canada, a later-day destination for East African Asians. The short-story collection *Uhuru Street* (1992) deals with specific

aspects of the Indian community's life in Dar es Salaam during the period between the 1950s and the 1980s. Vassanji is himself creating imaginative landscapes that future historians of culture will need to walk.

VATSA, Mamman Jiya (1944-86), Nigerian poet, was a major-general in the Nigerian army, minister of the new federal capital Abuja, and a member of the Supreme Military Council. He was executed following an abortive coup.

Vatsa's eight poetry collections for adults and eleven for children were mostly didactic or nationalistic, with titles such as *Back Again at Wargate* (1982), *Reach for the Skies* (1984) (subtitled *Patriotic Poems on Abuja*) and *Verses for Nigerian State Capitals* (1973). His best books are about ordinary people's lives and simple creatures: these include the *Pidgin collection *Tori for geti bow leg* (1981), his cultural picture book in *Hausa, *Bikin Suna*, and a charming picture storybook, *Stinger the Scorpion* (1979). This last reads well as prose. His literary importance derives from his role as facilitator and patron of the arts. He organized writing workshops for his fellow soldiers and their children and got their works published. He helped the Children's Literature Association of Nigeria with funds, built a Writers' Village for the Association of Nigerian Authors, and hosted or provided resources for their annual conferences. He was on the executive of both.

VERA, Yvonne (1954-), Zimbabwean short-story writer and novelist, was born in Bulawayo, Zimbabwe and educated at Luveve and Mzilikazi Secondary Schools. She holds a doctorate in literature from York University, Canada and was a writer-in-residence at Trent University, Canada in 1995. Since her return to Zimbabwe, she devotes most of her time to creative writing. Her first publication, *Why Don't You Carve Other Animals?* (1992), is a collection of short stories set in colonial Rhodesia during the liberation war. Caught in the conflict are a vulnerable people who have never had much control over their lives: men anxious to hold on to the little they have and women dreaming about fulfilment and achievement for their children. This collection, although uneven in its handling of the short-story form, is notable for its delicately chiselled poetic language. Her second publication, *Nehanda* (1993), is a novel based on the 1893 uprising in Zimbabwe. As the settlers gain a stranglehold on African land and invade African space, Nehanda becomes the centre of African resistance. She displays courage rooted in an African beliefs and values, in contrast to the materialistic outlook of her detractors. What emerges is an African world view rendered in a poetic style that captures African modes of expression and thought. Also implicit in Vera's creative reconstruction of the war is the central role played by women in the shaping of Zimbabwean history. In *Without a Name* (1994), a poetic novel in a surrealistic idiom, a woman who is raped during the liberation war later commits infanticide. *Under the Tongue* (1996), also written in a highly lyrical style, deals with a young girl's intense, painful relationship with her father. Her most recent work is *Butterfly Burning* (1998). Vera's work reveals a serious artist experimenting with the novel form and a poetic style.

VIEIRA, Arménio [See LUSOPHONE LITERATURE]

VILAKAZI, B(enedict) W(allet) (1906–47), Zulu poet; his works were originally written in the ★Zulu language and eventually translated into English. Like his fellow Zulu poet, Herbert I.E. ★Dhlomo, Vilakazi's poems were concerned with taking up the cause of the newly urbanized and consequently exploited mine workers. In this sense he, like Dhlomo, is an innovator in terms of South African poetry. To his concern for the exploited worker, Vilakazi brings a high moral purpose based on his adherence to Christian principles. Vilakazi joins these various elements to produce a poetry which defines social conflict in terms of class. Vilakazi's poetry for the most part lacks subtlety, the messages he seeks to convey being presented without ambiguity.

Visions and Reflections (1972) Poems by Frank ★Chipasula. The first collection of verse to appear from a Malawian poet, *Visions and Reflections* was written while Chipasula was still an undergraduate in Malawi but published during his exile in Zambia. Some of the poems exhibit Chipasula's nascent poetic strengths and carry youthful memories of Malawi's liberation struggle and innocent optimism about the promise of independence. However, the tone and posture change dramatically with exile and his commitment to a sustained attack on the excesses of the Banda regime.

VLADISLAVIĆ, Ivan (1957–), South African short-story writer and novelist, lives in Johannesburg, where he works as an editor. He has published a number of short stories, of which several have been translated into foreign languages. Individual stories, his collection *Missing Persons* (1989), and his novel, *The Folly* (1993), have won literary awards.

Vladislavić's post-modern style is seemingly effortless. He intermingles fantasy with references to historic events, enabling them to detonate with symbolic meanings both within a South African context and beyond it. The stories are a vision of the madness of South African life and a mordantly skilful send-up of pedantry which operates on the interface between the hugely comic and the tragic, a position no other writer in South Africa has so successfully explored. *The Folly*, situated in an apparently recognizable world, describes the building of a house, but the relevance extends to considerations of the imagination and to a satire of the political notion of constructing a new world. Vladislavić's is a distinctively individual voice.

Voice, The (1964) A novel by Gabriel ★Okara. This 'poetic novel' follows the hallucinatory wandering of Okolo (Ijo: the voice) through the corrupt city of Sologa (Lagos) as he denounces its encroaching materialism. Okolo's message about post-independence Nigeria is left unheeded and he is ultimately set adrift down the river. The metaphorical fight between Okolo's 'straight words' and the 'crooked words' of corrupt politics is linguistically sustained through the use of Ijo thought patterns that jostle the English word order. Although it is an unprecedented attempt at linguistic experimentation, the novel has been judged a stylistic dead end and the swan song of parabolic approaches to Nigerian fiction.

WACHIRA, Godwin (1936-), novelist, was born
and educated in Kenya before undertaking a B.Sc. at
Berlin University, Germany. He has worked variously
as a publisher (he founded Newsline Africa publishing
in 1975), an editor, a journalist, and an ostrich farmer.
His only novel, *★Ordeal in the Forest* (1967), belongs to
the body of historical fiction in Kenyan literature. Like
most of this writing, it deals with the Mau Mau struggle against colonialism. Written so closely upon the
events it describes, and being a trial work, the book
exhibits some obvious shortcomings. Thus, it presents
a stereotypical image of the settler community and
treats in a rather schematic manner the experience of
the common people under colonialism, the growth of
anti-colonial consciousness, and the formation of a
resistance movement. However, its strength lies in the
sobriety with which the novelist reveals the complexity of each fighter's story of participation in the liberation war.

WACIUMA, Charity (1936-), novelist, was born in
Naaro village, Fort Hall, Kenya, and trained as a
teacher in a college at Embu. She belongs among the
pioneers of indigenous writing for children, having
published *Mweru the Ostrich Girl*, her first book, in
1966. Her autobiographical novel of childhood and
adolescence, *★Daughter of Mumbi* (1969), gives an
ethnographic description of life among the Kikuyu
people and a historical account of a decade and a half
of colonial existence. The period ends with the worst
years of the emergency and the Mau Mau uprising in
the mid-1950s. What most impresses the child's imagination is the agonizing experience of fear, uncertainty
and humiliation, and the sudden rift that divided a
once united community. Having made a name for
herself as one of the earliest women writers in East
Africa, Waciuma remained silent after her promising
start.

Waiting for the Barbarians (1980) A novel by J.M.
★Coetzee. Like the poem by C.P. Cavafy from which
it takes its title, the novel is concerned with the way
'barbarians' are constructed as the necessary other in
any imperial project. Set on the remote frontier of an
unspecified empire, it traces the transition from a
phase of bureaucratized administrative control to a
phase of militarized totalitarian control that relies on
torture and terror. The narrator, an ageing magistrate
who has imagined he can see out his days peacefully as
chief official of the settlement, is caught up in the

transition and is powerless to resist it. By means of a
fetishistic attachment to a barbarian girl, the victim of
torture at the hands of the newly arrived colonel, he
attempts to expiate his guilt at being 'the lie which
Empire tells itself when times are easy.' The magistrate
is not a self-reflexive narrator in the manner of Coetzee's other narrators, but his present-tense narration
does draw attention to the constructedness of his
discourse. His attempts to decipher the hieroglyphics
of a previous empire in allegorical terms refers to the
allegorical structure of the novel itself, which can be
interpreted as dealing with the issue of the liberal
humanist response to the strategies of the South
African state in the 1970s.

Waiting Laughters (1990) Poems by Niyi ★Osundare.
The volume, a 'long song in many voices', is in four
parts and considers, as the title implies, the process of
waiting and the quality of humour. Osundare draws
on his Nigerian, especially his ★Yoruba, inheritance,
but there are poems that relate to other parts of Africa
and the wider black world. There are references to the
Niger, the Nile, the Limpopo, and the Atlantic; to the
events that comprised the freedom (and thus the
laughter) of African peoples – Langa, Sharpeville, and
Soweto; and to martyrs in the cause of African and
black freedom – Thomas Sankara, Steve Biko, Walter
Rodney, and Nelson Mandela – juxtaposed with references to apostates to the cause of freedom – Hitler,
Marcos, and Idi Amin. The poems are experimental in
nature and often require accompaniment by music:
flute, kora, Guangyuan, sekere, and the human voice,
often in medley.

Walk in the Night, A (1967) A novella by Alex ★La
Guma. The novella explores with compelling atmosphere and detail the expression of male rage and violence under conditions of police brutality, political
degradation, and inescapable poverty. The events of
the plot are played out in the course of one night,
beginning with the anger of the main character,
Michael Adonis, a 'coloured' (mixed race) man who
has unjustly lost his job. The scenes shift cinematically
from Michael to the other rooms in the tenement
where he lives to a police van driven by two white
policemen, revealing the potential for violence in all of
them. There is no overt political commentary in the
novel: there is no necessity for one. What is clear is
that without fair work, the just rule of law, decent
shelter, and the ability of people to look out for one

another, there can be no communal life and no human happiness.

Wall of the Plague, The (1984). A novel by André *Brink. Using cross-references with other 'plague literature', Brink engages in this novel with the metaphor of disease and the body politic to explore links between responses of people in medieval Europe to the plague and the *apartheid system in South Africa. The act of writing is linked with the walls built in a futile attempt to keep out the plague, yet the novel implies that writing can ultimately be seen as a legitimate form of political action. The narration itself raises the question of authorship and authority, as the male narrator appropriates the voice of his female subject, Andrea, an expatriate 'Cape coloured' (mixed race) woman who initially appears to be the one telling the story. Although often described by critics as clumsy and obvious, the plague metaphor can be seen to operate on a number of more subtle levels. The plot involves the increasing politicization of Andrea via her relationship with Mandla, an exiled black activist. After his murder she decides to return to South Africa to reclaim her identity.

WANGUSA, Timothy (1942-), Ugandan poet and novelist, was born in Bugisu, in eastern Uganda, studied English at Makerere University and the University of Leeds, UK, and has been Professor of Literature at Makerere as well an an administrator there and in the Ministry of Education. His collection of poems *Salutations: Poems 1965-1975* (1977), reissued with additional poems as *A Pattern of Dust: Selected Poems 1965-1990* (1994), reflects his rural origins. *Upon This Mountain* (1989), a novel, tells the story of Mwambu, who is determined to touch heaven, with a poetic lyricism that makes Mwambu's journey towards adulthood compelling. The novel combines African folktale and proverbs with Christian symbolism, reflecting Wangusa's profoundly felt Christian values.

WAR LITERATURE

East Africa: Perhaps as a result of a strongly Eurocentric bias in East African historiography, East African literature has been preoccupied with history. Most East African literary works that deal with history have as their subject matter the anti-colonial struggle, and some early publications belong equally to historiography and literature; memoirs, autobiography, and similar writings published by nationalist leaders soon after independence illuminate from different angles national liberation struggles. Such texts include, for example, Jomo Kenyatta's *Suffering without Bitterness* (1967), Julius Nyerere's *Uhuru na Umoja/Freedom and Unity* (1967), and Mutesa II, Kabaka of Buganda's *Desecration of My Kingdom* (1967). This category of writing also includes documentary reports written by partici-

pants in the liberation movement, particularly those involved in the events of the Mau Mau uprising of the 1950s in Kenya. Two examples are Waruhiu Itote's *'Mau Mau' General* (1967) and Gakaara wa Wanjau's *Mau Mau Author in Detention* (1988), which in the *Gikuyu original won the 1984 Noma Award. Two autobiographical works that come closer to fiction also refer to the Mau Mau, the great historical theme of most Kenyan writers: Muga Gakaru's *Land of Sunshine* (1958) ends with the outbreak of the uprising, and Mugo Gatheru's *Child of Two Worlds* (1964) shows the author persecuted as a student abroad because of his suspected political links. A third, Charity *Waciuma's *Daughter of Mumbi* (1969), covers a decade-and-a-half of colonialism, concentrating on the years of the emergency, which bring fear, humiliation, and division among the people.

Works of fiction proper differ in their historicity. Those whose aim is to re-create the general spirit of the time and to convey an impression of the military situation operate relatively freely with the historical material. Such are Godwin *Wachira's novel *Ordeal in the Forest* (1967), Meja *Mwangi's *Carcase for Hounds* (1974) and *Taste of Death* (1975), Muthoni *Likimani's *Passbook Number F. 47927: Women and Mau Mau in Kenya* (1985), Kenneth *Watene's play *My Son for My Freedom* (1973), and Micere Githae *Mugo's *The Long Illness of Ex-Chief Kiti* (1976). A stricter adherence to historical fact is evident in works that focus on concrete historical events or personalities. *Ngugi wa Thiong'o and Micere Mugo conducted research for their play *The *Trial of Dedan Kimathi* (1976), as did Samuel *Kahiga for his novel *Dedan Kimathi: The Real Story* (1990). Kenneth *Watene's play *Dedan Kimathi* (1974), however, demonstrates a different approach to dealing with the factual. The playwright's handling of his hero stems from a reality in which the historical and the legendary figures were almost indistinguishable in the minds of people.

Outside Kenya, episodes parallel to Mau Mau have inspired similar responses. Resistance to foreign invasion became a literary subject in the *utenzi* of Swahili literature. Some of these poems, though less well known, were written much earlier than their counterparts, in terms of historical content, in Kenya, and are of high literary value. Among them are Mwenyi Shomari bin Mwenyi Kambi's *Kufa kwa Mkwawa* [The death of Mkwawa] (1918), Abdul Karim bin Jamaliddini's *Utenzi wa Vita vya Maji-Maji* [A poem about the Maji-Maji war] (1957), Hemedi bin Abdallah bin Said Bin Abdalla bin Masudi el Buhry's *Utenzi wa Vita vya Wadachi kutamalaki Mrima 1307 A.H.* [A poem about the conquest of the East African coast by the Germans, 1891] (1971). Tanzanian playwright Ebrahim N. Hussein's play *Kinjeketile* (trans. 1970) is also set during the Maji-Maji anti-colonial uprising of 1905-7 in German East Africa. Tanzanian Ismael *Mbise's *Blood on Our*

Land (1974), which depicts an epoch that extends from 1896 to 1951, represents the first encounter of the Wameru with white settlers, the evolution of the colonial system, the growth of a peasant resistance movement, and the eviction of the people of Engare Nanyuki from their ancestral lands by the British government.

Important events in the post-colonial era are the subject matter of novels such as Robert *Serumaga's *Return to the Shadows* (1969), which gives a fictional account of the 1966 armed conflict in Uganda between the forces of the Kabaka of Buganda and those of President Milton Obote. Another is John *Nagenda's The *Seasons of Thomas Tebo* (1986), in the imaginary setting of which readers can recognize Uganda during the violent days of Idi Amin and the second presidency of Obote. For Marjorie Oludhe Macgoye and M.G. *Vassanji history is the reality against which, and as part of which, the life stories of their characters unfold. In *Coming to Birth* (1986) Macgoye skilfully merges the story of a raw peasant girl's development into a mature, self-reliant woman with that of the evolution of the Kenyan nation through the painful experiences of the emergency, the heady days of independence, and the subsequent struggle for power. *The Present Moment* (1987) and *Homing In* (1994), both of which employ the reminiscences of characters as the main tool of narration, reconstruct personal pasts and a national history that ranges from the early years of this century up to the present. Vassanji's characters in *The *Gunny Sack* (1989) and *The *Book of Secrets* (1994) purposefully search for a past and discover that the individual's past and that of his community are intertwined with the history of the whole country, and that the past never ends but is transformed in the present.

The author who has been most consistently concerned with history in East African literature is Ngugi wa Thiong'o. His first three novels, *Weep Not, Child* (1964), *The *River Between* (1965), and *A *Grain of Wheat* (1967), examine a past stretching from the anti-colonial resistance and death of the nationalist hero Waiyaki in the early 1890s, through Harry Thuku's campaign against colonial restrictions in 1921-1922, the controversy over female circumcision that came to a climax in 1929 and led to the setting up of Gikuyu independent schools, through the Mau Mau emergency, and up to the moment of independence. In these books Ngugi handles history with a sense of national commitment and a broad humanistic concern, subordinating historical concreteness and chronological accuracy to an idea of a people's history. In contrast, *Petals of Blood* (1975), dense with allusions to historical personages and events, moves in a panoramic manner to the distant, legendary past and to the African diaspora with a heightened awareness of history that has changed the aesthetics of his fiction.

The novel reads in parts like historical non-fiction, with pointed historical disquisitions that challenge the imperialist version of Kenya's history perpetuated by neo-colonialist professional historians.

The reaction of East African historians to literary treatments of history and conflict has been varied. Some, including N. Gatheru Wanjohi and Frank Furedi, have referred, for example, to Ngugi's novels for illustration of their theses. The predominant attitude, however, has been one of criticism and dismissal of literary writers as mythologizers and ideologues.

South Africa: Three wars in particular have produced South African writing of significance: the *Anglo-Boer war of 1899-1902, the Second World War, and the anti-*apartheid conflict of the 1970s and 80s. The Anglo-Boer war was the first major conflict to stimulate a significant literary response. Wide public interest in England created a ready market for war novels, in the main popular and superficial descriptions of some aspect of the campaign. *The Dop Doctor* (1910) by Richard Dehan (pseudonym for Clothilde Graves), although over-romanticized, gives some indication of the brutal reality of the war. Deneys Reitz's *Commando* (1929) is generally regarded as the most significant literary achievement of the period. Reitz's father had been a member of the Transvaal government during the war, and Reitz fought with the Boers from the age of seventeen, taking part in the commando raid into the Cape Colony led by General J.C. Smuts. *Commando* is an enthusiastic and vivid account of Reitz's experiences in the campaign. Other books that accurately reflect the Anglo-Boer war experience and have come to be regarded as classics are Sol T. *Plaatje's The *Mafeking Diary of Sol T. Plaatje* (1973; 1999) and Douglas *Blackburn's *A Burgher Quixote* (1903). Plaatje's book gives a unique view of the war from the perspective of a black person, while Blackburn's satirical novel strips away pretensions of honour and dignity both from the Boers and their British adversaries. Other accounts of the war are Edgar Wallace's *Unofficial Dispatches of the Anglo Boer War* (1901), Winston Churchill's *Young Winston's Wars* (1972) and Robert Baden-Powell's *Sketches in Mafeking and East Africa* (1907).

While the First World War produced little that is noteworthy, the Second World War inspired a number of new South African poets. Guy *Butler's collection *Stranger to Europe* (1952) typifies the effect that exposure to an international culture had on South African writers: it elicited a new sense of identity in artists who until then had considered themselves part of the European literary tradition. The poems and short stories of Uys Krige (for example *The Dream and the Desert*, 1953) reveal a similar sense of the discovery of a unique South African identity. Other notable poets of this period were Anthony Delius and F.T.

Prince. In the field of drama, the South African Department of Defence financed theatre entertainment, for example Arthur Ashdown's *Squadron X*, which toured South Africa in 1943. Madeleine Masson's plays *Passport to Limbo* (1942) and *Home Is the Hero* (1944) are further examples in the same genre.

From 1972, the South African Defence Force was involved externally in a war on the Namibia-Angola border against SWAPO, the South West African People's Organization, and in the townships in an undeclared civil war against the ANC, the African National Congress. The internal conflict reached a climax in the government's declaration of a state of emergency in 1986. These conflicts essentially constituted one war: a liberation struggle against the forces of apartheid. Literature of the time reflects a polarized apartheid society.

If this definition of war is used, virtually all the black South African writers of the 1970s and 1980s have to be seen as writing 'war literature' – especially when, as is frequently the case, novels, stories, poems, and plays deal with the experience of activists, or even 'innocent civilians', in potentially violent conflict with the state. Among the works which deal specifically with the guerilla war waged by the ANC and its allies, Mongane *Serote's *To Every Birth Its Blood* is probably the most faithful to the actual experiences of combatants at the time. The plays of Zakes *Mda in *We Shall Sing for the Fatherland and Other Plays* (1980) also explore the ambience of the war from the perspective of combatants, bringing out both its forceful necessity and the sacrifices it exacts from ordinary people who are caught in its labyrinth.

In some popular fiction by white writers, the border war provides a background to an unquestioning endorsement of the apartheid regime's negative stereotype of the liberation guerilla fighters as terrorists, while white soldiers are cast as heroes. An example is *The Exile* (1984) by Peter Essex. More reflective and honest accounts of the white experience of the war can be found in the anthology *Forces' Favourites* (1987). A successful fictionalized account of a guerilla fighter's experience is *Muzukuru: A Guerilla's Story* by Paul Hotz (1990).

Many South African novelists and playwrights have dealt directly or tangentially with the liberation war in their work, because apartheid was the common backdrop to South African life at this time; well-known examples include Nadine *Gordimer's *Burger's Daughter* (1979) and *July's People* (1981), as well as several of her stories, André *Brink's *A *Dry White Season* (1979) and J.M. *Coetzee's *Life & Times of Michael K.* (1983). International isolation and the effects of official *censorship and disinformation on writers themselves produced a recurring theme of white South Africans being under siege. Athol *Fugard's play *Playland* (1992), set in the final hours of the last decade of apartheid, depicts a symbolic encounter between a young white soldier recently returned from the border and a black nightwatchman. The action of the play reveals the soldier's remorse over his part in the killing of guerillas in Angola, and that of the nightwatchman, who has the murder of a white man on his conscience. In confronting the violence in their past lives, these representatives of the two sides of the liberation struggle seek a type of mutual redemption at the dawn of the post-apartheid 1990s.

South-Central Africa: The Zimbabwean war of liberation fought against the white Rhodesian regime lasted in its active military phase from 1972-1980. Written in England in 1977, Stanley *Nyamfukudza's *The Non-Believer's Journey* (1980), the first novel about the war, is marked by a pronounced scepticism towards the nationalist armed struggle. The euphoria of independence (April 1980) elicited a few idealized depictions of the freedom fighters and the just war they had fought, for example Edmund *Chipamaunga's *A Fighter for Freedom* (1983), Garikai Mutasa's *The Contact* (1985), and Spencer Tizora's *Crossroads* (1985). The anthology *And Now the Poets Speak* (1981) recorded the tribulations of the Zimbabwean people during the war and the hope for a future of peace and equality. A similar focus characterizes Chenjerai *Hove's war poetry.

A critical discourse about the war emerged from the political disillusionment that began in the mid-1980s. Ex-combatant writers Alexander Kanengoni and Isheunesu Mazorodze expose in their novels the opportunistic motives of some guerilla leaders. Younger writers such as Batisai Parwada in his often surrealistic short stories *Shreds of Darkness* (1987) and Gonzo Musengezi in his *Shona novel *Zvairwadza Vasara* [It hurts the survivors] reflect the traumatic effects of the war on the psyche of children. Dambudzo *Marechera's 'The Concentration Camp' (published posthumously as part of *Scrapiron Blues*, 1994) mirrors the emotional and physical trauma of the inhabitants of the restricted villages ('keeps') in which the Rhodesian army kept segments of the black population. In Hove's two novels *Bones* (1988) and *Shadows* (1991) the war serves as a backdrop and the characters are depicted as its victims.

The question of war and gender was first taken up by female ex-combatant Freedom *Nyamubaya. In her collection of poetry *On the Road Again* (1986) Nyamubaya deplores the war's failure to change the patriarchal structure of Zimbabwean society. *Mothers of the Revolution* (1990), a collection of interviews by Irene Staunton, illustrates women's support of the liberation war and their brutalization by both sides. A women's perspective on the war also dominates Yvonne *Vera's collection of short stories *Why Don't You Carve Other Animals?* (1992).

In Shimmer *Chinodya's war epic *Harvest of Thorns* (1989) as well as Charles Samupindi's novel *Pawns* (1992) the guerillas themselves are seen as victims who are psychologically damaged by the war. The fragmented narrative and absence of an authorial voice in these novels reflect the corrosion of a unified vision of national history.

Three novels by white Zimbabwean authors complement the black literary discourse on the war: Tim McLoughlin's *Karima* (1985), Bruce Moore-King's *White Man Black War* (1988), and Angus Shaw's *Kandaya: Another Time, Another Place* (1993). These books testify to the identity conflicts of white soldiers and officials fighting for the values of a society in which they no longer believe.

West Africa: Much of modern West African literature is a product of war. Guinea-Bissau's liberation war (1950s to 1974) released the poet in guerilla leader Amilcar Cabral. The Second World War features in Cyprian *Ekwensi's fiction ('Land of Sani' and 'Deserter's Dupe', 1947) and in Wole *Soyinka's drama (*Death and the King's Horseman*, (1975). None, however, has generated as much literature as the *Nigeria-Biafra war (1967-70). These texts cover all genres, though only Soyinka's existentialist *Madmen and Specialists* (1971) and the satirical comedy *Jero's Metamorphosis* (1973) are important dramatic achievements.

Through the activities of the University of Biafra's Odunke Community of Artists and Pro-Afrika's Ruth Bowert, Biafra's first war novel, Victor Uzoma Nwankwo's *The Road to Udima* (*Der weg nach Udima*, 1969) and poetry (Odunke's *Gedichte aus Biafra*, 1969) were published in Germany. Odunke's anthology *Nsukka Harvest* came later (1972). In *Beware, Soul Brother and Other Poems* (1971), Chinua *Achebe explores everyday life in Biafra and the war's historical ramifications. Nearly ten years later came Odia *Ofeimun's *The Poet Lied* (1980), which so scathingly critiques J.P. Clark *Bekederemo's *Casualties* (1970) that for several years Bekederemo gagged it with a libel threat. Soyinka's *Idanre and Other Poems* (1967) and *A Shuttle in the Crypt* (1971) and Christopher *Okigbo's 'Path of Thunder: Poems Prophesying War' (*Labyrinths, with Path of Thunder*, 1971) are the peak of poetic achievement.

Okigbo's death in Biafran military service has transformed him into a quasi-mythical figure who has received poetic tributes from his contemporaries, including a memorial anthology (*Don't Let Him Die*, ed. Chinua Achebe and Dubem Okafor, 1978). His continuing influence, both thematic and stylistic, is seen in Obiora *Udechukwu's *What the Madman Said* (1990).

Like the poetry, the prose explores various themes without showing any radical ideological or technical break with the past. Igbo writers explore such issues as the anti-Igbo pogrom in northern and western Nigeria (the direct cause of Biafra's secession from Nigeria), Biafra's heroism and internal contradictions, the difficulties of post-war rehabilitation, and neo-colonialism. Representative examples are S.O. *Mezu's *Behind the Rising Sun* (1970), Chinua Achebe's *Girls at War and Other Stories* (1972), I.N.C. *Aniebo's *The Anonymity of Sacrifice* (1974), John *Munonye's *A Wreath for the Maidens* (1973), Flora *Nwapa's *Never Again* (1975), Buchi *Emecheta's *Destination Biafra* (1982), and Ekwensi's *Survive the Peace* (1976) and *Divided We Stand* (1980). Ossie *Enekwe's *Come Thunder* (1984) is a *bildungsroman* in the manner of Stephen Crane's *The Red Badge of Courage*.

Of fiction written by non-Biafrans, Kole *Omotoso's allegorical *The Combat* (1972) and Festus *Iyayi's *Heroes* (1986) interpret the conflict in marxist terms, while Soyinka's *Season of Anomy* (1973) explores it through *Yoruba and Graeco-Asiatic mythology. Isidore *Okpewho's starkly realistic *The Last Duty* (1976) foregrounds the tragedy of people trapped between the combatants.

Contrary to prevailing criticism, the war literature does not represent a radically new artistic or *political consciousness. Writers have simply interpreted the raw experience, war, through the ideologies they already hold, which are products of the same neo-colonialist forces that led to the war itself.

WATENE, Kenneth (1944-), Kenyan playwright, was born in Central Province, Kenya and is a graduate of the National Theatre Drama School. He has contributed prose and poetry to *Ghala* magazine, he wrote articles for *Kenya Weekly News* in 1966, and he was a commentator on theatre for the *Daily Nation* in 1969. He has long since left the literary world and gone into business.

Watene's most important plays, *My Son for My Freedom* (1973) and *Dedan Kimathi* (1974), deal with the Mau Mau anti-colonial movement. The latter occupies a special place among Kenyan literary texts concerned with history, having ventured to look critically at an almost canonized national hero. This approach has not, however, distorted the dramatist's sense of measure, and the character that emerges illustrates an alternative, though not necessarily a more soundly proved, view of leadership and liberation struggle. *Sunset on the Manyatta* (1974) explores the themes of a young man's quest for fulfilment and a restored sense of completeness in a life disrupted by foreign education and culture.

WATSON, Stephen (1954-), South African poet, teaches English at the University of Cape Town. His poetry collections include *Poems 1977-1982* (1983), *In This City* (1986), *Cape Town Days* (1989), *Return of the*

Moon (1991), and *Presence of the Earth* (1995). He has also published a collection of essays, *Selected Essays: 1980-1990* (1990). He is an intensely regional poet in that he returns again and again in his poetry to Cape Town, the city in which he has lived most of his life. The view of Cape Town that he offers is, however, one that emphatically refuses the popular perception of the city as a tourist's delight, a bountiful place of sunshine, beach, mountain, and vineyard. Instead, Watson's Cape Town is a city of cold, mist, and rain. It is its sombreness, for the most part, that he traces. The personae who contend with this environment or flit through it tend to partake of this mood of disappointment or, at best, muted hope. A sad lyricism, a kind of curdled romanticism, runs through his work. In *Return of the Moon*, subtitled 'Versions from the /Xam', he draws on archival material, transcribed in the early years of the century by linguists who sought to record and preserve the culture of the /Xam (or Cape ★Bushmen). The poems are not translations: they seek to capture, instead, the essence of the vanished world of the /Xam. Watson is also a prominent critic and polemicist best known for his analysis of contemporary South African literature.

Weep Not, Child (1964), ★Ngugi's prize-winning novel, the first published in English by an East African. It tells the story of events leading up to, and the first years of, the Emergency situation in Kenya (Mau Mau) and their effects on the family of Ngotho as these are seen and experienced by Njoroge, Ngotho's youngest son. Njoroge believes he has a mission to serve his people and lead them to their enlightenment in the independence period, a belief inspired by the speeches of Kenyatta and fostered by his faith in Christian education. The novel describes Njorogo's progressive disaffection, leading through disillusionment to an eventual unsuccessful suicide attempt.

Njoroge's life is set against a complex pattern of relationships which affect the dramatic and tragic outcome of the novel. Njoroge's father, Ngotho, who served the British in the First World War, works as a *muhoi* (a bonded worker) on his own hereditary Kikuyu land, now owned by the white colonist Howlands and placed in the control of Jacobo who collaborates with the colonialist regimes.

As the Emergency develops Boro, Njoroge's older brother who has served the British in the Second World War (and seen his brother Kamau killed) joins the freedom fighters and kills Jacobo. Ngotho attempts to take the blame for his son, is tortured and dies. Boro then kills Howlands (who ironically has never attempted to understand the Kikuyu feeling for the land). Njoroge is tortured (castration is suggested) in turn by the white colonialists, expelled from the European school and in the end accepts work as a clerk in an Indian *duka*. His dream destroyed, in the end

Njoroge attempts suicide but is saved by his mother.

Ngugi's concern here, as in his subsequent novels, is Kikuyu preoccupations with ownership of the land as described in the Kikuyu founding religious myths in the legends of Mugo wa Kibiro and Mumbi. He is exploring parallels between Kikuyu and Christian founding legends, parallels which make the young Njoroge believe a Christian education can act as an agent for reconciliation between the races.

WERE, Miriam (1940-), Kenyan novelist and biographer. Born to a devoutly Christian family in Lugola, Kakamega District of northern Kenya, Were took degrees in the humanities and education at the universities of Pennsylvania (Philadelphia, USA) and Makerere (Kampala, Uganda), respectively, before training as a physician at the University of Nairobi, where she is a professor of community health. She represented Kenya at the 1985 UN Decade of Women Conference at Nairobi.

Were's novels, mostly published as secondary school readers by the East African Publishing House, deal with the familiar post-colonial theme of conflict between European and indigenous African ways of life. *The Boy in Between* (1969) and *High School Gent* (1969) are *Bildungsromane* that portray the struggles of an ambitious Kenyan boy. In *The Eighth Wife* (1972), the heroine, Kalimonje, marries a young war hero, Shalimba, resisting the lure of becoming the eighth wife of a chief who competes for her love with his own eldest son. Inter-ethnic marriage provides the major conflict in *Your Heart Is Your Altar* (1984). Were also wrote the biography of a nurse, Margaret Owanyoni, in *The Nurse with a Song* (1978).

WHALEY, Andrew (1958-), playwright, was born in Harare, Zimbabwe, and educated at Sir John Kennedy Primary in Kadoma and Prince Edward High School in Harare. He studied English literature at Bristol University, UK, and has since then written and directed plays for both stage and screen. His first play, *Platform 5* (1987), underscored the plight of street children when the Zimbabwe government dispersed them in order to host conference delegates of the Non-aligned Movement in 1986. *Platform 5* won a prize as the best new play and the best production during the 1987 Zimbabwe National Theatre Festival and was staged later that year at the Edinburgh Cultural Festival. *The Nyoka Tree* (1988), cast in the form of a fable, interrogates the semi-feudal relations of colonial Rhodesia, mockingly dubbed Paradise. *Chef's Breakfast* (1989) systematically underlines how the politically powerful betray their former ideals, their erstwhile comrades in war, as well as their own relatives. The play was inspired by the Sandura Commission, which investigated corruption in government circles in Zimbabwe in the late 1980s. *The Rise and Shine of Comrade*

Fiasco (1991) again dramatizes how ideals of the liberation struggle and the reality of post-independent Zimbabwe collide. The drama centres on an investigation of the past and the self in a context of disillusionment. The bold and original conception of the play, as well as its mixture of hilarity and seriousness, earned it the First Fringe Award during the 1990 Edinburgh Festival. In all the plays Whaley insists on the minimum number of characters, bare or rudimentary stagecraft, and choreography almost in the Samuel Beckett style. For him theatre is a social tool with which to raise questions and underline issues, however discomforting they may be.

WHEATLEY, Phillis (*ca.*1753–84), poet, the first black writer to publish a volume of poems, was taken from Africa to Boston in 1761 and became the slave of the Wheatley family. Frail but highly gifted, she made phenomenal progress in learning English and Latin. She became familiar with the Bible and the classics, which inspired her poetic imagination. She was the unofficial poet laureate of the Boston elite and addressed verses of sympathy and consolation to bereaved friends and families. Her first published poem, 'On the Death of George Whitefield' (1770), was an immediate success. She also addressed poems to King George III (1768), William Legge, the Earl of Dartmouth (1772), and George Washington (1775). In 1773, she visited England and published her *Poems on Various Subjects, Religious and Moral*. Wheatley has survived negative criticism, exemplified by Thomas Jefferson's laconic dismissal of her poetry as 'beneath the dignity of criticism' (1782) and J.S. Redding's (1939) censure of 'the negative, bloodless, unracial quality' of her poems. A fair assessment may be critical of her neoclassical and patriotic pretensions but it cannot ignore the fact that she was at heart an African; her work is one of the first examples of ★African-American literature. An anonymous volume of her poems and memoir appeared in 1834, and Charles Deane printed *The Letters of Phillis Wheatley* (1864). Collections of her work include Charles F. Heartman's *Poems and Letters* (1915) and Julian Mason's *Poems* (1966).

When Sunset Comes to Sapitwa (1980) Poems by Felix ★Mnthali. Only the second collection to be published by a Malawian poet (the first was Frank ★Chipasula's ★*Visions and Reflections*), it contains carefully crafted verse. With its pervading integrity, its celebration of life in the face of suffering, and its stoicism and dignity, it is an example of how Malawian writing at its best during the Banda period acted as a powerful moral counterstatement to the evil of the ruling regime.

Why Are We So Blest? (1972) A novel by Ayi Kwei ★Armah. Modin, a Ghanaian student, is bitterly disappointed with the supposed blessedness offered by

his scholarship at a university in the USA. The Eurocentric intellectual aridity he encounters, coupled with his sexual relationships with white women whom he mistakes for friends, cannot satisfy his craving for a revolutionary commitment to Africa. His latest girlfriend Aimée is self-centred and destructive towards both Modin and her African studies, thus embodying the typical Euro-American attitude to the African continent. They move together to North Africa, where they meet the translator Solo, formerly involved in the independence war of his African country, now living through a profoundly disillusioned exile. Solo is annoyed at Aimée's lip-service to the African revolution and feels sympathy for Modin. The latter is the victim of a gruesome assassination by some French soldiers, who also rape Aimée. The novel alternates narrations by all three characters, through Solo's reflections and extracts from the couple's notebooks.

WICOMB, Zoë (1949–), South African novelist and critic, grew up in rural Cape Province and studied English literature at the University of the Western Cape (BA 1968). In 1973 she left for exile in the UK, where she continued to study English literature and earned a master's degree (Strathclyde University, 1989). A founding editor of the *Southern Africa Review of Books*, she has taught literature, women's studies, and literary linguistics in South Africa and Britain, and she has served as writer-in-residence at Glasgow and Strathclyde universities.

A complex, dry irony characterizes Wicomb's single book-length fiction (★*You Can't Get Lost in Cape Town*, 1987), two stories in anthologies (1990, 1991), and twelve critical essays (1988–94), in accord with her demand that literature address power and its complexities. Whether writing fiction or analysing a family-planning advertisement, Wicomb insistently interrogates South African culture past and present; 'Another Story' (1990), for example, creates descendants of a 'coloured' (mixed race) character created by a white South African, Sarah Gertrude ★Millin, in ★*God's Step-Children* (1924). Well received in South Africa, *You Can't Get Lost in Cape Town* positions Wicomb (like Njabulo ★Ndebele) as a post-protest writer committed to democratic ideals, refusing a single ideological stance. Wicomb's own literary/cultural criticism assists in understanding her fiction.

WILHELM, Peter (1943–), South African novelist, poet, and journalist. Born in Cape Town, Wilhelm completed his schooling in the Transvaal, qualified as a teacher, and turned to journalism. He joined the *Financial Mail* in 1974 and has edited *Leadership* magazine, where he has written on the personalities and trends of the South African transition to democratic government.

Many of Wilhelm's novels and short stories reflect

colonial and post-colonial Africa as setting and as stark, lonely, alienated presence. *LM and Other Stories* (1975) comes out of his experiences in pre-independence Mozambique; two other collections of stories and the novel *The Dark Wood* (1977) explore colonialism's legacy of violence and terror. He demonstrates his interest in science fiction in some of the short stories and *Summer's End* (1984), a book for children. *The Mask of Freedom* (1994), a dystopian view of South Africa's destiny, is set in an indeterminate near future in which poverty, population growth, crime, and AIDS have determined social policy in a way that radically limits human freedom. Begun before the transition in South Africa, the novel is not a criticism of either that process or its possible outcome. However, certain underlying factors are seen as immutable, and he opposes to them the values of individual love, compassion, and the search for life's spiritual dimension. Wilhelm's poetry has been collected in *White Flowers* (1977) and *Falling into the Sun* (1993). He has won awards for his writing and reporting, including the Science Fiction Society of South Africa's prize and the Pringle Prize for reviews, and his stories and poems have been widely anthologized.

Will to Die, The (1972) Essays by Can *Themba. These essays appeared in *Drum, Golden City Post,* and other journals in Johannesburg in the 1950s and 60s. Themba could manipulate the English language with astonishing imaginativeness and facility, creating humorous coinages and stunning metaphors. The articles, all written with fast-paced energy and an exact mimicry of unusual speech patterns, deal with black township life in Johannesburg, particularly in Sophiatown, a vital, teeming Mecca for artists, writers, and musicians, later to be razed by the *apartheid regime to make way for a white suburb. The subjects range from his love affair with a white British girl, to accompanying his social worker sister to investigate starvation among black children, to government crackdowns on dissidents and the growth of ANC membership. He writes of the miseries that criminals visit on their own kind and of the daily dangers of having to commute by train from the townships to central Johannesburg. Particularly saddening are 'Requiem for Sophiatown' and his memorial to Nat *Nakasa, 'The Boy with the Tennis Racquet'. In 'The Suit', the most disturbing of the short stories, a man comes home early to find his wife in bed with another man, who hastily decamps in his underwear, leaving behind his suit. From then until his wife's suicide, the man insists that the suit accompany them everywhere, sit at table with them, and even be present at one of their parties. *The Will to Die* also includes Lewis *Nkosi's obituary for Can *Themba.

WILLIAMS, Adebayo (1951-), novelist and jour-

nalist, was born in Gbongan, Oyo State, Nigeria and received his post-secondary education (BA, 1975; MA, 1979; Ph.D., 1983) at the University of Ife (now Obafemi Awolowo University), where he also taught for many years. He lives in Birmingham, UK.

Williams wrote his first novel, *The Year of the Locusts,* while he was a teacher at the Federal Government College in Kaduna in 1978, but the manuscript was misplaced. When it was finally published it won the Association of Nigerian Authors (ANA) literary award in 1988. His second novel, *The Remains of the Last Emperor* (1994), was a joint winner of the 1995 ANA-Spectrum prize for prose fiction.

Williams is also a prolific literary and social critic whose scholarly articles have appeared in many prominent periodicals, including *Research in African Literatures, Présence africaine, Okike,* and *Africa Quarterly.* He has been a columnist for *Newswatch* (1985-91) and *African Concord* (1992) and an editor-at-large for *Africa Today* (since 1995), and he won the 1994 Diamond Award for Excellence in Journalism.

Witch-Herbalist of the Remote Town, The (1981) A novel by Amos *Tutuola. The source of this adventure is a tale about the *Yoruba trickster Ajapa, the tortoise. The hero journeys to the remote town to procure an antidote for his wife's barrenness from the witch-herbalist. Accompanied by his disembodied first, second, and third minds, he overcomes assorted adversaries along the way, all reminiscent of the weird and grotesque creatures that have become a Tutuola trademark. Having received the medicine from the most Christian witch-herbalist, he disobeys the injunction not to eat any of it and becomes pregnant. An undersea goddess relieves him in the end .

WOMEN IN LITERATURE
East Africa: *Feminism, understood as a concern with women, a probing into and representation of women's experience in literature, has been characteristic of East African creative writing from its beginning, preoccupying both male and female writers. While some works are entirely feminist in orientation, in most feminism constitutes an aspect of the many-faceted presentation of society, reflecting a view that women's issues are not separate from society's issues. In their exploration of women's position in society, East African writers lament the reduction of women's role to procreation and child rearing, which limits the realization of their potential. Nyapol, in Grace *Ogot's *The Promised Land* (1966), feels that 'marriage is a form of imprisonment'. Any attempt to venture beyond the established confines meets with opposition and rejection, as young Wairimu in Marjorie Oludhe Macgoye's *The Present Moment* (1987) discovers. Ogot's short stories 'The Middle Door' and 'Elizabeth' suggest that although modernization of traditional

society provides opportunities, especially for city women, old masculine attitudes continue, often in the form of sexist abuse.

East African feminist writing, however, asserts above all the indomitable will of women to participate fully in the life of their societies, led by their creativity and confidence in their own worth. Understandably, writers have focused on the best-known instances of such participation. *Ngugi wa Thiong'o and Micere *Mugo in The *Trial of Dedan Kimathi (1976), Ngugi in Petals of Blood (1977), and Muthoni *Likimani in Passbook Number F. 47927: Women and Mau Mau in Kenya (1985) are concerned with women's contribution to the anti-colonial movement. In Kenya Women Heroes and Their Mystical Power (1984) Rebeka *Njau searches history for stories of women of special merit. The heroines of Leonard *Kibera's Voices in the Dark (1970), Ngugi's *Devil on the Cross (1982) and *Matigari (1986), and John *Nagenda's The *Seasons of Thomas Tebo (1986) are involved in the struggle for justice during the independence era.

Others have written more generally about the undefeatable women of Africa. Asenath Odaga's The Shade Changes (1984), Marjorie Macgoye's Coming to Birth (1986), The Present Moment, and Homing In (1994), and Margaret Ogola's The River and the Source (1994) celebrate women's courage, dignity, intelligence, emotional depth, and inexhaustible capacity and thirst for growth. Ngugi's A *Grain of Wheat (1967), Peter *Palangyo's Dying in the Sun (1969), Samuel Kahiga's The Girl from Abroad (1974), and Rebeka Njau's *Ripples in the Pool (1975) portray women with complex characters whose actions are difficult to predict and yearnings hard to fathom. Also of interest is the recurrent image of the prostitute. In most cases she is seen as a victim, either of adverse material conditions in an unjust society (Ngugi's Petals of Blood) or of a forced marriage from which she desperately tries to escape, for example in Marjorie Macgoye's Murder in Majengo (1972).

Lastly, some texts are more intentionally feminist. Muthoni Likimani in What Does a Man Want? (1974), W.E. Mkufya in The Dilemma (1982), and Grace Ogot in 'The Other Woman' highlight the difficulties of establishing a satisfying heterosexual relationship. Agoro *Anduru in 'The Empty Heart', 'Loyalty to My Friend', and 'This Is Living' demonstrates the destructiveness of misconceived ideas about emancipation. Another examples of writing based on such misconceptions is Wanjira Muthoni's short story 'Why God Created Woman'. East African feminist writers have made a genuine contribution to literature and to the elucidation of some important issues affecting society.

South Africa: Before colonialism and the arrival of the written word in South Africa, many black women participated in the oral traditions of different ethnic groups. Contrary to conventional views about women's total exclusion from the public space, recent research shows that women played active roles in producing and performing these oral forms, and their relation to oral traditions shapes their status in contemporary literary practices. Oral performance was, however, emphatically male-centred in the region that came to be known as South Africa, and the male bias in pre-colonial South African literature continued into the period of literate culture. Black women, marginalized by gender and race from literary production, have therefore battled towards voice against multiple forms of oppression in a racist society where language, access to literary resources, literary standards, and available publishing outlets have been Western-, white-, and male-dominated.

Publication opportunities have played a considerable role in black women's writing. Although white patrons and publishers encouraged black men's writing from the early nineteenth century, not until the 1970s and 80s did prose fiction, journalism, and poetry by black women begin to appear, often strongly influenced by male protest traditions. The short-lived black women's publishing house Seriti Se Sechaba attempted to cultivate independent black women's writing in the 1980s, but its brief existence indicates the marginalization of black women's literary activity. In recent years, international and white-controlled publishers have shown considerable interest in black women's writing, an interest indicated by the recent upsurge of published autobiographies. Yet even when the publishing world is receptive to the voices and self-narratives of black women, it can inhibit more experimental and independent forms of creative expression.

During the late nineteenth and early twentieth centuries a handful of mission-educated black women were, like Daisy Makiwane, peripherally involved in journalism and an emerging black press, often producing columns and articles for a youthful readership both in the vernaculars and in English. During the 'Drum decade' (named after *Drum magazine) of the 1950s, however, black women journalists usually wrote minor pieces, their authority as writers undermined by the subjects they were commissioned to write. The dilemma of black women journalists in the vibrant although heavily androcentric world of black journalism is captured in Bessie *Head's novella The Cardinals.

Head was in fact the only woman writer who made a successful transition from journalism to creative writing. More recently black women journalists like Nomavenda Mathiane, whose selected writings are published as Beyond the Headlines: Truths of Soweto Life (1990), have found outlets for serious reporting, refreshingly approaching political events from perspectives influenced by their gendered status.

The short story has been a favoured genre for black women writers. Limited by lack of time and opportunity to write and marginalized by the publishing industry, black women writers have often produced short fiction, which since the early 1970s has been published in such popular and protest-oriented magazines as *Staffrider* and in anthologies like *Forced Landing* (1980). By the mid-1980s, a growing international feminist publishing industry, the proliferation of feminist literary theory, and interest in women's writing had led to black women's short stories appearing in such anthologies as *Unwinding Threads: Writing by Women in Africa* (1983), *Sometimes When It Rains: Writings by South African Women* (1987), edited by Ann Oosthuizen, *From the Heart* (1988), *Like a House on Fire* (1994), and *Raising the Blinds: A Century of South African Women's Stories* (1990), edited by Annemarie van Niekerk. Many black women's short stories followed the models of protest writing used by black male writers. Examples here would include Miriam *Tlali in *Footprints in the Quag* (1989) and Farida *Karodia in *Coming Home and Other Stories* (1988). A writer like Jayapraga Reddy (*On the Fringe of Dreamtime and Other Stories*, 1987) avoids the overtly political themes of Tlali and Karodia with her treatment of 'ordinary' lives. Other writers such as Zoë *Wicomb (*You Can't Get Lost in Cape Town*, 1987), Gladys *Thomas (in *Raising the Blinds*), Gcina *Mhlophe (in *Raising the Blinds* and *Sometimes When It Rains*), and Bessie Head (*The *Collector of Treasures*, 1977), have explicitly engaged with the intersection of gender and racial oppression; they represent relationships and interiority in ways that mark a shift from conventional social realism and the literary model that influenced women writers who are often considered more politically committed.

South African drama, especially at the height of 'resistance culture', has often been experimental, developing through workshops and allowing actors the opportunity to collaborate in directing and writing. The role of women in this process has been mainly as actors, rather than as dramatists or directors, but women actors have been co-authors in productions for which male dramatists have received international recognition. An interesting example is *Sarafina!* (1987) (written and produced by Mbongeni *Ngema), in which Leleti Khumalo played the central role. Black female dramatists who have received acclaim and worked independently are Fatima Dike (*The First South African*, 1979) and Gcina *Mhlophe (*Have You Seen Zandile?*, 1988).

A significant body of black women's written and published poetry emerged only in the 1970s, much of it reflecting the imperatives of national liberation and anti-apartheid protest. Often positioned as supporters in ancillary roles in the struggles against *apartheid,

many women poets consequently celebrated the figure of the strong black woman as mother (see, for example, *Breaking the Silence: A Century of South African Women's Poetry*, 1990). While this celebration seems to endorse male-centred struggles, women poets like Gcina Mhlophe, Gladys *Thomas, and Jennifer Davids (in *Raising the Blinds*) subtly introduce unique and often subversive elements into their representation of gender politics. The subversive strain in women's poetry has increased since the mid-1980s, with the emphasis on gender within the national liberation movement. Anthologies like *Siren Songs* (1989), *Breaking the Silence*, and Sobhna Poona's *In Search of Rainbows* (1990) point to the interest in feminist-oriented black women's poetry.

Although novels by black men flourished during the 1950s when there was a market for black writing, women's production of novels came erratically and in spurts: Ansuyah R. Singh (*Behold the Earth Mourns*, ca.1966) was the first South African of Indian origin to publish a novel in South Africa, yet did not publish further. Of the best-known black women novelists in South Africa, Miriam Tlali, Bessie Head, Farida Karodia, and Lauretta *Ngcobo (*Cross of Gold*, 1988), three have produced their work outside South Africa. Tlali is often considered a *Black Consciousness writer, but her work includes covert representation of women's position of silence and subjection in male-dominated society. Lauretta Ngcobo, along with Farida Karodia, illustrates the dilemmas of writers in exile trying to reclaim a sense of 'home'. Bessie Head, a prolific and idiosyncratic writer, departs interestingly from the perspective of Ngcobo and Karodia. After her move to Botswana, she published novels set in her country of exile, at the same time developing her insight into South Africa and claiming her country of exile as her home. Generally, women's novels are strongly autobiographical, a trend that has led critics to evaluate their works as straightforward documentary representation and to ignore their complex textual strategies.

The first wave of black South African autobiography emerged among men in the 1950s, the only female autobiographer among them Noni *Jabavu (*Drawn in Colour* and *The Ochre People*, 1963). The 1980s provided a receptive climate for black women's autobiographies, with international publishing houses such as Women's Press and local publishers like David Philip and Ravan Press actively seeking black women's literary productions. Most of these publishers encouraged autobiography, registering an international and local interest in documentation of the struggle against apartheid by its victims. While the interest in the 1950s centred around the black male intellectual the interest of the 1980s, largely because of the growing feminist movement, the new visibility of women in the national liberation movement, and the globally popularized interest in the anti-apartheid movement, focused on black women, seemingly the most victimized subjects of apartheid. The autobiographies, written in a mode of appeal and directed at an outside audience, tend to suppress explorations of interiority generally associated with women's writing. This trend is exemplified in Ellen *Kuzwayo's *Call Me Woman (1995), Emma Mashinini's Strikes Have Followed Me All My Life (1989), and Maggie Resha's My Life in the Struggle (1991). Collections of life narratives highlighting the struggles of ordinary black South African women proliferated in the 1980s as well. Examples are included in Belinda Bozzoli and Mmantho Nkotsoe's Women of Phokeng (1991), Jacklyn Cock's Maids and Madams (1980), and Barbara Schreiner's A Snake with Ice Water: Prison Writings of South African Women (1992). Since the beginning of the political changes of the 1990s, a heavily politicized approach has given way to an emphasis on personal and emotional relationships and a questioning of the androcentric legacy of the anti-apartheid movement and protest culture. Sindiwe *Magona's To My Children's Children and Forced to Grow (1992), Phyllis Ntantala's A Life's Mosaic (1992), and Mamphela Ramphele's A Life (1995) reflect the changing tenor of black women's autobiography.

Not only have black and white women writers in South Africa faced very different conditions regarding their racial, social, financial, and political status, but there have been divisions along national lines among white women as a group, particularly in regard to their classification as either English- or Afrikaans-speaking. From the beginning, the work of white women writers has been inscribed by ambivalences and contradictions largely associated with their position as both colonized (by male and national authority) and as colonizers (in their role as white 'madams'). Thus, South African women writers have not until recently been able to form an alliance to fight the gender issue, which has replaced the issue of race as a focus of literary and political attention.

White women's writing in English began in South Africa with the first British women settlers, mostly in the form of journals (such as that kept by Lady Anne Barnard) and letters, but much of it remained unpublished. An early attempt to link race and gender issues from a liberal-humanist perspective is seen in Olive *Schreiner's famous novel The *Story of an African Farm (1883). Schreiner, a committed feminist, believed that distinctions of race and colour were iniquitous and that 'any attempt to base our national life on [such] distinctions...will, after the lapse of many years, prove fatal to us'. While Schreiner advocated a celebration of racial and cultural diversity, Sarah Gertrude *Millin reflected the social Darwinism of her time by representing miscegenation as debasing and morally wrong, leading inevitably to the tainting of racial purity and the degeneration of the races. This idea is particularly

evident in her best-known novel, *God's Step-Children (1924). The novels of Pauline *Smith are South African pastoral romances in which the microcosm of the rural order is seen as a model for social stability. Whereas both Schreiner and Millin dealt directly in their novels with the issue of race, Smith suppresses the issue, focusing instead on an idealizing of rapidly disappearing rural values in her collections of short stories, The *Little Karoo (1925) and The *Beadle (1926). The best-known and most prolific of women novelists in South Africa is Nadine *Gordimer, whose work from the beginning engaged directly with issues of race. She acknowledged the inevitably split position of the white woman writer in an apartheid society, aware of the limitations of her speaking position while at the same time determined to speak out. Awarded the Nobel Prize for Literature in 1991, she also won the Booker Prize for her novel The *Conservationist (1974).

Women writers who left South Africa have still engaged with South African issues in their writing. Daphne Rooke's second novel Mittee (1951), set in the Transvaal before and during the *Anglo–Boer war, became an international bestseller; despite a well-established literary reputation in the 1950s and 60s in South Africa, she is only now being rediscovered. Like Rooke, Rose Zwi lives in Australia but continues to write about South Africa, as in her prize-winning first novel, Another Year in Africa (1980). Sheila *Roberts, who lives and teaches in the USA, has written short stories, novels, and poetry, and her first collection of stories, Outside Life's Feast (1975), was awarded the Olive Schreiner Prize. Among contemporary women writers within South Africa is Sheila *Fugard, who has written in a number of genres. Her first novel, The Castaways (1972), was regarded as technically innovative. Menán *du Plessis has written two well-received novels, A State of Fear (1983) and Longlive! (1989).

Women poets have been notably absent from South African poetry anthologies until recently. Cecily Lockett's Breaking the Silence seeks to redress this imbalance. Notable white women poets include Ruth *Miller, whose work was first published in 1965 and has only recently been collected (Ruth Miller: Poems, Prose, Plays, 1991), and, more recently, Ingrid de Kok, whose Familiar Ground was published in 1988.

Recent anthologies of South African women's writing have included writing in different genres by both black and white women, showing a concern to establish sisterhood. These include LIP from Southern African Women (1983), edited by Susan Brown, Isabel Hofmeyr and Susan Rosenberg and On Shifting Sands: New Art and Literature from South Africa, edited by Kirsten Holst Petersen and Anna Rutherford (1992).

Afrikaans women writers have inevitably been implicated in the nationalist and patriarchal discourses of Afrikanerdom. Elisabeth Eybers, an Afrikaans poet who wrote in the 1930s, was atypical in her challenge to some of these patriarchal stereotypes. The female experience has been a focus for much recent Afrikaans women's writing translated into English, marking its difference from earlier conservative Afrikaans womens' literature. Elsa Joubert, for example, relates a black woman's struggle in *Die swerfjare van Poppie Nongena* (1978; *The Long Journey of Poppie Nongena*, 1980). In her *Expedition to the Baobab Tree* (published in Afrikaans in 1981 and in English, translated by J.M. *Coetzee, in 1983), Wilma Stockenström explores feminist and post-colonial issues. Recent Afrikaans poetry has been dominated by women poets including Ingrid *Jonker, Antjie Krog, and Joan Hambidge. Jeanne Goosen is an Afrikaans writer who has written across the genres, with her novel *Ons is nie almal so nie* (1990) translated into English by André *Brink as *Not All of Us*.

South-Central Africa: As a result of social discrimination and lack of educational opportunity, writing by black Zimbabwean women lagged considerably behind that of men. Lassie Ndondo's *Ndebele novel *Quaphela Ingane* (1962) was the first published work by a black woman in what was then Rhodesia, followed by Jane Chifamba's collection of *Shona folk tales *Ngano dzepasi chigare* (1964). Further writing by women in the vernacular developed in the 1970s with the work by Joyce Simango, the first Shona novelist, and Ndebele novelist and playwright Barbara Makhalisa. Before Zimbabwe's independence in 1980, about ten books by black women were published. Major themes were polygamy, arranged marriages, the degeneration of morals in the cities, and the break-up of families. Since their publications were closely monitored by the colonial Literature Bureau, these authors had to avoid social and political controversy; their texts generally showed a strong Christian morality. After independence the number of women writers increased gradually. In the mid-1980s the first short publications in English appeared: Bertha Msora's play *I Will Wait* (1984), Kristina *Rungano's poetry collection *A Storm Is Brewing* (1984), Barbara Makhalisa's collection of short stories *The Underdog and Other Stories* (1984), and Freedom *Nyamubaya's poems *On the Road Again* (1986). As an ex-guerilla fighter, Nyamubaya deplores the betrayal of the revolutionary goals, especially in gender matters.

The publication of the first novel in English, *Nervous Conditions* by Tsitsi *Dangarembga (1988), was a breakthrough. This work has since gained critical attention within the international discourse on black *feminist writing. The second important English-language female voice appeared in the early 1990s. Yvonne *Vera published a volume of short stories, *Why Don't You Carve Other Animals?* (1992), and two

short novels, *Nehanda* (1993) and *Without a Name* (1994). Vera's imaginative style and unusual narrative structure made an immediate impact.

In 1990 a grassroots organization called Zimbabwean Women Writers (ZWW), with several hundred members throughout the country, formed in order to help its members gain self-confidence in a male-dominated society. ZWW's major goals are to teach writing skills, to improve literacy, to promote positive images of women in literature, and to develop a culture of reading among women. ZWW's writing groups hold writing workshops, record women's oral tales, organize public readings, and initiate library services and book selling in rural areas. Their writing is mostly concerned with the educational and professional disadvantages of women, gender discrimination, and changing gender roles. Living conditions and health issues are also central to their work. ZWW has been involved in publicity campaigns to prevent AIDS and to integrate people with AIDS into society. Writing by ZWW members is published in their newsletter and in the anthology *Zimbabwean Women Writers* (1994), edited by Norma Kitson. Anthologies in Shona and Ndebele will follow.

West Africa: The emergence of *feminist literary theory has made an impact on the West African scene. Feminist scholarship of West African literature accommodates liberal, socialist, and radical theoretical positions, inviting examination of the image of women in West African oral and popular literatures and the status of women in creative works by West African writers both male and female.

West African oral literature includes strong feminist content in some of its genres, such as maternity songs and other forms of oral performance by women. Essentially, however, the female presence in traditional literature is dominated by characters who are either dehumanized, for example the old woman in folktales and proverbs, or presented as caricatures, like the wives and co-wives in folktales whose survival is dependent on the whims and caprices of men. Where a woman is given some positive image, as in the folktale of the beautiful girl who rebels against her parents in order to choose her own suitor, the plot is so structured that the girl is the ultimate loser for daring to assert an identity in a basically patriarchal culture. Similarly, *Onitsha popular market literature, as a product of minds steeped in traditional African male chauvinistic values and the Victorian puritanism of a Euro-Christian colonialism, perpetuates the tradition of the woman as a male appendage. However, the market literature's affinity with the romance genre promotes a vision of the young couple who do marry out of genuine love, even if against parental opposition. The rebellious, ready-to-elope female lover of the Onitsha market literature could be a precursor of the modern feminist single woman who insists on a personal choice of marriage partner. This is the spirit of the heroines of modern popular (romantic) novels such as Helen Ovbiagele's *Evbu My Love* (1980) and *Forever Yours* (1982).

The study of the image of women in West African fiction written by males is an important aspect of feminist scholarship of West African literature. The attempt by some West African female literary scholars to show how Chinua *Achebe, Cyprian *Ekwensi, Wole *Soyinka, and others have canonized a tradition of the woman as appendage has given rise to a crop of West African female critics such as Juliet *Okonkwo, Helen Chukwuma, Molara *Ogundipe-Leslie, Chikwenye Okonjo-Ogunyemi, and others who have been instrumental in establishing a feminist reading of African literature. Their insights have encouraged some male authors to improve the humanity of their female characters, whose significance in the authors' earlier works had operated mainly on the level of the archetypal and mystical 'female essence'. Feminist literary scholarship has also contributed to the development of a generation of female novelists, playwrights, and poets who make the female character in literature the prime mover of events and initiator of heroic actions.

These women writers, many of whose works are, like Buchi *Emecheta's *In the Ditch* (1972), *Second Class Citizen* (1972), and *The Bride Price* (1975) and Rose Njoku's *Withstand the Storm* (1986), largely autobiographical, owe a substantial debt to the creative efforts of Nigerians Flora *Nwapa, and Zulu *Sofola, novelist and playwright respectively, and Ghanaian playwrights Ama Ata *Aidoo and Efua *Sutherland. Though the earlier works of these writers, for example Nwapa's *Efuru* (1966) and *Idu* (1970), Sofola's *King Ememe* (1975) and *Wedlock of the Gods* (1973), and Sutherland's *Edufa* (1967), were conceived within the framework of a patriarchal environment already represented in literature by their male counterparts, their attempt to draw attention to the predicament of women in that environment constitutes a shift of attention from the 'hero' to the 'heroine'. Although female characters in these works still help to sustain a male chauvinistic world, the authors succeed in showing that the male characters survive in that world at the expense of the female. These writers created a protest tradition in which what had been thought of as trivial female concerns assume major philosophical, economic, political, and sociocultural dimensions. Later works – by West African female novelists such as Mariama *Bâ, Buchi Emecheta, Hauwa Ali, Zaynab *Alkali, Ifeoma *Okoye, Rose Njoku, Leslie Jean Ofoegbu, Rosina *Umelo, Adaora *Ulasi, and others; playwright Tess *Onwueme; poets Molara Ogundipe-Leslie, Catherine *Acholonu, Mabel *Segun, Juliet Okonkwo, and Nina Mba – place women at the centre of fictional portrayal. Between 1966 and 1992, these

writers produced more than one hundred volumes of fiction, poetry, and drama. Their major themes are the effects on women of such conditions as poverty, educational constraints, child marriage, polygamy, sexual harassment, Muslim religious practices, divorce and the lack of it in a Euro-Christian connubial heritage, cultural legitimation of women's inferior status, corruption, and so on. Emecheta's *The *Joys of Motherhood* (1979), *Destination Biafra* (1981), and *Double Yoke* (1981), Alkali's *The Stillborn* (1984), Okoye's *Behind the Clouds* (1982), Nwapa's *One Is Enough* (1982), *Never Again* (1984), and *Women Are Different* (1986), Aidoo's **Our Sister Killjoy* (1977), and Onwueme's *The *Reign of Wazobia* (1988) are typical examples.

Feminist critical attention has also focused on essays and short stories published in magazines and newspapers edited by women. From pre-independence to modern times, women editors have played an important role not only in consciousness-raising but also in making the print medium available to women of all shades of gender conviction. No less important in portraying West African feminist thought is writing for children by Christy Ade-Ajayi, Mabel Segun, Ifeoma Okoye, Martina *Nwakoby, and many others. They recognize, as did such male writers as Achebe and Ekwensi, the part that literature plays in moulding young people's understanding of the world from the perspective of African values and needs. However, where children's literature written by men tends to perpetuate the marginalization of women, the special commitment of female writers is to balance male and female roles in writing for children.

West African feminism and the feminist spirit in West African literature argue for the liberated, self-reliant, and resourceful female person and for a complementarity of sex roles in a society where mutual obligations, multiple motherhood and kinship, and the centrality of children in a stable family form the cornerstone of inter-gender co-operation.

Wrath of the Ancestors, The (1980) A novel by A.C. *Jordan, translated from the *Xhosa (*Ingqumbo Yeminyanya*, 1940). Jordan depicts the struggle between maintaining the ancient customs of the Xhosa and accepting the advent of an industrial society. The heir to the chieftainship of the Mpondomise tribe, Zwelinzima, has studied at the Lovedale Institution and is a symbol of the new, educated generation of Africans. When he returns to reclaim his position, a conflict develops between him and his subjects over his resistance to a traditional marriage, and he marries the girl he met at Lovedale. The novel illustrates the importance of the ancestral spirits in Xhosa society when the community forces Zwelinzima to renounce his wife and take another designated by the ancestors. While the Western mind might see the subsequent suicides of the first wife and Zwelinzima as a triumph of evil forces, to the Mpondomise it is the inevitable retribution of the ancestors. *The Wrath of the Ancestors* is a rich, complex novel that affirmed the coming of age of Xhosa writing.

WRITING SYSTEMS IN AFRICA The study of writing systems in Africa has been impeded until recently by certain prejudices about the nature of writing. Much of what has been written on the subject is based on alphabetic scripts and has at its foundation the idea that writing is linked to speech. In this view writing is a secondary system of representation in which the letters of a script represent the sounds of speech, which in turn refer to an idea or thing. This narrow definition of writing has effectively denied the existence of any indigenous system of writing in sub-Saharan Africa. The attention lavished on the Egyptian hieroglyphics has tended to reinforce the stereotype of an Africa without writing by giving rise to spurious theories of the influence of hieroglyphics on other forms of writing on the continent as well as encouraging the notion that the hieroglyphics were in any case a Mediterranean phenomenon rather than an African one. A broad view of the different sorts of writing that have emerged at various times and places clearly indicates that they are connected not by their relationship to speech but rather by the way they are produced. Writing consists of durable inscriptions on some kind of surface, and it makes more sense to see it as an extension of drawing than of speech. Pictographic systems of writing are obviously much closer to the decorative arts than to other systems of representation, and in some cases it is not easy to determine whether an inscription should be described as drawing or as writing. To a certain extent these exist on a continuum and the boundaries between writing and other sorts of design are not at all clearly defined.

An approach to the question of writing in Africa with a more open definition of writing reveals that the continent has a large variety of graphic systems, many of which may best by understood as types of writing. Indeed it is possible that Southern Africa, which has *Bushmen rock inscriptions dating back some 2,700 years, may have furnished the world with the very first writing. There are however many writing systems that are still in use today in different parts of sub-Saharan Africa. The anthropologist Gerhard Kubik has attempted to catalogue the graphic systems that have already been described and has done important research on writing in Angola, Mozambique, Malawi, Tanzania, Zambia, and Cameroon. Writing systems that have been documented include the phonographic script of the Vai in Liberia, the *tusona* ideographs of southern Angola, the syllabic Igbo script of Ogbuefi Nwagu *Aneke, and the elaborate *inyago* pictographic system of the Yao in Malawi, but there is an urgent need for further research on these and other African graphic systems so that a proper history of writing on the African continent can be constructed.

X

XHOSA LITERATURE The task of developing a written form for the Xhosa language was begun by Anders Sparrman, who recorded about fifty-five Xhosa words as early as 1776, and Colonel Jacob Gordon, whose transcriptions of Xhosa words around the end of the eighteenth century anticipated contemporary practice. However, most of the pioneering work was essentially a collective effort by missionaries from British missionary societies, including John Bennie, who arrived at the mission station at Tyhume Valley in 1821, and John Ross, who carted a small printing press from Cape Town to the Tyhume Valley in 1823; the first printed text appeared the same year.

The publication of creative literature was preceded by a very productive period of newspaper and periodical publishing, beginning with *Umshumayeli wendaba* [The preacher of the news] in 1837 and ending with *Izwi labantu* [The voice of the people], 1897-1909. Several other periodicals appeared and disappeared between these two milestones, and many other recordings were made in the meantime, including Ntsikana's great hymn, 'UloThix' omkhulu' [Praise to the Great God], which was transcribed by John Brownlee and published in George Thompson's *Travels and Adventures in Southern Africa* (1827). Highly doxological and declamatory, it is a watershed in Xhosa poetry.

Because the primary objective of the missionaries was to spread the word of God, the early publications were religious and educational books. Several titles followed in quick succession as the earlier authors established themselves as creative writers. Although published overseas, W.B. Rubusana's *Zemk' inkomo magwalandini* paved the way in 1906, some years after the translation by Tiyo Soga of *The Pilgrim's Progress* as *Uhambo lomhambi* (1867); the Bible was translated into Xhosa in 1887. Both books had a tremendous influence on Xhosa literature and literacy.

The first novel to be produced locally, *USamson* (1906) by S.E.K. Mqhayi, was an adaptation of the biblical story of Samson and Delilah. The first original Xhosa novel was written by H.M. Ndawo and entitled *Uhambo lukaGqobhoka* [Christian's journey] (1909). Although it is to a large extent a parody of *The Pilgrim's Progress*, Ndawo succeeded in rooting the story in an African context. The book is still in circulation. The didacticism of early Xhosa literature is well illustrated by G.B. Sinxo's *UNomsa* (1922) and *Umzali wolahleko* (1933).

Among the early creative writers was Lillith Kakaza, whose novel *Intyatyambo yomzi* [The flower of the home] (1913) was the first to be written by a woman. She published a novelette, *UTandiwe wakwa Gcaleka* [Tandiwe the girl from Gcalekaland], the following year. Mqhayi's *Ityala lamawelw* [The lawsuit of the twins], modelled on a theme taken from the Bible, also appeared in 1914.

Mqhayi and J.J.R. Jolobe, the doyens of Xhosa literature, soon branched out to write on sociopolitical issues. In 1929 Mqhayi wrote his *Utopia, UDon Jadu*, which suggests ways of changing South African society. In 1936, Jolobe followed with poetry that made subtle but biting comment on the status quo. His collection of essays, *Amavo* [Essays] (1940), is full of ideas for reconstruction and development and characterized by a spirit of nationalism.

While it had unquestioned merits, missionary patronage of Xhosa literature had its disadvantages. Missionary objectives and church standards were not conducive to creativity, and as a result the departure of the missionaries left a stifled literature. For example Mqhayi's 'Ulwaluko' [Circumcision], a discussion of circumcision among the Xhosa, was considered inappropriate although it dealt with one of the fundamentals of Xhosa culture. Xhosa literature was hardly free of missionary constraints when state-controlled institutions introduced Bantu education, and institutional language boards were given strict instructions, which they followed enthusiastically, to weed out any attempt to represent political dissent, church conflict, or racial tensions in literature. Numerous efforts aborted at manuscript level, but those who could successfully disguise their criticism continued to write books that were fairly critical of the status quo. One of these is R. Siyongwana's *Ubulumko bezinja* [The wisdom of the dogs] (1962), a political satire published at the height of literary censorship and political oppression. Metaphor had become the key to publication, a trend that continued until recently, when P.T. Mtuze's *Alitshoni lingaphumi* (1986), later translated as *Waiting for Sunrise*, appeared with subtle but undisguised criticism of forced removals.

Three milestones in Xhosa literature are of interest. The first is G.I.M. Mzamane's provocative novel *Izinto zodidi* [Things of value] (1959), which openly champions the plight of women under both patriarchy and racial oppression. The second is a novel by R.L. Peteni entitled *Kwazidenge* (1980), a translation of his novel of racial tension in African society, *Hill of Fools* (1976). The third, G.S. Budaza's collection of short stories and essays entitled *Khawufan' ucinge* [Just imagine!] (1980), was the subject of bitter conflict with the education authorities of the past regime because of a story that reveals the atrocities purported to have been carried out on black workers by their former masters.

Xhosa creative writing, which has undertaken all genres with varying degrees of success, has recently expanded into radio drama. N. Saule's *Amaciko ethu* [Our eloquent speakers] (1988), followed L.K. Siwisa's *Uyinkulu kabani?* [Who's eldest son are you?] (1979) and laid the foundations for radio plays. Marcus Ngani's historical drama *Umkhonto kaTshiwo* [Tshiwo's spear] (1959) and Jolobe's *Elundini loThukela* [At the horizon of the Tugela River] (1958) are highly readable historical drama and novel, respectively.

Of the later generation of writers S.C. Satyo, in *Yivani ezi ndaba* [Listen to the news] (1990) and, with P.T. Mtuze, in *Uyavuth' umlilo* [The fire is raging] (1986), writes on political issues with great sensitivity and circumspection. B.B. Mkonto's *Inzonzobila* (1988) deals with social and moral issues of our times, a clear indication that politics is not the only subject of interest to young Xhosa writers, who continue along the lines followed by K.S. Bongela, one of the most prolific Xhosa writers of the contemporary period and the author of novels, drama, and essays, and W.K. Tamsanqa, whose drama *Buzani kubawo* [Ask father] (1958) is unrivalled.

Y

YIRENKYI, Asiedu (1946–), Ghanaian playwright, became involved in theatre through the Drama Studio Players, Accra, which he joined in the early 1960s. From there he went on to study drama at Legon and at Yale, in the USA, and to make a career as a lecturer in Nigeria and Ghana. He has been an actor, director, theatre company manager, and author of screenplays, and has held ministerial-level office. Since 1986 he has taught playwriting in the School of Performing Arts, Legon, but his most important contribution has been as a playwright. His collection *Kivuli and Other Plays* (1980) brings together texts written over an extended period and shows him working in a variety of styles: the earlier plays can be seen in relation to Efua *Sutherland's interest in drama based on the Ananse storytelling tradition. Others draw on his exposure to a variety of traditions of western theatre. In *Kivuli*, his major drama, he sets aside his usual subject matter, the urban middle classes, to examine the plight, arguably even the tragedy, of a villager, a litigious old man who, under the sway of his new young wife, fails to fulfil family responsibilities and is humiliated. The play is evidence of Yirenkyi's serious purpose and abilities.

YORUBA LITERATURE The history of Yoruba literature (as distinct from oral verbal art or *orature) parallels developments in *religion and literature elsewhere on the continent, where African-language writing resulted from Christian activities. The missionizing project needed Christianized and educated local Africans to supplement the few European missionaries available for the task and to produce the requisite texts, liturgical, hymnal, and instructional, in the pertinent local languages. One of the earliest Yoruba converts to Christianity was Samuel Ajayi Crowther. Released into Sierra Leone from a slave ship early in the nineteenth century, he was educated at Fourah Bay College and later ordained into the ministry by the Church Missionary Society (CMS). On returning to Nigeria, he produced an alphabet for the Yoruba language as well as a dictionary and grammar: *A Vocabulary of the Yoruba Language*, a Yoruba-English dictionary, was published in 1852. He also wrote primers for Yoruba instruction in the mission schools.

Literacy in Yoruba inevitably engendered literature in that language. Although today such literacy almost invariably presupposes prior literacy in English, it was not uncommon, up until the first and second decades of the twentieth century, for Yoruba-speaking individuals to be literate in that language only, their primary (or only) motivation being to read the Bible in their own language. That interest coincided with that of the missionaries, who, until pressured by the colonial administration to change their language policy, favoured local languages for both proselytization and instruction. The first popular missionary publications, for example, were Henry Townsend's bilingual *Iwe Irohin* [Newspaper] in 1859 and David Hinderer's *Ilosiwaju ero mimo* (1866), a Yoruba translation of John Bunyan's *The Pilgrim's Progress*. Crowther's Yoruba translation of the Bible, *Bibeli Mimo*, was published in 1900.

The earliest Yoruba creative writing was in verse, arguably because of the high incidence of poetic performance in traditional social and ritual functions. The pioneer was J. Sobowale Sobande, alias Sobo Arobiodu. A resident of Abeokuta, one of the most important bases of missionary effort in western Nigeria, he composed poetry in the style of traditional *oro* ritual chanting. His first volume of poems, *Iwe arofo orin* (1920) [Book of thoughtful verse], offered his readers sage commentary on human existence; five more were to follow. Also from Abeokuta came Kolawole Ajisafe, whose *Aiye akamara* [A treacherous world] (1921) enjoyed sustained popularity well into the 1940s. His *Gbadebo Alake* [Gbadebo, king of Ake-Abeokuta], a biography of the late king of that town, appeared in 1934.

Later Yoruba poets have, like Sobande, looked to traditional verse forms for inspiration. Thus Adetimkan Obasa compiled and published his *Akewi* series, collections of traditional *iwi* (traditional minstrelsy), some of it original, between 1924 and 1945; Adebayo Faleti composed such narrative poems as *Eda ko l'aropin* [No one may be written off] (1956); J.F. Odunjo's collection of original minstrelsy *Akojopo ewi aladun* [A collection of delightful poems] appeared in 1961. Other noteworthy poets include Afolabi Olabimtan and Olatunbosun Oladapo. Olabimtan released his anthology *Aadota arofo* [Fifty poems] in 1969, followed by *Ewi orisirisi* [Variations in minstrelsy] in 1975. Oladapo's collections *Aroye akewi, apa kiini* and *Aroye akewi, apa keji* [A minstrel's reflections, parts one and two] were published in 1974 and 1975 respectively.

Yoruba poetry is frequently more accessible on radio, television, and phonograph disc than in print. The printed versions, moreover, are mostly available in magazines and ephemeral publications. Poetry in contemporary Yoruba society is most alive in performance; while few buyers exist for books of poems, daily radio and television broadcasts of poetry attract large audiences, and poetry recordings on disc and tape enjoy brisk sales. Also, professional performances of *oriki* (praise poems) are a regular and popular feature of any worthwhile social occasion.

Yoruba creative prose dates from the early 1930s with the publication of the novels of Akintunde Akintan. *Igbehin a dun (tabi) omo orukan* [There will be sweetness at the last (or) The orphan], the rags-to-riches story of an orphan girl who eventually marries a king, came on the market in 1931. Akintan was soon eclipsed, however, by the genius who has endured as the all-time giant of Yoruba fiction, D.O. *Fagunwa. Employed as a mission school teacher, Fagunwa delved into the treasury of Yoruba folklore and cosmology for materials that he leavened with Christian precepts to create exciting adventure tales that entertain and edify. His novel *Ogboju ode ninu igbo irunmale* (1938) enjoyed immense success and has remained perhaps the greatest work of Yoruba fiction yet published. Wole *Soyinka translated it as *The *Forest of a Thousand Daemons* (1968). The rollicking adventure depicts the encounters of the intrepid hunter Akara-Ogun with unnaturally fearful animals and spirits in a forbidding forest. He triumphs over his adversaries, or escapes from them, thanks to his personal courage, powerful magical charms, and help from supernatural forces.

Fagunwa's later works, which generally follow the same pattern as the first, include *Igbo Olodumare* [Forest of the Almighty] (1949), *Ireke onibudo* [The gatekeeper's sugarcane] (1950), *Irinkerindo ninu igbo elegbeje* [Peregrinations in the forest of myriad wonders] (1954), and *Adiitu Olodumare* [God's unravellable knot] (1961). The last represents a departure from the rest; it is the story of Adiitu, who by persevering overcomes abject poverty to enjoy wealth.

Fagunwa's success and popularity have not been without some criticism of his sometimes obtrusive Christian bias and the heavy-handed moralizing in his novels. They are nevertheless rich examples of Yoruba verbal artistry, replete with proverbs, folktales, and the like. The English-language writer Amos *Tutuola has built a rather successful, if controversial, career on reworking Fagunwa's style and materials into spectacularly colourful sagas in his highly idiosyncratic language.

Fagunwa continues to influence later Yoruba fiction, such as that of Adekanmi Oyedele, whose *Aiye ree* [What a world] (1946) highlights traditional ways of life. Similarly, I.O. Delano's *Aiye d'aiye oyinbo* [It is now a white man's world] (1955) dramatizes the momentous changes in the life of a traditional ruler after the arrival of the white man. His second novel, *L'ojo ojoun* [In those long-ago days] (1963), recounts

the adventurous life of his father, featuring his conversion from traditional religion to Christianity. Ogunsina Ogundele's *Ibu Olokun* [The depths of the sea deity] (1956) and *Ejigbede lona isalu orun* [Ejigbede on the way to heaven] (1957) involve action that spans heaven, earth, and the depths of the seas.

By the mid-1950s a younger, better-educated generation of Yoruba writers began to crave greater creativity than characterized the earlier works, but the fiction that emerged in the following decade did not depart significantly from what went before, at least not thematically. For example, Femi Jeboda's *Olowolaiyemo* (1964) revisits the subject of the replacement of traditional values by crass materialism with the advent of Europeans. Originally written in 1960, it won the first prize in the literary competition organized by the Western Nigeria Ministry of Education to mark the country's attainment of independence that year. J.F. Odunjo's two novels, *Omo oku orun* [The orphan] and *Kuye*, both published in 1964, have as their heroes youthful characters who survive early deprivation to enjoy eventual prosperity, and D.J. Fatanmi returns in *Korimale ninu igbo adimula* [Korimale in the Adimula forest] (1967) to Fagunwa's tried and tested formula of human encounters with fantastic creatures in a forbidding forest.

The Yoruba poets Afolabi Olabimtan and Adebayo Faleti are also novelists. The former's *Kekere ekun* [The leopard cub] (1967) explores the tensions Christian converts endure in their effort to balance Christianity with traditional ways, while the latter's *Omo olokunesin* [The son of the keeper of the horse] (1970) is a historical narrative in three voices that resembles the Japanese *Rashomon*. Olabimtan released another novel, *Ayanmo* [Destiny], in 1973.

Yoruba drama is more a performance than a literary genre. It dates back to the waning years of the nineteenth century when the Yoruba elite of Lagos, and later the pupils in Christian mission schools, adapted folk material for stage entertainment and fund-raising. The Yoruba folk opera, pioneered by Hubert Ogunde in the 1930s, became world-famous in the 1960s and 70s, especially at the hands of Duro *Ladipo. Ogunde favoured biblical and folkloric materials, while Ladipo often had recourse to incidents from Yoruba history. Unfortunately, the texts of the operas were seldom transcribed and published, and the few that were are virtually inaccessible occasional publications of the Institute of African Studies at the University of Ibadan.

One of the earliest 'legitimate' Yoruba plays to be published was Adeboye Babalola's *Pasan sina* [The ship misses its way] (1956), a tale of misplaced justice. According to the dramatist, it shares with J.F. Odunjo's *Agbalowomeeri* [Despoiler of the destitute] (1958) the credit for laying the foundation for written Yoruba drama. Olanipekun Esan, a classics professor at the University of Ibadan, expanded the quarry for plot materials by turning to classical Greek drama and mythology. His *Teledalase* [The Creator's will is law] (1965) is an adaptation of Sophocles' *Oedipus Rex*; *Esin atiroja* [The lame fighting horse] (1966) is based on the tale of the Trojan horse; while *Orekelewa* [Consummate beauty] reworks Plautus' *Mercator*.

Adebayo Faleti published *Nwon ro pe were ni* [They took her for a mad person] in 1965, followed in 1974 by *Basorun Gaa* [Kingmaker Gaa], a historical drama about a notorious nineteenth-century chief. His other play is the detective intrigue *Idaamu paadi Minkailu* [The troubles of Father Michael] (1994). Afolabi Olabimtan's *Olorun l'o m'ejo da* [God alone is a true judge] (1966) is a murder mystery, but a more important achievement was *Olaore, afotejoye* [Olaore, who gains the throne through treachery] (1970), which poignantly dramatizes the 1960s political upheaval in the Yoruba world. Akinwunmi Isola earned fame for *Efunsetan Aniwura* (1970), a play about a nineteenth-century Ibadan chief; he later wrote the adventure *O le Ku* [He's so tough!] in 1974. T.A.A. Ladele's *Je ng lo'gba temi* [Let me live my life in peace] (1971) and Oladejo Okediji's tragedy *Rere Run* [A great disaster] (1973) are also of interest.

What is true about the relative vitality of printed (published) poetry and live performances is true also of drama. For example, while the market for published Yoruba drama is miniscule, Akinwunmi Isola reports that the live performance of *Efunsetan Aniwura* at the Liberty Stadium (Ibadan) in 1982 attracted an audience of 40,000.

Yoruba literature has not, as would have been expected, experienced continuous growth and development over the years, even despite the experience of favourable factors. For instance, Yoruba is taught throughout the educational system today, including some universities, where Ph.D. candidates write their dissertations in it. Public and private institutions have also promoted Yoruba language and literature: these include the Western Region Literature Committee of the Ministry of Education, Ibadan, inaugurated in

1944 and succeeded in 1954 by the General Publications Department (it inaugurated the periodical *Olokun*, a journal of modern Yoruba literature, in 1957); the Yoruba Language Society, formed in 1942; the Egbe Ijinle Yoruba [Society for authentic Yoruba], inaugurated in 1961; and the Yoruba Creative Writers Association, founded in 1982. However, Yoruba literature lost its momentum after the 1970s. That is not to say that no writing has been done since then, but that there has been little of significance. The decline is traceable mainly to Nigeria's political and social crises and the disarray of its economy and the infrastructure that would normally support literary activity such as universities. Moreover, the prospects for Yoruba literature are bedevilled by the same factors that plague African-language literatures generally, chief among them the defection of the best talents to more promising European-language writing. Such writers as Wole Soyinka, Ola ★Rotimi, Femi ★Osofisan, Bode ★Sowande, and Amos Tutuola would have contributed to an immensely rich tradition if they had chosen to write in Yoruba.

You Can't Get Lost in Cape Town (1987) Short stories by Zoë ★Wicomb. Begun as a 'compromise between novel and short story', the collection comprises ten stories, each complete in itself. Each also makes its own point, including language snobbery in anglophone colonial life, bitter race prejudice even for the relatively preferred 'coloureds' (individuals of mixed race) in South Africa, and an expatriate's glimpses of undercover unrest as she visits home. The threads are tied together in a continuous narrative depicting the protagonist, Frieda Shenton, as she evolves from a plump, gifted little girl, to the lone non-white student at boarding school, to a collegian at a protest demonstration, to an English teacher returning to Cape Town. Wicomb's style is compact, succinct, understated. Into a brief depiction of everyday events she injects a telling criticism of ★apartheid.

YULISA, Pat [See MADDY, Yulisa Amadu]

Z

ZELEZA, Paul Tiyambe (1955-), Zimbabwean short-story writer and novelist, was born in Salisbury, now Harare, and educated at the University of Malawi (BA), the University of London (MA), and Dalhousie University, Canada (Ph.D.). As an undergraduate he participated in the University of Malawi's Writers' Workshop, where he cultivated his interest in fiction. After doctoral studies, with the Banda regime still in power, he went to work at the University of the West Indies rather than return to Malawi. He is a professor of history at Trent University, Canada. In 1994 he won the prestigious Noma Award for his book *A Modern Economic History of Africa* (1993).

Zeleza's early short-story collection, *★Night of Darkness* (1976), blurs the boundaries between history and literature in a form that mines traditional oral material for its energy. His productivity appears to be increasing sharply. In 1992 he published his first novel, *Smouldering Charcoal*, about post-colonial Malawi, and then in 1994 a second collection of short stories, *The Joys of Exile*.

ZIMUNYA, Musaemura (1949-), Zimbabwean poet and short-story writer, was born in Mutare in the then Southern Rhodesia, now Zimbabwe, and educated in Rhodesia and at Kent University, UK, where he gained an MA in literature in 1979. Since 1980 he has been a teacher of literature at the University of Zimbabwe. Zimunya began publishing poems before he was an undergraduate at the University of Rhodesia in local literary periodicals, and later in journals and anthologies in Britain, the USA, and Yugoslavia, as well as in Kizito Muchemwa's *Zimbabwean Poetry in English* (1978) and in the collection he co-edited with Mudereri Khadani, *And Now the Poets Speak* (1981). The poems show an imagination keen to capture the beauty of nature almost in the tradition of the English romantics. His most outstanding book is *Thought Tracks* (1982), which fuses western literary techniques and African oral tradition to articulate the feelings of a generation that felt itself uprooted from its cultural past and marginalized by the colonial dispensation. In *Kingfisher, Jikinya, and Other Poems* (1982), the poet broadens his horizon and celebrates life, nature, and love, but the celebratory tone changes dramatically in *Country Dawns and City Lights* (1985), in which he sets out to de-mythologize rural life as idyllic while also portraying the city as a nightmare for the newly urbanized African. Its relaxed, conversational style and tone make the collection more accessible to a wider

readership than many of his earlier publications. *Country Dawns* was followed by the sombre *Perfect Poise* (1993) and *Selected Poems* (1995) as well as his first collection of short stories, *Nightshift* (1993), in which satire, pathos, and allegory underline the vulnerability and misery that haunt a once colonized people. He has also published a volume of literary criticism, *Those Years of Drought and Hunger: The Birth of African Fiction in English in Zimbabwe* (1982).

ZULU LITERATURE Zulu is a Bantu language spoken as a mother tongue by over eight million people in South Africa. It is beautifully expressive and melodic and has an extremely rich vocabulary to express its traditional hunting, gathering, pastoralist, and patriarchal cultural environment. The lexicon is enhanced by its tonal patterns, by a complex derivational system, and by the use of colourful ideophones to describe phenomena in sensual terms of sound and colour. Like the other languages in the Nguni subgroup, *★Xhosa, Swati and ★Ndebele, the Zulu phonetic system has adopted metallic click sounds from Khoisan in many words. Lexical wealth and variation is rendered necessary by the *ukuhlonipha* (avoidance and respect) custom, whereby a minor/female member of the family avoids the use of terms containing syllables encountered in the name and patronymic of male ascendants.

Social life is centred on the veneration of family, clan, and national ancestors and on allegiance to the royal house; both are considered the guardians of custom and religion and the sources of group strength and identity. The royal house acquired prominence through the wars of King ★Shaka (reigned 1816-1828), who forged the Zulu empire, and through the events associated with his two brothers and successors, Dingane (reigned 1828-1840) and Mpande (1840-1872). Mpande's son Cetshwayo (1872-1884) reached a pinnacle of national renown by defeating the British imperial army in 1879.

Zulu was reduced to writing towards the middle of the nineteenth century by missionaries. Previously literary expression had been purely oral and had reached its highest development in poetic eulogy (*izibongo*), in clan praises (*izithakazelo*), in the formulation of proverbial wisdom (*izaga*), and in a vast repertoire of prose narratives (*izinganekwane*). The missionaries devised a conjunctive orthographic system, analysed the grammatical structures, wrote dictionaries, and recorded oral literary forms. Subsequently the New

Testament was published in 1865 and the Bible in 1883, and Zulu texts were produced for use in mission schools. Newsletters and bulletins were also periodically issued by schools and missions and often contained contributions by native speakers. The weekly paper *Ilanga laseNatali* [The sun of Natal] appeared in 1904, closely followed by *UmAfrika*. Still enjoying wide circulation, these periodicals fostered talent in young Africans, who contributed creative writing, recordings of traditional literature, and lively debates on political and cultural events.

A link between the traditional and the modern was the prophet Isaiah Shembe, founder of the Church of the Nazarites, a syncretic mixture of Zulu and Christian symbolism and practices. Shembe composed a substantial number of hymns in the Zulu-Christian style that reflects messianic and nationalistic aspirations and embodies great respect for Zulu traditions.

During the 1920s Zulu texts by Zulu authors began to appear. Three Zulu plays based on Zulu history and folktale were published in the *Native Teachers' Journal*. The first Zulu book by a Zulu author, *Abantu Abamnyama Lapho Bavela Ngakhona* [The black people and their historical origins] (1922) by Magema Fuze, is a record of legends and oral traditions. Also in the 1920s some former students of the Mariannhill mission school formed companies that performed drama, dance, and music, creating the atmosphere of an African revival. English was widely used to cater for multilingual audiences, but many productions were in African languages and reflected the characteristics of oral performances, where word, rhythmic dance, and music are artistically blended.

Literary activity increased dramatically in the 1930s. John Langalibalele Dube, considered the father of Zulu fiction, published his novelette *Insila kaShaka* [Shaka's body servant] in 1933, and Violet Dube, the first Zulu woman writer, published *Woza Nazo* [Come with the stories] (1935), a collection of folktales that merge Zulu and European motifs in a lively style. In 1939 Nimrod Ndebele published the first full-length Zulu drama, *UGubudela Namazimuzimu* [Gubudela and the ogres], a famous folktale that deals with a cunning young man's destruction of the ogres who devoured his father. The play is a subtle sociopolitical protest against white oppression of blacks. Literature in Zulu becomes a considerable force with the publication of work by B.W. *Vilakazi and R.R.R. *Dhlomo.

Benedict Wallet Vilakazi published the first full-length Zulu novel and the first collection of Zulu poems in 1935. The novel, *Noma Nini* [No matter when], is a love story set in a mission station at the time of King Mpande. It defends the possibility of integrating the best of Zulu traditions with the new culture introduced by Christianity and school educa-

tion. The collection of poems, *Inkondlo kaZulu* [Zulu songs] draws its inspiration from *izibongo* and from the English Romantic poets and experiments with the incorporation of some western composition techniques. This experiment was harshly criticized, and in his second volume of poems, *Amal'Ezulu* (1945; *Zulu Horizons*, 1973), he presents a more genuine Zulu inspiration in both content and form. He published two further novels, *UDingiswayo kaJobe* (1939) and *Nje Nempela* [It is indeed so] (1947), in which he draws his inspiration from historical events and characters.

Following a novelette in English, *An *African Tragedy* (1928), R.R.R. Dhlomo wrote a series of semi-fictional biographies of Zulu kings in Zulu: *UDingane* (1936); *UShaka* (1937); *UMpande kaSenzangakhona* (1938); *UCetshwayo* (1952), and *UDinuzulu* (1968). He also wrote two novels, *UNomalanga ka-Ndengezi* [Nomalanga of Ndengezi] (1934), a love story set during Shaka's reign, and *Indlela Yababi* [The way of the wicked] (1946), which compares traditional and modern upbringing and portrays the city as a place of sin.

In the 1950s Zulu imaginative literature in most genres attained a high level of accomplishment and popularity. Often inspired by European texts read in schools, it was also strongly influenced by oral traditions in content and form: the dilemmas of modern and ancient, school and family education, Christianity and ancestor veneration supplied conflict, and motifs and images drawn from the oral repertoire provided metaphors to convey multivocal messages regarding present-day conditions and to criticize colonial authority. In addition, enforced mother-tongue education, the fruit of the Bantu Education Act of 1952, created the need for a large production of literature aimed at the school market. While some of the results are indifferent, many are of considerable literary value and reflect the themes and poles of conflict already mentioned.

In contemporary Zulu literature, the historical past is often portrayed as a lesson for the present, especially in drama and novels. Historical drama, sometimes seen as the modern counterpart of oral eulogies, reaches a high point in Elliot Zondi's *Ukufa kukaShaka* [Shaka's death] (1962); B.B. Ndelu's *Mageba Lazihlonza* [By Mageba the truth has been vindicated] (1962); Musa A.J. Blose's *Uqomisa mina-nje uqomisa iliba* [By courting me you court the grave] (1968); Chris Themba Msimang's *Izulu Eladuma eSandlwana* [The heavens that thundered at Sandlwana] (1979); and Elliot Zondi's 1986 *Insumansumane* [A mysterious flow of events]. Novels often use historical settings for stories that could happen at any time. Kenneth Bhengu has published a number of novels with either history or legend as a background. Muntu Xulu's *USimpofu* (1969) details the struggle between king Cetshwayo and the British governor Theophilus

Shepstone and highlights the struggle between Africa and the west. L.S. Luthango's *UMohloni* (1938) is a biographical sketch of Mohloni, a powerful adviser of the Sotho leader Moshoeshoe. M. Hlela and C. Nkosi's novel *Imithi Ephundliwe* [Barked trees] (1968) is based on the Zulu war of 1879. Themba Msimang's novel *Buzani kuMkabayi* [Ask Mkabayi] (1982) is about Shaka's kinswoman Mkabayi, who was the kingmaker during more than fifty years of Zulu history. Joice Jessie Gwayi has written three remarkable historical novels: *Bafa Baphela* [They all perished] (1973), *Shumpu* [Chopping off] (1974), and *Yekanini* [Oh my!] (1976).

The social opposition of the traditional and the modern is highlighted in a number of novels, short stories, and poems. The past is seen as a time of order and security compared with the turmoil of modern life, often identified with the city, where a person may be overwhelmed by crime and vice. The master of this genre is Cyril Lincoln Sibusiso Nyembezi, perhaps the best Zulu storyteller. His first novel, *Mntanami! Mntanami!* [My child! My child!] (1950), relates the adventures of a young man dissatisfied with rural life who runs off to Johannesburg, where a gang involves him in murder. It was followed by *Ubudoda abukhulelwa* [Manhood is not the result of age] (1954), which deals with the way a young man overcomes life's tragedies to become an outstanding member of society, and *Inkinsela yaseMgungundlovu* [The tycoon from Pietermaritzburg] (1962), which adopts the frame of a trickster folktale to portray a city slicker who tries to take advantage of the simple people of a rural village.

The theme of enforced marriage resulting from a father's greed for his daughter's dowry appears in a number of novels and short stories. Prominent among them is Jordan K. Ngubane's *Uvalo Lwezinhlonzi* [Fear of the frown], 1956), which satirizes dowry practice and points out its disruptive effects. Love and marital fidelity also feature in D.B.Z. Ntuli's novels *Ngiyoze Ngimthole* [I'll catch him one day] (1970), *Ithemba* [Hope] (1974) and *UBheka* [Bheka] (1977). Themba Msimang deals with problems in a polygamous marriage in his first novel, *Akuyiwe Emhlahlweni* [Let's consult the diviner] (1973).

The short story has become popular for its potential crisp narrative style and subtle sense of humour. Representative writers of this genre are D.B.Z. Ntuli, with *Izikhwili* [Short fighting sticks] (1969), *Uthingo Lwenkosazana* [The rainbow] (1971), and several publications into the late 1980s; W.M.B. Mkhize, with *Ezomhlaba Kazipheli* [Marvels never cease in the world] (1972) and *Emhlabeni Mntanomuntu* [Oh this world!] (1977); and Otty Nxumalo, who has published two novels, *Ikusasa Alaziwa* [Tomorrow is unknown] (1961) and *Ngisinga Empumalanga* [I gaze eastwards] (1969), in addition to two volumes of short stories with S.T.Z. Khwela, *Emhlabeni* [On earth]

(1962) and *Amanqampunqampu* [Headlines] (1966).

A promising new genre is the radio play, brief and to the point. Among the best collections are D.B.Z. Ntuli's *Woza Nendlebe* [Give me your ear] (1988) and *Ishashalazi* [The arena] (1988) (with N.F. Mbhele) and E.M. Damane's *Amavenge* [Lumps of meat] (1985) and *Awuthunyelwa Gundane* [Marriage is unpredictable] (1983).

Most published fiction writers (Nyembezi, Nxumalo, Ntuli, Msimang, etc.) have also published collections of poems, often in cooperation with other authors. Among the most original and powerful poets are J.C. Dlamini, O.H.E.M. Nxumalo, and, of course, Mazisi *Kunene. The latter, whose English translations of his own Zulu poems in both lyric and epic genres – written during long years of exile – have won a universal reputation, is Zulu literature's foremost practitioner, though the circumstances of its creation set his oeuvre apart.

The introduction in 1975 of folklore studies in schools has resulted in many anthologies of oral literature containing traditional and modern material. Among the most prolific folklore writers are C.T. Msimang, L.T.L Mabuya, and D.B.K. Mhlongo. Folkloristic material had been initially collected by Henry Callaway in 1868 and 1870; by James Stuart, who published a series of readers containing tales, legends, and poems in the 1920s; by Mbatha and Mdladla (1927 and 1937); and by C.L.S. Nyembezi, who published Zulu proverbs (1954) and royal praises (1958). The work of annotation and explanation of folklore has had many practitioners, chief among them A.T. Cope, *Izibongo: Zulu Praise Poems* (1968), David Rycroft, *The Praises of Dingana* (1988), and Elizabeth Gunner, *Musho! Zulu Popular Praises* (1994).

Zulu literature has become a very significant factor in South African life, with the publication of an average of 200 new titles a year. Its adult appeal is still limited, but growing.

ZUNGUR, Sa'ad (1915-58), Nigerian poet. The first northerner to gain admission to Yaba College, Lagos, he represented an early radicalism among the western-educated emirate elite. Endowed with a charismatic personality, in the immediate post-war years he was to influence the political thought of the first generation of *Hausa intellectuals, notably Aminu Kano, who formed the NEPU opposition party in the north and later wrote a memoir of Zungur (1973). In particular, two of Zungur's poems ensured his reputation: 'Maraba da Soja' [Welcome to the soldiers] (1946), where the discourse is of political values, and the influential 'Arewa: Jumhuriya ko Mulukiya?' [The north: republic or monarchy?] (*ca*.1949), in which he warned the Hausa-Fulani emirs to improve their governance or face political subjugation by the non-Hausa, non-Muslim southerners.

315

Suggested Further Reading

Allen, Roger. *The Arabic Novel: an historical and critical introduction*. Syracuse NY: Syracuse University Press, 1982.

Banham, Martin (ed.). *The Cambridge Guide to Theatre*. Cambridge University Press, 1988.

Banham, Martin, Errol Hill and George Woodyard (eds). *The Cambridge Guide to African and Caribbean Theatre*. Cambridge University Press, 1994.

Bertoncini, Elena. *Outline of Swahili Literature*. Leiden: E. J. Brill, 1989.

Boehmer, Elleke (ed.). *Altered State?: writing and South Africa*. Sydney: Dangaroo Press, 1994.

Booker, Keith M. *The African Novel in English*. Oxford: James Currey; Portsmouth, NH: Heinemann, 1998.

Brown, Duncan, and Bruno Van Dyk (eds). *Exchanges: South African writing in transition*. Pietermaritzburg: University of Natal Press, 1991.

Chapman, Michael, Colin Gardner and Es'kia Mphahlele (eds). *Perspectives on South African English Literature*. Johannesburg: Ad. Donker, 1992.

Chapman, Michael. *Southern African Literatures*. London and New York: Longman, 1996.

Chinweizu, Onwucheckwa Jemie, and Ihechuckwu Madubuike (eds). *Towards the Decolonization of African Literature*. Enugu: Fourth Dimension; Washington: Howard University Press, 1980.

Chipasula, Frank and Stella (eds). *The Heinemann Book of African Women's Poetry*. Oxford: Heinemann, 1995.

Coetzee, J.M. *White Writing: on the culture of letters in South Africa*. New Haven: Yale University Press, 1988.

Draper, James P. (ed.). *Black Literature Criticism: excerpts from criticism of the most significant works of black authors over the past 200 years*. Detroit: Gale, 1992, 3v.

Fuchs, Anne, and Geoffrey V. Davis. *Theatre and Change in South Africa*. Amsterdam: Harwood, 1996.

Gerard, Albert S. (ed.). *European-Language Writing in Sub-Saharan Africa*. Budapest: Akademiai Kiado, 1986, 2v.

Gikandi, Simon. *Reading the African Novel*. London: James Currey; Portsmouth, NH: Heinemann, 1987.

Gikandi, Simon. *Reading Chinua Achebe*. London: James Currey; Portsmouth, NH: Heinemann, 1991.

Gordimer, Nadine. *Writing and Being: the Charles Eliot Norton Lectures*. Cambridge, MA: Harvard University Press, 1995.

Gurnah, Abdulrazak (ed.). *Essays on African Writing: a re-evaluation*. Oxford: Heinemann, 1993.

Harrow, Kenneth W. (ed.) *Faces of Islam in African Literature*. Portsmouth, NH: Heinemann; London: James Currey, 1991.

Harrow, Kenneth W. *Thresholds of Change in African Literature: the emergence of a tradition*. Portsmouth, NH: Heinemann; London: James Currey, 1994.

Harrow, Kenneth W. (ed.). *The Marabout and the Muse: new approaches to Islam in African literature*. Portsmouth, NH: Heinemann; London: James Currey, 1996.

Herdeck, Donald E. (ed.). *African Authors: a companion to black African writing, Vol. I, 1300–1973*. Washington, DC: Black Orpheus Press, 1973.

Hunwick, J. O., and R. S. O'Fahey (eds). *Arabic Literature in Africa*. Leiden: Brill, 1994.

Jan Mohammed, Abdul R. *Manichean Aesthetics: the politics of literature in colonial Africa*. Amherst, MA: University of Massachasetts Press, 1983.

Jones, Eldred, Eustace Palmer, and Marjorie Jones (eds). *Critical Theory and African Literature Today* (ALT 15). London: James Currey; Trenton, NJ: Africa World Press, 1993.

Jones, Eldred, Eustace Palmer, and Marjorie Jones (eds). *The Question of Language in African Literature Today* (ALT 17). London: James Currey; Trenton, NJ: Africa World Press, 1991.

Julien, Eileen. *African Novels and the Question of Orality*. Bloomington: Indiana University Press, 1992.

Kannemeyer, J. C. *A History of Afrikaans Literature*. Pietermaritzburg: Shuter and Shooter, 1993.

Killam, G.D. (ed.) *The Writing of East and Central Africa*. Nairobi: Heinemann, 1984.

Knappert, Jan. *Four Centuries of Swahili Verse*. London and Nairobi: Heinemann Educational Books, 1979.

Kurtz, J. Roger, *Urban Obsessions, Urban Fears: the postcolonial Kenyan novel*. Oxford: James Currey; Trenton, NJ: Africa World Press, 1998.

Lazarus, Neil. *Resistance in Postcolonial African Fiction*. New Haven: Yale University Press, 1990

Lindfors, Bernth. *Comparative Approaches to African Literatures*. Amsterdam: Rodopi, 1994.

Lo Liyong, Taban. *Another Last Word*. Nairobi: Heinemann Kenya, 1990.

Maja-Pearce, Adewale (ed.). *The Heinemann Book of African Poetry in English*. Heinemann: Oxford, 1990.

Mayamba, N. *The East African Narrative Fiction: towards an aesthetic and a socio-political Uhuru*. Lagos: Cross

Continent, 1988.

Ndebele, Njabulo S. *Southern African Literature and Culture: rediscovery of the ordinary*. Manchester: Manchester University Press, 1991.

Ngara, Emmanuel. *Art and Ideology in the African Novel: a study of the influence of Marxism on African writing*. London: Heinemann, 1985.

—*Stylistic Criticism and the African Novel*. London: Heinemann, 1982.

Ngugi wa Thiong'o. *Decolonising the Mind: the politics of language in African literature*. London: James Currey; Portsmouth, NH: Heinemann, 1981.

Ngugi wa Thiong'o. *Moving the Centre: the struggle for cultural freedoms*. London: James Currey, 1993.

Ntuli, D. B. and Swanepoel, C.F. *South African Literature in African Languages: a concise historical perspective*. Pretoria: Acacia, 1993.

Ojaide, Tanure. *Poetic Imagination in Black Africa: essays on African poetry*. Carolina Academic Press, 1997.

Shava, Pineal Viriri. *A People's Voice: Black South African writing in the twentieth century*. London: Zed Books; Athens: Ohio University Press; Harare: Baobab Books, 1989.

Smith, M. van Wyk. *Grounds of Contest: a survey of South African English literature*. Cape Town: Jutalit, 1990.

Soyinka, Wole. *Art, Dialogue and Outrage. Essays on literature and culture*. Ibadan: New Horn, 1988. 2nd rev. ed. London: Methuen, 1990, edited by B. Jeyifo.

Trump, Martin (ed.). *Rendering Things Visible: essays on South African literary culture*. Johannesburg: Ravan Press; Athens: Ohio University Press, 1990.

Udenta, Udenta O. *Revolutionary Aesthetics and the African Literary Process*. Enugu: Fourth Dimension Publications, 1993.

Vera, Yvonne (ed.). *The Heinemann Book of Contemporary African Women's Writing*. Oxford: Heinemann, 1999.

White, Landeg, and Tim Couzens (eds). *Literature and Society in South Africa*. Cape Town: Maskew Miller Longman; London: Longman, 1984.

Wilentz, Gay Alden. *Binding Cultures: black women writers in Africa and the diaspora*. Bloomington: Indiana University Press, 1992.

Wilkinson, Jane (ed.). *Talking with African Writers: interviews with African poets, playwrights and novelists*. London: James Currey, 1992.

Zell, Hans, M., Carol Bundy and Virginia Coulon (eds). *A New Reader's Guide to African Literature*. London: Heinemann Educational Books, 1983.

Country–Author Guide

Algeria
Mohammed Dib
Assia Djebar
Touati Fettouma

Angola
Agostinho Neto

Benin
Félix Couchoro

Botswana
Bessie Head

Cameroon
Mongo Beti
Calixthe Beyala
Yodi Karone
Simon Njami
Ferdinand Oyono
Guillaume Oyono-Mbia

Central African Republic
Blaise N'Djehoya

Congo–Zaïre
Kama Kamanda
Sony Labou Tansi

Côte d'Ivoire
Bernard Dadié
Ahmadou Kourouma

Egypt
Andrée Chedid
Fathy Ghanem
Tewfiq al-Hakim
Naguib Mahfouz
Nawal el Saadawi

Ethiopia
Sahle Sellassie

Gambia
Lenrie Peters
Tijan M. Sallah

Ghana
Joseph Wilfred Abruquah
Kobena Eyi Acquah

Ama Ata Aidoo
Kofi Anyidoho
Ayi Kwei Armah
R.E.G. Armattoe
Kofi Awoonor
Mohammed Ben-Abdallah
J. Benibengor Blay
Yaw M. Boateng
Kwesi Brew
J. E. Casely-Hayford
Ottobah Cugoano
Joe de Graft
Michael Francis Dei-Anang
Cameron Duodu
Ferdinand Kwasi Fiawoo
Asare Konadu
B. Kojo Laing
Bill Okyere Marshall
Atukwei Okai
Martin Owusu
Kobina Sekyi
Francis Selormey
Efua Sutherland
Asiedu Yirenkyi

Guinea
Camara Laye
Williams Sassine

Kenya
Jared Angira
Khadambi Asalache
Francis Imbuga
Samuel Kahiga
Leonard Kibera
Muthoni Likimani
Charles Mangua
Ali A. Mazrui
Micere Githae Mugo
Meja Mwangi
Stephen N. Ngubiah
Ngugi wa Thiong'o
Rebeka Njau
Grace Ogot
Mwangi Ruheni
M. G. Vassanji
Godwin Wachira
Charity Waciuma
Kenneth Watene
Miriam Were

Lesotho
Thomas Mofolo
A. S. Mopeli-Paulus

Liberia
Bai T. J. Moore

Madagascar
Jean-Joseph Rabéarivelo
Jacques Rabémanajara

Malawi
Steve Chimombo
Frank Chipasula
Aubrey Kachingwe
Legson Kayira
Ken Lipenga
Jack Mapanje
Felix Mnthali
Edison Mpina
Anthony Nazombe
David Rubadiri

Mali
Amadou Hampâté Bâ

Mauritius
Edouard Maunick

Morocco
Tahar Ben Jelloun
Driss Chraïbi

Mozambique
Mia Couto
Lina Magaia

Namibia
Joseph Diescho
Dorian Haarhoff

Nigeria
Chinua Achebe
Catherine Obianuju Acholonu
Remi Aduke Adedeji
Frank Aig-Imoukhuede
Funso Aiyejina
Christie Ade Ajayi
Tolu Ajayi
Zaynab Alkali

T. M. Aluko
Elechi Amadi
Ogbuefi Nwagu Aneke
I.N.C. Aniebo
Seinde Arogbofa
Biyi Bandele-Thomas
J. P. Clark Bekederemo
Chinweizu
Michael J. C. Echeruo
T. Obinkaram Echewa
Obi B. Egbuna
Cyprian Ekwensi
Buchi Emecheta
Ossie Enekwe
Olaudah Equiano
D. O. Fagunwa
Tunde Fatunde
Harry Garuba
James Ene Henshaw
Chukwuemeka Ike
Eddie Iroh
Festus Iyayi
Duro Ladipo
Theresa Ekwutosi Meniru
S. Okechukwu Mezu
John Munonye
Pol Nnamuzikam Ndu
Emeka Nwabueze
Martina Awele Nwakoby
Nkem Nwankwo
Flora Nwapa
Onuora Nzekwu
Olu Obafemi
Odia Ofeimun
Olu Oguibe
Molara Ogundipe-Leslie
Wale Ogunyemi
Tanure Ojaide
Gabriel Okara
Christopher Okigbo
Akomaye Oko
Onookome Okome
Ifeoma Okoye
Isidore Okpewho
Ben Okri
Tayo Peter Olafioye
Kole Omotoso
Tess Akaeka Onwueme
Dillibe Onyeama
Dennis Osadebay
Naiwu Osahon
Femi Osofisan
Niyi Osundare
Sonny Oti
Helen Ovbiagele

Femi Oyebode
Segun Oyekunle
Ola Rotimi
Ken Saro-Wiwa
Mabel Segun
Zulu Sofola
Bode Sowande
Wole Soyinka
Ibrahim Tahir
Amos Tutuola
Obiora Udechukwu
Ada Ugah
Kalu Uka
Adaora Lily Ulasi
Rosina Umelo
Mamman Jiya Vatsa
Adebayo Williams
Sa'ad Zungur

Rwanda
Alexis Kagame

Senegal
Mariama Bâ
Alioune Diop
Birago Diop
Cheikh Anta Diop
David Diop
Malick Fall
Aminata Maiga Ka
Sembene Ousmane
L. S. Senghor

Sierra Leone
Adelaide Casely-Hayford
Gladys Casely-Hayford
Syl Cheney-Coker
William Conton
R. Sarif Easmon
Lemuel A. Johnson
Yulisa Amadu Maddy
Abioseh Nicol

Somalia
Nuruddin Farah

South Africa
Lionel Abrahams
Peter Abrahams
Tatamkhulu Ismail Afrika
Stephen Black
Douglas Blackburn
Harry Bloom
Elleke Boehmer
Dugmore Boetie

H. C. Bosman
Breyten Breytenbach
André Brink
Dennis Brutus
Guy Butler
Roy Campbell
Stuart Cloete
Sydney Clouts
J. M. Coetzee
Jack Cope
Patrick Cullinan
R. N. Currey
Achmat Dangor
H. I. E. Dhlomo
R. R. R. Dhlomo
Modikwe Dikobe
Menán du Plessis
Ahmed Essop
J. Percy Fitzpatrick
Athol Fugard
Sheila Meiring Fugard
Perceval Gibbon
Nadine Gordimer
Stephen Gray
Mafika Pascal Gwala
Bessie Head
Christopher Hope
Noni Jabavu
Dan Jacobson
Ingrid Jonker
A. C. Jordan
Farida Karodia
Gibson Kente
Keorapetse Kgositsile
Daniel P. Kunene
Mazisi Kunene
Ellen Kuzwayo
Alex La Guma
Douglas Livingstone
Donald Maclennan
Sindiwe Magona
Matsemele Manaka
Umaruiddin Don Mattera
James Matthews
Mzwakhe Mbuli
Zakes Mda
Gcina Mhlophe
Ruth Miller
Sarah Gertrude Millin
Bloke Modisane
Casey 'Kid' Motsisi
Es'kia Mphahlele
Mbuyiseni Mtshali
Mothobi Mutloatse
Mbulelo Mzamane

Nat Nakasa
Njabulo Ndebele
Lauretta Ngcobo
Mbongeni Ngema
Mike Nicol
Lewis Nkosi
Arthur Nortje
Alan Paton
Sol T. Plaatje
William Plomer
Thomas Pringle
Alfred Temba Qabula
Lesego Rampolokeng
Richard Rive
Sheila Roberts
Olive Schreiner
William Charles Scully
Sipho Sepamla
Mongane Wally Serote
Francis Carey Slater
Pauline Smith
Can Themba
Gladys Thomas
Miriam Tlali
Laurens van der Post
Christopher van Wyk
B. W. Vilakazi
Ivan Vladislavić
Stephen Watson
Zoë Wicomb
Peter Wilhelm

Sudan
Tayeb Salih

Tanzania
Agoro Anduru
Abdulrazak Gurnah
Ebrahim N. Hussein
Peter Palangyo
Prince Kagwema
Gabriel Ruhumbika

Tunisia
Albert Memmi

Uganda
Austin Bukenya
Barbara Kimenye
Bonnie Lubega
Lubwa p'Chong
John Nagenda
Peter Nazareth
Richard Carl Ntiru
Okello Oculi
Okot p'Bitek
John Ruganda
George Seremba
Eneriko Seruma
Robert Serumaga
Taban lo Liyong
Bahadur Tejani
Timothy Wangusa

Zambia
Dominic Mulaisho

Zimbabwe
N. H. Brettell
Samuel Chimsoro
Shimmer Chinodya
Edmund Chipamaunga
A. S. Cripps
Tsitsi Dangarembga
John Eppel
Chenjerai Hove
Wilson Katiyo
Doris Lessing
Nevanji Madanhire
Dambudzo Marechera
Timothy O. McLoughlin
Charles Mungoshi
Solomon Mutswairo
Geoffrey Ndhlala
Emmanuel Ngara
Stanley Nyamfukudza
Freedom Nyamubaya
Kristina Rungano
Stanlake Samkange
Ben Sibenke
T. K. Tsodzo
Lawrence Vambe
Yvonne Vera
Andrew Whaley
Paul Tiyambe Zeleza
Musaemura Zimunya

Guide to Readers

The Companion to African Literatures is an alphabetically organized, comprehensive guide to work written in English or widely available in translation from other languages. There are separate entries for selected African language literatures, with an emphasis on works available to readers of English.

Cross-referencing: ★Asterisks are used before the first appearance of a word within each entry to indicate that a separate related entry appears elsewhere in *The Companion*.

There are entries in the following categories:

Authors writing in English. Author entries include biographical information, details of major publications, and comment on their critical reputation.

Authors who write in an African or non-African language, but some of whose work is available in English translation.

Selected works of an author, giving brief descriptive entries.

Language entries distinguish *The Companion* from other reference works to the literature of the African continent. Selected African languages with published literatures (Gikuyu, Hausa, Igbo, Krio, Malagasy, Ndebele, Pidgin, Shona, Sotho, Swahili, Tsonga, Xhosa, Yoruba and Zulu). Entries on works which are written in Afrikaans, Portuguese (see *Lusophone Literature*), and French (see the *Novel, Francophone*), but which are mostly available in translation.

Themed entries as listed below are **further sub-divided alphabetically by region** (East Africa; South-Central Africa, South Africa and West Africa), categories which reflect differences in the literatures as shaped by their colonial and post-colonial experiences. (The literatures of North Africa, when available in translation from Arabic and French into English, are described through individual author entries).

> *Literary genres and sub-genres:* Drama, the Novel, Poetry, the Short Story, Popular Literature, Oral Tradition and Folklore, Anthologies, Biography and Autobiography, Children's Literature, Literary Magazines

> *Relations between literature and extra-literary influences:* Religion and Literature (Christianity, Islam, and Traditional African Religions), Politics and Literature, War Literature, Censorship, Women in Literature

Topics and Themes